Hall Caine

The Christian

A Story. Second Edition

Hall Caine

The Christian
A Story. Second Edition

ISBN/EAN: 9783337260941

Printed in Europe, USA, Canada, Australia, Japan

Cover: Foto ©Lupo / pixelio.de

More available books at **www.hansebooks.com**

The Christian

A Story

By

Hall Caine

Author of "The Manxman," etc. etc.

Second Edition

London
William Heinemann
1897

First Edition in One Volume, Six Shillings, consisting of 50,000 Copies, August 9, 1897; Second Edition, Fifty-first to Seventieth Thousand, August 25, 1897.

All rights reserved.

CONTENTS

FIRST BOOK
The Outer World . . . Page 1

SECOND BOOK
The Religious Life . 113

THIRD BOOK
The Devil's Acre . . . 226

FOURTH BOOK
Sanctuary . . . 359

The period of the story is the last quarter of the nineteenth century. No particular years are intended. The time occupied by the incidents of the First Book is about six months, of the Second Book about six months, of the Third Book about six months; then there is an interval of half a year, and the time occupied by the incidents of the Fourth Book is about six weeks. An Author's Note will be found at the end.

The Christian

FIRST BOOK—THE OUTER WORLD

I

On the morning of the 9th May 18—, three persons important to this story stood among the passengers on the deck of the Isle of Man steamship *Tynwald* as she lay by the pier at Douglas getting up steam for the passage to Liverpool. One of these was an old clergyman of seventy, with a sweet, mellow, childlike face; another was a young man of thirty, also a clergyman; the third was a girl of twenty. The older clergyman wore a white neckcloth about his throat, and was dressed in rather threadbare black, of a cut that had been more common twenty years before; the younger clergyman wore a Roman collar, a long clerical coat, and a stiff broad-brimmed hat with a cord and tassel. They stood amidships, and the Captain coming out of his room to mount the bridge, saluted them as he passed.

"Good morning, Mr. Storm."

The young clergyman returned the salutation with a slight bow and the lifting of his hat.

"Morning to you, Parson Quayle."

The old clergyman answered cheerily, "Oh, good morning, Captain, good morning."

There was the usual inquiry about the weather outside, and drawing up to answer it, the Captain came eye to eye with the girl.

"So this is the grand-daughter, is it?"

"Yes, this is Glory," said Parson Quayle. "She's leaving the old grandfather at last, Captain, and I'm over from Peel to set her off, you see."

"Well, the young lady has got the world before her at her feet, I ought to say. You're looking as bright and fresh as the morning, Miss Quayle."

The Captain carried off his compliment with a breezy laugh, and went along to the bridge. The girl had heard him only in a momentary flash of consciousness, and she replied merely with a side glance and a smile. Both eyes and ears, and every sense and every faculty, seemed occupied with the scene before her.

It was a beautiful spring morning, not yet nine o'clock, but the sun stood high over Douglas Head, and the sunlight was glancing in the harbour from the little waves of the flowing tide. Cars were rattling up the pier, passengers were trooping down the gangways, and the decks fore and aft were becoming thronged.

"It's beautiful!" she was saying, not so much to her companions as to herself, and the old parson was laughing at her bursts of rapture over the commonplace scene, and dropping out in reply little driblets of simple talk—sweet, pure nothings, the innocent babble as of a mountain stream.

She was taller than the common, and had golden red hair and magnificent dark grey eyes of great size. One of her eyes had a brown spot, which gave at the first glance the effect of a squint, at the next glance a coquettish expression, and ever after a sense of tremendous power and passion. But her most noticeable feature was her mouth, which was somewhat too large for beauty, and was always moving nervously. When she spoke her voice startled you with its depth, which was a kind of soft hoarseness, but capable of every shade of colour. There was a playful and impetuous raillery in nearly all she said, and everything seemed to be expressed by mind and body at the same time. She moved her body restlessly, and while standing in the same place her feet were always shuffling. Her dress was homely, almost poor, and perhaps a little careless. She appeared to smile and laugh continually, and yet there were tears in her eyes sometimes.

The young clergyman was of a good average height, but he looked taller from a certain distinction of figure. When he raised his hat at the Captain's greeting, he showed a forehead like an arched wall and a large close-cropped head. He had a well-formed nose, a powerful chin, and full lips, all very strong and set for one so young. His complexion was dark, almost swarthy, and there was a certain look of the gipsy in his big golden-brown eyes with their long black lashes. He was clean shaven, and the lower part of his face seemed heavy under the splendid fire of the eyes above it. His manner had a sort of diffident restraint; he stood on the same spot without moving, and almost without raising his drooping head; his speech was grave and usually slow and laboured, his voice was bold and full.

The second bell had rung, and the old parson was making ready to go ashore.

"You'll take care of this runaway, Mr. Storm, and deliver her safely at the door of the hospital?"

"I will."

"And you'll keep an eye on her in that big Babylon over there?"

"If she'll let me, sir."

"Yes, indeed, yes, I know; she's as unstable as water and as hard to hold as a puff of wind."

The girl was laughing again. "You might as well call me a tempest and have done with it, or," with a glance at the younger man, "say a storm—Glory St—— Oh!"

With a little catch of the breath she arrested the name before it was uttered by her impetuous tongue, and laughed again to cover her confusion. The young man smiled faintly and rather painfully, but the old parson was conscious of nothing.

"Well, and why not? A good name for you too, and you richly deserve it. But the Lord is lenient with such natures, John. He never tries them beyond their strength. She hasn't much leaning to religion, you know."

The girl recalled herself from the busy scene around and broke in again with a tone of humour and pathos mixed.

"There! call me an infidel at once, grandfather. I know what you mean. But just to show you that I haven't exactly registered a vow in heaven never to go to church in London because you've given me such a dose of it in the Isle of Man, I'll promise to send you a full and particular report of Mr. Storm's first sermon. Isn't that charming of me?"

The third bell was ringing, the blast of the steam-whistle was echoing across the bay, and the steamer was only waiting for the mails. Taking a step nearer to the gangway the old parson talked faster.

"Did Aunt Anna give you money enough, child?"

"Enough for my boat fare and my train."

"No more! Now Anna is so——"

"Don't trouble, grandfather. Woman wants but little here below—Aunt Anna excepted. And then a hospital nurse——"

"I'm afraid you'll feel lonely in that great wilderness."

"Lonely with five millions of neighbours!"

"You'll be longing for the old island, Glory, and I half repent me already———"

"If ever I have the blue-devils, grandpa, I'll just whip on my cape and fly home again."

"To-morrow morning I'll be searching all over the house for my runaway."

Glory tried to laugh gaily. "Upstairs, downstairs, and in my lady's chamber."

"'Glory,' I'll be crying. 'Where's the girl gone at all? I haven't heard her voice in the house to-day. What's come over the old place to strike it so dead?'"

The girl's eyes were running over, but in a tone of gentle raillery and heart's love she said severely, "Nonsense, grandfather; you'll forget all about Glory going to London before the day after to-morrow. Every morning you'll be making rubbings of your old runes, and every night you'll be playing chess with Aunt Rachel, and every Sunday you'll be scolding old Neilus for falling asleep in the reading-desk, and—and everything will go on just the same as ever."

The mails had come aboard, one of the gangways had been drawn ashore, and the old parson, holding his big watch in his left hand, was diving into his fob-pocket with the fingers of the right.

"Here"—panting audibly as if he had been running hard—"your mother's little pearl ring."

The girl drew off her slack, soiled glove and took the ring in her nervous fingers.

"A wonderful talisman is the relic of a good mother, sir," said the old parson.

The young clergyman bent his head.

"You're like Glory herself in that, though—you don't remember your mother either."

"No—no."

"I'll keep in touch with your father, John, trust me for that. You and he shall be good friends yet. A man can't hold out against his son for nothing worse than choosing the Church against the world. The old man didn't mean all he said; and then it isn't the thunder that strikes people dead, you know. So leave him to me; and if that foolish old Chalse hasn't been putting notions into his head——"

The throbbing in the steam-funnel had ceased, and in the sudden hush a voice from the bridge cried, "All ashore!"

"Good-bye, Glory! Good-bye, John! Good-bye both!"

"Good-bye, sir," said the young clergyman, with a long hand clasp.

But the girl's arms were about the old man's neck. "Good-bye, you dear old grandpa, and I'm ashamed I—I'm sorry I—I mean it's a shame of me to—good-bye!"

"Good-bye, my wandering gipsy, my witch, my runaway!"

"If you call me names I'll have to stop your mouth, sir. Again—another——"

A voice cried, "Stand back, there!"

The young clergyman drew the girl back from the bulwarks, and the steamer moved slowly away.

"I'll go below—no, I won't, I'll stay on deck. I'll go ashore—I can't bear it; it's not too late yet. No, I'll go to the stern and see the water in the wake."

The pier was cleared and the harbour was empty. Over the white churning water the seagulls were wheeling, and Douglas Head was gliding slowly back. Down the long line of the quay the friends of the passengers were waving adieus.

"There he is—on the end of the pier! That's grandpa waving his handkerchief! Don't you see it? The red and white cotton one! God bless him! How wae his little present made me! He has been keeping it all these years. But my silk handkerchief is too damp—it won't float at all. Will you lend me—— Ah, thank you! Good-bye! Good-bye! Good——"

The girl hung over the stern rail, leaning her breast upon it and waving the handkerchief as long as the pier and its people were in sight, and when they were gone from recognition she watched the line of the land until it began to fade into the clouds and there was no more to be seen of what she had looked upon every day of her life until to-day.

"The dear little island! I never thought it was so beautiful! Perhaps I might have been happy even there if I had tried. Now if I had only had somebody for company! How silly of me! I've been five years wishing and praying to get away, and now! . . . It *is* lovely though, isn't it? Just like a bird on the water! And when you've been born in a place . . . the dear little island! And the old folks, too! How lonely they'll be, after all! I wonder if I shall ever . . . I'll go below. The wind's freshening, and this water in the wake is making my eyes . . . Good-bye, little birdie! I'll come back—I'll . . . Yes, never fear, I'll——"

The laughter and impetuous talking, the gentle humour and pathos had broken at length into a sob, and the girl had wheeled about and disappeared down the cabin-stairs. John Storm stood looking after her. He had hardly spoken, but his great brown eyes were moist.

II

Her father had been the only son of Parson Quayle, and chaplain to the Bishop at Bishopscourt. It was there he had met her mother, who was lady's-maid to the bishop's wife. The maid was a bright young Frenchwoman, daughter of a French actress famous in her day, and of an officer under the Empire, who had never been told of her existence. Shortly after their marriage, the chaplain was offered a big mission station in Africa, and being a devotee, he clutched at it without fear of the fevers of the coast. But his young French wife was about to become a mother, and she shrank from the perils of his life abroad, so he took her to his father's house at Peel and bade her farewell for five years.

He lived four, and during that time they exchanged some letters. His final instructions were sent from Southampton: "If it's a boy, call him John (after the Evangelist), and if it's a girl, call her Glory." At the end of the first year she wrote: "I have shortened our darling, and you never saw anything so lovely! Oh, the sweetness of her little bare arms, and her neck, and her little round shoulders! You know she's red—I've really got a red one—a curly red one! Such big beaming eyes too! And then her mouth and her chin and her tiny red toes! I don't know how you can live without seeing her!" Near the end of the fourth year he sent his last answer: "Dear wife, this separation is bitter, but God has willed it, and we must not forget that the probabilities are that we may pass our lives apart." The next letter was from the English Consul on the Gaboon River, announcing the death of the devoted missionary.

Parson Quayle's household consisted only of himself and two maiden daughters, but that was too much for the lively young Frenchwoman. While her husband lived she suffocated under the old-maid *régime*, and when he was gone she made no more fight with destiny, but took some simple ailment and died suddenly.

A bare hillside frowned down on the place where Glory was born, but the sun rose over it, and a beautiful river hugged its sides. A quarter of a mile down the river there was a harbour, and beyond the harbour a bay, with the ruins of an old castle standing out on an islet rock, and then the broad sweep of the Irish Sea—the last in those latitudes to "parley with the setting sun." The vicarage was called Glenfaba, and it was half a mile outside the fishing-town of Peel.

Glory was a little red-headed witch from the first, with an air of general uncanniness in everything she did and said. Until after she was six there was no believing a word she uttered. Her conversation was bravely indifferent to considerations of truth or falsehood, fear or favour, reward or punishment. The parson used to say, " I'm really afraid the child has no moral conscience—she doesn't seem to know right from wrong." This troubled his religion, but it tickled his humour, and it did not disturb his love. "She's a perfect pagan—God bless her innocent heart!"

She had more than a child's genius for make-believe. In her hunger for child company, before the days when she found it for herself, she made believe that various versions of herself lived all over the place, and she would call them out to play. There was Glory in the river, under the pool where the perch swam, and Glory down the well, and Glory up in the hills, and they answered when she spoke to them. All her dolls were kings and queens, and she had a gift for making up in strange and grand disguises. It was almost as if her actress grandmother had bestowed on her from her birth the right to life and luxury and love.

She was a born mimic, and could hit off to a hair an eccentricity or an affectation. The frown of Aunt Anna, who was severe, the smile of Aunt Rachel, who was sentimental, and the yawn of Cornelius Kewley, the clerk, who was always sleepy, lived again in the roguish, rippling face. She remembered some of her mother's French songs, and seeing a street-singer one day, she established herself in the market-place in that character, with grown people on their knees around her, ready to fall on her and kiss her and call her Phonodoree, the fairy. But she did not forget to go round for the ha'pennies either.

At ten she was a tomboy and marched through the town at the head of an army of boys, playing on a comb between her teeth and flying the vicar's handkerchief at the end of his walking-stick. In these days she climbed trees and robbed orchards (generally her own) and imitated boys' voices and thought it tyranny that she might not wear trousers. But she wore a sailor's blue stocking-cap, and it brightened existence when, for economy's sake and for the sake of general tidiness, she was allowed to wear a white woollen jersey. Then somebody who had a dinghy that he did not want asked her if she would like to have a boat. Would she like to have paradise, or pastry cakes, or anything that was heavenly! After that she wore a sailor's jacket and a sou'wester when she was on the sea, and tumbled about the water like a duck.

At twelve she fell in love—with love. It was a vague passion interwoven with dreams of grandeur. The parson being too poor to send her to the girls' college at Douglas, and his daughters being too proud to send her to the dame's school at Peel, she was taught at home by Aunt Rachel, who read the poetry of Thomas Moore, knew the birthdays of all the royal family, and was otherwise meekly romantic. From this source she gathered much curious sentiment relating to some visionary world where young girls were held aloft in the sunshine of luxury and love and happiness. One day she was lying on her back on the heather of the Peel hill with her head on her arms, thinking of a story that Aunt Rachel had told her. It was of a mermaid who had only to slip up out of the sea and say to any man, "Come," and he came—he left everything and followed her. Suddenly the cold nose of a pointer rubbed against her forehead, a strong voice cried, " Down, sir !" and a young man of two-and-twenty, in leggings and a shooting-jacket, strode between her and the cliffs. She knew him by sight. He was John Storm, the son of Lord Storm, who had lately come to live in the mansion-house at Knockaloe, a mile up the hill from Glenfaba.

For three weeks thereafter she talked of nobody else, and even began to comb her hair. She watched him in church, and told Aunt Rachel she was sure he could see quite well in the dark, for his big eyes seemed to have the light inside of them. After that she became ashamed, and if anybody happened to mention his name in her hearing, she flushed up to the forehead and fled out of the room. He never once looked at her, and after a while he went away to Canada. She set the clock on the back-landing to Canadian time so that she might always know what he was doing abroad, and then straightway forgot all about him. Her moods followed each other rapidly, and were all of them overpowering and all sincere, but it was not until a year afterwards that she fell in love, in the church vestry, with the pretty boy who stood opposite to her in the Catechism class.

He was an English boy of her own age, and he was only staying in the island for his holidays. The second time she saw him it was in the grounds at Glenfaba, while his mother was returning a call indoors. She gave him a little tap on the arm, and he had to run after her—down a bank and up a tree, where she laughed and said, " Isn't it nice ?" and he could see nothing but her big white teeth.

His name was Francis Horatio Nelson Drake, and he was full of great accounts of the goings-on in the outer world, where his school was, and where lived the only "men" worth talking about. Of course he spoke of all this familiarly and with a convincing reality which wrapped Glory in the plumage of dreams. He was a wonderful being altogether, and in due time (about three days) she proposed to him. True, he did not jump at her offer with quite proper alacrity, but when she mentioned that it didn't matter to her in the least whether he wanted her or not, and that plenty would be glad of the chance, he saw things differently and they agreed to elope. There was no particular reason for this drastic measure, but as Glory had a boat it seemed the right thing to do.

She dressed herself in all her Confirmation finery and stole out to meet him under the bridge where her boat lay moored. He kept her half-an-hour waiting, having sisters and other disadvantages, but "once aboard her lugger" he was safe. She was breathless, and he was anxious, and neither thought it necessary to waste any time in kissing.

They slipped down the harbour and out into the bay, and then ran up the sail and stood off for Scotland. Being more easy in mind when this was done, they had time to talk of the future. Francis Horatio was for work—he was going to make a name for himself. Glory did not see it quite in that light. A name! yes, and lots of triumphal processions; but she was for travel—there were such lots of things people could see if they didn't waste so much time working.

"What a girl you are!" he said derisively; whereupon she bit her lip, for she didn't quite like it. But they were nearly half-an-hour out before he spoiled himself utterly. He had brought his dog, a she-terrier, and he began to call her by her kennel name and to say what a fine little thing she was, and what a deal of money they would make by her pups. That was too much for Glory. She couldn't think of eloping with a person who used such low expressions.

"What a girl you are!" he said again; but she did not mind it in the least. With a sweep of her bare arm she had put the tiller hard a port, intending to tack back to Peel, but the wind had freshened and the sea was rising, and by the swift leap of the boat the boom was snapped and the helpless sail came flapping down upon the mast. Then they tumbled into the trough, and Glory had not strength to pull them out of it, and the boy was of no more use than a tripper. She was in her white muslin dress, and he was nursing his dog, and the night was closing down on them, and they were wabbling about under a pole and a tattered rag. But all at once a great black yacht came heaving up in the darkness and a grown-up voice cried, "Trust yourself to me, dear."

It was John Storm. He had already awakened the young girl in her, and thereafter he awakened the young woman as well. She clung to him like a child that night, and during the four years following she seemed always to be doing the same. He was her big brother, her master, her lord, her sovereign. She placed him on a dizzy height above her, amid a halo of goodness and grandeur. If he smiled on her she flushed, and if he frowned she fretted and was afraid. Thinking to please him, she tried to dress herself up in all the colours of the rainbow, but he reproved her and bade her return to her jersey. She struggled to comb out her red curls until he told her that the highest ladies in the land would give both ears for them, and then she fondled them in her fingers and admired them in a glass.

He was a serious person, but she could make him laugh until he screamed. Excepting Byron and "Sir Charles Grandison," out of the vicar's library, the only literature she knew was the Bible, the Catechism, and the Church Service, and she used these in common talk with appalling freedom and audacity. The favourite butt of her mimicry was the parish clerk saying responses when he was sleepy.

The Parson: "O Lord, open Thou our lips" (no response). "Where are you, Neilus?"

The Clerk (awakening suddenly in the desk below): "Here I am, your reverence—and our mouth shall show forth Thy praise."

When John Storm did laugh he laughed beyond all control, and then Glory was entirely happy. But he went away again, his father having sent him to Australia, and all the light of her world went out.

It was of no use bothering with the clock on the back-landing, because things were different by this time. She was sixteen, and the only tree she climbed now was the tree of the knowledge of good and evil, and that tore her terribly. John Storm was the son of a lord, and he would be Lord Something himself some day. Glory Quayle was an orphan, and her grandfather was a poor country clergyman. Their poverty was sweet, but there was gall in it nevertheless. The little forced economies in dress, the frocks that had to be turned, the bonnets that were beauties when they were bought, but had to be worn until the changes of fashion made them frights, and then the mysterious parcels of left-off clothing from goodness knows where—how the independence of the girl's spirit rebelled against such humiliations.

The blood of her mother was beginning to boil over, and the old-maid *régime*, which had crushed the life out of the Frenchwoman, was suffocating the Manx girl with its formalism. She was always forgetting the meal-times regulated by the sun, and she could sleep at any time and keep awake until any hour. It tired her to sit demurely like a young lady, and she had a trick of lying down on the floor. She often laughed in order not to cry, but she would not even smile at a great lady's silly story, and she did not care a jot about the birthdays of the royal family. The old aunts loved her body and soul, but they often said, "Whatever is going to happen to the girl when the grandfather is gone?"

And the grandfather, good man, would have laid down his life to save her a pain in her toe, but he had not a notion of the stuff she was made of. His hobby was the study of the runic crosses with which the Isle of Man abounds, and when she helped him with his rubbings and his casts he was as merry as an old sand-boy. Though they occupied the same house, and her bedroom, that faced the harbour, was next to his little musty study that looked over the scullery slates, he lived always in the tenth century and she lived somewhere in the twentieth.

The imprisoned linnet was beating at the bars of its cage. Before she was aware of it she wanted to escape from the sleepy old scene, and had begun to be consumed with longing for the great world outside. On summer evenings she would go up Peel hill and lie on the heather, where she had first seen John Storm, and watch the ships weighing anchor in the bay beyond the old dead castle walls, and wish she were going out with them—out to the sea and the great cities north and south. But existence closed in ever-narrowing circles round her and she could see no way out. Two years passed, and at eighteen she was fretting that half her life had wasted away. She watched the sun until it sank into the sea, and then she turned back to Glenfaba and the darkened region of the sky.

It was all the fault of their poverty, and their poverty was the fault of the Church. She began to hate the Church; it had made her an orphan; and when she thought of religion as a profession, it seemed a selfish thing anyway. If a man was really bent on so lofty an aim (as her own father had been), he could not think of himself; he had to give up life and love and the world—and then these always took advantage of him. But people had to live in the world for all that, and what was the good of burying yourself before you were dead?

Somehow her undefined wishes took shape in visions of John Storm, and one day she heard he was home again. She went out on the hill that evening, and, being seen only by the gulls, she laughed and cried and ran. It was just like poetry, for there he was himself lying on the edge of the cliff, near the

very spot where she had been used to lie. On seeing him she
went more slowly, and began to poke about in the heather as
if she had seen nothing. He came up to her with both hands
outstretched, and then suddenly she remembered that she was
wearing her old jersey, and she flushed up to the eyes, and
nearly choked with shame. She got better by-and-by, and
talked away like a mill-wheel, and then fearing he might think
it was from something quite different, she began to pull the
heather, and to tell him why she had been blushing. He did
not laugh at all. With a strange smile he said something in
his deep voice that made her blood run cold.

"But I'm to be a poor man myself in future, Glory. I've
quarrelled with my father. I'm going into the Church."

It was a frightful blow to her, and the sun went down like a
shot. But it burst open the bars of her cage for all that. After
John Storm had found a curacy in London and taken Orders,
he told them at Glenfaba that among his honorary offices was
to be that of chaplain to a great West End hospital. This
suggested to Glory the channel of escape. She would go out
as a hospital nurse. It was easier said than done, for hospital
nursing was fashionable, and she was three years too young. With
great labour she secured her appointment as probationer, and
with greater labour still overcame the fear and affection of
her grandfather. But the old parson was finally appeased when
he heard that Glory's hospital was the same that John Storm
was to be chaplain of, and that they might go up to London
together.

III

Dear Grandfather of Me and Everybody at Glenfaba,—
Here I am at last, dear, at the end of my pilgrim's progress,
and the evening and the morning are the first day. It is now
eleven o'clock at night, and I am about to put myself to bed
in my own little room at the hospital of Martha's Vineyard,
Hyde Park, London, England.

The Captain was quite right; the morning was as fresh as
his flattery, and before we got far beyond the Head most of the
passengers were spread out below like the three legs of Man.
Being an old sea-doggie myself, I didn't give it the chance to
make me sick, but went downstairs and lay quiet in my berth,
and deliberated great things. I didn't go up again until we got
into the Mersey, and then the passengers were on deck, looking
like sour butter-milk spilt out of the churn.

What a glorious sight! The ships, the docks, the towers, the town! I couldn't breathe for excitement until we got up to the landing-stage. Mr. Storm put me into a cab, and, for the sake of experience, I insisted on paying my own way. Of course, he tried to trick me; but a woman's a woman for a' that. As we drove up to Lime Street Station there befell—a porter. He carried my big trunk on his head (like a mushroom), and when I bought my ticket, he took me to the train, while Mr. Storm went for a newspaper. Being such a stranger, he was very kind, so I flung the responsibility on Providence, and gave him sixpence.

There were two old ladies in the carriage beside ourselves, and the train we travelled by was an express. It was perfectly delightful, and for all the world like plunging into a stiff sou'-wester off the rocks at Contrary. But the first part of the journey was terrible. That tunnel nearly made me shriek. It was a misty day, too, at Liverpool, and all the way to Edge Hill they let off signals with a noise like battering-rams. My nerves were on the rack; so, taking advantage of the darkness of the carriage, I began to sing. That calmed me, but it nearly drove the old ladies out of their wits. *They* screamed if I didn't: and just as I was summoning the Almighty to attend to me a little in the middle of that inferno, out we came as innocent as a baby. There was another of these places just before getting into London; I suppose they are the purgatories through which you have to pass to get to these wonderful cities. Only if I had been consulted in the making of the Litany ("From sudden death, good Lord, deliver us"), I should have made an exception for people in tunnels.

You never knew what an absolute ninny Glory is! I was burning with such impatience to see London, that, when we came near it, I couldn't see anything for water under the brain. Approaching a great and mighty city for the first time must be like going into the presence of majesty. Only Heaven save me from such palpitation the day I become Songstress to the Queen!

Mercy! what a roar and boom—a deep murmur as of ten hundred million million moths humming away on a still evening in autumn. On a nearer view it is more like a Tower of Babel concern with its click and clatter. The explosion of voices, the confused clamour, the dreadful disorder—cars, waggons, omnibuses—it makes you feel religious and rather cold down the back. What a needle in a haystack a poor girl must be here if there is nobody above to keep track of her!

Tell Aunt Rachel they are wearing another kind of bonnet in London—more pokey in front—and say if I see the Queen I'll be sure to tell her all about it.

We didn't get to the hospital until nine, so I've not seen much of it yet. The housekeeper gave me tea and told me I might go over the house as I wouldn't be wanted to begin duty before morning. So for an hour I went from ward to ward like a female Wandering Jew. Such silence! I'm afraid this hospital nursing is going to be a lock-jaw business. And now I'm going to bed well, not homesick, you know, but just "longing a lil bit for all." To-morrow morning I'll waken up to new sounds and sights, and when I draw my blind I'll see the streets where the cars are for ever running and rattling. Then I'll think of Glenfaba and the birds singing and rejoicing.

Dispense my love throughout the island. Say that I love everybody just the same now I'm a London lady as when I was a mere provincial girl, and that when I'm a wonderful woman, and have brought the eyes of England upon me, I'll come back and make amends. I can hear what grandfather is saying: "Gough bless me, what a girl, though!" GLORY.

P.S.—I've not said much about Mr. Storm. He left me at the door of the hospital and went on to the house of his vicar, for that is where he is to lodge, you know. On the way up I expended much beautiful poetry upon him on the subject of love. The old girlies having dozed off, I chanced to ask him if he liked to talk of it, but he said no, it was a profanation. Love was too sacred, it was a kind of religion. Sometimes it came unawares, sometimes it smouldered like fire under ashes, sometimes it was a good angel, sometimes a devil making you do things and say things, and laying your life waste like winter. But I told him it was just charming, and as for religion there was nothing under heaven like the devotion of a handsome and clever man to a handsome and clever woman, when he gave up all the world for her, and his body and his soul and everything that was his. I think he saw there was something in that, for though he said nothing, there came a wonderful light into his splendid eyes, and I thought if he wasn't going to be a clergyman—but no matter. So long, dear!

IV

JOHN STORM was the son of Lord Storm (a peer in his own right), and nephew of the Prime Minister of England, the Earl of Erin. Two years before John's birth the brothers had quarrelled about a woman. It was John's mother. She had engaged herself to the younger brother, and afterwards fallen in love with the elder one. The voice of conscience told her that it was her duty to carry out her engagement, and she did so. Then the voice of conscience took sides with the laws of life, and told the lovers they must renounce each other, and they both did that as well. But the poor girl found it easier to renounce life than love, and after flying to religion as an escape from the conflict between conjugal duty and elemental passion, she gave birth to her child and died. She was the daughter of a rich banker, who had come from the soil, and she had been brought up to consider marriage distinct from love. Exchanging wealth for title, she found death in the deal.

Her husband had never stood in any natural affinity to her. On his part their marriage had been a loveless and selfish union, based on the desire for an heir that he might found a family and cancel the unfair position of a younger son. But the sin he committed against the fundamental law that marriage shall be founded only in love brought its swift revenge.

On hearing that the wife was dead the elder brother came to attend the funeral. The night before that event the husband felt unhappy about the part he had played. He had given no occasion for scandal, but he had never disguised, even from the mother of his son, the motives of his marriage. The poor girl was gone, he had only trained himself for the pursuit of her dowry, and the voice of love had been silent. Troubled by such thoughts, he walked about his room all night long, and somewhere in the first dead grey of dawn he went down to the death-chamber, that he might look upon her face again. Opening the door, he heard the sound of half-stifled sobs. Some one was leaning over the white face and weeping like a man with a broken heart. It was his brother.

From that time forward Lord Storm considered himself the injured person. He had never cared for his brother, and now he designed to wipe him out. His son would do it. He was the heir to the earldom, for the Earl had never married. But a posthumous revenge was too trivial. The Earl had gone into politics and was making a name. Lord Storm had missed his own opportunities, though he had got himself called to the Upper House, but his son should be brought up to eclipse everything.

To this end the father devoted his life to the boy's training. All conventional education was wrong in principle. Schools and colleges and the study of the classics were drivelling folly, with next to nothing to do with life. Travel was the great teacher. "You shall travel as far as the sun," he said; so the boy was taken through Europe and Asia, and learned something of many languages. He became his father's daily companion, and nowhere the father went was it thought wrong for the boy to go also. Conventional morality was considered mawkish. The chief aim of home training was to bring children up in total ignorance, if possible, of the most important facts and functions of life. But it was *not* possible, and hence suppression, dissimulation, lying, and, under the ban of secret sin, one half the world's woe. So the boy was taken to the temples of Greece and India, and even to Western casinos and dancing-gardens. Before he was twenty he had seen something of nearly everything the world has in it.

When the time came to think of his career, England was in straits about her Colonial Empire. The vast lands over sea wanted to take care of themselves. It was the moment of the " British North America Act," and that gave the father his cue for action. While his brother the Earl was fiddling the country to the tune of limited self-government for Crown Colonies, the father of John Storm conceived the daring idea of breaking up the entire empire, including the United Kingdom, into self-governing states. They were to be the "United States of Great Britain."

This was to be John Storm's policy, and to work it out Lord Storm set up a house in the Isle of Man, where he might always look upon his plan in miniature. There he established a bureau for the gathering of the data that his son would need to use hereafter. Newspapers came to him in his lonely retreat from all quarters of the globe, and he cut out everything relating to his subject. His library was a dusty room lined all round with brown paper packets which were labelled with the names of colonies and counties.

"It will take us two generations to do it, my boy, but we'll alter the history of England."

At fifty he was iron-grey and had a head like a big owl.

Meanwhile, the object of these grand preparations, the offspring of that loveless union, had a personality all his own. It seemed as if he had been built for a big man every way, and nature had been arrested in the making of him. When people looked at his head, they felt he ought to have been a giant, but he was far from rivalling the children of Anak. When they listened to his conversation, they thought he might turn out to be a creature of genius, but perhaps he was only a man of powerful moods. The best strength of body and mind seemed to have gone into his heart. It may be that the sorrowful unrest of his mother and her smothered passion had left their red stream in John Storm's soul.

When he was a boy, he would cry at a beautiful view in nature, at a tale of heroism, or at any sentimental ditty sung excruciatingly in the streets. Seeing a bird's nest that had been robbed of its eggs, he burst into tears; but when he came upon the bleeding, broken shells in the path, the tears turned to fierce wrath and mad rage, and he snatched up a gun out of his father's room, and went out to take the life of the offender.

On coming to the Isle of Man, he noticed, as often as he went to church, that a little, curly, red-headed girl kept staring at him from the vicar's pew. He was a man of two-and-twenty, but the child's eyes tormented him. At any time of day or night he could call up a vision of their gleaming brightness. Then his father sent him to Canada to watch the establishment of the Dominion, and when he came back he brought a Canadian canoe and an American yacht, and certain democratic opinions.

The first time he sailed the yacht in Manx waters he sighted a disabled boat and rescued two children. One of them was the girl of the vicar's pew, grown taller and more winsome. She nestled up to him when he lifted her into the yacht, and without knowing why he kept his arms about her.

After that he called his yacht the *Gloria* in imitation of her name, and sometimes took the girl out on the sea. Notwithstanding the difference of the years between them, they had their happy boy and girl days together. In her white jersey and stocking cap she looked every inch a sailor. When the wind freshened and the boat plunged, she stood to the tiller like a man, and he thought her the sweetest sight ever seen in a cockpit; and when the wind saddened and the boom came aboard, she was the cheeriest companion in a calm. She sang, and so did he, and their voices went well together. Her favourite song was "Come, lasses and lads," his was "John Peel," and they would sing them off and on for an hour at a spell. Thus on a summer evening, when the bay was lying like a tired monster asleep, and every plash of an oar was echoing on the hills, the people on the land would hear them coming around the castle rock with their

"D'ye ken John Peel, with his coat so gay?
D'ye ken John Peel at the break of day?
D'ye ken John P-e-e-l . . ."

For two years he amused himself with the child, and then realised that she was a child no longer. The pity of the girl's position took hold of him. This sunny soul, with her sportfulness, her grace of many gifts, with her eyes that flashed and gleamed like lightning, with her voice that was like the warble of a bird, this golden-headed gipsy, this witch, this fairy—what was the life that lay before her? Pity gave place to a different feeling, and then he was aware of a pain in the breast when he thought of the girl. As often as her eyes rested upon him he felt his face tingle and burn. He began to be conscious of an imprisoned side to his nature, the passionate side, and he drew back afraid. This wild power, this tempest, this raging fire within, God only knew whither it was to lead him. And then he had given a hostage to fortune, or his father had for him.

From his father's gloomy house at Knockaloe, where the winds were ever droning in the trees, he looked over to Glenfaba, and it seemed to him like a little white cloud lit up by the sunshine. His heart was for ever calling to the sunny spot over there, "Glory! Glory!" The pity of it was that the girl seemed to understand everything, and to know quite well what kept them apart. She flushed with shame that he should see her wearing the same clothes constantly, and with head aside and furtive glances she talked of the days when he would leave the island for good, and London would take him and make much of him, and he would forget all about his friends in that dead old place. Such talk cut him to the quick. Though he had seen a deal of the world, he did not know much about the conversation of women.

The struggle was brief. He began to wear plainer clothes— an Oxford tweed coat and a flannel shirt—to talk about fame as an empty word, and to tell his father that he was superior to all stupid conventions.

His father sent him to Australia. Then the grown-up trouble of his life began. He passed through the world now with eyes open for the privations of the poor, and he saw everything in a new light. Unconsciously he was doing in another way what his mother had done when she flew to religion from stifled passion. He had been brought up as a sort of Imperialist-democrat, but now he bettered his father's instructions. England did not want more parliaments; she wanted more apostles. It was not by giving votes to a nation, but by strengthening the soul of a nation that it became great and free. The man for the hour was not he who revolved schemes for making himself famous, but he who was ready to renounce everything, and, if he was great, was willing to become little, and, if he was rich, to become poor. There was room for an apostle—for a thousand apostles—who, being dead to the world's glory, its money or its calls, were prepared to do all in Christ's spirit, and to believe that in the renunciation which was the "secret" of Jesus lay the only salvation remaining for the world.

He tramped through the slums of Melbourne and Sydney, and afterwards through the slums of London, returned to the Isle of Man a Christian Socialist, and announced to his father his intention of going into the Church.

The old man did not fume and fly out. He staggered back to his room like a bullock to its pen after it has had its death-blow in the shambles. In the midst of his dusty old bureau, with its labelled packets full of cuttings, he realised that twenty years of his life had been wasted. A son was a separate being, of a different growth, and a father was only the seed at the root that must decay and die.

Then he made some show of resistance.

"But with your talents, boy, surely you are not going to throw away your chances of a great name?"

"I care nothing for a great name, father," said John. "I shall win a greater victory than any that Parliament can give me."

"But, my boy, my dear boy! one must either be the camel or the camel-driver; and then society——"

"I hate society, and society would hate me. It is only for the sake of the few godly men that God spares it, as He spared Sodom for Lot's sake."

Having braved this ordeal and nearly broken the heart of his old father, he turned for his reward to Glory. He found her at her usual haunt on the headlands.

"I was blushing when you came up, wasn't I?" she said. "Shall I tell you why?"

"Why?"

"It was this," she said, with a sweep of her hand across her bosom.

He looked puzzled.

"Don't you understand? This old rag—it's the one I was wearing before you went away."

He wanted to tell her how well she looked in it—better than ever now that her bosom showed under its seamless curves and her figure had grown so lithe and shapely. But though she was laughing, he saw she was ashamed of her poverty, and he thought to comfort her.

"I'm to be a poor man myself in future, Glory. I've quarrelled with my father. I'm going to take Orders."

Her face fell. "Oh, I didn't think anybody would be poor who could help it. To be a clergyman is all right for a poor man, perhaps, but I hate to be poor; it's horrid."

Then darkness fell upon his eyes and he felt sad and sick. Glory had disappointed him. She was vain, she was worldly, she was incapable of the higher things; she would never know what a sacrifice he had made for her; she would think nothing of him now; but he would go on all the same, the more earnestly because the devil had drawn a bow at him and the arrow had gone in up to the feathers.

"With God's help I shall nail my colours to the mast," he said.

Thus he made up his mind to follow the unrolling of the scroll. He had the strength called character. The Church had been his beacon before, but now it was to be his refuge.

He found no difficulty in making the necessary preparations. For a year he read the Anglican divines — Jeremy Taylor, Hooker, Butler, Waterland, Pearson, and Pusey,—and when the time came for his ordination, his uncle, the Earl of Erin, who was now Prime Minister, obtained him a title to a curacy under the popular and influential Canon Wealthy, of All Saints', Belgravia. The Bishop of London gave letters dimissory to the Bishop of Sodor and Man, by whom he was examined and ordained.

On the morning of his departure for London, his father, with whom there had in the meantime been trying scenes, left him this final word of farewell: "As I understand that you intend to lead the life of poverty, I presume that you do not need your mother's dowry, and I shall hold myself at liberty to dispose of it elsewhere, *unless* you require it for the use of the young lady who is, I hear, to go up with you."

V

"I WILL be a poor man among poor men," said John Storm to himself as he drove to his vicar's house in Eaton Place, but he awoke next morning in a bedroom that did not answer to his ideas of a life of poverty. A footman came with hot water and tea, and also a message from the Canon overnight, saying he would be pleased to see Mr. Storm in the study after breakfast.

The study was a sumptuous apartment immediately beneath, with soft carpets, on which his feet made no noise, and tigerskins over the backs of chairs. As he entered it, a bright-faced man in middle life, clean shaven, wearing a gold-mounted pince-nez, and bubbling over with politeness, stepped forward to receive him.

"Welcome to London, my dear Mr. Storm. When the letter came from the Prime Minister I said to my daughter Felicity—

you will see her presently—I trust you will be good friends—I said, 'It is a privilege, my child, to meet any wish of the dear Earl of Erin, and I am proud to be in at the beginning of a career that is sure to be brilliant and distinguished.'"

John Storm made some murmur of dissent.

"I trust you found your rooms to your taste, Mr. Storm?"

John Storm had found them more than he expected or desired.

"Ah, well, humble but comfortable, and in any case please regard them as your own, to receive whom you please therein, and to dispense your own hospitalities. This house is large enough. We shall not meet oftener than we wish, so we cannot quarrel. The only meal we need take together is dinner. Don't expect too much. Simple but wholesome—that's all we can promise you in a clergyman's family."

John Storm answered that food was an indifferent matter to him, and that half-an-hour after dinner he never knew what he had eaten. The Canon laughed and began again.

"I thought it best you should come to us, being a stranger in London, though I confess I have never had but one of my clergy residing with me before. He is here now. You'll see him by-and-by. His name is Golightly, a simple, worthy young man, from one of the smaller colleges, I believe. Useful, you know, devoted to me and to my daughter, but of course a different sort of person altogether, and—er——"

It was a peculiarity of the Canon that whatever he began to talk about he always ended by talking of himself.

"I sent for you this morning (not having had the usual opportunity of a meeting before) that I might tell you something of our organisation and your own duties. . . . You see in me the head of a staff of six clergy."

John Storm was not surprised; a great preacher must be followed by flocks of the poor; it was natural that they should wish him to help them and to minister to them.

"We have no poor in my parish, Mr. Storm."

"No poor, sir?"

"On the contrary, her Majesty herself is one of my parishioners."

"That must be a great grief to you, sir?"

"Oh, the poor! Ah, yes, certainly. Of course we have our associated charities, such as the maternity home founded in Soho by Mrs. Callender—a worthy old Scotswoman, odd and whimsical, perhaps, but rich, very rich and influential. My clergy, however, have enough to do with the various departments of our church work. For instance, there is the Ladies' Society, the Fancy Needlework classes, and the Decorative Flower Guild, not to speak of the daughter churches and the ministration in hospitals, for I always hold—er——"

John Storm's mind had been wandering, but at the mention of the hospital he looked up eagerly.

"Ah, yes, the hospital. Your own duties will be chiefly concerned with our excellent hospital of Martha's Vineyard. You will have the spiritual care of all patients and nurses—yes, nurses also—within its precincts, precisely as if it were your parish. 'This is my parish,' you will say to yourself, and treat it accordingly. Not yet being in full Orders, you will be unable to administer the sacrament, but you will have one service daily in each of the wards, taking the wards in rotation. There are seven wards, so there will be one service in each ward once a week, for I always say that fewer——"

"Is it enough?" said John. "I shall be only too pleased——"

"Ah, well, we'll see. On Wednesday evenings we have service in the church, and nurses not on night duty are expected to attend. Some fifty of them altogether, and rather a curious compound. Ladies among them? Yes, the daughters of gentlemen, but also persons of all classes. You will hold yourself responsible for their spiritual welfare. Let me see—this is Friday—say you take the sermon on Wednesday next, if that is agreeable. As to views, my people are of all shades of colour, so I ask my clergy to take strictly *via media* views—strictly *via media*. Do you intone?"

John Storm had been wandering again, but he recovered himself in time to say he did not.

"That is a pity; our choir is so excellent—two violins, a viola, clarinet, 'cello, double bass, the trumpets and drums, and of course the organ. Our organist himself——"

At that moment a young clergyman came into the room, making apologies and bowing subserviently.

"Ah, this is Mr. Golightly—the—h'm—Hon. and Rev. Mr. Storm. You will take charge of Mr. Storm, and bring him to church on Sunday morning."

Mr. Golightly delivered his message. It was about the organist. His wife had called to say that he had been removed to the hospital for some slight operation, and there was some difficulty about the singer of Sunday morning's anthem.

"Most irritating! Bring her up." The curate went out backwards. "I shall ask you to excuse me, Mr. Storm. My daughter, Felicity—ah, here she is."

A tall young woman in spectacles entered.

"This is our new housemate, Mr. Storm, nephew of dear Lord Erin. Felicity, my child, I wish you to drive Mr. Storm round and introduce him to our people, for I always say a young clergyman in London——"

John Storm mumbled something about the Prime Minister.

"Going to pay your respects to your uncle now? Very good and proper. Next week will do for the visits. Yes, yes. Come in, Mrs. Koenig."

A meek, middle-aged woman had appeared at the door. She was dark, and had deep luminous eyes with the moist look to be seen in the eyes of a tired old terrier.

"This is the wife of our organist and choir-master. Good day! Kindest greetings to the Prime Minister.... And by the way, let us say Monday for the beginning of your chaplaincy at the hospital."

The Earl of Erin, as First Lord of the Treasury, occupied the narrow, unassuming brick house which is the Treasury residence in Downing Street. Although the official head of the Church, with power to appoint its bishops and highest dignitaries, he was secretly a sceptic, if not openly a derider of spiritual things. For this attitude his early love passage had been chiefly accountable. That strife between duty and passion which had driven the woman he loved to religion, had driven him in the other direction and left a broad swath of desolation in his soul. He had seen little of his brother since that evil time, and nothing whatever of his brother's son. Then John had written, "I am soon to be bound by the awful tie of the priesthood," and he had thought it necessary to do something for him. When John was announced he felt a thrill of tender feeling to which he had long been a stranger. He got up and waited. The young man with his mother's face and the eyes of an enthusiast was coming down the long corridor.

John Storm saw his uncle first in the spacious old Cabinet room which looks out on the little garden and the Park. He was a gaunt old man with meagre moustache and hair and a face like a death's-head. He held out his hand and smiled. His hand was cold and his smile was half tearful and half saturnine.

"You are like your mother, John."

John never knew her.

"When I saw her last you were a child in arms and she was younger than you are now."

"Where was that, uncle?"

"In her coffin, poor girl."

The Prime Minister shuffled some papers and said—

"Well, is there anything you wish for?"

"Nothing. I've come to thank you for what you've done already."

The Prime Minister made a deprecatory gesture.

"I almost wish you had chosen another career, John; still the Church has its opportunities and its chances, and if I can ever——"

"I am satisfied—more than satisfied," said John. "My choice is based, I trust, on a firm vocation. God's work is great, sir; and greatest of all in London. That is why I am so grateful to you. Think of it, sir!"

John was leaning forward in his chair, with one arm stretched out.

"Of the five millions of people in this vast city, not one million cross the threshold of church or chapel. And then remember their condition. A hundred thousand live in constant want, slowly starving to death every day and hour, and a quarter of the old people of London die as paupers. Isn't it a wonderful scene, sir? If a man is willing to be spiritually dead to the world—to leave family and friends—to go forth never to return, as one might go to his execution——"

The Prime Minister listened to the ardent young man who was talking to him there with his mother's voice, and then said—

"I'm sorry."

"Sorry?"

"I'm afraid I've made a mistake."

John Storm looked puzzled.

"I've sent you to the wrong place, John. When you wrote, I naturally supposed you were thinking of the Church as a career, and I tried to put you in the way of it. Do you know anything of your vicar?"

John knew that fame spoke of him as a great preacher—one of the few who had passed through their Pentecost, and come out with the gift of tongues.

"Precisely!" The Prime Minister gave a bitter little laugh. "But let me tell you something about him. He was a poor curate in the country, where the lord of the manor chanced to be a lady. He married the lady of the manor. His wife died, and he bought a London parish. Then by the help of an old actor who gave lessons in elocution he—well, he set up his Pentecost. Since then he has been a fashionable preacher, and frequents the houses of great people. Ten years ago he was made an honorary canon, and when he hears of an appointment to a bishopric, he says in a tearful voice, 'I don't know what the dear Queen has got against me.'"

"Well, sir?"

"Well, if I had known you felt like that, I should scarcely

have sent you to Canon Wealthy. And yet I hardly know where else a young man of your opinions ... I'm afraid the Church has a good many Canon Wealthys in it."

"God forbid," said John. "No doubt there are Pharisees in these days just as in the days of Christ, but the Church is still the pillar of the State."

"The caterpillar, you mean, boy—eating out its heart and its vitals."

The Prime Minister gave another bitter little laugh, then looked quickly into John's flushed face and said—

"But it's poor work for an old man to sap away a young man's enthusiasm."

"You can't do that, uncle," said John, "because God is the absolute ruler of all things, good and bad, and He governs both to His glory. Let Him only give us strength to endure our exile——"

"I don't like to hear you talk like that, John. I think I know what the upshot will be. There's a gang of men about— Anglican Catholics they call themselves; well, remember the German proverb, 'Every priestling hides a popeling.' ... And if you *are* to be in the Church, John, is there any reason why you shouldn't marry and be reasonable? To tell you the truth, I'm rather a lonely old man, whatever I may seem; and if your mother's son would give me a sort of a grandson—eh?"

The Prime Minister was pretending to laugh again.

"Come, John, come, it seems a pity—a fine young fellow like you, too. Are there no sweet young girls about in these days? Or are they all dead and gone since I was a young fellow? I could give you a wide choice, you know, for when a man stands high enough ... in fact, you would find me reasonable—you might have anybody you liked, rich or poor, dark or fair——"

John Storm had been sitting in torment, and now he rose to go. "No, uncle," he said in a thicker voice, "I shall never marry. A clergyman who is married is bound to life by too many ties. Even his affection for his wife is a tie. And then there is her affection for the world, its riches, its praise, its honours——"

"Well, well, we'll say no more. After all, it's better than running wild, and that's what most young men seem to be doing now-a-days. But then your long education abroad, and your poor father left to look after himself! Good-day to you! Come and see me now and then. How like your mother you are sometimes! Good-day!"

When the door of the Cabinet room closed on John Storm the

Prime Minister thought, " Poor boy, he's laying up for himself a big heart-ache one of these fine days."

And John Storm, going down the street with uncertain step, said to himself, " How strange he should talk like that! But thank God, he didn't produce a flicker in me. I died to all that a year ago."

Then he lifted his head and his footstep lightened, and deep in some secret place the thought came proudly, " She shall see that to renounce the world is to possess the world—that a man may be poor and have all the kingdom of the world at his feet!"

He went back by the Underground from Westminster Bridge. It was mid-day and the train was crowded. His spirits were high and he talked with every one near him. Getting out at Victoria he came upon his Vicar on the platform and saluted him rather demonstratively. The Canon responded with some restraint and then stepped into a first-class carriage.

On turning into Eaton Place he came upon a group of people standing around something that lay on the pavement. It was an old woman, a tattered, bedraggled creature, with a pinched and pallid face. " Is it an accident ? " a gentleman was saying, and somebody answered, " No, sir, she's gorn off in a faint." " Why doesn't some one take her to the hospital ? " said the gentleman, and then, like the Levite, he passed by on the other side. The butcher's cart drew up at the curb, and the butcher jumped down, saying, " There never *is* no p'lice about when they're wanted for anythink."

" But they aren't wanted here, friend," said somebody from the outside. It was John Storm, and he was pushing his way through the crowd.

" Will somebody knock at that door, please ? " He lifted the old thing in his arms and carried her towards the Canon's house. The footman looked aghast. " Let me know when the Canon returns," said John, and then marched up the carpeted stairs to his rooms.

An hour afterwards the old woman opened her eyes and said, " Anythink gorn wrong ? Wot's up ? Is it the work'us ? "

It was a clear case of destitution and collapse. John Storm began to feed the old creature with the chicken and milk sent up for his own lunch.

Some time in the afternoon he heard the voice and step of the Vicar in the room below. Going down to the study, he was about to knock, but the voice continued in varying tones, now loud, now low. During a pause he rapped, and then with noticeable irritation the voice cried " Come in."

He found the Vicar, with a manuscript in hand, rehearsing his

Sunday's sermon. It was a shock to John, but it helped him to understand what his uncle had said about the Canon's Pentecost.

The Canon's brow was clouded. "Ah, is it you? I was sorry to see you getting out of a third-class carriage to-day, Mr. Storm."

John answered that it was the poor man's class, and therefore, he thought, it ought to be his.

"You do yourself an injustice, Mr. Storm. Besides, to tell you the truth, I don't choose that my assistant clergy——"

John looked ashamed. "If that is your view, sir," he said, "I don't know what you'll say to what I've been doing since."

"I've heard of it, and I confess I'm not pleased. Whatever your old *protégée* may be, my house is no place for her. I help to maintain charitable institutions for such cases, and I will ask you to lose no time in having her removed to the hospital."

John was crushed. "Very well, sir, if that is your wish; only I thought you said my rooms . . . Besides, the poor old thing fills her place as well as Queen Victoria, and perhaps the angels are watching the one as much as the other."

Next day John Storm called to see the old woman at Martha's Vineyard, and he saw the matron, the house-doctor, and a staff nurse as well. His adventure was known to everybody at the hospital. Once or twice he caught looks of amused compassion and heard a twitter of laughter. As he stood by the bed, the old woman muttered, " I knoo ez it wuzn't the work'us, my dear. He spoke to me friendly and squeedged my 'and."

Coming through the wards, he had looked for a face he could not see, but just then he was aware of a young woman, in the print dress and white apron of a nurse, standing in silence at the bed-head. It was Glory, and her eyes were wet with tears.

"You mustn't do such things," she said hoarsely; "I can't bear it," and she stamped her foot. "Don't you see that these people——"

But she turned about and was gone before he could reply. Glory was ashamed for him! Perhaps she had been taking his part! He felt the blood mounting to his face and his cheeks tingling. Glory! His eyes were swimming, and he dared not look after her, but he could have found it in his heart to kiss the old bag of bones on the bed.

That night he wrote to the parson in the island: "Glory has left off her home garments, and now looks more beautiful than ever in the white simplicity of the costume of the nurse. Her vocation is a great one. God grant she may hold on to it." Then something about the fallacy of ceremonial religion and the impossibility of pleasing God by such religious formalities. "But if we have publicans and Pharisees now, even as

they existed in Christ's time, all the more service is waiting for
that man for whom life has no ambitions, death no terrors. I
thank God I am in a great measure dead to these things. . . .
I will fulfil my promise to look after Glory. My constant prayer
is against Agag. It is so easy for him to get a foothold in a
girl's heart here. This great new world, with its fashions, its
gaieties, its beauty, and its brightness—no wonder if a beautiful
young girl, tingling with life and ruddy health, should burn with
impatience to fling herself into the arms of it. Agag is in
London, and as insinuating as ever."

VI

ON Sunday morning his fellow-curate came to his room to
accompany him to church. The Rev. Joshua Golightly was a
little man with a hook nose, small, keen eyes, scanty hair, and
a voice that was something between a whisper and a whistle.
He bowed subserviently, and made meek little speeches.

"I do trust you will not be disappointed with our church
and service. We do all we can to make them worthy of our
people."

As they walked down the streets he talked first of the
church officers—there were honorary wardens, gentlemen sides-
men, and lady superintendents of floral decorations; then of the
choir, which consisted of organist and choir-master, professional
members, voluntary members, and choir secretary. The anthem
was sung by a professional singer, generally the tenor from the
Opera; the Canon could always get such people—he was a
great favourite with artistes and "the profession." Of course
the singers were paid, and the difficulty this week had been
due to the exorbitant fee demanded by the Italian baritone
from Covent Garden.

Disappointment and disenchantment were falling on John
Storm at every step.

All Saints' was a plain dark structure with a courtyard in front.
The bells were ringing, and a line of carriages was drawing up
at the portico as at the entrance to a theatre, discharging their
occupants and passing on. Vergers in yellow and buff, with
knee-breeches, silk stockings, and powdered wigs, were receiving
the congregation at the doors.

"Let us go in by the west door—I should like you to see the
screen to advantage," said Mr. Golightly.

The inside of the church was gorgeous. As far up as the

clerestory every wall was frescoed, and every timber of the roof was gilded. At the chancel end there was a wrought-iron screen of delicate tracery, and the altar was laden with gold candlesticks. Above the altar and at either side of it were stained glass windows. The morning sun was shining through them, and filling the chancel with warm splashes of light. Ladies in beautiful spring dresses were following the vergers up the aisles.

"This way," the curate whispered, and John Storm entered the sacristy by a low doorway like the auditorium entrance to a stage. There he met some six others of his fellow-curates. They nodded to him and went on arranging their surplices. The choir were gathering in their own quarters, where the violins were tuning up, and the choir boys were laughing and behaving after their kind.

The bell slackened and stopped, and the organ began to play. When all were ready they stepped into a long corridor, and formed in line with their faces to the chancel and their backs to a little door at which a verger in blue stood guard.

"The Canon's room," whispered Mr. Golightly.

A prayer was said by some one, the choir sang the response, and then they walked in procession to their places in the chancel, the choir boys first, the Canon last. Seen through the tracery of the screen, the congregation appeared to fill every sitting in the church with a blaze of light and colour, and the atmosphere was laden with delicate perfume.

The service was choral. An anthem was sung at the close of the sermon, the collection being made during the hymn before it. The professional singer looked like any other chorister in his surplice, save for his swarthy face and heavy moustache.

The Canon preached. He wore his doctor's hood of scarlet cloth. His sermon was eloquent and literary, and it was delivered with elocutionary power. There were many references to great writers, painters, and musicians, including a panegyric on Michael Angelo and a quotation from Browning. The sermon concluded with a passage from Dante in the original.

John Storm was dazed and perplexed. When the service was over he came out alone, returning down the nave, which was now empty but still fragrant. Among other notices pasted on a board in the porch he found this one: "The Vicar and wardens, having learnt with regret that purses have been lost on leaving the church, recommend the congregation to bring only such money as they may need for the offertory."

Had he been to the house of God? No matter! God ruled the world in righteousness and wrought out everything to His own glory.

Next morning he began duty as chaplain at the hospital, and when he had finished the reading of his first prayers he could see that he had lived down some of the derision due to his adventure with the old woman. That poor old bag of bones was sinking and could not last much longer.

Going out by way of the dispensary, he saw Glory again, and heard that she had been to church the day before. It was lovely. All those hundreds of nice-looking people in gay colours, with the rustle of silk and the hum of voices—it was beautiful—it reminded her of the sea in summer. He asked what she thought of the sermon, and she said, " Well, it wasn't religion exactly—not what I call religion—not a 'reg'lar rousing rampage for sowls,' as old Chalse used to say, but——"

" Glory," he said impetuously, " I'm to preach my first sermon on Wednesday."

He did not ask her to come, but inquired if she was on night duty. She answered " no," and then somebody called her.

" She'll be there," he told himself, and he walked home with uplifted head. He would look for her; he would catch her eye; she would see that it was not necessary to be ashamed of him again.

And then close behind, very close, came recollections of her appearance. He could reconstruct her new dress by memory—her face was easy to remember. " After all, beauty is a kind of virtue," he thought; " and all natural friendship is good for the progress of souls if it is built upon the love of God."

He wrote nothing and learned nothing by heart. The only preparation he made for his sermon was thought and prayer. When the Wednesday night came he was very nervous. But the church was nearly empty, and the vergers, who were in their everyday clothes, had only partially lit up the nave. The Canon had done him the honour to be present; his fellow-curates read the prayers and lessons.

As he ascended the pulpit he thought he saw the white bonnets of a group of nurses in the dim distance of one of the aisles, but he did not see Glory, and he dared not look again. His text was " My kingdom is not of this world." He gave it out twice, and his voice sounded strange to himself—so weak and thin in that hollow place.

When he began to speak, his sentences seemed awkward and difficult. The things of the world were temporal, and the nations of the world were out of harmony with God. Men were biting and devouring each other who ought to live as brothers. " Cheat or be cheated," was the rule of life, as a modern philosopher had said. On the one side were the many dying of want, on the other side the few occupied with poetry and art, writing addresses to flowers, and peddling in the portraiture of the moods and methods of love, living lives of frivolity, taking pleasure in mere riches and the lusts of the eye, while thousands of wretched mortals were grovelling in the mire. . . . Then where was our refuge ? . . . The Church was the refuge of God's people . . . from Christ came the answer —the answer—the——"

His words would not flow. He fought hard, threw out another passage, then stammered, began again, stammered again, felt hot, made a fresh effort, flagged, rattled out some words he had fixed in his mind, perspired, lost his voice, and finally stopped in the middle of a sentence and said, "And now to God the Father—" and came down from the pulpit.

His sermon had been a failure, and he knew it. On going back to the sacristy the Reverend Golightly congratulated him with a simper and a vapid smile. The Canon was more honest but more vain. He mingled lofty advice with gentle reproof. Mr. Storm had taken his task too lightly. Better if he had written his sermon and read it. Whatever might serve for the country, congregations in London—at All Saints' especially— expected culture and preparation.

"For my own part I confess—nay, I am proud to declare— my watchword is Rehearse ! Rehearse ! Rehearse !"

As for the doctrine of the sermon it was not above question. It was necessary to live in the *nineteenth* century, and it was impossible to apply to its conditions the rules of life that had been proper to the first.

John Storm made no resistance. He slept badly that night. As often as he dozed off he dreamt that he was trying to do something he could not do, and when he awoke, he became hot as with the memory of a disgrace. And always at the back of his shame was the thought of Glory.

Next morning he was alone in his room and fumbling the toast on his breakfast-table, when the door opened and a cheery voice cried, " May I no come in, laddie ?"

An elderly lady entered. She was tall and slight, and had a long fine face with shrewd but kindly eyes and nearly snow-white hair.

"I'm Jane Callender," she said, "and I couldna wait for an introduction or sic bother, but must just come and see ye. Ay, laddie, it was a bonnie sermon yon ! I havena heard the match of it since I came frae Edinburgh and sat under the good Doctor Guthrie. Now *he* was nae slavish reader neither— none of your paper preachers was Thomas. My word, but you gave us the right doctrine, too! They're given over to the worship of Beelzebub—half these church-going folks. Oh, these Pharisees! They are enough to sour milk. I wish they had one neck, and somebody would just squeeze it. Now, where did you hear that, Jane? But no matter! And the lasses are worse than the men, with their fashions and foldolols. They love Jesus, but they like Him best in heaven, not bothering down in Belgravia. But I must be going my ways. I left James on the street, and there's no living with the man if you keep his horses waiting. Good morning till ye! . . . But eh, laddie, I'm afraid for ye: I'm thinking— I'm thinking . . . but come and see me at Victoria Square. Good morning!"

She had rattled this off at a breath, and had hardly given time for a reply when her black silk was rustling down the stairs.

John Storm remembered that the Canon had spoken of her. She was the good woman who kept the home for girls at Soho.

"The good creature only came to comfort me," he thought. But Glory! What was Glory thinking? That morning, after prayers at the hospital, he went in search of her in the outpatient department, but she pretended to be overwhelmed with work, and only nodded and smiled and excused herself.

"I haven't got a moment this morning, either for the king or his dog. I'm up to my eyes in bandages, and have fourteen plasters on my conscience, and now I must run away to my little boy whose leg was amputated on Saturday."

He understood her, but he came back in the evening and was resolved to face it out.

"What did you think of last night, Glory?" Then she put on a look of blank amazement.

"Why, what happened? Oh, of course—the sermon! How stupid of me! Do you know I forgot all about it?"

"You were not there, then?"

"Don't ask me. Really, I'm ashamed. After my promise to grandfather, too! But Wednesday doesn't count anyway, does it? You'll preach on Sunday . . . and then!"

His feeling of relief was followed by a sense of deeper humiliation. Glory had not even troubled herself to remember. Evidently he was nothing to her—nothing; while she——

He walked home through St. James's Park. Under the tall trees the peaceful silence of the night came down on him. The sharp clack of the streets was deadened to a low hum as of the sea afar off. Across the gardens he could see the clock in the tower of Westminster, and hear the great bell strike the quarters.

London! How little and selfish all personal thoughts were in the contemplation of the mighty city! He had been thinking only of himself and his own little doings. It was all so small and pitiful.

"Did my shame at my failure in the pulpit proceed solely from fear of losing the service of God, or did it proceed from wounded ambition, from pride, from thoughts of Glory——"

But the peaceful stars were over him It was a majestic night.

VII

MARTHA'S VINEYARD.

DEAR AUNTIE RACHEL,—Tell grandpa, to begin with, that John Storm preached his first sermon on Wednesday last, and according to programme I was there to hear it. Oh, God bless me, what a time I had of it! He broke down in the middle, taking stage fright or pulpit fright, or some such devilry, though there was nothing to be afraid of except a bandboxful of chattering girls who didn't listen, and a few old fogies with ear-trumpets. I was sitting in the darkness at the back, effectually concealed from the preacher by the broad shoulders of Ward Sister Allworthy, who is an example of "delicate femalism" just verging on old-maidenism. They tell me the "discoorse" was a short one, but I never got so many prayers into the time in all my born days, and my breath was coming and going so fast that the Sister must have thought they had set up a pumping engine in the pew behind her. Our poor heavy-laden Mr. Storm has been here since then with his sad and eager face, but I hadn't the stuff in me to tell him the truth about the sermon, so I told him I had forgotten to go and hear it, and may the Lord have mercy on my soul!

You want to know how I employ my time? Well, lest you should think I give up my days to dreams and my nights to idleness, I hasten to tell that I rise at 6, breakfast at 6.30, begin duty at 7, sup at 9.30 P.M., gossip till ten, and then go into my room and put myself to bed; and there I am at the end of it. Being only a probationer, I am chiefly in the out-patient department, where my duties are to collect the things wanted at the dispensary, make the patients ready to see the surgeon and pass them on to the dressers. My patients at present are the children, and I love them, and shall break my heart when I have to leave them. They are not always too well looked after by the surgeon, but that doesn't matter in the least, because, you see, they are constantly watched by the best and most learned doctor in the world—that's me.

Last Saturday I had my first experience of the operating theatre. Gracious goodness! I thought I shouldn't survive it. Fortunately I had my dressings and sponges to look after, so I just stiffened my back with a sort of imaginary six-foot steel bar, and went on "like blazes." But some of these staff nurses are just "ter'ble"; they take a professional pleasure in descending to that Inferno, and wouldn't miss a "theatre" for worlds. On Saturday it was a little boy of five who had his leg amputated, and now when you ask the white-faced darling where he's going to, he says he's going to the angels, and he'll get lots of gristly pork up there. He *is* too.

The *personnel* of our vineyard is abundant, but there are various sour grapes about. We have a medical school (containing lots of nice boys, only a girl may not speak to them even in the corridors), and a full staff of honorary and visiting physicians and surgeons. But the only doctor we really have much to do with is the house-surgeon, a young fellow who has just finished his student's course. His name is Abery, and since Saturday he has so much respect for Glory that she might even swear in his presence (in Manx), but Sister Allworthy takes care that she doesn't, having designs on his celibacy herself. He must have sung his *Te Deum* after the operation, for he got gloriously drunk, and wanted to inject morphia in a patient recovering from trouble of the kidney. It was an old hippopotamus of a German musician named Koenig, and he was in frantic terror. So I whispered to him to pretend to go to sleep, and then I told the doctor I had lost the syringe. But—"Gough bless me sowl!"—what a dressing the Sister gave me!

Yesterday was visiting-day, and when the friends of the patients come, even an hospital can have its humours. They try to sneak in little dainties, which may be delicious in themselves, but are deadly poison for the people they are intended for. Then we have to search under the bed-clothes of the patients and even feel the pockets of their visitors. The mother of my little boy came yesterday, and I noticed such a large protuberance at her bosom under her ulster that I began to foresee another operation. It was only a brick of currant cake paved with lemon peel. I hauled it out and moved round like a cloud of thunder and lightning. But she began to cry and to say she had made it herself for Johnnie, and then—well, didn't I just get a wigging from the Sister though!

But I don't mind what happens here, for I am in London, and to be in London is to live, and to live is to be in London. I've

not seen much of it yet, having only two hours off duty every
day, from ten to twelve, and then all I can do is to make little
dips into the Park and the district round about, like a new pigeon
with its wings clipped. But I watch the great new world from
my big box up here, and see the carriages in the Park, and the
people riding on horseback. They have a new handshake in
London. You lift your hand to the level of your shoulder, and
then waggle horizontally as if you had put your elbow out; and
when you begin to speak you say, "I—er," as if you had got the
mumps. But it is beautiful! The sound of the traffic is like
music, and I feel like a war-horse that wants to be marching to
it. How delightful it is to be young in a world so full of loveliness! And if you are not very ugly, it's none the worse.

All hospital nurses are just now basking in the sunshine of a
forthcoming ball. It is to be given at Bartimaeus's Hospital, where
they have a lecture-theatre larger than the common, and the
dancing there is for once to be to a happier tune. All the earth
is to be present—all the hospital earth; and if I could afford to
array myself in the necessary splendour, I should show this
benighted London what an absolute angel Glory is! But then
my first full holiday is to be on the 24th, when I expect to be
out from 10 A.M. until 10 P.M. I am nearly crazy whenever I
think of it; and when the time comes to make my first plunge
into London, I know I shall hold my breath exactly as if I were
taking a header off Creg Malin Rocks. . . .

GLORY.

VIII

ON the morning of the 24th Glory rose at five, that she might
get through her work and have the entire day for her holiday.
At that hour she came upon a rough-haired nurse, wearing her
cap a little on one side, and washing a floor with disinfectants.
Being in great spirits, Glory addressed her cheerfully.

"Are you off to-day, too?" she said.

The nurse gave her a contemptuous glance, and answered—

"I'm not one of your paying probationers, miss—playing probationers, *I* call them. We nurses are hard-working women,
whose life spells duty, and we've got no time for sight-seeing and
holiday-making."

"No, but you are one of those who ruin the profession altogether," said a younger woman who had just come up. "They
will expect everybody to do the same. This is my day off, but
I have to do the grate, and sweep the ward, and make the bed,

and tidy the Sister's room; and it's all through people like you. Small thanks you get for it either, for a girl may not even wear her hair in a fringe, and she is always expecting to hear the matron's, 'You're not fit for nursing, miss.'"

Glory looked at her. She was an exquisitely pretty girl, with dark hair, pink and ivory cheeks, and light grey eyes, but her hands were coarse, and her finger-nails flat and square; and when you looked again there was a certain blemished appearance about her beauty as of a Sèvres vase that is cracked somewhere.

"Do you say you are off to-day?" said Glory.

"Yes, I am; are you?"

"Yes, but I am strange to London. Could you take me with you, if you are going nowhere in particular?"

"Certainly, dear. I've noticed you before, and wanted to speak to you. You're the girl with the splendid name—Glory, isn't it?"

"Yes; what is yours?"

"Polly Love."

At ten o'clock that morning the two girls set out for their long day's jaunt.

"Now, where shall we go?" said Polly.

"Let us go where we can see a great many people," said Glory.

"That's easy enough, for this is the Queen's birthday, and——"

Glory thought of Aunt Rachel, and made a cry of delight.

"And now that I think of it," said Polly, as if by a sudden memory, "I've got tickets for the trooping of the colours—the Queen's colours, you know."

"Shall we see her?" said Glory.

"What a question! Why, no; but we'll see the soldiers and the generals, and perhaps the Prince. It's at 10.30, and only across the Park."

"Come along," said Glory; and she began to drag at her companion and to run.

"My gracious, what a girl you are, to be sure!"

But they were both running in another minute, and laughing and chattering like children escaped from school. In a quarter of an hour they were at the entrance to the Horse Guards. There was a crowd at the gates, and a policeman was taking tickets. Polly dived into her pocket.

"Where are mine? Oh, here they are. A great friend gave me them," she whispered. "He has a chum in one of those offices."

"A gentleman?" said Glory with studied politeness; but

they were crushing through the gate by that time, and thereafter she had eyes and ears for nothing but the pageant before her.

It was a beautiful morning, and the spring foliage of the Park was very green and fresh. Three sides of the great square were lined with redcoats; the square itself was thronged with people, and every window and balcony looking over it was filled. There were soldiers, sentries, policemen, the generals in cocked hats, and the Prince himself in a bearskin, riding by with the jingle of spurs and curb-chain. Then the ta-ra-ta-ta-ra of the bugle, the explosive voice crying "Escort for the colour," the officer carrying it, the white gloves of the staff fluttering up the salute, the flash of bayonets, the march round, and the band playing "The British Grenadiers." It was like a dream to Glory. She felt her bosom heaving and was afraid she was going to cry.

Polly was laughing and prattling merrily. "Ha, ha, ha! see that soldier chasing a sunshade? My! he has caught it with his sword."

"I suppose these are all great people," whispered Glory.

"I should think so," said Polly. "Do you see that gentleman in the window opposite?—that's the Foreign Office."

"Which?" said Glory, but her eyes were wandering.

"The one in the frock-coat and the silk hat talking to the lady in the green lawn and the black lace fichu and the spring bonnet."

"You mean beside that plain girl wearing the jungle of rhododendrons?"

"Yes; that's the gentleman who gave my friend the tickets."

Glory looked at him for a moment, and something very remote seemed to stir in her memory, but the band was playing once more and she was wafted away again. It was "God Save the Queen" this time, and when it ended and everybody cried "All over," she took a long, deep breath and said, "*Well!*"

Polly was laughing at her, and Glory had to laugh also. They set each other off laughing, and people began to look at them, and then they had to laugh again and run away.

"This Glory is the funniest girl," said Polly; "she is surprised at the simplest thing."

They went to look at the shops, passing up Regent Street, across the Circus, and down Oxford Street towards the City, laughing and talking nonsense all the time. Once when they made a little purchase at a shop the shopwoman looked astonished at the freedom with which they carried themselves, and after that they felt inclined to go into every shop in the street and behave absurdly everywhere. In the course of two hours they had accomplished all the innocent follies possible to the intoxication of youth, and were perfectly happy.

By this time they had reached the Bank and were feeling the prickings of hunger, so they looked out a restaurant in Cheapside and went in for some dinner. The place was full of men, and several of them rose at once when the two girls entered. They were in the outdoor hospital costume, but there was something showy about Polly's toilet, and the men kept looking their way and smiling. Glory looked back boldly, and said in an audible voice, "What fun it must be to be a barmaid, and to have the gentlemen wink at you, and be laughing back at them!" But Polly nudged her and told her to be quiet. She looked down herself, but nevertheless contrived to use her eyes as a kind of furtive electric battery in the midst of the most innocent conversation. It was clear that Polly had flown farthest in the ways of the world, and when you looked at her again you could see that the balance of her life had been deranged by some one.

After dinner the girls got into an omnibus and went still farther east, sitting at opposite sides of the car, and laughing and talking loudly to each other amid the astonishment of the other occupants. But when they came to mean and ugly streets with greengrocers' barrows by the curbstone, and weird and dreary cemeteries in the midst of gaunt green sticks that were trying to look like trees, Glory thought they had better return.

They went back by the Thames steamboat from some landing-stage among the docks. The steamer picked up passengers at every station on the river, and at London Bridge a band came aboard. As they sailed under St. Paul's the boat was crowded with people going west to see the celebrations in honour of the birthday, and the band was playing "And her golden hair was hanging down her back."

At one moment Glory was wild with delight, and at the next her gaiety seemed to be suddenly extinguished. The sun was setting behind the towers of Westminster in a magnificent lake of fire, and it seemed like the sun going down at Peel, except that the lights beneath, which glistened and flashed, were windows, not waves, and the deep hum was not the noise of the mighty sea, but the noise of mighty millions.

They landed at Westminster Bridge and went to a tea-room for tea. When they came out it was quite dark, and they got on to the top of an omnibus. But the town was now ablaze with gas and electric lights that were flinging out the initials of the Queen, and Whitehall was dense with carriages going to the official receptions. Glory wanted to be in the midst of so much life, so the girls got down and walked arm in arm.

As they passed through Piccadilly Circus they were laughing again, for the oppression of the crowds made them happy. The throng was greatest at that point and they had to push their way through. Among others, there were many gaily-dressed women who seemed to be waiting for omnibuses. Glory noticed that two of these women, who were grimacing and lisping, had spoken to a man who was also lounging about. She tugged at Polly's arm.

"That's strange! Did you see that?" she said.

"That! Oh, that's nothing. It's done every day," said Polly.

"What does it mean?" said Glory.

"Why, you don't mean to say . . . Well, this Glory . . . Really your friends ought to take care of you, my dear, you are so ignorant of the world."

And then suddenly, as by a flash of lightning, Glory had her first glimpse of the tragic issues of life.

"Oh, my gracious! come along," she whispered, and dragged Polly after her.

They were panting past the end of St. James's Street, when a man with an eyeglass and a great shield of shirt-front collided with them and saluted them. Glory was for forging ahead, but Polly had drawn up.

"It's only my friend," said Polly in another voice. "This is a new nurse. Her name is Glory."

The man said something about a glorious name and a glorious pleasure to be nursed by such a nurse, and then both the girls laughed. He was glad they had found his tickets useful, but sorry he could not see them back to the hospital, being dragged away to the bally Foreign Office reception in honour of the Queen's birthday.

"But I'm coming to the ball, you know, and," with a glance at Glory, "I've half a mind to bring my chum along with me."

"Oh, do," said Polly, partly covering the pupils of her eyes with her eyelids.

The man lowered his voice and said something about Glory which Glory did not catch, then waved his white kid glove, saying "Ta-ta," and was gone.

"Is he married?" said Glory.

"Married! Good gracious, no; what ridiculous ideas you've got!"

It was ten minutes after ten as the girls turned in at a sharp trot at the door of the hospital, still prattling and chattering and bringing some of the gaiety and nonsense of their holiday into the quiet precincts of the house of pain. The porter shook his finger at them with mock severity, and a ward Sister going through the porch in her white silence stopped to say that a patient had been crying out for one of them.

"It's me I know it's me," said Polly. "I've got a brother here out of a monastery, and he can't do with anybody else about him. It makes me tired of my life."

But it was Glory who was wanted. The woman whom John Storm had picked up out of the streets was dying. Glory had helped to nurse her, and the poor old thing had kept herself alive that she might deliver to Glory her last charge and message. She could see nobody, so Glory leaned over the bed and spoke to her.

"I'm here, mammie; what is it?" she said, and the flushed young face bent close above the withered and white one.

"He spoke to me friendly and squeedged my 'and, he did. S'elp me never, it's true. Gimme a black cloth on the corfin, my dear, and mind yer tell 'im to foller."

"Yes, mammie, yes; I will—be sure I—I—— Oh!"

It was Glory's first death.

IX

JOHN STORM had been through his first morning call that afternoon. For this ordeal he had presented himself in a flannel shirt in the hall, where the Canon was waiting for him in patent-leather boots and kid gloves, and his daughter Felicity in cream silk and white feathers. After they had seated themselves in the carriage, the Canon said, "You don't quite do yourself justice, Mr. Storm. Believe me, to be well dressed is a great thing to a young man making his way in London."

The carriage stopped at a house that seemed to be only round the corner.

"This is Mrs. Macrae's," the Canon whispered. "An American lady—widow of a millionaire. Her daughter—you will see her presently—is to marry into one of our best English families."

They were walking up the wide staircase behind the footman in blue. There was a buzz of voices coming from a room above.

"Canon—er—Wealthy, Miss Wealthy, and—er—the h'm . . . Rev. Mr. Storm!"

The buzz of voices abated, and a bright-faced little woman, showily dressed, came forward and welcomed them with a marked accent. There were several other ladies in the room, but only one gentleman. This person, who was standing, with teacup and saucer in hand, at the farther side, screwed an eyeglass in his eye, looked across at John Storm, and then said something to the lady in the chair beside him. The lady tittered a little. John Storm looked back at the man, as if by an instinctive certainty that he must know him when he saw him again. He was engulfed in a high, stiff collar, and was rather ugly; tall, slender, a little past thirty; fair, with soft, sleepy eyes, and no life in his expression, but agreeable; fit for good society, with the stamp of good-breeding, and capable of saying little humorous things in a thin "roofy" voice.

"I was real sorry I didn't hear Mr. Storm Wednesday evening," Mrs. Macrae was saying with a mincing smile. "My daughter told me it was just too lovely. Mercy, this is your great preacher. Persuade him to come to my 'At Home' Tuesday."

A tall, dark girl, with gentle manners and a beautiful face, came slowly forward, put her hand into John's, and looked steadily into his eyes without speaking. Then the gentleman with the eyeglass said suavely, "Have you been long in London, Mr. Storm?"

"Two weeks," John answered shortly, and half turned his head.

"How—er—interesting!" with a prolonged drawl and a little cold titter.

"Oh, Lord Robert Ure—Mr. Storm," said the hostess.

"Mr. Storm has done me the honour to become one of my assistant clergy, Lord Robert," said the Canon, "but he is not likely to be a curate long."

"That is charming," said Lord Robert. "It is always a relief to hear that I am likely to have one candidate the less for my poor perpetual curacy in Pimlico. They're at me like flies round a honey-pot, don't you know. I thought I had made the acquaintance of all the perpetual curates in Christendom. And what a sweet team they are, to be sure! The last of them came yesterday. I was out, and my friend Drake—Drake of the Home Office, you know—couldn't give the man the living, so he gave him sixpence instead, and the creature went away quite satisfied."

Everybody seemed to laugh except John (who only stared into the air), and the loudest laughter came from the Canon. But suddenly an incisive voice said—

"But why sharpen your teeth on the poor curates? Is there no a canon or a bishop handy that's better worth a bite?"

It was Mrs. Callender.

"I'll tell ye a story too, only *mine* shall be a true one."

"Jane! Jane!" said the hostess, shaking her fan as a weapon; and Lord Robert stretched his neck over his collar and made an amiable smile.

"A girl of eighteen came to me this morning at Soho, and she was in the usual trouble. The father was a wicked rector. He died last year leaving thirty-one thousand pounds, and the mother of his unfortunate child, that is to say his mistress, is now in the Union."

It was the first sincere word that had been spoken, where every tone had been wrong, every gesture false, and it fell on the company like a thunderclap. John Storm drew his breath hard, looked up at Lord Robert by a strange impulse, and felt himself avenged.

"What a beautiful day it has been," said somebody.

Everybody looked up at the maker of this surprising remark. It was a lady, and she blushed until her cheeks burned again.

A painful silence followed, and then the hostess turned to Lord Robert and said—

"You spoke of your friend Drake, didn't you? Everybody is talking of him, and as for the girls they seem to be crazy about the man. So handsome, they say, so natural, and such a splendid talker. But then girls are so quick to take fancies to people. You really must take care of yourself, my dear." (This to Felicity.) "Who is he? Lord Robert will tell you—an official of some kind, and son of Sir something Drake of one of the northern counties. He knows the secret of getting on in the world, though—he doesn't go about too much. But I've determined not to live any longer without making the acquaintance of this wonderful being, so Lord Robert must just bring him along Tuesday evening or else——"

John Storm escaped at last, without promising to come to the "At Home." He went direct to the hospital, and learned that Glory was out for the day. Where she could have gone, and what she could be doing, puzzled him grievously. That she had not put herself under his counsel and direction on her first excursion abroad hurt his pride and wounded his sense of responsibility. As the night fell his anxiety increased. Though he knew she would not return until ten he set out at nine to meet her.

At a venture he took the eastward course, and passed slowly down Piccadilly. The façade of nearly every club facing the Park was flaming with electric light. Young men in evening dress were standing on the steps, smoking, and taking the air after dinner, and pretty girls in showy costumes were promenading leisurely in front of them. Sometimes as a girl passed she looked sharply up, and the corner of her mouth would be raised a little, and when she had gone by there would be a general burst of laughter.

John's blood boiled, and then his heart sank; he felt so helpless, his pity and indignation were so useless and unnecessary. All at once he saw what he had been looking for. As he went by the corner of St. James's Street, he almost ran against Glory and another nurse in the costume of their hospital. They did not observe him, they were talking to a man; it was the man he had met in the afternoon, Lord Robert Ure.

John heard the man say, "Your Glory is such a glorious——" and then he lowered his voice, and appeared to say something that was very amusing, for the other girl laughed a great deal.

John's soul was now fairly in revolt, and he wanted to stop, to order the man off and to take charge of the two nurses, as his duty seemed to require of him. But he passed them, then looked back and saw the group separate, and as the man went by he watched the girls going westward. There was a glimpse of them under the gas-lamp as they crossed the street, and again a glimpse as they passed into the darkness under the trees of the Park.

He could not trust himself to return to the hospital that night, and his indignation was no less in the morning. But there was a letter from Glory saying that his poor old friend was dead, and had begged that he would bury her. He dressed himself in his best ("We can't take liberties with the poor," he thought) and walked across to the hospital at once. There he asked for Glory, and they went downstairs together to that chill chamber underground which has always its cold and silent occupant. It is only a short tenancy that anybody can have there, so the old woman had to be buried the same morning. The parish was to bury her, and the van was at the door.

He was standing with Glory in the hall, and his heart had softened to her.

"Glory," he said, "you shouldn't have gone out yesterday without telling me—the dangers of London are so great."

"What dangers?" she asked.

"Well, to a young girl, a beautiful girl——"

Glory peered up under her long eyelashes.

"I mean the dangers from—I'm ashamed in my soul to say it—the dangers from men."

She shot up a quick glance into his face and said in a moment, "You saw us, didn't you?"

"Yes, I saw you, and I didn't like your choice of company."

She dropped her head demurely and said, "The man?"

John hesitated. "I was speaking of the girl. I don't like the freedom with which she carries herself in this house. Among these good and devoted women is there no one but this . . . this——"

Glory's lower lip began to show its inner side. "She's bright and lively—that's all I care."

"But it's not all *I* care, Glory, and if such men as that are her friends outside ——"

Glory's head went up. "What is it to me who are her friends outside?"

"Everything, if you allow yourself to meet them again."

"Well," doggedly, "I *am* going to meet them again. I'm going to the nurses' ball on Tuesday."

John answered with deliberation, "Not in that girl's company."

"Why not?"

"I say *not* in that girl's company."

There was a short pause, and then Glory said with a quivering mouth, "You are vexing me, and you will end by making me cry. Don't you see you are degrading me too? I am not used to being degraded. You see me with a weak silly creature who hasn't an idea in her head, and can do nothing but giggle and laugh and make eyes at men, and you think I'm going to be led away by her. Do you suppose a girl can't take care of herself?"

"As you will, then," said John, with a fling of his hand, going off down the steps.

"Mr. Storm—Mr. Storm—Jo—Joh——"

But he was out on the pavement and getting into the workhouse van.

"Ah!" said a mincing voice beside her. "How jolly it is when anybody is suffering for your sake!" It was Polly Love, and again her eyelids were half covering her eyes.

"I'm sure I don't know what you mean," said Glory; her own eyes were swimming in big tear-drops.

"Don't you? What a funny girl you are! But your education has been neglected, my dear."

It was a combination van and hearse with the coffin under the driver's box, and John Storm (as the only discoverable mourner) with the undertaker on the seat inside.

"Will ye be willin' ter tyke the service at the cimitery, sir?" said the undertaker, and John answered that he would.

The grave was on the paupers' side, and when the undertaker, with his man, had lowered the coffin to its place, he said, "They've gimme abart three more funerals this morning, so I'll leave ye now, sir, to finish 'er off."

At the next moment John Storm in his surplice was alone with the dead, and had opened his book to read the burial service which no other human ear was to hear.

He read "Dust to dust, ashes to ashes," and then the bitter loneliness of the pauper's doom came down on his soul and silenced him.

But his imprisoned passion had to find a vent, and that night he wrote to the Prime Minister: "I begin to understand what you meant when you said I was in the wrong place. Oh, this London, with its society, its worldly clergy, its art, its literature, its luxury, its idle life, all built on the toil of the country and compounded of the sweat of the nameless poor! Oh, this 'Circe of cities,' drawing good people to it, decoying them, seducing them, and then turning them into swine! It seems impossible to live in the world and to be spiritually-minded. When I try to do so I am torn in two."

X

On the following Tuesday evening two young men were dining in their chambers in St. James's Street. One of them was Lord Robert Ure; the other was his friend and house-mate, Horatio Drake. Drake was younger than Lord Robert by some seven or eight years, and also beyond comparison more attractive. His face was manly and handsome, its expression was open and breezy; he was broad-shouldered and splendidly built, and he had the fair hair and blue eyes of a boy.

Their room was a large one, and it was full of beautiful and valuable things, but the furniture was huddled about in disorder. A large chamber-organ, a grand piano, a mandoline and two violins, pictures on the floor as well as on the walls, many photographs scattered about everywhere, and the mirror over the mantelpiece fringed with invitation cards, which were stuck between the glass and the frame.

Their man had brought in the coffee and cigarettes. Lord Robert was speaking in his weary drawl, which had the worn-out tone of a man who had made a long journey and was very sleepy.

"Come, dear boy, make up your mind, and let us be off."

"But I'm tired to death of these fashionable routs."

"So am I."

"They're so unnatural—so unnecessary."

"My dear fellow, of course they're unnatural—of course they're unnecessary; but what would you have?"

"Anything human and natural," said Drake. "I don't care a ha'p'orth about the morality of these things—not I—but I am dead-sick of their stupidity."

Lord Robert made languid puffs of his cigarette, and said, in a tearful drawl, "My dear Drake, of course it is exactly as you say. Who doesn't know it's so. It has always been so, and always will be. But what refuge is there for the poor leisured people but these diversions which you despise? And as for the poor titled classes—well, they manage to make their play their business sometimes, don't you know. Confess that they do sometimes, now, eh?"

Lord Robert was laughing with an awkward constraint; but Drake looked frankly into his face and said—

"How's that matter going on, Robert?"

"Fairly, I think, though the girl is not very hot on it. The thing came off last week, and when it was over I felt as if I had proposed to the girl and been accepted by the mother, don't you know. I believe this rout to-night is expressly in honour of the event, so I mustn't run away from my bargain."

He lay back, sent funnels of smoke to the ceiling, and then said, with a laugh like a gurgle, "I'm not likely to, though. That eternal dun was here again to-day. I had to tell him that the marriage would come off in a year certain. That was the only understanding on which he would agree to wait for his money. . . . Bad? Of course it's bad; but what would you have, dear boy?"

The men smoked in silence for a moment, and then Lord Robert said again, "Come, old fellow, for friendship's sake, if nothing else. She's a decent little woman, and dead bent on having you at her house to-night. And if you're badly bored we'll not stay long. We'll come away early, and . . . listen!—we'll slip across to the nurses' ball at Bartimæus's Hospital—there'll be fun enough there, at all events."

"I'll go," said Drake.

Half-an-hour later the two young men were driving up to the door of Mrs. Macrae's house in Belgrave Square. There was a line of carriages in front of it, and they had to wait their turn to approach the gate. Footmen in gorgeous livery were ready to open the cab-door, to help the guests across the red baize that lay on the pavement, to usher them into the hall, to lead them to the little marble chamber where they entered their names in a list intended for the next day's *Morning Post*, and finally to direct them to the great staircase where the general crush moved slowly up to the saloon above.

In the well of the stairs, half hidden behind a little forest of palms and ferns, a band in yellow and blue uniform sat playing the people in. On the landing the hostess stood waiting to receive, and many of the guests, by a rotary movement like the waters of a maelstrom, moved past her in a rapid and babbling stream, twisted about her and came down again. She welcomed Lord Robert effusively, and motioned to him to stand by her side. Then she introduced her daughter to Drake, and sent them adrift through the rooms.

The rooms were large ones with parquet flooring, from which all furniture had been removed, except the palms and ferns by the walls and the heavy chandeliers overhead. It was not yet ten o'clock, but already the house was crowded, and every moment there were floods of fresh arrivals. First came statesmen and diplomatists, then people who had been to the theatres, and towards the end of the evening some of the actors themselves. The night was close and the atmosphere hot and oppressive. At the farther end of the suite there was a refreshment-room, with its lantern lights pulled open; and there the crush was densest and the commotion greatest. The click-clack of many voices cut the thick air as with a thousand knives, and over the multitudinous clatter there was always the unintelligible boom of the band downstairs.

Most of the guests looked tired. The men made some effort to be cheerful, but the women were frankly jaded and fagged. Bedizened with diamonds, coated with paint and powder, laden with rustling silks, they looked weary and worn out. When spoken to they would struggle to smile, but the smiles would break down after a moment into dismal looks of misery and oppression.

"Had enough?" whispered Lord Robert to Drake.

Drake was satisfied, and Lord Robert began to make their excuses.

"Going already!" said Mrs. Macrae. "An official engagement, you say? Mr. Drake, is it? Oh, don't tell me! I know —*I* know! Well, you'll be married and settled one of these days—and then!"

They were in a hansom-cab driving across London in the direction of Bartimæus's Hospital. Drake was bareheaded and fanning himself with his crush-hat. Lord Robert was lighting a cigarette.

"Pshaw! What a stifling den! Did you ever hear such a clitter-clatter? A perfect Tower of Babel building company! What in the name of common sense do people suppose they're doing by penning themselves up like that on a night like this? What are they thinking about?"

"Thinking about, dear boy? You're unreasonable! Nobody wants to think about anything in such scenes of charming folly."

"But the women! Did you ever see such faded, worn-out dummies for the display of diamonds? Poor little women in their splendid misery! I was sorry for your *fiancée*, Robert. She was the only woman in the house without that hateful stamp of worldliness and affectation."

"My dear Drake, you've learned many things, but there's one thing you have not yet learned—you haven't learned how to take serious things as trifles and trifles as serious things. Learn it, my boy, or you'll embitter existence. You are not going to alter the conditions of civilisation by any change in your own particular life; so just look out the prettiest, wittiest, wealthiest little woman who is a dummy for the display of diamonds——"

"Me? Not if I know it, old fellow! Give me a little nature and simplicity, if it hasn't got a second gown to its back."

"All right—as you like," said Lord Robert, flinging out the end of his cigarette. "You've got the pull of some of us—you can please yourself. And here we are at old Bartimæus's, and this is a very different pair of shoes!"

They were driving out of one of London's main thoroughfares, through a groined archway, into one of London's ancient buildings with its quiet quadrangle where trees grow and birds sing. Every window of the square was lighted up, and there was a low murmur of music being played within.

"Listen," said Lord Robert. "I am here ostensibly as the guest of the visiting physician, don't you know, but really in the interests of the little friend I told you off."

"The one I got the tickets for last week?"

"Precisely."

At the next moment they were in the ball-room. It was the lecture-theatre for the students of the hospital school—a building detached from the wards, and of circular shape, with a gallery round its walls, which were festooned with flags and roofed with a glass dome. Some two hundred girls and as many men were gathered there; the pit was their dancing-ring and the gallery was their withdrawing-room. The men were nearly all students of the medical schools, the girls were nearly all nurses, and they wore their uniform. There was not one jaded face among them —not one weary look or tired expression. They were in the fulness of youth and the height of vigour. The girls laughed with the ring of joy, their eyes sparkled with the light of happiness, their cheeks glowed with the freshness of health.

The two men stood a moment and looked on.

"Well, what do you think of it?" said Lord Robert.
Drake's wide eyes were ablaze and his voice came in gusts.
"Think of it!" he said. "It's wonderful! It's glorious!"
Lord Robert's glass had dropped from his eye and he was laughing in his drawling way.
"What are you laughing at? Women like these are at least natural, and nature cannot be put on."
The mazurka had just finished and the dancers were breaking into groups.
"Robert, tell me, who is that girl over there—the one looking this way? Is it your friend?"
Lord Robert readjusted his glass.
"The pretty dark girl with the pink and white cheeks like a doll?"
"Yes, and the taller one beside her—all hair and eyes and bosom. She's looking across now. I've seen that girl before somewhere. Now, where have I seen her? Look at her—what fire and life and movement! The dance is over, but she can't keep her feet still."
"I see—I see. But let me introduce you to the matron and doctors first, and then——"
"I know now—I know where I've seen her! Be quick, Robert—be quick!"
Lord Robert laughed again in his tired drawl. He was finding it very amusing.

XI

When Glory learned that all nurses eligible to attend the ball were to wear hospital uniform, being on day duty, she decided to go to it. But then came John Storm's protest against the company of Polly Love, and she felt half inclined to give it up. As often as she remembered his remonstrance she was disturbed, and once or twice when alone she shed tears of anger and vexation.

Meantime Polly was full of arrangements, and Glory found herself day by day carried along in the stream of preparation. When the night came the girls dressed in the same cubicle. Polly was prattling like a parrot, but Glory was silent, and almost sad.

By help of the curling-tongs and a candle, Polly did up her dark hair into little knowing curls that went in and out on her temples and played hide-and-seek around the pretty shells of her pink and white ears. Glory was slashing the comb through her golden red hair by way of preliminary ploughing, when Polly cried, "Stop! Don't touch it any more, for goodness' sake! It's perfect! Look at yourself now."

Glory stood off from the looking-glass and looked. "Am I really so nice?" she thought; and then she remembered John Storm again, and had half a mind to tear down her glorious curls and go straight away to bed.

She went to the ball instead, and being there, she forgot all about her misgivings. The light, the colour, the brilliance, the perfume transported her to an enchanted world which she had never entered before. She could not control her delight in it. Everything surprised her, everything delighted her, everything amused her—she was the very soul of girlish joy. The dark-brown spot on her eye shone out with a coquettish light never seen in it until now, and the warble in her voice was like the music of a happy bird. Her high spirits were infectious—her light-hearted gaiety communicated itself to everybody. The men who might not dance with her were smiling at the mere sight of the sunshine in her face, and it was even whispered about that the President of the College of Surgeons, who opened the ball, had said that her proper place was not there—a girl like that young Irish nurse would do honour to a higher assembly.

In that enchanted world of music and light and bright and happy faces Glory lost all sense of time; but two hours had passed when Polly Love, whose eyes had turned again and again to the door, tugged at her sleeve and whispered, "They've come at last! There they are—there—directly opposite to us. Keep your next dance, dear. They'll come across presently."

Glory looked where Polly had directed, and, seeing again the face she had seen in the window at the Foreign Office, something remote and elusive once more stirred in her memory. But it was gone in a moment, and she was back in that world of wonders, when a voice which she knew and yet did not know, like a voice that called to her as she was awakening out of a sleep, said—

"Glory, don't you remember me? Have you forgotten me, Glory?"

It was her friend of the Catechism class—her companion of the adventure in the boat. Their hands met in a long handclasp with the gallop of feeling that is too swift for thought.

"Ah, I thought you would recognise me! How delightful!" said Drake.

"And you knew me again?" said Glory.

"Instantly—at first sight almost."

"Really! It's strange, though. Such a long, long time—ten years at least! I must have changed since then."

"You have," said Drake—"you've changed very much."

"Indeed, now! Am I really so much changed, for all? I've grown older, of course."

"Oh, terribly older!" said Drake.

"How wrong of me! But you have changed a good deal, too. You were only a boy in jackets then."

"And you were only a girl in short frocks."

They both laughed, and then Drake said, "I'm so glad we've changed together!"

"Are you?" said Glory.

"Why, yes," said Drake; "for if you had changed and I hadn't——"

"But what nonsense we're talking!" said Glory; and they both laughed again.

Then they told each other what had happened in that infinite cycle of time which had spun round since they parted. Glory had not much to narrate: her life had been empty. She had been in the Isle of Man all along, had come to London only recently, and was now a probationer-nurse at Martha's Vineyard. Drake had gone to Harrow and thence to Oxford, and being a man of artistic leanings, had wished to take up music, but his father had seen no career in it; so he had submitted—he had entered the subterranean catacombs of public life, and was secretary to one of the Ministers. All this he talked of lightly, as became a young man of the world to whom great things were of small account.

"Glory," said Polly at her elbow, "the waltz is going to begin."

The band was preluding. Drake claimed the dance, and Glory was astonished to find she had it free (she had kept it expressly).

When the waltz was over he gave her his arm and led her into the circular corridor to talk and to cool. His manners were perfect, and his voice, so soft and yet so manly, increased the charm. In passing out of the hot dancing-room she threw her handkerchief over her head, and, with the hand that was at liberty, held its ends under her chin. She wished him to look at her and see what change this had made; so she said, quite innocently—

"And now let me look at you again, sir!"

He recognised the dark-brown spot on her eye, and he could feel her arm through her thin print dress.

"You've told me a good deal," he said, "but you haven't said a syllable about the most important thing of all."

"And pray what is that?" said she.

"How many times have you fallen in love since I saw you last?"

"Good gracious, what a question!" said Glory.

His audacity was delightful. There was something so gracious and yet so masterful about him.

"Do you remember the day you carried me off—eloped with me, you know?" said Drake.

"I? How charming of me! But when was that, I wonder?" said Glory.

"Never mind; say, do you remember?"

"Well, if I do? What a pair of little geese we must have been in those days!"

"I'm not so sure of that—*now*," said he.

"You didn't seem very keen about me *then*, as far as I can remember," said she.

"Didn't I?" said he. "What a silly young fool I must have been!"

They laughed again. She could not keep her arm still, and he could almost feel its dimpled elbow.

"And do *you* remember the gentleman who rescued us?" she said.

"You mean the tall dark young man who kept hugging and kissing you in the yacht!"

"Did he?"

"Do you forget that kind of thing, then?"

"It was very sweet of him. But he's in the Church now, and the chaplain of our hospital."

"What a funny little romantic world it is, to be sure!" said Drake.

"Yes; it's like poetry, isn't it?" she answered.

Lord Robert came up to introduce Drake to Polly (who was not looking her sweetest), and he claimed Glory for the next dance.

"So you knew my friend Drake before?" said Lord Robert.

"I knew him when he was a boy," said Glory.

And then he began to sing his friend's praises; how he had taken a brilliant degree at Oxford, and was now private secretary to the Home Secretary, and would go into public life before long; how he could paint and act, and might have made a reputation as a musician; how he went into the best houses, and was a first-rate official; how, in short, he had the Promised Land before him, and was just on the eve of entering it.

"Then I suppose you know he is rich—enormously rich?" said Lord Robert.

"Is he?" said Glory, and something great and grand seemed to shimmer a long way off.

"Enormously," said Lord Robert; "and yet a man of the most democratic opinions."

"Really?" said Glory.

"Yes," said Lord Robert; "and all the way down in the hansom he has been trying to show me how impossible it is to him to marry a lady."

"Now why did you tell me that, I wonder?" said Glory; and Lord Robert began to fidget with his eyeglass.

Drake returned with Polly. He proposed that they should take the air in the quadrangle, and they went off for that purpose, the girls arm-in-arm some paces ahead.

"There's a dash of Satan himself in that red-headed girl," said Lord Robert. "She understands a man before he understands himself."

"She's as natural as nature," said Drake. "And what lips— what a mouth!"

"Irish, isn't she? Oh, Manx! What's Manx, I wonder?"

The night was very warm and close, and there was hardly more air in the courtyard. The sound of the band came to them there, and Glory, who had danced with nearly everybody within, must needs dance by herself without, because the music was more sweet and subdued out there, and dancing in the darkness was like a dream.

"Come and sit down on the seat, Glory," said Polly fretfully; "you are getting on my nerves, dear."

"Glory," said Drake, "how do the Londoners strike you?"

"Much like other mortals," said Glory—"no better, no worse —only funnier."

The men laughed at that description; and Glory proceeded to give imitations of London manners—the high handshake, the "ha-ha" of the mumps, the mouthing of the Canon, and the mincing of Mr. Golightly.

Drake bellowed with delight; Lord Robert drawled out a long owlish laugh; Polly Love said spitefully, "You might give us your friend the new curate next, dearest;" and then Glory went down like a shot.

"Really," began Drake, "it's not hospital nursing, you know——"

But there were low murmurings of thunder and some large splashes of rain, and they returned to the ball-room. The doctors and the matrons were gone by this time; only the nurses and the students remained, and the fun was becoming furious. One young student was pulling down a girl's hair, and another was waltzing with his partner carried bodily in his arms. Somebody lowered the lights, and they danced in a shadow-land; somebody began to sing, and they all sang in chorus: then somebody began to fling about paper bags full of tiny white wafers, and the bags burst in the air like shells, and their contents fell like stars from a falling rocket, and everybody was covered as with flakes of snow.

Meantime the storm had broken, and, above the clash and clang of the instruments of the band and the rhythmic shuffle of the feet of the dancers and the clear and joyous notes of their happy singing, there was the roar of the thunder that rolled over London and the rattle of the rain on the glass dome overhead.

Glory was in ecstasies; it was like a mist on Peel Bay at night with the moon shining through it and the waves dancing to a north-west breeze. It was like a black and stormy sea outside Contrary with the gale coming down from the mountains. And yet it was a world of wonder and enchantment and beauty and bright and happy faces.

It was morning when the ball broke up, and then the rain had abated, though the thunder was still rumbling. The men were to see the girls back to the hospital, and Glory and Drake sat in a hansom-cab together.

"So you always forget that kind of thing, do you?" he said.
"What kind of thing?" she asked.
"Never mind—*you* know!"

She had put up the hood of her outdoor cape, but he could still see the gleam of her golden hair.

"Give me that rose," he said—"the white one that you put in your hair."
"It's nothing," she answered.
"Then give it to me. I'll keep it for ever and ever!"

She put up her hand to her head.

"Ah, how sweet of you! And what a lovely little hand! But no; let me take it for myself."

He reached one arm around her shoulder, put his hand under her chin, tipped up her face, and kissed her on the lips.

"Darling!" he whispered.

Then in a moment she awoke from her world of wonder and enchantment, and the intoxication of the evening left her. She did not speak; her head dropped; she felt her cheeks burn red, and she hid her face in her hands. There was a momentary sense of dishonour, almost of outrage. Drake treated her lightly, and she was herself to blame.

"Forgive me, Glory!" he was saying, in a voice tremulous

and intense. "It shall never happen again—never, so help me God!"

The day was dawning and the last raindrops were splashing on the wet and empty pavement. The great city lay asleep, and the distant thunder was rolling away from it.

XII

THE chaplain of Martha's Vineyard had not been to the hospital ball. Before it came off he had thought of it a good deal, and as often as he remembered that he had protested to Glory against the company of Polly Love he felt hot and ashamed. Polly was shallow and frivolous, and had a little crab-apple of a heart, but he knew no harm of her. It was hardly manly to make a dead-set at the little thing because she was foolish and fond of dress, and because she knew a man who displeased him.

Then she was Glory's only companion, and to protest against Glory going in her company was to protest against Glory going at all. That seemed a selfish thing to do. Why should he deny her the delights of the ball? He could not go to it himself—he would not if he could; but girls liked such things—they loved to dance, and to be looked at and admired, and have men about them paying court and talking nonsense.

There was a sting in that thought, too; but he struggled to be magnanimous. He was above all mean and unmanly feelings —he would withdraw his objection.

He did not withdraw it. Some evil spirit whispered in his heart that Glory was drifting away from him. This was the time to see for certain whether she had passed out of the range of his influence. If she respected his authority she would not go. If she went, he had lost his hold of her and their old relations were at an end.

On the night of the ball he walked over to the hospital and asked for her. She had gone, and it seemed as if the earth itself had given way beneath his feet.

He could not help feeling bitterly about Polly Love, and that caused him to remember a patient to whom her selfish little heart had shown no kindness. It was her brother. He was some nine or ten years older, and very different in character. His face was pale and thin, almost ascetic, and he had the fiery and watery eyes of the devotee. He had broken a blood-vessel and was threatened with consumption, but his case was not considered dangerous. When Polly was about, his eyes would follow her round the ward with something of the humble entreaty of a dog. It was clear that he loved his sister and was constantly thinking of her; but she hardly ever looked in his direction, and when she spoke to him it was in a cold and fretful voice.

John Storm had observed this. It had brought him close to the young man, and the starved and silent heart had opened out to him. He was a lay-brother in an Anglican Brotherhood that was settled in Bishopsgate Street. His monastic name was Brother Paul. He had asked to be sent to that hospital because his sister was a nurse there. She was his only remaining relative. One other sister he had once had, but she was gone—she was dead—she died. . . . But that was a sad and terrible story; he did not like to talk of it.

To this broken and bankrupt creature John Storm found his footsteps turning on that night when his own heart lay waste. But on entering the ward he saw that Brother Paul had a visitor already. He was an elderly man in a strange habit a black cassock which buttoned close at the neck and fell nearly to his feet, and was girded about the waist by a black rope that had three great knots at its suspended ends. And the habit was not more different from the habit of the world than the face of the wearer was unlike the worldly face. It was a face full of spirituality, a face that seemed to invest everything it looked upon with a holy peace, a beautiful face, without guile or craft or passion, yet not without the signs of internal strife at the temples and under the eyes; but the battles with self had all been fought and won.

As John Storm stepped up the old man rose from his chair by the patient's bed.

"This is the Father Superior, sir," said Brother Paul.

"I've just been hearing of you," said the Father in a gentle voice. "You have been good to my poor brother."

John Storm answered with some commonplace--it had been a pleasure, a happiness; the brother would soon leave them; they would all miss him, perhaps himself especially.

The Father resumed his chair and listened with an earnest smile. "I understand you, dear friend," he said. "It is so much more blessed to give than to receive. Ah, if the poor blind world only knew! How it fights for its pleasures that perish, and its pride of life that passes away! Yet to succour a weaker brother or protect a fallen woman or feed a little child will bring a greater joy than to conquer all the kingdoms of the earth."

John Storm sat down on the end of the bed. Something

had gone out to him in a moment, and he was held as by a spell. The Father talked of the love of the world—how strange it was, how difficult to understand, how tragic, how pitiful. The lusts of the flesh, the lusts of the eye—how mean, how delusive, how treacherous. To think of the people of that mighty city day by day and night by night making themselves miserable in order that they might make themselves merry; to think of the children of men scouring the globe for its paltry possessions, that could not add one inch to the stature of the soul, while all the while the empire of peace and joy and happiness lay here at hand, here within ourselves, here in the little narrow compass of the human heart! To give, not to get, that was the great blessedness, and to give of yourself, of your heart's love, was the greatest blessedness of all.

John Storm was stirred. "The Church, sir," he said—"the Church itself has to learn that lesson."

And then he spoke of the hopes with which he had come up to London, and how they were being broken down and destroyed; of his dreams of the Church and its mission, and how they were dying or dead already.

"What liars we are, sir! How we colour things to justify ourselves! Look at our sacraments—are they a lie or are they a sacrilege? Look at our charities—are we Pharisees or are we hypocrites? And our clergy, sir—our fashionable clergy! Surely some tremendous upheaval will shake to its foundations the Church wherein such things are possible—a Church that is more worldly than the world! And then the woman-life of the Church, see how it is thrown away. That sweetest and tenderest and holiest power, how it goes to waste under the eye and with the sanction of the Church in the frivolities of fashion—in drawing-rooms, in gardens, in bazaars, in theatres, in balls——"

He stopped. His last word had arrested him. Had he been thinking only of himself and of Glory? His head fell, and he covered his face with his hand.

"You are right, my son," said the Father quietly, "and yet you are wrong, too. The Church of God will not be shaken to its foundations because of the Pharisees who stand in its public places, or because of the publicans who haunt its purlieus. Though the axe be laid to the rotten tree, yet the little seed will save its kind alive."

Then with an earnest smile and in a gentle voice he spoke of their little Brotherhood in Bishopsgate Street; how ten years ago they had founded it for detachment from earthly cares and earthly aims, and for hiddenness with God; how they had established it in the midst of the world's busiest highway, in the heart of the world's greatest market, to show that they despised gold and silver and all that the blind and cheated world most prizes, just as St. Philip and St. Ignatius had established the severest of modern rules in a profane and self-indulgent century to show that they could stamp out every suggestion of the flesh as a spark from the fires of hell.

And then he lifted his cord and pointed to the knots at the end of it, and told what they were—symbols of the three bonds by which he was bound—the three vows he had taken: the vow of poverty, because Christ chose it for Himself and His friends; the vow of obedience, because He had said, "He that heareth you heareth Me;" and the vow of chastity, because it was our duty to guard the gates of the senses, and to keep our eyes and ears and tongue from all inordinateness.

"But the lawful love of home and kindred," said John, "what of that?"

"We convert it into what is spiritual," said the Father. "All human love must be based on the love of God if it is to be firm and true and enduring, and the reason of so much failure of love in natural friendship is that the love of the creature is not built upon the love of the Creator."

"But the love, say, of mother and son—of brother and sister?"

"Ah, we have placed ourselves above the ordinary conditions of life, that none may claim our affections in the same way as Christ. Man has to contend with two sets of enemies—those from within and those from without—and no temptations are more subtle than those which come in the name of our holiest affections. But the sword of the Spirit must keep the tempter away. There is the Judas in all of us, and he will betray us with a kiss if he can."

John Storm's breast was heaving. He could scarcely conceal his agitation, but the Father had risen to go.

"It is eight o'clock, and I must be back to Compline," he said. And then he laughed and added, "We never ride in cabs, but I must needs walk across the Park to-night, for I have given away all my money."

At that the smile of an angel came into his old face, and he said with a sweet simplicity, "I love the Park. Every morning the children play there, and then it is the holy Catholic Church to me, and I like to walk in it and to lay my hands on the heads of the little ones, and to ask a blessing for them, and to empty myself. This morning as I was coming here I met a little boy carrying a bundle. 'And what is *your* name, my little man?' I said, and he told me what it was. 'And how old are you?' I asked. 'Twelve years,' he answered. 'And what have you got in your bundle?' 'Father's dinner, sir,' he said. 'And what is your father, my son?' 'A carpenter,' said the boy. And I thought if I had been living in Palestine nineteen hundred years ago I might have met another little Boy carrying the dinner of His father, who was also a carpenter, in a little bundle which Mary had made up for Him. So I felt in my pocket, and all I had was my fare home again, and I gave it to the little man as a thank-offering to God that He had suffered me to meet a sweet boy of twelve whose father was a carpenter."

John Storm's eyes were dim with tears.

"Good-bye, Brother Paul, and God send you back to us soon! Good-bye to you, dear friend, and when the world deals harshly with you, come to us for a few days in Retreat, that in the silence of your soul you may forget its vanities and vexations, and fix your thoughts above."

John Storm could not resist the impulse; he dropped to his knees at the Father's feet.

"Bless me also, Father, as you blessed the carpenter's boy."

The Father raised two fingers of his right hand and said—

"God bless you, my son, and be with you and strengthen you, and when He smiles on you, may the frown of man affect you not! Father in heaven, look down on this fiery soul and succour him! Help him to cast off every anchor that holds him to the world, and make him as a voice crying in the wilderness, 'Come out of her, my people, saith our God.'"

When John rose from his knees, the saintly face was gone, and all the air seemed to be filled with a heavenly calm.

While he had been kneeling for the Father's blessing, he had been aware of a step on the floor behind him. It was his fellow-curate, the Reverend Golightly, who was still waiting to deliver his message.

The Canon had been disappointed in one of his preachers for Sunday, and being himself engaged to preside over the annual dinner of a Dramatic Benevolent Fund to be held on the Saturday night, and therefore incapable of extra preparation, he desired that Mr. Storm should take the sermon on Sunday morning. John promised to do so. His fellow-curate smiled, bowed, coughed, and left him.

A small room was kept for the chaplain on the ground-floor of the hospital, and he went down to it and wrote a letter.

It was to the parson at Peel:—

"No doubt you hear from Glory frequently, and know all about her progress as a probationer. She seems to be very well, and certainly I have never seen her look so bright and so cheerful. At the moment of writing she is out at a ball given by some of the hospital authorities. Well, it is a perfectly harmless source of pleasure, and with all my heart I hope she is enjoying herself. No doubt, some form of amusement is necessary to a young girl in the height of her youth and health and beauty, and he would be only a poor sapless man who could not take delight in the thought that a good girl was happy. Her fellow-nurses, too, are noble and devoted women, doing true woman's work, and if there are some black sheep among them, that is no more than might be expected of the purest profession in the world.

"As for myself, I have tried to carry out my undertaking to look after Glory, but I cannot say how long I may be able to continue the task. Do not be surprised if I am compelled to give it up. You know I am dissatisfied with my present surroundings, and I am only waiting for the ruling and direction of the pillar of cloud and fire. God alone can tell how it will move, but God will guide me. I don't go out more than I can help, and when I do go I get humiliated and feel foolish. The life of London has been a great and painful surprise. I had supposed that I knew all about it, but I have really known nothing until now. Its cruelty, its deceit, and its treachery are terrible. London is the Judas that is for ever betraying with a kiss the young, the hopeful, the innocent. However, it helps one to know oneself, and that is better than lying wrapped in cotton wool. Give my kindest greetings to everybody at Glenfaba— my love to my father, too, if there are any means of conveying it."

The letter took him long to write, and when it was written he went out into the hall to post it. There he saw that a thunderstorm was coming, and he concluded to remain until it had passed over. He stepped into the library and selected a book, and returned to his room to read it. The book was "St. John Chrysostom on the Priesthood," and the subject was congenial, but he could not keep his mind on the printed page. He thought of the Father Superior, of the little Brotherhood in Bishopsgate, and then of Glory at the hospital ball, and again of Glory, and yet again and again of Glory. Do what he would he could not help but think of her.

The storm pealed over his head, and when he returned to the hall two hours later it was still far from spent. He stood at the open door and watched it. Forks of lightning lit up the Park, and floods of black rain made the vacant pavements like the surface of the sea. A tinkling cab slid past at intervals with its driver sheeted in oil-skins, and now and then there was an omnibus full within and empty without. Only one other living thing was to be seen anywhere. An Italian organ man had stationed himself in front of a mansion to the left and was playing vigorously.

John Storm walked through the hospital. It was now late, and the house was quiet. The house-doctor had made the last of his rounds and turned into his chambers across the courtyard, and the night nurses were boiling little kettles in their rooms between the wards. The surgical wards were darkened, and the patients were asleep already. In the medical wards there were screens about certain of the beds, and weary moans came from behind them.

It was after midnight when John Storm came round to the hall again, and then the rain had ceased, but the thunder was still rumbling. He might have gone home at length, but he did not go; he realised that he was waiting for Glory. Other nurses returned from the ball, and bowed to him and passed into the house. He stepped into the porter's lodge, and sat down and watched the lightning. It began to be terrible to him, because it seemed to be symbolical. What doom or what disaster did this storm typify and predict? Never could he forget the night on which it befell. It was the night of the nurses' ball.

He thought he must have slept, for he shook himself and thought, "What nonsense! Surely the soul leaves the body while we are asleep, and only the animal remains!"

It was now almost daylight, and two hansom cabs had stopped before the portico, and several persons who were coming up the steps were chattering away like wakened linnets. One voice was saying—

"Mr. Drake proposes that we should all go to the theatre, and if we can get a late pass I should like it above everything."

It was Glory; and a fretful voice answered her

"Very well, if *you* say so. It's all the same to *me*." It was Polly; and then a man's voice said—

"What night shall it be then, Robert?"

And a second man's voice answered, with a drawl, "Better let the girls choose for themselves, don't you know."

John Storm felt his hands and feet grow cold, and he stepped out into the porch. Glory saw him coming and made a faint cry of recognition.

"Ah, here is Mr. Storm! Mr. Storm, you should know Mr. Drake. He was in the Isle of Man, you remember——"

"I do *not* remember," said John Storm.

"But you saved his life, and you ought to know him——"

"I do *not* know him," said John Storm.

She was beginning to say, "Let me introduce——" But she stopped and stood silent for a moment, while the strange light came into her gleaming eyes of something no word could express, and then she burst into noisy laughter.

A superintendent Sister going through the hall at the moment drew up and said, "Nurse, I am surprised at you! Go to your room this instant;" and the girls whispered their adieux and went off giggling.

"What a glorious night it has been!" said Glory, going upstairs.

"I'm glad you think so," said Polly. "To tell you the truth, I found it dreadfully tiresome."

The two men lit their cigarettes and got back into one of the hansoms and drove away.

"What a bear that man is!" said Lord Robert.

"Rude enough certainly," said Drake; "but I liked his face for all that; and if the fates put it into his head to stand between me and death—well, I'm not going to forget it."

"Give him a wide berth, dear boy. The fellow is an actor—an affected fop. I met him at Mrs. Macrae's on Thursday. He is a religious actor and a *poseur*. He'll do something one of these days, take my word for it."

And meanwhile John Storm had buttoned his long coat up to his throat and was striding home through the echoing streets, with both hands clenched and his teeth set hard.

XIII

MARTHA'S.

Oh, Lord-a-massy! Oh, gough bless me sowl! Oh, my beloved grandfather! John Storm has done for himself at last! That man was never an author of peace and a lover of concord; but, my gracious, if you had heard his sermon in church on Sunday morning! Being a holy and humble woman of heart myself, I altered the Litany the smallest taste possible, and muttered away from beginning to end, "O Lord, close thou our lips;" but the Lord didn't heed me in the least, with the result that everybody on earth is now screaming and snarling at our poor Mr. Storm exactly as if he had been picking the pocket of the universe.

It was all about the morality of men. The text was as innocent as a baby, "Put ye on the Lord Jesus Christ, and make no provision for the flesh to fulfil the lusts thereof." And when he

began in the usual way, the dear old goodies in glasses thought
he had been wound up like the musical-box and had just turned
on the crank; so they cuddled in comfortably for forty winks
before the anthem. There were two natures in man, and man's
body might be good or bad according as spiritual or carnal
affections swayed it, and all the rest of the good old change-for-
sixpence-and-a-ha'penny-out, you know. But the lesson had
been from Isaiah, where the unreasonable old prophet is indignant with the ladies of Zion because they don't want to look
like dowdies, you remember: "Tremble, ye women that are at
ease; strip you, and make you bare, and gird sackcloth upon your
loins." And off he went like a comet, with the fashionable
woman for his tail. If matrimony nowadays didn't always mean
monogamy, who was chiefly to blame? Men were generally as
pure as women required that they should be; and if the lives of
men were bad, it was often because women did not demand that
they should be good. Tremble, ye women that are at ease, and
say why you allow your daughters to marry men who in fact and
effect are married already. Strip you, and be ashamed for the
poor women who were the first wives of your daughters' husbands, and for the children whom such men abandon and forget.
In leading your innocent daughters to courts and receptions, you
are only leading them to the auction-room, and in dressing and
decorating them you are preparing them for the market of base
men. Last week some titled philanthropist had hauled up a
woman in the East End of London for attempting to sell her
daughter. How shocking! everybody said. What a disgrace to
the nineteenth century! But the wretched creature had only
been doing the best according to her light for the welfare of her
miserable child, while here—with their eyes open, with their
cultured consciences—the wives of these same philanthropists
were doing the same thing every day—the very same!

Having gone for the mammies like this, he went for the dear
girls themselves one better. Let them gird sackcloth on their
loins and hide their faces. Why did they suffer themselves to
be sold? The woman who married a man for the sake of his
title or his position or any worldly advantage whatever was no
better than an outcast of the streets. Her act was the same,
and in all reason and justice her name should be the same also.

Hey, nonny, nonny! I told you how he broke down before;
but on Sunday morning, in spite of mine own amended Litany,
I had just as much hope of the breakdown of the falls of Niagara
or a nineteen-feet spring tide. You would have said his face was
afire, and those great eyes of his were lit up like the red lamps
on Peel pier.

Pulpit oratory! I don't know what it is, only I never heard the like of it in all my born days. I begin to think the real difference between preachers is the difference of the fire beneath the crust. In some it burns so low that it doesn't even warm the surface, and you couldn't get up enough puff to boil the kitchen-kettle; but in others—look out! It's a volcano, and the lava is coming down with a rush.

Mercy me, how I cried! "Oh, my daughter, oh, my child, what a ninny you are!" I told myself; but it was no use talking. His voice was as hoarse as a raven's, and sometimes you would have thought his very heart was breaking.

But the congregation! You should have seen the transformation scene! They had come in bowing and smiling and whispering softly until the church was a perfect sheet of sunshine, an absolute aurora borealis; but they went out like a north-east gale with mutterings of thunder and one man overboard.

And John Storm having put his foot in it, of course Glory Quayle had to get her toe in too. Coming down the aisle, some of the dear ladies of Zion, who looked as if they wanted to "swear in their wrath," were mumbling all the lamentations of Jeremiah. Who was he, indeed, to talk to people like that? Nobody had ever heard of him except his mother. And in the porch they came upon a fat old dump in a velvet dolman who declared it was perfectly scandalous, and she had had to come out in the middle. Whereupon Glory, *not* being delivered that day from all evil and mischief, said, "Quite right, ma'am, and you were not the only one who had to leave the church in the middle of that sermon." "Why, who else had to go?" said this female Pharisee. "The devil, ma'am," said Glory, and then left her with that bone to gnaw.

It turns out that the old girlie in the dolman is a mighty patron of this hospital, so everybody says I am in for nasty weather. But hoot! My heart's in the Hielan's, my heart is not here, my heart's in the Hielan's, sae what can I fear!

John Storm is in for it too, and they say his vicar waited for him in the vestry, but he looked like forked lightning coming out of the pulpit, so the good man thought it better to keep his rod in pickle awhile. It seems that the Lords of the Council and all the nobility were there, and it is a point of religious etiquette in London that in the hangman's house nobody speaks of the rope; but our poor John gave them the gibbet as well. It was a fearful thing to do, but nobody will make me believe he had not got his reasons. He hasn't been here since, but I am certain he has his eye on some fine folks, and whoever they are I'll bet "my bottom dollar" they deserved all they got.

But heigho! I haven't left myself breath to tell you about the ball. I was there! You remember I was lamenting that I hadn't got the necessary finery. In fact, I had put in a bit at the end of my prayers about it. "Oh, God, be good to me this once and let me look nice." And He *was*. He put it into the heads of the nabobs of this vineyard that nurses should "appear at the nurses' ball in regulation uniform only." So my cloak and my bonnet and my grey dress and my apron covered a multitude of sins.

You should have seen Glory that night, grandfather. She was a redder young lobster than ever, somehow; but she put a white rose in her carroty curls, and, gough bless me, what a bogh[1] she was, though! Of course, she made the acquaintance of the "higher ranks of society," and danced with all the earth. The great surgeon of something opened the ball with the matron of Bartimaeus's, and she went round on his arm like a dolly in a dolly-tub; but he soon saw what a marvellous and miraculous being Glory was, and, after I had waltzed so beautifully with the ancient personage, I had the hearts of all the young men flying round at the hem of my white petticoat—it was a nice new one for the occasion.

But the strangest thing was that somebody from the Isle of Man flopped down on me there just as if he had descended from the blue. It was that little English boy Drake, who used to come to the Catechism class, only now he is one of the smartest and handsomest young men in London. When he came up and announced himself, I am sure he expected me to expire on the spot or else go crazy, and of course I was trembling all over; but I behaved like a rational person, and stood my ground. He looked at me as much as to say, "Do you know you've grown to be a very fine young woman, and I admire you very much?" Whereupon I looked back as much as to reply, "That's quite right, my dear young sir, and I should have a poor opinion of you if you didn't." So being of the same opinion on the only subject worth thinking about (that's me), I behaved charmingly to him, and even forgave him when he carried off my white rose at the end.

Mr. Drake has a friend who is always with him. He is a willowy person, who owns sixteen setters and three church livings, they say, and wears (on week-days) a thunder-and-lightning suit of clothes—*you* know, a pattern so large that one man can't carry the whole of it and somebody else goes about with the rest. His name is Lord Robert Ure, and I intend to call him Lord Bob, for since he is such a frivolous person himself I must

[1] Dear.

make a point of being severe. I danced with him, of course, and he kept telling me what a wonderful future Mr. Drake had, and how the Promised Land was before him, and even hinting that it wouldn't be a bad thing to be Mrs. Joshua. Fancy Glory making a tremendous match with a leader of society! And if I hadn't gone to that hospital ball, no doubt the history of the nineteenth century would have been different!

They are going to take me next week to something far, far better than a ball, only I must not tell you anything about it yet, except that I keep awake all night sometimes to think of it. But thou sure and firmest earth, hear not my steps which way they walk!

It's late, and I'm just going to cuddle in. Good night! My kisses for the aunties and my love to everybody! In fact, you can serve out my love in ladles this time—being cheap at present, and plenty more where this is coming from.

Oh, I forgot to tell you what happened when we returned to the hospital! It was shockingly late, and the gentlemen had brought us back; but there was our John Storm with his sad and anxious face, waiting up to see us safely home. He was angry with me, and I didn't mind that in the least; but when I saw that he liked me well enough to be rude to the gentlemen, I fell a victim to the crafts and assaults of the devil, and couldn't help laughing out loud; and then Ward Sister Allworthy came along and lifted her lip and showed me her tusk.

It was a wonderful night altogether, and I was never so happy in my life; but all the same I had a good cry to myself alone before going to bed. Too much water had'st thou, poor Ophelia! Talk about two natures in one, I've got two hundred and fifty, and they all want to do different things! Ah me! the "ould Book" says that woman was taken out of the rib of a man, and I feel sometimes as if I want to get back to my old quarters.

GLORY.

P.S.—I'll write you a full and particular account of the great event of next week after it is over. Be innocent of the knowledge, dearest chuck, till thou applaud the deed. You see I don't want you to eat your meal in fear, or your porridge either. But I am burning with impatience for the night to come, and would like to run to it. Oh, if it were done when 'tis done, then 'twere well it were done quickly! See? I am going in for a course of Shakespeare!

XIV

A WEEK later Glory made her first visit to the theatre. Her companions were Drake, who was charmed with her naïveté, Lord Robert, who was amused by it, and Polly Love, who was annoyed and ashamed, and uttered little peevish exclamations.

As they entered the box which they were to occupy, the attendant drew back the curtain, and at sight of the auditorium she cried "Oh!" and then checked herself and coloured deeply.

With her eyes down she sat where directed in one of the three seats in front, Polly being on her right and Drake on her left, and Lord Robert at the back of the lace curtain. For some minutes she did not smile or stir, and when she spoke it was always in whispers. A great awe seemed to have fallen upon her, and she was behaving as she behaved in church.

Drake began to explain the features of the theatre. Down there were the stalls, and behind the stalls was the pit. The body? Well, yes—the body, so to speak. And the three galleries were the dress circle, the family circle, and the gallery proper. The organ-loft? No, there was no organ, but that empty place below was the well for the orchestra.

"And what is this little vestry?" she said.

"Oh, this is a private box where we can sit by ourselves and talk!" said Drake.

At every other explanation she had made little whispered cries of astonishment and delight; but when she heard that conversation was not forbidden she was entirely happy. She thought a theatre was even more beautiful than a church, and supposed an actor must have a wonderful living.

The house was filling rapidly, and as the people entered she watched them intently.

"What a beautiful congregation," she whispered—"audience, I mean!"

"Do you think so?" said Polly; but Glory did not hear her.

It was delightful to see so many lovely faces and listen to the low hum of their conversation. She felt happy among them already and quite kind to everybody, because they had all come together to enjoy themselves. Presently she bowed to some one in the stalls with a face all smiles, and then said to Polly—

"How nice of her! A lady moved to me from the body. How friendly they are in theatres!"

"But it was to Mr. Drake," said Polly; and then Glory could have buried her face in her confusion.

"Never mind, Glory," said Drake; "that's a lady who will like you the better for the little mistake. Rosa," he added, with a look towards Lord Robert, who smoothed his moustache and bent his head.

Polly glanced up quickly at mention of the name; and Drake explained that Rosa was a friend of his own—a lady journalist, Miss Rosa Macquarrie, a good and clever woman. Then, turning back to Glory, he said -

"She has been standing up for your friend Mr. Storm this week. You know there have been attacks upon him in the newspapers?"

"Has she?" said Glory, recovering herself and looking down again. "Which pew- stall, I mean——"

But the people were clapping their hands and turning their faces to the opposite side of the theatre. Some great personage was entering the royal box.

"My chief, the Home Secretary," said Drake; and, when the applause had subsided and the party were seated, the great man recognised his secretary and bowed to him; whereupon it seemed to Glory that every face in the theatre turned about and looked at her.

She did not flinch, but bore herself bravely. There was a certain thrill and a slight twitching of the head, such as a charger makes at the first volley in battle—nothing more, not even the quiver of an eyelid. This was the atmosphere in which Drake lived, and she felt a vague gratitude to him for allowing her to move in it.

"Isn't it beautiful!" she whispered, turning towards Polly; but Polly's face was hidden behind the curtain.

The orchestra was coming in, and Glory leaned forward and counted the fiddles, while Drake talked with Lord Robert across her shoulder.

"I found him reading Rosa's article this morning, and it seems he was present himself and heard the sermon," said Drake.

"And what's his opinion?" asked Lord Robert.

"Much the same as your own. Affectation—the man is suffering from the desire to be original—more egotism than love of truth, and so forth."

"Right, too, dear boy. All this vapouring is as much as to say, 'Look at me! I am the Hon. and Rev. Mr. Thingamy, nephew of the Prime Minister, and yet——'"

"I don't at all agree with the chief," said Drake, "and I told him so. The man has enthusiasm, and that's the very salt of the earth at present. We are all such pessimists in these days.

Thank God for anybody who will warm us up with a little faith, say I!"

Glory's bosom heaved, and she was just about to speak when there was a sudden clap as of thunder, and she leapt up in her seat. But it was only the beginning of the overture, and she sat down laughing. There was a tender passage in the music; and after it was over she was very quiet for a while, and then whispered to Polly that she hoped little Johnnie wasn't worse to-night, and it seemed wicked to enjoy oneself when any one was so poorly.

"Who is that?" said Drake.

"My little boy whose leg was amputated." said Glory.

"This Glory is so funny!" said Polly. "Fancy talking of that here!"

"Hush!" said Lord Robert, "the curtain is going up"—and the next moment Glory was laughing because they were all in the dark.

The play was "Much Ado about Nothing," and Glory whispered to Drake that she had never seen it before, but she had read "Macbeth," and knew all about Shakespeare and the drama. The first scene took her breath away, being so large and so splendid. It represented the outside of a gentleman's house, and she thought what a length of time it must have taken to build it, considering it was to last only a single night. But hush! The people were going indoors. No; they preferred to talk in the street. Oh, we were in Italy? Yes, indeed, that was different.

Leonato delivered his first speeches forcibly, and was rewarded with applause. Glory clapped her hands also, and said he was a very good actor for such a very old gentleman.

Then Beatrice made her entrance, and was greeted with cheers, whereupon Glory looked perplexed.

"It's Terry." whispered Polly; and Drake said "Ellen Terry;" but Glory still looked puzzled.

"They are calling her 'Beatrice,'" she said. Then, mastering the situation, she looked wise, and said, "Of course—the actress —I quite understand; but why do they applaud her she has done nothing yet?"

Drake explained that the lady playing Beatrice was a great favourite, and that the applause of the audience had been of the nature of a welcome to a welcome guest, as much as to say they had liked her before, and were glad to see her again. Glory thought that was beautiful, and, looking at the gleaming eyes that shone out of the darkness, she said—

"How lovely to be an actress!"

Then she turned back to the stage, where all was bright and brilliant, and said, "What a lovely frock, too!"

"Only a stage costume, my dear," said Polly.

"And what beautiful diamonds!"

"Paste," said Lord Robert.

"Hush!" said Drake; and then Benedick entered, and the audience received him with great cheering. "Irving," whispered Drake; and Glory looked more perplexed than before, and said—

"But you told me it was Mr. Irving's theatre, and I thought it would have been his place to welcome——"

The vision of Benedick clapping his hands at his own entrance set Lord Robert laughing in his cold way; but Drake said, "Be quiet, Robert!"

Glory, like a child, had ears for no conversation except her own, and she was immersed in the play in a moment. The merry war of Beatrice and Benedick had begun, and as she watched it her face grew grave.

"Now, that's very foolish of her," she said; "and if, as you say, she's a great actress, she shouldn't do such things. To talk like that to a man is to let everybody see that she likes him better than anybody else, though she's trying her best to hide it. The silly girl—he'll find her out!"

But the curtain had gone down on the first act, the lights had suddenly gone up, and her companions were laughing at her. Then she laughed also.

"Of course, it's only a play," she said largely, "and I know all about plays and about acting, and I can act myself, too."

"I'm sure you can," said Polly, lifting her lip. But Glory took no notice.

Throughout the second act she put on the same airs of knowledge, watching the masked ball intently, but never once uttering a laugh, and hardly ever smiling. The light, the colour, the dresses, the gay young faces, enchanted her; but she struggled to console herself. It was only her body that was up there, leaning over the front of the box with lips twitching and eyes gleaming; her soul was down on the stage, clad in a lovely gown, and carrying a mask, and laughing and joking with Benedick; but she held herself in, and when the curtain fell she began to talk of the acting.

She was still of opinion that Leonato was excellent for such an elderly gentleman, and when Polly praised Claudio, she agreed that he was good too.

"But Benedick is my boy for all," she said. In some way she had identified herself with Beatrice, and hardly ever spoke of her.

During the third act this air of wisdom and learning broke down badly. In the middle of the ballad, "Sigh no more, ladies, sigh no more," she remembered Johnnie, and whispered to Drake how ill he had been when they left the hospital. And when it was over, and Benedick protested that the song had been vilely sung, she sat back in her seat and said she didn't know how Mr. Irving could say such a thing, for she was sure the boy had sung it beautifully.

"But that's the author," whispered Drake; and then she said wisely—

"Oh, yes, I know—Shakespeare, of course."

Then came the liming of the two love-birds, and she declared that everybody was in love in plays of that sort, and that was why she liked them; but as for those people playing the trick, they were very simple if they thought Beatrice didn't know she loved Benedick. Claudio fell woefully in her esteem in other respects also, and when he agreed to spy on Hero, she said he ought to be ashamed of himself anyhow.

"How ridiculous you are!" said Polly. "It's the author, isn't it?"

"Then the author ought to be ashamed of himself also, for it is unjust and cruel and unnecessary," said Glory.

The curtain had come down again by this time, and the men were deep in an argument about morality in art, Lord Robert protesting that art had no morality, and Drake maintaining that what Glory said was right, and there was no getting to the back of it.

But the fourth act witnessed Glory's final vanquishment. When she found the scene was the inside of a church, and they were to be present at a wedding, she could not keep still on her seat for delight; but when the marriage was stopped, and Claudio uttered his denunciation of Hero, she said it was just like him, and it would serve him right if nobody believed him.

"Hush!" said somebody near them.

"But they *are* believing him," said Glory, quite audibly.

"Hush! hush!" came from many parts of the theatre.

"Well, that's shameful—her father, too——" began Glory.

"Hush, Glory!" whispered Drake; but she had risen to her feet, and when Hero fainted and fell she uttered a cry.

"What a girl!" whispered Polly. "Sit down—everybody's looking!"

"It's only a play, you know," whispered Drake; and Glory sat down and said—

"Well, yes, of course, it's only a play. Did you suppose——"

But she was lost in a moment. Beatrice and Benedick were

alone in the church now; and when Beatrice said "Kill Claudio," Glory leapt up again and clapped her hands. But Benedick would not kill Claudio, and it was the last straw of all. That wasn't what she called being a great actor, and it was shameful to sit and listen to such plays. Lots of disgraceful scenes happened in life, but people didn't come to the theatre to see such things, and she would go.

"How ridiculous you are!" said Polly; but Glory was out in the corridor, and Drake was going after her.

She came back at the beginning of the fifth act with red eyes and confused smiles, looking very much ashamed. From that moment onward she cried a good deal, but gave no other sign until the green curtain came down at the end, when she said—

"It's a wonderful thing! To make people forget it's not true is the most wonderful thing in the world!"

Lord Robert, standing behind the curtain at the back of Polly's chair, had been laughing at Glory with his long owlish drawl, and making cynical interjections by way of punctuating her enthusiasm; and now he said, "Would you like to have a nearer view of your wonderful world, Glory?"

Glory looked perplexed, and Drake muttered, "Hold your tongue, Robert!" Then, turning to Glory, he said shortly, "He only asked you if you would like to go behind the scenes; but I don't think——"

Glory uttered a cry of delight. "Like it? Better than anything in the world!"

"Then I must take you to a rehearsal somewhere," said Lord Robert; "and you'll both come to tea at the chambers afterwards."

Drake made some show of dissent; but Polly, with her most voluptuous look upwards, said it would be perfectly charming, and Glory was in raptures.

The girls, by their own choice, went home without escort by the Hammersmith omnibus. They sat on opposite sides and hardly talked at all. Polly was humming idly, "Sigh no more, ladies."

Glory was in a trance. A great, bright, beautiful world had that night swum into her view, and all her heart was yearning for it with vague and blind aspirations. It might be a world of dreams, but it seemed more real than reality, and when the omnibus passed the corner of Piccadilly Circus she forgot to look at the women who were crowding the pavement.

The omnibus drew up for them at the door of the hospital, and they took long breaths as they went up the steps.

In the corridor to the surgical ward they came upon John

Storm. His head was down and his step was long and measured, and he seemed to be trying to pass them in his grave silence; but Glory stopped and spoke, while Polly went on to her cubicle.

"You here so late?" she said.

He looked steadily into her face, and answered, "I was sent for—some one was dying."

"Was it little Johnnie?"

"Yes."

There was not a tear now—not the quiver of an eyelid.

"I don't think I care for this life," she said fretfully. "Death is always about you everywhere, and a girl can never go out to enjoy herself but——"

"It is true woman's work," said John hotly—"the truest, noblest work a woman can have in all the world!"

"Perhaps," said Glory, swinging on her heel. "All the same——"

"Good-night!" said John, and he turned on his heel also.

She looked after him and laughed. Then with a little hard lump at her heart she took herself off to bed.

Polly Love, in the next cubicle, was humming as she undressed—

"Sigh no more, ladies, sigh no more,
Men were deceivers ever."

That night Glory dreamt that she was back at Peel. She was sitting up on Peel hill, watching the big ships as they weighed anchor in the bay beyond the old dead castle walls, and wishing she were going out with them to the sea and the great cities so far away.

XV

John Storm was sitting in his room next morning fumbling the leaves of a book and trying to read, when a lady visitor was announced. It was Miss Macrae, and she came in with a flushed face, a quivering lip, and the marks of tears in her eyes. She held his hand with the same long hand clasp as before, and said in a tremulous voice—

"I am ashamed of coming, and mother does not know that I am here; but I am very unhappy, and if you cannot help me——."

"Please sit down," said John Storm.

"I have come to tell you," she said; and then her sad eyes moved about the room and came back to his face. "It is about Lord Robert Ure, and I am very wretched."

"Tell me everything, dear lady, and if there is anything I can do——"

She told him all. It was a miserable story. Her mother had engaged her to Lord Robert Ure (there was no other way of putting it) for the sake of his title, and he had engaged himself to her for the sake of her wealth. She had never loved him, and had long known that he was a man of scandalous reputation; but she had been taught that to attach weight to such considerations would be girlish and sentimental, and she had fought for a while and then yielded.

"You will reproach me for my feebleness," she said, and he answered haltingly—.

"No, I do not reproach you—I pity you!"

"Well," she said, "it is all over now, and if I am ruined, and if my mother——"

"You have told her you cannot marry him?"

"Yes."

"Then who am I to reproach you?" he said; and rising to his feet, he threw down his book.

Her dark eyes wandered about the room, and came back to his face again and shone with a new lustre.

"I heard your sermon on Sunday, Mr. Storm, and I felt as if there were nobody else in the church, and you were speaking to me alone. And last night at the theatre——"

"Well?"

He had been tramping the room, but he stopped.

"I saw him in a box with his friend and two—two ladies."

"Were they nurses from the hospital?"

She made a cry of surprise and said, "Then you know all about it, and the sermon *was* meant for me?"

He did not speak for a moment, and then he said, with a thick utterance—

"You wish me to help you to break off this marriage, and I will try. But if I fail, no matter what has happened in the past, or what awaits you in the future——"

"Oh," she said, "if I had your strength beside me I should be brave—I should be afraid of nothing."

"Good-bye, dear lady," said John Storm, and before he could prevent her she had stooped over his hand and kissed it.

John Storm had returned to his book, and was clutching it with nervous fingers, when his fellow-curate came with a message from the Canon to request his presence in the study.

"Tell him I was on the point of going down," said John; and the Reverend Golightly coughed and bowed himself out.

The Canon had also had a visitor that morning. It was Mrs.

Macrae herself. She sat on a chair covered with a tiger-skin, sniffed at her scented handkerchief, and poured out all her sorrows.

Mercy had rebelled against her authority, and it was entirely the fault of the new curate, Mr. Storm. She had actually refused to carry out her engagement with Lord Robert, and it all came of that dreadful sermon on Sunday. It was dishonourable, it was unprincipled, and it was a pretty thing to teach girls to indulge their whims without regard to the wishes of parents.

"Here have I been two years in London, spending a fortune on the girl, and trying to do my best for her, and the moment I fix her in one of the first English families, this young man—this curate—this . . . Upon my honour, it's real wicked, it's shameful!" And the handkerchief steeped in perfume went up from the nose to the eyes.

The Canon swung his pince-nez. "Don't put yourself about, my dear Mrs. Macrae. Leave the matter to me. Miss Macrae will give up her objections and———"

"Oh, you mustn't judge her by her quietness, Canon. You don't know her character. She's real stubborn when her mind's made up. But I'll be as stubborn as she is—I'll take her back to America—I'll never spend another penny———"

"And as for Mr. Storm," continued the Canon, "I'll make everything smooth in that quarter. You mustn't think too much about the unhappy sermon—a little youthful *esprit fort*— we all go through it, you know."

When Mrs. Macrae had gone he rang twice for Mr. Golightly, and said, "Tell Mr. Storm to come down to me immediately."

"With pleasure, sir," said the little man; and then he hesitated.

"What is it?" said the Canon, adjusting his glasses.

"I have never told you, sir, how I found him the night you sent me to the hospital."

"Well, how?"

"On his knees to a Catholic priest who was visiting a patient."

The Canon's glasses fell from his eyes and his broad face broke into strange smiles.

"I thought the Sorceress of Rome was at the bottom of it," he said. "His uncle shall know of this, and unless I am sadly deceived . . . But fetch him down."

John Storm was wearing his flannel shirt that morning, and he came downstairs with a heavy tread and swung himself, unasked, into the chair that had just before been occupied by Mrs. Macrae.

The perpendicular wrinkles came between the Canon's eyebrows, and he said: "My dear Storm, I have postponed as long as possible a painful interview. The fact is, your recent sermon has given the greatest offence to the ladies of my congregation, and if such teaching were persisted in we should lose our best people. Now, I don't want to be angry with you, quite the contrary, but I wish to put it to you, as your spiritual head and adviser, that your idea of religion is by no means agreeable to the needs and necessities of the nineteenth century. There is no freedom in such a faith, and St. Paul says, 'Where the spirit of the Lord is, there is liberty.' But the theory of your religion is not more unscriptural than its application is unwholesome. Yours is a gloomy faith, my dear Storm, and what did Luther say of a gloomy faith?—that the devil was very apt to be lurking behind it. As for himself, he married, you may remember; he had children, he played chess, he loved to see young people dancing——"

"I don't object to the dancing, sir," said John Storm. "I only object to the tune."

"What do you mean?" said the Canon, not without insolence, and the perpendicular wrinkles became large and heavy.

"I mean, sir," said John Storm, "that half the young people now-a-days—the young women in the West of London especially—are asked to dance to the 'Dead March.'"

And then he spoke of the infamous case of Mercy Macrae, how she was being bought and sold, and how scandalous was the reputation of the man she was required to marry.

"That was what I was coming down to speak about, sir—to ask you to save this innocent girl from such a mockery of holy wedlock. She is not a child, and the law cannot help her, but you can do so, because the power of the Church is at your back. You have only to set your face against this infamy and say——"

"My dear Mr. Storm" (the Canon was smiling condescendingly and swinging his glasses), "the business of the Church is to solemnise marriages, not to make them. But if the young lady comes to me I will say, 'My dear young lady, the conditions you complain of are more common than you suppose; put aside all foolish romantic notions, make a nest for yourself as comfortably as you can, and come back in a year to thank me.'"

John Storm was on his feet; the blood was mounting to his face and tingling in his fingers.

"And so these men are to make their wives of the daughters of the poor first, and then ask the Church to solemnise their polygamy——"

But the Canon had lifted his hand to silence him.

"My dear young friend, a policy like yours would decimate the House of Commons and abolish the House of Lords. Practical religion has a sweet reasonableness. We are all human, even if we are all gentlemen, and while silly young things——"

But John Storm was out in the hall and putting on his hat to see Glory.

Glory had not yet awakened from her trance. While others were living in to-day, she was still going about in yesterday. The emotion of the theatre was upon her, and the world of reality took the tone and colour of drama. This made her a tender woman but a bad nurse.

She began the day in the out-patient department, and a poor woman came with a child that had bitten its tongue. Its tongue had to be stitched, and the child's condition required that it should remain in the house a day or two. "Let me put the pore thing to bed, she's allus used to me," said the woman piteously. "Are you the mother?" said the Sister. "No, the grandmother." "The mother is the only person who can enter the wards except on visiting-day." The poor woman began to cry. Glory had to carry the child to bed, and she whispered to the grandmother, "Come this way," and the woman followed her. When they came to the surgical ward, she said to the nurse in charge, "This is the child's mother, and she has come to put the poor little thing to bed."

Later in the morning she was sent up to help in the same ward. A patient in great pain called to her and said, "Loosen this bandage for me, nurse—it is killing me." And she loosened it.

But the glamour of the theatre was upon her as well as its sentiment and emotion, and in the space before the bed of one of the patients, at a moment when the ward Sister was away, she began to make imitations of Beatrice and Benedick and the singer of "Sigh no more, ladies." The patient was Koenig, the choir-master of All Saints, a little fat German, with long moustaches, which he waxed and curled as he lay in bed. Glory had christened him "the hippopotamus," and at her mimicry he laughed so much that he rolled and pitched and dived among the bedclothes.

"Ach, Gott!" he cried, "vot a girl! Never—I haf never heard any one so goot on de stage. Vot a voice, too! A leetle vork under a goot teacher, and den, mine Gott! Vot is it de musicians say?—the genius has a Cremona inside of him on which he first composes his immortal vorks. You haf the Cremona, my dear, and I vill help you to bring it out. Vot you tink?"

It was the hour of the morning when the patients who can afford it have their newspapers brought up to them, but the newspapers were thrown aside, every eye was on Glory, and there was much laughter, and even some clapping of hands.

Ward Sister Allworthy entered with the house-doctor. "What's the meaning of this?" she demanded. Glory told the truth, and was reproved.

"Who has loosened this bandage?" said the doctor. The patient tried to prevaricate, but Glory told the truth again, and was reproved once more.

"And who permitted this woman to come into the ward?" said the nurse.

"I did," said Glory.

"You're not fit to be a nurse, miss, and I shall certainly report you as unfit for duty."

Glory laughed in the Sister's face.

It was at this moment that John Storm arrived after his interview with the Canon. He drew Glory into the corridor and tried to pacify her.

"Oh, don't suppose I'm going to do hospital nursing all my life," she said. "It may be good womanly work, but I want to be a human being with a heart, and not a machine called Duty. How I hate and despise my surroundings! I'll make an end of them one of these days. Sooner or later it must come to that."

"Your life has been deranged, Glory, and that is why you disdain your surroundings. You were at the theatre last night."

"Who told you that? . . . Well, what of it? Are you one of those who think the theatre——"

"I don't object to the theatre, Glory. It is the derangement of your life I am thinking of, and if anybody is responsible for that, he is your enemy, not your friend."

"You will make me angry again, as you did before," and she began to bite her quivering lip.

"I did not come to make you angry, Glory; I came to ask you, even to entreat you, to break off this hateful connection."

"Because you know nothing of this—this connection, as you say—you call it hateful."

"I know what I am talking about, my child. The life these men live is worse than hateful, and it makes my heart bleed to see you falling a victim to it."

"You are degrading me again. You are always degrading me. Other men try to be agreeable to me, but you . . . Besides, I cannot hear my friends abused. Yes, they *are* my friends. I *was* at the theatre with them last night, and I am going to take tea at their chambers on my next holiday. So please——"

"Glory!"

With one plunge of his arm he had gripped her by the wrist.

"You are hurting me."

"You are never to set foot in the rooms of those men."

"Let me go."

"You are inexperienced as a child, Glory, and it is my duty to protect you against yourself."

"Let go, I say!"

"Don't destroy yourself. Think while there's time; think of your good name, your character."

"I shall do as I please."

"Listen! If I have chosen to be a clergyman, it's not because I've lived all my life in cotton-wool. Let me tell you what the lives of such men really are—the best of them, the very best. He gets up at noon, walks in the Park, takes tea with some one, grunts and groans that he must go to somebody's dinner-party, escapes to the Gaiety Theatre, sups at a so-called club——"

"You mean Lord Robert, but what right have you to say——"

"The right of one who knows him to be as bad as this, and worse—ten times worse. Such a man thinks he has a right to play with a girl if she is poor. She may stake her soul, her salvation, but he risks nothing. To-day he trifles with her, to-morrow he marries another, and flings her to the devil."

"There's something else in this. What is it?"

But John Storm had swung about and left her.

As soon as she was at liberty Glory went in search of Polly Love, expecting to find her in her cubicle, but the cubicle was empty. Coming out of the little room she saw a piece of paper lying on the floor. It was a letter, carefully folded. She picked it up, unfolded it, and read it, hardly knowing what she was doing, for her head was dizzy and her eyes were swimming in unshed tears. It ran—

"You ask, do I mean to adopt entirely? Yes, to bring up just the same as if it were born to me. I hope yours will be a strong and healthy boy, but if it is a girl——"

Glory could not understand what she was reading. Whose letter could it be? It was addressed "X.Y.Z., office of *Morning Post*."

There was a hurried footstep approaching, and Polly came in, with her eyes on the ground as if looking for something she had dropped. At the next moment she had snatched the letter out of Glory's hand and was saying—

"What are you doing in my room? Has your friend the chaplain told you to spy upon me?"

The expression on her face was appalling, and Glory, who had flushed up with shame, turned away without a word.

When John Storm got back to his room he found the following letter from the Canon on his table:—

"Since our interview of this morning (so strangely abridged) I have had the honour to visit your dear uncle, the Prime Minister, and he agrees with me that the strain of your recent examinations and the anxieties of a new occupation have probably disturbed your health, and that it will be prudent of you to take a short vacation. I have therefore the greatest pleasure in assuring you that you are free from duty for a week, a fortnight, or a month, as your convenience may determine, and during your much-regretted absence I will do my best to sustain the great loss of your invaluable help."

On reading the message John Storm flung himself into a chair and burst into a long peal of bitter laughter. But when the laughter was spent there came a sense of great loneliness. Then he remembered Mrs. Callender, and went across to her little house in Victoria Square, showed her the Canon's letter, and told her everything.

"Lies, lies, lies!" she said. "Ah, laddie, laddie, to lie, to know you lie, to be known to lie, and yet to go on lying—that is the whole art of life with these fashionable shepherds and their fashionable flock. As for that woman—ugh! She was separated from her husband for two years before his death, and he died in a hotel abroad without kith or kin to comfort him, and now she wears his hair in a gold locket on her bosom. That's what she is! But all's well that ends well, laddie. The holly will do ye good, for you were killing yerself with work. You'll no be spending it in your little island now, eh?"

John Storm was sitting with one leg across the other, and his head on his hand and his elbow on his knee.

"I shall spend it," he said, "in retreat at the Brotherhood in Bishopsgate."

"God bless me, man, is that the change of air ye'll be going to gie yoursell? It may be well enough for men with water in their veins; but you have blood, laddie, blood! Tak' care, tak' care!"

XVI

STILL AT MARTHA'S.

QUITE right, dear Aunt Anna, the terms "authority" and "obedience" must be known and honoured. Only when it is a case of put a penny in the slot and out comes the word of command, you can't exactly feel that way. The Board of Directors put the penny into the slot of this institution, and the word of command, so far as I am concerned, comes out of the mouth of Ward Sister Allworthy. I call her the White Owl. She is five feet ten, and has big round cheeks, which sometimes I should dearly love to slap—as mothers slap their "childers" when they administer a humiliating punishment.

So you think you notice "a certain want of aptitude?" Well, I don't think I am naturally a bad nurse, Aunt Anna. The patients like me, and they don't die of the dumps while I am about. Only I can't practise nursing by the rule of three, and as a consequence I get myself reported. Sister Allworthy has reported me three times, bless her! Thrice the brinded cat hath mew'd, and now she threatens to have me up before the matron. That dear soul has difficulties of locomotion, being buried under the Pelion on Ossa of a mountain of fat. She inhabits a cave of Adullam on the edge of the Inferno (*i.e.* the "theatre") below-stairs, and has a small dog with a bad heart and broken wind always nagging on her knee. I call her the Chief Broker in Breakages and Head Dealer in Diseases, and she is only seen once a day when she comes round to take stock. You have to be nice with her majesty, for she can haul you up at the weekly Board, and put a score against you in the black book, and send you away without a certificate. If that happens, a girl who expects to earn her living as a nurse has never any particular need to pray, "In all time of our wealth, Good Lord, deliver us."

But oh, my dear grandfather, what do you think of our John Storm now? After uttering the lamentations of Jeremiah and predicting all the plagues of Egypt, he has gone off to hold his peace, that is to say, he has gone to make his "Retreat," which being interpreted means praying without ceasing, and also without speaking, eighteen hours a day, six days at a spell, and sometimes sixty. When he comes back, reeking with all that holiness, I shall feel myself such a miserable sinner. . . .

Soberly, I could cry to think of it, though, and when I remember that perhaps I was partly to blame . . .

It was this way. In that "ter'ble discoorse" I told you he had scotched the snake, not killed it, and his vicar (I call him Mr. Worldly Wiseman), finding that his ladies and nobility went out, like the Pharisees, one by one, told our poor John he was ill and stood in need of instant rest. It looked like it, certainly, and the trouble must have been a sort of human rabies, in which the poor victim bites at his best friends first. He came here with his lower lip hanging like an old dog's, and I was so stupid as not to see that he was being hunted like a dog too, and only told myself how ugly and untidy he had grown of late. But the Sister had just before been showing me her tusks again, and being possessed with a fury, I gave it him world without end. He was very unreasonable, though, and seemed to say that I must have no friends and no amusements that were not of his choosing, and that after spending my days walking through the inside of this precious hospital, I must spend my nights walking round the outside of it. Being a woman of like passions with himself, I had a "ter'ble dust" with him on the subject, and the next I heard was that he was going to make "Retreat" in a kind of English Church monastery somewhere in the city, where he would "try to disentangle" himself "from the world" and see what he "ought to do next." He sent me his blessing with this message, and I sent him back mine—a less holy one, but he'll make it do.

I thought you would remember Mr. Drake's mother, dear Auntie Rachel. Yes, he is fair also, and wears his hair brushed across his forehead, much as you see in the portraits of Napoleon. In fact, he is a sort of fair-haired Napoleon in nature as well.

He took me to the theatre the other evening, and that was the great event I intended to tell you about. It was quite a proper sort of place, and nobody behaved badly except Glory, who kept talking and preaching and going silly with excitement all the evening through—with the result that everybody was staring me-wards and wanting to turn me out.

Since then Mr. Drake's friend, Lord Bob, who knows all the actors on earth seemingly, has taken us "behind," and we have seen a rehearsal. Things don't look quite the same behind as before, but nothing in the world does that, and I wasn't a bit disenchanted. In fact, I found everything delightfully romantic and amusing—and really I do not think it *can* be so very wicked to be an actress. Do you?

My friend, Polly Love, was with us—Polly is a probationer also, and sleeps in the cubicle next to mine,—and after the rehearsal we went to the gentlemen's chambers to tea. I can hear what Aunt Anna is saying, "Goodness gracious! you didn't do that, girl?" Well, yes, I did, though. In the interests of my sex I wanted to see how two boys could live in rooms all by themselves, and it's perfectly shocking how well they get on without a woman. Of course I wasn't such a silly as to let wit about that; but after I had examined their sitting-room, and cross-examined its owners on its numerous photographs (chiefly feminine), and tried how it feels to hold their big pipes between one's teeth, I whipped off my hat at once and began to put things straight for them, and then I made the tea.

By this time the gentlemen had changed into their jackets, and I sent them flying around for cups and saucers and sugar basins. It turned out that they had only one teaspoon in the place, and when anybody wanted to stir her tea, she said " Will you oblige me with *the* spoon, please?" What fun it was! We laughed until we cried—at least one of us did—and eventually we managed to break the teapot and a slop basin and to overturn a standing lamp. It was perfectly delightful.

But the best sport was after tea was over, and Glory was called on for imitations of the people we had seen at the theatre. Of course she couldn't imitate a man when she was in a woman's frock, so, being as bright as diamonds that night and twice "as impudent as a white stone,"[1] she actually conceived the idea of dressing up in man's clothes. Naturally the gentlemen were enchanted, so I hope Auntie Rachel isn't terribly shocked. Mr. Drake lent me his knickerbockers and a velvet jacket, and Polly and I went into the bedroom, where she helped me to find the way to put them on. With my own blouse and my own hat (I am wearing a felt one now with a broad brim and a feather), and, *of course*, my own slippers and stockings, I made a bogh of a boy, I can tell you. I thought Polly would have died of delight in the bedroom, but when we came out, she kept covering her face and crying, "Glory, how *can* you?"

I'm afraid I sang and talked more than was good for the soul, but it was all Mr. Drake's doing. He declared I was such a marvellous mimic that it was simply a waste of time and the good gifts of God to go on hospital nursing any longer. And I do believe that if anything happened, and the need arose, he would . . .

Only fancy Glory a public person, and all the world and his wife going down on their knees to her! But then it is fearful to think of being an actress, isn't it?

After all such glorious "outs" I have to go "in" to the

[1] A Manx proverb.

hospital, and then comes my fit again. Do you remember my little boy who said he was going to the angels, and he would get lots of gristly pork up there? He has gone, and I don't think I like nursing children now. Oh, how I long to go out into the world! I want to shine in it! I want to become great and glorious. I could do it too I know I could. I have got it in me, I am sure I have. Yet here I am in a little dark corner crying for the sunshine!

How silly this is, isn't it? It sounds like madness. My dears, allow me to introduce you to some one—

GLORY QUAYLE,
March Hare and Madwoman.

XVII

THE Board-room of the Hospital of Martha's Vineyard was a large and luxurious chamber, with an oval window at its farther end, and its two side-walls panelled with portraits of former chairmen and physicians. In great oaken arm-chairs, behind ponderous oaken tables, covered with green cloth and furnished with writing-pads, the Board of Governors sat in three sides of a square, leaving an open space in the middle. This open space was reserved for patients seeking admission or receiving discharge, and for officers of the hospital presenting their weekly reports.

On a morning in August the matron's report had closed with a startling item. It recommended the immediate suspension of a nurse on the ground of gross impropriety of conduct. The usual course in such a case was for the Board of the hospital to depute the matron to act for them in private, but the chairman in this instance was a peppery person, with a stern mouth and a solid under-jaw.

"This is a most serious matter," he said. "I think—this being a public institution—I really think the Board should investigate the case for itself. We ought to assure ourselves that—that, in fact, no other irregularity is going on in the hospital."

"May it please your lordship," said a rotund voice from one of the side-tables, "I would suggest that a case like this of grievous moral delinquency comes directly within the dispensation of the chaplain, and if he has done his duty by the unhappy girl (as no doubt he has), he must have a statement to make to the Board with regard to her."

It was Canon Wealthy.

"I may mention," he added, "that Mr. Storm has now returned to his duties and is at present in the hospital."

"Send for him," said the chairman.

When John Storm entered the Board-room, it was remarked that he looked no better for his holiday. His cheeks were thinner, his eyes more hollow, and there was a strange pallor under his swarthy skin.

The business was explained to him, and he was asked if he had any statement to make with regard to the nurse whom the matron had reported for suspension.

"No," he said, "I have no statement."

"Do you mean to tell the Board," said the chairman, "that you know nothing of this matter—that the case is too trivial for your attention—or perhaps that you have never even spoken to the girl on the subject?"

"That is so; I never have," said John.

"Then you shall do so now," said the chairman, and he put his hand on the bell beside him, and the messenger appeared.

"You cannot intend, sir, to examine the girl here," said John.

"And why not?"

"Before so many—and all of us men save one. Surely the matron——"

The Canon rose to his feet again. "My young brother is naturally sensitive, my lord, but I assure him his delicate feelings are wasted on a girl like this. He forgets that the shame lies in the girl's sin, not in her just and necessary punishment."

"Bring her in," said the chairman. The matron whispered to the messenger, and he left the room.

"Pardon me, sir," said John Storm; "if it is your expectation that I should question the nurse on her sin, as the Canon says, I cannot do so."

"Cannot?"

"Well, I will not."

"And is that your idea of your duty as a chaplain?"

"It is the matron's duty, not the chaplain's, to——"

"The matron! the matron! This is your parish, sir, your parish! A great public institution is in danger of a disgraceful scandal, and you, who are responsible for its spiritual welfare . . . Really, gentlemen——"

Again the Canon rose with a conciliatory smile. "I think I understand my young friend," said he, "and your lordship and the Board will appreciate his feelings however you may disapprove of his judgment. What generous heart cannot sympathise with the sensitive spirit of the youthful clergyman who shrinks from the spectacle of guilt and shame in a young, and perhaps beautiful, woman. But if it will relieve your lordship from an embarrassing position, I am myself willing——"

"Thank you," said the chairman, and then the girl was brought into the room in charge of Sister Allworthy.

She was holding her head down and trying to cover her face with her hands.

"Your name, girl?" said the Canon.

"Mary Elizabeth Love," she faltered.

"You are aware, Mary Elizabeth Love, that our excellent and indulgent matron" (here he bowed to a stout lady who sat in the open space) "has been put to the painful duty of reporting you for suspension, which is equivalent to your immediate discharge. Now, I cannot hold out a hope that the Board will not ratify her recommendation, but it may perhaps qualify the terms of your 'character' if you can show these gentlemen that the unhappy lapse from good conduct which brings you to this position of shame and disgrace is due in any measure to irregularities practised perhaps within this hospital, or to the temptations of any one connected with it."

The girl began to cry.

"Speak, nurse; if you have anything to say, the gentlemen are willing to hear it."

The girl's crying deepened into sobs.

"Useless!" said the chairman.

"Impossible!" said the Canon.

But some one suggested that perhaps the nurse had a girl friend in the hospital who could throw light on the difficult situation. Then Sister Allworthy whispered to the matron, who said, "Bring her in."

John Storm's face had assumed a fixed and absent expression, but he saw a girl of larger size than Polly Love enter the room with a gleam, as it were, of sunshine on her golden red hair. It was Glory.

There was some preliminary whispering, and then the Canon began again—

"You are a friend and companion of Mary Elizabeth Love?"

"Yes," said Glory.

Her voice was full and calm, and a look of quiet courage lit up her girlish beauty.

"You have known her other friends, no doubt, and perhaps you have shared her confidence?"

"I think so."

"Then you can tell the Board if the unhappy condition in

which she finds herself is due to any one connected with this hospital."

"I think not."

"Not to any officer, servant, or member of any school attached to it?"

"No."

"Thank you," said the chairman, "that is quite enough," and down the tables of the governors there were nods and smiles of satisfaction.

"What have I done?" said Glory.

"You have done a great service to an ancient and honourable institution," said the Canon, "and the best return the Board can make for your candour and intelligence is to advise you to avoid such companionship for the future and to flee such perilous associations."

A certain desperate recklessness expressed itself in Glory's face, and she stepped up to Polly, who was now weeping audibly, and put her arm about the girl's waist.

"What are the girl's relatives?" said the chairman.

The matron replied out of her book. Polly was an orphan, both her parents being dead. She had a brother, who had lately been a patient in the hospital, but he was only a lay helper in the Anglican monastery at Bishopsgate Street, and therefore useless for present purposes.

There was some further whispering about the tables. Was this the girl who had been recommended to the hospital by the coroner who had investigated a certain notorious and tragic case? Yes.

"I think I have heard of some poor and low relations," said the Canon; "but their own condition is probably too needy to allow them to help her at a time like the present."

Down to this moment Polly had done nothing but cry, but now she flamed up in a passion of pride and resentment.

"It's false!" she cried. "I have no poor and low relations, and I want nobody's help. My friend is a gentleman—as much a gentleman as anybody here—and I can tell you his name if you like. He lives in St. James's Street, and he is Lord——"

"Stop, girl!" said the Canon in a loud voice. "We cannot allow you to compromise the honour of a gentleman by mentioning his name in his absence."

John stepped to one of the tables of the governors and took up a pamphlet which lay there. It was the last annual report of Martha's Vineyard, with a list of its governors and subscribers.

"The girl is suspended," said the chairman, and reaching for the matron's book, he signed it and returned it.

"This," said the Canon, "appears to be a case for Mrs.

Callender's Maternity Home at Soho, and with the consent of the Board I will request the chaplain to communicate with that lady immediately."

John Storm had heard, but he made no answer; he was turning over the leaves of the pamphlet.

The Canon hemmed and cleared his throat. "Mary Elizabeth Love," he said, "you have brought a stain upon this honourable and hitherto irreproachable institution, but I trust and believe that ere long, and before your misbegotten child is born, you may see cause to be grateful for our forbearance and our charity. Speaking for myself, I confess it is an occasion of grief to me, and might well, I think, be a cause of sorrow to him who has had your spiritual welfare in his keeping" (here he gave a look towards John), "that you do not seem to realise the position of infamy in which you stand. We have always been taught to think of a woman as sweet and true and pure, a being hallowed to our sympathy by the most sacred associations and endeared to our love by the tenderest ties, and it is only right" (the Canon's voice was breaking), "it is only right, I say, that you should be told at once and in this place, though tardily and too late, that for the woman who wrongs that great ideal, as you have wronged it, there is but one name known among persons of good credit and good report—a hard name, a terrible name, a name of contempt and loathing—the name of *prostitute*."

Crushing the pamphlet in his hand, John Storm had taken a step towards the Canon, but he was too late. Some one was there before him. It was Glory. With her head erect and her eyes flashing she stood between the weeping girl and the black-coated judge, and everybody could see the swelling and heaving of her bosom.

"How dare you!" she cried. "You say you have been taught to think of a woman as sweet and pure. Well, *I* have been taught to think of a *man* as strong and brave, and tender and merciful to every living creature, but most of all to a woman if she is erring and fallen. But you are not brave and tender; you are cruel and cowardly, and I despise you and hate you!"

The men at the tables were rising from their seats.

"Oh, you have discharged my friend," she said, "and you may discharge me too if you like—if you *dare!* But I will tell everybody that it was because I would not let you insult a poor girl with a cruel and shameful name, and trample upon her when she was down. And everybody will believe me, because it is the truth; and anything else you may say will be a lie, and all the world will know it!"

The matron was shambling up also.

"How dare you, Miss! Go back to your ward this instant! Do you know whom you are speaking to?"

"Oh, it's not the first time I've spoken to a clergyman, ma'am. I'm the daughter of a clergyman, and the granddaughter of a clergyman, and I know what a clergyman is when he is brave and good, and gentle and merciful to all women, and when he is a man and a gentleman—not a Pharisee and a crocodile!"

"Please, take that girl away," said the chairman.

But John Storm was by her side in a moment.

"No, sir," he said, "nobody shall do that."

But now Glory had broken down too, and the girls, like two lost children, were crying on each other's breasts. John opened the door, and led them up to it.

"Take your friend to her room, nurse; I shall be with you presently."

Then he turned back to the chairman, still holding the crumpled pamphlet in his hand, and said calmly and respectfully—

"And now that you have finished with the woman, sir, may I ask what you intend to do with the man?"

"What man?"

"Though I did not feel myself qualified to sit in judgment on the broken heart of a fallen girl, I happen to know the name which she was forbidden to mention, and I find it here, sir—here in your list of subscribers and governors."

"Well, what of it?"

"You have wiped the girl out of your books, sir. Now I ask you to wipe the man out also."

"Gentlemen," said the chairman, rising, "the business of the Board is at an end."

XVIII

JOHN STORM wrote a letter to Mrs. Callender, explaining Polly Love's situation, and asking her to call on the girl immediately; and then he went out in search of Lord Robert Ure at the address he had discovered in the report.

He found the man alone on his arrival, but Drake came in soon afterwards. Lord Robert received him with a chilly bow; Drake offered his hand coldly; neither of them requested him to sit.

"You are surprised at my visit, gentlemen," said John, "but I have just now been present at a painful scene, and I thought it necessary that you should know something about it."

Then he described what had occurred in the Board-room, and in doing so dwelt chiefly on the abjectness of the girl's humiliation. Lord Robert stood by the window rapping a tune on the window-pane, and Drake sat in a low chair with his legs stretched out and his hands in his trouser-pockets.

"But I am at a loss to understand why you have thought it necessary to come here to tell that story," said Lord Robert.

"Lord Robert," said John, "you understand me perfectly."

"Excuse me, Mr. Storm, I do not understand you in the least."

"Then I will not ask you if you are responsible for the girl's position."

"Don't."

"But I will ask you a simpler and easier question."

"What is it?"

"When are you going to marry her?"

Lord Robert burst into ironical laughter, and faced round to Drake.

"Well, these men—these curates—their assurance, don't you know. . . . May I ask your reverence, what is *your* position in this matter—your standing, don't you know?"

"That of chaplain of the hospital."

"But you say she has been turned out of it."

"Very well, Lord Robert, merely that of a man who intends to protect an injured woman."

"Oh, I know," said Lord Robert drily; "I understand these heroics. I've heard of your sermons, Mr. Storm—your interviews with ladies, and so forth."

"And I have heard of your doings with girls," said John. "What are you going to do for this one?"

"Exactly what I please."

"Take care. You know what the girl is. It's precisely such girls . . . At this moment she is tottering on the brink of hell, Lord Robert. If anything further should happen—if you should disappoint her . . . she is looking to you and building up hopes —if she should fall still lower and destroy herself body and soul——"

"My dear Mr. Storm, please understand that I shall do everything or nothing for the girl exactly as I think well, don't you know, without the counsel or coercion of any clergyman."

There was a short silence, and then John Storm said quietly, "It is no worse than I expected. But I had to hear it from your own lips, and I have heard it. Good-day."

He went back to the hospital and asked for Glory. She was banished with Polly to the housekeeper's room. Polly was catching flies on the window (which overlooked the Park) and humming "Sigh no more, ladies." Glory's eyes were red with weeping. John drew Glory aside.

"I have written to Mrs. Callender, and she will be here presently," he said.

"It is useless," said Glory. "Polly will refuse to go. She expects Lord Robert to come for her, and she wants me to call on Mr. Drake."

"But I have seen the man myself."

"Lord Robert?"

"Yes. . . . He will do nothing."

"Nothing!"

"Nothing, or worse than nothing."

"Impossible!"

"Nothing of that kind is impossible to men like those."

"They are not so bad as that, though; and even if Lord Robert is all you say, Mr. Drake——"

"They are friends and housemates, Glory, and what the one is the other must be also."

"Oh, no; Mr. Drake is quite a different person."

"Don't be misled, my child. If there were any real difference between them——"

"But there is; and if a girl were in trouble or wanted help in anything——"

"He would drop her, Glory, like an old lottery ticket that has drawn a blank and is done for."

She was biting her lip, and it was bleeding slightly.

"You dislike Mr. Drake," she said, "and that is why you cannot be just to him. But he is always praising and excusing you, and when any one——"

"His praises and excuses are nothing to me. I am not thinking of myself. I am thinking——"

He had a look of intense excitement, and his speaking was abrupt and disconnected.

"You were splendid this morning, Glory, and when I think of the girl who defied that Pharisee being perhaps herself the victim . . . The man asked me what my standing was, as if that . . . But if I had really had a right, if the girl had been anything to me, if she had been somebody else, and not a light, shallow, worthless creature, do you know what I should have said to him? 'Since things have gone so far, sir, you must marry the girl now, and keep her, and be faithful to her, and love her, or else I——'"

"You are flushed and excited, and there is something I do not understand——"

"Promise me, Glory, that you will break off this bad connection."

"You are unreasonable. I cannot promise."

"Promise that you will never see these men again."

"But I must see Mr. Drake at once and arrange about Polly."

"Don't mention the man's name again; it makes my blood boil to hear you speak it."

"But this is tyranny, and you are worse than the Canon, and I cannot bear it."

"Very well; as you will. It's of no use struggling. . . . What is the time?"

"Six o'clock, nearly."

"I must see the Canon before he goes to dinner."

His manner had changed suddenly. He looked crushed and benumbed.

"I am going now," he said, turning aside.

"So soon? When shall I see you again?"

"God knows . . . I mean . . . I don't know," he answered in a helpless way.

He was looking around as if taking a mental farewell of everything.

"But we cannot part like this," she said. "I think you like me a little still, and——"

Her supplicating voice made him look up into her face for a moment. Then he turned away, saying "Good-bye, Glory." And with a look of utter exhaustion he went out of the room.

Glory walked to a window at the end of the corridor, that she might see him when he crossed the street. There was just a glimpse of his back as he turned the corner with a slow step and his head on his breast. She went back crying.

"I could fancy a fresh herring for supper, dear," said Polly. "What do you say, housekeeper?"

John Storm went back to the Canon's house a crushed and humiliated man. "I can do no more," he thought. "I will give it up." His old influence with Glory must have been lost. Something had come between them—something or some one. "Anyhow, it is all over, and I must go away somewhere."

To go on seeing Glory would be useless. It would also be dangerous. As often as he was face to face with her he wanted to lay hold of her and say, "You must do this and this, because it is my wish and direction and command, and it is *I* that say so." In the midst of God's work how subtle were the temptations of the devil!

But with every step that he went plodding home there came other feelings. He could see the girl quite plainly, her fresh young face, so strong and so tender, so full of humour and heart's love, and all the sweet beauty of her form and figure. Then the old pain in his breast came back again, and he began to be afraid.

"I will take refuge in the Church," he thought. In prayer and penance and fasting he would find help and consolation. The Church was peace—peace from the noise of life, and strength to fight and to vanquish. But the Church must be the Church of God—not of the world, the flesh, and the devil.

"Ask the Canon if he can see me immediately," said John Storm to the footman, and he stood in the hall for the answer.

The Canon had taken tea that day in the study with his daughter Felicity. He was reclining on the sofa, propped up with velvet cushions, and holding the teacup and saucer like the wings of a butterfly in both hands.

"We have been deceived, my dear" (sip, sip), "and we must pay the penalty of the deception. Yet we have nothing to blame ourselves for—nothing whatever. Here was a young man from heaven knows where, bent on entering the diocese. True, he was merely the son of a poor lord who had lived the life of a hermit, but he was also the nephew, and presumably the heir, of the Prime Minister of England." (Sip, sip, sip.) "Well, I gave him his title. I received him into my house. I made him free of my family—and what is the result? He has disregarded my instructions, antagonised my supporters, and borne himself towards me with an attitude of defiance, if not disdain."

Felicity poured out a second cup of tea for her father, sympathised with him, and set forth her own grievances. The young man had no conversation, and his reticence was quite embarrassing. Sometimes when she had friends and asked him to come down, his silence—well, really——

"We might have borne with these little deficiencies, my dear, if the Prime Minister had been deeply interested. But he is not. I doubt if he has ever seen his nephew since that first occasion. And when I called at Downing Street about the time of the sermon, he seemed entirely undisturbed. 'The young man is in the wrong place, my dear Canon; send him back to me.' That was all."

"Then why don't you do it?" said Felicity.

"It is coming to that, my child; but blood is thicker than water, you know, and after all——"

It was at this moment the footman entered the room to ask if the Canon could see Mr. Storm.

"Ah, the man himself!" said the Canon, rising. "Jenkyns,

remove the tray." Dropping his voice, "Felicity, I will ask you to leave us together. After what occurred this morning at the hospital anything like a scene . . ." Then aloud, "Bring him in, Jenkyns. . . . Say something, my dear. Why don't you speak? . . . Come in, my dear Storm. You'll see to that matter for me, Felicity. Thanks, thanks! Sorry to send you off, but I'm sure Mr. Storm will excuse you. Good-bye for the present."

Felicity went out as John Storm came in. He looked excited, and there was an expression of pain in his face.

"I am sorry to disturb you, but I need not detain you long," he said.

"Sit down, Mr. Storm, sit down," said the Canon, returning to the sofa.

But John did not sit. He stood by the chair vacated by Felicity, and kept beating his hat on the back of it.

"I have come to tell you, sir, that I wish to resign my curacy."

The Canon glanced up with a stealthy expression and thought, "How clever of him! To resign before he is told plainly that he has to go—that is very clever."

Then he said aloud, "I am sorry, very sorry. I'm always sorry to part with my clergy. Still—you see I am entirely frank with you—I have observed that you have not been comfortable of late, and I think you are acting for the best. When do you wish to leave me?"

"As soon as convenient—as early as I can be spared."

The Canon smiled condescendingly. "That need not trouble you at all. With a staff like mine, you see . . . Of course you are aware that I am entitled to three months' notice?"

"Yes."

"But I will waive it; I will not detain you. Have you seen your uncle on the subject?"

"No."

"When you do so, please say that I always try to remove impediments from a young man's path if he is uncomfortable—in the wrong place, for example."

"Thank you," said John Storm, and then he hesitated a moment before stepping to the door.

The Canon rose and bowed affably. "Not an angry word," he thought. "Who shall say that blood does not count for something?"

"Believe me, my dear Storm," he said aloud, "I shall always remember with pride and pleasure our early connection. Perhaps I think you are acting unwisely, even foolishly, but it will continue to be a source of satisfaction to me that I was able to give you your first opportunity, and if your next curacy should chance to be in London, I trust you will allow us to maintain the acquaintance."

John Storm's face was twitching and his pulses were beating violently, but he was trying to control himself.

"Thank you," he said; "but it is not very likely——"

"Don't say you are giving up orders, dear Mr. Storm, or perhaps that you are only leaving our Church in order to unite yourself to another. Ah! have I touched on a tender point? You must not be surprised that rumours have been rife. We cannot silence the tongues of busybodies and mischief-makers, you know. And I confess, speaking as your spiritual head and adviser, it would be a source of grief to me if a young clergyman who has eaten the bread of the Establishment, and my own as well, were about to avow himself the subject and slave of an Italian bishop."

John Storm came back from the door.

"What you are saying, sir, requires that I should be plain-spoken. In giving up my curacy I am not leaving the Church of England, I am only leaving you."

"I am so glad, so relieved."

"I am leaving you because I cannot live with you any longer, because the atmosphere you breathe is impossible to me, because your religion is not my religion or your God my God!"

"You surprise me. What have I done?"

"A month ago I asked you to set your face as a clergyman against the shameful and immoral marriage of a man of scandalous reputation, but you refused; you excused the man and sided with him. This morning you thought it necessary to investigate in public the case of one of that man's victims, and you sided with the man again—you denied to the girl the right even to mention the scoundrel's name."

"How differently we see things! Do you know I thought my examination of the poor young thing was merciful to the point of gentleness. And that I may tell you—notwithstanding the female volcano who came down on me—was the view of the Board and of his lordship the chairman."

"Then I am sorry to differ from them. I thought it unnecessary and unmanly and brutal, and even blasphemous."

"Mr. Storm! Do you know what you are saying?"

"Perfectly, and I came to say it."

His eyes were wild, his voice was hoarse; he was like a man breaking the bonds of a tyrannical slavery.

"You called that poor child a prostitute because she had

wasted the good gifts which God had given her. But God has given good gifts to you also—gifts of intellect and eloquence with which you might have raised the fallen and supported the weak, and defended the down-trodden and comforted the broken-hearted—and what have you done with them? You have bartered them for benefices, and peddled them for popularity; you have given them in exchange for money, for houses, for furniture, for things like this—and this—and this. You have sold your birthright for a mess of pottage, therefore *you* are the prostitute."

"You're not yourself, sir; leave me," and crossing the room the Canon touched the bell.

"Yes, ten thousand times more the prostitute than that poor fallen girl with her taint of blood and will. There would be no such women as she is to fall victims to evil companionship if there were no such men as you are to excuse their betrayers and to side with them. Who is most the prostitute—the woman who sells her body or the man who sells his soul?"

"You're mad, sir! But I want no scene——"

"You are the worst prostitute on the streets of London, and yet you are in the Church, in the pulpit, and you call yourself a follower of the One who forgave the woman and shamed the hypocrites, and had not where to lay His head!"

But the Canon had faced about and fled out of the room.

The footman came in answer to the bell, and finding no one but John Storm, he told him that a lady was waiting for him in a carriage at the door.

It was Mrs. Callender. She had come to say that she had called at the hospital for Polly Love and the girl had refused to go to the home at Soho.

"But whatever's amiss with ye, man?" she said. "You might have seen a ghost!"

He had come out bareheaded, carrying his hat in his hand.

"It's all over," he said. "I've waited weeks and weeks for it, but it's over at last. It was of no use mincing matters, so I spoke out."

His red eyes were ablaze, but a great load seemed to be lifted off his mind, and his soul seemed to exult.

"I have told him I must leave him, and I am to go immediately. The disease was dire and the remedy had to be dire also."

The old lady was holding her breath and watching his flushed face with strained attention.

"And what may ye be going to do now?"

"To become a religious in something more than the name;

to leave the world altogether, with its idleness and pomp and hypocrisy and unreality."

"Get yoursel some flesh on your bones first, man. It's easy to see ye've no been sleeping or eating these days and days together."

"That's nothing—nothing at all. God cannot take half your soul. You must give yourself entirely."

"Eh, laddie, laddie, I feared me this was what ye were coming till. But a man cannot bury himsel before he is dead. He may bury the half of himsel, but is it the better half? What of his thoughts—his wandering thoughts? Choose for yoursel, though, and if you must go—if you must hide yoursel for ever, and this is the last I'm to see of ye . . . ye may kiss me, laddie—I'm old enough, surely . . . Go on James, man; what for are ye sitting up there staring?"

When John Storm returned to his room he found a letter from Parson Quayle. It was a good-natured, cackling epistle, full of sweet nothings about Glory and the hospital, about Peel and the discovery of ancient runes in the graveyards of the treen chapels, but it closed with this postscript:—

"You will remember old Chalse, a sort of itinerant beggar and the privileged pet of everybody. The silly old gawk has got hold of your father, and has actually made the old man believe that you are bewitched! Some one has put the evil eye on you—some woman, it would seem, and that is the reason why you have broken away and behaved so strangely! It is most extraordinary. That such a foolish superstition should have taken hold of a man like your father is really quite astonishing; but if it will only soften his rancour against you and help to restore peace, we may perhaps forgive the distrust of Providence and the outrage on common-sense. All's well that ends well, you know, and we shall all be happy."

XIX

MARTHA'S.

LOST, STOLEN, OR STRAYED—a man, a clergyman, answers to the name of John Storm. Or rather he does not answer, having allowed himself to be written to twice without making so much as a yap or a yowl by way of reply. Last seen six days ago, when he was suffering from the sulks, after being in a de'il of a temper with a helpless and innocent maiden who "doesn't know nothin'" that can have given him offence. Any one giving information of his welfare and whereabouts to the said H. and I. M. will be generously and appropriately rewarded.

But soberly, my dear John Storm, what has become of you? Where are you, and whatever have you been doing since the day of the dreadful inquisition? Frightful rumours are flying through the air like knives, and they cut and wound a poor girl woefully. Therefore be good enough to reply by return of post—and in person.

Meantime please accept it as a proof of my eternal regard that, after two knock-down blows received in silence, I am once more coming up smiling. Know then that Mr. Drake has justified all expectations, having compelled Lord Robert to provide for Polly, who is now safely ensconced in her own country castle somewhere in St. John's Wood, furnished to hand with servants and vassals complete. Thus you will be charmed to observe in me the growth of the prophetic instinct, for you will remember my positive prediction, that if a girl were in trouble, and the necessity arose, Mr. Drake would be the first to help her. Of course he had a great deal to say that was as sweet as sirup on the loyalty of my own friendship also, and he expended much beautiful rhetoric on yourself as well. It seems that you are one of those who follow the impulse of the heart entirely, while the rest of us divide our allegiance with the head; and if you display sometimes the severity of a tyrant of our sex, that is only to be set down as another proof of your regard, and of the elevation of the pedestal whereon you desire us to be placed. Thus he reconciles me to the harmony of the universe and makes all things easy and agreeable.

This being the case, I have now to inform you that Polly's baby has come, having hastened his arrival (it is a man, bless it!) owing either to the tears or the terrors of the crocodile. And being on night duty now, and therefore at liberty from 6.30 to 8.30, I intend to pay him my first call of ceremony this evening, when anybody else would be welcome to accompany me who might be willing to come to his shrine of innocence and love in the spirit of the wise men of the East. But lest anybody *should* inquire for me at the hospital at the first of the hours aforesaid, this is to give warning that the White Owl has expressly forbidden all intercourse between the members of her staff and the discharged and dishonoured mother. Set it down to my spirit of contradiction that I intend to disregard the mandate, though I am only too well aware that the poor discharged and dishonoured one has no other idea of friendship than that of a loyalty in which she shares but is not sharing. Of course woman is born to such selfishness as the sparks fly upward; but if I should ever meet with a man who isn't, I will just give myself up to him, body and soul and belongings, unless he has a wife or other encumbrance already and is booked for this world, and in that event I will enter into my own recognisances and be bound over to him for the next. GLORY.

At 6.30 that evening Glory stood waiting in the portico of the hospital, but John Storm did not come. At 7 she was ringing at the bell of a little house in St. John's Wood that stood behind a high wall and had an iron grating in the garden door. The bell was answered by a good-natured, slack-looking servant, who was friendly, and even familiar in a moment.

"Are you the young lady from the hospital? The Missis told me about you. I'm Liza, and come upstairs. . . . Yes, doing nicely, thank you, both of 'em is—and mind your head, Miss."

Polly was in a little bandbox of a bedroom, looking more pink and white than ever against the linen of her frilled pillow-slips. By the bedside a woman of uncertain age in deep mourning, with little twinkling eyes and fat cheeks, was rocking the baby on her knee and babbling over it in words of maudlin endearment.

"Bless it, 'ow it do notice! Boo-loo-loo!"

Glory leaned over the little one and pronounced it the prettiest baby she had ever seen.

"Syme 'ere, Miss. There ain't sech another in all London! It's jest the sort of baby you can love. Pore little thing, it's quite took to me already, as if it wanted to enkirridge you, my dear."

"This is Mrs. Jupe," said Polly, "and she's going to take baby to nurse."

"Boo-loo-loo-loo! And a nice new cradle's awaiting of it afront of the fire in my little back-parlour. Boo-loo!"

"But surely you're never going to part with your baby!" said Glory.

"Why, what do you suppose, dear? Do you think I'm going to be tied to a child all my days, and never be able to go anywhere or do anything or amuse myself at all?"

"Jest that. It'll be to our mootual benefit, as I said when I answered your advertisement."

Glory asked the woman if she was married and had any children of her own.

"Me, Miss? I've been married eleven years, and I've allwiz prayed the dear Lord to gimme childring. Got any? On'y one little girl; but I want to adopt another from the birth, so as to have something to love when my own's growd up."

Glory supposed that Polly could see her baby at any time, but the woman answered doubtfully—

"Can she see baby? Well, I would rather not, certingly. If I tyke it, I want to feel it is syme as my very own and do my dooty by it, pore thing; and if the mother were coming and going, I should allwiz feel as she 'ad the first claim."

Polly showed no interest in the conversation until Mrs. Jupe asked for the name of her "friend," in lieu of eighty pounds that were to be paid down on delivery of the child.

"Come, myke up your mind, my dear, and let me tyke it away at onct. Give me 'is name, that's good enough for me."

After some hesitation Glory gave Lord Robert's name and address, and the woman prepared the child for its departure.

"Don't tyke on so, my dear. 'Tain't seeh a great crime, and many a laidy of serciety 'as done worse."

At the street door Glory asked Mrs. Jupe for her own address, and the woman gave her a card, saying if she ever wanted to leave the hospital it would be easy to help such a fine-looking young woman as she was to make a bit of living for herself.

Polly recovered speedily from the trouble of the child's departure, and presently assumed an easy and almost patronising tone towards Glory, pretending to be amused, and even a little indignant, when asked how soon she expected to be fit for business again, and able to do without Lord Robert's assistance.

"To tell you the truth," she said, "I was as much to blame as he was. I wanted to escape from the drudgery of the hospital, and I knew he would take me when the time came."

Glory left early, vowing in her heart she would come no more. When she changed her omnibus at Piccadilly the Circus was very full of women.

"Letter for you, nurse," said the porter as she entered the hospital. It was from John Storm :—

DEAR GLORY,—I have at length decided to enter the Brotherhood at Bishopsgate Street, and I am to go into the monastery this evening. It is not as a visitor that I am going this time, but as a postulant or novice, and in the hope of becoming worthy in due course to take the vows of life-long consecration. Therefore I am writing to you probably for the last time, and parting from you perhaps for ever.

Since we came up to London together I have suffered many shocks and disappointments, and I seem to have been torn in ribbons. My cherished dreams have proved to be delusions; the palaces I had built up for myself have turned out to be pasteboard, gilt, and rubbish; I have been robbed of all my jewels, or they have shown themselves to be shingle stones. In this condition of shame and disillusionment I am now resolved to escape at the same time from the world and from myself, for I am tired of both alike, and already I feel as if a great weight had been lifted off me.

But I wish to speak of you. You must have thought me cantankerous, and so I have been sometimes, but always by conviction and on principle. I could not countenance the fashionable morality that is corrupting the manhood of the laity, or endure the toleration that is making the clergy thoroughly wicked. I could not without a pang see you cater to the world's appetites or be drawn into its gaieties and frivolities; and it was agony to me to fear that a girl of your pure if passionate nature might perhaps fall a victim to a gamester in life's follies—an actor indulging a pastime—a mere cheat.

And what you tell me of your friend's altered circumstances does not relieve me of such anxieties. The man who has deceived a girl once is likely to deceive her again. Short of marriage itself, such connections should be cut off entirely, whatever the price. When they are maintained in relations of liberty, the victim is sure to be further victimised, and her last state is always worse than the first.

However, I do not wish to blame anybody, least of all you, who have done everything for the best, and especially now when I am parting from you for ever. You have never realised how much you have been to me, and I doubt if I knew it myself until to-day. You know how I was brought up—with a solitary old man—God be with him—who tried to be good to me for the sake of his ambitions, and to love me for the sake of his revenge. I never knew my mother, I never had a sister, and I can never have a wife. You were all three to me, and yourself besides. There were no women in our household, and you stood for woman in my life. I have never told you this before, but now I tell it as a dying man whispers his secret with his parting breath.

I have written my letters of farewell—one to my father, asking his forgiveness if I have done him any wrong, one to my uncle with my love and thanks, and one to your good old grandfather, giving up my solemn and sacred trust of you. My conduct will, of course, be condemned as weak and foolish from many points of view; but by my departure some difficulties will be removed, and for the rest I have come to see that everything is done by the spirit and nothing by the flesh, and that by prayer and fasting I can help and protect you more than by counsel and advice. Thus everything is for the best.

The Rule under which the Brothers live in community forbids them to write and receive letters without special permission, or even to think too constantly of the world outside; and now that I am on the eve of that new life, memories of the old one keep crowding on me as on a drowning man. But they are all of one period—the days when we were at Peel in your sweet little island, before the vain and cruel world came in between us, when you were a simple, merry girl, and I was little more than a happy boy, and we went plunging and laughing through your bright blue sea together.

But earth's joys grow very dim and its glories are fading. That also is for the best. I have my Koh-i-noor—my desire to depart and surrender my life to God.   JOHN STORM.

"Anything wrong, nurse? Feeling ill, ain't ye? Only dizzy a bit? Unpleasant news from home, perhaps?"

"No, something else. Let me sit in your room, porter."

She read the letter again and again, until the words seemed blurred and the lines irregular as a spider's web. Then she thought, "We cannot part for ever like this. I must see him again, whatever happens. Perhaps he has not yet gone."

It was now half-past eight and time to go on duty, but she went upstairs to Sister Allworthy and asked for an hour's further leave. The request was promptly refused. She went downstairs to the matron, and asked for half-an-hour only that she might see a friend away on a long journey, and that was refused too. Then she tightened her quivering lips, returned to the porter's room, fixed her bonnet on before the scratched pier-glass, and boldly walked out of the hospital.

It was now quite dark and the fashionable dinner-hour of Belgravia, and as she hurried through the streets many crested and coroneted carriages drew up at the great mansions and discharged their occupants in evening dress. The Canon's house was brilliantly lighted, and when the door was opened in answer to her knock, she could see the Canon himself at the head of his own detachment of diners coming downstairs with a lady in white silk chatting affably on his arm.

"Is Mr. Storm at home?"

The footman, in powdered wig and white cotton gloves, answered haltingly, "If it is—er—anything about the hospital, Miss, Mr.—er—Golightly will attend."

"No, it is Mr. Storm himself I wish to see."

"Gorn!" said the footman, and he shut the door in her face.

She had an impulse to hammer on the door with her hand,

and command the flunkey to go down on his knees and beg her pardon. But what was the good? She had no time to think of herself now.

As a last resource she would go to Bishopsgate. How dense the traffic seemed to be at Victoria! She had never felt so helpless before.

It was better in the City, and as she walked eastward in the direction indicated by a policeman, every step brought her into quieter streets. She was now in that part of London which is the world's busiest market-place by day but is shut up and deserted at night. Her light footsteps echoed against the shutters of the shops. The moon had risen and she could see far down the empty street.

She found the place at last. It was one of London's weather-beaten old churches, shouldered by shops on either hand, and almost pushed back by the tide of traffic. There was an iron gate at the side, leading by an arched passage to a little court-yard which was bounded by two high blank walls, by the back wall of the church, and by the front of a large house with a small doorway and many small windows. In the middle of the courtyard there was a tree with a wooden seat round its trunk.

And being there, she felt afraid and almost wished she had not come. The church was dimly lighted, and she thought perhaps the cleaners were within. But presently there was a sound of singing, in men's voices only, and without any kind of musical accompaniment. Just then the clock in the steeple struck nine and chimes began to play—

"Days and moments quickly flying."

The singing came to an end, and there was some low in-articulate droning and then a general "Amen." The hammer of the bell continued to beat out its hymn, and Glory stood under the shadow of the tree to collect her thoughts.

Then the sacristy door opened and a line of men came out. They were in long black cassocks, and they crossed the court-yard from the church to the house with the measured and hasty step of monks, and with their hands clasped at their breasts. Almost at the end of the line, walking with an old man whose tread was heavy, there was a younger one who was bare-headed, and who did not wear the cassock. The moon threw a light on his face, which looked pale and worn. It was John Storm.

Glory gave a faint cry, a gasp, and he turned round as if startled.

"Only the creaking of the sycamore," said the Superior.

And then the mysterious shadows took them; they passed into the house, the door was closed, and she was alone with the chimes—

"Days and moments quickly flying,
Blend the living with the dead."

Glory's strength had deserted her, and she went away as she came. When she got back to Victoria, she felt for the first time as if her own little life had been swallowed up in the turmoil of London, and she had gone down to the cold depths of an icy sea.

It was a quarter to ten when she returned to the ward, and the matron, with her dog on her lap, was waiting to receive her.

"Didn't I tell you that you could not go out to-night?"

"Yes, ma'am," said Glory.

"Then how did you dare to go?"

Glory looked at her unwaveringly with glittering eyes that seemed to smile, whereupon the matron picked up her dog, gathered up her train, and swept out of the ward, saying—

"Nurse, you can leave me at the end of your term, and you need never cross the doors of this institution again."

Then Glory, who had all night wanted to cry, burst into laughter. The ward Sister reproved her, but she laughed in the woman's fat face, and would have given worlds to slap it.

There was not a nurse in the hospital who showed more bright and cheerful spirits when the patients were being prepared for the night. But next morning, in the grey dawn, when she had dragged herself to bed, and was able at length to be alone, she beat the pillows with both hands and sobbed in her loneliness and shame.

XX

But youth is rich in hope, and at noon, when Glory awoke, the thought of Drake flashed upon her like light in a dark place. He had compelled Lord Robert to assist Polly in a worse extremity, and he would assist her in her present predicament. How often he had hinted that the hospital was not good enough for her, and that some day and somewhere Fate would find other work for her and another sphere. The time had come; she would appeal to him, and he would hasten to help her.

She began to revive the magnificent dreams that had floated in her mind for months. No need to tell the people at home of her dismissal and disgrace; no need to go back to the island. She would be somebody in her own right yet. Of course she would have to study, to struggle, to endure disappointments, but she would triumph in the end. And when at length she was great and famous she would be good to other poor girls; and as often as she thought of John Storm in his solitude, in his cell, though there might be a pang, a red stream running somewhere within, she would comfort herself with the thought that she too was doing her best, she too had her place, and it was a useful and worthy one.

Before that time came, however, there would be managers to influence and engagements to seek, and perhaps teachers to pay for. But Drake was rich and generous and powerful; he had a great opinion of her talents, and he would stop at nothing.

Leaping out of bed, she sat down at the table as she was and wrote to him.

"DEAR MR. DRAKE,—Try to see me to-night. I want your advice immediately. What do you think? I have got myself 'noticed' at last, and as a consequence I am to leave at the end of my term. So things are urgent, you see. I 'wave my lily hand' to you.
GLORY.

"P.S.—To save time I suggest the hour and the place: eight o'clock—St. James's Park—by the bridge going down from Marlborough House."

Drake received this note as he was sitting alone in his chambers, smoking a cigarette after drinking a cup of tea, in that hour of glamour that is between the lights. It seemed to bring with it a secret breath of passion out of the atmosphere in which it had been written. At the first impulse it went up to his lips, but at the next moment he was smitten by the memory of something, and he thought, "I will do what is right; I will play the game fair."

He dined that night with a group of Civil servants at his club in St. James's Street, but at a quarter to eight, notwithstanding some playful bantering, he put on his overcoat and turned towards the Park. The autumn night was soft and peaceful; the stars were out and the moon had risen; a fragrant mist came up from the lake, and the smoke of his cigar was hardly troubled by the breeze that pattered the withered tassels of the laburnums. Big Ben was striking eight as he reached the end of the little bridge, and almost immediately afterwards he was aware of soft and hurrying footsteps approaching him.

Glory had come down by the Mall. The whispering of the big white trees in the moonlight was like company, and she sang to herself as she walked. Her heart seemed to have gone into her heels since yesterday, for her step was light, and sometimes she ran a few paces. She arrived out of breath as the great clock was striking, and seeing the figure of a gentleman in evening dress by the end of the bridge, she stopped to collect herself.

Her hand was hot and a little damp when Drake took it, and her face was somewhat flushed. She had all at once become ashamed that she had come to ask him for anything, and she took out her pocket-handkerchief and began to roll it in her palms. He misunderstood her agitation, and trying to cover it, he offered his arm and took her across the bridge, and they turned westward down the path that runs along the margin of the lake.

"Mr. Storm has gone," she said, thinking to explain herself.

"I know," he answered.

"It is generally known, then?"

"I had a letter from him yesterday."

"Was it about me?"

"Yes."

"You must not mind if he says things, you know."

"I don't, Glory. I set them down to the egotism of the religious man. The religious man cannot believe that anybody can live a moral life and act on principle except from the religious impulse. . . . I suppose he has warned you against me, hasn't he?"

"Well—yes."

"I'm at a loss to know what I've done to deserve it. But time must justify me. I am not a religious man myself, you know, though I hate to talk of it. To tell you the truth, I think the religious idea a monstrous egotism altogether, and the love of God merely the love of self. Still, you must judge for yourself, Glory."

"Are we not wasting our time a little?" she said. "I am here—isn't that proof enough of my opinion?" And then in an agitated whisper she added, "I have only half-an-hour, the gates will be closing, and I want to ask your advice, you know. You remember what I told you in my letter?"

He patted the hand on his arm and said, "Tell me how it happened."

She told him everything, with many pauses, expecting every moment that he would break in upon her and say, "Why didn't you box the woman's ears?" or perhaps laugh and assure her that it did not matter in the least, and she was making too much of a mere bagatelle. But he listened to every syllable, and after she had finished there was silence for a moment. Then he said, "I'm sorry—very sorry; in fact, I am much troubled about it."

Her nerves were throbbing hard and her hand on his arm was twitching.

"If you had left of your own accord after that scene in the Board-room it would have been so different—so easy for me to help you."

"How?"

"I should have gone to my chief—he is a governor of many hospitals—and said, 'A young friend of mine, a nurse, is uncomfortable in her present place and would like to change her hospital.' It would have been no sooner said than done. But now—now there is the black book against you, and God knows if . . . In fact, somebody has laid a trap for you, Glory, intending to get rid of you at the first opportunity, and you seem to have walked straight into it."

She felt stunned. "He has forgotten all he has said to me," she thought. In a feeble, expressionless voice she asked—

"But what am I to do now?"

"Let me think."

They walked some steps in silence. "He is turning it over," she thought. "He will tell me how to begin."

He stopped, as if seized by a new idea.

"Did you tell them where you had been?"

"No," she replied, in the same weak voice.

"But why not do so? There is hope in that. The chaplain was your friend—your only friend in London, so far as they know. Surely that is an extenuating circumstance so plausible——"

"But I cannot——"

"I know it is bitter to explain—to apologise—and if I can do it for you——"

"I will not allow it," she said. Her lips were set and her breath was coming through them in gusts.

"It is a pity to allow the hospitals to be closed against you. Nursing is a good profession, Glory—even a fashionable one. It is true womanly work and——"

"That was what he said."

"Who? John Storm? He was right. Indeed he was an entirely honourable and upright man, and——"

"But *you* always seemed to say there were other things more worthy of a girl, and if she had a mind to . . . But no matter.

We needn't talk about the hospitals any longer. I am not fit for them and shall never go back to them, whatever happens."

He looked down at her. She was biting her lips, and the tears were gathering in her eyes.

"Well, well, never mind, dear," he said, and he patted her hand again.

The moon had begun to wane, and out of the dark shadows they walked in they could see the lines of houses lit up all around.

"Look," she said, with a feeble laugh, "in all this great busy London is there nothing else I'm fit for?"

"You are fit for anything in the world, my dear," he answered.

Her nerves were throbbing harder than ever. "Perhaps he doesn't remember," she thought. Should she tell him what he said so often about her talents, and how much she might be able to make of them?

"Is there nothing a girl can do except go down on her knees to a woman?"

He laughed and talked some nonsense about the kneeling. "Poor little woman! she doesn't know what she is doing," he thought."

"I shouldn't mind what people thought of me," she said, "not even my own people, who have been brought up with such narrow ideas, you know. They might think what they liked, if I felt I was in the right place at last—the right place for me, I mean."

Her nervous fingers were involuntarily clutching at his coat sleeve. "Now any other man . . ." he thought.

She began to cry. "He *won't* remember," she told herself. "It was only his way of being agreeable when he praised me and predicted such wonderful things. And now his good breeding will not allow him to tell me there are hundreds, thousands, tens of thousands of girls in London as likely to . . ."

"Come, you mustn't cry, Glory. It's not so bad as that."

She had never seemed to him so beautiful, and he wanted to take her in his arms and comfort her.

"I had no one but you to come to," she murmured in her confusion. But she was thinking, "Why didn't you stop me before? Why have you let me go on all these months?"

"I must try to think of something, and I'll speak to my friend Rosa—Miss Macquarrie, you know."

"You are a man," said Glory, "and I thought perhaps . . ." But she could not speak of her fool's paradise now, she was so deeply ashamed and abased.

"That's just the difficulty, my dear. If I were not a man I might so easily help you."

What did he mean? The frogs kept croaking at the margin of the lake, disturbed by the sounds of their footsteps.

"Whatever you were to tell me to do I should do it," she said, in the same confused murmur. She was ruining herself with every word she uttered.

He drew up and stood before her so close that she could feel his breath on her face.

"My dear Glory," he said passionately, "don't think it isn't terrible to me to renounce the happiness of helping you; but I must not, I dare not, I will not take it."

She could scarcely breathe for the shame that took sudden hold of her.

"Heaven knows I would give anything to have the joy of looking after your happiness, dear; but I should despise myself for ever if I took advantage of your circumstances."

Good God! what did he think she had been asking of him?

"I am thinking of yourself, Glory, because I want to esteem you and honour you, and because your good name is above everything else—everything else in the world."

Her shame was now abject. It stifled her, deafened her, blinded her. She could not speak or hear or see.

He took her hand and pressed it.

"Let me go," she stammered.

"Stay—do not go yet!"

"Let me go, will you?"

"One moment——"

But with a cry like the cry of a startled bird she disappeared in the shadow of the trees.

He stood a moment where she had left him, tingling in every nerve, wanting to follow her, and overtake her, and kiss her, and abandon everything. But he buttoned up his overcoat and turned away, telling himself that whatever another man might have done in the same case, he at least had done rightly, and that men like John Storm were wrong if they thought it was impossible to act on principle without the impulse of religion.

Meanwhile Glory was flying through the darkness, and weeping in the bitterness of her disappointment and shame. The big trees overhead were all black now, and very gaunt and grim, and the breeze was moaning in their branches.

"I had disgrace enough already," she thought; "I might have spared myself a degradation like this."

Drake had supposed that she came to plead for herself to-night as she had pleaded for Polly a week ago. How natural that he should think so! How natural, and yet how hideous!

"I hate him! I hate him!" she thought.

John Storm had been right. In their heart of hearts these men of society had only one idea about a girl, and she had stumbled on it unawares. They never thought of her as a friend and an equal, but only as a dependant and a plaything, to be taken or left as they liked.

"Oh, how shameful to be a woman! how shameful, how shameful!"

And Drake had renounced her! In the hideous tangle of his error he had renounced her! For honour's sake, and her own sake, and for the sake of his character as a gentleman—renounced her! Oh, there was somebody who would never have renounced her whatever had happened, and yet she had driven him away, and he was gone for ever.

"I hate myself! I hate myself!"

She remembered how often out of recklessness and daring and high spirits, but without a thought of evil, she had broken through the barrier of manners, and given Drake occasion to think lightly of her—at the ball, at the theatre, at tea in his chambers, and by dressing herself up as a man.

"I hate myself! I hate myself!"

John Storm was right, and Drake in his different way was right too, and she alone had been to blame. But Fate was laughing at her, and the jest was very, very cruel.

"No matter. It is all for the best," she thought. She would be the stronger for this experience—the stronger and the purer too, to stand alone and to face the future.

She got back to the hospital just as the great clock of Westminster was chiming the half-hour, and she stood a moment on the steps to listen to it. Only half an-hour had passed, and yet all the world had changed!

XXI

It was the last day of Glory's probation, and, dressed in the long blue ulster in which she came from the Isle of Man, she was standing in the matron's room waiting for her wages and discharge. The matron was sitting sideways at her table, with her dog snarling in her lap. She pointed to a tiny heap of gold and silver and to a foolscap paper which lay beside it.

"That is your month's salary, nurse, and that is your 'character.' The 'character' has given me a deal of trouble. I have done all I could for you. I have said you were bright and cheerful, and that the patients liked you. I trust I have not committed myself too far."

Glory gathered up the money, but left the "character" untouched.

"You need not be anxious, ma'am; I shall not require it."

"Have you got a situation?"

"No."

"Then where are you going next?"

"I don't know—yet."

"How much money have you saved?"

"About three months' wages."

"Only three pounds altogether!"

"It will be quite sufficient."

"What friends have you got in London?"

"None—that is to say—no, none whatever."

"Then why don't you go back to your island?"

"Because I don't wish to be a burden upon my people, and because earning my living in London doesn't depend on the will or the whim of any woman."

"That's just like you. I might have dismissed you instantly, but, for the sake of the chaplain, I've borne with your rudeness and irregularities, and even tried to be your friend, and yet . . . I dare say you've not even told your people why you are leaving the hospital."

"I haven't—I haven't told them yet that I'm leaving at all."

"Then I've a great mind to do it for you. A venturesome, headstrong girl who flings herself on London is in danger of ruin."

"You needn't trouble yourself, ma'am," said Glory, opening the door to go.

"Why so?" said the matron.

Glory stood at her full height and answered—

"Because if you said that of me, there is nobody in the world would believe you."

Her box had been brought down to the hall, and the porter, who wished to be friendly, was cording it.

"May I leave it in your care, porter, until I am able to call for it?"

"Certingly, nurse. Sorry you're goin'. I'll miss your face, too."

"Thank you. I'll call for my letters also."

"There's one just come."

It was from Aunt Anna, and was full of severe reproof and

admonition. Glory was not to think of leaving the hospital; she must try to be content with the condition to which God had called her. But why had her letters been so few of late? and how did it occur that she had never told them about Mr. Storm? He had gone for good into that strange Brotherhood, it seemed. Not Catholic, and yet a monastery. Most extraordinary! They were all eagerly waiting to hear more about it; besides, the grandfather was anxious on Glory's account. If half they heard was true, the dangers of London . . .

The house-surgeon came down to say good-bye. He had always been as free and friendly as Sister Allworthy would allow. They stood a moment at the door together.

"Where are you going to?" he asked.

"Anywhere—nowhere—everywhere; to 'all the airts the wind can blaw.'"

It was a clear bright morning with a light keen frost. On looking out, Glory saw that flags were flying on the public buildings.

"Why, what's going on?" she said.

"Don't you know? It's the 9th of November—Lord Mayor's Day."

She laughed merrily. "A good omen. I'm the female Dick Whittington! Here goes for it! Good-bye, hospital nursing. Bye-bye, doctor."

She dropped him a playful curtsy at the bottom of the steps, and then tripped along the street.

"What a girl it is!" he thought. "And what is to become of her in this merciless old London?"

She had taken less than a score of steps from the hospital when great blinding tear-drops leapt from her eyes and ran down her cheeks, but she only dropped her veil and walked on boldly.

END OF FIRST BOOK.

SECOND BOOK.—THE RELIGIOUS LIFE

I

THE Society of the Holy Gethsemane, popularly called the Bishopsgate Fathers, was one of the many conventual institutions of the English Church which came as a sequel to the great upheaval of religious feeling known as the Tractarian or Oxford movement. Most of them gave way under the pressure of external opposition, some of them broke down under the strain of internal dissension, and a few lived on as secret brotherhoods, in obedience to a rule which was never divulged by their members, who were said to wear a hair-shirt next the skin, and to scourge themselves with the lash of discipline.

Of these conventual institutions, the Society of the Holy Gethsemane had been one of the earliest, and it was now quite the oldest, although it had challenged not only the traditions of the Reformed Church, but the spirit of the age itself, by establishing its place of prayer at the very doors of the Stock Exchange—that crater of volcanic emotions, that generating house for the electric currents of the world.

Its founder and first Superior had been a man of iron will, who had fought his way through ecclesiastical courts and popular anger, and even family persecution, which had culminated in an effort of his own brother to shut him up as a lunatic. His first disciple and most stanch supporter had been the Rev. Charles Frederic Lamplugh, a Fellow of Corpus, newly called to orders after an earlier career which had been devoted to the world, and, according to rumour, nearly wrecked in an affair of the heart.

When the community had proved its legal right to exist within the Establishment, and public clamour had subsided, this disciple was despatched to America, and there he established a branch brotherhood and became great and famous. At the height of his usefulness and renown he was recalled, and this exercise of authority provoked a universal outcry among his admirers. But he obeyed: he left his fame and glory in America and returned to his cell in London, and was no more heard of by the outer world, until the founder of the Society died, when he was elected by the brothers to the vacant place of Superior.

Father Lamplugh was now a man of seventy, so gentle in his manner, so sweet in his temper, so pious in his life, that, when he stepped out of his room to greet John Storm on his arrival in Bishopsgate Street, it seemed as if he brought the air of heaven in the rustle of his habit and to have come from the holy of holies.

"Welcome! welcome!" he said. "I knew you would come to us; I have been expecting you. The first time I saw you I said to myself, 'Here is one who bears a burden; the world cannot satisfy the cravings of a heart like that; he will surrender it some day.'"

Having been there before, though in "Retreat" only, John entered at once into the life of the brotherhood. It was arranged that he was to spend some two or three months as a postulant, then to take the vow of a novice for one year, and finally, if he proved his vocation, to seal and establish his calling by taking the three life vows of poverty, chastity, and obedience.

The home of the brotherhood was one of those old London mansions in the heart of the city, which were built perhaps for the palaces of dignitaries of the Church, and were afterwards occupied as the houses and offices of London merchants and their apprentices, and have eventually descended to the condition of warehouses and stores, and tenement dwellings for the poor. Its structure remained the same, but the brothers made no effort to support its ancient grandeur. Nothing more simple could be imagined than the appointments of their monastery. The carved oak staircase was there, but the stairs were carpetless, and the panelled and parqueted hall was bare of ornament, except for a picture, in a pale oaken frame, of the head of Christ in its crown of thorns. A plain clock in a deal case was nailed up under the floral cornice, and beneath it there hung the text, "Lord, who shall dwell in Thy tabernacle, or who shall rest upon Thy holy hill? Even he that leadeth an uncorrupt life." The old dining-room was now the community-room, the old kitchen was the refectory, the spacious bedrooms were partitioned into cells, and the corridors, which had once been covered with tapestry, were now coated with whitewash, and bore the inscription, "Silence in the passages."

In this house of poverty and dignity, of past grandeur and present simplicity, the brothers lived in community. They were forty in number, consisting of ten lay brothers, ten novices, and twenty professed fathers. The lay brothers, who were under the special direction of their own Superior, the Father Minister, and were rarely allowed to go into the streets, had to clean the house and bake the bread, and cook and serve the food which was delivered at the door, and thus, in that narrow circle of duty, they proved their piety by their devotion to a lot which condemned them to scour and scrub to the last day of life. The clerical brothers, who were nearly all in full orders, enjoyed a more varied existence, being confined to the precincts only during a part of their novitiate, and then sent out at the will of the Superior to preach in the churches of London or the country, and even despatched on expeditions to establish missions abroad.

The lay brothers had their separate retiring-room, but John Storm met his clerical house-mates on the night of his arrival. It was the hour of evening recreation, and they were gathered in the community-room for reading and conversation. The stately old dining-room was as destitute as the corridors of adornments or even furniture. Straw arm-chairs stood on the clean white floor, a bookcase, containing many volumes of the Fathers, lined one of the panelled walls, and over the majestic fireplace there was a plain card with the inscription, "There be eunuchs which have made themselves eunuchs for the kingdom of heaven's sake."

The brothers gathered about him and examined him with a curiosity which was more than personal. To this group of men detached from life the arrival of some one from the outer world was an event of interest. He knew what wars had been waged, what epidemics were raging, what Governments had risen and fallen. He might not speak of these things in casual talk, for it was against rule to discuss, for its own sake, what had been seen or heard outside, but they were in the air about him, and they were happening on the other side of the wall.

And he on his part also examined his house-mates and tried to guess what manner of men they were and what had brought them to that place. They were men of all ages, and nearly every school of the Church had sent its representatives. Here was the pale face of the ascetic and there the guileless eyes of the saint. Some were keen and alert, others were timid and slow. All wore the long black cassock of the community, and many wore the rope with three knots. They spoke little of the world outside, but it was clear that they could not dismiss it from their thoughts. Their talk was cheerful, and the Father told stories of his preaching expeditions which provoked some laughter. They had no newspapers (except one well-known High Church organ) and no games, and there was no smoking.

The bell rang for supper and they went down to the refectory. It was a large apartment in the basement, and it still bore the emblems of its ancient service. Over the great kitchen ingle there was yet another card with the inscription, "Neither said any of them that aught of the things which he possessed was his own, but they had all things in common." A table scoured white ran round three sides of the room, the seats were forms without backs, and there was one chair—the Superior's chair— in the middle.

The supper consisted of porridge and milk and brown bread, and it was eaten out of plates and cans of pewter. While it lasted, one of the brothers, seated at a raised desk, read first a few passages of Scripture and then some pages of a secular book which the religious were thus hearing at their meals. The supper was hardly over when the bell rang again. It was time for Compline, the last service of the day, and the brothers formed in procession and passed out of the house across the courtyard into the little church.

The old place was dimly lighted, but the brothers occupied the chancel only. They sat in two companies on opposite sides of the choir, in three rows of stalls, the lay brothers in front, the novices next, and the Fathers at the back. Each side had its leader in the recitation of the prayers. The Miserere was said kneeling, the Psalms were sung with frequent pauses, each of the duration of the words "Ave Maria," producing the effect of a broken wail. The service was short, and it ended with "May the Lord Almighty grant us a quiet night and a perfect end." There was another stroke of the bell and the brothers returned to the house in silence.

John Storm walked with the Superior, and passing through the courtyard, in the light of the moon that had risen while they were at prayers, he was startled by the sound of something.

"Only the creaking of the sycamore," said the Father.

He had thought it was the voice of Glory, but he had been hearing her cry throughout the service, so he dismissed the circumstance as a dream. Half-an-hour later the household had retired for the night, the lights were put out, and the Society of the Gethsemane was at rest.

John's cell was on the topmost floor, next to the quarters of the lay brothers. There was nothing above it but a high lead flat, which was sometimes used by the religious as watch-tower and breathing-place. The cell was a narrow room with bare floor, a small table, one chair, a praying-stool, a crucifix, and a stump bed, having a straw pillow and a crimson coverlet marked with a large white cross.

"Here," he thought, "my journey is at an end. This is my

resting-place for life." The mighty hand of the Church was on him, and he felt a deep peace. He was like a ship that had been tossed at sea and was lying quiet in harbour at last.

Without was the world, the fantastic world, for ever changing; within were gentle if strict rules and customs securely fixed. Without was the ceaseless ebb and flow of the financial tide; within were content and sweet poverty and no disturbing fears. Without were struggle and strife and the fever of gain; within were peace and happiness and the grand mysteries which God reveals to the soul in solitude.

He began to pass his life in review and to think, " Well, it is all over, at all events. I shall never leave this place. Friends who forgive me, good-bye! and foes who are unforgiving, good-bye to you too!"

And the world, the great, vain, cruel, hypocritical world, farewell to it also! Farewell to its pomp and its glory! Farewell to life and liberty and—love!

The wind was rustling the leaves of the tree in the courtyard, and he could not help but hear again the voice he had heard when crossing from the church. His eyes were closed, but Glory's face, with its curling and twitching lip and its laughing and liquid eyes, was printed on the darkness.

" Ave Maria," he murmured, and saying this again and again, he fell asleep.

Next morning the daylight had not quite dawned when he was awakened by a knock at his door, and a low voice saying, " Benedicamus Domino!"

It was the Father Superior, who made it his rule to rouse the household himself, on the principle of " Whosoever will be chief among you, let him be your servant."

" Deo Gratias," he answered, and the voice went on through the corridor. Then the bell rang for Lauds and Prime, and John left his cell to begin his life as Brother Storm.

II

Though it was against the rule of the Order to indulge in particular friendships, yet, in obedience to the rule of Nature, he made friends among the brothers. His feeling for the Superior became stronger than love and approached to adoration, and there were certain of the Fathers to whom his heart went out with a tender sympathy. The Father Minister was a man of a hard, closed soul, very cantankerous and severe, but the rest were gentle and timid men for the most part, with a wistful outlook on the world.

It was due in part to the proximity of his cell to the quarters assigned to the lay brothers that his two closest friendships were made among them. One was with a great creature, like an overgrown boy, who kept the door to the monastery by day, and alternated that duty with another by night. He was called Brother Andrew—for the lay brothers were known by their Christian names—and he was one of those characterless beings who are only happy when they have merged their individuality in another's and joined their fate to his. He attached himself to John from the first, and as often as he was at liberty he was hanging about him, ready to fetch and carry in his shambling gait, which was like the roll of an old dog. The expression of his beardless face was that of a boy, and he had no conversation, for he always agreed with everything that was said to him.

The other of John's friendships was with the lay brother whom he had known outside, the brother of Polly Love; but this was a friendship of slower growth, impeded by a tragic obstacle. John had seen him first in the refectory on the night of his arrival, and observed in his face the marks of suffering and exhaustion. At various times afterwards he had seen him in the church and encountered him in the corridors, and had sometimes bowed to him and smiled, but the brother had never once given sign of recognition. At length he had begun to doubt his identity, and one morning, going upstairs from breakfast side by side with the Superior, he said—

"Father, is the lay brother with the melancholy eyes and the pale face the one whom I knew at the hospital?"

"Yes," said the Father, "but he is under the rule of silence."

"Ah! Does he know what has become of his sister?"

"No."

It was the morning hour of recreation, and the Father drew John into the courtyard and talked of Brother Paul.

He was much tormented by thoughts of the world without, and being a young man of a weak nervous system and a consumptive tendency, such struggles with the evil one were hurtful to him. Therefore, though it was the rule that a lay brother should not be consecrated until after long years of service, it had been decided that he should take the vows immediately, in order that Satan might yield up his hold of him and the world might drag at him no more.

"Is that your experience?" said John. "When a religious has taken the vows are his thoughts of the world all conquered?"

"He is like the sailor making ready for his voyage. As long as he lies in harbour, his thoughts are of the home he has left behind him, but when he has once crossed the bar and is out on the ocean, he thinks only of the haven where he would be."

"But are there no backward glances, Father? The sailor may write to the friends he has parted from—surely the religious may pray for them."

"As brothers and sisters of the spirit, yes, always and at all times; as brothers and sisters of the flesh, no, never save in hours of especial need. He is the spouse of Christ, my son, and all Christ's children are his kindred equally."

As a last word the Father begged of John to abstain from reference to anything that had happened at the hospital, lest Brother Paul might hear of it and manifold evils be the result.

The warning seemed needless. From that day forward John tried to avoid Brother Paul. In church and in the refectory he kept his eyes away from him. He could not see that worn face with its hungry look and not think of a captured eagle with a broken wing. It was with a shock that he discovered that their cells were side by side. If they came near to each other in the corridors, he experienced a kind of terror and was thankful for the rule of silence which forbade them to speak. Under the smouldering ashes there might be coals of fire which only wanted a puff to fan them into flame.

They came face to face at last. It was on the lead flat of the tower above their cells. John had grown accustomed to go there after Compline that he might look on London from that eminence and thank God that he had escaped from its clutches. The stars were out and the city lay like a great monster around and beneath. Something demoniacal had entered into his view of it. Down there was the river winding like a serpent through its sand, and here and there were the bridges like the scales across it, and farther west was the head of the great creature, just beginning to be ablaze with lights.

"She is there," he thought, and then he was startled by a sound. Had he uttered the words aloud? But it was some one else who had spoken. Brother Paul was standing by the parapet with his eyes in the same direction. When he became conscious that John was behind him, he stammered something in his confusion and then hurried away as if he had been detected in a crime.

"God pity him!" thought John. "If he only knew what has happened!"

Going back to his cell, he began to think of Glory. By the broken links of memory he remembered for the first time since coming into the monastery the condition of insecurity in which he had left her. How uncertain her position at the hospital, how perilous her relations with her friend!

The last prayer of the day for the brothers of the Gethsemane was the prayer before the crucifix by the side of the bed, "Thanks be to God for giving me the trials of this day." To this he added another petition, "And bless and protect her wheresoever she may be."

He ceased to frequent the tower after that, and did not go up to it again until the morning of the day on which he was to make his vows. By this time his soul had spent itself so prodigally in prayer that he had almost begun to regard himself as one already in another world. The morning was clear and frosty, and he could see that something unusual was taking place on the earth below. Traffic was stopped, the open spaces were crowded, and processions were passing through the streets with bands of music playing and banners flying. Then he remembered what day it was—it was Lord Mayor's Day, the 9th of November—and once again he thought of Glory. She would be there, for her heart was light and she loved the world and all its scenes of gaiety and splendour.

It was the day of his final preparation, and he was under the rule of silence, so he returned to his cell and shut the door. But he could not shut out the sounds of the streets. All day long the bands were playing and the horses prancing, and there was the tramp of many feet. And even in the last hour before the ceremony, when he was on his knees in front of the crucifix and the palms of his hands were placed against his face, he could see the gay spectacle and the surging throngs—the men, the women, the children in every window, on every parapet, and Glory in the midst of them with her laughing lips and her sparkling eyes.

Night brought peace with it at length, and then the bell rang and he went down to service. The brothers were waiting for him in the hall, and they formed into line and passed into the church; first Brother Andrew with the cross, then Brother Paul with the incense, and the other lay brothers with the candles, then the religious in their cassocks, and the Superior in his cope, and John Storm last of all.

The altar was decorated as for a feast and the service was strange but solemn. John had drawn up in writing a promise of stability and obedience, and this he placed with his own hand on the altar. Down to that moment he had worn his costume as a secular priest, but now he was to be robed in the habit of the Order.

The Father stood on the altar steps with the habit lying at his feet. He took it up and blessed it and then put it on John, saying as he bound it with the cord, "Take this cord and wear it in memory of the purity of heart wherewith you must ever hereafter seek to abide in the love and service of our Lord Jesus."

At that moment a door was suddenly and loudly slammed, to signify that the world was being shut out, the choir said the Gloria Patri and then sang a hymn beginning—

> "Farewell, thou world of sorrow,
> Unrest, and schism, and strife!
> I leave thee on the threshold
> Of the celestial life."

It was the occasion of Brother Paul's life vows also, and as John stood back from the altar steps the lay brother was brought up to them. He was very pale and nervous, and he would have stumbled but for the help of the Father Minister and Brother Andrew, who walked on either side of him.

Then the same ceremony was gone through again, but with yet more solemn accessories. The Burial Service was read, the De Profundis was sung, the bell was tolled, the "Ecce quam bonum" was intoned, and finally the chant was chanted—

> "Dead to Him, then death is over,
> Dead and gone are death's dark fears."

John Storm was profoundly stirred. The heavens seemed to open and all the earth to pass away. It was difficult to believe that he was still in the flesh.

When he was able to collect himself, he was on the tower again, but in his cassock now and gripping the cord by which it was tied. The frosty air of the morning had thickened to a fog, the fog-signals were sounding, and the mighty monster below seemed to be puffing fire from a thousand nostrils and bellowing from a thousand throats.

Some one had come up to him. It was Brother Paul. He was talking nervously, and even pretending to laugh a little.

"I am so happy to see you here. And I am glad the silence is at an end and I am able to tell you so."

"Thank you," said John, and he tried to pass him.

"I always knew you would come to us, that is to say, after the night I heard you at the hospital—the night of the nurses' ball, you remember, and the Father's visit, you know. Still, I trust there was nothing wrong—nothing at the hospital, I mean——"

John was fumbling for the door to the dormer.

"Everybody loved you, too—the patients and the nurses and everybody! How they will miss you there! I trust you left everybody well—and happy and . . . eh?"

"Good-night," said John from the head of the stair.

There was silence for a moment, and then the brother said in another voice—

"Yes, I understand you. I know quite well what you mean. It is a fault to speak of the outer world except on especial need. We have taken the vows, too, and are pledged for life—I am, at all events. Still, if you could have told me anything. . . . But I am much to blame. I must confess my fault and do my penance."

John was diving down the stair and hurrying into his room.

"God help him!" he thought. "And me too! God help both of us! How am I to live if I have to hide this secret? Yet how is he to live if he learns it?"

He sat on the bed and tried to compose himself. Yes, Brother Paul was an object for pity. In all the moral universe there was no spectacle more pitiable than that of a man who had left the world while his heart was still in it. What was he doing here? What had brought him? What business had such an one in such a place? And then his pitiful helplessness for all the uses of life and duty! Could it be right, could it be necessary, could it be God's wish and will?

Here was a man whose sister was in the world. She was young and vain, and the world was gay and seductive. Without a hand to guide and guard her, what evils might not befall? She was sunk already in shame and degradation, and he had put it out of his power to save her. Whatever had happened in the past, whatever might happen in the future, he was lost to her for ever. The captured eagle with the broken wing was now chained to the wall as well. But prayer! Prayer was the bulwark of chastity, and God was in need of no man's efforts.

John fell on his knees before the crucifix. With the broken logic of reverie he was thinking of Glory, and Brother Paul, and Polly and Drake. They crossed his brain and weighed upon it, and went out and returned. The night was cold, but the sweat stood on his brow in beads. In the depths of his soul something was speaking to him, and he was trying not to listen. He was like a blind man who had stumbled to the edge of a precipice, and could hear the waves breaking on the rocks beneath.

When he said his last prayer that night he omitted the petition for Glory (as duty seemed to require of him), and then found that all life and soul and strength had gone out of it. In the middle of the night he awoke with a sense of fright. Was it only a dream that he was dead and buried? He raised his head in the darkness and stretched out his hand. No, it was true. Little by little he pieced together the incidents of the previous day. Yes, it had really happened.

"After all, I am not like Paul—I am not bound for life," he told himself, and then he lay back like a child and was comforted.

He was ashamed, but he could not help it. He was feeling already as if he were a prisoner in a dungeon looking forward to his release.

III

5A LITTLE TURNSTILE,
HIGH HOLBORN, LONDON, W.C.,
November 9th, 18—.

Oh yiz, oh yiz, oh yiz! This is to announce to you, with due pomp and circumstance, that I, Glory Quayle, am no longer at the hospital—for the present. Did I never tell you? Have you never noticed it in the regulations? Every half-year a nurse is entitled to a week's holiday, and as I have been exactly six months to-day at Martha's Vineyard, and as a week is too short a time for a trip to the "oilan,"[1] and as a good lady whose acquaintance I have made here had given me a pressing invitation to visit her . . . See?

Being the first day since I came up to London that I have been sole mistress of my will and pleasure, I have been letting myself loose like "Cæsar" does the moment his mad little hoofies touch the grass. I must tell you all about it. The day began beautifully. After a spell of laughing and crying weather, and all the world sneezing and blowing its nose, there came a frosty morning with the sun shining and the air as bright as diamonds. I left the hospital between eleven and twelve o'clock, and crossing the Park by Birdcage Walk, I noticed that flags were flying on Buckingham Palace and church-bells ringing everywhere. It turned out to be the birthday of the Prince of Wales and the Lord Mayor's Day as well, and by the time I got to Storey's Gate, bands of music were playing and people were scampering towards the Houses of Parliament. So I ran too, and from the gardens in front of Palace Yard I saw the Lord Mayor's Show.

Do you know what that is, good people? It is a civic

---
[1] Island.

pageant. Once a year the City King makes a royal procession through the streets, with his soldiers and servants and keepers and pipers and retainers, bewigged and bepowdered and be-stockinged pretty much as they used to be in the days before the Flood. There have been seven hundred of him in succession, and his particular vanity is to show that he is wearing the same clothes still. But it was beautiful altogether, and I could have cried with delight to see those grave-looking signiors forgetting themselves for once and pretending they were big boys over again.

Such a sight! Flags were flying everywhere and festoons were stretched across the streets with mottoes and texts such as "Unity is strength" and "God save the Queen," and other amiable if not original ideas. Traffic was stopped in the main thoroughfares, and the 'buses were sent by devious courses, much to the astonishment of the narrow streets. Then the crowds, the dense layers of potted people with white upturned faces, for all the world like the pictures of the round stones standing upright at the Giant's Causeway—it was wonderful!

And then the fun! Until the procession arrived the policemen were really obliging in that way. The one nearest me was as fat as Falstaff, and a slim young Cockney in front kept addressing intimate remarks to him and calling him Robert. The young impudence himself was just as ridiculous, for he wore a fringe which was supported by hair-oil and soap, and rolled carefully down the right side of his forehead so that he could always keep his left eye on it. And he did too.

But the pageant itself! My gracious! how we laughed at it! There were Epping Forest verderers, and beefeaters from the Tower, and pipers of the Scots Guards, and ladies of the ballet shivering on shaky stools and pretending to be "Freedom" and "Commerce," and last of all the City King himself, smiling and bowing to his subjects, and with his liegemen behind him in yellow coats and red silk stockings. Perhaps the most popular character was a Highlander in pink tights, where his legs ought to have been, walking along as solemnly as if he thought it was a sort of religious ceremony and he was an idol out for an airing.

And then the bands! There must have been twenty of them, both brass and fife, and they all played the "Washington Post," but no two had the luck to fall on the same bar at the same moment. It was a medley of all the tunes in music, an absolute kaleidoscope of sounds, and meantime there was the clash of bells from the neighbouring belfries in honour of the Prince's birthday and the rattle of musketry from the Guards, so that when the double event was over I felt like the man whose wife presented him with twins—I wouldn't have lost either of them for a million of money, but I couldn't have found it in my heart to give a bawbee for another one.

The procession took half-an-hour to pass, and when it was gone, remembering the ladies in lovely dresses who had rolled by in their gorgeous carriages, looking not a bit cleverer or handsomer than other people, I turned away with a little hard lump at my heart and a limp in my left foot—the young Cockney with the fringe had backed on to my toe. I suppose they are feasting with the lords and all the nobility at the Guildhall to-night, and no doubt the crumbs that fall from the rich man's table will go in pies and cakes to the alleys and courts where hunger walks, and I dare say little Lazarus in the Mile-End Road is dreaming at this very moment of Dick Whittington and the Lord Mayor of London.

It must have been some waking dream of that sort which took possession of me also, for what do you suppose I did? Shall I tell you? Yes, I will. I said to myself, "Glory, my child, suppose you were nearly as poor as he was in this great, glorious, splendid London; suppose—only suppose—you had no home and no friends, and had left the hospital, or perhaps even been turned away from it, and hadn't a good lady's door standing open to receive you, what would you do first, my dear?" To all of which I replied promptly, "You would first get yourself lodgings, my child, and then you would just go to work to show this great, glorious London what a woman can do to bring it to her little feet."

I know grandfather is saying, "Gough bless me, girl! you didn't try it though?" Well, yes, I did—just for fun, you know, and out of the spirit of mischief that's born in every daughter of Eve. Do you remember that Manx cat that wouldn't live in the house, notwithstanding all the bribes and corruption of Aunt Rachel's new milk and softened bread, but went off by the back-yard wall to join the tribe of pariah pussies that snatch a living how they may? Well, I felt like Rumpy for once, having three "goolden sovereigns" in my pocket and a mind superior to fate.

It was glorious fun altogether, and the world is so amusing that I can't imagine why anybody should go out of it before he must. I hadn't gone a dozen yards in my new character as Dick Whittington *fille* before a coachman as fat as an elephant was shouting, "Where d'ye think yer going ter?" and I was nearly run down in the Broad Sanctuary by a carriage containing two brazen women in sealskin jackets, with faces so thick with powder and paint that you would have thought they had been quarrelling on washing-day and thrown the blue bag at each other's eyes. I recognised one of them as a former nurse who had left the hospital in disgrace, but happily she didn't see me, for the little hard lump at my heart was turning as bitter as gall at that moment, so I made some philosophical observations to myself and passed on.

Oh, my gracious, these London landladies! They must be female Shylocks, for the pound of flesh is the badge of all their tribe. The first one I boarded asked two guineas for two rooms, and lights and fires extra. "By the month?" says I. "Yus, by the month, if ye like," says she. "Two guineas a month?" says I. Marry come up! I was out of that house in a twinkling.

Then I looked out a group of humbler thoroughfares, not far from the Houses of Parliament, where nearly every house had a card fixed up on a little green blind. At last I found a place that would do—for my week, only my week, you know. Ten shillings, and no extras. "I'll take them," said I, with a lofty air, and thereupon the landlady, a grim person, with the suspicion of a moustache, began to cross-examine me. Was I married? Oh, dear no. Then what was my business? Fool that I was, I said I had none, being full of my Dick Whittingtonism, and not choosing to remember the hospital, for I was wearing my private clothes, you know. But hoot! She didn't take unmarried young ladies without businesses, and I was out in the street once more.

I didn't mind it, not I indeed, and it was only for fun after all; but since people objected to girls without businesses, I made up my mind to be a singer, if anybody asked me the question again. My third landlady had only one room, and it was on the second floor back; but before I got the length of mounting to this eyry, I went through my examination afresh. "In the profession, Miss?" "What profession?" "The styge, of course." "Well, ye—yes, something of that sort." "Don't tyke anybody that's on the styge."

Oh dear! oh dear! I could have screamed, it was so ridiculous. But time was getting on; Big Ben was striking four, and the day was closing in. Then I saw a sign, " Home for Girls." "Wonder if it is a charity," thinks I; but no, it didn't look like that, so in I went as bold as brass and inquired for the manageress. "Is it the matron you mean, Miss?" "Very well, the matron then," said I, and presently she came up—no, not smiling, for she wasn't an amiable-looking Christian; but I thought she would smother me with mysterious questions. "Tired of the life, are you, my dear? It *is* a cruel one, isn't it?" I stood my ground for some minutes, and then, feeling dreadfully thick in the throat, and cold down the back, I asked her what she was talking about, whereupon she looked bewildered, and inquired if I was a good girl, and being told that I hoped so, she said she couldn't take me in there, and then pointed to a card on the wall, which, simpleton that I was, I hadn't read before: "A home and rescue is offered to women who desire to leave a life of misery and disgrace."

I *did* scream that time, the world was so nonsensical. At one place, being "on the styge," I was not good enough to be taken in, at another I was not bad enough, and what in the name of all that was ridiculous was going to happen next? But it was quite dark by this time, the air was as black as a northwest gale, and I was "aweary for all my wings;" so forgetting Dick Whittington *fille*, and only remembering the good female Samaritan who had asked me to stay with her, I made a dart for Victoria Street, and jumped into the first 'bus that came along, just as the hotels and the clubs and the great buildings were putting out the Prince of Wales's feathers as sign and symbol of the usual rejoicings within.

It was an "Atlas" omnibus, and it took me to Piccadilly Circus, and that being the wrong direction, I had to change. But a fog had come down in the meanwhile, and lo, there I was in the middle of it!

O Ananias, Azarias, and Misael! Do you know what a London fog is? It's smoke, it's soot, it's sulphur. It is darker than night, for it extinguishes the lights, and denser than the mist on the Curragh, and filthier than the fumes of the brickkiln. It makes you think the whole round earth must be a piggery copper, and that London has lifted the lid off. In the midst of this inferno the cabs crawl and the 'buses creep, and foul fiends, who turn out to be men merely, go flitting about with torches, and you grope and croak and cough, and the most innocent faces come puffing and snorting down on you like the beasts in the Apocalypse.

I thought it good fun at first, but presently I could only keep from crying by having a good laugh, and I was doing that, and asking somebody the way to the Holborn omnibus, when a policeman pushed me and said, "Come, move on, none of yer lyterin' abart here!"

I could have choked, but remembering something I had seen on that very spot on the night of my first day out, I dived across the street and ran, in spite of curses and collisions. But the "somebody," whoever he was, had followed me, and he put me into the right 'bus, so I got here at last. It took two mortal hours to do it, and after that spell of purgatory this house is like a blessed paradise, peopled with angels of mercy and grace, as paradise ought to be.

The good Samaritan was very kind, and she made tea for me in a twinkling and slaughtered the fatted calf in the shape of a pot of raspberry jam. Her name is Mrs. Jupe, and her husband is something in a club, and she has one child of eleven, whose bedfellow I am to be, and here I am now with Miss Slyboots in our little bedroom, feeling safe and sound and monarch of all I survey!

Good-night, good people! Half-an-hour hence I'll be going through a mad march of the incidents of the day, turned topsy-turvy according to the way of dreams. But wae's me! wae's me! If it had all been true—if I had been really homeless and friendless and penniless, instead of having three "goolden" pounds in my purse, and Providence, in the person of Mrs. Jupe, to fall back upon! When I grow to be a wonderful woman and have brought the eyes of all the earth upon me, I am going to be good to poor girls who have no anchorage in London. John Storm was right; this great, glorious, brilliant, delightful London can be very cruel to them sometimes. It calls to them, beckons to them, smiles on them, makes them think there must be joy in the blaze of so much light and luxury and love by the side of so many palaces, and then . . .

But perhaps the mischief lies deeper down; and though I'm not going to cut my hair and wear a waistcoat and stand up for the equal rights of the sexes, I feel at this moment that if I were only a man I should be the happiest woman in the world, God bless me! Not that I'm afraid of London—not I indeed; and to show you how I long to take a header into its turbulent tides, I hereby warn and apprise and notify you that perhaps I may use my week's holiday to find a more congenial employment than that of deputy White Owl at the hospital. I am not in my right place yet, Aunt Anna notwithstanding; so look out for revelations! To be or not to be? that is the question. Just say the word and I'll leave it to Providence, which is always a convenient legatee, and in any case . . . But wait, only wait and see what a week will bring forth!

Greet the island for me to the inmost core of its being. The dear little "oilan"! Now that I am so far away I go over it in my mind's eye with the idiotic affection of a mother who knows every inch of her baby's body and would like to gobble it. The leaves must be down by this time, and there can be nothing on the bare boughs but the empty nests where the little birdies used to woo and sing. My love to them, and three tremendous kisses for yourselves! GLORY.

P.S.—Oh, haven't I given you the "newses" about John Storm? There are so many things to think about in a place like London, you see. Yes, he has gone into a monastery—communication cut off—wires broken down by the "storm," &c. Soberly, he has gone for good seemingly, and to talk of it lightly is like picking a penny out of a blind man's hat. Of course it was only to be expected that a man with an upper lip like that should come to grief with all those married old maids and elderly women of the opposite sex. Canons to right of him, canons to left of him, canons in front of him—but rumour says it was John himself who volleyed and thundered. He wrote me a letter when he was on the point of going, saying how London had shocked and disappointed him, and how he longed to escape from it and from himself at the same time, that he might dedicate his life to God. It was right and true, no doubt; but wherefore could not I pronounce Amen? He also mentioned something about myself, how much I had been to him; for he had never known his mother, and had never had a sister, and could never have a wife. All which was excellent; but a mere woman like Glory doesn't want to read that sort of thing in a letter, and would rather have five minutes of John Storm the man than a whole eternity of John Storm the saint. His letter made me think of Christian on his way to the eternal city, but that person has always seemed to me a doubtful sort of hero anyway, taking Mrs. Christian into account and the various little Christians, and I can't pity him a pin about his bundle, for he might just as well have left behind him what he couldn't enjoy of God's providence himself.

But this is like hitting a cripple with his crutch, John being gone and past all defending himself; and when I think of it in the streets, I have to run to keep myself from doing something silly, and then people think I'm chasing an omnibus when I'm really only chasing my tears. I can't tell you much about the Brotherhood. It looks like a cross between a palace and a penitentiary, and it appears that Ritualism has gone one better than High Churchmanship and is trying to introduce the monastic system, which, to an ordinary woman of the world, seems well enough for the man in the moon, though the man in the moon might have a different way of looking at things. They say the brothers are all celibates and live in cells, but I think I've seen a look in John Storm's eyes that warns me that he wasn't intended for "the lek o' that" exactly. To tell you the truth, I half blame myself for what has happened, and I am ashamed when I remember how jauntily I took matters all the time our poor John was fighting with beasts at Ephesus. But I am vexed with him, too; and if only he had waited patiently before taking such a serious step in order to hear *my* arguments . . . But no matter. A jackdaw isn't to be called a religious bird because it keeps a-cawing on the steeple, and John Storm won't make himself into a monk by shutting himself up in a cell. Good-night.

IV

THE house to which Glory had fled out of the fog was a little dingy tobacconist's shop opening on a narrow alley that runs from Holborn into Lincoln's Inn Fields. It was kept by the baby-farmer whom she had met at the house of Polly Love, and the memory of the address thrust upon her there had been her only resource on that day of crushing disappointment and that night of peril. Mrs. Jupe's husband, a waiter at a West End club, was a simple and helpless creature, very fond of his wife, much deceived by her and kept in ignorance of the darker side of her business operations. Their daughter, familiarly called "Booboo," a silent child with cunning eyes and pasty cheeks, was being brought up to help in the shop and to dodge the inspector of the School Board.

On coming downstairs next morning to the close and dingy parlour at the back, Glory had looked about her as one who had expected something she did not see, whereupon Mrs. Jupe, who was at breakfast with her husband, threw up her little twinkling eyes and said—

"Now I know what she's a-looking for—it's the byeby."

"Where is it?" said Glory.

"Gorn, my dear."

"Surely you don't mean——"

"No, not dead, but I 'ad to put it out, pore thing."

"Ye see, Miss," said Mr. Jupe with his mouth full, "my missus couldn't nurse the byeby and 'tend to the biziniss as well; so, as reason was——"

"It brikes my 'eart to think it; but it made such a n'ise, pore darling——"

"Does the mother know?" said Glory.

"That wasn't necessary, my dear. It's gorn to a pusson I can trust to tyke kear of it, and I'm trooly thenkful——"

"It jest amarnts to this, Miss—the biziniss is too much for the missus as things is——"

"I wouldn't keer if my 'ealth was what it used to be in the dyes when I 'ad Booboo."

"But it ain't, and she's often said as how she'd like a young laidy to live with her and 'elp her with the shop."

"A nice-lookin' girl might 'ave a many chawnces in a place syme as this, my dear."

"Lawd, yus; and when I seen the young laidy come in at the door, 'strike me lucky!' thinks I, 'the very one.'"

"Syme 'ere, my dear. I reckkernized ye the minute I seen ye; and if ye want to leave the hospital and myke a stawt, as you were saying last night——"

Glory stopped them. They were on the wrong track entirely. She had merely come to lodge with them, and if that was not agreeable——

"Well, and so ye shell, my dear; and if ye don't like the shop all at onct, there's Booboo,—she wants lessons——"

"But I can pay," said Glory, and then she was compelled to say something of her plans. She wanted to become a singer, perhaps an actress, and, to tell them the truth, she might not be staying long, for when she got engagements——

"Jest as you like, my dear; myke yerself at 'ome. On'y don't be in a nurry about engygements. Good ones ain't tots picked up by the childring in the streets these dyes."

Nevertheless it was agreed that Glory was to lodge at the tobacconist's, and Mr. Jupe was to bring her box from the hospital on coming home that night from his work. She was to pay ten shillings a week, all told, so that her money would last four or five weeks, and leave something to spare. "But I shall be earning long before that," she thought, and her resources seemed boundless. She started on her enterprise instantly, knowing no more of how to begin than that it would first be necessary to find the office of an agent. Mr. Jupe remembered one such place.

"It's in a street off of Waterloo Road," he said, "and the name on the windows is Josephs."

Glory found this person in a fur-lined coat and an opera-hat sitting in a room which was papered with photographs, chiefly of the nude and the semi-nude, intermingled with sheafs of playbills that hung from the walls like ballads from the board of the ballad-monger.

"Vell, vot's your line?" he asked.

Glory answered nervously and indefinitely.

"Vot can you do, then?"

She could sing and recite and imitate people.

The man shrugged his shoulders. "My terms are two guineas down and ten per cent. on salary."

Glory rose to go. "That is impossible. I cannot——"

"Vait a minute. How much have you got?"

"Isn't that my business, sir?"

"Touchy, ain't ye, Miss? But if you mean bizness, I'll tyke a guinea and give you the first chawnce what comes in."

Reluctantly, fearfully, distrustfully, Glory paid her guinea and left her address.

"Daddle doo," said the agent.

Then she found herself in the street. "Two weeks less for lodgings," she thought, as she returned to the tobacconist's. But Mrs. Jupe seemed entirely satisfied.

"What did I tell ye, my dear? Good engygements ain't chasing nobody abart the streets these dyes, and there's that many girls now as can do a song and a dance and a recitashing."

Three days passed, four days, five days, six days, a week, and still no word from Mr. Josephs. Glory called on him again. He counselled patience. It was the dead season at the theatres and music-halls, but if she only waited——

She waited a week longer, and then called again, and again, and yet again. But she brought nothing back except her mimicry of the man's manner. She could hit him off to a hair— his raucous voice, his guttural utterance, and the shrug of his shoulders that told of the Ghetto.

Mrs. Jupe shrieked with laughter. That lady's spirits were going up as Glory's came down. At the end of the third week she said, "I can't a bear to tyke yer money no longer, my dear, you not doing nothink."

Then she hinted at a new arrangement. She had to be much from home. It was necessary; her health was poor—an obvious fiction. During her absence she had to leave Booboo in charge.

"It ain't good for the child, my dear, and it ain't good for the shop; but if anybody syme as yerself would tyke a turn behind the counter——"

Having less than ten shillings in her pocket, Glory was forced to submit.

There was a considerable traffic through the little turnstile. Lying between Bedford Row and Lincoln's Inn, it was the usual course of lawyers and lawyers' clerks passing to and from the courts. They were not long in seeing that a fresh and beautiful face was behind the counter of the dingy little tobacco shop. Business increased, and Mrs. Jupe became radiant.

"What did I tell ye, my dear? There's more real gentlemen a mooching rahnd here in a day than a girl would have a chawnce of meeting in a awspital in a twelvemonth."

THE RELIGIOUS LIFE

Glory's very soul was sickening. The attentions of the men, their easy manners, their little liberties, their bows, their smiles, their compliments—it was gall and wormwood to the girl's unbroken spirit. Nevertheless she was conscious of a certain pleasure in the bitterness. The bitterness was her own; the pleasure some one else's, so to speak, who was looking on and laughing. She felt an unconquerable impulse to sharpen her wit on Mrs. Jupe's customers, and even to imitate them to their faces. They liked it, so she was good for business both ways.

But she remembered John Storm and felt suffocated with shame. Her thoughts turned to him constantly, and she called at the hospital to ask if there were any letters. There were two, but neither of them was from Bishopsgate Street. One was from Aunt Anna. Glory was not to dream of leaving the hospital. With tithes going down every year and everything else going up, how could she think of throwing away a salary and adding to their anxieties? The other was from her grandfather :—

"Glad to hear you have had a holiday, dear Glory, and trust you are feeling the better for the change. Must confess to being a little startled by the account of your adventure on Lord Mayor's Day, with the wild scheme for cutting adrift from the hospital and taking London by storm. But it was just like my little witch, my wandering gipsy, and I knew it was all nonsense; so when Aunt Anna began to scold, I took my pipe and went upstairs. Sorry to hear that John Storm has gone over to Popery, for that is what it comes to, though he is not under the Romish obedience. I am the more concerned because I failed to make his peace with his father. The old man seems to blame me for everything, and has even taken to passing me on the road. Give my best respects to Mrs. Jupe when you see her again, with my thanks for taking care of you. And now that you are alone in that great and wicked Babylon, take good care of yourself, my dear one. To know that my runaway is well and happy and prosperous is all I have left to reconcile me to her absence. Yes, the harvest is over and threshed and housed, and we have fires in the parlour nearly every day, which makes Anna severe sometimes, coals being so dear just now and the turf no longer allowed to us."

It was ten days overdue. That night, in her little bedroom, with its low ceiling and sloping floor, Glory wrote her answer:—

"But it isn't nonsense, my dear grandfather, and I really have left the hospital. I don't know if it was the holiday and the liberty or what, but I felt like that young hawk at Glenfaba—do you remember it? —the one that was partly snared, and came dragging the trap on to the lawn by a string caught round its leg. I had to cut it away—I had to, I had to! But you mustn't feel one single moment's uneasiness about me. An able-bodied woman like Glory Quayle doesn't starve in a place like London. Besides, I am provided for already, so you see my bow abides in strength. The first morning after my arrival Mrs. Jupe told me that if I cared to take to myself the style and title of teacheress to her little Slyboots, I had only to say the word, and I should be as welcome as the flowers in May. It isn't exactly first fiddling, you know, and it doesn't bring an ambassador's salary, but it may serve for the present, and give me time to look about. You mustn't pay too much attention to my lamentations about being compelled by nature to wear a petticoat. Things being so arranged in this world, I'll make them do. But it does make one's head swim and one's wings droop to see how hard Nature is on a woman compared to a man. Unless she is a genius or a jellyfish, there seems to be only one career open to her, and that is a lottery, with marriage for the prizes, and for the blanks—oh dear, oh dear! Not that I have anything to complain of, and I hate to be so sensitive. Life is wonderfully interesting, and the world is such an amusing place that I have no patience with people who run away from it, and if I were a man . . . But wait, only wait, good people!"

V

JOHN STORM had made one other friend at Bishopsgate Street—the dog of the monastery. It was a half-bred bloodhound, and nobody seemed to know whence he came and why he was there. He was a huge, ungainly, and most forbidding creature, and partly for that reason, but chiefly because it was against rule to fix the affections on earthly things, the brothers rarely caressed him. Unnoticed and unheeded, he slept in the house by day and prowled through the court by night, and had hardly ever been known to go out into the streets. He was the strictest monk in the monastery, for he eyed every stranger as if he had been Satan himself, and howled at all music except the singing in the church.

On seeing John for the first time, he broadened his big flews and stiffened his thick stern, according to his wont with all intruders, but in this instance the intruder was not afraid. John patted him on the peaked head and rubbed him on the broad nose, then opened his mouth and examined his teeth, and finally turned him on his back and tickled his chest, and they were fast friends and comrades for ever after.

Some weeks after the dedication they were in the courtyard together, and the dog was pitching and plunging and uttering deep bays, which echoed between the walls like thunder at play. It was the hour of morning recreation, between Terce and Sext, and the religious were lolling about and talking, and one lay brother was sweeping up the leaves that had fallen from the tree, for the winter had come and the branches were bare. The lay brother was Brother Paul, and he made sidelong looks at John, but kept his head down, and went on with his work without speaking. One by one the brothers went back to the house, and John made ready to follow them, but Paul put himself in his way. He was thinner than before, and his eyes were red and his respiration difficult. Nevertheless, he smiled in a childlike way and began to talk of the dog. What life there was in the old creature still! and nobody had known there was so much play in it.

"You are not feeling so well, are you?" said John.

"Not quite so well," he answered.

"The day is cold, and this penance is too much for you."

"No, it's not that. I asked for it, you know, and I like it. It's something else. To tell you the truth, I'm very foolish in some ways. When I've got anything on my mind, I'm always thinking. Day and night it's the same with me, and even work——"

His breathing was audible, but he tried to laugh.

"Do you know what it is this time? It's what you said on the tower on the night of the vows, you remember. What you didn't say, I mean, and that's just the trouble. It was wrong to talk of the world without great necessity; but if you had been able to answer me in a word, if you had been able to say 'Yes' when I asked if everybody was well, you would have done it, wouldn't you?"

"We'll not talk of that now," said John.

"No, it would be the same fault as before. Still——"

"How keen the air is! And your asthma is so troublesome! You must really let me speak to the Father."

"Oh, that's nothing; I'm used to it. But if you know yourself what it is to be always thinking of anybody——"

John called to the dog, and it capered about him. "Good morning, Brother Paul." And he went into the house. The lay brother leaned on his besom and drew a long sigh, that seemed to come from the depth of his chest.

John had hastened away lest his voice should betray him.

"Awful!" he thought. "It must be awful to be always thinking of somebody, and in fear of what has happened to her. Poor little Polly! She's not worthy of it; but what does that matter? Blood is blood and love is love, and only God is stronger."

A few days afterwards the air darkened and softened, and snow began to fall. Between Vespers and Evensong John went up to the tower to see London under its mantle of white. It was like an Eastern city now under an Eastern moonlight, and he was listening to the shouts and laughter of people snowballing in the streets, when he heard a laboured step on the stair behind him. It was Brother Paul coming up with a spade to shovel away the snow. His features were pinched and contracted, and his young face was looking old and worn.

"You really must not do it," said John. "To work like this is not penance but suicide. I'll speak to the Father, and he'll——"

"Don't, for mercy's sake, don't. Have some pity, at all events. If you only knew what a good thing work is for me—how it drives away thoughts and stifles——"

"But it's so useless, Brother Paul. Look! the snow is still falling, and there's more to come yet."

"All the same, it's good for me. When I'm very tired, I can sleep sometimes; and then God is good to you if you don't spare yourself. Some day perhaps He'll tell me something."

"He'll tell us everything in His own good time, Brother Paul."

"It's easy to counsel patience. If I were like you are, I should be counting the days until my time was over, and that would help me to bear things. But when you are dedicated for life——"

He stopped at his work and looked over the parapet, and seemed to be gazing into the weary days to come.

"Have you anybody of your own out there?"

"You mean any——"

"Any relative—any sister?"

"No."

"Then you don't know what it is; that's why you won't give me an answer."

"Don't ask me, Brother Paul."

"Why not?"

"It might only make you the more uneasy if I told you what——"

The lay brother let his spade fall, then slowly, very slowly, picked it up again and said—

"I understand. You needn't say any more. I shall never ask you again."

The bell rang for Evensong and John hurried away. "If it were only some one who was deserving of it!" he thought. "Some one who was worthy that a man should risk his soul to save her!"

At supper and in church he saw Brother Paul going about like a man in a waking dream, and when he went up to bed he heard him moving restlessly in the adjoining cell. The fear of betraying himself was becoming unbearable, and he leaped up and stepped out into the corridor intending to ask the Superior to give him another room elsewhere. But he stopped and came back. "It's not brave," he thought, "it's not kind, it's not human," and saying this again and again, as one whistles when going by a haunted house, he covered his ears and fell asleep.

In the middle of the night, while it was still quite dark, he was awakened by a light on his face and the sense of some one looking down on him in his sleep. With a shudder he opened his eyes and saw Brother Paul, candle in hand, standing by the bed. His eyes were red and swollen, and when he spoke his voice was full of tears.

"I know it's a fault to come into anybody else's cell," he said; "but I would rather do my penance than endure this torture. Something has happened—I can see that quite well; but I don't know what it is, and the suspense is killing me. The certainty would be easier to bear; and I swear to you by Him who died for us that if you tell me I shall be satisfied. Is she dead?"

"Not that," said John by a sudden impulse, and then there was an awful silence.

"Not dead!" said Paul. "Then would to God that she were dead, for it must be something worse, a thousand times worse!"

John felt as if the secret had been stolen from him in his sleep; but it was gone, and he could say nothing. Brother Paul's lips trembled, his respiration quickened, and he turned away and smote his head against the wall and sobbed.

"I knew it all the time," he said. "Her sister went the same way, and I could see that she was going too, and that was why I was so anxious. Oh, my poor mother! my poor mother!"

For two days after that John saw no more of Brother Paul. "He is doing his penance somewhere," he thought.

Meanwhile the snow was still falling, and when the brothers went out to Lauds at 6 A.M., they passed through a cutting of snow which was banked up afresh every morning, though the day had not then dawned. On the third day John was the first to go down to the hall, and there he met Brother Paul, with his spade in his hands, coming out of the courtyard. He looked like a man who was melting before a fire as surely as a piece of wax.

"I am sorry now that I told you," said John.

Brother Paul hung his head.

"It is easy to see that you are suffering more than ever, and it is all my fault. I will go to the Father and confess."

Between breakfast and Terce John carried out his intention. The Superior was sitting before a handful of fire in a little room that was darkened by leather-bound books and by the flakes of snow which were falling across the window-panes.

"Father," said John, "I am a cause of offence to another brother, and it is I who should be doing his penance." And then he told how he had broken the observance which forbids any one to talk of his relations with the world without.

The Father listened with great solemnity. "My son," he said, "your temptation is a testimony to the reality of the religious life. Satan's rage against the home of consecrated souls is terrible, and he would fain break in upon it if he could with worldly thoughts and cares and passions. But we must conquer him by his own weapons. Your penance, my son, shall be of the same kind with your offence. Go to the door and take the place of the doorkeeper, and stay there day and night until the end of the year. Thus shall the evil one be made aware that you are the guardian of our house, to be tampered with no more."

Brother Andrew was troubled when John took his place at the door that night, but John himself was unconcerned. He was doorkeeper to the household, so he began on the duties of his menial position. As the brothers passed in and out on their mission errands, he opened the door and closed it. If any one knocked, he answered "Praise be to God," then slid back the little grating in the middle panel of the door and looked out at the stranger. The hall was a chill place with a stone floor, and he sat on a form that stood against one of its walls. His bed was in an alcove which had formerly been the cloak-room, and a card hung over it with the inscription, "Children, obey your parents in the Lord." He had no company except big Brother Andrew, who stole down sometimes to cheer him with his speechless presence, and the dog, which was always hanging about him.

VI

It was at least some comfort to be out of the proximity of Brother Paul. The sounds of the lay brother in the neighbouring cell had brought back recollections of Glory, and he had more than he could do to conquer his thoughts of her. Since he had taken his vows, and had ceased to mention her in his prayers, she had been always with him, and his fears for her fate had been pricked and goaded by the constant presence of Brother Paul's anxieties.

On the other hand, it was some loss that he could not go to the church; and he remembered with a pang how happy he had been after a night of terrors when he had gone into God's house in the morning and cast his burden on Him with one yearning cry of "God bless all women and young children!"

It was now the Christmas season, and his heart tingled and thrilled as the brothers passed through the door at midday, and talked of the women who attended the Christmas services. Were they really so calm as they seemed to be, and had they conquered their natural affections?

Sometimes during the midday service he would slide back the grating and listen for the women's voices. He heard one voice in all of them, but he knew it was only a dream. Then he would watch the snow falling from the little patch of dun-coloured sky crossed by bars, and tell himself that that was all he was to see of the world henceforth.

The sky emptied itself at last, and Brother Paul came again to shovel away the snow. He was weaker than ever, for the wax was melting away. When he began to work, his chest was oppressed and his face was feverish. John snatched the spade out of his hand, and fell to doing his work instead of him.

"I can't bear to see it, and I won't," he said.

"But the Father——"

"I don't care; you can tell him if you like. You are killing yourself by inches, and you are a failing man anyway."

"Am I really dying?" said Brother Paul, and he staggered away like one who had heard his sentence.

John looked after him, and thought—"Now, what should I do if I were in that man's place? If the case were Glory's, and I fixed here as in a vice?"

He was ashamed when he thought of Glory like that, and he dismissed the idea; but it came back with mechanical obstinacy, and he was compelled to consider it. His vows? Yes, it would be death to his soul to break them. But if she were lost, who had no one but him to look to—if she went down to wreck and ruin—then the fires of hell would be as nothing to his despair.

Brother Paul came to him next day, and sat on the form by his side, and said—

"If I'm really dying, what am I to do?"

"What would you like to do, Brother Paul?"

"I should like to go out and find her."

"What good would there be in that?"

"I could say something that would stop her and put an end to everything."

"Are you sure of it?"

A wild light came into his eyes, and he answered, "Quite sure."

John played the hypocrite, and began to counsel patience.

"But a man can't live without hope and not go mad," said Brother Paul.

"We must trust and pray," said John.

"But God never answers us. If it were your own case, what would you do? If some one outside were lost——"

"I should go to the Father and say, 'Let me go in search of her.'"

"I'll do it," said Brother Paul.

"Why not? The Father is kind and tender, and he loves his children."

"Yes, I *will* do it," said Paul, and he made for the Father's room.

He got to the door of the cell, and then came back again. "I can't," he said. "There's something you don't know. I can't look in his face and ask."

"Stay here, and I'll ask for you," said John.

"God bless you!" said Paul.

John made three hasty strides, and then stopped.

"But if he will not——"

"Then God's will be done!"

It was morning, and the Superior was reading in his room.

"Come in, my son," he said, and he laid his book on his lap. "This is a book you must read some day, the 'Inner Life of Père Lacordaire.' Most fascinating! An inner life of intolerable horror until he had conquered his natural affections."

"Father," said John, "one of our lay brothers has a little sister in the world and she has fallen into trouble. She has gone from the place where he left her, and God only knows where she is now. Let him go out and find her."

"Who is it, my son?"

"Brother Paul—and she is all he has, and he cannot help but think of her."

"This is a temptation of the Evil One, my son. Brother Paul has newly taken the vows, and so have you. The vows are a challenge to the powers of evil, and it is only to be expected that he who takes them will be tested to the uttermost."

"But, Father, she is young and thoughtless. Let him go out and find her and save her, and he will come back and praise God a thousand times the more."

"The temptations of Satan are very subtle; they come in the guise of duty. Satan is tempting our brother through love, and you also through pity. Let us turn our backs on him."

"Then it is impossible?"

"Quite impossible."

When John returned to the door, Brother Paul was standing by the alcove gazing with wet eyes on the text hanging above the bed. He saw his answer in John's face, and they sat down on the form without speaking.

The bell rang for service, and the religious began to pass through the hall. As the Father was crossing the threshold, Brother Paul flung himself down at his feet and clutched his cassock and made a frantic appeal for pity.

"Father, have pity upon me and let me go!"

The Father's eyes became moist, but his will remained unshaken. "As a man I ought to have pity," he said, "and as the father of all of you I should be kind to my children; but it is not I who refuse you—it is God, and I should be guilty of a sin if I let you go."

Then Paul burst into mad laughter, and the religious gathered round and looked at him in astonishment. There was foam on his lips and fire in his eyes, and he threw up his hands and fell back fainting.

The Father made the sign of the cross on his breast and his lips moved in silence for a moment. Then he said to John, who had raised the lay brother in his arms—

"Leave him there. Damp his forehead and hold his hands."

And turning to the religious he added, "I ask the prayers of the community for our poor brother. Satan is fighting for his soul. Let us wrestle in prayer that we may expel the spirit that possesses him."

At the next moment John was alone with the unconscious man, except for the dog which was licking his forehead. And looking after the Superior, he told himself that such unlimited power over the body and soul of another the Almighty could have meant for no man. The love of God and the fear of the devil had swallowed up the love of man and stifled all human affections. Such religion must have hardened the best man ever born. As for the poor broken creature lying there so still, his vows had been made to Heaven, and to Heaven alone his obedience was due. The nature within him had spoken too loudly, but there were laws of nature which it was a sin to resist. Then why should he resist them? The cry of blood was the voice of God, or God had no voice and He could speak to no man. Then why should he not listen?

Brother Paul recovered consciousness and raised his head. The waves of memory flowed back upon him and his eyes flamed and his lip trembled.

"I will go if I have to break my vows," he said.

"No need for that," said John.

"Why so?"

"Because I will let you out at night and let you in again in the morning."

"You?"

"Yes, I. Listen!"

And then these two crushed and fettered souls, bound by no iron bonds, confined by no bolts and bars, but only under the shadow of the supernatural, sat together like prisoners in a dungeon concocting schemes for their escape.

"The Father locks the outer gate himself," said John. "Where does he keep the key?"

"In his own room on a nail above his bed," said Paul.

"Who is the lay brother attending to him now?"

"Brother Andrew."

"Brother Andrew will do anything for me," said John.

"But the dog?" said Paul. "He is always in the court at night, and he barks at the sound of a step."

"Not my step," said John.

"I'll do it," said Paul.

"I will send you to some one who can find your sister. You'll tell her you come from me and she'll take you with her."

They could hear the singing in the church, and they paused to listen.

"When I come back in the morning I'll confess everything and do my penance," said Paul.

"And I too," said John.

The sun had come out with a sudden gleam, and the thawing snow was dripping from the trees in drops like diamonds. The singing ceased, the service ended, and the brothers came back to the house. When the Father entered, Paul was clothed and in his right mind, and sitting quietly on the form.

"Thank God for this answer to our prayers!" said the Father. "But you must pray without ceasing lest Satan should conquer you again. Until the end of the year say your Rosary in the church every night alone from Compline to midnight."

Then turning to John he said with a smile, "And you shall be like the anchoret of old to this household, my son. We monks pray by day, but the anchoret prays by night. Unless we know that in the dark hours the anchoret guards the house, who shall rest on his bed in peace?"

VII

AT the end of the fourth week after Glory had paid her fee to the agent, she called on him again. It was Saturday morning, and the vicinity of his office was a strange and surprising scene. The staircase and passages to the house as well as the pavement of the streets, as far as to the public-house at the corner, were thronged with a gaudy but shabby army of music-hall artistes of both sexes. When Glory attempted to pass through them she was stopped by a cry of "Tyke yer turn on treasury day, my dear," and she fell back and waited.

One by one they passed upstairs, came down again with cheerful faces, shouted their adieux and disappeared. Meanwhile they amused themselves with salutations, all more or less lively and familiar, told stories and exchanged confidences, while they danced a step or stamped about to keep away the cold. "You've chucked the slap[1] on with a mop this morning, my dear," said one of the girls. "Have I, my love? Well, I was a bit thick about the clear, so I thought it would keep me warm." "It ain't no use facing the doner of the casa with that," said a man who jingled a few coins as he came downstairs, and away went two to the public-house. Sometimes a showy brougham would drive up to the door, and a magnificent person in a fur-lined coat with diamond rings on both hands would sweep through the lines and go upstairs. When he came down again his carriage door would be opened by half a dozen "pros" who would call him "dear old cully," and tell him they were "down on their luck" and hadn't "done a turn for a fortnight." He would distribute shillings and half-crowns among them, cry "Ta-ta, boys," and drive away, whereupon his pensioners would

[1] Rouge.

stroke their cuffs and collars of threadbare astracan, tip winks after the carriage and say, "That's better than crying cabbages in Covent Garden, ain't it?" Then they would all laugh knowingly, and one would say, "What's it to be, cully?" and somebody would answer, "Come along to Poverty Point then," and a batch of the waiting troop would trip off to the corner.

One of the gorgeous kind was coming down the stairs when his eye fell on Glory as she stood in a group of girls who were decked out in rose pink and corresponding finery. He paused, turned back, re-opened the office-door, and said in an audible whisper, "Who's the pretty young ginger you've got here, Josephs?" A moment afterwards the agent had come out and called her upstairs.

"It's salary day, my dear, vait there," he said, and he put her into an inner room, which was tawdrily furnished in faded red plush, with a piano and coloured prints of ballet-girls and boxing men, and was full of the odour of stale tobacco and bad whisky.

She waited half-an-hour, feeling hot and ashamed and troubled with perplexing thoughts, and listening to the jingle of money in the adjoining room, mingled with the ripple of laughter and sometimes the exchange of angry words. At length the agent came back, saying, "Vell, vhat can I do for you to-day, my dear?"

He had been drinking; his tone was familiar, and he placed himself at the end of the sofa upon which Glory was seated.

Glory rose immediately. "I came to ask if you have heard of anything for me," she said.

"Sit down, my dear."

"No, thank you."

"Heard anything? Not yet, my dear. You must vait——"

"I think I've waited long enough, and if your promises amount to anything you'll get me an appearance, at all events."

"So I vould, my dear; I vould get you an extra turn at the Vashington, but it is very expensive, and you've got no money."

"Then why did you take what I had if you can do nothing? Besides, I don't want anything but what my talents will earn. Give me a letter to a manager—for mercy's sake do something for me!"

There was the shrug of the Ghetto as the man rose and said, "Very vell; if it's like that, I'll give you a letter and velcome."

He sat at the table and wrote a short note, sealed it carefully in an envelope which was backed with advertisements, then gave it to Glory and said, "Daddle doo. You'll not require to come again."

Going downstairs she looked at the letter. It was addressed to an acting-manager at a theatre in the farthest west of London. The passages of the house and the pavements outside were now empty; it was nearly two o'clock and snow was beginning to fall. She was feeling cold and a little hungry, but making up her mind to deliver the letter at once, she hastened to the Temple Station.

There was a *matinée*, so the acting-manager was "in front." He took the letter abruptly, opened it with an air of irritation, glanced at it, glanced at Glory, looked at the letter again, and then said in a strangely gentle voice, "Do you know what's in this, my girl?"

"No," said Glory.

"Of course you don't—look," and he gave her the letter to read. It ran:—

"DEAR ——,—This wretched young ginger is worrying me for a shop. She isn't worth a ——. Get rid of her, and oblige,

"JOSEPHS."

Glory flushed up to the forehead and bit her lip, then a little nervous laugh broke from her throat, and two great tears came rolling from her eyes. The acting-manager took the letter out of her hands and tapped her kindly on the shoulder.

"Never mind, my child. Perhaps we'll disappoint him yet. Tell me all about it."

She told him everything, for he had bowels of compassion. "We can't put you on at present," he said, "but our saloon contractor wants a young lady to give out programmes, and if that will do to begin with——"

It was a crushing disappointment, but she was helpless. The employment was menial, but it would take her out of the tobacco shop and put her into the atmosphere of the theatre, and bring fifteen shillings a week as well. She might begin on Monday if she could find her black dress, white apron, cap, and cuffs. The dress she had already, but the apron, cap, and cuffs would take the larger part of the money she had left.

By Sunday night she had swallowed her pride with one great gulp, and was writing home to Aunt Anna:—

"I'm as busy as Trap's wife these days—indeed that goddess of industry is nothing to me now; but Christmas is coming, and I shall want to buy a present for grandfather (and perhaps for the aunties as well), so please send me a line in secret saying what he is wanting most. Snow! snow! snow! The snow it snoweth every day."

On the Monday evening she presented herself at the theatre,

and was handed over to another girl to be instructed in her duties. The house was one of the best in London, and Glory found pleasure in seeing the audience assemble. For the first half-hour the gorgeous gowns, the beautiful faces, and the distinguished manners excited her and made her forget herself. Then little by little there came the pain of it all, and by the time the curtain had gone up her gorge was rising, and she crept out into the quiet corridor, where her colleague was seated already under an electric lamp reading a penny number.

The girl was a little tender black and white thing, looking like a dahlia. In a quarter of an hour Glory knew all about her. During the day she served in a shop in the Whitechapel Road. Her name was Agatha Jones—they called her Aggie. Her people lived in Bethnal Green, but Charlie always came to the theatre to take her home. Charlie was her young man.

In the intervals between the acts Glory assisted in the cloakroom, and there the great ladies began to be very amusing. After the tinkle of the electric bell announcing the second act she returned to the deserted corridor, and before her audience of one gave ridiculous imitations in dead silence of ladies using the puff and twiddling up their front hair.

"My! It's you as oughter be on the styge, my dear," said Aggie.

"Do you think so?" said Glory.

"I'm going on myself soon. Charlie's getting me on the clubs."

"The clubs?"

"The foreign clubs in Soho. More nor one has begun there."

"Really?"

"The foreigners like dancing best. If you can do the splits and shoulder the leg it's the mykings of you for life."

When the performance was over they found Charlie waiting on the square in front of the house. Glory had seen him before, and she recognised him immediately. He was the young Cockney with the rolled fringe who had bantered the policeman by Palace Yard on Lord Mayor's Day. They got into the Underground together, and when Glory returned to the subject of the foreign clubs Charlie grew animated and eloquent.

"They give ye five shillings a turn, and if yer good for anythink ye may do six turns of a Sunday night, not ter speak of special nights and friendly leads and sech."

When Glory got out at the Temple, Aggie's head was resting on Charlie's shoulder and her little gloved fingers were lightly clasped in his hand.

On the second night Glory had conquered a good deal of her

pride. The grace of her humour was saving her. It was almost as if somebody else was doing servant's duty and she was looking on and laughing. After all, it was very funny that she should be there, and what delicious thoughts it would bring later! Even Nell Gwynn sold oranges in the pit at first; and then, some day, when she had risen above all this ...

It must have been a great night of some sort. She had noticed red baize and an awning outside, and the front of one of the boxes was laden with flowers. When its occupants entered, the orchestra played the national anthem and the audience rose to their feet. It was the Prince with the Princess and their daughters. The audience was only less distinguished, and something far off and elusive moved in her memory when a lady handed her a check and said in a sweet voice—

"A gentleman will come for this seat."

Glory's station was in the stalls, and she did not go out when the lights went down and the curtain rose. The play was a modern one—the story of a country girl who returned home after a life of bitterness and shame.

It moved her and thrilled her and stirred the smouldering fires of her ambition. She was sorry for the actress who played the part, the poor thing did not understand, and she would have given worlds to pour her own voice through the girl's mouth. Then she was conscious that she was making a noise with her hands, and looking down at them she saw the crumpled programmes and her white cuffs, and remembered where she was and what, and she murmured, "O God, do not punish me for these vain thoughts!"

All at once a light shot across her face as she stood in the darkness. The door of the corridor had been opened and a gentleman was coming in. He stood a moment beside her with his eyes on the stage and said in a whisper—

"Did a lady leave a seat?"

It was Drake! She felt as if she would suffocate, but answered in a strained voice—

"Yes, that one—programme, please."

He took the programme without looking at her, put his fingers into his waistcoat pocket, and slid something into her hand. It was sixpence.

She could have screamed. The humiliation was too abject. Hurrying out, she threw down her papers, put on her cloak and hat, and fled.

But next morning she laughed at herself, and when she took out Drake's sixpence she laughed again. With the poker and a nail she drove a hole through the coin, and then hung it up by a

string to a hook over the mantelpiece, and laughed (and cried a
little) every time she looked at it. Life was so funny! Why
did people bury themselves before they were dead? She
wouldn't do it for worlds. But she did not go back to the
theatre for all that, and neither did she return to the counter.

Christmas was near, the shops became bright and gay, and
she remembered what beautiful presents she had meant to send
home out of the money she had hoped to earn. On Christmas
Eve the streets were thronged with little family groups out
shopping, and there were many amusing sights. Then she
laughed a good deal—she could not keep from laughing.

Christmas Day opened with a rimy, hazy morning, and the
business thoroughfares were deserted. They had sucking-pig
for dinner, and Mr. Jupe, who was at home for the holiday,
behaved like a great boy. It was afternoon before the postman arrived with a bag as big as a creel, full of Christmas cards
and parcels. There was a letter for Glory. It was from Aunt
Anna.

"We are concerned about the serious step you have taken,
but trust it is for the best, and that you will give Mrs. Jupe
every satisfaction. Don't waste your savings on us. Remember
there are post-office savings banks everywhere, and that there is
no friend like a little money."

At the bottom there was a footnote from Aunt Rachel: "Do
you ever see the Queen in London, and the dear Prince and
Princess?"

She went to service that night at St. Paul's Cathedral. Entering by the west door, a verger in a black cloak directed her to
a seat in the nave. The great place was dark and chill and half
empty. All the singing seemed to come from some unseen
regions far away, and when the preacher got into the curious
pulpit, he looked like a Jack-in-the-box, and it seemed to be a
drum that was speaking.

Coming out before the end, she thought she would walk to
the Whitechapel Road, of which Aggie had told her something.
She did so, going by Bishopsgate Street, but turning her head
away as she passed the church of the Brotherhood. The motley
crowd of Polish Jews, Germans, and Chinamen, in the most
interesting street in Europe, amused her for a while, and then
she walked up Houndsditch and passed through Bishopsgate
Street again.

At the Bank she took an omnibus for home. The only other
fare was a bouncing girl in a big hat with feathers.

"Going to the market, my dear? No? I hates it myself,
too, so I goes to the 'alls instead. Come from the country, don't

ye? Same here. Father's a farmer, but he's got sixteen besides me, so I won't be missed. Live? I live at Mother Nan's dress-house now. Nice gloves, ain't they? My hat? Glad you like the style. I generally get a new hat once a week, and as for gloves, if anybody likes me——"

That night in her musty bedroom Glory wrote home while little Slyboots slept:—

"'The best laid schemes o' mice and men gang aft aglee.'

"Witness me!

"I intended to send you some Christmas presents, but the snow has been so industrious that not a mouse has stirred if he could help it. However, I send three big kisses instead and a pair of mittens for grandfather, worked with my own hands, because I wouldn't allow any good Brownie to do it for me. Tell Aunt Rachel I *do* see the Prince and Princess sometimes. I saw them at the theatre the other night. Yes, the theatre! You must not be shocked—we are rather gay in London—we go to the theatre occasionally. It is so interesting to meet all the great people. You see I am fairly launched in fashionable society, but I love everybody just the same as ever, and the moment the candle is out I shall be thinking of Glenfaba and seeing the 'Waits,' and 'Oiel Verree,' and 'Hunting the Wren,' and grandfather smoking his pipe in the study by the light of the fire, and Sir Thomas Traddles, the tailless, purring and blinking at his feet. Merry Christmas to you, my dears. Bye-bye!"

VIII

"'Where's that bright young Irish laidy?' the gentlemen's allwiz sayin', my dear," said Mrs. Jupe; and for very shame's sake, having no money to pay for board and lodgings, Glory returned to the counter.

A little beyond Bedford Row, in a rookery of apartment houses in narrow streets, there lives a colony of ballet-girls and chorus-girls who are employed at the lighter theatres of the Strand. They are a noisy, merry, reckless, harmless race, free of speech, fond of laughter, wearing false jewellery, false hair, and false complexions, but good boots always, which they do their utmost not to conceal.

Many of these girls pass through the Turnstile on their way to their work, and towards seven in the evening the tobacconist's would be full of them. Nearly all smoked, as the stained forefinger of their right hands showed, and while they bought their cigarettes they chirruped and chirped until the little shop was like a tree full of linnets in the spring.

Most of them belonged to the Frailty Theatre, and their usual talk was of the "stars" engaged there. Chief among these were the "Sisters Bellman," a trio of singers in burlesque, and a frequent subject of innuendo and repartee was one Betty, of that ilk, whose name Glory could remember to have seen blazing in gold on nearly every hoarding and sign.

"Says she was a governess in the country, my dear." "Oh yus, I dare say. Came out of a slop-shop in the Mile-End Road though, and learnt 'er steps with the organ-man in the court a-back of the jam-factory." "Well, I never! She's a wide un, she is!" "About as wide as Broad Street, my dear. Use ter sell flowers in Piccadilly Circus till somebody spoke to 'er, and now she rides 'er brougham, doncher know." Then the laughter would be general, and the girls would go off with their arms about each other's waists, and singing, in the street substitute for the stage whisper, "And 'er golden 'air was 'anging dahn 'er back!"

This yellow-haired and yellow-fingered sisterhood saw the game of life pretty clearly, and it did not take them long to get abreast of Glory. "Like this life, my dear!" "Go on! Do she look as if she liked it?"

"Perhaps I do, perhaps I don't," said Glory.

"Tell that to the marines, my dear. I use ter be in a shop myself, but I couldn't a-bear it. Give me my liberty, I say; and if a girl's got any sort of figure——Unnerstand, my dear?"

Late that night one of the girls came in breathless and cried, "Hooraa! What d'ye think? Betty wants a dresser, and I've got the shop for ye, my dear. Guinea a week and the pickings, and you go to-morrow night on trial. Bye-bye!"

Glory's old infirmity came back upon her, and she felt hot and humiliated. But her vanity was not so much wounded by the work that she was offered, as her honour was hurt by the work she was doing. Mrs. Jupe's absences from home were now more frequent than ever. If the business that took her abroad was akin to that which had taken her to Polly Love——

To put an end to her uneasiness, Glory presented herself at the stage-door.

"You the noo dresser, miss?" said the doorkeeper. "Collins has orders to look after you. Collins!"

A scraggy, ugly, untidy woman who was passing through an inner door looked back and listened.

"Come along of me, then," she said, and Glory followed her, first down a dark passage, then through a dusty avenue between stacks of scenery, then across the open stage, up a flight of stairs and into a room of moderate size, which had no window and no ventilation, and contained three cheval glasses, a couch, four cane-bottom chairs, three small toilet-tables with gas jets suspended over them, three large trunks, some boxes of cigarettes, and a number of empty champagne bottles. Here there was another woman, as scraggy and untidy as the first, who bobbed her head at Glory and then went on with her work, which was that of taking gorgeous dresses out of one of the trunks and laying them on the end of the couch.

"She told me to show you her first act," said the woman called Collins, and throwing open another of the trunks, she indicated some of the costumes contained in it.

It was a new world to Glory, and there was something tingling and electrical in the atmosphere about her. There were the shouts and curses of the scene-shifters on the stage, the laughing voices of the chorus-girls going by the door, and all the multitudinous noises of the theatre before the curtain rises. Presently there was a rustle of silk, and two young ladies came bouncing into the room. One was tall and pink and white, like a scarlet runner, the other was little and dainty. They stared at Glory, and she was compelled to speak.

"Miss Bellman, I presume?"

"Ye mean Betty, down't ye?" said the tall lady, and at that moment Betty herself arrived. She was a plump person with a kind of vulgar comeliness, and Glory had a vague sense of having seen her before somewhere.

"So ye've came," she said, and she took possession of Glory straightway. "Help me off of my sealskin."

Glory did so, the others were similarly disrobed, and in a few moments their three ladyships were busy before the toilet-tables with their grease and rose pink and black pencils.

Glory was taking down the hair of her stout ladyship, and her stout ladyship was looking at Glory in the glass.

"Not a bad face, girls, eh?"

The other two glanced at Glory approvingly. "Not bad," they answered, and then hummed or whistled as they went on with their making-up.

"Oh, *thank* you," said Glory with a low curtsy, and everybody laughed. It was really very amusing. Suddenly it ceased to be so.

"And what's its nyme, my dear?" said the little lady.

A sort of shame at using in this company the name that was sacred to home, to the old parson, and to John Storm, came creeping over Glory like a goosing of the flesh, and by the inspiration of a sudden memory she answered, "Gloria."

The little lady paused with the black pencil at her eyebrows and said—

"My! What a nyme for the top line of a bill!"

"Ugh! Mykes me feel like Sundays, though," said the tall lady with a shudder.

"Irish, my dear?"

"Something of that sort," said Glory.

"Brought up a laidy, I'll be bound?"

"My father was a clergyman," said Glory, "but——"

A sudden peal of laughter stopped her, whereupon she threw up her head and her eyes flashed, but her stout ladyship patted her hand and said—

"No offence, Glo, but you really mustn't—they're *all* clergymen's daughters, doncher know."

A sharp knock came to the door, followed by the first call of the call-boy, "Half-hour, ladies." Then there was much bustle and some irritation in the dressing-room, and the tuning up of the orchestra outside. The knock came again, "Curtain up, please." The door was thrown open, the three ladies swept out—the tall one in tights, the little one in a serpentine skirt, the plump one in some fancy costume—and Glory was left to gather up the fragments, to listen to the orchestra, which was now in full power—to think of it all and to laugh.

The ladies returned to the dressing-room again and again in the course of the performance, and when not occupied with the changing of their dresses they amused themselves variously. Sometimes they smoked cigarettes, sometimes sent Collins for brandy and soda, sometimes talked of their friends in front—"Lord Johnny's 'ere again. See 'im in the prompt box? It's 'is sixtieth night this piece, and there's only been sixty-nine of the run"—and sometimes they discussed the audience generally—"Don't know what's a matter with 'em to-night; ye may work yer eyes out, and ye can't get a 'and."

The curtain came down at length, the outdoor costumes were resumed, the call-boy cried "Carriages, please," the ladies answered "Right ye are, Tommy," her plump ladyship nodded to Glory, "You'll do middling, my dear, when ye get yer 'and in;" and then nothing was left but the dark stage, the blank house, and the "Good night, Miss," of the porter at the stage-door.

So these were favourites of the footlights! And Glory Quayle was dressing and undressing them and preparing them for the stage! Next morning before rising Glory tried to think it out. Were they so very beautiful? Glory stretched up in bed to look at herself in the glass, and lay down again with a smile. Were they so much cleverer than other people? It was foolishness to think of it, for they were as empty as a drum. There must be some explanation, if a girl could only find it out.

The second night at the theatre passed much like the first, except that the ladies were visited between the acts by a group of fellow-artistes from another company, and then the free-and-easy manners of familiar intercourse gave way to a style that was most circumspect and precise, and, after the fashion of great ladies, they talked together of morning calls and leaving cards and five-o'clock tea.

There was a scene in the performance in which the three girls sang together, and Glory crept out to the head of the stairs to listen. When she returned to the dressing-room her heart was bounding, and her eyes, as she saw them in the glass, seemed to be leaping out of her head. It was ridiculous! To think of all that fame, all that fuss about voices like those, about singing like that, while she . . . If she could only get a hearing!

But the cloud had chased the sunshine from her face in a moment, and she was murmuring again, " O God, do not punish a vain presumptuous creature!"

All the same she felt happy and joyous, and on the third night she was down at the theatre earlier than the other dressers, and was singing to herself as she laid out the costumes, for her heart was beginning to be light. Suddenly she became aware of some one standing at the open door. It was an elderly man with a bald head and an owlish face. He was the stage-manager; his name was Sefton.

" Go on, my girl," he said. " If you've got a voice like that why don't you let somebody hear it?"

Her plump ladyship arrived late that night, and her companions were dressed and waiting when she swept into the room like a bat with outstretched wings, crying, " Out o' the wy! Betty Bellman's coming! She's lyte."

There were numerous little carpings, backbitings, and hypocrisies during the evening, and they reached a climax when Betty said, " Lord Bobbie is coming round to-night, my dear." " Not if *I* know it, my love," said the tall lady. " We are goin' to supper at the Nell Gwynn club, my dearest." " Surprised at ye, my darling." " *You* are a nice one to preach, my pet!"

After that encounter two of their ladyships, who were kissing and hugging on the stage, were no longer on speaking terms in the dressing-room, and as soon as might be after the curtain had fallen, the tall lady and the little one swept out of the place with mysterious asides about a " friend being a friend," and " not staying there to see nothing done shabby."

"If she don't like she needn't, my dear," said the boycotted one, and then she dismissed Glory for the night with a message to the friend who would be waiting on the stage.

The atmosphere of the dressing-room had become oppressive and stifling that night, and, notwithstanding the exaltation of her spirits since the stage-manager had spoken to her, Glory was sick and ashamed. The fires of her ambition were struggling to burn under the drenching showers that had fallen upon her modesty, and she felt confused and compromised.

As she stepped down the stairs the curtain was drawn up, the auditorium was a void, the stage was dark, save for a single gas jet that burned at the prompter's wing, and a gentleman in evening dress was walking to and fro by the extinguished footlights. She was about to step up to the man when she recognised him, and turning on her heel she hurried away. It was Lord Robert Ure, and the memory that had troubled her at the first sight of Betty was of the woman who had ridden with Polly Love on the day of the Lord Mayor's Show. Feeling hot and foolish and afraid, she was scurrying through the dark passages when some one called to her. It was the stage-manager.

"I should like to hear your voice again, my dear. Come down at eleven in the morning sharp. The leader of the orchestra will be here to play."

She made some confused answer of assent, and then found herself in the back street, panting audibly and taking long breaths of the cold night air. She was dizzy and was feeling, as she had never felt before, that she wanted some one to lean upon. If anybody had said to her at that moment, "Come out of the atmosphere of that hot-bed, my child, it is full of danger and the germs of death," she would have left everything behind and followed him, whatever the cost or sacrifice. But she had no one, and the pain of her yearning and the misery of her shame were choking her.

Before going home she walked over to the hospital; but no, there was still no letter from John Storm. There was one from Drake, many days overdue :—

"DEAR GLORY,—Hearing that you call for your letters, I write to ask if you will not let me know where you are and how the world is using you. Since the day we parted in St. James's Park I have often spoken of you to my friend Miss Macquarrie, and I am angry with myself when I remember what remarkable talents you have, and that they are only waiting for the right use to be made of them. Yours most kindly,
"F. H. N. DRAKE."

"Many thanks, good Late-i'-th'-day," she thought, and she was crushing the letter in her hand when she saw there was a postscript:—

"*P.S.*—This being the Christmas season, I have given myself the pleasure of sending a parcel of Yule-tide goodies to your dear old grandfather and his sweet and simple household; but as they have doubtless long forgotten me, and I do not wish to embarrass them with unnecessary obligations, I will ask you not to help them to the identification of its source."

She straightened out the letter and folded it, put it in her pocket and returned home. Another letter was waiting for her there. It was from the Parson:—

"So you sent us a Christmas-box after all! That was just like my runaway, all innocent acting and make-believe. What joy we had of it!—Rachel and myself, I mean, for we had to carry on the fiction that Aunt Anna knew nothing about it, she being vexed at the thought of our spendthrift spending so much money. Chalse brought it into the parlour while Anna was upstairs, and it might have been the ark going up to Jerusalem, it entered in such solemn stillness. Oh dear! oh dear! The bun-loaf, and the almonds, and the cheese, and the turkey, and the pound of tobacco and the mull of snuff! On account of Anna everything had to be conducted in great quietness, but it was a terribly leaky sort of silence, I fear, and there were hot and hissing whispers. God bless you for your thought and care of us! Coming so timely, it is like my dear one herself, a gift that cometh from the Lord; and when people ask me if I am not afraid that my granddaughter should be all alone in that great and wicked Babylon, I tell them 'No; you don't know my Glory! she is all courage and nerve and power, a perfect bow of steel, quivering with sympathy and strength.'"

IX

CHRISTMAS had come and gone at the Brotherhood, and yet the project was unfulfilled. John himself had delayed its fulfilment from one trivial cause after another. The night was too dark or not dark enough; the moon shone or was not shining. His real obstacle was his superstitious fear. The scheme was very easy of execution, and the Father himself had made it so. This and the Father's trust in him had almost wrecked the enterprise. Only his own secret anxieties, which were interpreted to his consciousness by the sight of Brother Paul's wasting face, sufficed to sustain his purpose.

"The man's dying. It cannot be unpleasing to God."

He said this to himself again and again, as one presses the pain in one's side to make sure it is still there. Under the shadow of the crisis his character was going to ruin. He grew cunning and hypocritical, and could do nothing that was not false in reality or appearance. When the Father passed him he would drop his head, and it was taken for contrition, and he was commended for humility.

It was now the last day of the year, and therefore the last of his duty at the door.

"It must be to-night," he whispered, as Paul passed him.

Paul nodded. Since the plan of escape had been projected he had lost all will of his own, and become quite passive and inert.

How the day lingered! And when the night came it dragged along with feet of lead. It seemed as if the hour of evening recreation would never end. Certain of the brothers who had been away on preaching missions throughout the country had returned for the Feast of the Circumcision, and the house was bright with fresh faces and cheerful voices. John thought he had never before heard so much laughter in the monastery.

But the bell rang for Compline, and the brothers passed into church. It was a cold night, the snow was trodden hard, and the wind was rising. The service ended, and the brothers returned to the house with clasped hands, and passed up to their cells in silence, leaving Brother Paul at his penance in the church.

Finally the Father put up his hood and went out to lock the gate, and the dog, who took this for his signal, shambled up and followed him. When he returned he shuddered and shrugged his shoulders.

"A bitter night, my son," he said. "It's like courting death to go out in it. Heaven help all homeless wanderers on a night like this."

He was wiping the snow from his slippers.

"So this is the last day of your penance, Brother Storm, and to-morrow morning you will join us in the community-room. You have done well; you have fought a good fight and resisted the assaults of Satan. Good-night to you, my son, and God bless you!"

He took a few steps forward and then stopped. "By the

way, I promised you the 'Life of Père Lacordaire,' and you might come to my room now and fetch it."

The Father's room was on the ground-floor to the left of the staircase, and it was entered from a corridor which cut the house across the middle. The rooms that opened out of this corridor to the front looked on the courtyard, and those to the back looked across the City in the direction of the Thames. The Father's room opened to the back. It was as bare of ornament as any of the cells, but it had a small fire and a writing-table on which a lamp was burning.

As they entered the room together the Father hung the key of the gate on one of many hooks above the bed. It was the third hook from the end nearest the window, and the key was an old one with very few wards. John watched all this, and even observed that there were books on the floor, and that a man might stumble if he did not walk warily. The Father picked up one of them.

"This is the book, my son. A most precious document, the very mirror of a living human soul. What touched me most perhaps were the Father's references to his mother. A monk may not have his mother to himself, and if the love of woman is much to him, he is miserable indeed until he has fixed his eyes on the most blessed among women. But the religious life does not destroy natural affection. It only kills in order to bring forth new life. The corn of wheat dies that it may live again. That is the true Christian asceticism, my son, and so it is with our vows. Good-night!"

As John was coming out of the Father's room he met Brother Andrew going into it with clean linen over one arm and a ewer of water in the other hand. He threw on his bed in the alcove the book which the Father had given him, and sat down on the form at the door and tried to strengthen himself in his purpose.

"The man is dying for the sight of his sister. He can save her soul if he can only see her. It cannot be displeasing to the Almighty."

When he lifted his head the house was silent, except for the wind that whistled outside. Presently there was a scarcely perceptible click, as of a door closing, and Brother Andrew came from the direction of the Superior's room. John called to him and he stepped up on tiptoe, for the monk hates noise as an evil spirit. The sprawling features of the big fellow were all smiles.

"Has the Father gone to bed?" said John.

"Yes."

"Just gone?"

"No—half-an-hour ago."

"Then he will be asleep by this time."

"He was asleep before I left him."

"So he doesn't lock his door on the inside?"

"No, never."

"Does the Father sleep soundly?"

"Sometimes he does and sometimes a cat would waken him."

"Brother Andrew ——"

"Yes."

"Would you do something for me if I wanted it very much?"

"You know I would."

"Even if you had to run some risk?"

"I'm not afraid of that."

"And if I got you into trouble perhaps?"

"But you wouldn't. You wouldn't get anybody into trouble."

John could go no further. The implicit trust in the simple face was too much for him.

"What is it?" said Brother Andrew.

"Oh, nothing—nothing at all," said John. "I was only trying you, but you are too good to be tempted, and I am ashamed. You must go to bed now."

"Can I put out the lights for you?"

"No, I'm not ready yet. Ugh! what a cruel wind. A cold night for Brother Paul in the church."

"Tell me, Brother Storm, what is the matter with Brother Paul? He makes me think of my mother, I don't know why."

John made no answer, and the lay brother began to go upstairs. Two steps up he stopped and whispered—

"Won't you let me do something for you, then?"

"Not to-night, Brother Andrew."

"Good-night, Brother Storm."

"Good-night, my lad."

John listened to his footsteps until they stopped far overhead, and then all was quiet. Only the whistling of the wind broke the stillness of the peaceful house. He slid back the grating and looked out. All was darkness except for the tiny gleam of coloured light that came from the church, where Brother Paul sat to say his Rosary.

This fortified his courage, and he got up to put out the lamps in the staircase and corridors. He began at the top, and as he came down he listened on every landing and looked carefully around. There was no sound anywhere except the light fall of his own deadened footstep. His superstitious fears came back upon him and his restless conscience created terrors. The old London mansion, with its mystic cells, seemed full of strange shadows, and the wind howled around it like a fiend. One by one he extinguished the lamps. The last of them hung in the hall under the picture of Christ in His crown of thorns. As he put it out he thought the eyes looked at him, and he shuddered.

It was now half-past ten, and time to carry out his project. The back of his neck was aching, and his breath was coming quick. With noiseless steps he walked to the door of the Father's room and listened again. Hearing nothing, he opened the door wide and stepped into the room.

The fire was slumbering out, but it cast a faint red glow on the ceiling and on the bed. A soft light rested on the Father's face and he was sleeping peacefully. There was no sound except the wind in the chimney and a whistle sounding from a steamer in the river.

To reach the key where it hung above the bed it was necessary to step between the fire and the sleeping man. As John did so his black shadow fell on the Father's face. He stretched out his hand for the key and found that a bunch of other keys were now hanging over it. When he removed them they jingled slightly, and then his heart stood still, but the Father did not stir, and he took the key of the gate off the hook, put the other keys back in their place, and turned to go.

The dog began to howl—somebody was playing music in the street—and the open door made the wind to roar in the chimney. The Father sighed, and John stood with a quivering heart and looked over his shoulder. But it was only a deep human sigh uttered in sleep.

At the next moment John had returned to the corridor and closed the door behind him. His throat was parched, his eyelids were twitching, and his temples were beating like drums. He went gliding along like a thief, and as he passed the picture of Christ in the darkness the wind seemed to be crying "Judas!"

Back in the hall, he dropped on to the form, for his knees could support him no longer. Love and conscience, humanity and religion, clamoured loud in his heart and tore him to pieces. "Traitor!" cried one. "But the man's dying," cried another. "Judas!" "She is hovering on the brink of hell and he may save her soul from death and damnation!" When the struggle was over, conscience and religion were worsted and he was more cunning than before.

Then the clock chimed the three-quarters and he raised his head. The streets, usually so quiet at that hour, were becoming noisy with traffic. There were the shuffling of many feet on the hard snow and the sharp crack of voices.

He opened the great door of the house with as little noise as possible and stepped out into the courtyard. The bloodhound started from its quarters and began to growl, but he silenced it with a word, and the creature came up and licked his hand. He crossed the court with quick and noiseless footsteps, lifted the latch of the sacristy and pushed through to the church.

There was a low droning sound in the empty place. It ran a space and was then sucked in like the sound of the sea at the harbour steps. Brother Paul was sitting in the chancel with a lamp on the stall by his side. His head leaned forward, his eyes were closed, and the light on his thin face made it look pallid and lifeless. John called to him in a whisper.

"Paul!"

He rose quickly and followed John into the courtyard, looking wild and weak and lost.

"But the lamp—I've forgotten it," he said. "Shall I go back and put it out?"

"How simple you are," said John. "Somebody may be lying awake in the house. Do you want him to see that you've left your penance an hour too soon?"

"True."

"Come this way—quietly."

They passed on tiptoe into the passage leading to the street, where some flickering gleams of the light without fell over them.

"Where's your hat?" said John.

"I forgot that too—I left it in the church."

"Take mine," said John, "and put up your hood and button your cassock—it's a cruel night."

"But I'm afraid," said Paul.

"Afraid of what?"

"Now that the time has come, I'm afraid to learn the truth about her. After all, uncertainty is hope, you know, and then——"

"Tut! Be a man! Don't give way at the last moment. Here, tie my handkerchief about your neck! How helpless you are, though. I've half a mind to go myself instead."

"But you don't know what I want to say, and if you did you couldn't say it."

"Then listen! Are you listening?"

"Yes."

"Go to the hospital where your sister used to be a nurse."

"Martha's Vineyard?"

"Ask for Nurse Quayle—will you remember?"

"Nurse Quayle."

"If she is on night duty she will see you at once. But if

she is on day duty, she may be in bed and asleep, and in that case——"

"What?"

"Here, take this letter. Have you got it?"

"Yes."

"Give it to the porter. Tell him it comes from the former chaplain—you remember. Say it concerns a matter of great importance, and ask him to send it up to the dormitories immediately. Then——"

"Well?"

"Then *she* must tell you what to do next."

"But if she is out?"

"She may be—this is New-Year's Eve."

"Ah!"

"Wait in the porch till she comes in again."

John's impetuous will was carrying everything before it, and the helpless creature began to overwhelm him with grateful blessings.

"Pooh! We'll not talk of that . . . Have you any money?"

"No."

"Neither have I. I brought nothing here except the little in my purse, and I gave that up on entering."

"I don't want any—I can walk."

"It will take you an hour, then."

A clock was striking somewhere. "Hush! One, two, three . . . eleven o'clock. It will be midnight when you get there. Now go."

The key was grating in the lock of the gate. "Remember! Lauds, at six in the morning."

"I'll be back at five."

"And I'll open the gate at 5.30. Only six hours to do everything."

"Good-night, then."

"Wait!"

"What is it?"

Paul was in the street, but John was in the darkness of the passage.

"Very likely you'll cross London in a cab with her."

"My sister?"

"Your sister went to live somewhere in St. John's Wood, I remember."

"St. John's Wood?"

"Tell her"—John was striving to keep his voice firm—"Tell her I am happy—and cheerful—and looking strong and well, you know."

L

"But you're not. You're too good, and you're wearing yourself away in my——"

"Tell her I am often thinking of her, and if she has anything to say—anything to send—any word—any message . . . It can't be displeasing to the Almighty . . . But no matter! Go, go!"

The key had grated in the lock again, the lay brother was gone, and John was left alone.

"God pity and forgive me!" he muttered, and then he turned away.

The traffic in the streets was increasing every moment, and as he stumbled across the courtyard a drunken man going by the gate stopped and cried into the passage, "Helloa, there! I'm a watchin' of ye!" The bloodhound leapt up and barked, but John hurried into the house and clashed the door.

He sat on the form and tried to compose himself. He thought of Paul as he had seen him at the last moment—the captured eagle with the broken wing scudding into the night, the night of London, but free, free!

In his mind's eye he followed him through the streets—down Bishopsgate Street into Threadneedle Street, and along Cheapside to St. Paul's Churchyard. Crowds of people would be there to-night waiting for the striking of the clock at midnight, that they might raise a shout and wish each other a happy New Year.

That made him think of Glory. She would be there too, for she loved a rich and abounding life. He could see her quite plainly in the midst of the throng with her sparkling eyes and bounding step. It would be so new to her, so human and so beautiful. Glory! Always Glory!

He thought he must have been dreaming, for suddenly the clocks were all striking, first the clock in the hall, then the clocks of the churches round about, and finally the great clock of the Cathedral. Almost at the same moment there was a distant sound like the rattle of musketry, and then the church-bells began to ring.

The noises in the streets were now tumultuous. People were shouting and laughing. Some of them were singing. At one moment it was a Salvation chorus, at the next a music-hall ditty, First, "At the Cross, at the Cross," then "Mr. 'Enry 'Awkins," and then an unfamiliar ditty. With measured steps over the hardened snow of the pavement, there came tramping along a line of boys and girls crying—

"D'ye ken John Peel with his coat so gay?
D'ye ken John Peel at the break of day?
D'ye ken John P-e-e-l . . ."

Their shrill trebles broke like a rocket on the topmost note, and there was loud laughter.

"Glory again. Always, always Glory!"

Then the scales fell from his eyes, and he saw himself as he was, a self-deluded man and a cheat. The impulses that had prompted him to this night's work had really centred in Glory. It had been Glory first and Glory last, and his pity for Brother Paul and his fear for the fate of Polly had been only a falsehood and pretence.

The night wind was still howling about the house. Its noise mingled with the peal of the church-bells, and together they seemed to utter the voices of mocking fiends: Judas! Traitor! Fool! Fool! Traitor! Judas!

He covered his ears with his hands, and his head fell into his breast.

X

THE LITTLE TURNSTILE,
New Year's Eve.

Hooraa! hooraa!

Feeling like bottled yeast this evening and liable to go off, I thank my stars I have three old babies at home to whom I am bound to tell everything. So lizzen, lizzen, for all! Know ye, then, all men (and women), by these presents, that there is a gentleman in London who predicts wonderful things for Glory. His name is Sefton, and I came to know him through three ladies—I call them the Three Graces—whose acquaintance I have made by coming to live here. He is only an old mushroom, with a bald, white head; and if I believed everything their ladyships say, I should conclude that he is one of those who never sin except twice a year, and that is all the time before Christmas and all the time after it. But their Graces belong to that saintly sisterhood who would take away the devil's character if they needed it (they don't), and though the mushroom's honour were as scarce as the middle cut in salmon, yet in common loyalty Glory would have to believe in it.

It is all about my voice. Hearing it by accident when I was humming about the house like a blue-bottle, he asked me to let him hear it again in a place where he could judge of it to more advantage. That turned out to be a theatre—yes, indeed, a theatre—but it was the middle of the morning, and nobody was there except ourselves and a couple of cleaners, so Aunt Anna needn't be afraid. Yes, the chief of the orchestra was present, and he sat before a piano on the edge of the maelstrom, in what we should call the High Bailiff's pews—but they call them the stalls—while the mushroom himself went back to the cavernous depths of the body, which in a theatre they have properly christened the pit, and this morning it looked like the bottomless one.

Lor'-a-massey! Ever see the inside of a theatre in the daytime? Of course you've not, my dears. It is what the world itself was the day before the first day—without form and void, and darkness on the face of the deep. Not a ray of daylight anywhere, except the adulterated kind that comes mooching round corridors and prowling in at half-open doors, and floating through the sepulchral gloom like the sleepy eyes of the monsters that terrified me in the caves at Gob-ny-Deigan when I used to play pirate, you remember.

The gentlemen had left me alone on the stage with five or six footlights—which they ought to call face-lights—flashing in my eyes, and when the pianist began to vamp and I to sing, it was like pitching my voice into a tunnel, and I became so dreadfully nervous that I was forced to laugh. That seemed to vex my unseen audience, who thought me "rot"; so I said, "Let there be more light, then," and there was more light, "and let the piano cease from troubling," and it was so. Then I just stiffened my back and gave them one of mother's French songs, and after the first verse I called out to the manager at the back, "Can you hear me?" and he called back, "Go on; it's splendid!" So I did "Mylecharaine" in the Manx, and I suppose I acted both of my songs; but I was only beginning to be aware that my voice in that great place was a little less like a barrel-organ than usual, when suddenly there came a terrific clatter, such as comes with the ninth wave on the shingle, and my two dear men in the dark were clapping the skin of their hands off!

Oh, my dears, my dears! If you only knew how for weeks and weeks I had been moaning and lamenting that it was because I wasn't clever that people took no notice of me, you would forgive a vain creature when she said to herself, "My daughter, you are really somebody after all—you, you, you!" It was a beautiful moment though, and when the old mushroom came back to the stage saying, "What a voice! What expression! What nature!" I felt like falling on his bald head and kissing it, not being able to speak for lumps in the throat, and feeling like the Methodist lady who poured out whisky for the class-leaders after they had presented her with a watch, and then told the reporters to say she had suitably responded.

Heigho! I have talked about the fashionable people I meet in London, but I don't want to be one of them. They do nothing but rush about, dress, gossip, laugh, love, and plunge into all the delights of life. That is not my idea of existence. I am ambitious. I want to do something. I am tired in my soul of doing nothing. Yes, it *has* been that all along, though I didn't like to tell you so before. There are people who are born in the midst of greatness and they don't know how to use it. But to be one of the world's celebrities, that is so different. To have won the heart of the world, so that the world knows you and thinks of you and loves you! Say it is by your voice you do it and that your world is the concert-hall, or even the music-hall - what matter? You needn't *live* music-hall, whatever the life inside of it. And then that great dark void peopled with faces that laugh or cry just as you please to make them—confess that it would be magnificent, my dear ones!

I am to go again to-night to hear what Mr. Sefton has to propose, but already this dingy little bedroom smiles upon me, and even the broken tiles in the backyard might be the pavement of Paradise! If it is true what he tells me . . . Well, he that hath the bride is the bridegroom, and if my doings hereafter don't make your hair curl, I will try to show the inhabitants of this stupid old earth what a woman can do in spite of every disadvantage. I shall not be sorry to leave this place either. The rats in these old London houses (judging by the cries of woe) hold a nightly carnival for the eating up of the younger members of the family. And then Mrs. Jupe and Mr Jupe—Mr. Dupe I call him; she deceives him so dreadfully with her gadding about. . . . But anon, anon, good people!

It is New Year's Eve to-day, and nearly nine months since I came up to London. *Tempus fugit!* In fact, *tempus* is *fugit*-ing most fearfully, considering that I am twenty-one on Sunday next, you know, and that I haven't begun to do anything really. The snowdrops must be making a peep at Glenfaba by this time, and Aunt Rachel will be cutting slips of the rose-trees and putting them in pots. Yandher place must be *urromassy*[1] nice though, with snow on the roof and the sloping lawn, and the windows glistening with frost, just like a girl in her Confirmation veil, as she stands back to look at herself in the glass. I intend to see the New Year in this time on the outside of St. Paul's Cathedral, where people congregate in thousands as twelve o'clock approaches, to carry on the beautiful fiction that there is still only one clock in London, and they have to hold their noses in the air to watch for the moment when it is going to strike. But in the midst of the light and life of this splendid city, I know my heart will go back with a tender twinge to the little dark streets

[1] Out of mercy.

on the edge of the sea, where the Methodist choirs will be singing "Hail, smiling morn," preparatory to coffee and currant-cake.

Who will be your "first foot" this year, I wonder? It was John Storm last year, you remember, and being as dark as a gipsy, he made a perfect *qualtagh*.[1] And how we laughed when, disguised in the snow that was falling at the time, he pretended to be a beggar, and came in just as grandfather was reading the bit about the Good Shepherd, and how He loved His lambs; and then I found him out! Ah me!

I am looking perfectly dazzling in a new hat to-day, having been going about hitherto in one of those little frights that used to be cocked up on the top of your hair like a hen on a cornstack. But now I am carrying about the Prince of Wales's feathers, and if he could only see me himself in them——

You see what a scatter-brained creature I am! Leaving the hospital has made me grow so much younger every day, that I am almost afraid I may come to contemplate short frocks. But really it's the first time I've looked nice for an eternity, and now I entirely retract and repent me of all I said about wishing to be a man. Being a girl, I'll put up with it; and if all the old mushroom says on that head also is true . . . But then men are such funny things, bless them!   GLORY.

P.S.—No word from John Storm yet. Apparently he never thinks of us now—of me, at all events; and I suppose he has resigned himself and taken the vows. That's one kind of religion, I dare say, but I can't understand it; and I don't know how a dog even can be nailed up to a wall and not go mad. In the night, lying in bed, I sometimes think of him. A dark cell, a bench for a bed, a crucifix, and no other furniture, praying with trembling limbs and chattering teeth. No; such things are too high for me; I cannot reach to them.

It seems impossible that *he* can be in London too. What a place this London is! Such a mixture! Fashion, religion, gaiety, devotion, pride, depravity, wealth, poverty! I find that, for a girl to succeed in London, her moral colour must be heightened a little. *Pinjane*[2] alone won't do. Give her a slush of *pissaves*,[3] and she'll go down sweeter. Angels are not wanted here at all. The only angels there are in London are kept framed in the church windows, and I half suspect that even they were women once, and liked bread and butter. And then Nell Gwynne's flag floats from the steeple of St. Martin's-in-the-Fields, and now and again they ring the bells for her!

[1] Manx for "first foot."
[2] Manx dish, like Devonshire junket.
[3] Preserves.

XI

At eleven o'clock that night Glory was putting on her hat and cloak to return home when the call-boy came to the dressing-room door to say that the stage-manager was waiting to see her. With a little catch in her breast, and then with a tightening of the heart-strings, she followed him to the stage-manager's office. It was a stuffy place over the porter's lodge, approached by a flight of circular iron stairs and lumbered with many kinds of theatrical property.

"Come in, my dear," said the stage-manager, and pushing away some models of scenery he made room for her on a sofa which stood by a fast-dying fire. Then shutting the door, he bobbed his head at her and winked with both eyes, and said in a familiar whisper—

"It's all right, my dear. I've settled that little matter for you."

"Do you mean . . ." began Glory, and then she waited with parted lips.

"It's as good as done, my dear. Sit down." Glory had risen in her excitement. "Sit down and I'll tell you everything."

He had spoken to his management. "Gentlemen," he had said, "unless I'm mistaken, I've found a prize." They had laughed. He was always finding prizes. But he knew what he was talking about, and they had given him *carte blanche*.

"You think there is really some likelihood, then . . ." began Glory, with the catch in her breath again, for her throat was thick and her breast was heaving,

"Sit down, now, do sit down, my dear, and listen."

He was suave, he was flattering, he was intimate, he was coaxing. She was to leave everything to him. Of course there was much to be done yet. She had a wonderful voice; it was finer than music. She had style as well; it was astonishing how she had come by it. Only a dresser too—not even in the chorus. But stars were never turned out by nature. She had many things to learn, and would have to be coached up carefully before she could be brought out. He had done it for others, though, and he could do it for her, and if——

Glory's eyes were shining and her heart was beating like a drum.

"Then you think that eventually, if I work hard—after years perhaps——"

"You can't do it on your own, my dear, so leave yourself in my hands entirely, and don't whisper a word about it yet."

"Ah!" It was like a dream coming true; she could scarcely believe in it. The stage-manager became still more suave, and flattering, and familiar. If she "caught on" there was no knowing what he might not get for her—ten pounds a week—fifteen, twenty, twenty-five, even fifty perhaps.

Glory's palpitation was becoming painful, and at the bottom of her heart there was a certain fear of this sudden tide of fortune, as if Providence had somehow made a mistake and would as suddenly find it out. To appease her conscience she began to think of home and how happy she might make everybody there if God was really going to be so good to her. They should want for nothing; they should never know a poor day again.

Meantime the stage-manager was painting another picture. A girl didn't go a-begging if he once took her up. There was S——. She was only an "auricomous" damsel, serving in a tobacconist's shop in the Haymarket when he first found her, and now where was she?

"Of course I've no interest of my own to serve, my dear—none whatever. And there'll be lots of people to tempt you away from me when your name is made."

Glory uttered some vehement protest and then was lost in her dreams again.

"Well, well, we'll see," said the stage-manager. He was looking at her with glittering eyes.

"Do you know, my dear, you are a very fine-looking young woman?"

Glory's head was down, her face was flushed, and she was turning her mother's pearl ring around her finger. He thought she was overwhelmed by his praises, and coming closer, he said—

"Dare say you've got a good stage-figure too, eh? Pooh! Only business, you know! But you mustn't be shy with me, my dear. And besides, if I am to do all this for you, you must do something for me sometimes."

She hardly heard him. Her eyes were still glistening with the far-off look of one who gazes on a beautiful vision. "You are so good," she said. "I don't know what to say or how to thank you."

"This way," he whispered, and leaning over to her he lifted her face and kissed her.

Then her poor dream of glory and grandeur and happiness was dispelled in a moment, and she awoke with a sense of outrage and shame. The man's praises were flattery; his predictions were a pretence: he had not really meant it at all, and she had been so simple as to believe everything.

"Oh!" she said, with the feeble, childish cry of one who has received a pistol-wound in battle. And then she rose and turned to go. But the stage-manager, who was laughing noisily out of his hot red face, stepped between her and the door.

"My dear child, you can't mean . . . A trifle like that——"

"Open the door, please," she said in her husky voice.

"But surely you don't intend . . . In the profession we think nothing, you know——"

"Open the door, sir!"

"Really! upon my word——"

When she came to herself again she was out in the dark back street, and the snow was hard and dirty under foot, and the wind was high and cold, and she was running along and crying like a disappointed child.

The bitterest part of it all was the crushing certainty that she had no talents and no chances of success, and that the man had only painted up his fancy picture as a means of deceiving her. Oh, the misery of being a woman! Oh, the cruelty of this great, glorious, devilish London, where a girl, if she was poor and alone, could live only by her looks!

With God knows what lingering remnant of expectation, but feeling broken and beaten after her brave fight for life, and with the weak woman uppermost at last, she had turned towards the hospital. It was nearly half-past eleven when she got there, and Big Ben was chiming the half-hour as she ascended the steps. Bracing herself up, she looked in at the porter's door with a face that was doing its best to smile.

"Any letters to-night, porter?"

"Not to-night, Miss."

"No? Well, none to get, none to answer, you know. Happy New Year to you!"

But there was the sob in her laughter, and the man said, "I'd be sorry to miss your face, nurse, but if you'll leave your address I'll send your letters on and save you the journey so late at night."

"Oh, no—no, there'll be no more letters now, porter, and—I'll not come again. Here!"

"No, no, Miss."

"Yes, yes, you must!"

She forced a shilling into the porter's hand in spite of his protests and then fled from the look in his face, which seemed to her to say that he would like to return her sixpence.

John Storm was lost to her. It was foolishness to go on

expecting to hear from him. Had he not told her that the rule under which the brothers lived in community forbade them to write and receive letters except by special permission? But she had expected that something would happen—some accident, some miracle, she hardly knew what. That dream was over now; she was alone; it was no use deceiving herself any longer.

She went home by the back streets, for people were peering into her face, and she thought perhaps she had been crying. Late as it was, being New Year's Eve, there were groups about every corner, and in some of the flagged courts and alleys little girls were dancing to the music of the Italian organ-man or turning catherine-wheels. As she was going down Long Acre a creachy voice saluted her.

"Evening, Miss! Going home early, ain't ye?"

It was a miserable-looking woman in clothes that might have been stolen from a scarecrow.

"Market full to-night, my dear? Look as if the dodgers had been at ye. Live? I live off of the Lane. But lor' bless ye, I've lived in a many places! Seen the day I lived in Soho Square. I was on the 'alls then. Got a bit quisby on my top-notes, you know, and took the scarlet fever—soldier, I mean, my dear. But where's the use of frettin? I likes to be jolly, and I allwiz is. Doing now? Selling flowers outside the theatres—police is nasty if you've got nothink. Ain't I going home? Soon as I get a drain of white satin. Wish you luck, my dear! S'long!"

As she came up to the shop in the Turnstile, she could hear that it was noisy with the voices of men and girls, so she turned back through Lincoln's Inn Fields and passed down to Fleet Street. It was approaching twelve o'clock by this time, and streams of people were flowing in the direction of St. Paul's Cathedral. Glory turned eastward also, and allowed herself to be carried along with the current which babbled and talked like a river in the night.

Immediately in front of her there was a line of girls walking arm-in-arm across the width of the pavement. They were factory girls in big hats with ostrich feathers, and as they skipped along with their free step they sang snatches of Salvation hymns and music-hall songs. All at once they gave a shrill peal of laughter, and one of them cried, "Tell me what it is and I'll give it a nyme." At the next moment a strange figure was forging past their line, going westward with long strides. It was a man in the habit of a monk, with long black cassock and broad-brimmed hat. Glory caught a glimpse of his face as he passed her. It was a hungry, eager face, with

THE RELIGIOUS LIFE

big melancholy eyes, and it seemed to her that she must have seen it before somewhere. The wind was very cold and the great cross on the dome of the Cathedral stood out like a beacon against flying clouds.

St. Paul's Churchyard was thronged with noisy, happy people, and down to the last minute before the hour they shouted and joked and laughed. Then there was a hush, the great crowds seemed to hold their breath as if they had been a single living creature, and every face was turned upwards to the clock. The clock struck, the bells of the Cathedral began to ring, the people cheered and saluted each other and shook hands on every side, and then the dense mass broke up.

Glory could have cried for joy of it all—it was so simple, so human, so childlike. But she listened to the laughter and salutations of the people about her and felt "more lonely than the Bedouin in the desert;" she remembered the bubbling hopes that had carried her through the day, and her heart fell low; she thought of the letter which she had posted home on her way to the theatre, and two great tears came rolling from her eyes.

The face of the monk tormented her, and suddenly she bethought herself whose face it must have been. It must have been the face of Polly Love's brother. He belonged to the Bishopsgate Fathers, and had once been a patient in the hospital, and perhaps he was going there now on some errand or urgent message—to the doctors or to——

"It was foolish not to leave my address when the porter asked me," she thought. She would go back and do so. There could be no harm in that; and if anything had really happened, if John——

"Happy New Year to you, my dear!"

Somebody in the drifting crowd was standing before her and blocking the way. It was Agatha Jones in a mock sealskin coat and big black hat surmounted by black feathers, and with Charlie Wilkes (with his diminutive cap pushed back from his oily fringe and pimpled forehead) leaning heavily on her arm.

"Well, I never! Who'd have thought of meeting you in St. Paul's Churchyawd!"

Glory tried to laugh and to return the salutation over the noises of the people and the clangour of the bells. And then Aggie put her face close, as women do who are accustomed to talking in the street, and said, "Thought we'd seen the lahst of you, my dear, when you went off that night sudden. Selling programmes somewhere else now?"

"Something of that sort," said Glory.

"I'm not. I've left the old red church this fortnight and more. Charlie's got me on the clubs. But my word!" turning to Charlie, "it's her as oughter be there, my dear!"

"She cheeks me 'out," said Charlie, "as you'll knock the stuffing out of Betty Bellman 'erself if you once myke a stawt."

And Aggie said, "I might get you to do a turn almost any Sunday if you like, my dear. There's always somebody as downt come, and they're glad of an extra turn to tyke the number, if she's only clever enough to get a few 'ands. Going 'ome, dear?"

"Yes," said Glory.

"Where d'ye live?" said Aggie, and Glory told her.

"I'll call for you Sunday night at eight, and if you downt tyke your chawnce when you get it, you're a foolisher woman than I thought you were, that's str'ight! Bye-bye!"

XII

ALWAYS at half-past five in the morning the Father Superior began to awaken the Brotherhood. It took him a quarter of an hour to pass through the house on that errand, for the infirmities of his years were upon him. During this interval John Storm had intended to open the gate to Paul and then return the key to its place in the Father's room. The time was short, and, to lose no part of it, he had resolved to remain awake the whole night through.

There was little need to make a call on that resolution. With fear and remorse he could not close his eyes, and from hour to hour he heard every sound of the streets. At one o'clock the voices singing outside were strained and cracked and out of tune; at two, they were brutish and drunken, and mingled with shrieks of quarrelling; at three, there was silence; at four, the butchers' waggons were rattling on the stones from the shambles across the river to the meat markets of London, with the carcasses of the thousands of beasts that were slaughtered over-night to feed the body of the monster on the morrow; and at five, the postal vans were galloping from the railway stations to the post-office with the millions of letters that were to feed its mind.

At half-past five the Father had come out of his room and passed slowly upstairs, and John Storm was in the courtyard opening the lock of the outer gate. Although there was a feeling of morning in the freezing air, it was still quite dark.

"Paul," he whispered, but there was no answer.

"Brother Paul!" he whispered again, and then waited, but there was no reply.

It was not at first that he realised the tremendous gravity of what had occurred—that Brother Paul had not returned, and that he must go back to the house without him. He kept calling into the darkness until he remembered that the Father would be down in his room again soon, and looking for the key where he had left it.

Back in the hall, he reproached himself with his haste, and concluded to return to the gate. There would be time to do it; the Father was still far overhead; his "Benedicamus Domino" was passing from corridor to corridor, and Paul might be coming down the street.

"Paul! Paul!" he cried again, and opening the gate he looked out. But there was no one on the pavement except a drunken man and a girl, singing themselves home in the dead waste of the New Year's morning.

Then the truth fell on him like a thunder-clap, and he hurried back to the house for good. By this time the Father was coming down the stairs, and had reached the landing of the first storey. Snatching up from the bed in the alcove the book which had been lying there all night unregarded, he crept into the Father's room. He was coming out of it when he came face to face with the Father himself, who was on the point of going in.

"I have been returning the book you lent me," he said, and then he tried to steal away in his shame. But the Father held him awhile with playful remonstrance. The hours were not all saved that were stolen from the night, and his swelled eyes this morning were a testimony to the musty old maxim. Still, with a book like that, his diligence was not to be wondered at, and it would be interesting to hear what he thought of it. He couldn't say as yet? That wasn't to be wondered at either. Somebody had said that a great book was like a great mountain —not to be seen to the top while you were still too near to it.

John's duplicity was choking him. His eyes were averted from the Father's face, for he had lost the power of looking straight at any one, and he could see the key of the gate still shaking from the hook on which his nervous fingers had placed it. When he escaped at length, the Father asked him to ring the bell for Lauds, as Brother Andrew, whose duty it was, had evidently overslept himself.

John rang the bell, and then took his lamp and some tapers from a shelf in the hall, and went out to the church to light the candles, for that also was Brother Andrew's duty. As he was crossing the courtyard on his way back to the house, he passed the Father going to open the gate.

"But what has become of your hat?" said the Father, and then, for the first time, John remembered what he had done with it.

"I've lent—that is to say, I've lost it," he answered, and then stood with his eyes on the ground, while the Father reproved him for heedlessness of health and so forth.

It is part of the perversity of circumstance that, while an incident of the greatest gravity is occurring, its ridiculous counterpart is usually taking place by the side of it. When the religious had gathered in the church, it was seen that three of the stalls were vacant—Brother Paul's, Brother Andrew's, and the Father Minister's. The service had hardly begun when the bell was heard to ring again, and with a louder clangour than before, whereupon the religious concluded that Brother Andrew had awakened from his sleep, and was remembering with remorse his belated duty.

But it was the Father Minister. That silent and severe person had oftentimes rebuked the lay brother for his sleepiness, and this morning he had himself been overcome by the same infirmity. Awakening suddenly a little after six by the watch that hung by his bed, he had thought, "That lazy fellow is late again—I'll teach him a lesson." Leaping to his feet (the monk sleeps in his habit), he had hastened to the bell and rung it furiously, and then snatched up a taper and hurried down the stairs to light the candles in the church. When he appeared at the sacristy door with a lighted taper in his hand and confusion on his face, the brothers understood everything at a glance, and not even the solemnity of the service could smother the snufflings of their laughter.

The incident was a trivial one, but it diverted attention for a time from the fact of Paul's absence; and when the religious went back to the house and found Brother Andrew returned to his old duty as doorkeeper, the laughter was renewed and there was some playful banter.

The monk is so far a child that the least thing happening in the morning is enough to determine the temper of the day, and as late as the hour for breakfast the house was still rippling with the humour of the Father Minister's misadventure. There was one seat vacant in the refectory—Brother Paul's—and the Superior was the first to observe it. With a twinkle in his eye, he said—

"I feel like Boy Blue this morning. Two of my stray sheep

have come home, bringing their tails behind them. Will anybody go in search of the third?"

John Storm rose immediately, but a lay brother was before him, so he sat down again with his white cheeks and quivering lips, and made an effort to eat his breakfast.

The reader for the week recited the Scripture for the day, and then took up the book which the brothers were hearing at their meals. It was the "Life and Death of Father Ignatius of St. Paul," and the chapter they had come to dealt with certain amusing examples of vanities and foibles. An evil spirit might have selected it with special reference to the incidents of the morning, for at every fresh illustration the Father Minister squirmed on his seat, and the brothers looked across at him, and laughed with a spice of mischief, and even a touch of malice.

John's eyes were on the door and his heart was quivering, but the messenger did not return during breakfast; and when it was over the Superior rose without waiting for him, and led the way to the community-room.

A fire was burning in the wide grate, and the room was cheerful with reflected sun-rays, for the sun was shining in the courtyard and glistening on the frosty boughs of the sycamore. It was a beautiful New Year's morning, and the Father began to tell some timely stories. In the midst of the laughter that greeted them the lay brother returned and delivered his message: Brother Paul could not be found, and there was not a sign of him anywhere in the house.

"That's strange!" said the religious.

"Perhaps he is in his cell," said the Father.

"No, he is not there," said the messenger; "and his bed has not been slept in."

"Now, that explains something," said the Father. "I thought he didn't answer when I knocked at his door in the morning; but my ears grow dull and my eyes are failing me, and I told myself perhaps——"

"It's very strange!" said the religious, with looks of astonishment.

"But perhaps he stayed all night at his penance in the church," said the Father.

"Apparently his hat did so, at all events," said one of the brothers. "I saw it lying with his lamp on the stall in front of me."

There was silence for a moment, and then the Father said, with a smile—

"But my children are so amusing in such matters. Only this

morning I had to reprove Brother Storm for losing his hat somewhere, and now Brother Paul——"

By an involuntary impulse, obscure to themselves, the brothers turned towards John, who was standing in the recess of one of the windows, with his pale face looking out on the sunshine.

John was the first to speak.

"Father," he said, "I have something to say to you."

"Come this way," said the Superior, and they passed out of the room together.

The Father led the way to his room and closed the door behind them. But there was little need for confession; the Father seemed to know everything in an instant. He sat in his wicker chair before the fire and rocked himself and moaned.

"Well, well, God's wrath comes up against the children of disobedience, but we must do our best to bear our punishment."

John Storm made no excuses. He had stood by the Father's chair and told his story simply, without fear or remorse, only concealing that part of it which concerned himself in relation to Glory.

"Yes, yes," said the Father, "I see quite plainly how it has been. He was like tinder, ready to take fire at a spark, and you were thinking I had been hard and cruel and inhuman."

It was the truth; John could not deny it; he held down his head and was silent.

"But shall I tell you why I refused that poor boy's petition? Shall I tell you who he was and how he came to be here? Yes, I will tell you. Nobody in this house has heard it until now, because it was his secret and mine and God's alone—not given me in confession, no, or it would have to be locked in my breast for ever. But you have thrust yourself in between us, so you must hear everything, and may the Lord pity and forgive you and help you to bear your burden."

John felt that a cold damp was breaking out on his forehead, but he clenched his moist hands and made ready to control himself.

"Has he ever spoken of another sister?"

"Yes, he has sometimes mentioned her."

"Then perhaps you have been told of the painful and tragic event that happened?"

"No," said John; but something that he had heard at the Board meeting at the hospital returned at that moment with a stunning force to his memory.

"His father, poor man, was one of my own people—one of the lay associates of our Society in the world outside. But his health gave way, his business failed him, and he died in a madhouse, leaving his three children to the care of a friend. The friend was thought to be a worthy and even a pious man, but he was a scoundrel and a traitor. The younger sister—the one you know—he committed to an orphanage, the elder one he deceived and ruined. As a sequel to his sin she lived a life of shame on the streets of London, and died by suicide at the end of it."

John Storm put up one hand to his head as if his brain was bursting, and with the other hand he held on to the Father's chair.

"That was bad enough, but there was worse to follow. Our poor Paul had grown to be a man by this time, and Satan put it into his heart to avenge his sister's dishonour. 'As the whirlwind passeth, so the wicked are no more.' The betrayer of his trust was found dead in his room, slain by an unknown assassin. Brother Paul had killed him."

John Storm had fallen to his knees. If hell itself had opened at his feet he could not have been stricken with more horror. In a voice strangled by fear he stammered, "But why didn't you tell me this before? Why have you hidden it until now?"

"Passions, my son, are the same in a monastery as outside of it, and I had too much reason to fear that the saintliest soul in our Brotherhood would have refused to live and eat and sleep in the same house with a murderer. But the poor soul had come to me like a hunted beast, and who was I that I should turn my back upon him? Before that he had tramped through the streets and slept in the parks, under the impression that the police were pursuing him, and thereby he contracted the lung disease from which he suffers still. What was I to do? Give him up to the law? Who shall tell me how I could have held the balance level? I took him into my house; I sheltered him; I made him a member of our community; Heaven forgive me, I suffered myself to receive his vows. It was for me to comfort his stricken body, for the Church to heal his wounded soul; and as for his crime, that was in God's hands, and God alone could deal with it."

The Father had risen to his feet, and he spoke the last words with uplifted hand.

"Now you know why I refused that poor boy's petition. I loved him as a son, but neither the disease of his body nor the weakness of his mind could break the firmness of the rule by which I held him. I knew that Satan was dragging him away from me, and I would not give him up to the sufferings and dangers which the Evil One was preparing for him in the world. But how subtle are the temptations of the devil! He found the weak place in my armour at last. He found you, my son—you;

and he tempted you by all your love, by all your pity, by all your tenderness, and you fell, and this is the consequence."

The Father clasped his hands at his breast and walked to and fro in the little room.

"The bitterness of the world against religious houses is great already, but if anything should happen now, if a crime should be committed, if our poor brother, clad in the habit of our Order——"

He stopped and crossed himself and lifted his eyes, and said in a tremulous whisper, "O God, whom have I in heaven but Thee? My flesh and my heart faileth; but God is the strength of my heart, and my portion for ever.'"

John had staggered to his feet like a drunken man. "Father," he said, "send me away from you. I am not fit to live by your side."

The Father laid both hands on his shoulders. "And shall I lower my flag to the enemy like that? There is only one way to defeat the devil, and that is to defy him. No, no, my son; you shall remain with me to the last."

"Punish me, then. Give me penance. Let me be the lowest of the low and the meanest of the mean. Only tell me what I am to do and I will do it."

"Go back to the door and resume your duty as doorkeeper."

John looked at the Father with an expression of bewilderment.

"I thought you had done with it, my son, but Heaven knew better. And promise that when you are there you will pray for our wandering brother, that he may not be allowed to fulfil the errand on which you sent him out; pray that he may never find his sister, or anybody who knows her and can tell him where she is and what has become of her; pray that she may never cross his path to the last hour of life and the first of death's sundering; promise to pray for this, my son, night and day, morning and evening, with all your soul and strength, as you would pray for God's mercy and your soul's salvation."

John did not answer; he was like a man in a stupor. "Is it possible?" he said. "Are you sending me back to the door? Can you trust me again?"

The Father stepped to the side of the bed and took the key of the gate from its place under the shelf. "Take this key with you too, because for the future you are to be the keeper of the gate as well."

John had taken the key mechanically, hardly hearing what was being said.

"Is it true, then?—have you got faith in me still?"

The Father put both hands on his shoulders again and

looked into his face. "God has faith in you, my child, and who am I that I should despair?"

When John Storm returned to the door, his mind was in a state of stupefaction. Many hours passed during which he was only partly conscious of what was taking place about him. Sometimes he was aware that certain of the brothers had gathered around, with a tingling, electrical atmosphere among them, and that they were asking questions about the escape, and whispering together as if it had been something courageous and almost commendable, and had set their hearts beating. Again, sometimes he was aware that big Brother Andrew was sitting by his side on the form, stroking his arm from time to time, and talking in his low voice and aimless way about his mother and the last he saw of her. "She followed me down the street crying," he said, "and I have often thought of it since and been tempted to run away." Also he was aware that the dog was with him always, licking the backs of his stiff hands and poking up a cold muzzle into his downcast face.

All this time he was doing his duties automatically, and apparently without help from his consciousness, opening and closing the door as the brothers passed in and out on their errands to the dead and dying, and saying "Praise be to God!" when a stranger knocked. It may be that his body was merely answering to the habits of his intellect, and that his soul, which had sustained a terrible blow, was lying stunned and swooning within.

When it revived and he began to know and to feel once more, there was no one with him, for the brothers were asleep in their beds, and the dog was in the courtyard and the house was very quiet, for it was the middle of the night. And then it came back to him, like a dream remembered in the morning, that the Father had asked him to pray for Brother Paul that he might fail in the errand on which he had sent him out into the world, and though with his lips he had not promised, yet in his heart he had undertaken to do so.

And being quite alone now, with no one but God for company, he went down on his knees in his place by the door and clasped his hands together.

"O God," he prayed, "have pity on Paul, and on me, and on all of us! Keep him from all danger and suffering, and from the snares and assaults of the Evil One. Grant that he may never find his sister—or anybody who knows her—or anybody who can tell him where she is and what has become of her . . ."

But having got so far he could get no further, for suddenly it occurred to him that this was a prayer which concerned Glory and himself as well. It was only then that he realised the magnitude and awfulness of the task he had undertaken. He had undertaken to ask God that Paul might not find Glory either, and therefore that he on his part might never hear of her again. When he put it to himself like that, the sweat started from his forehead and he was transfixed with fear.

He rose from his knees and sat on the form, and for a long hour he laboured in the thought of a thousand possibilities, telling himself of the many things which might befall a beautiful girl in a cruel and wicked city. But then again he thought of Paul, and of his former crime and present temptation, and remembered the shadow that hung over the Brotherhood.

"O God, help me," he cried; "strengthen me, support me, guide me!"

He tried to frame another prayer, but the words would not come; he tried to kneel as before, but his knees would not bend. How could he pray that Glory also might be lost—that something might have happened to her—that somewhere and in some way unknown to him——?

No, no, a thousand times no! The prayer was impossible. Let come what would, let the danger to Paul and to the Brotherhood be what it might, let Satan and all his legions fall on him, yet he could not and would not utter it.

XIII

The stars were paling, but the day had not yet dawned when there came a knock at the door. John started and listened. After an interval the knock was repeated. It was a timid, hesitating tap, as if made with the tips of the fingers low down on the door.

"Praise be to God!" said John, and he drew the slide of the grating. He had expected to see a face outside, but there was nothing there.

"Who is it?" he asked, and there came no answer.

He took up the lamp that was kept burning in the hall and looked out through the bars. There was nothing in the darkness but an icy mist which appeared to be rising from the ground.

"Only another of my dreams," he thought, and he laid his hand on the slide to close it.

Then he heard a sigh that seemed to rise out of the ground,

and at the same moment the dog uttered a deep bay. He laid hold of the door and pulled it quickly open. At his feet the figure of a man was kneeling, bent double and huddled up.

"Paul!" he cried in an excited whisper.

Brother Paul raised his head. His face was frightfully changed. It was grey and wasted. His eyes wandered, his lips trembled, and he looked like a man who had been flogged.

"Good Lord! what a wreck!" thought John. He helped him to rise and enter. The poor creature's limbs were stiff with cold, and he stumbled from weakness as he crossed the threshold.

"But, thank God, you are back, and no harm done!" said John. "How anxious we've been! You must never go out again—never! There, brother, sit there."

The wandering eyes looked up with a supplicating expression.

"Forgive me, Brother Storm——"

But John would not listen. "Hush, brother! what have I to forgive? How cold you are! Your hands are like ice. What can I do? There's no fire in the house at this time of night— even in the kitchen it will be out now. But wait; I can rub you with my hands. See, I'm warm and strong. There's a deal of blood in me yet. That's better, isn't it? Tingling, eh? That's right—that's good! Now for your feet—your feet will be colder still."

"No, brother, no. I ought to be kissing the feet of everybody in the house and asking the prayers of the community, and yet you——"

"Tut! what nonsense! Let me take off this shoe. Dear me! how it sticks! Why, you've worn it through and through. Look! What a mercy the snow was hard! If there had been thaw, now! How far you must have walked!"

"Yes, I've wandered a long way, brother."

"You shall tell me all about it. I want to hear everything— every single thing."

"There's nothing to tell. I've failed in my errand, that's all."

John, who was on his knees, drew back and looked up. "Do you mean, then . . . Have you not seen your sister?"

"No, she's gone, and nobody knows anything about her."

"Well, perhaps it's for the best, brother. God's will be done, you know. If you had found her who knows?—you might have been tempted . . . But tell me everything."

"I cannot do that, I'm so weak, and it's not worth while."

"But I want to hear all that happened. See, your feet are all right now—I've rubbed them warm again. Though I fast so much and look so thin, I've a deal of life in me. And I've been pouring it all into you, haven't I? That's because I want you to revive and be strong and tell me everything. Hush! Speak low; don't waken anybody! Did you find the hospital?"

"Yes."

"Then Nurse Quayle sees nothing of your sister now! That's the pity of the life she is leading, poor girl! No friends, no future——"

"It wasn't that, brother."

"What, then?"

"The nurse was not there."

A silence followed, and then John said in another voice, "I suppose she was on holiday. It was very stupid of me; I didn't think of that. Twice a year a hospital nurse is entitled to a week's holiday, and no doubt——"

"But she was gone."

"Gone? You mean left the hospital?"

"Yes."

"Well," in a husky voice, "that isn't to be wondered at either. A high-spirited girl finds it hard to be bound down to rule and regulation. But the porter—he is an intelligent man—he would tell you where she had gone to."

"I asked him; he didn't know. All he could say was that she left the hospital on the morning of the Lord Mayor's Show-day."

"That would be the 9th of November—the day we took our vows."

There was another pause. The big dark eyes were wandering vacantly.

"After all, he is only a porter. You asked for the matron, didn't you?"

"Yes; I thought she might know what had become of my sister. But she didn't. As for Nurse Quayle, she had been dismissed also, and nobody knew anything about her."

John had seated himself at Paul's side, and the form itself was quivering.

"Now that's just like her," he said hoarsely. "That matron was always a hard woman. And to think that in that great house of love and pity nobody——"

"I am forgetting something, brother."

"What is it?"

"The porter told me that the nurse called for her letters from time to time. She had been there that night—not half an hour before."

"Then you followed her, didn't you? You asked which way she had gone, and you hurried after her?"

"Yes; but half-an-hour in London is a week anywhere else. Let anybody cross the street and he is lost—more lost to sight than a ship in a storm on the ocean. And then it was New Year's Eve, and the thoroughfares were crowded, and thousands of women were coming and going—and . . . What could I do?" he said helplessly.

John answered scornfully, "What could you do? Do you ask me what you could do?"

"What would you have done?"

"I should have tramped every street in London and looked into the face of every woman I met until I had found her. I should have worn my shoes to the welt and my skin to the bone before I would have come crawling home like a snail with my shell broken over my head."

"Don't be hard on me, brother, least of all now, when I have come home, like a snail, as you say, with my shell broken. I was very tired and ill, and did all I could. If I had been strong like you, and brave-hearted, I might have struggled longer. But I *did* tramp the streets and look into the women's faces. She must have been among them, if she's living the life you speak of, but God would not let me find her. Why was it that my search was fruitless? Perhaps there was evil in my heart at first—I don't mind telling you that now—but I swear to you by Him who died for us that at last I only wanted to find my sister, that I might save her. But I am such a helpless creature, and . . ."

John put his arm about Paul's shoulders.

"Forgive me, brother. I was mad to talk to you like that— I who sent you out on that cruel night and stayed at home myself. You did what you could . . ."

"You think that—really?"

"Yes, only at the moment it seemed as if we had changed places somehow, and it was I who had lost a sister and been out to find her, and given up the search too soon, and come home empty and useless and broken-spirited and . . ."

Paul was looking up at him with a face full of astonishment.

"Do you really think I did all I could to find her—the nurse, I mean?"

But John had turned his own face away, and there was no answer. Paul tried to say something, but he could not find the words. At last in a choked voice he murmured, "We must keep close together, brother; we are in the same boat now."

And feeling for John's hand, he took it and held it, and they sat some minutes with bowed heads, as if a ghost were going by.

"There's nothing but prayer and penance and fasting left to us, is there?"

Still John made no reply, and the broken creature began to comfort him.

"We have peace here, at all events, and you wouldn't think what temptations come to you in the world when you've lost somebody, and there seems to be nothing left to live for. Shall I tell you what I did? It was in the early morning and I was standing in a doorway in Piccadilly. The cabs and the crowds were gone, and only the nightmen were swilling up the dirt of the pavements with their hose-pipes and water. 'My poor girl is lost,' I thought. 'We shall never see one another again. This wicked city has ruined her, and our mother, who was so holy, was fond of her when she was a little child.' And then my heart seemed to freeze up within me . . . and I did it. You'll think I was mad—I went to the police station and told them I had committed a crime. Yes, indeed, I accused myself of murder and began to give particulars. It was only when they noticed my habit that I remembered the Father, and then I refused to answer any more questions. They put me in a cell, and that was where I spent the night, and next morning I denied everything and they let me go."

Then, dropping his voice to a hoarse whisper, he said, "That wasn't what brought me back, though. It was the vow. You can't think what a thing the vow is until you've broken it. It's like a hot iron searing your very soul, and if you were dying and at the farthest ends of the earth, and you had to crawl on your hands and knees, you would come back . . ."

He would have said more, but an attack of coughing silenced him, and when it was over there was a sound of some one moving in the house.

"What is that?"

"It is the Father," said John. "Our voices have wakened him."

Paul struggled to his feet.

"It's only a life of penance and suffering you've come back to, my poor lad."

"That's nothing—nothing at all . . . But are you sure you think I did everything?"

"You did what you could. Are you going somewhere?"

"Yes, to the Father."

"God bless you, my lad!"

"And God bless you too, brother!"

Half an-hour later, by order of the Superior, John Storm, with the help of Brother Andrew and the Father Minister, carried

Brother Paul to his cell. The bell had been rung for Lauds, and going up the stairs they passed the brothers coming down to service. News of Paul's return had gone through the house like a cutting wind, and certain of the brothers who had gathered in groups on the landings were whispering together, as if the coming back had been a shameful thing which cast discredit on all of them. It wasn't love of rule that had brought the man home again, but broken health and the want of a bed to die upon! Thus they talked under their breath, unconscious of the secret operation of their own hearts. In a monastery, as elsewhere, failure is the worst disgrace.

John Storm returned to the hall with a firm step and eyes full of resolution. Hardly answering the brothers, who plied him with questions, he pushed through them with long strides, and taking the key of the outer gate from the place in the alcove where he had left it, he turned towards the Father's room.

The day had dawned, and through the darkness which was lifting in the little room he could see the Father rising from his knees.

"Father!" he cried in an excited voice, and his words, like his breath, came in gusts.

"What is it, my son?"

"Take this key back again. The world is calling me, and I cannot trust myself at the door any longer. Put me under the rule of silence and solitude and shut me up in a cell, or I shall break my obedience and run away as sure as heaven is over us!"

XIV

GLORY awoke on New Year's morning with a little hard lump at her heart and thought, "How foolish! Am I to give up all my cherished dreams because one man is a scoundrel?"

The struggle might be bitter, but she would not give in. London was the mother of genius. If she destroyed, she created also. It was only the weak and the worthless she cast away. The strong she made stronger, the great she made greater. "O God, give me the life I love!" she thought; "give me a chance; only let me begin— no matter how, no matter where!"

She remembered her impulse of the night before to follow Brother Paul, and the little hard lump at her heart grew bitter. John Storm had gone from her, forgotten her, left her to take care of herself. Very well, so be it! What was the use of thinking? "I hate to be sentimental," she thought.

If Aggie called on Sunday night she would go with her, no matter if it was beginning at the bottom. Others had begun there, and what right had she to expect to begin anywhere else? For the future she would take the world on its own terms and force it to give way. She would conquer this great cruel London and yet remain a good girl in spite of all.

Such was the mood in which she came down to breakfast, and the first thing that met her eyes was a letter from home. At that her face burned for a moment and her breath came in gusts, but she put the letter into her pocket unopened and tossed her head a little and laughed. "I hate to be so sensitive," she thought, and then she began to tell Mrs. Jupe what she intended to do.

"The clubs!" cried Mrs. Jupe. "I thought you didn't tyke to the shop because you fancied yerself above present company. But the foreign clubs! My gracious!"

The hissing of Mrs. Jupe's taunting voice followed her about all that day, and late at night, when they were going to bed and the streets were quiet, and there was only the jingle of a passing hansom or a drunken shout or the screech of a concertina, she could hear it again from the other side of the plaster partition, interrupted occasionally by the sound of Mr. Jupe's attempts to excuse and apologise for her. No matter! Anything to escape from the atmosphere of that woman's house, to be free of her and quit of her for ever.

Towards eight o'clock on Sunday evening she went up to her bedroom to put on her hat and ulster, and being alone there, and waiting for Aggie, she could not help but open her letter from home.

"Sunday next is your birthday, my dear one," wrote the Parson, "so we send you our love and greetings. This being the first of your twenty-one that you have spent from home, I will be thinking of you all the day through, and when night comes, and I smoke a pipe by the study fire, I know I shall be leaving the blind up that I may see the evening star and remember the happy birthdays long ago, when somebody who was so petted and spoiled used to say she had just come down from it, having dressed herself in some strange and grand disguises, and told us she was Phonodoree the fairy. You will be better employed than that, Glory, and as long as my dear one is well and happy and prosperous in the great city where she so loves to be——"

The candle was shaking in Glory's hands, and the little half-lit bedroom seemed to be blinking in and out.

Aunt Anna had added a postscript: "Glad to hear you are enjoying yourself in London, but rather alarmed at your frequent mention of theatres. Take care you don't go too often, child, and mind you send us the name of the vicar of the parish you are living in, for I certainly think grandfather ought to write to him."

To this again there was a footnote by Aunt Rachel: "You say nothing of Mr. Drake now-a-days. Is he one of Mrs. Jupe's visitors? And is it he who takes you to theatre?"

Then there was a New Year's card enclosed, having a picture of an Eastern shepherd at the head of his flock of sheep, and bearing the inscription, "Follow in his footsteps."

But the hissing sound of Mrs. Jupe's voice came up from below, and Glory's tears were dried in an instant. On going downstairs, she found Aggie in her mock sealskin and big black feathers sitting in the parlour at the back of the shop, and Mrs. Jupe talking to her in whispers, with an appearance of knowledge and familiarity. She caught the confused look of the one and the stealthy glances of the other, and the hard lump at her heart grew harder.

"Come on," said Glory, and a few minutes afterwards the girls were walking towards Soho. The little chapels in the quieter streets were dropping out their driblets of people and the lights in the church windows were being extinguished one by one. Aggie had recovered her composure, and was talking of Charlie as she skipped along with a rapid step, swinging her stage-box by her side. Charlie was certain to be at one of the clubs, and he would be sure to see them home. He wasn't out of his time yet, and that was why her father wouldn't allow him about. But he was in an office at a foundry, and his people lived in a house, and perhaps one of these days——"

"Did you say that some of the people who are on the stage now began at the clubs?" said Glory.

"Plenty, my dear. There's Betty Bellman for one. She was at a club in Old Compton Street when Mr. Sefton found her out."

Aggie had to "work a turn" at each of three clubs that night, and the girls were now at the door of the first of them. It stood at the corner of a reputable square, and was like any ordinary house on the outside. But people were coming and going constantly, and the doorkeeper was kept opening and closing the door. In the middle of the hall a clerk stood at a desk, having a great book in front of him, and making a show of challenging everybody as he entered. He recognised Aggie as an artiste, but passed Glory also on the payment of twopence and the signing of her name in the book.

The dining-room of the house had been converted into a

bar, with counter and stillage, and after the girls had crushed through the crowds that stood there they came into a large and shabby chamber, which had the appearance of having been built over the space which had once been the backyard. This room had neither windows nor skylights; its walls were decorated with portraits of Garibaldi and Victor Emanuel in faded colours, and there was a stage and proscenium at its farther end.

It was an Italian club that met there on Sunday nights, and some two or three hundred hairdressers and restaurant-keepers of swarthy complexion sat in groups at little round tables with their wives and sweethearts (chiefly Englishwomen), smoking and drinking and laughing at the performance on the stage.

Aggie went down to her dressing-room under the floor, and Glory sat at a table with a yellow-haired lady and a dark-eyed man. A negro without the burnt cork was twanging a banjo and cracking the jokes of the corner-man.

"That's my style—a merry touch-and-go," said the lady. And then, glancing at Glory, "Singing to-night, my dear?"

Glory shook her head.

"Thort you might be a pro' p'rhaps. Use ter be myself when I was in the bally at the Lane. Married now, my dear; but I likes to come of a Sunday night when the kids is got to bed."

Then Aggie danced a skirt-dance, and there were shouts of applause for her, and she came back and danced again. When she reappeared in jacket and hat, and with her stage-box in her hand, the girls crushed their way out. Going through the bar they were invited to drink by several of the men who were standing there, but they got into the street at last.

"They're rather messy, those bars," said Aggie; "but managers like you to come round and tyke something after you've done your turn —if it's only a cup of cawfy."

"Do you like this life?" said Glory, taking a long breath.

"Yes, awfully!" said Aggie.

Their next visit was to a Swiss club, which did not greatly differ from the Italian one, except that the hall was more shabby, and that the audience consisted of French and Swiss waiters and skittish young English milliners. The girls had taken their hats and cloaks off and sat dressed like dolls in white muslin with long streamers of bright ribbon. A gentleman sang the "Postman's Knock," with the character accompaniment of a pot-hat and a black-edged envelope; a lady sang "Maud" in silk tights and a cloak; Aggie danced her skirt-dance, and then the floor was cleared for a ball.

"They're going to dance the Swiss dance," said Aggie, "and

the M.C. wants me to tyke a place; but I hate these fellows to be hugging me. Will you be my partner, dear?"

"Well, just for a minute or two," said Glory with nervous gaiety. And then the dance began.

It proved to be a musical version of "odd man out," and Glory soon found herself being snapped up by other partners and addressed familiarly by the waiters and their women. She could feel the moisture of their hands and smell the oil of their hair, and a feeling like a spasm of physical pain came over her.

"Let us go," she whispered.

"Yes, it's getting lyte," said Aggie, and they pressed through the crowded bar and out into the street.

The twanging of the fiddles, the thud of the dancing, and the peals of coarse laughter followed them from the stifling atmosphere within, and Glory felt sick and faint.

"Do you say that managers of good places call at these clubs sometimes?"

"Often," said Aggie; and she hummed a music-hall tune as she skipped and tripped along.

The streets, which had been dark and quiet when they arrived in Soho, were now ablaze with lights in every window and noisy with people on every pavement. The last club they had to visit was a German one, and as they came near it they saw that a man was standing at the door bareheaded, and looking out for somebody.

"It's Charlie," said Aggie with a little jump of joy. But when they came up to him a scowl darkened his dark face, and he said—

"Lyte as usual! Two of the bloomin' turns not come, and me looking up and dahn the bloomin' street for you every minute and more!"

The girl's eyes blinked as if he had struck her, but she only tossed her head and stiffened her under lip and said—

"Jawing again, are ye? I'd chuck it for once, Charlie, if it was only for sake of company."

With that she disappeared to the dressing-room, and Charlie took charge of Glory, pushed a way for her through the refreshment-room, offered her a "glaws of somethink," and, with an obvious pride of possession, introduced her to admiring acquaintances as "a friend o' mine." "Like yer style, Charlie," said some of them. "Oh, yus! Dare say!" said Charlie.

The proscenium was surmounted by the German and English flags intertwined, the walls were adorned with oleograph portraits of the Kaiser, his father and grandfather, Bismarck and Von Moltke, and the audience consisted largely of lively young

German Jews and Jewesses in evening dress, some Polish Jews, and a sprinkling of other foreigners.

During Aggie's turn Glory was conscious that two strangers out of another world altogether had entered the club and were standing at the back.

"Toffs," said Charlie, looking at them over her shoulder, and then, answering to himself the meaning of their looks, "No, my lads! 'Tain't the first we've seen of sech!"

Then Aggie came up with an oily person in a flowered waistcoat and said—

"This is my friend, guv'nor; and she wouldn't mind doing a turn if you asked her."

"If de miss vill oblige," began the oily one; and then the blood rushed to Glory's face, and before she knew what else had happened, her hat and ulster were in Aggie's hands, and she was walking up the steps to the stage.

There was some applause when she went on, but she was in a dazed condition, and it all seemed to be taking place a hundred miles away. She heard her own voice saying, "Ladies and gentlemen, with your kind permission I will endeavour to give you an imitation . . ." and something more. Down to that moment her breath had been coming and going in hot gasps, and she had felt a dryness in the throat; but every symptom of nervousness suddenly disappeared, and she threw up her head like a charger in battle.

Then she sang. It was only a common street song, and everybody had heard it a thousand times. She sang, "And her golden hair was hanging down her back," after the manner of a line of factory girls going home from work at night. Arm in arm, decked in their Vandyke hats, slashed with red ribbon and crowned with ostrich feathers, with their free step, their shrill voices—they were there before everybody's eyes; everybody could see them, everybody could recognise them, and before the end of the first verse there were shouts and squeals of laughter.

Glory felt dizzy yet self-possessed; she gave a little audible laugh while she stood bowing between the verses. In a few minutes the song was finished, and the people were stamping, whistling, uttering screeching cat-calls, and shouting "Brayvo." But Glory was sitting at the foot of the stage by this time, with a face contorted as in physical pain. After the first thrill of success, the shame of it all came over her, and she saw how low she had fallen, and felt horrified and afraid. The clamour, the clapping of hands, the vulgar faces, the vulgar laughter, the vulgar song, Sunday night, her own birthday! It all passed before her like the incidents in some nightmare, and at the back of it came other memories—Glenfaba, the sweet and simple household, the old Parson smoking by the study fire and looking up at the evening star, and then John Storm and the church chimes at Bishopsgate! One moment she sat there with her burning face, staring helplessly before her, while people crowded round to shake hands with her, and cried into her ears above the deafening tumult, "You'll have to tyke another turn, dear;" and then she burst into passionate weeping.

"Stand avay! De lady's not fit to sing again," said some one, and she opened her eyes.

It was one of the two gentlemen who had been standing at the back.

"Ach Gott! Is it you? Don't you know me, nurse?"

It was Mr. Koenig, the organist.

"My gracious! Vot are you doing here, my child? Two monts ago I haf ask for you at de hospital, and haf write to de matron, but you vere gone. Since den I haf look for you all over London. Vhere do you lif?"

Glory told him, and he wrote down the address.

"Ugh! A genius and lif in a tobacco-shop! My vife vill call on you and fetch you avay. She is a goot woman, and vhatever she tell you to do you must do it; but not musical and clever same like as you. Bless mine soul! Singing in a Sunday club! Do you know, my child, you haf a voice, and talents, great talents! Vants training—yes. But vhat vould you haf? Here am I, Carl Koenig! I speak ver' bad de Englisch, but I know ver' goot to teach music. I vill teach you same like I teach oder ladies who pay me many dollare. Do you know vhat I am?"

Yes, she knew what he was—he was the organist at All Saints, Belgravia.

"Pooh! I am a composer as vell. I write songs, and all your countrymen and countryvomen sing dem. I haf a choral company, too, and it is for dat I vant you. I go to de first houses in de land, de lords, de ministers, de princes. You shall come vith me. Your voice is soprano—no, mezzo-soprano—and it vill grow. I vill pitch it, and vhen it is ready I vill bring you out. But now get away from dis place, and naivare come back, or I vill be more angry as before."

Then Glory rose and he led her to the door. Her heart felt big and her eyes were glistening. Aggie was in the refreshment-room. Having finished for the night, the girl had resumed her outdoor costume without removing her make-up, and was laughing merrily among a group of men, and playing them off against Charlie, who was still in the sulks and drinking at the bar. When Glory appeared Aggie fidgeted with her glove and said, "Aren't you going to see us home, Charlie?"

"No," said Charlie.

"Where are you going to?"

"Nowhere as you can come."

Aggie's eyes watered, and she wrenched a button off, but she only laughed and answered, "Don't think as we're throwing ourselves at *your* head, my man. We only wanted to *know*. Ta-ta!"

It was now midnight, and the streets were thin of people, but sounds of music and dancing came from nearly every open window and door.

Aggie was crying. "That's the worst of the clubs," she said, "they lead 'em to the gambling hells. And then a young man always knows when he can tyke advantage."

As they returned past the Swiss club, somebody who was being thrown out into the street was shouting in a gurgling voice, "Let go o' my throat or I'll corpse ye!" And farther on two or three girls in their teens, with their arms about the necks of twice as many men, were reeling along the pavement and singing in a tuneless wail.

XV

Towards the middle of Lent the Society of the Holy Gethsemane was visited by its ecclesiastical Visitor. This was the Bishop of the diocese, a liberal-minded man, and not a very rigid ecclesiastic, abrupt, brusque, business-like, and a good administrator. When the brothers had gathered in the community-room, he took from the Superior the leather-bound volume containing the rule of the Brotherhood, and read aloud the text of it.

"And now, gentlemen," he said, "whether I approve of your rule or not is a matter with which we have no concern at present. My sole duty is to see that it is lawfully administered. Are you satisfied with the administration of it and willing to remain under its control?"

There was only one response from the brothers—they were entirely satisfied.

The Bishop rose with a smile and bowed to the brothers, and they began to leave the room.

"There are two of my people whom you have not yet seen," said the Father.

"Where are they?"

"In their cells."

"Why in their cells?"

"One of them is ill; the other is under the rule of silence and solitude."

"Let us visit them," said the Bishop, and they began to ascend the stairs.

"I may not agree with your theory of the religious life, Father, but when I see your people giving up the world and its comforts, its joys and possessions, its ties of blood and affection——"

They had reached the topmost storey, and the Father had paused to recover breath. "This cell to the right," said he, "is occupied by a lay brother who was tempted by the Evil One to a grievous act of disobedience, and the wrath of God has fallen on him. But Satan has over-reached himself for once, and by that very act grace has triumphed. Not a member of our community rejoices more in the blessed sacrament, and when I place the body of our Lord——"

"May we go in to him?"

"Certainly; he is dying of lung disease, but you shall see with what patience he possesses his soul."

Brother Paul was sitting before a small fire in an arm-chair padded with pillows, holding in his dried-up hands a heavy crucifix which was suspended from his neck.

"How lightsome and cosy we are up here," said the Bishop. "A long way up, certainly, but no doubt you get everything you require."

"Everything," said Paul.

"I dare say the brothers are very good to you—they usually are so to the weak and ailing in a monastery."

"Too good, my lord."

"Of course you see a doctor occasionally?"

"Three times a week, and if he would only let me escape from an evil and troublesome world——"

"Hush! It's not right to talk like that, my son. Whatever happens, it is our duty to live, you know."

"I've lost all there was to live for, and besides——"

"Then there is nothing you wish for?" said the Bishop.

"Nothing but death," said Paul, and lifting the crucifix, he carried it to his lips.

"Thank God we are born to die," said the Bishop, and they stepped back to the corridor and closed the door.

"This next cell," said the Father, "is occupied by such a one as you were thinking of—one who was born to possess the world and to achieve its sounding triumphs, but——"

"Has he given it up entirely?"

"Entirely."

"Is he young?"

"Quite young, and he has left the world, not as Augustine did, after learning by bitter experience the deceitfulness of sin——"

"Then why is he here?"

"He cannot trust himself yet. He feels the inward strivings and struggles of our rebellious nature and——"

"Then his solitude and silence are voluntary?"

"Now they are. See," said the Father, and stooping to the floor he picked up a key that lay at his feet.

"What does that mean?"

"He locks himself in and pushes the key under the door."

When they entered the cell, John Storm was standing by the window in a stream of morning sunlight, looking out on the world below with fixed and yearning eyes.

"This is our Visitor," said the Father. "The rule of silence is relaxed in his case!"

"Have I not seen you before?" said the Bishop.

"I think not, Father," said John.

"What is your name and where did you live before you came here?"

John told him.

"Then I have both seen and heard you. But I perceive that the world has gone on a little since you left it—your Canon is an Archdeacon now and one of the chaplains to the Queen as well. How long have you been in the Brotherhood?"

"Since the 14th of August."

"And how long have you kept your cell?"

"Since the Octave of Epiphany."

"But this is Lent—rather a long penance, Father."

"I have often urged our dear brother . . ." began the Father.

"You carry your fastings and prayers too far, Mr. Storm," said the Bishop. He was picking up one by one some black-letter books that were lying on the table and on the bed. "I know that divines in all ages tell us that the body is evil, and that its desires and appetites must be eradicated; but they also teach us that the perfect Christian character is the blending of the two lives, the life of nature and the life of grace. Don't despise your humanity, my son. Your Master did not despise it. He came down from heaven that He might live and work among the sinful brotherhood of man. And don't pray for death, or fast as if you wished for it. You would have no right to do that even if you were like your poor neighbour next door, whom death smiles on and beckons to repose. But you are young and you are strong. Who knows what good work your Heavenly Father holds in store for you yet?"

John had returned to the window and was looking out with vacant eyes.

"But all this is beside my present business," said the Bishop. "There is nothing you wish to complain of?"

"Nothing whatever."

"You are content to live in this house, under the laws and statutes of this society, and in voluntary obedience to its Superior?"

"Yes."

"That is enough."

The Bishop was leaving the cell when his eye was arrested by some writing in pencil on the wall. It ran, "9th of November—Lord Mayor's Day;" and under it were short lines such as a prisoner makes when he keeps a reckoning.

"What is the meaning of this date?" said the Bishop.

John was silent, but the Father answered with a smile, "That is the date of his vow, my lord. It is part of the discipline of his life of grace to keep count of the days of his novitiate, so eager is he for the time when he may dedicate his whole life to God."

Back at the head of the stairs the Father paused again and said "Listen!"

There was the sound as of a trembling hand turning the key in the lock of the door they had shut behind them, and at the next moment the key itself came out of the aperture under it.

When the door closed on the Bishop and John Storm was alone in his cell, one idea was left with him—the idea of work. He had tried everything else, and everything had failed.

He had tried solitude. On asking to be shut up in a cell he had said to himself, "The thought of Glory is a temptation of my unquickened and unspiritual nature. It has already betrayed me into an act of cowardice and inhumanity, and it will drive me out into the world and fling me back again as it drove out and flung back Brother Paul." But the result of solitude was specious and deceitful. As pictures seem to float before the eyes after the eyelids are closed, so his past life, now that it was over, seemed to rise up before him with awful distinctness. Sitting alone in his cell, every event of his life with Glory passed before him in review and harassed him with pitiless condemnation. Why had he failed to realise the essential difference of temperament between himself and that joyous creature? Why had he hesitated to gratify her natural and innocent love of mere life?

Why had he done this? Why had he not done that? If Glory were lost, if the wicked and merciless world had betrayed her, the fault was his, and God would surely punish him. Thus would solitude enervate his soul by frightening it, and the temptation he had hoped to vanquish became the more strong and tyrannical.

He had tried reading. The Fathers told him that God allowed ascetics to keep the keys of their nature in their own hands; that they had only to think of woman as more bitter than death, and of her beauty as a cause of perdition, and that if any woman's face tormented them, they were to picture it to the eye of the mind as old and wrinkled, defaced by disease, and even the prey of the worm. He tried to think of Glory as the Fathers directed, but when darkness fell and he lay on his bed, with the first dream of the night the strong powers of nature, that had no mind to surrender, swept down the pitiful bulwarks of religion, and Glory was smiling upon him in her youth, her beauty, her sweetness, her humour, and all the grace of her countless gifts.

He had tried fasting. Three times a day Brother Andrew brought him his food, and twice a day, when the lay brother had left him, he opened the window and spread the food on the sill for the birds to take it. But the results of fasting were the reverse of his expectations. At one moment he was uplifted by strong emotions, at the next moment he was in collapse. Visions began to pass before him. His father's face tormented him constantly, and sometimes he was conscious of the face of his mother, though he had never known her. But above all and through all there came the face of Glory. Fasting had only extended his dreams about her. He was dreaming both by day and by night now, and Glory was with him always.

He had tried prayer. Hitherto he had said his offices regularly, but now he would say special prayers as well. To get the victory over his lawless and rebellious nature he would turn his eyes to the Mother of the Lord. But when he tried to fix his mind on Mary there was nothing to answer to it. All was shadowy and impalpable. There was only a vague, empty cloud before his eyes, until suddenly a luminous face glided into the vacant place, and it was full of tenderness, of sweetness, of charm, of pity and womanly love—but it was the face of Glory.

Despair laid hold of him. His attempts to overcome nature were clearly rejected by the Almighty. Winter passed with its foggy days. The Father wished him to return to the ordinary life of the community, yet he begged to be allowed to remain.

But the spring came and diffused its joy throughout all nature. He listened to the leaves, he watched the birds threading their way in the clear air, he caught glimpses of the yellow flowers, and strained his eyes for the green country beyond. The young birds began to take wing, and one little sparrow came hopping into his room as often as he opened his window in the morning, and played about his feet like a mouse, and then was gone to the mother-bird that called to it from the tree.

Little by little hope grew to impatience, and impatience rose to fever-heat, but he remembered his vow, and to put himself out of temptation he locked the door of his cell and pushed the key through the aperture under it. But he could not lock the door of his soul, and his old trouble came up again with the throb of a stronger and fresher life. Every morning when he awoke he thought of Glory. Where was she now? What had become of her by this time? He wrote on the wall the date of her disappearance from the hospital—"9th of November—Lord Mayor's Day"—and tried to keep pace in his mind with the chances of her fate. "I am guilty of a folly," he thought. The pride of his reason revolted against what he was doing. Nevertheless he knew full well it would be the same to-morrow, and the next day, and the next year, for his human passions would not yield, and his vow still clutched him as with fangs.

He was standing one morning by the window looking through an opening between high buildings to the river, with its hay-barges gliding down the glistening water-way, and its little steamers with their spirals of smoke ascending, when everything in the world began in a moment to bear another moral interpretation. The lesson of life was work. Man could not exist without it. If he departed from that condition, no matter how much he fasted and meditated and prayed, he was useless and miserable and depraved.

Then the lock turned in the door of his cell and the Father and the Bishop entered. When they were gone, he felt suffocated by their praises of his piety, and asked himself, "What am I doing here?" He was a hypocrite. Ten thousand other men whom the Church called saints had been hypocrites before him, and as they paced their cloisters they had asked themselves the same question. But the mighty hand of the Church was over him still, and with trembling fingers he turned the key again and pushed it under the door. Then he knew that he was a coward also, and that religion had deprived him of his will, of his manhood, and enervated his soul itself.

Brother Paul was moving about in the adjoining cell. The lay brother had become very weak; his step was slow, his feet dragged along the floor; his breath was audible, and sometimes his cough was long and raucous. John had heard these sounds every day and had tried not to listen, but now he strained his ears to hear. A new thought had come to him: he would ask to be allowed to nurse Brother Paul; that should be his work, for work alone could save him.

Next morning he leapt up from sleep at the first syllable of "Benedicamus Domino" and cried "Father!" But when the door opened in answer to his call it was the Father Minister who entered. The Superior had gone to give a Retreat to a sisterhood in York and would be absent until the end of Lent. John looked at the hard face of the deputy, the very mirror of its closed and frozen soul, and he could say nothing.

"Is it anything that I can do for you?" said the Father Minister.

"No that is to say—no, no," said John.

When he opened his window that day he could hear the Lenten services in the church. The prayers, the responses, the psalms, and the hymns woke to fresh life the memory of things long past, and for the first time he became oppressed with a great loneliness. The near neighbourhood of Brother Paul intensified that loneliness, and at length he asked for an indulgence and spoke to the Father Minister again.

"Brother Paul is ill; let me attend to him," he said.

The Father Minister shook his head. "The brother gets all he wants. He does not wish for constant attendance."

"But he is a dying man, and somebody should be with him always."

"The doctor says nothing can be done for him. He may live months. But if he is dying, let us leave him to meditate on the happiness and glory of another world."

John made no further struggle. Another door had closed on him. But it was not necessary to go to Brother Paul that he might be with him always. The spiritual eye could see everything. Listening to the sounds in the adjoining cell, it was the same at length as if the wall between them had fallen down and the two rooms were one. Whatever Brother Paul did John seemed to see, whatever he said in his hours of pain John seemed to hear; and when he lifted his scuttle of coal from the place at the door where the lay brother left it, John's hand seemed to bear up the weight.

It was a poor, pathetic folly, but it brought the comfort of company, and John thought with a pang of the time when he had wished to be separated from Paul, and had all but asked for a cell elsewhere. Paul had a fire, and John could hear him build and light and stir it; and sometimes when this was done he would sit down himself before his own empty grate on his own side of the wall, and fancy they were good comrades sitting side by side.

As the day passed, he thought that Brother Paul on his part also was touched by the same sense of company. His silence at certain moments, his half-articulate salutations, his repetition of the sounds that John himself made, seemed to be the dumb expression of a sense that, in spite of the wall that divided them, and the rule of silence and solitude that separated them on John's side, they were nevertheless together.

Brother Paul's cough grew rapidly worse, and at last it burst into a fit so long and violent as to seem as if it would never end. John held his breath and listened. "He'll suffocate," he thought; "he'll never live through it." But the spasm passed, and there was a prolonged hush, a dead stillness, that was not broken by so much as the sound of a breath. Was he gone? By a sudden impulse, in the agony of his suspense, John stretched out his hand and knocked three times on the wall.

There was a short silence, and then faintly, slowly, and irregularly three other knocks came back to him.

Paul had understood, and John shouted in his joy. But even on top of his relief came his religious fears. Had he broken the rule of silence? Were they guilty of a sin?

Nevertheless, for many days thereafter, though they knew it was a fault, in this vague and dumb and feeble fashion they communicated constantly. On going to bed they rapped "Good-night"; on rising for the day they rapped "Good-morning." They rapped when the bell rang for mid-day service, and again when the singing came up through the courtyard. And sometimes they rapped from sympathy, and sometimes from pity, and sometimes from mere human loneliness and the love of company.

Thus did these exiles from life, struggling to live under the eye of God in obedience to their earthly vow, try to cheer their crushed and fettered souls, and to comfort each other like imprisoned children.

XVI

THE PRIORY, ST. JOHN'S WOOD,
LONDON.

BEHOLD, all men and women at Glenfaba, I have made one further change in my rôle of female Wandering Jew! You have to think of Glory now, dear people, in a nice house in St. John's Wood, though there is no wood anywhere visible except the Park, where they keep all the wild beasts in

London—all that go on four legs, you know. The master of the mansion is Mr. Carl Koenig, a dear old hippopotamus, who is five-feet-nothing in his boots, and has piercing black eyes and an electro plated moustache. He is a sort of an English-German-Dutch-Polish musician. When he talks of himself as an organist, he is always a little John Bull, being F.R.C.O. and lots of things besides; when he speaks of "Vaterland," he is a German; when he mentions the sea, he is a Dutchman; and when he is in good spirits (or they are in him), he sings "Poland is not lost for ever!" all over the house until you sometimes wish it were.

His wife is an Englishwoman, about forty or more, with big, moist, doggy eyes, that give you an idea of slave-humility and an unappreciated and undeveloped soul. There never were two married folk less alike, she being one of those silent creatures who come into a room and sit and listen and never speak, except to give instructions to the maids, while he is always cackling like an old hen who can never lay an egg without letting the whole world know all about it. They have two female servants, both beautiful Cockneys, besides a boy in the garden, and a parrot that holds forth all over the place; and their house is the rendezvous of all kinds and conditions of great people, for Mr. Koenig himself is a sort of Gideon's lamp among "pros." of nearly every order.

And now you want to know how I come to be here. You are to learn then that Mr. Koenig happened to be one of my patients in the hospital, he having gone there for a slight operation, and I having helped to nurse him through what he calls his "operatic cure." In the course of that ordeal he had music of a less excruciating kind sometimes, it seems, and after his return home he searched for me all over London on account of my voice, and finding me unexpectedly at last, he sent his wife to Mrs. Jupe's to fetch me, and—and here I am in a dainty little dimity room, whose walls are covered with portraits of well-known singers, violinists, pianists, and composers, with their affectionate inscriptions underneath.

But you want to learn why I am here. Well, you must know that Mr. Koenig (although a foreign musician) is organist of All Saints, Belgravia, where they sing a solo anthem at nearly every Sunday morning service; and having had various disappointments at the hands of vocal soloists from the Opera, whose "professional engagements suddenly intervened," he conceived the audacious idea of "intervening" a woman to do their duty permanently. So this is my position in the church at which John Storm used to be curate, and once a week I pipe that his old enemy the Canon may play. But as that good man is of St. Paul's opinion about women holding their tongues in the synagogue, and is blest with just enough ear to know a contralto from a cornerake, I have to be hidden away behind a screen in order that his reverence may have all the fun to himself of believing me to be a boy.

So you see, my dearies, you needn't be anxious about me "at all at all," seeing that I am living in this atmosphere of art and the odour of sanctity, and that I have kept only one tiny little thing back, and I am going to tell you that now. You were afraid that I might go too often to the theatre, Aunt Anna. Never mind, auntie, I shall not be going so very often now, and in proof thereof permit me to introduce myself in my future style and character—Miss Glory Quayle, the eminent social entertainer! You don't know what that is, dear people? It is quite simple and innocent nevertheless. I am to go to the houses of smart people when they give their grand parties and sing and recite, and so forth. Nothing wrong, you see—only what I used to do at Glenfaba.

You must know that, just as in the country the men go to the smithy when they have nothing more pressing on hand than to settle the affairs of the universe, and the women to the mangle-house when they have to mangle other things besides clothes, so in the towns the poor rich people have their own particular diversion, which they call their "At Homes." Mr. Drake used to tell me they were terrible Tower-of-Babel concerns, at which everybody talked at once, and all the tongues in the place went 'click-clack world without end.' But they must be perfectly charming for all that; and when I think of the dresses and the diamonds and the titles as long as your breath—oh dear! oh dear!

I shall see it all soon, I suppose, for to supply the place of the hammer and the anvil the smart folks always add musical accompaniment to the confusion of tongues, and Mr. Koenig, who has a choral company, goes to the cream of the cream of such gatherings, and sings and plays from Grieg and Schumann, and Liszt and Wagner, and Chopin and Paderewski, and the place intended for me in this grand organisation would appear to be that of jester to my lords and ladies. "Ach Gott!" says Mr. Koenig, who "speaks ver' bad de Englisch," "your great people vant de last new ting. One lady she say to me, 'Dear Mr. Koenig, I tink I shall not ask you dis season. I hear you everyvheres I go to, and I get so tired of peoples.' But vhen I takes anoder wis me I am a new beesness. You shall sing and recite your leetle funny tings. Your great people tink dey loof music, but dey loof better to laugh. 'For mercy's sake, make dem laugh, Mr. Koenig'—dat's vhat a great man say to me. But, my gootness, how can I? I am a musician, I am a composer, I am an arteeste!"

For this high and noble office I have been going through a purgatory of preparation in which I have sometimes hardly known whether I was a hurdy-gurdy or an explosion of cats, and the future female jester has even been known to lie down on the floor and cry in her dumps of despair or some such devilry. However Mr. Koenig begins to believe that I am passable, and my first appearance is to be made immediately after Easter, at the house of the Home Secretary, where it is not improbable, dear Aunt Rachel, that I may meet Mr. Drake, although that is no part of my programme.

Of course I shall have to look charming in any case, and I am already busy with my dress. It is a black silk gown with a tight-fitting bodice. The bodice has windbag sleeves, formed of shawl pieces of guipure lace, and some lilies of the valley on the breast, finished with a waistband of heliotrope velvet, and I am going to wear long black gloves all the way up my arms, which are growing round and plump and lovely enough for anything. The skirt is my old one, and I got the lace for three-and-six, so I am not ruining myself, you see; and though my hair is getting redder than ever, red is the fashionable colour in London now, therefore I shan't waste much money on dyes.

But for all this brave exterior, when the time comes I know that down in my heart I shall be terrified. It will be like the first dive of the year. "One plunge, Glory, my child," and then over I'll go! I partly realise already what it will be like by my experiences on Sunday evenings when the celebrities come here after church, and Mr. Koenig exhibits me to admiring friends, and tells them how I brought him "goot look," and I overhear them say, "That girl will show them all something yet." Oh, this London is adorable, my dears, with its wit and fashion, and gaiety and luxury; and I have concluded that to live in the world is the best thing one can do after all. Some people say hard things about it, and want to reform it, or even to leave it altogether; but I love it, I love it, and think it just charming!

And now spring is here, and the world is lovely in its yellow and green. It must be *urromassy* nice over yandher in the "oilan" too, with the primroses and the violets and the gorse in the glen. Oh dear! oh dear! I can smell it all three hundred miles away! The lilacs will be out at Glenfaba now, and Aunt Anna will be collecting her Easter eggs. Well, wait a whiley and I'll come to thee, my dears!

Not a word from John Storm, of course. No doubt he is fighting with shadows while other people are struggling with realities. They tell me these Brotherhoods are common in the Church now, though most of them are secret societies; but the more I think of that kind of religion the more it looks like setting tasks to try faith, as if God were a coquettish woman. That reminds me that Mr. Worldly-Wealthy-Wiseman is no longer a Canon, having got himself made Archdeacon, and as such he looks more than ever like a black Spanish cock, being clad, of course, in those funny clothes, like the bishops, which always make one think their lordships must be in doubt on getting up in the morning whether they ought to wear a schoolboy's knickerbockers or a ballet-girl's skirt, so they settle the difficulty by putting on both. For this reason I try to avoid him when on duty at the church, lest I should be suddenly possessed of a devil and behave badly to his face. But this being Lent, and there being special preachers every day, it chanced on Sunday morning that I came upon three of him all in a row, and oh, my gracious! Solomon in all his glory was not arrayed like one of these!

It is too bad, though, to think that men like John Storm can't find room in the Church for the sole of their foot, while this archdemon is flourishing in it like a green bay-tree. Forgive me, grandfather; I can't help it. But then the church in the country doesn't seem the same thing as in town. *There* you are somehow made to feel that man does a little and God does all the rest, while *here* we reverse that order of things, with the result that this seed of the Amalekite . . . But never mind!

I went to the Zoo this morning. There was a lion shut up in a cage all by himself. Such a solemn, splendid, silent fellow; I could have cried.

But it is the witching hour of night, my daughter, and you must put yourself to bed. "Goot look!" GLORY.

XVII

IN the middle of the night of Good Friday, John Storm was awakened by noises in the adjoining cell. There seemed to be the voices of two men in angry and violent altercation, the one threatening and denouncing, the other protesting and supplicating.

"The girl is dead—isn't that proof enough?" said one voice.

"It's a lie! It's a false accusation!" said the other voice. "Paul, what are you going to do?" "Put this bullet in your brain." "But I'm innocent. I take the Almighty to witness that I am innocent. Put the pistol down. Help! help!" "No use calling—there's nobody in the house." "Mercy! mercy! I haven't much money about me, but you shall have it all. Take everything—everything—and if there's anything I can do to start you in life . . . I'm rich, Paul—I have influence . . . only spare me!" "Scoundrel, do you think you can buy me as you bought my sister?" "And if I did, I was not the only one." "Liar! Tell that to herself when you meet her at the judgment!" "Assassin!" "Too late—you've met her."

John Storm listened and understood. The two voices were one voice, which was the voice of Brother Paul. The lay brother was delirious. His poor broken brain was rambling in the ways of the past. He was re-enacting the scene of his crime.

John hesitated. His impulse was to fly into Paul's room and lay hold of him, that he might prevent him from doing himself any injury. But he remembered the law of the community that no member of it should go into the cell of another under pain of grievous penance. And then there was the rule of silence and solitude, which had not yet been lifted away.

But monks are great sophists, and at the next moment John Storm had told himself that it was not Brother Paul who was in the adjoining room, but only his poor perishing body, labouring through the last sloughs of the twilight land of death. Paul himself, his soul, his spirit, was far away. Hence it could be no sin to go into the cell of one whose senses were not there.

His own door was locked, but he scraped back the key and lit his candle, and stepped into the passage. The voices were still loud in Paul's room, but no one seemed to hear them. Not another sound broke the silence of the sleeping house. The cell beyond Paul's was empty. It was Brother Andrew's cell, and Andrew was at the door downstairs.

When John Storm entered the dark room, candle in hand, Brother Paul was standing in the middle of the floor, with one hand outstretched, and a ghastly and appalling smile upon his face. He was pale as death, his eyes were ablaze, his forehead was streaming with perspiration, and he was breathing from the depths of his chest. He wiped the dews from his brow and said in a choking voice, " He has died as he lived—a liar and a scoundrel!"

John took him by the hand and drew him to the bed, and putting him to sit there, he tried to soothe and comfort him. He was terrified at first by the sound of his own voice, but the sophism that had served to bring him served to support him also, and he told himself it could be no breach of the rule of silence to speak to one who was not there. The delirium of the lay brother spent itself at length, and he fell into a deep sleep.

Next day, when Brother Andrew came to John's cell with the food, he began to sing, as if to himself, while he bustled about the room.

"Brother Paul is sinking—he is sinking rapidly—Father Jerrold has confessed him—he has taken the sacrament—and is very patient."

This, as if it had been a Gregorian chant, the great fellow had hit upon as a means of communicating with John, without breaking rule and committing sin.

John did not lock his door on the following night. On going to bed he listened for the noises he had heard before, half fearing and yet half wishing that he might hear them again. But he heard nothing; and towards midnight he fell asleep. Something made him shudder, and he awoke with the sensation of moonlight on his face. The moon was indeed shining, and its sepulchral light was on a figure that stood by the foot of the bed. It was Paul, with a livid face, murmuring his name in a voice almost as faint as a breath.

John leapt up, and put his arms about him.

"You are ill, brother—very ill."

"I am dying."

"Help! help!" cried John, and he made for the door.

"Hush, brother, hush!"

"Oh, I don't care for rule. Rule is nothing in a case like this. And besides, it is an understood thing . . . Help!"

"I implore you, I conjure you," said Paul, in a voice strangled by weakness. "Let them leave us together a little longer. It was by my own wish that I was left alone. I have something to say to you, something to confess. I have to ask your pardon."

In two strides John had reached the door, but he came back without opening it.

"Why, my poor lad, what have you done to me?"

"When you let me out of the house to go in search of my sister——"

"That was long ago—we'll not talk of it now, brother."

"But I cannot die in peace without telling you. You remember that I had something to say to her?"

"Yes."

"It was a threat. I was going to tell her that unless she gave up her way of life, I should find the man who had been the cause of it, and follow him up and kill him."

"It was only a temptation of the devil, brother, and it is past, and now——"

"Don't you see what I was going to do? I was going to bring trouble and disgrace upon you also as my comrade and accomplice. That's what a man comes to when Satan——"

"But God willed it otherwise, brother—let us say no more about it."

"You forgive me, then?"

"Forgive? It is I who ought to ask for your forgiveness, and perhaps if I told you everything——"

"There is something else. Listen! The Almighty is calling me—I have no time to lose."

"But you are so cold, brother. Lie on the bed, and I'll cover you with the bedclothes. Oh, never fear—they shan't separate us again. If the Father were at home—he is so good and tender-hearted—but no matter. There, there!"

"You will despise and hate me—you who are so holy and brave, and have given up everything and conquered the world, and even triumphed over love itself."

"Don't say that, brother."

"It's true, isn't it? Everybody knows what a holy life you live."

"Hush!"

"But I have never lived the religious life at all, and I only came to it as a refuge from the law and the gallows, and if the Father hadn't——"

"Another time, brother."

"Yes, the story I told the police was true, and I had really——"

"Hush, brother, hush! I won't hear you. What you are saying is for God's ear only, and whatever you have done God will judge your soul in mercy. We have only to ask Him——"

"Quick, then; the last sands are running out," and he strove to rise and kneel.

"Lie still, brother; God will accept the humiliation of your soul."

"No, no, let me up; let me kneel beside you. The prayer for the dying—say it with me, Brother Storm; let us say it together. 'O Lord, save——'

"'O Lord, save Thy servant,
"'Which putteth his trust in Thee.
"'Send him help from Thy holy place.
"'And . . . evermore . . . mightily defend him.
"'Let the enemy have no advantage over him.
"'Nor the . . . wicked——

"'Be unto him, O Lord, a strong tower.
"'From the——
"'O Lord, hear our prayers.
"'And——'"
"Paul! Paul! Speak to me! Speak! Don't leave me. We will console and support each other. You shall come to me, I will go to you. No matter about the religious life. One word! My lad, my lad!"

But Brother Paul had gone. The captured eagle with the broken wing had slipped its chain at last.

In the terrible peace which followed the air of the room seemed to become empty. John Storm felt chill and dizzy, and a great awe fell upon him The courage which he had built up in sight of Brother Paul's sufferings ebbed rapidly away, and his old fear of rule flowed back. He must carry the lay brother to his cell; he must be ignorant of his death; he must conceal and cover up everything. The moon had gone by this time, for it was near to morning, and the shadows of night were contending with the leaden hues of dawn.

He opened the door and listened. The house was still quite silent. He walked on tiptoe to the end of the corridor, pausing at every cell. There was no sound anywhere, except the sonorous breathing of some heavy sleeper and the ticking of the clock in the hall.

Then he returned to the chamber of death, and lifting the body in his arms, he carried it back to the room which it had so recently left as a living man. He scarcely felt its weight, for the limbs under the cassock had dried up like withered twigs. He stretched them out on the bed that they might be fit for death's composing hand, and then closed the eyes and laid the hands together on the breast, and took the heavy cross that hung about the neck and put it as well as he could into the nerveless fingers. By this time the daylight had overcome the shadows of the fore-dawn, and the ruddy glow of morning was gliding into the room. Traffic was beginning to stir in the sleeping city and a cart was rattling down the street.

One glance more he gave at the dead brother's face, and going down on his knees beside it, he said a prayer and crossed himself. Then he rose and stole back to his room and shut the door without a sound.

There was a boundless relief when this was done, and partly from relief and partly from exhaustion he fell asleep. He slept for a few minutes only, but sleep knows no time, and a moment in its garden of forgetfulness will wipe out the bitterness of a life. When he awoke he stretched out his hand as he was accustomed to do and rapped three times on the wall. But the tide of consciousness returned to him even as he did so, and in the dead silence that followed his very heart grew cold.

Then the Father Minister began to awaken the household. His deep call and the muffled answer which followed it rose higher and higher and came nearer and nearer, and every step as he approached seemed to beat upon John Storm's brain. He had reached the topmost storey— he was coming down the corridor —he was standing before the door of the dead man's cell.

"Benedicamus Domino," he called, but no answer came back to him. He called again, and there was a short and terrible silence.

John Storm held his breath and listened. By the faint click of the lock he knew that the door had been opened and that the Father Minister had entered the room. There was a muttered exclamation and then another short silence, and after that there came the click of the lock again. The door had been closed and the Father Minister had resumed his rounds. When he called at the door of John Storm's cell, not a tone of his voice would have told that anything unusual had taken place.

The bell rang and the brothers trooped down the stairs. Presently the low droning sound of their voices came up from the chapel where they were saying Lauds. But the service had scarcely ended when the Father Minister's step was on the stair again. This time another was with him. It was the doctor. They entered the brother's room and closed the door behind them. From the other side of the wall John Storm followed every movement and every word.

"So he has gone at last, poor soul."

"Is he long dead, doctor?"

"Some hours certainly. Was there nobody with him then?"

"He didn't wish for anybody. And then you told us that nothing could be done, and that he might live a month."

"Still, a dying man, you know . . . But how strangely composed he looks! And then the cross on his breast as well!"

"He was very devout and penitent. He made his last devotion yesterday, with an intensity of joy such as I have rarely witnessed."

"His eyes closed, too! You are sure there was nobody with him?"

"Nobody whatever."

There was a moment's silence and then the doctor said, "Well, he has slipped his anchor at last, poor soul."

"Yes, he has launched on the ocean of the love of God. May we all be as ready when our call comes."

They came back to the corridor, and John heard their footsteps going downstairs. Then for some minutes there were unusual noises below. Rapid steps were coming and going, the hall bell was ringing and the front door was opening and shutting.

An hour later Brother Andrew came with the breakfast. He was obviously excited, and putting down the tray he began to busy himself in the room, and to sing, as before, in his pretence of a Gregorian chant—

"Brother Paul is dead—he died in the night—there was nobody with him—we are sorry he has left us, but glad he is at peace—God rest the soul of our poor Brother Paul!"

It was Easter Day. At mid-day service in the church the brothers sang the Easter Hymn, and a mighty longing took hold of John Storm for his own resurrection from his living grave.

Next day there was much coming and going between the world outside and the adjoining cell, and late at night there were heavy and shambling footsteps, and even some coarse and ribald talk.

"Bear a 'and, myte."

"Well, they won't have their backs broke as carry this one downstairs. He ain't a Danny Lambert, anyway."

"No, they don't feed ye on Bovril in plyces syme as this. I'll lay ye odds yer own looking-glass wouldn't know ye arter three months 'ard on religion and dry tommy."

"It pawses me 'ow people tyke to it. Gimme my pint of 'our-half, and my own childring to foller me."

Early on the following morning a stroke rang out on the bell, then another stroke, and again another. "It is the knell," thought John.

A group of the lay brothers came up and passed into the room. "Now," said one, as if giving a signal, and then they passed out again with the measured steps of men who bear a burden. "They are taking him away," he thought.

He listened to their retreating footsteps. "He has gone," he murmured.

The passing bell continued to ring out minute by minute, and presently there was the sound of singing. "It is the service for the dead," he told himself.

After a while both the bell and the singing ceased, and then there was no sound anywhere except the dull rumble of the traffic in the city outside—the deep murmur of the mighty sea that flows on for ever.

"What am I doing?" he asked himself. "What bolts and

bars are keeping me? I am guilty of a folly. I am degrading myself."

At mid-day Brother Andrew came with his food. "Brother Paul is buried," he sang, "the coffin was beautiful—it was covered with flowers—we buried him in his cassock, with his beads and psalter— we left the cross on his breast—he loved it and died with it in his hands—the Father has come home—he said mass this morning."

John Storm could bear no more. He pushed the lay brother aside and made straight for the Superior's room.

The Father was sitting before the fire, looking sad and low and weary. He rose to his feet with a painful smile as John broke into his cell with blazing eyes and cried in a choking voice—

"Father, I cannot live the religious life any longer. I have tried to—with all my soul and strength I've tried to, but I cannot—I cannot. This life of prayer and penance and meditation is stifling me and corrupting me and crushing the man out of me, and I cannot bear it."

"What are you saying, my son?"

"I have been deceiving you, and myself, and everybody."

"Deceiving me?"

"It was for my own ends, and not Brother Paul's, that I helped him to break obedience, and so injure his health and hasten his death."

"Your own?"

"I, too, had a sister in the world, and my heart was hungry for news of her."

"A sister?"

"Some one nearer than a sister,—and all my spiritual life has been a sham."

"My son, my son!"

"Forgive me, Father. I shall love you and honour you and revere you always; but I must break my obedience and leave you, or I shall be a hypocrite and a liar and a cheat."

XVIII

THE dinner-party at the Home Secretary's took place on a Wednesday in the week after Easter. It had rained during the day but cleared up towards night. Glory and Koenig had taken an omnibus to Waterloo Place, and then walked up the wide street that ends with the wide steps going down to the Park. Two lines of lofty stone houses go off to right and left, and the house they were going to was one of them.

A footman received them with sombre but easy familiarity. The artistes? Yes. They were shown into the library, and light refreshments were brought in to them on a tray. Three other members of the choral company were there already. Glory was seeing it all for the first time, and Koenig was describing and explaining everything in broken whispers.

A band was playing in the well of the circular staircase, and a second footman stood in an alcove behind an outwork of hats and overcoats. The first footman reappeared. Were the artistes ready to go to the drawing-room?

They followed him upstairs. The band had stopped, and there was the distant hum of voices and the crackle of plates. Waiters were coming and going from the dining-room, and the butler stood at the door giving instructions. At one moment there was a glimpse within of ladies in gorgeous dresses, and a table laden with silver and bright with fairy lamps. When the door opened the voices grew louder, when it closed the sounds were deadened.

The upper landing opened on to a salon which had three windows down to the ground, and half of each stood open. Outside there was a wide terrace lit up by Chinese and Moorish lanterns. Beyond was the dark patch of the Park, and farther still the towers of the Abbey and the clock of Westminster, but the great light was not burning to-night.

"De House naivare sits on Vednesday night," said Koenig.

They passed into the drawing-room, which was empty. The standing lamps were subdued by coverings of yellow silk lace. There was a piano and an organ.

"Ve'll stay here," said Koenig, opening the organ, and Glory stood by his side.

Presently there were ripples of laughter, sounds of quick indistinguishable voices, waves of heliotrope, and the rustle of silk dresses on the stairs. Then the ladies entered. Two or three of them who were elderly leaned their right hands on the arms of younger women, and walked with ebony sticks in their left. An old lady wearing black satin and a large brooch came last. Koenig rose and bowed to her. Glory prepared to bow also, but the lady gave her a side inclination of the head as she sat in a well-cushioned chair under a lamp, and Glory's bow was abridged.

The ladies sat and talked, and Glory tried to listen. There were little nothings, punctuated by trills of feminine laughter. She thought the conversation rather silly. More than once the ladies lifted their lorgnettes and looked at her. She set her lips hard and looked back without flinching.

A footman brought tea on a tray, and then there was the tinkle of cup and saucer and more laughter. The lady in satin looked round at Koenig, and he began to play the organ. He played superbly, but nobody seemed to listen. When he finished there was a pause, and everybody said, "Oh, thank you; we're all—er——" and then the talk began again. The vocal soloist sang some ballad of Schumann, and as long as it lasted an old lady with an ear-trumpet sat at the foot of the piano, and a young girl spoke into it. When it was over, everybody said, "Ah, that dear old thing!" Then there was an outbreak of deeper voices from the stairs, with lustier laughter and heavier steps.

The gentlemen appeared, talking loudly as they entered. Koenig was back at the organ, and playing as if he wished it were the 'cello and the drum and the whole brass band. Glory was watching everything; it was beginning to be very funny. Suddenly it ceased to be so. One of the gentlemen was saying in a tired drawl, "Old Koenig again! How the old boy lasts! Seem to have been hearing him since the Flood, don't you know."

It was Lord Robert Ure. Glory caught one glimpse of him, then looked down at her slipper and pawed at the carpet. He put his glass in his eye, screwed up the left side of his face, and looked at her.

An elderly man with a leonine head came up to the organ and said, "Got anything comic, Mr. Koenig? All had the influenza last winter, you know, and lost our taste for the classical."

"Vith pleasure, sir," said Koenig, and then turning to Glory he touched her wrist. "How's de pulse? Ach Gott! beating same like a child's! Now is your turn."

Glory made a step forward, and the talk grew louder as she was observed. She heard fragments of it. "Who is she?" "Is she a professional?" "Oh no—a lady." "Sing, does she, or is it whistling?" "No, she's a professional; we had her last year; she does conjuring." And then the voice she had heard before said, "By Jove, old fellow, your young friend looks like a red standard rose!" She did not flinch. There was a nervous tremor of the lip, a scarcely perceptible curl of it, and then she began.

It was "Mylecharaine," a Manx ballad in the Anglo-Manx, about a farmer who was a miser. His daughter was ashamed of him, because he dressed shabbily and wore yellow stockings; but he answered that if he didn't the stocking wouldn't be yellow that would be forthcoming for her dowry.

She sang, recited, talked, acted, lived the old man, and there was not a sound until she finished, except laughter and the clapping of hands. Then there was a general taking of breath and a renewed outbreak of gossip. "Really, really! How— er—natural!" "Natural—that's it, natural. I never— er——" "Rather good, certainly; in fact, quite amusing." "What dialect is it?" "Irish, of course." "Of course, of course," with many nods and looks of knowledge, and a buzz and a flutter of understanding. "Hope she'll do something else." "Hush! she's beginning."

It was "Ny Kiree fo Niaghtey," a rugged old wail of how the sheep were lost on the mountains in a great snowstorm; but it was full of ineffable melancholy. The ladies dropped their lorgnettes, the men's glasses fell from their eyes and their faces straightened, the noisy old soul with the ear-trumpet sitting under Glory's arm was snuffling audibly, and at the next moment there was a chorus of admiring remarks. "'Pon my word, this is something new, don't you know!" "Fine girl too!" "Fine! Irish girls often run to it." "That old miser—you could see him!"

"What's her next piece?—something funny, I hope."

Koenig's pride was measureless, and Glory did not get off lightly. He cleared the floor for her, and announced that with the indulgence, &c., the young artiste would give an imitation of common girls singing in the street.

The company laughed until they screamed, and when the song was finished Glory was being overwhelmed with congratulations and inquiries. "Charming! All your pieces are charming! But really, my dear young lady, you must be more careful about our feelings. Those sheep now—it was really quite too sad." The old lady with the ear-trumpet asked Glory whether she could go on for the whole of an afternoon, and if she felt much fatigued sometimes, and didn't often catch cold.

But the lady in satin came to her relief at last. "You will need some refreshment," she said. "Let me see now if I cannot . . ." and she lifted her glass and looked round the room. At the next moment a voice that made a shudder pass over her said—

"Perhaps *I* may have the pleasure of taking Miss Quayle down?"

It was Drake. His eyes were as blue and boyish as before, but Glory observed at once that he had grown a moustache, and that his face and figure were firmer and more manlike. A few minutes afterwards they had passed through one of the windows on to the terrace, and were walking to and fro.

It was cool and quiet out there after the heat and hubbub of the drawing-room. The night was soft and still. Hardly a breath of wind stirred the leaves of the trees in the Park below. The rain had left a dewy moistness in the air, and a fragrant mist was lying over the grass. The stars were out, and the moon had just risen behind the towers of Westminster.

Glory was flushed with her success. Her eyes sparkled and her step was light and free. Drake touched her hand as it lay on his arm and said—

"And now that I have got you to myself, I must begin by scolding you."

They looked at one another and smiled.

"Have I displeased you so much to-night?" she said.

"It's not that. Where have you been all this time?"

"Ah, if you only knew!" She had stopped, and was looking into the darkness.

"I *want* to know. Why didn't you answer my letter?"

"Your letter?" She was clutching at the lilies of the valley in her bosom.

He tapped her hand lightly, and said, " Well, we'll not quarrel this time, only don't do it again, you know, or else——"

She recovered herself and laughed. Her voice had a silvery ring, and he thought it was an enchanting smile that played upon her face. They resumed their walk.

"And now about to-night. You have had a success, of course."

"Why of course?"

"Because I always knew you must have."

She was proud and happy. He began to be grave and severe.

"But the drawing-room after dinner is no proper scene for your talents. The audience is not in the right place or the right mood. Guests and auditors—their duties clash. Besides, to tell you the truth, art is a dark continent to people like these."

"They were kind to me, at all events," said Glory.

"To-night, yes. The last new man—the last new monkey——"

She was laughing again, and swinging along on his arm as if her feet hardly touched the ground.

"What is the matter with you?"

"Nothing; I am only thinking how polite you are;" and then they looked at each other again and laughed together.

The mild radiance of the stars was dying into the brighter light of the moon. A bird somewhere in the dark trees below had mistaken the moonlight for the dawn, and was making its early call. The clock at Westminster was striking eleven, and there was the deep rumble of traffic from the unseen streets round about.

"How beautiful!" said Glory. "It's hard to believe that this can be the same London that is so full of casinos and clubs and . . . monasteries.

"Why, what does a girl like you know about such places?"

She had dropped his arm, and was looking over the balcony. The sound of voices came from the red windows behind them. Then the soloist began to sing again. His second ballad was the "Erl King"—

"Du liebes Kind, komm' geh' mit mir!
Gar schöne Spiele spiel' ich mit dir."

"Any news of John Storm?" said Drake.

"Not that I know of."

"I wonder if you would like him to come out again—now."

"I wonder!"

At that moment there was a step behind them, and a soft voice said, "I want you to introduce me, Mr. Drake."

It was a lady of eight or nine-and-twenty, wearing short hair brushed upwards and backwards in the manner of a man.

"Ah, Rosa—Miss Rosa Macquarrie," said Drake. "Rosa is a journalist, and a great friend of mine, Glory. If you want fame, she keeps some of the keys of it, and if you want friendship . . . But I'll leave you together."

"My dear," said the lady, "I want you to let me know you."

"But I've seen you before—and spoken to you," said Glory.

"Why, where?"

Glory was laughing awkwardly. "Never mind now! Some other time perhaps."

"The people inside are raving about your voice. 'Where does it come from?' they are saying—'from a palace or Ratcliffe Highway?' But I think I know. It comes from your heart, my dear. You have lived and loved and suffered—and so have I. Here we are in our smart frocks, dear, but we belong to another world altogether and are the only working women in the company. Perhaps I can help you a little, and you have helped me already. I may know you, may I not?"

There was a deep light in Glory's eyes and a momentary quiver of her eyelids. Then without a word she put her arms about Rosa's neck and kissed her.

"I was sure of you," said Rosa. Her voice was low and husky. "Your name is Glory, isn't it? It wasn't for nothing you were given that name. God gave it you!"

The party was breaking up and Koenig came for "his star." "I vill give you an engagement for one, two, tree year, upon my vord I vill," he said as they went downstairs. While the butler took him back to the library to sign his receipt and receive his cheque, Glory stood waiting by the billiard-table in the hall, and Drake and Lord Robert stepped up to her.

"Until when?" said Drake with a smile, but Glory pretended not to understand him. "I dare say you thought me cynical to-night, Glory. I only meant that if you are to follow this profession I want you to make the best of it. Why not look for a wider scene? Why not go directly to the public?"

"But de lady is engaged to me for tree years," said Koenig, coming up.

Drake looked at Glory, who shook her head, and then Koenig made an effort at explanation. It was an understood thing. He had taught her, taken her into his house, found her in a Sunday——

But Drake interrupted him. If they could help Miss Quayle to a better market for her genius, Mr. Koenig need be no loser by the change. Then Koenig was pacified, and Drake handed Glory down to a cab.

"We're good friends again, aren't we?" he said, touching her hand lightly.

"Yes," she answered.

There was a letter from Aunt Rachel waiting for her at the Priory. Anna didn't like these frequent changes, and she had no faith in music or musicians either, but the Parson thought Anna too censorious, and as for Mr. Koenig's Sunday evening companies, he had no doubt they were of Germans chiefly, and that they came to talk of Martin Luther and to sing his hymn. Sorry to say his infirmities were increasing; the burden of his years was upon him, and he was looking feeble and old.

Glory slept little that night. On going to her room, she threw up the window and sat in front of it, that the soft night breeze might play on her hot lips and cheeks. The moon was high and the garden was slumbering under its gentle light. Everything around was hushed, and there was no sound anywhere except the far-off rumble of the great city as of the wind in distant trees. She was thinking of a question which Drake had put to her.

"I wonder if I should?" she murmured.

And through the silence there was the unheard melody of the German song—

"Du liebes Kind, komm' geh' mit mir!
Gar schöne Spiele spiel' ich mit dir."

XIX

THE PRIORY, *May Day.*

DEAR AUNTIE RACHEL,—The great evening is over! Such dresses, such diamonds—you never saw the like! The smart folks are just like other human beings, and I was not the tiniest bit afraid of them. My own part of the programme went off pretty well, I think. Mr. Koenig had arranged the harmonies and accompaniments of some of our old Manx songs, so I sang "Mylecharaine," and they listened and clapped, and then "Ny Kiree fo Niaghtey," and they cried (and so did I), and then I imitated some work-girls singing in the streets, and they laughed and laughed until I laughed too, and then they laughed because I was laughing, and we all laughed together. It was over and done before I knew where I was, and everybody was covering me with—well, no, not kisses, as grandfather used to do, but the society equivalent—ices and jellies, which the gentlemen were rushing about wildly to get for me.

But all this is as nothing compared to what is to happen next. I mustn't whisper a word about it yet, so false face must hide what the false heart doth know. You'll *have* to forgive me if I succeed, for nothing is wicked in this world except failure, you know, and a little sin must be a great virtue if it has grown to be big enough, you see. There! How sagacious of me! You didn't know what a philosopher you had in the family, did you, my dears?

It is to be on the 24th of May. That will be the Queen's birthday over again; and when I think of all that has happened since the last one, I feel as romantic as a schoolgirl and as sentimental as a nursery-maid. Naturally I am in a fearful flurry over the whole affair, and, to tell the truth, I have hied me to the weird sisters on the subject; that is to say, I have been to a fortune-teller and spent a "goolden" half-sovereign on the creature at one fell swoop. But she predicts wonderful things for me, so I am satisfied. The newspapers are to blaze with my name, I am to have a dazzling success and become the idol of the hour, all of which is delightful and entrancing, and quite reasonable at the money. Grandfather will reprove me for tempting Providence, and of course John Storm, if he knew it, would say that I shouldn't do such things under any circumstances; yet to tell me I oughtn't to do this and I oughtn't to do that is like saying I oughtn't to have red hair and I oughtn't to catch the measles. I can't help it! I can't help it! So what's the good of breaking one's heart about it?

But I hadn't got to wait for *Hecate et cie* for what related to
the newspapers. You must know, dear Aunt Rachel, that I *did*
meet Mr. Drake at the house of the Home Secretary, and he
introduced me to a Miss Rosa Macquarrie, who is no longer
very young or beautiful, but a dear for all that! and she, being
a journalist, has bruited my praises abroad, with the result that
all the world is ringing with my virtues. Listen, all men and
women, while I sound mine own glory out of a column as long
as the Duke of York's: –

"She is young and tall, and has auburn hair" (always thought
it was red myself) "and large grey eyes, one of which seems at
a distance to be brown" (it squints), "giving an effect of humour
and coquetry and power rarely, if ever, seen in any other face.
... Her voice has startling varieties of tone, being at one
moment soft, cooing, and liquid, and at another wild, weird, and
plaintive, and her face, which is not strictly beautiful" (Oh!),
"but striking and unforgettable, has an extraordinary range of
expression. ... She sings, recites, speaks, laughs, and cries
(literally), and some of her selections are given in a sort of Irish
patois" (Oh, my beloved Manx!) "that comes from her girlish
lips with charming vivacity and drollness." All of which,
though it is quite right, and no more than my due, *of course*,
made me sob so long and loud that my good little hippopotamus
came upstairs to comfort me, but finding me lying on the floor,
he threw up his hands and cried, "Ach Gott! I t'ought it vas a
young lady, but vhatever is it?"

Yet wae's me! Sometimes I think how many poor girls there
must be who have never had a chance, while I have had so many
and such glorious ones; who cannot get anybody to listen to
them, while I am so pampered and praised; who live in narrow
alleys and serve in little dark shops, where men and men-things
talk to them as they can't talk to their sisters and wives, while
I am held aloft in an atmosphere of admiration and respect;
who earn their bread in clubs and casinos, where they breathe
the air of the hotbeds of hell, while I am surrounded by everything that ennobles and refines! O God, forgive me if I am a
vain presumptuous creature, laughing at everything and everybody, and sometimes forgetting that many a poor girl who is
being tossed about in London is just as good as me, and as
clever and as brave!

But hoot! "I likes to be jolly and I allus is." So Aunt
Anna doesn't like this Wandering Jew existence! Well, do you
know I always thought I should love a gipsy life. It has a sense
of movement that must be delightful, and then I love going
fast. Do you remember the days when "Cæsar" used to take

the bit in his teeth and bolt with me? Lo, there was little me, astride on his bare back, with nothing to trust to but Providence and a pair of rope reins: but, oh my! I couldn't breathe for excitement and delight! Dear old maddest of created "Cæsars," I feel as if I were whacking at him yet! What do you think of me? But we "that be females are the same craythurs alwis," as old Chalse used to say, and what a woman is in the cradle she continues to be to the end. There again! I wonder who told you that, young lady!

But to tell you the truth at last, dear Aunt Rachel, there is something I have kept back until now, because I couldn't bear the thought of any of you being anxious on my account, especially grandfather, who thinks of Glory so much too often as things are. Can't you guess what it is? I couldn't help taking up my life of Wandering Jew, because I was *dismissed* from the hospital! Didn't you understand that, my dears? I thought I was telling you over and over again. Yes, dismissed as unfit to be a nurse; and so I was, according to the order of the institution first, and human love and pity last. But all's well that ends well, you know, and now that my wanderings seem to be over and I am in my right place at length, I feel like one who is coming out of a long imprisonment, a great peril, a darkness deeper even than John Storm's cell. And if I ever become a famous woman, and good men will listen to me, I will tell them to be tender and merciful to poor girls who are trying to live in London and be good and strong, and that the true chivalry is to band themselves together against the other men who are selfish and cruel and impure. Oh, this great, glorious, devilish, divine, London! It must stand to the human world as the seething, boiling, bubbling waters of Niagara do to the world of nature. Either a girl floats over its rapids like a boat, and in that case she draws her breath and thanks God, or she is tossed into its whirlpool like a dead body and goes round and round until she finds the vortex and is swallowed up!

There! I have blown off my steam, and now to business. Mr. Drake is to give a luncheon-party in his rooms on the twenty-fourth, in honour of my experiment, but the great event itself will not come off until nearly half-past nine that night. By that time the sun will have set over the back of the sea at Peel, the blackbird will have given you his last "guy-smook," and all the world will be dropping asleep. Now, if you'll only remember to say just then, 'God bless Glory!' I'll feel strong and big and brave.

Your poor, silly, sentimental girlie,   GLORY.

XX

SOME weeks had passed, and it was the morning of the last day of John Storm's residence at Bishopsgate Street. After calling the Brotherhood, the Father had entered John's room, and was resting on the end of the bed.

"You are quite determined to leave us?"

"Quite determined, Father."

The Father sighed deeply and said in broken sentences—

"Our house is passing through terrible trials, my son. Perhaps we did wrong to come here. There is no cross in our foundations, and we have built on a worldly footing. 'Unless the Lord build the house. . . .' It was good of you to delay the execution of your purpose, but now that the time has come . . . I had set my heart on you, my son. I am an old man now, and something of the affection of the natural father——"

"Father, if you only knew——"

"Yes, yes; I know, I know. You have suffered, and it is not for me to reproach you. The novitiate has its great joys, but it has its great trials also. Self has to be got rid of, faith has to be exerted, obedience has to be learned, and, above all, the heart has to be detached from its idols in the world—a devoted mother, it may be—a dear sister—perhaps a dearer one still."

There was silence for a moment. John's head was down; he could not speak.

"That you wish to return to the world only shows that you came before you heard the call of God. Some other voice seemed to speak to you, and you listened and thought it was God's voice. But God's voice will come to you yet, and you will hear it and answer it, and not another. . . . Have you anywhere to go to when you leave this house?"

"Yes, the home of a good woman. I have written to her; I think she will receive me."

"All that you brought with you will be returned, and if you want money——"

"No, I came to you as a beggar; let me leave you as a beggar, too."

"There is one thing more, my son."

"What is it, Father?"

The old man's voice was scarcely audible. "You are breaking obedience by leaving us before the end of your novitiate, and the community must separate itself from you, though you are only a novice, as from one who has violated his vow and cast himself off from grace. This will have to be done before you cross our threshold. It is our duty to the Brotherhood; it is also our duty to God. You understand that?"

"Yes."

"It will be in the church a few minutes before mid-day service."

The Father rose to go. "Then that is all?"

"That is all."

The Father's voice was breaking. "Good-bye, my son."

"Good-bye, Father, and God forgive me!"

A leather trunk which John had brought with him on the day he came to the Brotherhood was returned to his room, containing the clothes he had worn in the outer world, as well as his purse and watch and other belongings. He dressed himself in his habit as a clergyman, and put the cassock of the Society over it, for he knew that to remove that must be part of the ordeal of his expulsion. Then the bell rang for breakfast, and he went down to the refectory.

The brothers received him in silence, hardly looking up as he entered, though by their furtive glances he could plainly see that he was the only subject that occupied their thoughts. When the meal was over he tried to mingle among them, that he might say farewell to as many as were willing that he should do so. Some gave him their hands with prompt goodwill, some avoided him, some turned their backs upon him altogether.

But if his reception in the refectory was chilling, his welcome in the courtyard was warm enough. At the first sound of his footstep on the paved way, the dog came from his quarters under the sycamore. One moment the creature stood and looked at him with its sad and bloodshot eyes, then with a bound it threw its fore-paws on his breast, and then plunged around him and uttered deep bays that were like the roar of thunder.

He sat on the seat and caressed the dog, and his heart grew full and happy. The morning was bright with sunshine, the air was fragrant with the leafage of spring, and birds were singing and rejoicing in the tree.

Presently Brother Andrew came and sat beside him. The lay brother, like a human dog, had been following him about all the morning, and now in his feeble way he began to talk of his mother, and to wonder if John would ever see her. Her name was Pincher, and she was a good woman. She lived in Crook Lane, Crown Street, Soho, and kept house for his brother, who was a pawnbroker. But his brother, poor fellow, was much given to drink, and perhaps that had been a reason why he himself had left home. John promised to call on her, and then

Brother Andrew began to cry. The sprawling features of the great fellow were almost laughable to look upon.

The bell rang for Terce. While the brothers were at prayers, John took his last look over the house. With the dog at his heels—the old thing seemed determined to lose sight of him no more—he passed slowly through the hall and into the community-room and up the stairs and down the top corridor. He looked again at every inscription on the wall, though he knew them all by heart and had read them a hundred times. When he came to his own cell, he was touched by a strange tenderness. Place where he had thought so much, prayed so much, suffered so much - it was dear to him after all! He went up on to the tower. How often he had been drawn there as by a devilish fascination! The great city looked innocent enough now under its mantle of sunlight, dotted over with green; but how dense, how difficult! Then the bell rang for midday service, though it was not yet noon, and he went down to the hall. The brothers were there, preparing to go into the church. The order of the procession was the same as on the day of his dedication, except that Brother Paul was no longer with them Brother Andrew going first with the cross, then the lay brothers, then the religious, then the Father, and John Storm last of all.

Though the courtyard was full of sunshine, the church looked dark and gloomy. Curtains were drawn across the windows, and the altar was draped as for a funeral. As soon as the brothers had taken their places in the choir the Father stood on the altar steps and said —

"If any member of this community has one unfaithful thought of going back to the outer world, I charge him to come to this altar now. But woe to him through whom the offence cometh! Woe to him who turns back after taking up the golden plough!"

John was kneeling in his place in the second row of the choir. The eyes of the community were upon him. He hesitated a moment, then rose and stepped up to the altar.

"My son," said the Father, "it is not yet too late. I see your fate as plainly as I see you now. Shall I tell you what it is? Can you bear to hear it? I see you going out into a world which has nothing to satisfy the cravings of your soul. I see you foredoomed to failure and suffering and despair. I see you coming back to us within a year with a broken and bleeding heart. I see you taking the vows of life-long consecration. Can you face that future?"

"I must."

The Father drew a long breath. "It is inevitable," he said,

and taking a book from the altar he read the awful service of the degradation:—

"By the authority of God Almighty, Father (✠), Son and Holy Ghost, and by our own authority, we the members of the Society of the Holy Gethsemane do take away from thee the habit of our Order, and depose and degrade and deprive thee of all rights and privileges in the spiritual goods and prayers which, by the grace of God, are done among us."

"Amen! Amen!" said the brothers.

During the reading of the service John had been kneeling. The Father motioned to him to rise, and proceeded to remove the cord with which he had bound him at his consecration. When this was done he signalled to Brother Andrew to take off the cassock.

The bell was tolled. The Father dropped on his knees. The brothers, hoarse and husky, began to sing *In exitu Israel de Ægypto*. Their heads were down, their voices seemed to come up out of the earth.

It was all over now. John Storm turned about, hardly able to see his way. Brother Andrew went before him to open the door of the sacristy. The lay brother was crying audibly.

The sun was still shining in the courtyard, and the birds were still singing and rejoicing, The first thing of which John was conscious was that the dog was licking his rigid fingers.

A moment later he was in the little covered passage to the street, and Brother Andrew was opening the iron gate.

"Good-bye, my lad."

He stretched out his hand, then remembered that he was an excommunicated man, and tried to draw it back, but the lay brother had snatched at it and lifted it to his lips.

The dog was following him into the street.

"Go back, old friend."

He patted the old creature on the head, and Brother Andrew laid hold of it by the loose skin at its neck. A hansom was waiting for him with his trunk on the top.

"Victoria Square, Westminster," he called. The cab was moving off, when there was a growl and a lurch—the dog had broken away and was running after it.

How crowded the streets were! How deafening was the traffic! The church-bell was ringing for mid-day service. What a thin tinkle it made out there, yet how deep was its boom within! Stock Exchange men, with their leisurely activity, were going in by their seven doorways to their great market-place in Capel Court.

He began to feel a boundless relief. How his heart was

beating! With what a strange and deep emotion he found himself once more in the world! Driving in the dense and devious thoroughfares was like sailing on a cross sea outside a difficult headland. He could smell the brine, and feel the flick of the foam on his lips and cheeks. It was liberty, it was life!

Feeling anxious about the dog, he drew up the cab for a moment. The faithful creature was running under the driver's seat. Before the cab could start again, a line of sandwich-men had passed in front of it. Their boards contained a single word. The word was " GLORIA."

He saw it, yet it barely arrested his consciousness. Somehow it seemed like an echo from the existence he had left behind.

The noises of life were as wine in his veins now. He was burning with impatience to overtake his arrears of knowledge, to see what the world had gone through in his absence. Leaning over the door of the hansom, he read the names of the streets and the signs over the shops, and tried to identify the houses which had been rebuilt and the thoroughfares which had been altered. But the past was the past, and the clock would turn back for no man. These men and women in the streets knew all that had happened. The poorest beggar on the pavement knew more than he did. Nearly a year of his life was gone—in prayer, in penance, in fasting, in visions, in dreams—dropped out, left behind, and lost for ever.

Going by the Bank, the cab drew up again to allow a line of omnibuses to pass into Cheapside. Every omnibus had its board for advertisements, and nearly every board contained the word he had seen before—" GLORIA."

" Only the name of some music-hall singer," he told himself. But the name had begun to trouble him. It had stirred the fibres of memory, and made him think of the past -- of his yacht, of Peel, of his father, and finally of Glory—and again of Glory—and yet again of Glory.

He saw that flags were flying on the Mansion House and on the Bank, and pushing up the trap of the hansom, he asked if anything unusual was going on.

" Lawd, down't ye know what day it is terday, sir? It's the dear ole laidy's birthday. That's why all the wimming's going abart in their penny carridges. Been through a hillness, sir?"

" Yes, something of that sort."

" Thort so, sir."

When the cab started afresh, he began to tell himself what he was going to do in the future. He was going to work among the poor and the outcast, the oppressed and the fallen. He was going to search for them and find them in their haunts of sin and misery. Nothing was to be too mean for him. Nothing was to be common or unclean. No matter about his own good name! No matter if he was only one man in a million! The kingdom of heaven was like a grain of mustard-seed.

When he came within sight of St. Paul's, the golden cross on the dome was flashing like a fiery finger in the blaze of the mid-day sun. That was the true ensign! That was the great example! It was a monstrous and wicked fallacy, a gloomy and narrow formula, that religion had to do with the affairs of the other world only. Work was religion! Work was prayer! Work was praise! Work was the love of man and the glory of God!

Glorious gospel! Great and deathless symbol!

END OF SECOND BOOK

THIRD BOOK.—THE DEVIL'S ACRE

I

BEHIND Buckingham Palace there is a little square of modest houses, standing back from the tide of traffic, and nearly always as quiet as a cloister. At one angle of the square is a house somewhat larger than the rest, but just as simple and unassuming. In the dining-room of this house an elderly lady was sitting down to lunch alone, with the covers laid for another at the opposite end of the table.

"Hae ye the spare room ready, Emma?"

"Yes, ma'am," said the maid.

"And the sheets done airing? And baith the pillows? And the pillow-slips—and everything finished?"

The maid was answering "Yes" to each of these questions when a hansom-cab came rattling up to the front of the house, and the old lady leapt out of her seat.

"It's himsel'," she cried, and she ran like a girl to the hall.

The door had been opened before she got there, and a deep voice was saying, "Is Mrs Callender——"

"It's John! My gracious! It's John Storm!" the old woman cried, and she lifted both hands as if to fling herself into his arms.

"My guidness, laddie, but you gave puir auld Jane sic a start! Expected ye? To be sure we expected ye, and terribly thrang we've been all morning making ready. Only my daft auld brain must have been a wee ajee. But," smiling through her tears, "has a body never a cheek that you must be kissing at her hand? And is this your dog?" looking down at the bloodhound. "Welcome? Why, of course, it's welcome. What was I saying the day, Emma? 'I'd like fine to have a dog,' didn't I? and here it is to our hand. Awa' wi' ye, James, man, and show Mr. Storm to his room, and then find a bed for the creature somewhere. Letters for ye, laddie? Letters enough, and you'll find them on the table upstairs. Only, mind ye, the lunch is ready, and your fish is getting cold."

John Storm opened his letters in his room. One of them was

from his uncle, the Prime Minister: "I rejoice to hear of your most sensible resolution. Come and dine with me at Downing Street this day week at seven o'clock. I have much to say and much to ask, and I expect to be quite alone."

Another was from his father: "I am not surprised at your intelligence; but if anything could exceed the folly of going into a monastery it is the imbecility of coming out of it. The former appears to be a subject of common talk in this island already, and no doubt the latter will soon be so."

John flinched as at a cut across the face, and then smiled a smile of relief. Apparently Glory was writing home, wherever she was, and there was good news in that, at all events. He went downstairs.

"Come your ways in, laddie, and let me look at ye again. Man, but your face is pale, and your bonnie eyes are that sunken. But sit ye down and eat. They've been starving ye, I'm thinking, and miscalling it religion. It's enough to drive a reasonable body to drink. Carnal I am, laddie, and I just want to put some flesh on your bones. Monks indeed! And in this age of the world too! Little Jack Horners sitting in corners saying, 'Oh, what a good boy am I!'"

John defended his late brethren. They were holy men; they lived a holy life; he had not been good enough for their company.

"But I feel like a sailor home from sea," he said; "tell me what has happened."

"Births, marriages, and deaths? I suppose ye're like the lave of the men and think nothing else matters to a woman. But come now, more chicken? No? A wee bitty! Aye, but ye're sair altered, laddie. Weel, where can a body begin?"

"The Canon—how is he?"

"Fine as fi'pence. Guid as ever in the pulpit? Aye, but it's a pity he doesna bide there, for he's mething to be windy of when he comes out of it. Deacon now, bless ye, or archdeacon, or some sic botherment, and his daughter is to be married to yon slip of a curate with the rabbit mouth and the heather legs. Weel, she wasna for all markets, ye ken."

"And Mrs. Macrae?"

"Gone over to the angels. Dead? Nae, ye're too expecting altogether. She's got religion though, and holds missionary meetings in her drawing-room of a Monday, and gives lunches to actor folk of a Sunday, and now a poor woman that's been working for charity and Christianity all her days has no chance with her anyway."

"And Miss Macrae?"

"Poor young leddy, they're for marrying her at last! Aye, to that Ure man, that lord thing, with the eyeglass. I much misdoubt but her heart's been somewhere else, and there's ane auld woman would a hantle rather have heard tell of her getting the richt man than seeing the laddie bury himsel' in a monastery. She's gi'en in at last though, and it's to be a grand wedding, they're telling me. Some of your Americans are kittle cattle— just the Jews of the West seemingly- and they must do everything splendiferously. There are to be jewels as big as walnuts, and bouquets five feet in diameter, and a rope of pearls for a necklace, and a rehearsal of the hale thing in the church. Aye, indeed, a rehearsal; and the 'deacon, honest man, in the middle of the magnificence."

John Storm's pale face was twitching. "And the hospital," he said; "has anything happened there?"

"Nothing."

"No other case such as the one——"

"Not since yon poor bit lassie."

"Thank God!"

"It was the first ill thing I had heard tell of for years, and the nurses are good women for all that. High-spirited? Aye, but dear, bright, happy things, to think what they have to know and to be present at! Lawyers, doctors, and nurses see the worst of human nature, and she'd be a heartless woman who'd no make allowance for them, poor creatures!"

John Storm had risen from the table with a flushed face, making many excuses. He would step round to the hospital; he had questions to ask there, and it would be a walk after luncheon.

"Do," said Mrs. Callender; "but remember dinner at six. And, hark ye, hinny, this house is to be your hame until you light on a better one, so just sleep saft in it and wake merrily. And Jane Callender is to be your auld auntie until some ither body tak's ye frae her, and then it'll no be her hand ye'll be kissing for fear of her wrinkles, I'm thinking."

The day was bright, the sun was shining, and the streets were full of well-groomed horses in gorgeous carriages, with coachmen in splendid liveries, going to the Drawing-room in honour of the royal birthday. As John went by the palace the approaches to it were thronged. The band of the Household Cavalry was playing within the rails, and officers in full-dress uniform, members of the diplomatic service with swords and cocked hats, and ladies in gorgeous brocades, carrying bouquets of orchids, and wearing tiaras of diamonds and large white plumes, were filing through the gates towards the Throne-room.

The hospital looked strangely unfamiliar after so short an absence, and there were new faces among the nurses who passed to and fro in the corridors. John asked for the matron, and was received with constrained and distant courtesy. Was he well? Quite well? They had a resident chaplain now, and being in priest's orders, he had many opportunities where death was so frequent. Was he sure he had not been ill? John understood—it was almost as if he had come out of some supernatural existence, and people looked at him as if they were afraid.

"I came to ask if you could tell me anything of Nurse Quayle?"

The matron could tell him nothing. The girl had gone; they had been compelled to part with her. Nothing serious? No; but totally unfit to be a nurse. She had some good qualities certainly — cheerfulness, brightness, tenderness — and for sake of these, and his own interest in the girl, they had put up with inconceivable rudeness and irregularities. What had become of her? She really could not say. Nurse Allworthy might know—and the matron took up her pen.

John found the ward sister with the house-surgeon at the bed of a patient. She was short, even curt, said over her shoulder she knew nothing about the girl, and then turned back to her work. As John passed out of the ward the doctor followed him, and hinted that perhaps the porter might be able to tell him something.

The porter was difficult at first, but seeing his way clearer after a while, he admitted to receiving letters for the nurse, and delivering them to her when she called. That was long ago, and she had not been there since New Year's Eve. Then she had given him a shilling, and said she would trouble him no more.

John gave him five shillings, and asked if anybody ever called for her. Yes, once. Who was it? A gentleman. Had he left his name? No, but he had said he would write. When was that? A day or two before she was there the last time.

Drake! There could not be a doubt of it. John Storm looked at the clock. It was 3.45. Then he buttoned his coat and crossed the street to the Park, with his face in the direction of St. James's Street.

Horatio Drake had given a luncheon in his rooms that day in honour of Glory's first public appearance. The performance was to come off at night, but in the course of the morning there had been a dress rehearsal in the salon of the music-hall. Twenty men and women, chiefly journalists and artists, had assembled there to get a first glimpse of the *débutante*, and cameras had lurked behind portières and in alcoves to catch her poses, her expressions, her fleeting smiles and humorous grimaces. Then the company had adjourned to Drake's chambers. The luncheon was now over, the last guest had gone, and the host was in his dining-room alone.

Drake was standing by the chimney-piece, holding at arm's length a pencil sketch of a woman's beautiful face and lithe figure. "Like herself, alive to the finger-tips," he thought, and then he propped it against the pier-glass.

There was a sound of the opening and closing of the outer door downstairs, and Lord Robert entered the room. He looked heated, harassed, and exhausted. Shaking out his perfumed pocket-handkerchief, he mopped his forehead, drew a long breath, and dropped into a chair.

"I've done it," he said; "it's all over."

Polly Love had lunched with the company that day, and Lord Robert had returned home with her in order to break the news of his approaching marriage. While the girl had been removing her hat and jacket he had sat at the piano and thumbed it, hardly knowing how to begin. All at once he had said, "Do you know, my dear, I'm to be married on Saturday?" She had said nothing at first, and he had played the piano furiously. Heavens! what a frame of mind to be in! Why didn't the girl speak? At last he had looked round at her, and there she stood grinning, gasping, and white as a ghost. Suddenly she had begun to cry. Good God! such crying! Yes, it was all over. Everything had been settled somehow.

"But I'll be in harder condition before I tackle such a job again."

There was silence for a moment. Drake was leaning on the mantelpiece, his legs crossed, and one foot beating on the hearthrug. The men were ashamed, and they began to talk of indifferent things. Smoke? Don't mind. Those Indian cigars were good. Not bad, certainly.

At length Drake said in a different voice, "Cruel but necessary, Robert—necessary to the woman who is going to be your wife, cruel to the poor girl who has been."

Lord Robert rose to his feet impatiently, stretched his arm and shot out his striped cuff, and walked to and fro across the room.

"'Pon my soul, I believe I should have stuck to the little thing but for the old girl, don't you know. She's made such good social running lately . . . And then she's started this evangelical craze, too . . . No, Polly wouldn't have suited her book anyhow."

Silence again, and then further talk on indifferent things.

"Wish Benson wouldn't sweep the soda-water off the table."

"Ring for it."

"The little thing really cares for me, don't you know. And it isn't my fault, is it? I had to hedge. Frank, dear boy, you're always taunting me with the treadmill we have to turn for the sake of society and so forth, but with debts about a man's neck like a millstone, what could one do?"

"I don't mean that you're worse than others, old fellow, or that sacrificing this one poor child is going to mend matters much."

"No, it isn't likely to improve my style of going, is it?"

"But that man John Storm was not so far wrong after all, and for this polygamy of our 'lavender glove tribe' the nation itself will be overtaken by the judgment of God one of these days."

Lord Robert broke into a peal of derisive laughter. "Go on," he cried. "Go on, dear boy! It's funny to hear you, though—after to-day's proceedings, too," and he glanced significantly around the table.

Drake brought down his fist with a thump on to the mantelpiece. "Hold your tongue, Robert. How often am I to tell you this is a different thing entirely? Because I discover a creature of genius, and try to help her to the position she deserves——"

"You hypocrite! if it had been a man instead of a charming little woman with big eyes, don't you know——"

But there had been a ring at the outer door, and Benson came in to say that a clergyman was waiting downstairs.

"Little Golightly again!" said Lord Robert wearily. "Are these everlasting arrangements never——"

The man stopped him. It was not Mr. Golightly; it was a stranger; would not give his name; looked like a Catholic priest; had been there before, he thought.

"Can it be—talk of the devil——"

"Ask him up," said Drake. And while Drake bit his lip and clenched his hands, and Lord Robert took up a scent-bottle and sprayed himself with eau de Cologne, they saw a man clad in the long coat of a priest come into the room—calm, grave, self-possessed, very pale, with hollow and shaven cheeks, and dark and sunken eyes which burned with a sombre fire, and head so closely cropped as to seem to be almost bald.

John Storm's anger had cooled. As he crossed the Park the heat of his soul had turned to fear, and while he stood in the hall below, with an atmosphere of perfume about him, and even a delicate sense of a feminine presence, his fear had turned to terror. On that account he had refused to send up his name, and on going up the staircase lined with prints, he had been tempted to turn about and fly lest he should come upon Glory face to face. But finding only the two men in the room above, his courage came back, and he hated himself for his treacherous thought of her.

"You will forgive me for this unceremonious visit, sir," he said, addressing himself to Drake.

Drake motioned him to be seated. He bowed but continued to stand.

"Your friend will remember that I have been here before."

Lord Robert bent his head and went on trifling with the spray.

"It was a painful errand, relating to a girl who had been nurse at the hospital. The girl was nothing to me, but she had a companion who was very much."

Drake nodded and his lips stiffened, but he did not speak.

"You are aware that since then I have been away from the hospital. I wrote to you on the subject; you will remember that."

"Well?" said Drake.

"I have only just returned, and have come direct from the hospital now."

"Well?"

"I see you know what I mean, sir. My young friend has gone. Can you tell me where to find her?"

"Sorry I cannot," said Drake coldly, and it stung him to see a look of boundless relief cross the grave face in front of him.

"Then you don't know——"

"I didn't say that," said Drake, and then the lines of pain came back.

"At the request of her people I brought her up to London, sir. Naturally they will look to me for news of her, and I feel responsible for her welfare."

"If that is so, you must pardon me for saying you've taken your duty lightly," said Drake.

John Storm gripped the rail of the chair in front of him and there was silence for a moment.

"Whatever I may have to blame myself with in the past, it would relieve me to find her well and happy and safe from all harm."

"She *is* well and happy and safe too—I can tell you that much."

There was another moment of silence, and then John Storm said in broken sentences and in a voice that was struggling to control itself, "I have known her since she was a child, sir . . . You cannot think how many tender memories . . . It is nearly a year since I saw her, and one likes to see old friends after an absence."

Drake did not speak, but he dropped his head, for John's eyes had begun to fill.

"We were good friends too. Boy and girl comrades almost. Brother and sister, I should say, for that was how I liked to think of myself—her elder brother, bound to take care of her."

There was a little trill of derisive laughter from the other side of the room, where Lord Robert had put the spray down noisily, and turned to look out into the street. Then John Storm drew himself up and said in a firm voice—

"Gentlemen, why should I mince matters? I will not do so. The girl we speak of is more to me than anybody else in the world besides. Perhaps she was one of the reasons why I went into that monastery. Certainly she is the reason I have come out of it. I have come to find her. I *shall* find her. If she is in difficulty or danger I intend to save her. Will you tell me where she is?"

"Mr. Storm," said Drake, "I am sorry, very sorry, but what you say compels me to speak plainly. The lady is well and safe and happy. If her friends are anxious about her, she can reassure them for herself, and no doubt has already done so. But in the position she occupies at present, you are a dangerous man. It might not be her wish, and it would not be to her advantage, to meet with you, and I cannot allow her to run the risk."

"Has it come to that? Have you a right to speak for her, sir?"

"Perhaps I have——" Drake hesitated, and then said with a rush, "the right to protect her against a fanatic."

John Storm curbed himself; he had been through a long schooling. "Man, be honest," he said. "Either your interest is good or bad, selfish or unselfish. Which is it?"

Drake made no answer.

"But it would be useless to bandy words. I didn't come here to do that. Will you tell me where she is?"

"No."

"Then it is to be a duel between us—is that so? You for the girl's body and I for her soul? Very well, I take your challenge."

There was silence once more, and John Storm's eyes wandered about the room. They fixed themselves at length on the sketch by the pier-glass.

"On my former visit I met with the same reception. The girl could take care of herself. It was no business of mine. How that relation has ended I do not ask. But this one——"

"This one is an entirely different matter," said Drake, "and I will thank you not to ——"

But John Storm was making the sign of the cross on his breast, and saying, as one who was uttering a prayer, "God grant it is and always may be!"

At the next moment he was gone from the room. The two men stood where he had left them until his footsteps had ceased on the stairs and the door had closed behind him. Then Drake cried, "Benson—a telegraph form! I must telegraph to Koenig at once."

"Yes, he'll follow her up on the double-quick," said Lord Robert. "But what matter? His face will be enough to frighten the girl. Ugh! It was the face of a death's-head."

At dinner that night John Storm was more than usually silent. To break in upon his gravity, Mrs. Callender asked him what he intended to do next.

"To take priest's orders without delay," he said.

"And what then?"

"Then," he said, lifting a twitching and suffering face, "to make an attack on the one mighty stronghold of the devil's kingdom, whereof woman is the direct and immediate victim; to tell Society over again it is an organised hypocrisy for the pursuit and demoralisation of woman, and the Church that bachelorhood is not celibacy, and polygamy is against the laws of God; to look and search for the beaten and broken who lie scattered and astray in our bewildered cities, and to protect them and shelter them whatever they are, however low they have fallen, because they are my sisters and I love them."

"God bless ye, laddie! That's spoken like a man," said the old woman, rising from her seat.

But John Storm's pale face had already flushed up to the eyes, and he dropped his head as one who was ashamed.

II

At eight o'clock that night John Storm was walking through the streets of Soho. The bell of a jam-factory had just been rung, and a stream of young girls in big hats with gorgeous flowers and sweeping feathers were pouring out of an archway and going arm-in-arm down the pavement. Men standing in groups at street ends shouted to them as they passed, and they shouted back in shrill voices and laughed with wild joy. In an alley round one corner an organ-man was playing "Ta-ra-ra-boom-de-ay," and some of the girls began to dance and sing around him. Coming to the main artery of traffic, they were almost run down by a splendid equipage which was cutting across two thoroughfares into a square, and they screamed with mock terror as the fat coachman in tippet and cockade bellowed to them to get out of the way.

The square was a centre of gaiety. Theatres and music-halls lined two of its sides, and the gas on their façades and the beacons on their roofs were beginning to burn brightly in the fading daylight. With skips and leaps the girls passed over to the doors of these palaces, and peered with greedy eyes through lines of policemen and doorkeepers in livery at gentlemen in shields of shirt-front and ladies in light cloaks and long white gloves, stepping in satin slippers and patent leather shoes out of gorgeous carriages into gorgeous halls.

John Storm was looking on at this masquerade when suddenly he became aware that the flare of coarse lights on the front of the building before him formed the letters of a word. The word was "GLORIA." Seeing it again as he had seen it in the morning, but now identified and explained, he grew hot and cold by turns, and his brain, which refused to think, felt like a sail that is flapping idly on the edge of the wind.

There was a garden in the middle of the square, and he walked round and round it. He gazed vacantly at a statue in the middle of the garden and then walked round the rails again. The darkness was gathering fast, the gas was beginning to blaze, and he was like a creature in the coil of a horrible fascination. That word, that name over the music-hall, fizzing and crackling in its hundred lights, seemed to hold him as by an eye of fire. And remembering what had happened since he left the monastery—the sandwich-men, the boards on the omnibuses, the hoardings on the walls—it seemed like a fiery finger which had led him to that spot. Only one thing was clear—that a supernatural power had brought him there, and that it was intended he should come. Fearfully, shamefully, miserably, rebuking himself for his doubts, yet conquered and compelled by them, he crossed the street and entered the music-hall.

He was in the pit, and it was crowded, not a seat vacant anywhere, and many persons standing packed in the crush-room at the back. His first sensation was of being stared at. First the man at the pay-box and then the cheek-taker had looked at him, and now he was being looked at by the people about him. They were both men and girls. Some of the men wore light frock-coats and talked in the slang of the racecourse; some of the girls wore noticeable hats and showy flowers in their bosoms, and were laughing in loud voices. They made a way for him of themselves, and he passed through to a wooden barrier that ran round the last of the pit seats.

The music-hall was large, and to John Storm's eyes, straight from the poverty of his cell, it seemed garish in the red and gold of its Eastern decorations. Men in the pit seats were smoking pipes and cigarettes, and waiters with trays were hurrying up and down the aisles serving ale and porter, which they set down on ledges like the book-rests in church. In the stalls in front, which were not so full, gentlemen in evening dress were smoking cigars, and there was an arc of the tier above in which people in fashionable costumes were talking audibly. Higher yet, and unseen from that position, was a larger audience still, whose voices rumbled like a distant sea. A cloud of smoke filled the atmosphere, and from time to time there was the sound of popping corks and breaking glasses and rolling bottles.

The curtain was down, but the orchestra was beginning to play. Two men in livery came from the sides of the curtain and fixed up large figures in picture-frames that were attached to the wings of the proscenium. Then the curtain rose and the entertainment was resumed. It was in sections, and after each performance the curtain was dropped and the waiters went round with their trays again.

John Storm had seen it all before in the days when, under his father's guidance, he had seen everything—the juggler, the acrobat, the step-dancer, the comic singer, the tableaux and the living picture. He felt tired and ashamed, yet he could not bring himself to go away. As the evening advanced he thought, "How foolish! What madness it was to think of such a thing!" He was easier after that, and began to listen to the talk of the people about him. It was free, but not offensive. In the frequent intervals some of the men played with the girls, pushing and nudging and joking with them, and the girls laughed and answered back. Occasionally one of them would turn her head aside and look into John's face with a saucy smile. "God forbid that I should grudge them their pleasure," he thought. "It's all they have, poor creatures."

But the audience grew noisier as the evening went on. They called to the singers, made inarticulate squeals, and then laughed at their own humour. A lady sang a comic song. It described her attempt to climb to the top of an omnibus on a windy day. John turned to look at the faces behind him, and every face was red and hot, and grinning and grimacing. He was still half-buried in the monastery he had left that morning, and he thought, "Such are the nightly pleasures of our people. To-night, to-morrow night, the night after! Oh, my country, my country!"

He was awakened from these thoughts by an outburst of applause. The curtain was down and nothing was going on except the putting up of a new figure in the frames. The figure was 8. Some one behind him said, "That's her number!" "The new *artiste?*" said another voice. "Gloria," said the first.

John Storm's head began to swim. He looked back—he was in a solid block of people. "After all, what reasons have I?" he thought, and he determined to stand his ground.

More applause. Another leader of the orchestra had appeared. Baton in hand, he was bowing from his place before the footlights. It was Koenig, the organist, and John Storm shuddered in the darkest corner of his soul.

The stalls had filled up unawares to him, and a party was now coming into a private box which had hitherto been empty. The late-comers were Drake and Lord Robert Ure, and a lady with short hair brushed back from her forehead.

John Storm felt the place going round him, yet he steadied and braced himself. "But this is the natural atmosphere of such people," he thought. He tried to find satisfaction in the thought that Glory was not with them. Perhaps they had exaggerated their intimacy with her.

The band began to play. It was music for the entrance of a new performer. The audience became quiet, there was a keen, eager, expectant air, and then the curtain went up. John Storm felt dizzy. If he could have escaped he would have turned and fled. He gripped with both hands the rail in front of him.

Then a woman came gliding on to the stage. She was a tall girl in a dark dress and long black gloves, with red hair and a head like a rose. It was Glory! A cloud came over John Storm's eyes and for a few moments he saw no more.

There was some applause from the pit and the regions overhead. The people in the stalls were waving their handkerchiefs, and the lady in the box was kissing her hand. Glory was smiling, quite at her ease, apparently not at all nervous, only a little shy and with her hands interlaced in front of her. Then there was silence again and she began to sing

It is the moment when prayers go up from the heart not used to pray. Strange contradiction! John Storm found himself praying that Glory might do well, that she might succeed and eclipse everything! But he had turned his eyes away, and the sound of her voice was even more afflicting than the sight of her face. It was nearly a year since he had heard it last, and now he was hearing it under these conditions, in a place like this! He must have been making noises by his breathing. "Hush! hush!" said the people about him, and somebody tapped him on the shoulder.

After a moment he regained control of himself, and he lifted his head and listened. Glory's voice, which had been quavering at first, gathered strength. She was singing "Mylecharaine," and the wild, plaintive harmony of the old Manx ballad was floating in the air like the sound of the sea. After her first lines a murmur of approval went round, the people sat up and leaned forward, and then there was silence again, dead silence, and then loud applause.

But it was only with the second verse that the humour of her song began, and John Storm waited for it with a trembling heart. He had heard her sing it a hundred times in the old days, and she was singing it now as she had sung it before. There were the same tricks of voice, the same tricks of gesture, the same expressions, the same grimaces. Everything was the same and yet everything was changed. He knew it. He was sure it must be so. So artless and innocent then, now so subtle and significant. Where was the difference? The difference was in the place, in the people. John Storm could have found it in his heart to turn on the audience and insult them. Foul-minded creatures, laughing, screaming, squealing, punctuating their own base interpretations, and making evil of what was harmless. How he hated the grinning faces round about him!

When the song was finished Glory swept a gay curtsey, lifted her skirts and tripped off the stage. Then there were shouting, whistling, stamping, and deafening applause. The whole house was unanimous for an encore, and she came back smiling and bowing with a certain look of elation and pride. John Storm was becoming terrified by his own anger. "Be quiet there," said some one behind him. "Who's the josser?" said somebody else, and then he heard Glory's voice again.

It was another Manx ditty. A crew of young fishermen are going ashore on Saturday night after their week on the sea after the herring. They go up to the inn; their sweethearts meet them there; they drink and sing. At length they are so overcome by liquor and love that they have to be put to bed in their big sea-boots. Then the girls kiss them and leave them. The singer imitated the kissing, and the delighted audience repeated the sound. Sounds of kissing came from all parts of the hall, mingled with loud acclamations of laughter. The singer smiled and kissed back. Somehow she conveyed the sense of a confidential feeling, as if she were doing it for each separate person

in the audience, and each person had an impulse to respond.
It was irresistible, it was maddening, it swept over the whole
house.

John Storm felt sick in his very soul. Glory knew well what
she was doing. She knew what these people wanted. His
Glory! Glory of the old, innocent, happy days! O God!
O God! If he could only get out! But that was impossible.
Behind him the dense mass was denser than ever, and he was
tightly wedged in by a wall of faces—hot, eager, with open
mouths, teeth showing, and glittering and dancing eyes. He
tried not to listen to what the people about were saying, yet he
could not help but hear.

"Tasty, ain't she?" "Cerulean, eh?" "Bit 'ot, certinly!"
"Well, if I was a Johnny, and had got the oof, she'd have a
brougham and a sealskin to-morrow." "To-night, you mean,"
and then there were significant squeaks and trills of laughter.

They called her back again, and yet again, and she returned
with unaffected cheerfulness and a certain look of triumph. At
one moment she was doing the gaiety of youth, and at the next
the crabbedness of age, now the undeveloped femininity of the
young girl, then the volubility of the old woman. But John
Storm was trying to hear none of it. With his head on his
breast and his eyes down he was struggling to think of the
monastery and to imagine that he was still buried in his cell.
It was only this morning that he left it, yet it seemed to be a
hundred years ago. Last night the Brotherhood, the singing
of Evensong, Compline, the pure air, silence, solitude, and the
atmosphere of prayer; and to-night the crowds, the clouds of
smoke, the odour of drink, the meaning laughter, and Glory as
the centre of it all!

For a moment everything was blotted out, and then there was
loud hand-clapping and cries of "Bravo!" He lifted his head.
Glory had finished and was bowing herself off. The lady in the
private box flung her a bouquet of damask roses. She picked it
up and kissed it, and bowed to the box, and then the acclamations
of applause were renewed.

The crush behind relaxed a little, and he began to elbow his
way out. People were rising or stirring everywhere, and the
house was emptying fast. As the audience surged down the
corridors to the doors they talked and laughed and made inarticulate
sounds. "A tricky bit of muslin, eh?" "Yus; she's
thick." "She's my dart, anyhow." Then the whistling of a
tune. It was the chorus of "Mylecharaine." John Storm felt
the cool air of the street on his hot face at last. The policemen
were keeping a way for the people coming from the stalls, the

doorkeepers were whistling or shouting for cabs, and their cries were being caught up by the match-boys, who were running in and out like dogs among the carriage wheels and the horses' feet. "En-sim!" "Four-wheel-er!"

In a narrow court at the back, dimly lit and not much frequented, there was a small open door under a lamp suspended from a high blank wall. This was the stage-door of the music-hall, and a group of young men, looking like hairdressers' assistants, blocked the pavement at either side of it. "Wonder what she's like off." "Like a laidy, you bet." "Yus; but none o' yer bloomin' hamatoors." "Gawd, here's the josser again!"

John Storm pushed his way through to where a commissionaire sat behind a glass partition in a little room walled with pigeon-holes.

"Can I see Miss Quayle?" he asked.

The porter looked blank.

"Gloria, then," said John Storm with an effort.

The porter looked at him suspiciously. Had he an appointment? No; but could he send in his name? The porter looked doubtful. Would she come out soon? The porter did not know. Would she come this way? The porter could not tell. Could he have her address?

"If ye want to write to the laidy, write here," said the porter, with a motion of his hand to the pigeon-holes.

John Storm felt humiliated and ashamed. The hairdressers' assistants were grinning at him. He went out feeling that Glory was farther than ever from him now, and if he met her they might not speak. But he could not drag himself away. In the darkness under a lamp at the other side of the street he stood and waited. Shoddy broughams drove up, with drivers in shabby livery, bringing "turns" in wonderful hats and overcoats, over impossible wigs, whiskers, and noses—niggers, acrobats, clowns, and comic singers, who stepped out, shook the straw of their carriage carpets off their legs, and passed in at the stage entrance.

At length the commissionaire appeared at the door and whistled, and a hansom-cab rattled up to the end of the court. Then a lady muffled in a cape, with the hood drawn over her head, and carrying a bouquet of roses, came out leaning on the arm of a gentleman. She stood a moment by his side and spoke to him and laughed. John heard her laughter. At the next moment she had stepped into the hansom, the door had fallen to, the driver had turned, the gentleman had raised his hat, the light had fallen on the lady's face, and she was leaning forward and smiling. John saw her smiles.

At the next moment the hansom had passed into the illuminated thoroughfares and the group of people had dispersed. John Storm was alone under the lamp in the little dark street, and somewhere in the dark alleys behind him the organ-man was still grinding out " Ta ra-ra-boom-de-ay."

" Weel, what luck on your first night out ? " said Mrs. Callender at breakfast in the morning. " Found any of the poor lost things yet ? "

" One," said John, with a rueful face, " Lost enough, though she doesn't know it yet, God help her ! "

" They never do at first, laddie. Write to her friends if she has any."

" Her friends ? "

" Nothing like home influences, ye ken."

" I will—I must ! It's all I can do now."

III

THE PRIORY, *Friday morning.*

On, my dear aunties, don't be terrified, but Glory has had a kind of a wee big triumph ! Nothing very awful, you know, but on Monday night, before a rather larger company than usual, she sang and recited and play-acted a little, and as a result all the earth—the London earth—is talking about her, and nobody is taking any notice of the rest of the world. Every post is bringing me flowers with ribbons and cards attached, or illustrated weeklies with my picture and my life in little, and I find it's wonderful what a lot of things you may learn about yourself if you'll only read the papers. My room at this moment is like a florist's window at nine o'clock on Saturday morning, and I have reason to suspect that mine host and teacher, Carl Koenig, F.R.C.O., exhibits them to admiring neighbours when I am out. The voice of that dear old turtle has ever since Monday been heard in the land, and besides telling me about Poland day and night from all the subterranean passages of the house, he has taken to waiting on me like a nigger and ordering soups and jellies for me as if I had suddenly become an invalid. Of course I am an able-bodied woman just the same as ever, but my nerves have been on the rack all the week, and I feel exactly as I did long ago at Peel when I was a little naughty minx and got up into the tower of the old church and began pulling at the bell rope, you remember. Oh dear ! Oh dear ! My frantic terror at the noise of the big bells and the vibration of the shaky old walls! Once I had begun I couldn't leave off for my life, but went on tugging and tugging and quaking and quaking until - have you forgotten it? - all the people came running helter-skelter under the impression that the town was afire. And then, behold, it was only little me, trembling like a leaf and crying like a ninny! I remember I was scolded and smacked and dismissed into outer darkness (it was the chip vault, I think), for that first outbreak of fame, and now, lest you should want to mete out the same punishment to me again . . .

Aunt Anna, I'm knitting the sweetest little shawl for you, dear—blue and white to suit your complexion—being engaged in the evening only, and most of the day sole mistress of my own will and pleasure. How charming of me, isn't it? But I'm afraid it isn't, because you'll see through me like a colander, for I want to tell you something which I have kept back too long, and when I think of it I grow old and wrinkled like a Christmas apple. So you must be a pair of absolute old angels, aunties, and break the news to grandfather.

You know I told you, Aunt Rachel, to say something for me at nine o'clock on the Queen's birthday. And you remember that Mr. Drake used to think pearls and diamonds of Glory and predict wonderful things for her. Then you don't forget that Mr. Drake had a friend named Lord Robert Ure, commonly called Lord Bob. Well, you see, by Mr. Drake's advice and Lord Bobbie's influence and agency, and I don't know what, I have made one more change—it's to be the last, dears, the very last—in my Wandering Jew existence, and now I am no longer a society entertainer, because I am a music-hall art——

Glory had written so far when she dropped the pen and rose from the table wiping her eyes.

"My poor child, you can't tell them, it's impossible; they would never forgive you!"

Then a carriage stopped before the house, the garden-bell was rung, and the maid came into the room with a lady's card. It was inscribed "Miss Polly Love," with many splashes and flourishes.

"Ask her up," said Glory. And then Polly came rustling up the stairs in a silver-grey silk dress and a showy hat, and with a pug-dog tucked under her arm. She looked older and less beautiful. The pink and ivory of her cheeks was coated with powder, and her light grey eyes were pencilled. There was the same blemished appearance as before, and the crack in the vase was now plainly visible. Glory had met the girl only once since they parted after the hospital, but Polly kissed her effusively. Then she sat down and began to cry.

"Perhaps you wouldn't think it, my dear, but I'm the most miserable girl in London. Haven't you heard about it? I thought everybody knew. Robert is going to be married. Yes, indeed, to-morrow morning to that American heiress, and I hadn't an idea of it until Monday afternoon. That was the day of your luncheon, dear, and I felt sure something was going to happen, because I broke my looking-glass dressing to go out. Robert took me home, and he began to play the piano, and I could see he was going to say something. 'Do you know, little woman, I'm to be married on Saturday?' I wonder I didn't drop, but I didn't, and he went on playing. But it was no use trying, and I burst out and ran into my room. After a minute I heard him coming in, but he didn't lift me up as he used to do. Only talked to me over my back, telling me to control myself, and what he was going to do for me, and so on. He used to say a few tears made me nicer looking, but it was no good crying—and then he went away."

She began to cry again, and the dog in her lap began to howl.

"O God! I don't know what I've done to be so unfortunate. I've not been flash at all, and I never went to cafés at night, or to Sally's or Kate's, as so many girls do, and he can't say I ever took notice of anybody else. When I love anybody I think of him last thing at night and first thing in the morning, and now to be left alone . . . I'm sure I shall never live through it!"

Glory tried to comfort the poor broken creature. It was her duty to live. There was her child—had she never even seen it since she parted with it to Mrs. Jupe? It must be such a darling by this time, creeping about and talking a little, wherever it was. She ought to have the child to live with her, it would be such company.

Polly kissed the pug to stop its whining, and said, "I don't want company. Life isn't the same thing to me now. He thinks because he is marrying that woman . . . What better is she than me, I would like to know? She's only snapping at him for what he is, and he is only taking her for what she's got, and I've a great mind to go to All Saints and shame them? You wouldn't? Well, it's hard to hide one's feelings, but it would serve them right if—if I did it."

Polly had risen with a wild look and was pressing the pug so hard that it was howling again.

"Did what?" said Glory.

"Nothing . . . that is to say——"

"You mustn't dream of going to the church. The police——"

"Oh, it isn't the police I'm afraid of," said Polly, tossing her head.

"What then?"

"Never mind, my dear," said Polly. On the way downstairs she reproached herself for not seeing what was coming. "But girls like us never do, now do we?"

Glory coloured up to her hair, but made no protest. At the gate Polly wiped her eyes and drew down her veil and said, "I'm sorry to say it to your face, my dear, but it's all been that Mr. Drake's doings, and a girl ought to know he'd do as much himself, and worse. But you're a great woman now, and in everybody's mouth, so you needn't care. Only——"

Glory's face was scarlet and her under lip was bleeding. Yet she kissed the poor shallow thing at parting, because she was down, and did not understand, and lived in another world entirely. But going back to where her letter lay unfinished, she thought, "Impossible! If this girl, living in an atmosphere so different, thinks that . . ." Then she sat at the table and forced herself to tell all.

She had got through the red riot of her confession and was writing, "I don't know what he would think of it, but do you know I thought I saw his face on Wednesday night. It was in the dark and I was in a cab driving away from the stage-door. But so changed! oh, so changed! It must have been a dream, and it was the same as if his ghost had passed me."

Then she became aware of voices in dispute downstairs. First, a man's voice, then the voices of two men, one of them Koenig's, the other with a haunting ring in it. She got up from the table and went to the door of her room, going on tiptoe, yet hardly knowing why. Koenig was saying, "No, sair, de lady does not lif here." Then a deep, strong chest-voice answered, "Mr. Koenig, surely you remember me?" and Glory's heart seemed to beat like a watch. "No-o, sair. Are you . . . Oh, yes; vhat am I tinking of? . . . But de lady——"

"Mr. Koenig," Glory called, cried, gasped over the stair-rail, "ask the gentleman to come up, please."

She hardly knew what happened next, only that Koenig seemed to be muttering confused explanations below, and that she was back in her sitting-room giving a glance into the looking-glass and doing something with her hair. Then there was a step on the stairs, on the landing, at the threshold, and she fell back a few paces from the door that she might see him as he came in. He knocked. Her heart was beating so violently that she had to keep her hand over it. "Who's there?"

"It is I."

"Who's I?"

Then she saw him coming down on her, and the very sunlight seemed to wave like the shadows on a ship. He was paler and thinner, his great eyes looked weary though they smiled, his hand felt bony though firm, and his head was closely cropped.

She looked at him for a moment without speaking, and with a sensation of fulness at her heart that was almost choking her.

"Is it you? I didn't know it was you . . . I was just thinking . . ." She was talking at random and was out of breath as if she had been running.

"Glory, I have frightened you."

"Frightened? Oh, no! Why should you think so? Perhaps I am crying, but then I'm always doing that nowadays. And besides, you are so——"

"Yes, I am altered," he said in the pause that followed.

"And I?"

"You are altered too." He was looking at her with an earnest and passionate gaze. It was she—herself—Glory—not merely a vision or a dream. Again he recognised the glorious eyes with their brilliant lashes and the flashing spot in one of them that had so often set his heart beating. She looked back at him and thought, "How ill he must have been!" and then a lump came into her throat, and she began to laugh that she might not have to cry, and broke out into broad Manx lest he should hear the tremor in her voice.

"But you're coming-to, aren't ye? And you've left that theer . . . Aw, it's glad ter'ble I am, as our people say, and it's longin' mortal you'd be for all, boy."

Another trill of nervous laughter and then a burst of earnest English. "But tell me, you've come for good; you are not going back to ——."

"No, I am not going back to the Brotherhood, Glory." How friendly his low voice sounded!

"And you?"

"Well, I've left the hospital, you see."

"Yes, I see," he said. His weary eyes were wandering about the room, and for the first time she felt ashamed of its luxuries and its flowers.

"But how did you find me?"

"I went to the hospital first——"

"So you hadn't forgotten me? Do you know, I thought you had quite . . . But tell me at once, where did you go then?"

He was silent for a moment, and she said, "Well?"

"Then I went to Mr. Drake's chambers."

"I don't know why everybody should think that Mr. Drake——"

His great eyes were fixed on her face and his mouth was quivering, and to prevent him from speaking, she put on a look of forced gaiety and said—

"But how did you light on me at last?"

"I meant to find you, Glory, if I tramped all London over and everybody denied you to me"—the lump in her throat was hurting her dreadfully—"but I chanced to see the name over the music-hall."

She saw it coming and broke into laughter. "The music-hall! Only think! You looking at music-halls!"

"I was there on Monday night."

"You? Monday? Then perhaps it was not my fancy that I saw you by the stage-do . . ." Her nerves were getting more and more excited, and to calm them she crossed her arms above her head. "So they gave you my address at the stage-door, did they?"

"No, I wrote for it to Peel."

"Peel?" She caught her breath and her arms came down. "Then perhaps you told them where——"

"I told them nothing, Glory."

She looked at him through her eyelashes, her head held down.

"Not that it matters, you know. I've just been writing to them, and they'll soon . . . But oh, I've so much to say, and I can't say it here. Couldn't we go somewhere? Into the Park or on to the Heath, or farther—much farther—the room is so small, and I feel as if I've been suffocating for want of air."

"I've something to say, too, and if——"

"Then let it be to-morrow morning, and we'll start early, and you'll bring me back in time for the theatre. Say Paddington Station at eleven—will that do?"

"Yes."

She saw him to the gate, and when he was going she wanted him to kiss her hand, so she pretended to do the high handshake, but he only held it for a moment and looked steadily into her eyes. The sunshine was pouring into the garden, and she was bare-headed. Her hair was coiled up, and she was wearing a light morning blouse. He thought she had never looked so beautiful.

On getting into the omnibus at the end of the street, he took a letter out of his breast-pocket, and, being alone, he first carried it to his lips, then reopened and read it:—

"See her at once, dear John, and keep in touch with her, and I shall be happy and relieved. As for your father, that old Chalse is going crazy, and is sending Lord Storm crazy too. He has actually discovered that the dust the witch walks on who has cast the evil eye on you lies in front of Glenfaba gate, and he has been sweeping it up o' nights, and scattering it in front of Knockaloe! What simplicity! There are only two women here. Does the silly old gawk mean Rachel? or is it perhaps Aunt Anna?"

And while the omnibus joggled down the street, and the pale young clergyman with the great weary eyes was poring over his letter, Glory was sitting at her table and writing with flying fingers and a look of enthusiastic ecstasy :—

"I've had three bites at this cherry. But who do you think has just been here? John—John Storm! But then you know that he is back, and it wasn't merely my fancy that I saw him by the stage-door. It seems as if people had been denying me to him, and he has been waiting for me and watching over me" (blot). "His voice is so low, but I suppose that comes to people who are much alone, and he is so thin and so pale, and his eyes are so large, and they have that deep look that cuts into the heart. He knew he was changed, and I think he was ashamed" (blot), "but of course I didn't let wit that I was taking notice, and I'm so happy for his sake, poor fellow, that he has escaped from his cage in that Salvation Zoo, that I know I shall make them split their sides in the theatre to-night" (blot, blot). "How tiresome! This ink must have got water in it somehow, and then my handwriting is such a hop-skip-and-a-jump anyway. But hoots!

'Why shouldn't I love Johnny?
And why shouldn't Johnny love me?'

GLORY.

IV

IT was a beautiful May morning, and standing outside Paddington Station with the dog at his feet, he felt her approach instinctively as she came towards him with her free step, in her white cambric dress under the light parasol fringed with lace. Her face was glowing with the fresh air, and she looked happy and bright. As they walked into the station she poured out a stream of questions about the dog, took possession of him straightway, and concluded to call him Don.

They agreed to spend the day at Burnham Beeches, and while he went for the tickets she stepped on to the platform. It was Saturday, the bookstall was ablaze with the picture papers, and one of them was prominently displayed at a page containing her own portrait. She wanted John to see this, so she invented an excuse for bringing him face to face with it, and then she laughed, and he bought the paper.

The clerk recognised her—they could see that by the smile he kept in reserve,—and a group of officers in the Guards, in flannels and straw hats, going down to their club at Maidenhead, looked at her and nudged each other, as if they knew who she was. Her eyes danced, her lips smiled, and she was proud that John should see the first-fruits of her fame. She was proud of him, too, with his bold walk and strong carriage, as they passed the officers, in their negligent dress, with their red and blue neckties. But John's heart was aching, and he was wondering how he was to begin on the duty he had to do.

From the moment they started she gave herself up to the delights of their holiday, and even the groaning and cranking and joggling of the train amused her. When the Guards got into their first-class carriage, they had glanced at the open window where her brilliant eyes and rosy lips were gleaming behind a veil. John gazed at her with his slow and tender looks, and felt guilty and ashamed.

They left the train at Slough, and a wave of freshness with an odour of verdure and sap blew into their faces. The dog leaped and barked, and Glory skipped along with it, breaking every moment into enthusiastic exclamations. There was hardly any wind, and the clouds, which were very high overhead, were scarcely moving. It was a glorious day, and Glory's face wore an expression of perfect happiness.

They lunched at the old hotel in the town, with the window open, and the swallows darting in the air outside, and Glory, who took milk "for remembrance," rose and said, " I looks towards Mr. Storm," and then drank his health and swept him the prettiest curtsy. All through lunch she kept feeding the dog from her own fingers, and at the end rebuked him for spreading his bones in a half-circle across the carpet, a thing which was never done, she said, in the best society, this side the Cannibal Islands.

" By-and-by," he thought; " time enough by-and-by," for the charm of her joy was infectious.

The sun was high when they started on their walk, and her face looked flushed and warm. But through the park-like district to the wood she raced with Don, and made him leap over her sunshade and roll over and over on the bright green grass. The larks were trilling overhead, everything was humming and singing.

"Let her have one happy day," he thought, and they began to call and shout to each other.

Then they came to the beeches, and being sheltered from the fiery rays of the sun, she put down her sunshade and John took off his hat. The silence and gloom, the great gnarled trees with their thews and sinews, their arms and thighs and loins, the gentle rustle of the breeze in the branches overhead, the deep accumulation of dead leaves underfoot, the fluttering of wings, the low cooing of pigeons, and all the mystery and wonder of the wood brought a sense of awe as on entering a mighty minster in the dusk. But this wore away presently, and Glory began to sing. Her pure voice echoed in the fragrant air, and the happiness so long pent up and starved seemed to bubble in every word and note.

"Isn't this better than singing in music-halls?" he thought, and then he began to sing too, just like any happy boy, without thinking of yesterday or to-morrow, of before or after. She smiled at him. He smiled back. It was like a dream. After his long seclusion it was difficult to believe it could be true. The open air, the perfume of the leaves they were wading through, the silver bark of the birches and the blue peeps of the sky between, and then Glory walking with her graceful motion, and laughing and singing by his side! "I shall wake up in a minute," he thought, "I'm sure I shall!"

They sang one song together. It was "Lasses and Lads," and, to make themselves think it was the old time back again, they took each other's hands and swung them to the tune. He felt her clasp like milk coursing through his body, and a great wave of tenderness swept up his hard resolve, as sea-wrack is thrown up after a storm. "She is here; we are together; why trouble about anything more?" and the time flew by.

But their voices went wrong immediately, and they were soon in difficulties. Then she laughed, and they began again, but they could not keep together, and as often as they tried they failed. "Ah, it's not like the old days," he thought, and a mood of sadness came over him. He had begun to observe in Glory the trace of the life she had passed through—words, phrases, ideas, snatches of slang, touches of moods which had the note of a slight vulgarity. When the dog took a bone uninvited she cried, "It's a click; you've sneaked it;" when John broke down in the singing, she told him to "chuck it off the chest," and when he stopped altogether she called him glum and said she would "do it on her own."

"Why does he look so sorrowful?" she thought, and telling herself that this came to people who were much alone, she rattled on more recklessly than before.

She talked of the life of the music-hall, the life at the "back," glorifying it by a tone of apology. It was all hurry-scurry, slap-dash-and-drive, no time to consider effects, a succession of last acts and first nights; so it was really harder to be a music-hall woman than a regular actress. And the music-hall woman was no worse than other women considering. Had he seen their ballet? It was fetching. Such pages! Simply darlings! *They* were the proud young birds of paradise whom toffs like those Guards came to see, and it was fun to see them pluming and preening themselves at the back, each for the eyes of her own particular lord in the stalls. Thus she flung out unfamiliar notes, hardly knowing their purport, but to John they were as slimy creatures out of the social mire she had struggled through. Oh, London! London! Its shadow was over them even there, and go where they would, they could never escape from it.

His former thought began to hang about him again, and he asked her to tell him what had happened to her during his absence.

"Shall I?" she said. "Well, I brought three golden sovereigns out of the hospital to distribute among the people of London, but, bless you, they went nowhere."

"And what then?"

"Then—then Hope was a good breakfast but a bad supper, you know. But shall I tell you all? Yes, yes, yes, I will."

She told him of Mrs. Jupe's, and of the deception she had practised upon her people, and he turned his head that he might not see her tears. She told him of the "Three Graces," and of the stage-manager—she called him the "stage-damager"—and then *she* turned her head that she might hide her shame. She told him of Josephs, the bogus agent, and his face grew hard and his brown eyes looked black.

"And where did you say his place was?" he asked in a voice that vibrated and broke.

"I didn't say," she answered with a laugh and a tear.

She told him of Aggie, and of the foreign clubs, and of Koenig, and of the dinner-party at the Home Secretary's, and then she skipped a step and cried—

"Ding, dong, dended,
My tale's ended."

"And was it there you met Mr. Drake again?"

She replied with a nod.

"Never having seen him in the meantime?"

She pursed her lips and shook her head. "That's all over now, and what matter? 'I likes to be jolly and I allwis is!'"

"But is it all over?" he said, and he looked at her again with the deep look that had cut into her heart.

"He's going to say something," she thought, and she began to laugh, but with a faint tremor, and giving the dog her parasol to carry in his mouth, she took off her hat, swung it in her hand by the brim and set off to run.

There was the light shimmer of a pool at a level below, where the water had drained to a bottom and was enclosed by beeches. The trees seemed to hang over it with outstretched wings, like birds about to alight, and round its banks there were plots of violets which filled the air with their fragrance. It was a Godblest bit of ground, and when he came up with her she was standing at the edge of the marshy mere panting and on the point of tears, and saying in a whisper, "Oh, how beautiful!"

"But however am I to get across?" she cried, looking with mock terror on the two inches of water that barely covered the grass, and at the pretty red shoes that peeped from under her dress.

Then something extraordinary occurred. She hardly knew what was happening until it was over. Without a word, without a smile, he lifted her up in his arms and carried her to the other side. She felt helpless like a child—as if suddenly she belonged to herself no longer. Her head had fallen on his shoulder and her heart was beating against his breast. Or was it *his* heart that was beating? When he put her down she was afraid she was going to cry, so she began to laugh and to say they mustn't lose that 7.30 to London or the "rag" would be rolling up without her and the "stage-damager" would be using "cuss words."

They had to pass the old church of Stoke Pogis on the way back to the town, and after looking at its timber belfry and steeple, John suggested that they should see the inside. The sexton was found working in the garden at the side of his house, and he went indoors for the keys. "Here they be, sir, and you being a pa'son I'll bide in the orchet. You and your young missus can look at the church without me. 'A b'lieve 'a hev seed it afore," he said with a twinkle.

The church was dark and cool. There was a window representing an angel ascending to heaven against a deep-blue sky, and a squire's pew furnished like a box at the theatre with a carpet, and even a stove. The chairs in the front bore family crests, and behind them were inferior chairs, without crests, for the servants. John had opened the little modern organ and begun to play. After a while he began to sing. He sang "Nazareth," and his voice filled the empty church and went up into the gloom of the roof, and echoed and returned, and it was almost as if another voice were singing there.

Glory stood by his side and listened; a wonderful peace had come down on her. Then the emotion that vibrated in his deep voice made something surge up to her throat. "Life for evermore! Life for evermore!" All at once she began to weep, to sob, and to laugh in a breath, and he stopped.

"How ridiculous I am to-day! You'll think me a maniac," she said. But he only took her hand as if she had been a child and led her out of the church.

Insensibly the day had passed into evening, and the horizontal rays of the sun were dazzling their eyes as they returned to the hotel for tea. In giving orders for this meal they had left the illustrated weekly behind, and it was now clear from the easy smiles that greeted them that the paper had been looked at and Glory identified. The room was ready, with the table laid, the window closed, and a fire of wood in the doggrate, for the chill of evening was beginning to be felt. And to make him forget what had happened at the church she put on a look of forced gaiety and talked rapidly, frivolously, and at random. The fresh air had given her such a colour that they would "fairly eat her to-night." How tired she was, though! But a cup of tea would exhilarate her "like a Johnnie's first whisky and soda in bed."

He looked at her with his grave face; every word was cutting him like a knife. "So you didn't tell the old folks at Glenfaba about the hospital until later?"

"No. Have a cup of 'the girl'? They call champagne 'the boy' at 'the back,' so I call tea 'the girl,' you know."

"And when did you tell them about the music-hall?"

"Yesterday. Muffins?" and as she held out the plate, she waggled the wrist of her other hand and mimicked the cry of the muffin-man.

"Not until yesterday?"

She began to excuse herself. What was the use of taking people by surprise? And then good people were sometimes so easily shocked. Education and upbringing and prejudices, and even blood——

"Glory," he said, "if you are ashamed of this life, believe me it is not a right one."

"Ashamed? Why should I be ashamed? Everybody is saying how proud I should be."

She spoke feverishly, and by a sudden impulse she plucked up the paper, but as suddenly let it drop again, for, looking at his grave face, her little fame seemed to shrivel up. "But give a dog a bad name, you know . . . You were there on Monday night. Did you see anything, now—anything in the performance——"

"I saw the audience, Glory; that was enough for me. It is impossible for a girl to live long in an atmosphere like that and be a good woman. Yes, my child, impossible! God forbid that I should sit in judgment on any man, still less on any woman; but the women of the music-hall, do they *remain* good women? Poor souls! they are placed in a position so false that it would require extraordinary virtue not to become false along with it! And the whiter the soul that is dragged through that -that mire, the more the defilement. The audiences at such places don't want the white soul, they don't want the good woman; they want the woman who has tasted of the tree of good and evil. You can see it in their faces, and hear it in their laughter, and measure it in their applause. Oh, I'm only a priest, but I've seen these places all the world over, and I know what I'm saying, and I know it's true, and you know it's true, Glory——"

Glory leapt up from the table, and her eyes seemed to emit fire. "I know it's hard and cruel and pitiless, and since you were there on Monday, and saw how kind the audience was to *me*, it's personal and untrue as well."

But her voice broke, and she sat down again, and said in another tone, "But, John, it's nearly a year, you know, since we saw each other last, and isn't it a pity? Tell me, where are you living now? Have you made your plans for the future? Oh, who do you think was with me just before you called yesterday? Polly!—Polly Love, you remember? She's grown stout and plainer, poor thing, and I was so sorry . . . Her brother was in your Brotherhood, wasn't he? Is he as strangely fond of her as ever? Is he? Eh? Don't you understand? Polly's brother, I mean?"

"He's dead, Glory. Yes, dead. He died a month ago. Poor boy! he died broken-hearted. He had come to hear of his sister's trouble at the hospital. I was to blame for that. He never looked up again."

There was silence; both were gazing into the fire, and Glory's mouth was quivering. All at once she said, "John—John Storm, why can't you understand that it's not the same with me as with other women? There seem to be two women in me always. After I left the hospital I went through a good deal. Nobody will ever know how much I went through. But even at the worst somehow I seemed to enjoy and rejoice in everything. Things happened that made me cry, but there was another *me* that was laughing. And that's how it is with the life I am living now. It is not I myself that go through this—this mire, as you call it; it's only my other self, my lower self, if you like; but I am not touched by it at all. Don't you see that? Don't you, now?"

"There are professions which are a source of temptation, and talents that are a snare, Glory——"

"I see, I see what you mean. There are not many ways a woman can succeed in—that's the cruelty of things. But there are a few, and I've chosen the one I'm fit for. And now—now that I've escaped from all that misery, that meanness, and have brought the eyes of London upon me, and the world is full of smiles for me, and sunshine, and I am happy, you come at last— you that I couldn't find when I wanted you so much, oh, so much! because you had forgotten me—you come to me out of a darkness like the grave, and tell me to give it all up. Yes, yes, yes, that's what you mean—give it all up! Oh, it's cruel!"

She covered her face with her hands and sobbed. He bent over her with a sorrowful face, and said, "My child, if I have come out of a darkness as of the grave, it is because I had *not* forgotten you there, but was thinking of you every day and hour."

Her sobbing ceased, but the tears still flowed through her fingers.

"Before that poor lad abandoned hope he came out into the world too—stole out—thinking to find his lost one. I told him to look for you first, and he went to the hospital."

"I saw him."

"You?"

"It was on New Year's Eve. He passed me in the street."

"Ah! . . . Well, he came back anyway, and said you were gone, and all trace of you was lost. Did I forget you after that, Glory?"

His husky voice broke off suddenly, and he rose with a look of wretchedness. "You are right, there are two selves in you, and the higher self is so pure, so strong, so unselfish, so noble . . . Oh, I am sure of it, Glory! Only there's no one to speak to it, no one. I try, but I cannot."

She was still crying behind her hands.

"And meanwhile the lower self—there are only too many to speak to *that*——"

Her hands came down from her disordered face and she said, "I know whom you mean."

"I mean the world."

"No, indeed; you mean Mr. Drake. But you are mistaken.

Mr. Drake has been a good friend to me, but he isn't anything else, and doesn't want to be. Can't you see that when you think of me and talk of me as you would of some other women, you hurt me and degrade me, and I cannot bear it? You see I am crying again—goodness knows why. But I shan't give up my profession. The idea of such a thing! It's ridiculous! Think of Glory in a convent! One of the Poor Clares, perhaps!"

"Hush!"

"Or back in the island serving out sewing at a mothers' meeting! Give it up! Indeed I won't!"

"You shall and you must!"

"Who'll make me?"

"I will!"

Then she laughed out wildly, but stopped on the instant, and looked up at him with glistening eyes. An intense blush came over her face, and her looks grew bright as his grew fierce. A moment afterwards the waiting-maid, with an inquisitive expression, was clearing the table, and keeping a smile in reserve for "the lovers' quarrel."

Some of the Guardsmen were in the train going back, and at the next station they changed to the carriage in which Glory and John were sitting. Apparently they had dined before leaving their club at Maidenhead, and they talked at Glory with covert smiles. "Going to the Colosseum to-night?" said one. "If there's time," said another. "Oh, time enough. The attraction doesn't begin till ten, don't you know, and nobody goes before." "Tell me she's rippin'." "Good, deuced good."

Glory was sitting with her back to the engine, drumming lightly on the window, and looking out at the setting sun. At first she felt a certain shame at the obvious references, but, piqued at John's silence, she began to take pride in them, and shot glances at him from under her half-closed eyelids. John was sitting opposite with his arms folded. At the talk of the men he felt his hands contract and his lips grow cold with the feeling that Glory belonged to everybody now and was common property. Once or twice he looked at them, and became conscious of an impression which had floated about him since he left the Brotherhood, that nearly every face he saw bore the hideous stamp of self-indulgence and sensuality.

But the noises of the train helped him not to hear, and he looked out for London. It lay before them under a canopy of smoke, and now and then a shaft from the setting sun lit up a glass roof, and it glittered like a sinister eye. Then there came from afar, above the creaking and groaning of the wheels and

the whistle of the engine, the deep multitudinous murmur of
that distant sea. The mighty tide was rising and coming up to
meet them. Presently they were dashing into the midst of it,
and everything was drowned in the splash and roar.

The Guardsmen, being on the platform side, alighted first,
and on going off they bowed to Glory with rather more than
easy manners. A dash of the devil prompted her to respond
demonstratively, but John had risen and was taking off his hat
to the men, and they were going away discomfited. Glory was
proud of him—he was a man and a gentleman.

He put her into a hansom under the lamps outside the station,
and her face was lit up, but she patted the dog and said, "You
have vexed me, and you needn't come to see me again. I shall
not sing properly this evening or sleep to-night at all, if that is
any satisfaction to you, so you needn't trouble to inquire."

When he reached home, Mrs. Callender told him of a shocking
occurrence at the fashionable wedding at All Saints that morning.
A young woman had committed suicide during the ceremony,
and it turned out to be the poor girl who had been dismissed
from the hospital.

John Storm remembered Brother Paul. "I must bury her,"
he thought.

V

GLORY sang that night with extraordinary vivacity and charm, and
was called back again and again. Going home in the cab, she tried
to live through the day afresh—every step, every act, every
word, down to that triumphant "*I* will." Her thoughts swayed as
with the swaying of the hansom, but sometimes the thunderous
applause of the audience broke in, and then she had to remember
where she had left off. She could feel that beating against her
breast still, and even smell the violets that grew by the pool.
He had told her to give up everything, and there was an ex-
quisite thrill in the thought that perhaps some day she would
annihilate herself and all her ambitions, and . . . Who knows
what then?

This mood lasted until Monday morning, when she was sitting
in her room, dressing very slowly and smiling at herself in the
glass, when the cockney maid came in with a newspaper which
her master had sent up on account of its long report of the
wedding.

"The church of All Saints was crowded with a fashionable congregation, among whom were many notable persons in the world of politics and society, including the father of the bridegroom, the Duke of ——, and his brother, the Marquis of ——. An arch of palms crossed the nave at the entrance to the chancel, and festoons of rare flowers were suspended from the rails of the handsome screen. The altar and the table of the commandments were almost obscured by the wreaths of exotics that hung over them, and the columns of the colonnade, the font, and the offertory boxes were similarly buried in rich and lovely blossom . . .

"Thanks to an informal rehearsal some days before, the ceremony went off without a hitch. The officiating clergy were the Venerable Archdeacon Wealthy, D.D., assisted by the Rev. Josiah Golightly and other members of the numerous staff of All Saints. The service, which was fully choral, was under the able direction of the well-known organist and choir-master, Mr. Carl Koenig, F.R.C.O., and the choir consisted of twenty adult and forty boy voices. On the arrival of the bride a procession was formed at the west entrance, and proceeded up to the chancel, singing, 'The voice that breathed o'er Eden.'"

"Poor Polly!" thought Glory.

"The bride wore a duchess satin gown trimmed with chiffon and Brussels lace, and having a long train hung from the shoulders. Her tulle veil was fastened with a ruby brooch and with sprays of orange blossom sent specially from the Riviera, and her necklace consisted of a rope of graduated pearls fully a yard long, understood to have belonged to the jewel-case of Catherine of Russia. She carried a bouquet of flowers (the gift of the bridegroom) ordered from Florida, the American home of her family. The bride's mother wore . . . The bridesmaids were dressed . . . Mr. Horatio Drake acted as best man . . ."

Glory drew her breath as with a spasm, and threw down the newspaper. How blind she had been, how vain, how foolish! She had told John Storm that Drake was only a good friend to her, meaning him to understand that thus far she had allowed him to go and no farther. But there was a whole realm of his life into which he did not ask her to enter. The "notable persons in politics and society," "the bridesmaids," these made up his real sphere, his serious scene. Other women were his friends, companions, equals, intimates, and when he stood in the eye of the world it was they who stood beside him. And she? She was his hobby. He came to her in his off hours. She filled up the under side of his life.

With a crushing sense of humiliation she was folding up the newspaper to send it downstairs when her eye was arrested by a paragraph in small type in the corner. It was headed, "Shocking occurrence at a fashionable wedding."

"Oh, good gracious!" she cried. A glance had shown her what it was. It was a report of Polly's suicide.

"At a fashionable wedding at a West-End church on Saturday" (no names), "a young woman who had been sitting in the nave was seen to rise and attempt to step into the aisle, as if with the intention of crushing her way out, when she fell back in convulsions, and on being removed was found to be dead. Happily the attention of the congregation was at that moment directed to the bride and bridegroom, who were returning from the vestry with the bridal party behind them, and thus the painful incident made no sensation among the crowded congregation. The body was removed to the parish mortuary, and from subsequent inquiries it transpired that death had been due to poison self-administered, and that the deceased was Elizabeth Anne Love (24), of no occupation, but formerly a nurse—a circumstance which had enabled her to procure half an ounce of liquor strychniae on her own signature at a chemist's where she had been known.

"Oh, God! Oh, God!" Glory understood everything now. "I've a great mind to go to All Saints and shame them." . . . "Oh, it isn't the police I'm afraid of." Polly's purpose was clear. She had intended to fall dead at the feet of the bride and bridegroom and make them walk over her body. Poor, foolish, ineffectual Polly! Her very ghost must be ashamed of the failure of her revenge. Not a ripple of sensation on Saturday, and this morning only a few obscure lines in little print!

Oh, it was hideous! The poor thing's vengeance was theatrical and paltry; but what of the man, wherever he was? What did he think of himself now, with his millions and his murder?—yes, his murder, for what else was it?

An hour later Glory was ringing the bell of a little house in St. John's Wood whereof the upper blinds were drawn. The grating of the garden door slid back and an untidy head looked out.

"Well, ma'am?"

"Don't you remember me, Liza?"

"Lawd, yus, Miss!" and the door was opened immediately; "but I was afeared you was one o' them reportin' people, and my orders is not to answer no questions."

"Has *he* been here then?"

"Blesh ye, no, Miss! He's on 'is way to the Continents. But 'is friend 'as, and he's settled everything 'andsome—I will say that for the gentleman."

Glory felt her gall rising; there was something degrading, almost disreputable, even in the loyalty of Drake's friendship.

"Fancy my not knowing you, Miss, and me at the Moosic 'All a Tuesday night! I 'ope you'll excuse the liberty, but I did laugh, and I won't say but I shed a few tears too. Arranged? Yes, the jury and the coroner and everythink. It's to be at twelve o'clock, so you may think I've 'ad my 'ands full. But you'll want to look at 'er, pore thing! Go up, Miss, and mind yer 'ead; there's nobody but 'er friends with 'er now."

The friends proved to be Betty Belmont and her dressing-room companions. When Glory entered they showed no surprise. "The pore child told us all about you," said Betty; and the little one said, "It's your nyme that's caught on, dear. The minute I heard it I said what a top-line for a bill!"

It was the same little bandbox of a bedroom, only now it was darkened, and Polly's troubles were over. There was a slightly-convulsed look about the mouth, but the features were otherwise calm and childlike, for all the dead are innocent.

The three women with demure faces were sipping Benedictine and talking among themselves, and Polly's pug-dog was coiled up on the bare bolster and snoring audibly.

"Pore thing! I don't know how she could 'a done it. But there, that's the worst of this life! It's all in the present and leads to nothing and ain't got no future." "What could the pore thing do? She wasn't so wonderful pretty; and then men like . . ." "She was str'ight with him, say what yer like. Only she ought to been more patienter, and she needn't 'a been so hard on the laidy neither." "She had everything the heart could wish. Look at her rooms! I wonder who'll——"

Carriages were heard outside, and two or three men came in to do the last offices. Glory had turned her face away, but behind her the women were still talking. "Wait a minute, mister! . . . What a lovely ring! . . . I wish I had a keepsake to remember her by." "Well, and why not? She won't want——"

Glory felt as if she was choking, but Polly's pug-dog had been awakened by the commotion and was beginning to howl, so she took up the little mourner and carried it out. An organ-man somewhere near was playing "Sweet Marie."

The funeral was at Kensal Green, and the four girls were the only followers. The coroner's verdict being *felo-de-se*, the body was not taken into the chapel, but a clergyman met it at the gate and led the way to the grave. Walking with her head down and the dog under her arm, Glory had not seen him at first, but when he began with the tremendous words, "I am the resurrection and the life," she caught her breath and looked up. It was John Storm.

While they were in the carriage the clouds had been gathering, and now some spots of rain were falling. When the bearers had laid down their burden, the spots were large and frequent, and all save one of the men turned and went back to the shelter of the porch. The three women looked at each other, and one of them muttered something about "the dead and the living," and then the little lady stole away. After a moment the tall one followed her, and from shame of being ashamed the third one went off also.

By this time the rain was falling in a sharp shower and John Storm, who was bareheaded, had opened his book and begun to read: "Forasmuch as it hath pleased Almighty God of His great mercy to take unto Himself the soul of our dear sister departed——"

Then he saw that Glory was alone by the grave-side, and his voice faltered and almost failed him. It faltered again and he halted when he came to the "sure and certain hope," but after a moment it quivered and filled out, and seemed to say, "Which of us can sound the depths of God's design?" After the "maimed rites" were over, John Storm went back to the chapel to remove his surplice, and when he returned to the grave Glory was gone.

She sang as usual at the music-hall that night, but with a heavy heart. The difference communicated itself to the audience, and the unanimous applause which had greeted her before frayed off at length into separate hand-claps. Crossing the stage to her dressing-room, she met Koenig, who came to conduct for her, and he said—

"Not quite yourself to-night, my dear, eh?"

Going home in the hansom Polly's dog cuddled up with the old sympathy to the new mistress, and seemed to be making the best of things. The household was asleep, and Glory let herself in with a latch-key. Her cold supper was laid ready, and a letter was lying under the turned-down lamp. It was from her grandfather, and had been written after church on Sunday night.

"It is now so long—more than a year—since I saw my runaway and truant, that, notwithstanding the protests of Aunt Anna and the forebodings of Aunt Rachel, I have determined to give my old legs a journey and my old eyes a treat. Therefore, take warning that I intend to come up to London forthwith, that I may see the great city for the first time in my life, and—which is better—my little granddaughter among all her new friends, and in the midst of her great prosperity."

At the foot of this there was a postscript from Aunt Rachel hastily scrawled in pencil :—

"Take no notice of this. He is far too weak to travel, and indeed he is really failing; but your letter, which reached us last night, has so troubled him ever since, that he can't take rest for thinking of it."

It was the last straw. Before finishing the letter or taking off her hat, Glory took up a telegraph form and wrote, "Postpone journey — am returning home to-morrow." Then she heard Koenig letting himself into the house, and going downstairs she said —

"Will you take this message to the telegraph office for me, please?"

"Vhy, of course I vill, and den ve'll have supper togeder—look!" and he laughed and opened a paper, and drew out a string of sausages.

"Mr. Koenig," she said, "you were right. I was not myself to-night. I want a rest, and I propose to take one."

As Glory returned upstairs she heard stammerings, sputterings, and swearings behind her about managers, engagements, announcements, geniuses, children, and other matters. Back in her room she lay down on the floor, with her face in her hands, and sobbed. Then Koenig appeared, panting and saying, "Dere! I knew vhat vhould happen! Here's a pretty ting! And dat's vhy Mr. Drake told me to deny you to de man. De brute, de beast, de dirty son of a monk!"

But Glory had leapt up with eyes of fire and was crying, "How dare you, sir? Out of my room this instant."

"Mein Gott! It's a divil!" Koenig was muttering like a servant as he went downstairs. He went out to the telegraph office and came back, and then Glory heard him frying his sausages on the dining-room fire.

The night was far gone when she pushed aside her untouched supper, and wiping her eyes that she might see properly, sat down to write a letter :—

"DEAR JOHN STORM (monk, monster, or whatever it is!),—I trust it will be counted to me for righteousness that I am doing your bidding and giving up my profession—for the present.

'Between a woman's 'yes' and 'no,'
There isn't room for a pin to go,'

which is very foolish of her in this instance, considering that she is earning various pounds a night and has nothing but Providence to fall back upon. I have told my jailer I must have my liberty, and, being a man of like passions with yourself, he has been busy blaspheming in the parlour downstairs. I trust virtue will be its own reward, for I dare say it is all I shall ever get. If I were Narcissus I should fall in love with myself to-day, having shown an obedience to tyranny which is beautiful and worthy of the heroic age. 'But to-morrow morning I go back to the 'oilan,' and it will be so nice up there without anybody and all alone."

She was laughing softly to herself as she wrote and catching her breath with a little sob at intervals.

"A letter now and then is profitable to the soul of man—and woman—but you must not expect to hear from *me*, and as for you, though you *have* resurrected yourself, I suppose a tyrant of your opinions will continue the Benedictine rule which compels you to hold your peace—and other things. I am engaged to breakfast with a nice girl named Glory Quayle to-morrow morning—that is to say, *this* morning—at Euston Station at a quarter to seven, but happily this letter won't reach you until 7.30, so I'll just escape interruption."

The house was still and the streets were quiet, not even a cab going along.

"Good-bye! I've realised—a dog! It's a pug, and therefore, like somebody else, it always looks black at me, though I suspect its father married beneath him, for it talks a good deal and evidently hasn't been brought up in a Brotherhood. Therefore, being a 'female,' I intend to call it Aunt Anna—except when the original is about. Aunt Anna has been hopping up and down the room at my heels for the last hour, evidently thinking that a rational woman would behave better if she went to bed. Perhaps I shall take a leaf out of your book and 'comb her hair' when I get her all alone in the train to-morrow, that she may be prepared for the new sphere to which it has pleased Providence to call her.

"Good-bye again! I see the lamps of Euston running after each other, only it's the *other* way this time. I find there is something that seizes you with a fiercer palpitation than coming *into* a great and wonderful city, and that is going out of one. Dear old London! After all, it has been very good to me. No one, it seems to me, loves it as much as I do. Only somebody thinks . . . Well, never mind! Good-bye 'for all.'

GLORY."

At seven next morning, on the platform at Euston, Glory was standing with melancholy eyes at the door of a first-class compartment watching the people sauntering up and down, talking in groups and hurrying to and fro, when Drake stepped up to her. She did not ask what had brought him—she knew. He looked fresh and handsome, and was faultlessly dressed.

"You are doing quite right, my dear," he said in a cheerful voice. "Koenig telegraphed and I came to see you off. Don't bother about the theatre, leave everything to me ; take a rest after your great excitement and come back bright and well."

The locomotive whistled and began to pant, the smoke rose to the roof, the train started, and before Glory knew she was going she was gone.

Then Drake walked to his club and wrote this postscript to a letter to Lord Robert Ure at the Grand Hotel, Paris : "The Parson has drawn first blood, and Gloria has gone home."

VI

ON the Sunday evening after Glory's departure John Storm, with the bloodhound running by his side, made his way to Soho in search of the mother of Brother Andrew. He had come to a corner of a street where the walls of an ugly brick church ran up a narrow court and turned into a still narrower lane at the back. The church had been for some time disused, and its façade was half covered with hoardings and plastered with placards : " Brighton and Back, 3s." " Lloyd's News." " Coals, 1s. a cwt." and " Barclay's Sparkling Ales."

There was a tumult in the court and lane. In the midst of a close-packed ring of excited people, chiefly foreigners, shouting in half the languages of Europe, a tall young cockney, with bloated face and eyes aflame with drink, was writhing and wrestling and cursing. Sometimes he escaped from the grasp of the man who held him, and then he flung himself against the closed door of a shop which stood opposite, with the three balls of the pawnbroker suspended above it. Somebody within the shop was howling for help. It was a woman's voice, and the louder she screamed the more violent were the man's efforts to beat down the door between them.

As John Storm stood a moment looking on, some one on the street beside him said, "It's a d—— shyme." It was a man with a feeble, ineffectual face, and the appearance of a waiter. Seeing he had been overheard, the man stammered, " Beg parding, sir ; but they may well say ' When the Devil can't come hisself 'e sends 'is brother Drink.' " Having said this he began to move along, but stopped suddenly on seeing what the clergyman with the dog was doing.

John Storm was pushing his way through the crowd, and his black figure in that writhing ring of undersized foreigners looked big and commanding. "What's this?" he was saying in a husky voice that rose clear above the clamour. The shouting and swearing subsided, all save the howling from the inside of the shop, and the tumult settled down in a moment to mutterings and gnashings and a broken and irregular silence.

Then somebody said, "It's nothink, sir." And somebody else said, "'E's on'y drunk, and wantin' to pench 'is mother." Without listening to this explanation John Storm had laid hold of the young man by the collar and was dragging him, struggling and fuming, from the door.

"What's going on?" he demanded. "Will nobody speak?"

Then a poor swaggering imitation of a man came up out of the cellar of a house that stood next to the disused church, and a comely young woman carrying a baby followed close behind him. He had a gin-bottle in his hands, and with a wink he said, "A christenin'—that what's goin' on. 'Ave a kepple o' pen'orth of 'ollands, old gel?"

At this sally the crowd recovered its audacity and laughed, and the drunken man began to say that he could "knock spots out of any bloomin' parson, 'en no bloomin' erer."

But the young fellow with the gin-bottle broke in again. "What's yer gyme, mister? Preach the gawspel? Give us treeks? This is my funeral, down't ye know, and I'd jest like to hear."

The little foreigners were enjoying the parson-baiting, and the drunken man's courage was rising to fever heat. "I'll give 'im one-two between the eyes if 'e touches me again." Then he flung himself on the pawnshop like a battering-ram, the howling inside, which had subsided, burst out afresh, and finally the door was broken down.

Half-a-minute afterwards the crowd was making a wavering dance about the two men. "Look out, ducky," the young fellow shouted to John. The warning came too late—John went reeling backwards from a blow.

"Now, my lads, who says next?" cried the drunken ruffian. But before the words were out of his mouth there was a growl, a plunge, a snarl, and he was full length on the street with the bloodhound's muzzle at his throat.

The crowd shrieked and began to fly. Only one person seemed to remain. It was an elderly woman, with dry and straggling grey hair. She had come out of the pawnshop and thrown herself on the dog in an effort to rescue the man underneath, crying, "My son—oh, my son! It'll kill him! Tyke the beast away!"

John Storm called the dog off, and the man got up unhurt and nearly sober. But the woman continued to moan over the ruffian and to assail John and his dog with bitter insults. "We want no truck with parsons 'ere," she shouted.

"Stou thet, mother. It was my fault," said the sobered man, and then the woman began to cry; and the next minute John Storm was going with mother and son into the shut-up pawnshop, and the unhinged door was being propped behind them.

The crowd was trailing off when he came out again half-an-hour afterwards, and the only commotion remaining was caused by a belated policeman asking, "Wot's bin the matter 'ere?" and by the young fellow with the gin-bottle performing a step dance on the pavement before the entrance to the cellar. The old woman stood at her door wiping her eyes on her apron, and her son was behind with a face that was now red from other causes than drink and rage.

"Good-bye, Mrs. Pincher; I may see you again soon."

Hearing this, the young swaggerer stopped his step-dancing and cried, "What cheer, myte? Was it a blowter and a cup of cawfy?"

"For shyme, Charlie!" cried the girl with the baby, and the young fellow answered, "Shut yer 'ead, Aggie!"

The waiter was still at the corner of the court, and when John came up he spoke again. "There must be sem amoosement knockin' women abart, but I can't see it myself." Then in a simple way he began to talk about his "missis," and what a good creature she was, and finally announced himself "gyme" to help a parson "as stood up to that there drunken bloke for sake of a woman."

"What's your name?" said John.

"Jupe," said the man, and then something stirred in John's memory.

On the following day John Storm dined with his uncle at Downing Street. The Prime Minister was waiting in the library. In evening dress, with his back to the fireplace and his hands enlaced behind him he looked even more thin and gaunt than before. He welcomed John with a few familiar words and a smile. His smile was brief and difficult, like that which drags across the face of an invalid. Dinner was announced immediately, and the old man took the young one's arm and they passed into the dining-room.

The panelled chamber looked cold and cheerless. It was lighted by a single lamp in the middle of the table. They took their seats at opposite sides. The statesman's thin hair shone on his head like streaks of silver. John exercised a strong physical influence upon him, and all through the dinner his bleak face kept smiling.

"I ought to apologise for having nobody to meet you, but I had something to say—something to suggest—and I thought perhaps——"

John interrupted with affectionate protestations, and a tremor passed over the wrinkles about the old man's eyes.

"It is a great happiness to me, my dear boy, that you have turned your back on that Brotherhood, but I presume you intend to adhere to the Church?"

John intended to take priest's orders without delay, and then go on with his work as a clergyman.

"Just so, just so"—the long tapering fingers drummed on the table—"and I should like to do something to help you."

Then sipping at his wine-glass of water, the Prime Minister, in his slow, deep voice and official tone, began to detail his scheme. There was a bishopric vacant. It was only a colonial one—the Bishopric of Colombo. The income was small, no more than seventeen hundred pounds, the work was not light, and there were eighty clergy. Then a colonial bishopric was not usually a stepping-stone to preferment at home, yet still——

John interrupted again. "You are most kind, uncle, but I am only looking forward to living the life of a poor priest, out of sight of the world and the Church."

"Surely Colombo is sufficiently out of sight, my boy?"

"But I see no necessity to leave London."

The Prime Minister glanced at him steadily, with the concentrated expression of a man who is accustomed to penetrate the thoughts and feelings of another.

"Why then—why did you——"

"Why did I leave the monastery, uncle? Because I had come to see that the monastic system was based on a faulty ideal of Christianity, which has been tried for the greater part of nineteen hundred years and failed. The theory of monasticism is that Christ died to redeem our carnal nature, and all we have to do is to believe and pray. But it is not enough that Christ died once. He must be dying always—every day—and in every one of us. God is calling on us in this age to seek a new social application of the Gospel, or, shall I say, to go back to the old one."

"And that is?"

"To present Christ in practical life as the living Master and King and example, and to apply Christianity to the life of our own time."

The Prime Minister had not taken his eyes off him. "What

does this mean?" he had asked himself, but he only smiled his difficult smile and began to talk lightly. If this creed applied to the individual, it applied also to the State; but think of a Cabinet conducting the affairs of a nation on the charming principles of "taking no thought for the morrow," and "loving your enemies," and "turning the other cheek," and "selling all and giving to the poor"!

John stuck to his guns. If the Christian religion could not be the ultimate authority to rule a Christian nation, it was only because we lacked faith and trusted too much to mechanical laws made by statesmen rather than to moral laws made by Christ. "Either the life of Christ, as the highest standard and example, means something or it means nothing. If something, let us try to follow it; but if nothing, then, for God's sake, let us put it away as a cruel, delusive, and damnable mummery."

The Prime Minister continued to ask himself, "What is the key to this?" and to look at John as he would have looked at a problem that had to be solved, but he only went on smiling and talking lightly. It was true we said a prayer and took an oath on the Bible in the Houses of Parliament, but did anybody think for a moment that we intended to trust the nation to the charming romanticism of the politics of Jesus? As for the Church, it was founded on Acts of Parliament; it was endowed and established by the State; its head was the Sovereign, its clergy were Civil servants who went to levées and hung on the edge of drawing-rooms and troubled the knocker of No. 10 Downing Street. And as for Christ's laws, in this country they were interpreted by the Privy Council and were under the direct control of a State department. Still, it was a harmless superstition that we were a Christian nation. It helped to curb the masses of the people, and if that was what John was thinking of——

The Prime Minister paused and stopped.

"Tell me, my boy," touching John's arm, "do you intend yourself to live . . . in short, the . . . well, after the example of the life of Christ?"

"As far as my weak and vain and sinful nature will permit, uncle!"

"And in what way would you propose to apply your new idea of Christianity?"

"My experiment would be made on a social basis, sir, and first of all in relation to woman." John was hot all over, and his face had flushed up to the eyes.

The Prime Minister glanced stealthily across the table, passed his thin hand across his forehead and thought, "So that's how it is!" But John was deep in his theme and saw nothing. The present position of women was intolerable. Upon the wellbeing of women, especially of working women, the whole welfare of society rested. Yet what was their condition? Think of it—their dependence on man, their temptations, their rewards, their punishments! Three-halfpence an hour was the average wage of a working woman in England!—and that in the midst of riches, in the heart of luxury, and with one easy and seductive means of escape from poverty always open. Ruin lay in wait for them, and was beckoning them and enticing them in the shape of dancing-houses and music-halls and rich and selfish men.

"Not one man in a million, sir, would come through such an ordeal unharmed. And yet what do we do?—what does the Church do for these brave creatures on whose virtue and heroism the welfare of the nation depends? If they fall, it cuts them off, and there is nothing before them but the streets or crime or the Union or suicide. And meanwhile it marries the men who have tempted them, to the snug and sheltered darlings for whose wealth or rank or beauty they have been pushed aside. Oh, uncle, when I walk down Regent Street in the daytime I am angry, but when I walk down Regent Street at night I am ashamed. And then to think of the terrible solitude of London to working girls who want to live pure lives—the terrible spiritual loneliness!"

John's voice was breaking, but the Prime Minister had almost ceased to hear. Thinking he had realised the truth at last, his own youth seemed to be sitting before him and he felt a deep pity.

"Coffee here or in the library, your Lordship?" said the man at his elbow.

"The library," he answered, and taking John's arm again he returned to the other room. There was a fire burning now, and a book lay under the lamp on a little table, with a silver papercutter through the middle to mark the page.

"How you remind me of your mother sometimes, John! That was just like her voice, do you know—just!"

Two hours afterwards he led John Storm down the long corridor to the hall. His bleak face looked soft and his deep voice had a slight tremor. "Good-night, my dear boy, and remember your money is always waiting for you. Until your Christian Social State is established you are only an advocate of Socialism, and may fairly use your own. If yours is the Christianity of the first century it has to exist in the nineteenth, you know. You can't live on air or fly without wings. I shall be curious to see what approach to the Christian ideal the condition of civilisation admits of. Yet I don't know what your religious friends and the humdrum herd will think of you—mad probably, or at least weak and childish, and perhaps even a hunter after easy popularity. But good-night, and God bless you in your people's church and Devil's Acre."

John was flushed and excited. He had been talking of his plans, his hopes, his expectations. God would provide for him in this as in everything, and then God's priest ought to be God's poor. Meantime two gentlemen in plush waited for him at the door. One handed him his hat, the other his stick and gloves.

Then with regular steps, and his hands behind him, the Prime Minister paced back through the quiet corridors. Returning to the library, he took up his book and tried to read. It was a novel, but he could not attend to the incidents in other people's lives. From time to time he said to himself, "Poor boy! Will he find her? Will he save her?" One pathetic idea had fixed itself on his mind—John Storm's love of God was love of a woman, and she was fallen and wrecked and lost.

A fortnight later John wrote to Glory:—

"Fairly under weigh at last, dear Glory! Taken priest's orders, got the Bishop's 'licence to officiate,' and found myself a church. It is St. Mary Magdalene's, Crown Street, Soho, a district that has borne for three hundred years the name of the 'Devil's Acre,' bears it still, and deserves it. The church is an old proprietary place, licensed, not consecrated, formerly belonging to Greek, or Italian, or French, or some other refugees, but long shut up and now much out of repair. Present owners, a company of Greek merchants, removed from Soho to the City, and being too poor (as trustees) to renovate the structure, they have forced me to get money for that purpose from my uncle, the Prime Minister. But the money is my own, apparently, my uncle having in my interest demanded from my father ten thousand pounds out of my mother's dowry, and got it. And now I am spending two thousand pounds on the repair of my church buildings, notwithstanding the protests of the Prime Minister, who calls me 'chaplain to the Greek-Turks,' and of Mrs. Callender, who has discovered that I am a 'maudlin, sentimental, daft young spendthrift.' Dare say I am all that and a good deal more, as the wise world counts wisdom—but it matters little.

"Have not waited for the workmen, though, to begin operations. Took first services last Sunday. No organist, no choir, no clerk, and next to no congregation. Just the church cleaner, a good, simple old soul named Pincher, her son, a reformed drunkard and pawnbroker, and another convert who is a club waiter. Nevertheless I went through the whole service, morning and evening, prayers, psalms, and sermon. God will be the more glorified.

"Have started my new crusade on behalf of women, too, and made various processions of three persons through the streets of Soho. First, my pawnbroker bearing the banner (a white cross, the object of various missiles), next, my waiter carrying a little harmonium, and familiarly known as the 'organ-man,' and finally myself in my cassock. Last mentioned proves to be a highly popular performance, being generally understood to be a man in a black petticoat. We have had the nightly accompaniment of a much larger procession, though, calling themselves 'Skellingtons,' otherwise the 'Skeletons,' an army of low women and roughs who live vulture lives on this poor, soiled, grimy, forgotten world. Thank God, the ground of evil-doers is in danger, and they know it!

"Behind my church, in a dark unwholesome alley called Crook Lane, we have a clergy-house, at present let out in tenements, the cellar being occupied as a gin-shop. As soon as these premises can be cleared of their encumbrances I shall turn them into a club for working girls. Why not? In the old days the Church came to the people: let it come to the people now. Here we are in the midst of this mighty stronghold of the devil's kingdom of sin and crime. Foreign clubs, casinos, dancing academies and gambling houses are round about us. What are we to do? Put up a forest of props (as at the Abbey) and keep off touch and contamination? God forbid! Let us go down into these dens of moral disease and disinfect them. The poor working girls of Soho want their Sunday: give it them. They want music and singing: give it them. They want dancing: give them that also; for God's sake give it them in your churches, or the devil will give it them in his hells!

"Expect to be howled at, of course. Some good people will think I am either a fanatic or an artful schemer, while the clerical place-seekers, who love the flesh-pots of Egypt and have their eyes on the thrones of the Church and the world, will denounce my 'secularity,' and tell me I am feeding the 'miry troughs' of the publican and sinner. No matter, if only God is pleased to vouchsafe 'signs following.' And one weary-faced lonely girl grown fresh of countenance and happy of mien, or one bright little woman snatched from the brink of perdition, will be a better fruit of religion than some of them have seen for many a year.

"As soon as the workmen have cleared out I am going to establish a daily service, and keep the church open always.

Still at Mrs. Callender's, you see; but I am refusing all invitations, except as a priest, and already I don't seem to have time to draw my breath. No income connected with St. Mary Magdalene's, or next to none, just enough to pay the caretaker; but I must not complain of that, for it is the accident to which I owe my church, nobody else wanting it under the circumstances. I had begun to think my time in the monastery wasted, but God knew better. It will help me to live the life of poverty, of purity, of freedom from the world.

"Love to the grandfather and the ladies. How I wish you were with me in the thick of the fight! Sometimes I dream you are, too, and I fancy I see you in the midst of these bright young things, with their flowers and feathers—they will make beautiful Christians yet! Oddly enough, on the day you travelled to the island, every hour that took you farther away seemed to bring you nearer. Greetings!"

VII

GLENFABA, "THE OILAN."

OH, gracious and grateful friend, at length you have remembered the existence of the "poor lone critter" living in dead-alive land! Only that I lack gall to make oppression bitter, I should of course return your belated epistle by the Dead Letter Office, marked "Unknown" across your "Dear Glory," there being no longer anybody in these regions who has a plausible claim to that dubious title. But, alas! I am not my own woman now, and with tears of shame I acknowledge that *any* letter from London comes like an angel's whisper breathed to me through the air.

I dare say you have been unreasonable enough to think that I ought to have written to tell you of my arrival; and knowing that man is born to vanity as the sparks fly upwards, I have more than once intended to take pen in hand and write; but there is something so sleepy in this island atmosphere that my good resolution has hitherto been a still-born babe that has breathed but never cried!

Know, then, that my journey hither was performed with due celerity, and no further disaster than befalls me when, as usual, I have *done* those things which I ought not to have done, and left *undone* those things which I ought to have done—the former, in this instance, having reference to various bouts of crying, which drew forth the sympathy of a compassionate female sharper in the train—and the latter to the catch of my satchel, which enabled that obliging person to draw forth my embroidered pocket-handkerchief in exchange.

I was in good time for the steamboat at Liverpool, and it was crowded, according to its wont, with the Lancashire lads and lasses, in whom affection is as contagious as the mumps. Being in the dumps myself on sailing out of the river, and thinking of the wild excitement with which I had sailed into it, I think I should have found that I had not *done* crying, in both senses, but for the interest of watching an amiable Bob Brierley, who, with his arm about the waist of the person sitting next to him, kept looking round at the rest of the world, from time to time, with the innocence of one whose left hand didn't know what his right hand was doing.

But we had hardly crossed the bar when the prince of the powers of the air began to envy the happiness of these dear young goodies; and if you had seen the weather for the next four hours, you would have agreed that the devil must have had a hand in it! Up came a wave over the after quarter, and down went the passengers below decks, staggering and screaming like brewery rats, and then on we came, like the Israelites out of Egypt, on eagles' wings! Having lost my own sea-legs a little, I thought it prudent to go down too, with my doggie tucked under my arm, and finding a berth in the ladies' cabin, I fell asleep and didn't awake until we were on the cross current just off the island, when, amid moans and groans and other noises, I heard the tearful voice of a sick passenger asking, "Is there any hope, stewardess?"

The train got to Peel as the sun was setting behind the grim old castle walls, and when I saw the dear little town again I dropped half a tear, and even felt an insane desire to run out to meet it. Grandfather was at the station with old "Cæsar" and the pony carriage, and when I had done kissing him and he had done panting and puffing and talking nonsense, as if I had been Queen Victoria and the Empress of the French rolled into one, I could have cried to see how small and feeble he had become since I went away. We could not get off immediately, for in his simple joy at my return he was hailing everybody and everybody was hailing him, and the dear old Pharisee was sounding his trumpet so often in the market-place, that he might have glory of men, that I thought we should never get up to Glenfaba that night. When we did so at length, the old aunties were waiting at the gate, and then he broke into exclamations again. "Hasn't she grown tall? Look at her! Hasn't she now?" Whereupon the aunties took up their parable with, "Well, well! Aw, well! Aw, well now! Well, ye navar!" So that by the time I got through I had kissed everybody a dozen times, and was as red over the eyes as a grouse.

Then we went into the house, and for the first five minutes I couldn't tell what had come over the old place to make it look so small and mean. It was just as if the walls of the rooms had been the bellows of a concertina and somebody had suddenly shut them. But there was the long clock clucking away on the landing, and there was Sir Thomas Traddles purring on the hearthrug, and there were the same plates on the dresser, and the same map of Africa over the fireplace, with a spot of red ink where my father died.

The moon was glistening on the sea when I went to bed that night, and when I got up in the morning the sun was shining on it, and a crow cut across my window cawing, and I heard grandfather humming to himself on the path below. And after my long spell in London, and my railway journey of the day before, it was the same as if I had fallen asleep in a gale on the high seas and awakened in a quiet harbour somewhere.

So here I am, back at Glenfaba, in my old little room with my old little bed, and everything exactly as it used to be; and I begin to believe that when you went into that monastery you only just got the start of me in being dead. There used to be a few people in this place, but now there doesn't seem to be a dog left. All the youngsters have " gone foreign," and all the oldsters have gone to—" goodness knows which." Sometimes we hear the bleat of sheep on the mountains, and sometimes the scream of seagulls overhead, and sometimes we hold a convocation of all living rooks in the elms on the lawn. We take no thought for the morrow, what we shall eat or what we shall put on, and on Sundays when the church-bell rings we go out, like the Israelites in the wilderness, in clothes which wax not old after forty years. During the rest of the week we watch the blue-bottles knocking their stupid heads against the ceiling, and listen to the grasshoppers whispering in the grass, and fall asleep to the hum of the bees, and awake to the *hee-haw* of old Neilus's " canary."[1] Such is the dead-alive life we live at Glenfaba, and the days of our years are threescore years and ten, and if . . . Ohoy! (A yawn.)

I suppose it is basely ungrateful of me to talk like this, for the dear place itself is lovely enough to disturb one's hope of paradise, and this very morning is as fresh as the dew on the

[1] Donkey.

grass, with the larks singing above, and the river singing below, and clouds like little curls of foam hovering over the sea. And as for my three dear old dunces, who love me so much more than I deserve, I am ashamed in my soul when I overhear them planning good things for me to eat, and wild excitements for me to revel in, that I may not be dull or miss the luxuries I am accustomed to. "Do you know I'm afraid Glory doesn't care so much for pinjane after all," I heard grandfather whispering to Aunt Anna one morning, and half an hour afterwards he was reproving Aunt Rachel for pressing me too hard to serve at the soup-kitchen.

They govern me like a child in pinafores, and of course like a child I revenge myself by governing all the house. But, oh dear, oh dear! gone are the days when I could live on water-gruel and be happy in a go-cart. Yes, the change is in me, not in them or in the old home, and what's the good of putting back the clock when the sun is so stubbornly keeping pace? I might be happy enough at Glenfaba still, if I could only bring back the days when the garden trees were my gymnasium, and I used to rock myself and sing like a bird on a bough in the wind, or when I led a band of boys to rob our own orchard—a bold deed, for which Bishop Anna oft times launched at me and all her suffragans her severest censure—it was her slipper, I remember. But I can't run barefoot all day long on the wet sand now, with the salt spray blowing in my face, and a young lady of one-and-twenty seldom or never rushes out to play dumps and baggy-mug in public with little girls of ten.

As a result, my former adventures are now limited to careering on the back of little "Cæsar," who has grown so ancient and fat that he waddles like an old duck, and riding him is like working your passage. So I confine myself to sitting on committees, and being sometimes sat upon, and rubbing the runes for grandfather, and cleaning the milk-pails for Aunt Anna, and even such holy kill-times as going to church regularly, and watching Neilus when he is passing round the plate after "Let your light so shine before men"—light to his practical intellect being clearly a synonym for silver in the shape of threepenny bits!

But, oh my! oh my! I am a dark character in this place for all that. The dear old goodies have never yet said a syllable about my letter announcing that I had gone over to the enemy (*i.e.* Satan and the music-hall), and there is a dead hush in the house as often as the wind of conversation veers in that direction. This is nothing, though, to the white awe in the air when visitors call and I am questioned how I earn my living in London.

I hardly know whether to laugh or cry at the long-drawn breath of relief when I wriggle out of a tight place without telling a lie. But you can't hide an eel in a sack, and I know the truth will pop out one of these days. Only yesterday I went district-visiting with Aunt Rachel, and one of the Balaams of life, who keeps a tavern for fishermen, lured us into his bar parlour to look at a portrait of "Gloria" which he had cut out of an illustrated paper and pinned up on the wall "because it resembled me so much!" Oh dear, oh dear! I could have found it in my heart to brazen it out on the spot at this sight of my evil fame; but when I saw poor little auntie watching me with fearful eyes, I talked away like a mill-wheel, and went out thanking God that the rest of the people of Peel were not as other men are, or even as this publican.

I have been getting newspapers myself, though, sent by my friend Rosa; and as long as the mis-reporters concerned themselves with my own doings and failures to do, and lied as tenderly as an epitaph about my disappearance from London, I cut them up and burnt them. But when they forgot me, and began to treat of other people's triumphs, I made Neilus my waste-paper basket, on the understanding that the papers were to go to the fishermen just home from Kinsale. Then from time to time he told me they were "goin' round, Miss, goin' round," and gave me other assurances of "the greatest circulation in the world," which was true enough certainly, though the old thief omitted to say it was at the paper-mill, where they were being turned into pulp.

But, heigho! I don't need newspapers to remind me of London. Like St. Paul, I have a devil that beats me with fists, and as often as a clear day comes, and one can see things a long way off, he makes me climb to the top of Slieu Whallin,[1] that I may sit on the beacon by the hour and strain my eyes for a glimpse of England, feeling like Lot's wife when she looked back on her old home, and then coming down with a heavy heart and a taste of tears in my mouth as if I had been turned into a pillar of salt. Dear old London! But I suppose it is going on its way just as it used to do, with its tides of traffic and its crowds and carriages, and wandering merchants and hawkers crying their wares, and everything the same as ever, just the same, although Glory isn't there!

10.30 P.M.—I had to interrupt the writing of my letter this morning owing to an alarm of illness seizing grandfather. He had been taken with a sudden faintness. Of course we sent

[1] A mountain in Man.

for the doctor, but before he arrived the faintness had passed; so he looked wise at us, like a prize-riddle which had to be guessed before his next visit, left us his autograph (a wonderful hieroglyphic), and went away. Since then grandfather has been in the hands of a less taciturn practitioner, whom he calls the "flower of Glenfaba" (that's me), and after talking nonsense to him all day, and playing chess with him all the evening, I have put him to bed laughing, and come back to my own room to finish my letter with an easier mind. For the last half-hour the aurora has been pulsing in the northern sky, and I have been thinking that the glorious phantasmagoria must be the sign of a gale in heaven, just as sleet and mist and black wind are the signs of a gale on earth. But it has tripped off into nothingness, and only the dark night is left, through which the dogs at Knockaloe are keeping up their private correspondence with the dogs at Ballamoar by the medium of their nightly howls.

Oh dear! Only 10.30! And to know that while we are going to bed by country hours, with nearly everything still and dead around us, London is just beginning to bestir itself! When I lie down and try to sleep, I shall see the wide squares, with their statues of somebody inside, and the blaze of lights over the doors of the theatres, and all the tingling life of the great and wonderful city. Ugh! It makes one feel like one's own ghost wandering through the upper rooms and across the dark landings, and hearing the strains of the music and the sounds of the dancing from the ballroom below-stairs!

But, my goodness! (I can still swear on that, you see, and not be forsworn!) "What's the odds if you're jolly?—and I allus is!" How's your dog? Mine would write you a letter, only her heart is moribund, and if things go on as they are going she must set about making her will. In fact, she is now lying at the foot of my bed thinking matters out, and bids me tell you that after various attempts to escape Home Rule, not being (like her mistress) one of those natures made perfect through suffering, she is only "kept alive by the force of her own volition" in this house that is full of old maids, and has nothing better in it than one old cat, and he isn't worth hunting, being destitute of a tail. Naturally she is doing her best (like somebody else) to keep herself unspotted from that world which is a source of so much temptation, but she is bound to confess that a little "divilment" now and then would help her to take a more holy and religious view of life.

I "wish you happy" in your new enterprise; but if you are going in for being the champion of woman in this world—of her wrongs—I warn you not to be too pointed in your moral, for there is a story here of a handsome young curate who was so particular in the pulpit with "Lovest thou me?" that a lady followed him into the vestry and admitted that she did. Soberly, it is a great and noble effort, and I've half a mind to love you for it. If men want women to be good they *will* be good, for women dance to the tune that men like best, and always have done so since the days of Adam—not forgetting that gentleman's temptation, nor yet his excuse about " the woman *Thou gavest me*," which shows he wasn't much of a husband anyway, though certainly he hadn't much choice of a wife.

My love to dear old London! Sometimes I have half a mind to skip off and do my wooing myself. Perhaps I should do so, only that Rosa writes that she would like to come and spend her summer holiday in Peel. Haven't I told you about Rosa? She's the lady journalist that Mr. Drake introduced me to.

"But let's to bed,
Said Sleepyhead."

GLORY.

P.S.—IMPORTANT.—Ever since I left London I have been tormented with the recollection of poor Polly's baby. She put him out to nurse with the Mrs. Jupe you heard of, and that person put him out to somebody else. While the mother lived I had no business to interfere, but I can't help thinking of the motherless mite now, and wondering what has become of him. I suppose that like Jeshurun he waxeth fat and kicketh by this time, yet it would be the act of a man and a clergyman if anybody would take up my neglected duty and make it his business to see that there is somebody to love the poor child. Mrs. Jupe's address is 5A The Little Turnstile, going from Holborn into Lincoln's Inn Fields.

VIII

IT was on a Saturday morning that John Storm received Glory's letter, and on the evening of the same day he set out in search of Mrs. Jupe's. The place was not easy to find, and when he discovered it at length, he felt a pang at the thought that Glory herself had lived in this dingy burrowing. As he was going up to the door of the little tobacco-shop a raucous voice within was saying, "That's what's doo on the byeby, and until you can pye up you needn't be a-kemmin' 'ere no more." At the next moment a young woman crossed him on the threshold. She was a little slender thing, looking like a flower that has been broken by the wet. He recognised her as the girl who had nursed the baby in Crook Lane on the day of his first visit to Soho. She was crying, and to hide her swollen eyes she dropped her head at passing, and he saw her faded ribbons and soiled straw hat.

A woman of middle age behind the counter was curtsying to his clerical attire, and a little girl at the door of an inner room was looking at him out of the corner of her eyes, with head aslant.

"Father Storm, I think, sir. Come in and set you down, sir. Mind the shop, Booboo. My 'usband 'as told me about ye, sir. 'You'll know 'im at onct, Lidjer,' 'e sez, siz 'e. No, 'e ain't 'ome from the club yet, but 'e might be a-kemmin' in any time now, sir."

John Storm had seated himself in the little dark parlour, and was looking round and thinking of Glory. "No matter; my business is with you, Mrs. Jupe," he answered, and at that the twinkling eyes and fat cheeks, which had been doing their best to smile, took on a look of fear.

"Wot's the metter?" she asked, and she closed the door to the shop.

"Nothing, I trust, my good woman," and then he explained his errand.

Mrs. Jupe listened attentively and seemed to be asking herself who had sent him.

"The poor young mother is dead now, as you may know, and——"

"But the father ain't," said the woman sharply, "and, begging your parding, sir, if 'e want's ter know where the byeby is 'e can come 'isself and not send sembody else!"

"If the child is well, my good woman, and well cared for——"

"It *is* well keared for, and it's gorn to a pusson I can trust."

"Then what have you got to conceal? Tell me where it is, and——"

"Not me! If it's 'is child, and 'e wants it, let 'im pye for it, and interest ep ter dite. Them swells is too fond of gettin' parsons to pull their chestnuts out o' the fire."

"If you suppose I am here in the interests of the father, you are mistaken, I do assure you."

"Ow, you do, do yer?"

Matters had reached this pass when the door opened and Mr. Jupe came in. Off went his hat with a respectful salutation, but seeing the cloud on his wife's face, he abridged his greeting. The woman's apron was at her eyes in an instant.

"Wot's gowin' on?" he asked. John Storm tried to explain, but the woman contented herself with crying.

"Well, it's like this, don'tcher see, Father. My missis is that fond of childring, and it brikes 'er 'art——"

Was the man a fool or a hypocrite?

"Mr. Jupe," said John, rising, "I'm afraid your wife has been carrying on an improper and illegal business——"

"Now stow thet, sir," said the man, wagging his head. "I respects the Reverend Jawn Storm a good deal, but I respects Mrs. Lidjer Jupe a good deal more, and when it comes to improper and illegal bizinss——"

"Down't mind 'im, 'Enery," said the wife, now weeping audibly.

"And down't you tyke on so, Lidjer," said the husband, and they looked as if they were about to embrace.

John Storm could stand no more. Going down the court he was thinking with a pang of Glory—that she had lived months in the atmosphere of that impostor—when somebody touched his arm in the darkness. It was the girl. She was still crying.

"I reckerleck seeing you in Crook Lane, sir, the day we christened my byeby, and I waited, thinking p'raps you could help me."

"Come this way," said John, and walking by his side along the blank wall of Lincoln's Inn Fields, the girl told her story. She lived in one room of the clergy-house at the back of his church. Having to earn her living, she had answered an advertisement in a Sunday paper, and Mrs. Jupe had taken her baby to nurse. It was true she had given up all claim to the child, but she could not help going to see it—the little one's ways were so engaging. Then she found that Mrs. Jupe had let it out to somebody else. Only for her "friend" she might never have heard of it again. He had found it by accident at a house in Westminster. It was a fearful place, where men went for gambling. The man who kept it had just been released from eighteen months' imprisonment, and the wife had taken to nursing while the husband was in prison. She was a frightful woman, and he was a shocking man, and "they knocked the children about cruel." The neighbours heard screams and slaps and moans, and they were always crying "Shame!" She had wanted to take her own baby away, but the woman would not give it up because there were three weeks' board owing, and she could not pay.

"Could you take me to this house, my child?"

"Yes, sir."

"Then come round to the church after service to-morrow night."

The girl's tearful face glistened like April sunshine. "And will you help me to get my little girl? Oh, how good you are! Everybody is saying what a Father it is that's come to . . ." She stopped, then said quite soberly, "I'll get somebody to lend me a shawl to bring 'er 'ome in. People say they pawn everything, and perhaps the beautiful white perlice I bought for 'er . . . Oh, I'll never let 'er out of my sight again, never!"

"What is your name, my girl?"

"Agatha Jones," the girl answered.

It was nearly eleven o'clock on Sunday night before they were ready to start on their errand. Meantime Aggie had done two turns at the foreign clubs, and John Storm had led a procession through Crown Street, and been hit by a missile thrown by a "Skeleton," whom he declined to give in charge. At the corner of the alley he stopped to ask Mrs. Pincher to wait up for him, and the girl's large eyes caught sight of the patch of plaster above his temple.

"Are you sure you want to go, sir?" she said.

"There's no time to lose," he answered. The bloodhound was with him; he had sent home for it since the attempted riot.

As they walked towards Westminster she told him where she had been, and what money she had earned. It was ten shillings, and that would buy so many things for baby.

"To-morrow I'll get a cot for her—one of those wicker ones; iron is so expensive. She'll want a pair o' socks, too; and by-and-by she'll 'ave to be shortened."

John Storm was thinking of Glory. He seemed to be re-treading the steps of her life in London. The dog kept close at his heels.

"She'll 'a bin a month away now—a month to-morrow. I wonder if she's growed much—I wonder! It's wrong of people letting their childring go away from them. I'll never go out at nights again—not if I 'ave to tyke in sewing for the slop-shops. See this!" laughing nervously, and showing a shawl that hung on her arm. "It's to bring 'er 'ome in—the nights is so chill for a byeby."

John's heart was heavy at sight of these little preparations, but the young mother's face was radiant.

As they went by the Abbey, under its forest of scaffolding, and, walking towards Millbank, dipped into the slums that lie in the shadow of the dark prison, they passed soldiers from the neighbouring barracks going arm-in-arm with girls, and this made Aggie talk of her "friend," and cry a little, saying it was a week since she had seen him, and she was afraid he must have 'listed. She knew he was rude to people sometimes, and she asked pardon for him, but he wasn't such a bad boy after all, and he never knocked you about except when he was drinking.

The house they were going to was in Angel Court, and having its door only to the front, it was partly sheltered from observation. A group of women with their aprons over their heads stood talking in whispers at the corner. One of them recognised Aggie, and asked if she had got her child yet, whereupon John stopped and made some inquiries. The goings-on at the house were scandalous. The men who went to it were the lowest of the low, and there was scarcely one of them who hadn't "done time." The man's name was Sharkey, and his wife was as bad as he was. She insured the children at seven pounds apiece, and "Lawd love ye, sir, at that price the poor things is worth more dead nor alive!"

Aggie's face was becoming white, and she was touching John Storm's elbow as if pleading with him to come away, but he asked further questions. Yes, there were several children. A twelve months' baby, a boy, was fretful with his teething, and on Sunday nights, when the woman was wanted downstairs, she just put the poor darling to bed and locked the room. If you lived next door you could hear his crying through the wall.

"Agatha," said John, as they stepped up to the door, "get us both into this house as best you can, then leave the rest to me. Don, lie close."

Aggie tapped at the door. A little slide in it was run back, and a voice said, "Who's there?"

"Aggie," the girl answered.

"Who's that with you?"

"A friend of Charlie's," and then the door was opened.

John crossed the threshold first, the dog followed him, the girl entered last. When the door had closed behind them, the doorkeeper, a young man holding a candle in his hand, was staring at John with his whole face open.

"Hush! Not a word! Don, watch that man!"

The young man looked at the dog and turned pale.

Where is Mrs. Sharkey?"

"Downstairs, sir."

There were sounds of men's voices from below, and from above there came the convulsive sobs of a child, deadened as by a door between.

"Give me your candle."

The man gave it.

"Don't speak or stir, or else——"

John glanced at the dog, and the man trembled.

"Come upstairs, child," and the girl followed him to the upper floor.

On reaching the room in which the baby was crying they tried the door. It was locked. John attempted to force it, but it would not yield. The child's sobs were dying down to a sleepy moan.

Another room stood open and they went in. It was the living-room. A kettle on the fire was singing and puffing steam. There was no sign of a key anywhere. Only a table, some chairs, a disordered sofa, certain sporting newspapers lying about, and a few pictures on the walls. Some of the pictures were of racehorses, but all the rest were memorial cards, and one bore the text, " He shall gather them in His arms." Aggie was shuddering as with cold, being chilled by some unknown fear.

"We must go down to the cellar—there's no help for it," said John.

The man in the hall had not spoken or stirred. He was still gazing in terror on the bloodshot eyes looking out of the darkness. John gave the candle to the girl, and began to go noiselessly downstairs. There was not a movement in the house now. Big Ben was striking. It was twelve o'clock.

At the next moment John Storm was midway down, and had full view of the den. It was a washing cellar, with a coal vault going out of it under the street. Some fifteen or twenty men, chiefly foreigners, were gathered about a large table covered with green baize, on which a small lamp was burning. A few of the men were seated on chairs ranged about, the others were standing at the back in rows two deep. They were gambling. The game was faro. Rows of lucifer matches were laid on the table, half-crowns were staked on them, and cards were cut and dealt. Except the banker, a middle-aged man with the wild eye of the hard spirit-drinker, everybody had his face turned away from the cellar stairs.

They did not smoke or drink, and they only spoke to each other when the stakes were being received or paid. Then they quarrelled and swore in English. After that there was a chilling and hideous silence, as if something awful were about to occur. The lamp cast a strong light on the table, but the rest of the room was darkened by patches of shadow.

The coal vault had been turned into a drinking bar, and behind the counter there was a well-stocked stillage. In the depths of its shade a woman sat knitting. She had a gross red and white face, and in the arch above her was the iron grid in the pavement. Somebody on the street walked over it, causing a hollow sound, as of soil falling on a coffin.

John Storm was no coward, but a certain tremor passed over him on finding himself in this subterranean lurking-place of men who were as beasts. He stood a full minute unseen. Then he heard the woman say in a low hiss, "Cat's mee-e-et!" and he knew he had been observed. The men turned and looked at him, not suddenly or all at once, but furtively, cautiously, slowly. The banker crouched at the table with an astonished face, and tried to smuggle the cards out of sight.

John stood calmly, his whole figure displaying courage and confidence. The group of men broke up. "He's got the coppers," said one. Nobody else spoke, and they began to melt away. They disappeared through a door at the back, which led into a yard, for, like rats, the human vermin always have a second way out of their holes.

In half a minute the cellar was nearly empty. Only the banker and the woman and one young man remained. The young man was Charlie.

"What cheer, myte?" he said with an air of unconcern. "Is it treeks ye want, sir? Here ye are then," and he threw a pack of cards at John's feet.

"It's that gel o' yawn that's done this," said the woman.

"So it's a got-up thing, is it," said Charlie, and, stepping to the counter, he took up a drinking-glass, broke it at the rim and holding its jagged edges outwards, turned to use it as a weapon.

John Storm had not yet spoken, but a magnetic instinct warned him. He whistled, and the dog bounded down. The young man threw his broken glass on the floor and cried to the keeper of the house, "Don't stir, you! First, you know, the beast will be at yer throat."

Hearing Charlie's voice, Aggie was creeping down the stairs. "Charlie!" she cried. Charlie threw open his coat, stuck his fingers in the armholes of his waistcoat, said in a voice of hatred, passion, and rage, "Go and pawn yourself!" and then swaggered out at the back-door. The keeper made show of following, but John Storm called on him to stop. The man looked at the dog and obeyed. "Wot d'ye want o' me?" he said.

"I want this girl's baby. That's the first thing I want. I'll tell you the rest afterwards."

"Oh, that's it, is it?" The man's grimace was frightful.

"It's gone, sir. We've lost it," said the woman, with a hideous expression.

"That story will not pass with me, my good woman. Go upstairs and unlock the door! You too, my man—go on!"

A minute later they were in the bedroom above. Three neglected children lay asleep on bundles of rags. One of twelve months old was in a wicker cradle, one of three years was in a wooden cot, and a younger child was in a bed. Aggie had come up behind, and stood by the door trembling and weeping.

"Now, my girl, find your baby," said John, and the young mother hurried with eager eyes from the cradle to the cot, and from the cot to the bed.

"Yes, here it is," she cried. "No—oh no, no!" and she began to wring her hands.

"Told yer so," said the woman, and with a wicked grin she pointed to a memorial card which hung on the wall.

Aggie's child was dead and buried. Diarrhœa! The doctor at the dispensary had given a certificate of death, and Charlie had shared the insurance money. "Wish to Christ it was ended," he had said. He had been drunk ever since.

The poor girl was stunned. She was no longer crying. "Oh, oh, oh! What shall I do?" she said.

"Who's child is this?" said John, standing over the wicker cradle. The little sufferer from inflamed gums had sobbed itself to sleep.

"A real laidy's," said the woman. "Mrs. Jupe told us to tyke great kear of it. The father is Lord something."

"My poor girl," said John, turning to Aggie, "could you carry this child home for me?"

"Oh, oh, oh!" said the girl, but she wrapped the shawl about the child and lifted it up sleeping.

"Now, you down't!" said the man, putting himself on guard before the door. "That child is worth undrids of pounds to me, and——"

"Stand back, you brute!" said John, and with the girl and her burden he passed out of the house.

The front door stood open and the neighbourhood had been raised. Trollopy women in their under-petticoats and with their hair hanging about their necks were gathered at the end of the court. Aggie was crying again, and John pushed through the crowd without speaking.

They went back by Broad Sanctuary, where a solitary policeman was pacing to and fro on the echoing pavement. Big Ben was chiming the half-hour after midnight. The child coughed like a sheep constantly, and Aggie kept saying, "Oh, oh, oh!"

Mrs. Pincher, in her widow's cap and white apron, was waiting up for them, and John committed the child to her keeping. Then he said to Aggie, who was turning away, "My poor child, you have suffered deeply, but if you will leave this man I will help you to begin life again, and if you want money I will find it."

"Well, he *is* a Father and no mistake!" said Mrs. Pincher, but the girl only answered in a hopeless voice—

"I don't want no money, and I don't want to begin life again."

As she crossed the court to her room in the tenement house they heard her "Oh, oh, oh!"

Before going to bed that night John Storm wrote to Glory:—
"Hurrah! Have got poor Polly's baby, so you may set your heart at ease about it. All the days of my life I have been thought to be a dreamer, but it is surprising what a man can do when he sets to work for somebody else! Your former landlady turns out to be the wife of my 'organ-man,' and it was pitiful to see the dear old simpleton's devotion to his bogus little baggage. I have lost him, of course, but that was unavoidable.

"It was by help of another victim that I traced the child at last. She is a ballet-girl of some sort, and it was as much as I could stand to see the poor young thing carrying Polly's baby, her own being dead and buried without a word said to her. Short of the grace of God she will go to the bad now. Oh, when will the world see that in dealing with the starved hearts of these poor fallen creatures God Almighty knows best how to do His own business? Keep the child with the mother, foster the maternal instinct, and you build up the best womanhood. Drag them apart, and the child goes to the dogs and the mother to the devil.

"But Polly's baby is safely lodged with Mrs. Pincher, a dear old grandmotherly soul who will love it like her own, and all the way home I have been making up my mind to start baby-farming myself on fresh lines. He who wrongs the child commits a crime against the State. However low a woman has fallen she is a subject of the Crown, and if she is a mother she is the Crown's creditor. These are my first principles, the application will come anon. Meantime you have given me a new career, a glorious mission! Thank God and Glory Quayle for it for ever and ever! Then—who knows?—perhaps you will come back and take it up yourself some day. When I think of the precious time I spent in that monastery . . . But no, only for that I should not be here.

"Oh, life is wonderful! But I feel afraid that I shall wake up—perhaps in the street somewhere—and find I have been dreaming. Deeply grieved to hear of the grandfather's attack.

Trust it has passed. But if not, certain I am that all is well with him, and that he is stayed only on God.

"I hope you are well and plodding through this wilderness in comfort, avoiding the thorns as well as you can. Glenfaba may be dull, but you do well to keep out of the whirlpool of London for the present. Yours is a snug spot, and when storms are blowing even the seagulls shelter about your house, I remember. ... But why Rosa? Is Peel the only place for a summer holiday?"

IX

GLENFABA.

Oh, my dear John Storm, is it coals of fire you are heaping on my head, or fire of brimstone? Your last letter with its torrents of enthusiasm came sweeping down on me like a flood. What work you are in the midst of! What a life! What a purpose! While I—I am lying here like an old slipper thrown up on the sea-beach. Oh, the pity of't, the pity of't! It must be glorious to be in the rush and swirl of all this splendid effort, whatever comes of it! One's soul is thrilled, one's heart expands! As for me, the garden of my mind is withering, and I am consuming the seed I ought to sow.

Rosa has come. She has been here a month nearly, and is just charming, say what you will. Her thoughts have the dash of the great world, and I love to hear her talk. True, she troubles me sometimes, but that's only my envy and malice and all uncharitableness. When she tells of Betty-this and Ellen-that, and their wonderful successes and triumphs, I'm the meanest sinner that crawls.

It's funny to see how the old folk bear themselves towards her. Aunt Rachel regards her as a sort of an artist, and is clearly afraid that she will break out into madness in spots somewhere. Aunt Anna disapproves of her hair, which is brushed up like a man's, and of her skirt, which "would be no worse if it were less like a pair of breeches," for she has brought her "bike." She talks on dangerous subjects also, and nobody did such things in auntie's young days. Then she addresses the old girlies as I do, and calls grandfather "Grand-dad," and, like the witch of Endor generally, is possessed of a familiar spirit. Of course I give her various warning looks from time to time lest the fat should be in the fire, but she's a woman, bless her! and it's as true as ever it was that a woman can keep the secret she doesn't know.

Yes, the ideal of womanhood has changed since the old aunties were young; but when I listen to Rosa, and then look over at Rachel with her black ringlets, and at Anna with her old-fashioned "front," I shudder and ask myself, "Why do I struggle?" What is the reward if one gives up the fascination of life and the world? There is no reward. Nothing but solitary old maidism, unless two of you happen to be sisters, for who else will join her shame to yours? Dreams, dreams, only dreams! Dreams of the dearest thing that ever comes into a woman's arms—and then you awake and there is no one there. A dame's school when the old father is gone, but no children of your own to love you, nobody to think of you, scraping a little here, pinching a little there, growing older and smaller year by year, looking yellow and craned like an apple that has been kept on the top shelf too long, and then . . . the end.

Oh, but I'm trying so hard, so very hard, to be "true to the higher self in me," because somebody says I must. What do you think I did last week? In my character of Lady Bountiful I gave an old folks' supper in the soup-kitchen, understood to be in honour of my return. Roast beef and plum-duff, not to speak of pipes and 'baccy, and forty old people of both sexes sitting down to "the do." After supper there was a concert, when Chalse (the fat old thief!) overflowed the "elber" chair, and alluded to me as "our beautiful donor," and lured me into singing "Mylecharaine," and leading the company when we closed with the doxology.

But "it was not myself at all, Molly dear, 'twas my shadow on the wall," and in any case man can't live by soup-kitchens alone—nor woman either. And knowing what a poor, weak, vain woman I am at the best, I ask myself sometimes would it not be a thousand times better if I yielded to my true nature instead of struggling to realise a bloodless ideal that is not me in the least, but only my picture in the heart of some one who thinks me so much better than I am?

Not that anybody ever sees what a hypocrite I can be, though I came near to letting the cat out of the bag as lately as last night. You must know that when I turned my back on London at the command of John Knox the second, I brought all my beautiful dresses along with me, except such of them as were left at the theatre. Yet I daren't lay them out in the drawers, so I kept them under lock and key in my boxes. There they lurked like evil spirits in ambush, and as often as their perfume escaped into the room my eyes watered for another sight of them! But in spite of all temptation I resisted, I conquered, I triumphed—until last night, when Rosa talked of Juliet, what a glorious creature she was, and how there was nobody on the stage who could "look" her and "play" her too!

What do you think I did? Shall I tell you? Yes, I will. I crept upstairs to my quiet little room, tugged the box from its hiding-place under the bed, drew out my dresses—my lovely, lovely brocades—and put them on! Then I spoke the potion speech, beginning in a whisper, but getting louder as I went on, and always looking at myself in the glass. I had blown out the candle, and there was no light in the room but the moon that was shining on my face; but I was glowing, my very soul was afire, and when I came to the end I drew myself up with eyes closed and head thrown back and heart that paused a beat or two and said, "*I—I* am Juliet, for I am a great actress!"

Oh, oh, oh! I could scream with laughter to think of what happened next! Suddenly I became aware of somebody knocking at my door (I had locked it) and of a thin voice outside saying fretfully, "Glory, whatever is it? Aren't you well, Glory?" It was the little Auntie; and thinking what a shock she would have if I opened the door and she came upon this grand Italian lady instead of poor little me, I had to laugh and to make excuses while I smuggled off my gorgeous things and got back into my plain ones!

It was a narrow squeak; but I had a narrower one some days before. Poor grandfather! He regards Rosa as belonging to a superior race, and loves to ask her what she thinks of Glory. He has grown quite simple lately, and as soon as he thinks my back is turned he is always saying, "And what is your opinion of my granddaughter, Miss Macquarrie?" To which she answers, "Glory is going to make your name immortal, Mr. Quayle." Then his eyes sparkle and he says, "Do you think so?—do you really think so?" Whereupon she talks further balderdash, and the dear old darling smiles a triumphant smile!

But I always notice that not long afterwards his eyes look wet and his head hangs low, and he is saying to the aunties, with a crack in his voice, "She'll go away again. You'll see she will. Her beauty and her talents belong to the world." And then I burst in on them and scold them, and tell them not to talk nonsense.

Nevertheless he is beginning to regard Rosa with suspicion, as if she were a witch luring me away, and one evening last week we had to steal into the garden to talk that we might escape from his watchful eyes. The sun had set—there was the red glow behind the castle across the sky and the sea, and we were walking on the low path by the river under the fuchsia hedge that hangs over from the lawn, you know. Rosa was talking with her impetuous dash of the great career open to any one who could win the world in London, how there were people enough to help her on, rich men to find her opportunities, and even to take theatres for her, if need be. And I was hesitating and halting and stammering, "Yes, yes, if it were the *regular* stage . . . who knows? . . . perhaps it might not be open to the same objections . . ." when suddenly the leaves of the fuchsia rustled as with a gust of wind, and we heard footsteps on the path above.

It was the grandfather, who had come out on Rachel's arm and overheard what I had said! "It's Glory!" he faltered, and then I heard him take his snuff and blow his nose as if to cover his confusion, thinking I was deceiving them and carrying on a secret intercourse. I hardly know what happened next, except that for the five minutes following "the great actress" had to talk with the tongues of men and angels (Beelzebub's) in order to throw dust in the dear old eyes and drive away their doubts. It was a magnificent performance, "you go bail." I'll never do the like of it again, though I had only one old man and one old maid and one young woman for audience. The house "rose" at me too, and the poor old grandfather was appeased. But when we were back indoors I overheard him saying, "After all, there's no help for it. She's dull with us—what wonder! We can't cage our linnet, Rachel, and perhaps we shouldn't try. A song-bird came to cheer us, but it will fly away. We are only old folks, dear—it's no use crying." And on going to his room that night he closed his door and said his prayers in a whisper that I might not hear him when he sobbed.

He hasn't left his bed since. I fear he never will. More than once I have been on the point of telling him there is no reason to think the deluge would come if I *did* go back to London; but I will never leave him now. Yet I wish Aunt Rachel wouldn't talk so much of the days when I went away before. It seems that every night, on his way to his own room, he used to step into my empty one and come out with his eyes dim and his lips moving. I am not naturally hard-hearted, but I can't love grandfather like that. Oh, the cruelty of life! . . . I know it ought to be the other way about . . . but I can't help it.

All the same I could cry to think how short life is, and how little of it I can spare. "Cling fast to me and hold me," my heart is always saying, but meantime London is calling to me, calling to me like the sea, and I feel as if I were a wandering mermaid, and she were my ocean home.

T

LATER.

Poor, poor grandfather! I was interrupted in the writing of my letter this morning by another of those sudden alarms. He had fainted again, and it is extraordinary how helpless the aunties are in a case of illness. Grandfather knows it too; and after I had done all I could to bring him round, he opened his eyes and whispered that he had something to say to me alone. At that the poor old things left the room with tears of woe and a look of understanding. Then fetching a difficult breath, he said, "*You* are not afraid, Glory, are you?" and I answered him "No," though my heart was trembling. And then a feeble smile struggled through the wan features of his drawn face, and he told me his attack was only another summons. "I'll soon die for good," he said, "and you must be strong and brave, my child, for death is the common lot, and then what is there to fear?" I didn't try to contradict him—what was the good of doing that? And after he had spoken of the coming time he talked quietly of his past life, how he had weathered the storm for seventy odd years, and his Almighty Father was bringing him into harbour at last. "I can't pray for life any longer, Glory. Many a time I did so in the old days when I had to bring up my little granddaughter, but my task is over now, and after the day is done, where is the tired labourer who does not lie down to his rest with a will?"

The doctor has been and gone. There is no ailment, and nothing to be done or hoped. It is only a general failure and a sinking earthwards of the poor worn-out body as the soul rises to the heaven that is waiting to receive it. What a pagan I feel beside him! And how glad I am that I didn't talk of leaving him again when he was on the eve of his far longer journey! I have sent the aunties to bed, but Rosa has made me promise to waken her at four that she may take her turn at his bedside.

NEXT MORNING.

Rosa relieved me during the night, and I came to my room and lay down in the chillness of the dawn. But now I am sorry that I allowed her to do so, for I did not sleep, and grandfather appears to have been troubled with dreams. I fancied he shuddered a little as I left them together, and more than once through the wall I heard him cry, "Bring him back," in the toneless voice of one who is labouring under the terrors of a nightmare. But each time I heard Rosa comforting him, so I lay down again without going in.

Being stronger this morning, he has been propped up in bed

writing a letter. When he called for the pens and paper, I asked if I couldn't write it for him, but the old darling made a great mystery of the matter, and looked artful, and asked if it was usual to fight your enemy with his own powder and shot. Of course I humoured him and pretended to be mighty curious, though I think I know who the letter was written to, all the same that he kept the address side of the envelope hidden even when the front of it was being sealed. He sealed it with sealing-wax, and I held the candle while he did so, with his poor trembling fingers in danger from the light, and then I stamped it with my mother's pearl ring, and he smuggled it under the pillow.

Since breakfast he has shown an increased inclination to doze, but there have been visits from the wardens and from neighbouring parsons, for a *locum tenens* has had to be appointed. Of course they have all inquired where his pain is, and on being told that he has none, they have gone downstairs cackling and clucking and crowing in various versions of "Praise God for that!" I hate people who are always singing the Doxology.

NOON.

Condition unchanged, except that in the intervals of drowsiness his mind has wandered a little. He appears to live in the past. Looking at me with conscious eyes, he calls me "Lancelot"— my father's name. It has been so all the morning. One would think he was walking in a twilight land where he mistakes people's faces and the dead are as much alive as the living.

They all think I am brave, oh, so brave! because I do not cry now, as everybody else does—even Aunt Anna behind her apron —although my tears can flow so easily, and at other times I keep them constantly on tap. But I am really afraid, and down at the bottom of my heart I am terrified. It is just as if *something* were coming into the house slowly, irresistibly, awfully, and casting its shadow on the floor already.

I have found out the cause of his outcries in the night. Aunt Rachel says he was dreaming of my father's departure for Africa. That was twenty-two years ago, but it seems that the memory of the last day has troubled him a good deal lately. "Don't you remember it?" he has been saying. "There were no railways in the island then, and we stood at the gate to watch the coach that was taking him away. He sat on the top and waved his red handkerchief. And when he had gone and it was no use watching, we turned back to the house—you and Anna and poor, pretty young Elise. He never came back, and when Glory goes again she'll never come back either."

In the intervals of his semi-consciousness, when he mistakes me for my father, my wonderful bravery often fails me, and I find excuses for going out of the room. Then I creep noiselessly through the house and listen at half-open doors. Just now I heard him talking quite rationally to Rachel, but in a voice that seemed to speak inwardly, not outwardly, as before. "She can't help it, poor child," he said. "Some day she'll know what it is, but not yet, not until she has a child of her own. The race looks forward, not backward. God knew when he created us that the world couldn't go on without that bit of cruelty, and who am I that I should complain?"

I couldn't bear it any longer, and with a pain at my heart I ran in and cried, "I'll never leave you, grandfather." But he only smiled and said, "I'll not be keeping you long, Glory, I'll not be keeping you long," and then I could have died for shame.

EVENING.

All afternoon he has been like a child, and everything present to his consciousness seems to have been reversed. The shadow of eternity appears to have wiped out time. When I have raised him up in bed he has delighted to think he was a little boy in his young mother's arms. Oh, sweet dream! The old man, with his furrowed forehead and beautiful white head and all the heavy years rolled back! More than once he has asked me if he may play till bedtime, and I have stroked his wrinkled hands and told him "Yes," for I pretend to be his mother, who died when she was old.

But the "part" is almost too much for me, and lest I should break down under the strain of it, I am going out of his room constantly. I have just been into his study. It is as full as ever of his squeezes and rubbings and plaster casts and dusty old runes. He has spent all his life away back in the tenth century, and now he is going farther, farther. . . .

Oh, I am aweary, aweary! If anything happens to grandfather I shall soon leave this place; there will be nothing to hold me here any longer, and besides I could not bear the sight of these evidences of his gentle presence, so simple, so touching. But what a vain thing London is with all its vast ado—how little, how pitiful!

LATER.

It is all over. The curtain has fallen, and I am not crying. If I did cry, it would not be from grief, but because the end was so beautiful, so glorious! It was at sunset, and the streamers of the sun were coming horizontally into the room. He awoke from a long drowsiness, and a serenity almost angelic overspread his face. I could see that he was himself once again. Death had led him back through the long years since he was a child, and he knew he was an old man and I a young woman. "Have the boats gone yet?" he asked, meaning the herring-boats that go at sunset. I looked out, and told him they were at the point of going. "Let me see them sail," he said; so I slipped my arms about him, and raised him until he was sitting up and could see down the length of the harbour and past the castle to the sea. The reflection of the sunlight was about his silvery old head, and over the damps and chills of death it made a radiance on his face like a light from heaven. There was hardly a breeze, and the boats were dropping down from their berths with their brown sails half set. "Ah," he said, "it's the *other* way with me, Glory. I'm coming in, not going out. I've been beating to windward all my life, but I see the harbour on my lee-bow at last as plainly as I ever saw Peel, and now I'm only waiting for the top of the tide and the master of the port to run up the flag!"

Then his head fell gently back on my arm and his lips changed colour, but his eyes did not close, and over his saintly face there passed a fleeting smile. Thus died a Christian gentleman—a simple, sunny, merry, happy, child-like creature, and of such are the kingdom of heaven. GLORY.

Parson Quayle's Letter.

DEAR JOHN,—Before this letter reaches you, or perhaps along with it, you will receive the news that tells you what it is. I am "in," John; I can say no more than that. The doctor tells me it may be now or then or at any time. But I am looking for my enlargement soon, and whether it comes to-morrow sunset or with to-day's next tide, I leave myself in His hands in whose hands we all are. Well has the wise man said, "The day of our death is better than the day of our birth," so with all good-will, and what legacy of strength old age has left to me, I send you my last word and message.

My poor old daughters are sorely stricken, but Glory is still brave and true, being, as she always was, a quivering bow of steel. People tell me that the poor mother is strong in the girl, and the spirit of the mother's race; but well I know the father's stalwart soul supports her; and I pray God that when my dark hour comes her loving and courageous arms may be around me.

That brings me to the object of my letter. This living will soon be vacant, and I am wondering who will follow in my feeble steps. It is a sweet spot, John! The old church does not look so ill when the sun shines on it, and in the summertime this old garden is full of fruit and flowers. Did I ever tell you that Glory was born here? I never had another grandchild, and we were great comrades from the first. She was a wise and winsome little thing, and I was only an old child myself, so we had many a run and romp in these grounds together. When I try to think of the place without her, it is a vain effort and a painful one; and even while she was away in your great and wicked Babylon, with its dangers and temptations, her little ghost seemed to lurk at the back of every bush and tree, and sometimes it would leap out on me and laugh.

It is months since I saw your father, but they tell me he has lately burnt his bureau, making one vast bonfire of the gatherings of twenty years. That is not such ill news either; and maybe, now the great ado that worked such woe is put by and gone, he would rejoice to see you back at home, and open his hungering arms to you.

But my eyes ache and my pen is shaking. Farewell! Farewell! Farewell! An old man leaves you his blessing, John. God grant that in His own good time we may meet in a blessed paradise, rejoicing in His gracious mercy, and all our sins forgiven! ADAM QUAYLE.

X

GLORY's letter and its enclosure fell on John Storm like rain in the face of a man on horseback—he only whipped up and went faster.

"How can I find words," he wrote, "to express what I feel at your mournful news? Yet why mournful? His life's mission was fulfilled, his death was a peaceful victory, and we ought to rejoice that he was so easily released. I trust you will not mourn too heavily for him, or allow his death to stop your life. It would not be right. No trouble came near his stainless heart, no shadow of sin; his old age was a peaceful day which lasted until sunset. He was a creature that had no falsetto in a single fibre of his being, no shadow of affectation. He kept like this through all our complicated existence in this artificial world, absolutely unconscious of the hollowness and pretension and sham that surrounded him—tolerant, too, and kind to all. Then why mourn for him? He is gathered in—he is safe.

"His letter was touching in its artful simplicity. It was intended to ask me to apply for his living. But my duty is here, and London must make the best of me. Yet more than ever now I feel my responsibility with regard to yourself. The time is not ripe to advise you. I am on the eve of a great effort. Many things have to be tried, many things attempted. It is a gathering of manna—a little every day. To God's keeping and protection meantime I commit you. Comfort your aunts, and let me know if there is anything that can be done for them."

The ink of this letter was hardly dry when John Storm was in the middle of something else. He was in a continual fever now. Above all, his great scheme for the rescue and redemption of women and children possessed him. He called it Glory's scheme when he talked of it to himself. It might be in the teeth of nineteenth-century morality, but what matter about that? It was on the lines of Christ's teaching when He forgave the woman and shamed the hypocrites. He would borrow for it, beg for it, and there might be conditions under which he would steal for it too.

Mrs. Callender shook her head.

"I much misdoubt there'll be scandal, laddie. It's a woman's work, I'm thinking."

"'Be thou as chaste as ice,' auntie, 'as pure as snow' . . . But no matter! I intend to call out the full power of a united Church into the warfare against this high wickedness. Talk of the union of Christendom! If we are in earnest about it we'll unite to protect and liberate our women."

"But where's the siller to come frae, laddie?"

"Anywhere—everywhere! Besides, I have a bank I can always draw on, auntie."

"You're no meaning the Prime Minister again, surely?"

"I mean the King of Kings. God will provide for me in this as in everything."

Thus his reckless enthusiasm bore down everything, and at the back of all his thoughts was the thought of Glory. He was preparing a way for her; she was coming back to a great career, a glorious mission; her bright soul would shine like a star; she would see that he had been right and faithful, and then . . . then . . . But it was like wine coursing through his veins—he could not think of it.

Three thousand pounds had to be found to buy or build homes with, and he set out to beg for the money. His first call was at

Mrs. Macrae's. Going up to the house, he met the lady's poodle in a fawn-coloured wrap coming out in charge of a footman for its daily walk round the square.

He gave the name of "Father Storm," and after some minutes of waiting he was told that the lady had a headache and was not receiving that day.

"Say the nephew of the Prime Minister wishes to see her," said John.

Before the footman had returned again there was the gentle rustle of a dress on the stairs, and the lady herself was saying, "Dear Mr. Storm, come up. My servants are real tiresome, they are always confusing names."

Time had told on her; she was looking elderly, and the wrinkles about her eyes could no longer be smoothed out. But her "front" was curled, and she was still saturated in perfume.

"I heard of your return, dear Mr. Storm," she said in the languid voice of the great lady, but the accent of St. Louis, as she led the way to the drawing-room. "My daughter told me about it. She was always interested in your work, you know . . . Oh yes, quite well, and having a real good time in Paris. Of course you know she has been married. A great loss to me naturally, but being God's will, I felt it was my duty as a mother . . ." and then a pathetic description of her maternal sentiments, consoled by the circumstance that her son-in-law belonged to "one of the best families," and that she was constantly getting newspapers from "the other side" containing full accounts of the wedding and of the dresses that were worn at it.

John twirled his hat in his hand and listened.

"And what are your dear devoted people doing down there in Soho?"

Then John told of his work for working girls, and the great lady pretended to be deeply interested. "Why, they'll soon be better than the upper classes," she said.

John thought it was not improbable, but he went on to tell of his scheme, and how small was the sum required for its execution.

"Only three thousand! That ought to be easily fixed up. Why, certainly!"

"Charity is the salt of riches, madam, and if rich people would remember that their wealth is a trust——"

"I do—I always do. 'Lay not up for yourselves treasure on earth'—what a beautiful text *that* is!"

"I'm glad to hear you say so, madam. So many Christian people allow that God is the God of the widow and fatherless, while the gods they really worship are the gods of silver and gold."

" But I love the dear children, and I like to go to the institution to see them in their nice white pinafores making their curtsies. But what you say is real true, Mr. Storm; and since I came from Sent Louis I've seen considerable people who are that silly about cats . . ." and then a long story of the folly of a lady friend who had once had a pet Persian, but it died, and she wore crape for it, and you could never mention a cat in her hearing afterwards.

At that moment the poodle came back from its walk, and the lady called it to her, fondled it affectionately, said it was a present from her poor dear husband, and launched into an account of her anxieties respecting it, being delicate and liable to colds, notwithstanding the trousseau (it was a lady poodle) which the fashionable dog tailor in Regent Street had provided for it.

John got up to take his leave. "May I then count on your kind support on behalf of our poor women and children of Soho?"

"Ah, of course, that matter . . . Well, you see, the Archdeacon kindly comes to talk 'City' with me—in fact, I'm expecting him to-day—and I never do anything without asking his advice, never, in my present state of health—I have a weak heart, you know," with her head aside and her saturated pocket-handkerchief at her nose. " But has the Prime Minister done anything?"

"He has advanced me two thousand pounds."

"Really?" rising and kicking back her train. "Well, as I say, we ought to fix it right away. Why not hold a meeting in my drawing-room? All denominations, you say? I don't mind —not in a cause like that," and she glanced round her room as if thinking it was always possible to disinfect it afterwards.

Somebody was coughing loudly in the hall as John stepped downstairs. It was the Archdeacon coming in. "Ah," he exclaimed with a flourish of the hand, greeting John as if they had parted yesterday and on the best of terms. Yes, there *had* been changes, and he was promoted to a sphere of higher usefulness. True, his good friends had looked for something still higher, but it was the premier archdeaconry at all events, and in the Church, as in life generally, the spirit of compromise ruled everything. He asked what John was doing, and on being told, he said with a somewhat more worldly air, " Be careful, my dear Storm, don't encourage vice. For my part, I am tired of the 'fallen sister.' To tell you the truth, I deny the name. The painted Jezebel of the Piccadilly pavement is no sister of mine."

"We don't choose our relations, Archdeacon," said John. "If God is our Father, then all men are our brothers, and all women are our sisters whether we like it or not."

"Ah! The same man still, I see. But we will not quarrel about words. Seen the dear Prime Minister lately? Not *very* lately? Ah, well"—with a superior smile—"the air of Downing Street, it's *so* bad for the memory, they say," and coughing loudly again, he stepped upstairs.

John Storm went home that day light-handed but with a heavy heart.

"Begging is an ill trade on a fast day, laddie," said Mrs. Callender. "Sit you down and tak' some dinner."

"How dare these people pray, 'Our Father which art in heaven'? It's blasphemy! It's deceit!"

"Aye, and they would deceive God about their dividends if He couldn't see into their safes."

"Their money is the meanest thing heaven gives them. If I asked them for their health or their happiness, Lord God, what would they say?"

On the Sunday night following, John Storm preached to an overflowing congregation from the text, "This people draweth nigh unto me with their mouth, and honoureth me with their lips, but their heart is far from me."

But a few weeks afterwards his face was bright and his voice was cheery, and he was writing another letter to Glory:—

"In full swing at last, Glory. To carry out my new idea, I had to get three thousand pounds more of my mother's money from my uncle. He gave it up cheerfully, only saying he was curious to see what approach to the Christian ideal the situation of civilisation permitted. But Mrs. Callender is *dour*, and every time I spend sixpence of my own money on the Church she utters withering sarcasms about being only a 'daft auld woman hersel',' and then I have to caress and coax her.

"The newspapers were facetious about my 'Baby Houses' until they scented the Prime Minister at the back of them, and now they call them the 'Storm Shelters,' and christen my nightly processions 'The White-cross Army.' Even the Archdeacon has begun to tell the world how he 'took an interest' in me from the first, and gave me my title. I met him again the other day at a rich woman's house, where we had only one little spar, and yesterday he wrote, urging me to 'organise my great effort,' and have a public dinner in honour of its inauguration. I did not think God's work could be well done by people dining in herds and drinking bottles of champagne, but I showed no malice. In fact, I agreed to hold a meeting in the lady's drawing-room, to which clergymen, laymen, and members of all denominations are being invited, for this is a cause that rises above all differences of dogma, and I intend to try what can be done towards a union of Christendom on a social basis. Mrs. Callender is *dour* on that subject too, reminding me that where the carcass is, there will the eagles be gathered together. The Archdeacon thinks we must have the meeting before the twelfth of August, or not until after the middle of September, and Mrs. Callender understands this to mean that 'the Holy Ghost always goes to sleep in the grouse season.'

"Meantime, my Girls' Club goes like a forest fire. We are in our renovated clergy-house at last, and have everything comfortable. Two hundred members already, chiefly dressmakers and tailors, and girls out of the jam and match factories. The bright, merry young things, rejoicing in their brief blossoming time between girlhood and womanhood, I love to be among them and to look at their glistening eyes! Mrs. Callender blows withering blasts on this head also, saying it is no place for a 'laddie,' whereupon I lie low and think much, but say nothing.

"Our great night is Sunday night after service. Yes, indeed, Sunday! That's just when the devil's houses are all open round about us, and why should God's house be shut up? It is all very well for the people who have only one Sabbath in the week to keep it wholly holy—I have seven, being a follower of Jesus, not of Moses. But the rector of the parish has begun to complain of my 'intrusion,' and to tell the bishop I ought to be 'mended or ended.' It seems that my 'doings' are 'indecent and unnecessary,' and my sermons are 'a violation of all the sanctities, all the modesties of existence.' Poor dumb dog, teaching the Gospel of Don't! The world has never been reformed by 'resignation' to the evils of life, or converted by 'silence' either.

"How I wish you were here in the midst of it all! And— who knows?—perhaps you will be some day yet. Do not trouble to answer this—I will write again soon, and may then have something practical to say to you. *Au revoir!*"

XI

On the day of the drawing-room meeting, a large company gathered in the hall at Belgrave Square. Lady Robert Ure, back from the honeymoon, received the guests for her mother, whose weak heart and a headache kept her upstairs. Her husband stood aside, chewing the end of his moustache and looking through his eyeglass with a gleam of amused interest in his glittering eye. There were many ladies, all fashionably dressed, and one of them wore a sea-gull's wing in her hat, with part of the root left visible, and painted red to show that it had been torn out of the living bird. The men were nearly all clergymen, and the cut of their cloth and the fashions of their ties indicated the various complexions of their creeds. They glanced at each other with looks of embarrassment, and Mrs. Callender, who came in like a breeze off a Scottish moor, said audibly that she had never seen "sae many craws on one tree before." The Archdeacon was there with his head up, talking loudly to Lady Robert. She stood motionless in her place, never turning her head towards John Storm, though it was plain that she was looking at him constantly. More than once he caught an expression of pain in her face, and felt pity for her as one of the brides who had acted the lie of marrying without love. But his spirits were high. He welcomed everybody, and even bantered Mrs. Callender when she told him she "objected to the hale thing," and said "Weel, weel, wait a wee."

The Archdeacon gave the signal and led the way with Lady Robert to the drawing-room, where Mrs. Macrae, redolent of perfume, was reclining on a sofa with the "lady poodle" by her side. As soon as the company were seated the Archdeacon rose and coughed loudly.

"Ladies and gentlemen," he said, "we have no assurance of a blessing except 'Ask and ye shall receive.' Therefore, before we go further, it is our duty, as brethren of a common family in Christ, to ask the blessing of Almighty God on this enterprise."

There was a subdued rustle of drooping hats and bonnets, when suddenly a thin voice was heard to say, "Mr. Archdeacon, may I inquire first who is to ask the blessing?"

"I thought of doing so myself," said the Archdeacon with a meek smile.

"In that case, as a Unitarian, I must object to an invocation in which I do not believe."

There was a half-suppressed titter from the wall at the back, where Lord Robert Ure was standing with his face screwed up to his eyeglass.

"Well, if the name of our Lord is a stumbling-block to our Unitarian brother, no doubt the prayer in this instance would be acceptable without the customary Christian benediction."

"That's just like you," said a large man near the door, with whiskers all round his face. "You've been trimming all your life, and now you are going to trim away the name of our Lord Jesus Christ."

"If our Low Church brother thinks he can do better . . . "

But John Storm intervened. He had looked icy cold, though the twitching of his lower lip showed that he was red hot within.

"Ladies and gentlemen," he said in a quavering voice, "I apologise for bringing you together. I thought if we were in earnest about the union of Christendom we might at least unite in the real contest with evil. But I find it is a dream; we have only been trifling with ourselves, and there is not one of us who wants the union of Christendom, except on the condition that his rod shall be like Aaron's rod which swallowed up all the rest. It was a mistake, and I beg your pardon."

"Yes, sir," said the Archdeacon, "it *was* a mistake; and if you had taken my advice from the first, and asked the blessing of God through good High Churchmen alone——"

"God doesn't wait for any asking," said John, now flushing up in the eyes. "He gives freely to High Churchmen, Low Churchmen, and No Churchmen alike."

"If that is your opinion, sir, you are no better than some of your friends, and, for my part, I will never darken your door again!"

"*Darken* is a good word for it, Archdeacon," said John, and with that the company broke up.

Mrs. Macrae looked like a thunder-cloud as John bowed to her on passing out, but Mrs. Callender cried in a jubilant voice, "Be skipper of your ain ship, laddie!" and added (being two yards behind the Archdeacon's broad back going down the stairs), "If some folks are to be inheritors of the kingdom of heaven there'll be a michty crush at the pearly gates, I'm thinking!"

John Storm went back to Soho with a heavy heart. Going up Victoria Street he passed a crowd of ragged people who were ploughing their way through the carriages. Two constables were taking a man and a woman to the police court in Rochester Row. The prisoners were Sharkey, the keeper of the gambling house, and his wife the baby-farmer.

But within a week John Storm, in greater spirits than ever, was writing to Glory again:—

"The Archdeacon has deserted me, but no matter! My uncle has advanced me another thousand of my mother's money, so the crusade is *self*-supporting in one sense, at all events. What a fool I am! Ask Aunt Anna her opinion of me, or say old Chalse or the village natural. But never mind! Folly and wisdom are relative terms, and I don't envy the world its narrow ideas of either. You would be amused to see how the women of the West End are taking up the movement—Lady Robert Ure among the rest! They have banded themselves into a Sisterhood, and christened our clergy-house a 'Settlement.' One of my Greek owners came in the other evening to see the alterations.

His eyes glistened at the change, and he asked leave to bring a friend. I trust you are well and settling things comfortably, and that Miss Macquarrie has gone. It is raining through a colander here, but I have no time to think of depressing weather. Sometimes when I cross our great squares, where the birds sing among the yellowing leaves, my mind goes off to your sweet home in the sunshine; and when I drop into the dark alleys and lanes, where the pale-faced children play in their poverty and rags, I think of a day that is coming, and, God willing, is now so near, when a ministering angel of tenderness and strength will be passing through them like a gleam. But I am more than ever sure that you do well to avoid for the present the pompous joys of life in London, where for one happy being there are a thousand pretenders to happiness."

On the Sunday night following, Crook Lane, outside the clergy-house, was almost blocked with noisy people of both sexes. They were a detachment of the 'Skeletons,' and the talk among them was of the trial of the Sharkeys, which had taken place the day before. "They've 'ed six months," said one. "And it's all along o' minjee parsons," said another; and Charlie Wilkes, who had a certain reputation for humour, did a step-dance and sang some doggerel beginning—

"Father Storm is a werry good man,
'E does you all the 'arm 'e can."

Through this crowd two gentlemen pushed their way to the clergy-house, which was brilliantly lit up. One of them was the Greek owner, the other was Lord Robert Ure. Entering a large room on the ground floor, they first came upon John Storm, in cassock and biretta, standing at the door and shaking hands with everybody who came in and went out. He betrayed no surprise, but greeted them respectfully and then passed them on. Every moment of his time was occupied. The room was full of the young girls of the district, with here and there a Sister out of another world entirely. Some were reading, some conversing, some laughing, some playing a piano, and some singing. Their voices filled the air like the chirping of birds, and their faces were bright and happy. "Good-evening, Father," they said on entering, and "Good-night, Father," as they went away.

The two men stood some minutes and looked round the room. It was observed that Lord Robert did not remove his hat. He kept chewing the end of a broken cigarette, whereof the other end hung down his chin. One of the Sisters heard him say, "It will do with a little alteration, I think." Then he went off alone, and the Greek owner stepped up to John Storm.

It was not at first that John could attend to him, and when he was able to do so he began to rattle on about his own affairs. "See," he said with a delighted smile and a wave of the arm, "see how crowded we are! We'll have to think of taking in the next door soon."

"Father Storm," said the Greek, "I have something serious to say, though the official notification will of course reach you by another channel."

John's face darkened as a ripe cornfield does when the sun dies away from it.

"I am sorry to tell you that the trustees, having had a favourable offer for this property——"

"Well?" His great staring eyes had stopped the man.

"—— have decided to sell."

"Sell? Did you say so . . .? To whom? . . . What?"

"To tell you the truth, to the syndicate of a music-hall."

John staggered back, breathing audibly. "Now if a man had to believe that . . . Do you know, if I thought such a thing could happen——"

"I'm sorry you take the matter so seriously, Father Storm. It's true you've spent money on the property, but, believe me, the trustees will derive no profit——"

"Profit? Money? Do you suppose I'm thinking of that, and not of the desecration, the outrage, the horror? But who are they? Is that man . . . Lord——"

The Greek had nodded his head, and John flung open the door. "Out of this! Out of it, you Judas!" And almost before the Greek had crossed the threshold the door was banged at his back.

The incident had been observed, and there was dead silence in the club-room, but John only cried, "Let's sing something, girls," and when a Sister struck up his favourite "Nazareth" there was no voice so loud as his.

But he had realised everything. "Gloria" was coming back, and the work of months was overthrown!

When he was going home groups of the girls were talking in whispers in the hall, and Mrs. Pincher, who was wiping her eyes at the door, said, "I wonder you don't drown yourself, I do."

At the corner of the lane Mr. Jupe was waiting for him, to beg his pardon and to ask his advice. What he had said of Mrs. Jupe had turned out to be true. The Sharkeys had "split" on her, and she had been arrested. "It was all in the evenin' paipers last night," the weak creature whimpered, "and to-day my manager told me I 'ad best look out for another place. Oh, my poor Lidjer! What am I to do?"

"Do? Cut her off like a rotten bough!" said John scornfully, and with that he strode down the street. The human sea roared around him, and he felt as if he wanted to fling himself into the midst of it and be swallowed up.

On reaching Victoria Square he told Mrs. Callender the news —flung it out at her with a sort of triumphant shout. His church had been sold over his head, and being only "Chaplain to the Greek-Turks," he was to be turned into the streets. Then he laughed wildly, and by some devilish impulse began to abuse Glory. "The next chaplain is to be a girl," he cried, "one of those creatures who throw kisses at gaping crowds, and sweep curtsies for their dirty crusts."

But all at once he turned white as a ghost and sat down trembling. Mrs. Callender's face was twitching, and to prevent herself from crying she burst into scorching satire. "There!" she said, sitting in her rocking-chair and rocking herself furiously, "I ken'd weel what it would come til! Adversity mak's a man wise, they say, if it doesna mak' him rich. But it's the Prime Minister I blame for this. The auld dolt! he must be fallen to his dotage. It's enough to mak' a reasonable body go out of her mind to think of sic wise asses. I told you what to expect, but you were always miscalling me for a suspicious auld woman. Oh, it's a thing ye'd no suspect; but Jane Callender is only a daft auld fool, ye see, and doesna ken what she's saying!"

But the next moment she had jumped up and flung her arms about John's neck, and was crying over him like a girl. "Oh, my son! my ain son! And is it for me to fling out at ye? Aye, aye, it's a heartless world, laddie!"

He kissed the old woman, and then she tried to coax him to eat. "Come, come, a wee bittie, just a wee bittie. We must eat our supper, anyway."

"God seems dead, and heaven a long way off," he murmured.

"And a drap o' whisky will do no harm—a wee drappie."

"There's only one thing clear—God sees I'm unfit for the work, so He has taken it away from me."

She turned aside from the table, and the supper was left untouched.

The first post next morning brought a letter from Glory.

THE GARDEN HOUSE,
CLEMENT'S INN, W.C.

Forgive me! I have returned to town! I couldn't help it, I couldn't, I couldn't. London dragged me back. What was I to do after everything was settled and the aunties provided for?

—assist in a dame's school, and wage war with pothooks and hangers? Oh! I was simply dying of weariness—dying, dying, dying!

And then they made me such tempting offers. Not the music-hall—don't think that. I dare say you were quite right there. No, but the theatre, the regular theatre! Mr. Drake has bought some broken-down old place, and is to turn it into a beautiful theatre expressly for me. I am to play Juliet. Only think— Juliet!—and in my own theatre! Already I feel like a liberated slave who has crossed her Red Sea.

And don't think a woman's mourning is like the silly old laws which lasted but three days. *He* is buried in my heart, not in the earth, and I shall love him and revere him always! And then didn't you tell me yourself it wouldn't be right to allow his death to stop my life?

Write and say you forgive me, John. Reply by return, and make yourself your own postman—registered. You'll find me here at Rosa's. Come, come, come! I'll never forgive you if you don't come soon—never, never! GLORY.

XII

A FORTNIGHT had passed, and John Storm had not yet visited Glory. Nevertheless he had heard of her from day to day through the medium of the newspapers. Every morning he had glanced down the black columns for the name that stood out from them as if its letters had been printed in blood. The reports had been many and mysterious. First, the brilliant young artiste, who had made such an extraordinary impression some months before, had returned to London and would shortly resume the promising career which had been interrupted by illness and family bereavement. Next, the forthcoming appearance would be on the regular stage, and in a Shakspearean character which was always understood to be a crucial test of histrionic genius. Then, the revival of "Romeo and Juliet," which had formerly been in contemplation, would probably give way to the still more ambitious project of an entirely new production by a well-known Scandinavian author, with a part peculiarly fitted to the personality and talents of the débutante. Finally, a syndicate was about to be formed for the purchase of some old property, with a view to its reconstruction as a theatre, in the interest of the new play and the new player.

John Storm laughed bitterly. He told himself that Glory

was unworthy of the least of his thoughts. It was his duty to go on with his work and think of her no more.

He had received his official notice to quit. The church was to be given up in a month, the clergy-house in two months, and he believed himself to be immersed in preparations for the rehousing of the club and home. Twenty young mothers and their children now lived in the upper rooms, under obedience to the Sisterhood, but Polly's boy had remained with Mrs. Pincher. From time to time he had seen the little one tethered to a chair by a scarf about its waist, creeping by the wall to the door, and there gazing out on the world with looks of intelligence, and babbling to it in various inarticulate noises. "Boo-loo! Lal-la! Mum-um!" The little dark face had the eyes of its mother, but it represented Glory for all that. John Storm loved to see it. He felt that he could never part with it, and that if Lord Robert Ure himself came and asked for it he would bundle him out of doors.

But a carriage drew up at Mrs. Callender's one morning, and Lady Robert Ure stepped out. Her pale and patient face had the feeble and nervous smile of the humiliated and unloved.

"Mr. Storm," she said in her gentle voice, "I have come on a delicate errand. I cannot delay any longer a duty I ought to have discharged before."

It was about Polly's baby. She had heard of what had happened at the hospital, and the newspapers which had followed her to Paris, with reports of her wedding, had contained reports of the girl's death also. Since her return she had inquired about the child, and discovered that it had been rescued by him and was now in careful keeping.

"But it is for me to look after it, Mr. Storm, and I beg of you to give it up to me. Something tells me that God will never give me children of my own, so I shall be doing no harm to any one, and my husband need never know whose child it is I adopt. I promise you to be good to it. It shall never leave me. And if it should live to be a man, and grow to love me, that will help me to forget the past and to forgive myself for my own share in it. Oh, it is little I can do for the poor girl who is gone—for after all, she loved him, and I took him from her. But this is my duty, Mr. Storm, and I cannot sleep at night or rest in the day until it is begun."

"I don't know if it is your duty, dear lady, but if you wish for the child it is your right," said John Storm, and they got into the carriage and drove to Soho.

"Boo-loo! Lal-la! Mum-um!" The child was tethered to

the chair as usual and talking to the world according to its wont. When it was gone, and the women on the doorsteps could see no more of the fine carriage of the great lady who had brought the odour of perfume and the rustle of silk into the dingy court, and Mrs. Pincher had turned back to the house with red eyes and her widow's cap awry, John Storm told himself that everything was for the best. The last link with Glory was broken! Thank God for that! He might go on with his work now and need think of her no more!

That day he called at Clement's Inn.

The Garden House was a pleasant dwelling, fronting on two of its sides to the garden of the ancient Inn of Chancery, and cosily furnished with many curtains and rugs. The cockney maid who answered the door was familiar in a moment, and during the short passage from the hall to the floor above she communicated many things. Her name was Liza; she had heard him preach; he had made her cry; "Miss Gloria" had known her former mistress, and Mr. Drake had got her the present place.

There was a sound of laughter from the drawing-room. It was Glory's voice. When the door opened she was standing in the middle of the floor in a black dress and with a pale face, but her eyes were bright and she was laughing merrily. She stopped when John Storm entered and looked confused and ashamed. Drake, who was lounging on the couch, rose and bowed to him, and Miss Macquarrie, who was correcting long slips of printer's proofs at a desk by the window, came forward and welcomed him. Glory held his hand with her long hand-clasp and look steadfastly into his eyes. His face twitched and her own blushed deeply, and then she talked in a nervous and jerky way, reproaching him for his neglect of her.

"I have been busy," he began, and then stopped with a sense of hypocrisy. "I mean worried and tormented," and then stopped again, for Drake had dropped his head.

She laughed, though there was nothing to laugh at, and proposed tea, rattling along in broken sentences that were spoken with a tremulous trill, which had a suggestion of tears behind it. "Shall I ring for tea, Rosa? Oh, you *have* rung for tea! Ah, here it comes! Thank you, Liza. Set it here," seating herself. "Now who says 'the girl'? Remember?" and then more laughter.

At that moment there was another arrival. It was Lord Robert Ure. He kissed Rosa's hand, smiled on Glory, saluted Drake familiarly, and then settled himself on a low stool by the tea-table, pulled up the knees of his trousers, relaxed the congested muscles of one-half of his face and let fall his eyeglass.

Drake was handing out the cups as Glory filled them. He was looking at her attentively, vexed at the change in her manner since John Storm entered. When he returned to his seat on the sofa he began to twitch the ear of her pug, which lay coiled up asleep beside him, calling it an ugly little pestilence, and wondering why she carried it about with her. Glory protested that it was an angel of a dog, whereupon he supposed it was now dreaming of paradise—listen!—and then there were audible snores in the silence, and everybody laughed, and Glory screamed.

"I declare on my honour, my dear," said Drake with a mischievous look at John, "the creature is uglier than the beast that did the business on the day we eloped."

"Eloped!" cried Rosa and Lord Robert together.

"Why, did you never hear that Glory eloped with me?"

Glory was trying to drown his voice with hollow laughter.

"She was seven and I was six and a half, and she had proposed to me in the orchard the day before!"

"Anybody have more tea? No? Some sally-lunn, perhaps?" and then more laughter.

"Hold your tongue, Glory! Nobody wants your tea! Let us hear the story," said Rosa.

"Why, yes, certainly," said Lord Robert, and everybody laughed again.

"She was all for travel and triumphal processions in those days——"

Glory stopped her ears and began to sing—

"'Willy, Willy Wilkin,
Kissed the maid a-milkin
Fa, la, la!'

"There were so many things people could do if they wouldn't waste so much time working——

'Willy, Willy Wilkin,
Kissed the maid——'"

"Glory, if you don't be quiet we'll turn you out!" and Rosa got up and flourished her proofs.

"I had brought my dog, and when I called her a——"

But Glory had leapt to her feet and fled from the room. Drake had leapt up also, and now, putting his back against the door, he raised his voice and went on with his story.

"Somebody saved us, though, and she lay in his arms and kissed him all the way home again."

Glory was strumming on the door and singing to drown his

voice. When the story was ended and she was allowed to come back, she was panting and gasping with laughter, but there were tears in her eyes for all that, and Lord Robert was saying, with a sidelong look towards John Storm, "Really, this ought to be a scene in the new 'Sigurdsen,' don't you know!"

John had retired within himself during this nonsense. He had been feeling an intense hatred of the two men, and was looking as gloomy as deep water. "All acting, sheer acting," he thought, and then he told himself that Glory was only worthy of his contempt. What could attract her in the society of such men? Only their wealth and their social station. Their intellectual and moral atmosphere must weary and revolt her.

Rosa had to go to her newspaper office, and Drake saw her to the door. John rose at the same time, and Glory said, "Going already?" but she did not try to detain him. She would see him again; she had much to say to him. "I suppose you were surprised to hear that I had returned to London?" she said, looking up at his knitted brows.

He did not answer immediately, and Lord Robert, who was leaning against the chimneypiece, said in his cold drawl, "Your friend ought to be happy that you have returned to London, seems to me, my dear, instead of wasting your life in that wilderness."

John drew himself up. "It's not London I object to," he said; "that was inevitable, I dare say."

"What then?"

"The profession she has come back to follow."

"Why, what's amiss with the profession?" said Lord Robert, and Drake, who returned to the room at the moment, said, "Yes, what's amiss with it? Some of the best men in the world have belonged to it, I think."

"Tell me the name of one of them, since the world began, who ever lived an active Christian life?"

Lord Robert made a kink of laughter, and turning to the window began to play a tune with his finger-tips on the glass of a pane. Drake struggled to keep a straight face, and answered, "It is not their *rôle*, sir."

"Very well, if that's too much to ask, tell me how many of them have done anything in real life, anything for the world, for humanity—anything whatever, I don't care what it is."

"You are unreasonable, sir," said Drake, "and such objections could as properly apply to the professions of the painter and the musician. These are the children of joy. Their first function is to amuse. And surely amusement has its place in real life, as you say?"

"On the contrary," said John, following his own thought, for he had not listened, "how many of them have lived lives of reckless abandonment, self-indulgence, and even scandalous licence?"

"Those are abuses that apply equally to other professions, sir. Even the Church is not free from them. But in the view of reasonable beings, one clergyman of evil life—nay, one hundred, would not make the profession of the clergy bad."

"A profession," said John, "which appeals above all to the senses and lives on the emotions, and fosters jealousy and vanity and backbiting, and develops duplicity and exists on lies, and does nothing to encourage self-sacrifice or to help suffering humanity, is a bad profession and a sinful one!"

"If a profession is sinful," said Drake, "in proportion as it appeals to the senses, and lives on the emotions, and develops duplicity, then the profession of the Church is the most sinful in the world, for it offers the greatest temptations to lying, and produces the worst hypocrites and impostors!"

"That," said John, with eyes flashing and passion vibrating in his voice, "that, sir, is the great Liar's everlasting lie—and you know it!"

Glory was between them with uplifted hands. "Peace, peace! Blessed is the peacemaker! But tea! Will nobody take more tea? Oh, dear! oh dear! Why can't we have tea over again?"

"I know what you mean, sir," said Drake. "You mean that I have brought Glory back to a life of danger and vanity, and sloth and sensuality. Very well. I deny your definition. But call it what you will, I have brought her back to the only life her talents are fit for, and if that's all——"

"Would you have done the same for your own sister?"

"How dare you introduce my sister's name in this connection?"

"And how dare you resent it? What's good for one woman is good for another."

Glory was turning aside, and Drake was looking ashamed. "Of course . . . naturally . . . all I meant," he faltered . . . "if a girl has to earn her living, whatever her talents, her genius . . . that is one thing. But the upper classes, I mean, the leisured classes——"

"Damn the leisured classes, sir!" said John, and in the silence that followed the men looked round, but Glory was gone from the room.

Lord Robert, who had been whistling at the window, said to Drake in a cynical undertone, "The man is hipped and sore.

He has lost his challenge, and we ought to make allowances for him, don't you know."

Drake tried to laugh. "I'm willing to make allowances," he said lightly; "but when a man talks to me as if . . . as if I meant to . . ." but the light tone broke down, and he faced round upon John and burst out passionately, "What right have you to talk to me like this? What is there in my character, in my life, that justifies it? What woman's honour have I betrayed? What have I done that is unworthy of the character of an English gentleman?"

John took a stride forward, and came face to face and eye to eye with him. "What have you done?" he said. "You have used a woman as your decoy to win your challenge, as you say, and you have struck me in the face with the hand of the woman I love. That's what you've done, sir, and if it's worthy of the character of an English gentleman, then God help England!"

Drake put his hand to his head and his flushed face turned pale. But Lord Robert Ure stepped forward and said with a smile, "Well, and if you've lost your church, so much the better. You are only an outsider in the ecclesiastical stud anyway. Who wants you? Your rector doesn't want you; your bishop doesn't want you. Nobody wants you, if you ask me."

"I don't ask you, Lord Robert," said John. "But there's somebody who does want me for all that. Shall I tell you who it is? It's the poor and helpless girl who has been deceived by the base and selfish man, and then left to fight the battle of life alone, or to die by suicide, and go shuddering down to hell! That's who wants me, and, God willing, I mean to stand by her."

"Damme, sir, if you mean *me*, let me tell you what *you* are," said Lord Robert, screwing up his eyeglass. "You"—shaking his head right and left—"you are a man who takes delicately-nurtured ladies out of sheltered homes and sends them into holes and hovels in search of abandoned women and their misbegotten children! Why"—turning to Drake—"what do you think has happened? My wife has fallen under this gentleman's influence—the poor simpleton!—and not an hour before I left my house she brought home a child which he had given her to adopt. Think of it!—out of the shambles of Soho, and God knows whose brat and bastard!"

The words were hardly out of his mouth when John Storm had taken him by both shoulders. "God *does* know," he said, "and so do I. Shall I tell you whose child that is? Shall I? It's yours." The man saw it coming and turned white as a ghost. "Yours! and your wife has taken up the burden of your sin and shame, for she's a good woman, and you are not fit to live on the earth she walks upon!"

He left the two men speechless, and went heavily down the stairs. Glory was waiting for him at the door. Her eyes were glistening after recent tears.

"You will come no more?" she said. She could read him like a book. "I can see that you intend to come no more."

He did not deny it, and after a moment she opened the door, and he passed out with a look of utter weariness. Then she went back to her room and flung herself on the bed face downwards.

The men in the drawing-room were beginning to recover themselves. Lord Robert was humming a tune, Drake pacing to and fro.

"Buying up his church to make a theatre for Glory was the very refinement of cruelty!" said Drake. "Good heavens! what possessed me?"

"Original sin, dear boy!" said Lord Robert, with a curl of the lip.

"Original? A bad plagiarism, you mean!"

"Very well. If *I* helped you to do it, shall I help you to give it up? Withdraw the prospectus and return the deposits on shares, the dear Archdeacon's among the rest."

Drake took up his hat and left the house. Lord Robert followed him presently. Then the drawing-room was empty, and the hollow sound of sobbing came down to it from the bedroom above.

Father Storm read prayers in church that night with a hard and absent heart. A terrible impulse of hate had taken hold of him. He hated Drake, he hated Glory, he hated himself most of all, and felt as if seven devils had taken possession of him, and he was a hypocrite, and might fall dead at the altar.

"But what a fate the Almighty has saved me from!" he thought. Glory would have been a drag on his work for life. He must forget her. She was only worthy of his contempt. Yet he could not help but remember how beautiful she had looked in her mourning dress, with that pure pale face and its signs of suffering! Or how charming she had seemed to him even in the midst of all that deception! Or how she had held him as by a spell!

Going home, he came upon a group of men in the Court. One of them planted himself full in front, and said with an insolent swagger, "Me and my mytes thinks there's too many parsons abart 'ere. What do you think, sir?"

"I think there are more gamblers and thieves, my lad," he answered, and at the next instant the man had struck him in the face. He closed with the ruffian, grappled him by the throat, and flung him on his back. One moment he held him there, writhing and gasping, then he said, "Get up and get off, and let me see no more of you."

"No, sir, not this time," said a voice above his back. The crowd had melted away, and a policeman stood beside them. "I've been waiting for this one for weeks, Father," he said, and he marched the man to jail.

It was Charlie Wilkes. At the trial of Mrs. Jupe that morning, Aggie, being a witness, had been required to mention his name. It was all in the evening papers, and he had been dismissed from his time-keeping at the foundry.

XIII

A WEEK passed. Breakfast was over at Victoria Square, and John Storm was glancing at the pages of a weekly paper. "Listen!" he cried, and then read aloud in a light tone of mock bravery, which broke down at length into a husky gurgle—

"'The sympathy which has lately been evoked by the announcement that a proprietary church in Soho has been sold for secular uses is creditable to public sentiment——'"

"Think of that, now!" interrupted Mrs. Callender.

"'——and no doubt the whole community will agree to hope that Father Storm will recover from the irritation natural to his eviction——'"

"Aye, we can all get over another body's disappointment, laddie."

"'But there is a danger that in this instance the altruism of the time may develop a sentimentality not entirely good for public morals——'"

"When the ox is down, there are lots of butchers, ye ken!"

"'With the uses to which the fabric is to be converted it is no part of our purpose to deal, further than to warn the public not to lend an ear to the all too prurient purity of the amateur moralist; but considering the character of the work now carried on in Soho, no doubt with the best intentions——'"

"Aye, aye, it's easy to steal the goose and give the giblets in alms."

"'——it behoves us to consider if the community is not to be congratulated on its speedy and effectual ending. Father Storm is a young man of some talents and social position, but without any special experience or knowledge of the world: in fact, a weak, over-sanguine, and rather foolish fanatic——'"

"Oh, aye, he's down; down with him!"

"'——and therefore it is monstrous that he should be allowed to subvert the order of social life or disturb the broad grounds of the reasonable and the practical——'"

"Never mind. High winds only blaw on high hills, laddie!"

"'——As for the "fallen sister" whom he has taken under his special care, we confess to a feeling that too much sympathy has been wasted on her already. Her feet take hold of hell, her house is the way of the grave, going down to the chamber of death——'"

Mrs. Callender leapt to her feet. "That's the 'deacon-man; I ken the cloven hoof!"

John Storm had flung the paper away. "What a cowardly world it is!" he said. "But God wins in the end, and by God he shall!"

"Tut, man, don't tak' on like that. You can't climb the Alps on roller-skates, you see! But as for the Archdeacon, pooh! I'm no windy about your 'Sisters' and 'Settlements' and sic like, but if there had been Society papers in the Lord's time, Simon the Pharisee would have been a namby-pamby critic compared to some of them."

A moment afterwards she was looking out of the window and holding up both hands. "My gracious! It's himsel'! It's the Prime Minister!"

A gaunt old gentleman with a meagre moustache, wearing a broad-brimmed hat and unfashionable black clothes, was stepping up to the door.

"Yes, it's my uncle," said John, and the old lady fled out of the room to change her cap.

"I have heard what has happened, John, so I have come to see you," said the Prime Minister.

Was he thinking of the money? John felt uneasy and ashamed.

"I'm sorry, my boy, very sorry!"

"Thank you, uncle."

"But it all comes, you see, of the ridiculous idea that we are a Christian nation! Such a thing couldn't have occurred at the shrine of a pagan god!"

"It was only a proprietary church, uncle. I was much to blame."

"I do not deny that you have acted unwisely, but what difference does that make, my boy? To sell a church seems like the climax of irreverence; but they are doing as bad every day. If you want to see what times the Church has fallen on, look at the advertisements in your religious papers—your Benefice and Church Patronage Gazettes, and so forth. A traffic, John, a slave traffic, worse than anything in Africa, where they sell bodies, not souls!"

"It is a crime which cries to the avenging anger of heaven," said John, "but it is the Establishment that is to blame, not the Church, uncle."

"We are a nation of money-lenders, my boy, and the Church is the worst usurer of them all, with its learned divines in scarlet hoods who hold shares in music-halls, and its Fathers in God living at ease and leasing out public-houses. *You* have been lending money on usury too, and on a bad security. What are you going to do now?"

"Go on with my work, uncle, and do two hours where I did one before."

"And get yourself kicked where you got yourself kicked before!"

"Why not? If God puts ten pounds on a man, He gives him strength to bear twenty."

"John, John, I am feeling rather sore, and I can't bear much more of it. I'm growing old, and my life is rather lonely too. Except your father, you are my only kinsman now, and it seems as if our old family must die with you. But come, my boy, come, throw up all this sorry masquerade. Isn't there a woman in the world who can help me to persuade you? I don't care who she is, or what, or where she comes from."

John had coloured to the eyes, and was stammering something about the true priest cut off from earthly marriage, therefore free to commit himself completely to his work, when Mrs. Callender came back, spruce and smart, with many smiles and curtsies. The Prime Minister greeted her with the same old-fashioned courtesy, and they cooed away like two old doves, until a splendid equipage drove up to the door, and the plain old gentleman drove away in it.

"Wasn't he nice with me, wasn't he now?" the old lady kept saying, and John being silent—"Tut! you young men are just puir loblollyboys with a leddy when the auld ones come."

Going to Soho that day John Storm felt a sudden thrill at seeing on the street in front of him, walking in the same direction, an elderly figure in cassock and cord. It was the Father Superior of the Brotherhood. John overtook him and greeted him.

"Ah, I was on my way to see you, my son."

"Then you have heard what has happened"

"Yes. Satan's shafts fly fast." Then taking John's arm as they walked, "Earthly blows are but reminders of Him, my son, like the hair-shirt of the monk, and this trouble of yours is God's reminder of your broken obedience. What did I tell you when you left us—that you would come back within a year? And you will! Leave the world, my son. It treats you badly. The human spirit reigns over it, and even the Church is a Christian society out of the sphere and guidance of the Divine Spirit. Leave it and return to your unfinished vows."

John shook his head, and took the Father into the clergy-house, where the girls were gathering for the evening. "How can I leave the world, Father, when there's work like this to do? Society presents to a large proportion of these bright creatures the alternative, 'Sell yourself or starve.' But God says, 'Live, work, and love.' Therefore society is doomed, and that dead man's sepulchre, the Establishment, is doomed, but the Church will live, and become the corner-stone of the new order, and stand between woman and the world, as it stood of old between the poor and the rich."

The Father preached for John that night, taking for his text, "The flesh lusteth against the Spirit, and the Spirit against the flesh." And on parting from him at the door of the sacristy he said, "Religious work can only be good, my son, if it concerns itself first of all with the salvation of souls. Now what if it pleased God to remove you from all this—to call you to a work of intercession—say to the mission-field?"

John's face turned pale. "There can be no need to fly," he said with a frightened look. "Surely London is a mission-field wide enough for any man."

"Yet, who knows? Perhaps for your own soul's sake, lest vanity should take hold of you, or the love of fame, or—or any of the snares of Satan! But good-bye, and God be with you!"

When John Storm reached home he found a letter awaiting him. It was from Glory.

"Are you dead and buried? If so, send me word, that I may compose your epitaph. 'Here lies' . . . *Lies* is good, for though you didn't promise to come back you ought to have done so, therefore it comes to the same thing in the end. You must not think too ill of Mr. Drake. I call him the milk of human kindness, and his friend Lord Robert the oil thereof—I mean the oil of vitriol. But his temper is like the Caspian Sea, having neither ebb nor flow, while yours is like the Bay of Biscay-Oh! so I can't expect you to agree. As for poor me, I may be guilty of all the seven deadly sins, but I can't see why I should be boycotted on that account. There is something I didn't know when you were here, and I want to explain about it. Therefore come 'right away' (Lord Bob Americanised). Being slow to anger and plenteous in mercy, I will forgive you if you come soon. If you don't, I'll—I'll go on the bike—feminine equivalent to the drink. To tell you the truth, I've done so already, having been careering round the gardens of the Inn during the early hours of morning, clad in Rosa's 'bloomers,' in which I make a picture and a sensation at the same time, she being several sizes larger round the hips, and fearfully and wonderfully made. If that doesn't fetch you, I'll go in for boxing next, and in a pair of four-ounce gloves I'll cut a *striking* figure, I can tell you.

" But, John Storm, have you cast me off entirely? Do you intend to abandon me? Do you think there is no salvation left for me? And are you going to let me sink in all this mire without stretching out a hand to help me? Oh dear! oh dear! I don't know what has come over the silly old world since I came back to London. Think it must be teething, judging by the sharpness of its bite, and feel as if I should like to give it a dose of sirup of squills."

As John read the letter his eyelids quivered and his mouth relaxed. Then he glanced at it again and his face clouded.

"I cannot leave her entirely to the mercy of men like these," he thought.

This innocent daring, this babe-like ripping up of serviceable conventions—God knows what advantage such men might take of it. He must see her once again, to warn, to counsel her. It was his duty—he must not shrink from it.

It had been a day of painful impressions to Glory. Early in the morning Lord Robert had called to take her to the "reading" of the new play. It took place in the saloon of an unoccupied Strand theatre, of which the stage also had been engaged for rehearsal. The company were gathered there, and being more or less experienced actors and actresses, they received her with looks of courteous indulgence, as one whose leading place must be due to other things than talent. This stung her; she felt her position to be a false one, and was vexed that she had permitted Lord Robert to call for her. But her humiliation had yet hardly begun.

While they stood waiting for the manager, who was late, a gorgeous person with a waxed moustache and in a fur-lined coat, redolent of the mixed odour of perfume and stale tobacco, forced his way up to her and offered his card. She knew the man in a moment.

"I'm Josephs," he said in a confidential undertone, "and if there's anything I can do for you—acting management—anything—it vill give me pleesure."

Glory flushed up and said, "But you don't seem to remember, sir, that we have met before."

The man smiled blandly. "Oh, yes. I've kept track of you ever since, and know all about you. You hadn't made your appearance then, and naturally I couldn't do much. But now —*now* if you vill give me de pleesure——"

"Then an agent is one who can do nothing for you when you want help, but when you don't want it——"

The man laughed to carry off his audacity. "Vell, you know vhat they say of us—agent from *agere*, ' to do,' and we're always ' doing.' Ha, ha! But if you are villing to let bygones be bygones, I am, and velcome."

Glory's face was crimson. "Will somebody go for the stage doorkeeper?" she said, and one of the company went out on that errand. Then raising her voice, so that everybody listened, she said, "Mr. Josephs, when I was quite unknown, and trying to get on, and finding it very hard, as we all do, you played me the cruellest trick a man ever played on a woman. I don't owe you any grudge, but for the sake of every poor girl who is struggling to live in London, I am going to turn you out of the house."

"Eh? Vhat?"

The stage doorkeeper had entered. "Porter, do you see this gentleman? He is never to come into this theatre again as long as we are here, and if he tries to force his way in, you are to call a policeman and have him bundled back into the street!"

"Daddle do," and the waxed moustache over the grinning mouth seemed to cut the face across.

When Josephs had gone, Glory could see that the looks of indulgence on the faces of the company had gone also. "She'll do!" said one. "She's got the stuff in her!" said another; but Glory herself was now quaking with fear, and her troubles were not yet ended.

A little stout gentleman entered hurriedly with a roll of papers in his hand. He stepped up to Lord Robert, apologised for being late, and mopped his bald crown and red face. It was Sefton.

"This is to be our manager," said Lord Robert, and Mr. Sefton bobbed his head, winked with both eyes, and said, "Charmed, I'm sure, charmed!"

Glory could have sunk into the earth for shame, but in a moment she had realised the crushing truth that when a woman has been insulted in the deepest place—in her honour—the best she can do is to say nothing about it.

The company seated themselves around the saloon and the reading began. First came the list of characters, with the names of the cast. Glory's name and character came last, and her nerves throbbed with sudden pain when the manager read, "and Gloria—Miss Glory Quayle."

There was a confused murmur, and then the company composed themselves to listen. It was Gloria's play. She was rather scandalous. After the first act Glory thought it was going to be the story of Nell Gwynne in modern life; after the second, of Lady Hamilton; and after the third, in which the woman wrecks and ruins the first man in the country, she knew it was only another version of the "Harlot's Progress," and must end as that had ended.

The actors were watching their own parts, and pointing and punctuating with significant looks the places where the chances came, but Glory was overwhelmed with confusion. How was she to play this evil woman? The poison went to the bone, and to get into the skin of such a creature a good woman would have to dispossess herself of her very soul. The reading ended, every member of the company congratulated some other member on the other's opportunities, and Sefton came up to Glory to ask if she did not find the play strong and the part magnificent.

"Yes," she said; "but only a bad woman could play that part properly."

"You'll do it, my dear, you'll do it on your own!" he answered gaily, and she went home perplexed, depressed, beaten down, and ashamed.

A newspaper had been left at the door. It was a second-rate theatrical journal, still damp from the press. The handwriting on the wrapper was that of Josephs, and there was a paragraph marked in blue pencil. It pretended to be a record of her short career, and everything was in it—the programme selling, the dressing, the foreign clubs—all the refuse of her former existence, set in a sinister light, and leaving the impression of an abject upbringing, as of one who had been *in* the streets if not on them.

Well, she had chosen her life, and must take it at its own price. But oh, the cruelty of the world to a woman, when her very success could be her shame! She felt that the past had gripped her again—the pitiless past—she could never drag herself out of the mire.

That night she wrote to John Storm, and next morning before Rosa had risen—her duties kept her up late—she heard a voice downstairs. Her dog also heard it, and began to bark. At the next moment John was in the room, and she was laughing up into his splendid black eyes, for he had caught her down at the sofa holding the pug's nose and trying to listen.

"Is it you? It's so good of you to come early. But this dog"—breaking into the Manx dialect—"she's ter'ble, just ter'ble!" Then rising and looking serious, "I wished to tell you that I knew nothing about the church, nothing whatever. If I'd had the least idea . . . But they told me nothing—it was very wrong—nothing. And the first thing I knew was when I saw it in all the newspapers."

He was leaning on the end of the mantelpiece. "If they deceived you like that, how can you go on with them?"

"You mean" (she was leaning on the other end, and speaking falteringly)—"you mean that I ought to give it all up. But it's too late for that now. It was too late when I came to know. Besides, it would do no good; you would be in the same position still, and as for me—well, somebody else would have the theatre, so where's the use?"

"I was thinking of the future, Glory, not the past. People who deceive us once are capable of doing so again."

"True—that's true—only—only——"

She was breaking down, and he turned his eyes away from her, saying, "Well, it's all over now, and there's no help for it."

"No, there's no help for it."

He tried to think what he had come to say, but do what he would he could not remember. The moment he looked at her the thread of his thoughts was lost, and the fragrance of her presence, so sweet, so close, made him feel as if he wanted to touch her. There was an awkward silence, and then he fidgeted with his hat and moved.

"Are you going so soon?"

"I'm busy, and——"

"Yes, you must be busy now."

"And then why . . . Why should we prolong a painful interview, Glory?"

She shot up a look under her eyebrows. His eyes had a harassed expression, but there was a gleam in them that set her heart beating.

"Is it so painful? Is it?"

"Glory, I meant to tell you I could not come again."

"No! You're not so busy as all that, are you? Surely" (the Manx again, only she seemed to be breathless now), "surely you're not so ter'ble busy but you can just put a sight on a girl now and again, for all?"

He made a gesture with his hand. "It disturbs—it distracts——"

"Oh, is that all? Then," with a forced laugh, "I'll come to see you instead. Yes, I will, though."

"No, you mustn't do that, Glory. It would only torment——"

"Torment! Gough bless me! Why torment?" and a fugitive flame shot up at him.

"Because," he stammered, and she could see that his lips quivered; then calmly, very calmly, pronouncing the words slowly, and in a voice as cold as ice, "because I love you!"

"You!"

"Didn't you know that?" His voice was guttural. "Haven't you known it all along? What's the use of pretending? You've dragged it out of me. Was that only to show your power over me?"

"Oh!"

She had heard what her heart wanted to hear, and not for worlds would she have missed hearing it, yet she was afraid, and trembling all over.

"We two are of different natures, Glory, that's the trouble between us—now, and always has been. We have nothing in common—absolutely nothing. You have chosen your path in life, and it is not my path. I have chosen mine, and it is not yours. Your friends are not my friends. We are two different beings altogether, and yet—and yet I love you! And that's why I cannot come again."

It was sweet, but it was terrible. So different from what she had dreamt of: "I love you!—you are my soul!—I cannot live without you." Yet he was right. She had slain his love before it was born to her—it was born dead. In an unsteady voice, which had suddenly become husky, she said—

"No doubt you are right. I must leave you to judge. Perhaps you have thought it all out."

"Don't suppose it will be easy for me, Glory. I've suffered a good deal, and I dare say I shall suffer more yet. If so, I'll bear it. But for the sake of my work——"

"Ah! . . . But of course I can't expect . . . Naturally you love your work also——"

"I *do* love my work also, and therefore it's no use trifling. 'If thine eye offend——'"

She was stung. "Well, since there's no help for it, I suppose we must shake hands and part."

Not until then—not until he had pronounced his doom and she had accepted it did he realise how beautiful she seemed to him. He felt as if something in his throat wanted to cry out.

"It isn't what I expected, Glory—what I dreamt of for years."
"But it's best—it seems best."
"I tried to make a place for you too, but you wouldn't have it—you let it go; you preferred this other lot in life."

She remembered Josephs, and Sefton, and the newspaper, and the part, and she covered her face with her hands.

"How can I go on, Glory, to the peril of my . . . It's dangerous, even dangerous."

"Yes, you are a clergyman and I am an actress. You must think of that. People are so ignorant, so cruel, and I dare say they are talking already."

"Do you think I should care for that, Glory?" Her hands came down from her face. "Do you think I should care one jot if all the miserable scandal-mongering world thought——"

"You'll think the best of me, then?"

"I'll think of both of us as we used to be, my child, before the world came between us, before you——"

She was fighting against an impulse to fling herself into his arms, but she only said in a soft voice, "You are quite right, quite justified. I have chosen my lot in life, and must make the best of it."

"Well . . ." He was holding out his hand.

But nevertheless she put her hand behind her, thinking, "No; if I shake hands with him it will be the end of everything."

"Good-bye!" and with an expression of utter despair he left her.

She did not cry, and when Rosa came down immediately afterwards she was smiling and her eyes were very bright.

"Was that your friend Mr. Storm? Yes? You must beware of him, my dear. He would stop your career and think he was doing God's service."

"There's no danger of that, Rosa. He only came to say he would come no more," and then something flashed in her eyes and died away, and then flashed again.

"Yes," thought Rosa, "there's an extraordinary attraction about her that makes all other women seem tame." And then Rosa remembered somebody else and sighed.

John Storm went back to Soho by way of Clare Market, and when people saluted him in the streets with "Good-morning, Father," he did not answer because he did not see them. On going to church that night, he came upon a group of Charlie's cronies betting six to one against his getting off, and a girl in gay clothes was waiting to speak to him. It was Aggie. She had come to plead for Charlie.

"It's the drink, sir. 'E's a good boy when 'e's not drinking. But I ask pardon for 'im; and if you would only not prosecute——"

John was ashamed of himself at sight of the girl's fidelity to her unworthy lover.

"And you, my child—what about you?"

"Oh, I'm all right. What's broken can't be mended."

And meanwhile the church-bells were ringing, and the cabs were running to the theatres.

XIV

THE rehearsals began early in the morning and usually lasted until late in the afternoon. Glory found them wearisome, depressing, and often humiliating. The body of the theatre was below the level of the street, and in the daytime was little better than a vast vault. If she entered by the front, she stumbled against seats and saw the figures of men and women silhouetted in the distance, and heard the echo of cavernous voices. If by the back, she came upon the prompter's table set midway across the stage, with a twin gas-bracket shooting up behind it like a geyser, and an open space of some twenty feet by twenty in front, whereon the imaginary passions were to disport themselves at play.

Glory found real ones among them, and they were sometimes in hideous earnest. Jealousy, envy, uncharitableness, and all the rancour of life where the struggle for it is bitterest, attempts to take advantage of her inexperience, to rob her of the best positions on the stage, to cut out her lines which "scored;" these, with the weary waits, the half darkness, the chill atmosphere, the void in front, with its seats in linen covers, suggesting an audience of silent ghosts, and then the sense of the bright, busy, bustling, rattling, real world above, sent her home day after day with a headache, a heartache, and tears bubbling out of her eyes.

And when she had conquered these conditions or settled down to them, and had made such progress with her part as to throw away her scrip, the old horror of the woman she was to make herself into came back as a new terror. The visionary Gloria was very proud and vain and selfish, and trampled everything under foot that she might possess the world and the things of the world.

Meantime the real Gloria had a far different part to play.

Every morning, with a terrible reality at her heart, she glanced over the newspapers for news of John Storm. She had not far to look. A sort of grotesque romance had gathered about him, as of a modern Don Quixote tilting at windmills. His name was the point of a pun; there were cartoons, caricatures, and all other forms of the joke that is not a joke because it is an insult.

Sometimes she took stolen glances at his work. On Sunday morning she walked through Soho, past the people sitting on their doorsteps reading the sporting intelligence in the Sunday papers, with their larks in cages hung on nails overhead, until she came to the church, and heard the singing inside, and saw chalked up on the walls the legend, " God bless the Farver!"

" Strange charge against a clergyman!" It was a low-class paper, and the charge was a badge of honour. A young ruffian (it was Charles Wilkes) had been brought up on remand on a charge of assaulting Father Storm, and being sentenced to a week's imprisonment, notwithstanding the Father's appeal and offer of bail, he had accused the clergyman of relations with his sweetheart (it was Agatha Jones).

Glory's anger at the world's treatment of John Storm deepened to a great love of the misunderstood and down-trodden man. She saw an announcement of his last service, and determined to go to it. The church was crowded, chiefly by the poor, and the air was heavy with the smell of oranges and beer. It was a week-day evening, and when the choir came in, followed by John Storm in his black cassock, Glory could not help a thrill of physical joy at being near him.

The text was, " Woe unto you, Scribes and Pharisees, hypocrites! for ye are like unto whited sepulchres, which indeed appear beautiful outside, but are within full of dead men's bones and all uncleanness!" The first half of the sermon was a denunciation of the morality of men. We made clean the outside of the platter, but the so-called purity of England was a smug sham built upon rottenness and sin! There were men among us, damned sensualists, left untouched by the idleness of the public conscience, who did not even know where their children were to be found. Let them go down into the gutters of life and look for their own faces, and—God forgive them!—their mothers' faces, among the outcast and the criminal. The second half was a defence of woman. The sins of the world against women were the most crying wrongs of the time. Had they ever reflected on the heroism of women, on their self-denying, unrewarded labour! Oh, why was woman held so cheap as in this immoral London of to-day? There had been scarcely a breach of the law of nature by women, and not one that men were not chiefly to blame for. Men tempted them by love of dress, of ease, of money, and of fame, to forget their proper vocation; but every true woman came right in the end, and preferred to the false and fictitious labour for worldly glory a mother's silent and unseen devotion, counting it no virtue at all. "Yes, women, mothers, girls, in your hands lies the salvation of England. May you live in this prospect, and may God and His ever-blessed Mother be your reward all through this weary life and in glory everlasting."

There was a procession with banners, cross, stars, green and blue fleur-de-lis, but Glory saw none of it. She was kneeling with head down and heart choked with emotion. The next she knew the service was over, the congregation was gone; only one old woman in widow's weeds was left, jingling a bunch of keys.

"Has the Father gone?"

"No, ma'am; he is still in the sacristy."

"Show me to it."

At the next moment, with fluttering throat and a look of mingled love and awe, she was standing eye to eye with John Storm in the little bare chamber of the church.

"Glory, why do you come here?"

"I can't help it."

"But we said good-bye and parted."

"*You* did; I didn't. It was not so easy——"

"Easy? I told you it wouldn't be easy, my child; and it hasn't been. I said I should suffer, and I have suffered. But I've borne it—you see I've borne it. Don't ask me at what cost."

"Oh, oh, oh!" and she covered her face.

"Yes, the devil tortured me with love first. I was seeing you and hearing you everywhere and in everything, Glory. But I got over that, and then he tortured me with remorse. I had left you to the mercy of the world. It was my duty to watch over you. I did it too."

She glanced up quickly.

"Ah! you never knew that! But no matter! It's all over now, and I'm a different man entirely. But why do you come and torment me again? It's nothing to you, nothing at all. You can shake it off in a moment. That's your nature, Glory; you can't help it. But have you no pity? You find me here, trying to help the helpless—the brave girls who have the virtue to be poor, and the strength to be weak, and the courage to be friendless. Why can't you leave me alone? What am I to you? Nothing at all! You care nothing for me, nothing whatever."

She glanced up again, and the look of love in her eyes was stronger now than the look of awe. He saw it, and could not help knowing how strongly it worked upon his feelings.

"Go back to your own world, unhappy girl! You love it—you must; you have sacrificed the best impulses of your heart to it!"

She was smiling now. It was the old radiant smile, but with a gleam of triumph in it that he had never seen before. It worked like madness upon him, and he tried to insult her again.

"Go back to your own company, to the people who *play* at real life, and build toy-houses, and give themselves away body and soul for the clapping of hands in a theatre! Go back to the lies and hypocrisies of society, and the brainless mashers who adorn it! They dance superbly and are at home in drawing-rooms, and know all about sporting matters and theatrical affairs! I know none of these things, and I am kicked and cuffed, and ridiculed and hounded down as an indecent man or shunned as a moral leper! Why do you come to me?" he cried, hoarse and husky.

But she only stretched out her hands to him and said, "Because I love you!"

"What are you saying?" He was quivering with pain.

"I love you, and have always loved you, and you love me—you know you do—you love me still!"

"Glory!"

"John!"

"For God's sake! Glory!"

With a wild shout of joy he rushed upon her, flung his arms about her, and covered her face and hands with kisses. After a moment he whispered, "Not here, not here;" and she felt, too, that the room was suffocating them, and they must go out into the open air, the fields, the Park.

Somebody was knocking at the door. It was Mrs. Pincher. A man was waiting to speak to the Father. They found him in the lane. It was Jupe, the waiter. His simple face wore a strange expression of joy and fear, as if he wished to smile and dare not.

"My pore missis 'as got off and wants to come 'ome, sir, and I thought as you'd tell me what I oughter do."

"Take her back and forgive her, my man; that's the Christian course."

His love was now boundless; his large charity embraced everything, and going off he saluted everybody. "Good-evening, Mrs. Pincher. Good-night, Lydia."

"Well, 'e *is* a Father, too, and no mistake!" somebody was saying behind him as he went away with Glory.

The moon was at the full, and while they were passing through the streets it struggled with the gas from the shop windows as the flame of a fire struggles with the sunshine, but when they passed under the trees it shone out in its white splendour like a bride. The immeasurable vault above was silvered with stars, too, through depth on depth of space, and all the glorious earth and heaven seemed to smile the smile of love. A strong south breeze was blowing, and as it shook the trees of the Park, that blessed patch of nature in the midst of the toiling city seemed to sing the song of love!

Their hands found each other, and they walked along almost in silence, afraid to break the spell of their dream lest they should awake and find it gone. It seemed wonderful to him that they were together, and he could hardly believe it was reality, though the touch of her hand filled him with a strange physical exultation which he had never felt before. He seemed to be walking on the clouds, and she too was swaying by his side as if her blood was dancing. Sometimes she dried her glistening eyes, and once she stopped and swung in front of him and looked long at him, and then raised her face to his and kissed him.

"Whether you like it or not, your life is bound up with mine for ever and ever!" she whispered.

"It had to be," he answered. "I know it now. I can no longer deceive myself."

"And we shall be happy? In spite of all you said, we shall be very happy, eh?"

"Yes; that will be quite forgotten, Glory."

"And forgiven," she said, and then between a sigh and a blush she asked him to kiss her again.

"My love!"

"My soul!"

The wind swept the hood of her cape about her head and he could smell the fragrance of her hair.

He tried to think what he had done to deserve such happiness, but all the suffering he had gone through seemed as nothing compared to a joy like this. The great clock of Westminster swung its hollow sounds into the air, which went riding by on the wind like the notes of an organ, now full and now as soft as a baby's whisper. They could hear the far-off rumble of the vast city which fringed their blessed island like a mighty sea, and through the pulse of their clasped hands it seemed as if they felt the pulse of the world. An angel had come down and breathed on the face of the waters, and it was God's world after all.

He took her home, and they parted at the door. "Don't come in to-night," she whispered. She wished to be alone, that she might think it all out and go over it again, every word, every look. There was a lingering hand-clasp and then she was gone.

He returned through the Park and tried to step over the very places where her feet had trod. On reaching Buckingham Gate, he turned back and walked round the Park, and again round it, and yet again. The bells tolled out the hours, the cabs went westward with ladies in evening wraps going home from theatres, the tide of traffic ebbed farther and farther and died down, but still he walked and the wind sang to him.

"God cannot blame us," he thought. "We were made to love each other." He uncovered his head to let the wind comb through his hair, and he was happy, happy, happy! Sometimes he shut his eyes, and then it was hard to believe that she was not walking by his side, a fragrant presence in the moonlight, going step by step with him.

When the day was near the wind had gone, the little world of wood was silent, and his footsteps crunched on the gravel. Then a yellow gleam came in the sky to the east, and a chill gust swept up as a scout before the dawn, the trees began to shiver, the surface of the lake to creep, the birds to call, and the world to stretch itself and yawn.

"Peace in her chamber, wheresoe'er
It be—a holy place."

As he went home by Birdcage Walk the Park was still heavy with sleep, and its homeless wanderers had not yet risen from their couches on the seats. A pale mist was lying over London, but the towers of the Abbey stood clear above it, and pigeons were wheeling around them like sea-fowl about rocks in the sea. What a night it had been! A night of dreams, of love, of rapture!

The streets were empty and very quiet—only the slow rattle of the dust-cart and the measured step of policemen changing beats. Long blue vistas and a cemetery silence as of a world under the great hand of the gentle brother of Death, and then the clang of Big Ben striking six.

A letter was waiting for John in the breathless hall. It was from the Bishop of London: "Come and see me at St. James's Square."

XV

SUDDENLY there sprang out to Glory the charm and fascination of the life she was putting away. Trying to be true to her altered relations with John Storm, she did not go to rehearsal the next morning, but not yet having the courage of her new position, she did not tell Rosa her true reason for staying away. The part was exhausting—it tried her very much; a little break would do no harm. Rosa wrote to apologise for her on the score of health, and thus the first cloud of dissimulation rose up between them.

Two days passed, and then a letter came from the manager: "Trust you are rested and will soon be back. The prompter read your lines, but everything has gone to pieces. Slack, slovenly, spiritless, stupid, nobody acting, and nobody awake, it seems to me. 'All right at night, governor,' and the usual nonsense. Shows how much we want you. But envious people are whispering that you are afraid of the part. The blockheads! If you succeed this time you'll be made for life, my dear. And you *will* succeed!—Yours merrily," &c.

With this were three letters addressed to the theatre. One of them was from a press-cutting agency asking to be allowed to supply all newspaper articles relating to herself, and enclosing a paragraph as a specimen: "A little bird whispers that 'Gloria' as 'Gloria' is to be a startling surprise. Those who have seen her rehearse . . . But mum's the word—an' we could an we would." &c. Another of the letters was from the art editor of an illustrated weekly asking for a sitting to their photographer for a full-page picture, and the third enclosed the card of an interviewer on an evening paper. Only three days ago Glory would have counted all this as nothing, yet now she could not help but feel a thrilling, joyous excitement.

Drake called after the absence of a fortnight. He had come to speak of his last visit. His face was pale and serious, not fresh and radiant as usual, his voice was shaking and his manner nervous. Glory had never seen him exhibit so much emotion, and Rosa looked on in dumb astonishment.

"I was to blame," he said, "and I have come to say so. It was a cowardly thing to turn the man out of his church, and it was worse than cowardly to use you in doing it. Everything is fair, they say, in . . ." But he flushed up like a girl and stopped, and then faltered, "Anyhow I'm sorry—very sorry; and if there is anything I can do——"

Glory tried to answer him, but her heart was beating violently, and she could not speak.

"In fact, I've tried to make amends already. Lord Robert has a living vacant in Westminster, and I've asked him to hand it over to the Bishop with the request that Father Storm——"

"But will he?"

"I've told him he must. It's the least we can do if we are to have any respect for ourselves. And anyhow, I'm about tired of this anti-Storm uproar. It may be all very well for men like me to object to the man—I deny his authorities, and think him a man out of his century and country—but for these people with initials, who write in the religious papers, to rail at him, those shepherds who live on five thousand a year and pretend to follow One who hadn't a home or a second coat, and whose friends were harlots and sinners, though He was no sinner Himself—it's infamous, it's atrocious, it raises my gorge against their dead creeds and paralytic churches. Whatever his faults, he is built on a large plan; he has the Christ idea, and he is a man and a gentleman, and I'm ashamed that I took advantage of him. That's all over now, and there's no help for it; but if I might hope that you will forgive—and forget——"

"Yes," said Glory in a low voice, and then there was silence, and when she lifted her head Drake was gone and Rosa was wiping her eyes.

"It was all for love of you, Glory. A woman can't hate a man when he does wrong for love of herself."

John Storm came in later the same day, when Rosa had gone out, and Glory was alone. He was a different man entirely. His face looked round and his dark eyes sparkled. The clouds of his soul seemed to have drifted away, and he was boiling over with enthusiasm. He laughed constantly, and there was something almost depressing in the lumbering attempts at humour of the serious man.

"What do you think has happened? The Bishop sent for me and offered me a living in Westminster. It turns out to be in the gift of Lord Robert Ure; but no thanks to him for it. Lady Robert was at the bottom of everything. She had called on the Bishop. He remembered me at the Brotherhood, and told me all about it. St. Jude's, Brown's Square, on the edge of the worst quarter in Christendom! It seems the Archdeacon expected it for Golightly, his son-in-law. The Reverend Joshua called on me this morning and tried to bully me, but I soon bundled him off to Botany Bay. Said the living had been promised to him—a lie, of course. I soon found that out. A lie is well named, you know—it hasn't a leg to stand upon. Ha, ha, ha!"

Nothing would serve but that they should go to look at the scene of their future life, and with Don—he had brought his dog; it had to be held back from the pug under the table— they set off immediately. It was Saturday night, and as they dipped down into the slums that lie under the shadow of the Abbey, Old Pye Street, Peter's Street, and Duck Lane were aflare with the coarse lights of open naphtha lamps, and all but impassable with costers' barrows. There were the husky voices of the street hawkers, the hoarse laughter, the quarrelling, the oaths, the rasping shouts of the butcher selling chunks of dark joints by auction, the screeches of the roast-potato man, and the smell of stale vegetables and fried fish. "Jow, 'ow much a pound for yer turmaters?" "Threepence? I gave mor'n that for 'em myself." "Garn!" "S'elp me Gawd, I did, mum!"

"Isn't it a glorious scene?" said John; and Glory, who felt chilled and sickened, recalled herself from some dream of different things altogether, and said, "Isn't it?"

"Sanctuary, too! What human cats we are! The poor sinners cling to the place still!"

He took her into the alleys and courts that score and wrinkle the map of Westminster like an old man's face, and showed her the "model" lodging-houses and the gaudily-decorated hells where young girls and soldiers danced and drank.

"What's the use of saying to these people, 'Don't drink; don't steal'? They'll answer, 'If you lived in these slums you would drink too.' But we'll show them that we can live here and do neither—that will be the true preaching."

And then he pictured a life of absolute self-sacrifice, which she was to share with him. "You'll manage all money matters, Glory. You can't think how I'm swindled. And then I'm such a donkey as far as money goes—that's not far with me, you know. Ha, ha, ha! Who's to find it? Ah, God pays His own debts. He'll see to that."

They were to live under the church itself; to give bread to the hungry and clothes to the naked; to set up their Settlement in the gaming-house of the Sharkeys, now deserted and shut up; to take in the *un*deserving poor—the people who had nothing to say for themselves, precisely those; and thus they were to show that they belonged neither to the publicans and sinners nor to the Scribes and Pharisees.

"Only let us get rid of self. Only let us show that self-interest never enters our head in one single thing we do . . ." And meantime Glory, who had turned her head aside with a lump in her throat, heard some one behind them saying—

"Lawd, Jow, that's the curick and his dorg—'im as got pore Sharkey took! See 'im with the laidy?"

"S'elp me, so it is! Another good man gorn to 'is gruel, and all 'long of a bloomin' dorg."

They walked round by the church. John was talking rapturously at every step, and Glory was dragging after him like a criminal going to the pillory. At last they came out by Great Smith Street, and he cried, "See, there's the house of God under its spider's web of scaffolding, and here's Broad Sanctuary—broad enough in all conscience! Look!"

A crowd of girls and men were trooping out of a place of entertainment opposite, and there were screams and curses. "Look at 'im!" cried a woman's voice. "There 'e is, the swine! And 'e was the ruin of me, and now 'e's 'listed for a soldier, and goin' off with another woman!"

"You're bleedin' drunk, that's what you are," said a man's voice, "and if you down't take kear I'll send ye 'ome on a dawer!"

"Strike me, will ye, ye dog? Do it! I dare you!"

"She ain't worth it, soldier—come along," said another female voice, whereupon the first broke into a hurricane of oaths; and a little clergyman going by at the moment—it was the Rev. J. Golightly—said, "Dear, dear! Are there no policemen about?" and so passed on with his tall wife tucked under his arm.

John Storm pressed through the crowd and came between the two who were quarrelling. By the light of the lamp he could see them. The man was Charlie Wilkes, in the uniform of a soldier; the woman, with the paint running on her face, her fringe disordered, and her back hair torn down, was Aggie Jones.

"We down't want no religion 'ere," said Charlie, sneering.

"You'll get some, though, if you're not off quick!" said John. The man looked round for the dog and a moment afterwards he had disappeared.

Glory came up behind. "Oh, Aggie, woman, is it you?" she said, and then the girl began to cry in a drunken sob.

"Girls is cruel put upon, mum," said one of the women; and another cried, "Nix, the slops!" and a policeman came pushing his way and saying, "Now, then, move on! We ain't going to stand 'ere all night."

"Call a cab, officer," said John.

"Yes, sir—certainly, Father. Four-wheeler!"

"Where do you live, Aggie?" said Glory; but the girl, now sobbing drunk, was too far gone to follow her.

"She lives in Brown's Square, sir," said the woman who had

spoken before, and when the cab came up she was asked to get in with the other three.

It was a tenement house, fronting to one façade of St. Jude's, and Aggie's room was on the second storey. She was helpless, and John carried her up the stairs. The place was in hideous disorder, with clothing lying about on chairs, underclothing scattered on the floor, the fire out, many cigarette ends in the fender, a candle stuck in a beer bottle, and a bunch of withered roses on the table.

As John laid the girl on the bed she muttered, "Lemme alone!" and when he asked what was to happen to her when she grew old if she behaved like this when young, she mumbled, "Don't want to be old. Who's goin' to like me then, d'ye think?"

Half-an-hour afterwards Glory and John were passing through the gates into Clement's Inn, with its moonlight and silence, its odour of moistened grass, its glimpse of the stars, and the red and white blinds of its windows lit up round about. John was still talking rapturously. He was now picturing the part which Glory was to play in the life they were to live together. She was to help and protect their younger sisters, the child-women, the girls in peril, to enlist their loyalty and filial tenderness for the hour of temptation.

"Won't it be glorious? To live the life, the real life of warfare with the world's wickedness and woe. Won't it be magnificent? You'll do it too! You'll go down into those slums and sloughs which I've shown you to-night—they are the cradle of shame and sin, Glory, and this wicked London rocks it! —you'll go down into them like a ministering angel to raise the fallen and heal the wounded! You'll live in them, revel in them, rejoice in them; they'll be your battle-field. Isn't that better, far better, a thousand times better than *playing* at life, and all its fashions and follies and frivolities?"

Glory struggled to acquiesce, and from time to time in a trembling voice she said, "Yes," and "Oh yes," until they came to the door of the Garden House, and then a strange thing happened. Somebody was singing in the drawing-room to the music of the piano. It was Drake. The window was open and his voice floated over the moonlit gardens—

"Du liebes Kind, komm' geh mit mir!
Gar schöne Spiele spiel' ich mit dir."

Suddenly it seemed to Glory that two women sprang into life in her—one who loved John Storm and wished to live and work beside him, the other who loved the world and felt that she could never give it up. And these two women were fighting for her heart, which should have it and hold it and possess it for ever.

She looked up at John and he was smiling triumphantly. "Are you happy?" she asked.

"Happy! I know a hundred men who are a hundred times as rich as I, but not one who is a hundredth part as happy!"

"Darling!" she whispered, holding back her tears. Then looking away from him she said, "And do you really think I'm good enough for a life of such devotion and self-sacrifice?"

"Good enough!" he cried, and for a moment his merry laughter drowned the singing overhead.

"But will the world think so?"

"Assuredly. But who cares what the world thinks?"

"We do, dear we must!"

And then while the song went on she began to depreciate herself in a low voice and with a creeping sense of hypocrisy— to talk of her former life in London as a danger, of the tobacco-shop, the foreign clubs, the music-hall, and all the mire and slime with which she had been besmirched. "Everything is known now, dear. Have you never thought of this? It is your duty to think of it."

But he only laughed again with a joyous voice. "What's the odds?" he said. "The world is made up for the most part of low, selfish, sensual beings, incapable of belief in noble aims. Every innovator in such a world exposes himself to the risk of being slandered or ridiculed, or even shut up in a lunatic asylum. But who wouldn't rather be St. Theresa in her cell than Catherine of Russia on her throne? And in your case, what does it come to anyway? Only that you have gone through the fiery furnace and come out unscathed. All the better— you'll be a living witness, a proof that it is possible to pass through this wicked Babylon unharmed and untouched."

"Yes, if I were a man—but with a woman it is so different. It is an honour to a man to have conquered the world, but a disgrace to a woman to have fought with it. Yes, believe me, I know what I'm saying. That's the cruel tragedy in a woman's life, do what you will to hide it. And then you are so much in the eye of the world; and besides your own position there is your family's, your uncle's. Think what it would be if the world pointed the finger of scorn at your—at your mission —at your high and noble aims—and all on account of me! You would cease to love me—and I—I ——"

"Listen!" He had been shuffling restlessly on the pavement before her. "Here I stand! Here are you! Let the waves of public opinion dash themselves against us, we stand or fall together!"

"Oh, oh, oh!"

She was crying on his breast, but with what mixed and conflicting feelings! Joy, pain, delight, dread, hope, disappointment. She had tried to dishonour herself in his eyes, and it would have broken her heart if she had succeeded. But she had failed and he had triumphed, and that was harder still to bear

From overhead they heard the last lines of the song—

"Erreicht den Hof mit Müh und Noth
In seinen Armen das Kind war todt."

"Good-night," she whispered, and fled into the house. The lights in the dining-room were lowered, but she found a telegram that was waiting on the mantelpiece. It was from Sefton, the manager: "Author arrived in London to-day. Hopes to be at rehearsal Monday. Please be there certain."

The world was seizing her again, the imaginary Gloria was dragging her back with visions of splendour and success. But she crept upstairs, and went by the drawing-room on tiptoe. "Not to-night," she thought. "My face is not fit to be seen to-night."

There was a dying fire in her bedroom, and her evening gown had been laid out on a chair in front of it. She put the gown away in a drawer, and out of a box which she drew from beneath the bed she took a far different costume. It was the nurse's outdoor cloak, which she had bought for use at the hospital. She held it a moment by the tips of her fingers and looked at it, and then put it back with a sigh.

"Gloria! is that you?" Rosa called up the stairs; and Drake's cheery voice cried, "Won't our nightingale come down and give us a stave before I go?"

"Too late! Just going to bed. Good-night," she answered. Then she lit a candle, and sat down to write a letter.

"It's no use, dear John, I cannot! It would be like putting bad money into the offertory to put me into that holy work. Not that I don't admire it, and love it, and worship it. It is the greatest work in the world, and last week I thought I could count everything else as dross, only remembering that I loved you, and that nothing else mattered. But now I know that this was a vain and fleeting sentiment, and that the sights and scenes of your work repel me on a nearer view, just as the hospital repelled me in the early mornings, when the wards were being cleaned and the wounds dressed, and before the flowers were laid about.

"Oh, forgive me, forgive me! But if I am fit to join your life at all, it cannot be in London. That 'old serpent called the devil and Satan' would be certain to torment me here. I could not live within sight and sound of London and go on with the life you live. London would drag me back. I feel as if it were an earlier lover, and I must fly away from it. Is that possible? Can we go elsewhere? It is a monstrous demand, I know. Say you cannot agree to it. Say so at once—it will serve me right."

The stout watchman of the New Inn was calling midnight when Glory stole out to post her letter. It fell into the letter-box with a thud, and she crept back like a guilty thing.

XVI

NEXT morning Mrs. Callender heard John Storm singing to himself before he left his bedroom, and she was standing at the bottom of the stairs when he came down three steps at a time.

"Bless me, laddie," she said, "to see your face shining, a body would say that somebody had left ye a legacy or bought ye a benefice instead of taking your church frae ye!"

"Why, yes, and better than both, and that's just what I was going to tell you."

"You must be in a hurry to do it too, coming downstairs like a cataract."

"You came down like a cataract yourself once on a time, auntie; I'll lay my life on that."

"Aye, did I, and not sae lang since neither. And fools and prudes cried 'Oh!' and called me a tomboy. But, hoots! I was nought but a body born a wee before her time. All the lasses are tomboys now, bless them, the bright heartsome things!"

"Auntie," said John softly, seating himself at the breakfast table, "what d'ye think?"

She eyed him knowingly. "Nay, I'm ower thrang working to be bothered thinking. Out with it, laddie."

He looked wise. "Don't you remember saying that work like mine wanted a woman's hand in it?"

Her old eyes blinked. "Maybe I did, but what of it?"

"Well, I've taken your advice, and now a woman's hand *is* coming into it to guide it and direct it."

"It must be the right hand though, mind that."

"It *will* be the right hand, auntie."

"Weel, that's grand," with another twinkle. "I thought it might be the *left*, ye see, and ye might be putting a wedding-ring on it!" And then she burst into a peal of laughter.

"However did you find it out?" he said with looks of astonishment.

"Tut, laddie! love and a cough cannot be hidden. And to think a woman couldna see through you too! But come," tapping the table with both hands, "who is she?"

"Guess."

"Not one of your Sisters—no?" with hesitation.

"No," with emphasis.

"Some other simpering thing, na doot—they're all alike these days."

"But didn't you say the girls were all tomboys now?"

"And if I did, d'ye want a body to be singing the same song always? But come, what like is she? When I hear of a lassie I like fine to know her colour first. What's her complexion?"

"Guess again."

"Is she fair? But what a daft auld dunce I am!—to be sure she's fair."

"Why, how did you know that, now?"

"Pooh! They say a dark man is a jewel in a fair woman's eye, and I'll warrant it's as true the other way about. But what's her name?"

John's face suddenly straightened and he pretended not to hear.

"What's her name?" stamping with both feet.

"Dear me, auntie, what an ugly old cap you're wearing."

"Ugly?" reaching up to the glass. "Who says it's ugly?"

"I do."

"Tut! you're only a bit boy born yesterday. But, man, what's all this botherment about telling a lassie's name?"

"I'll bring her to see you, auntie."

"I should think you will indeed, and michty quick too!"

This was on Sunday, and by the first post on Monday John Storm received Glory's letter. It fell on him like a blast out of a cloud in the black north-east and cut him to the heart's core. He read it again, and being alone, he burst into laughter. He took it up a third time, and when he had finished there was something at his throat that seemed to choke him. His first impulse was fury. He wanted to rush off to Glory and insult her, to ask her if she was mad or believed him to be so. Because she was a coward herself, being slave-bound to the world and afraid to fight it face to face, did she wish to make a coward of him also—to see him sneak away from the London that had kicked him, like a cur with its tail between its legs?

After this there came an icy chill and an awful consciousness that mightier forces were at work than any mere human weakness. It was the world itself, the great pitiless world, that was dividing them again as it had divided them before, but irrevocably now—not as a playful nurse that puts petted children apart, but as a torrent that tears the cliffs asunder. "Leave the world, my son, and return to your unfinished vows." Could it be true that this was only another reminder of his broken obedience?

Then came pity. If Glory was slave-bound to the world, which of us was not in chains to something? And the worst slavery of all was slavery to self. But that was an abyss he dared not look into; and he began to think tenderly of Glory, to tell himself how much she had to sacrifice, to remember his anger and to be ashamed.

A week passed, and he went about his work in a helpless way, like a derelict without rudder or sail, and with the sea roaring about it. Every afternoon when he came home from Soho Mrs. Callender would trip into the hall wearing a new cap with a smart bow, and finding that he was alone she would say, "Not to-day, then?"

"Not to-day," he would answer, and they would try to smile. But seeing the stamp of suffering on his face, she said at last, "Tut, laddie! they love too much who die for love."

On the Sunday afternoon following he turned again towards Clement's Inn. He had come to a decision at last, and was calm, and even content, yet his happiness was like a gourd which had grown up in a day, and the morrow's sun had withered it.

Glory had been to rehearsal every day that week. Going to the theatre on Monday night she had said to herself, "There can be no harm in rehearsing—I'm not compelled to play." Notwithstanding her nervousness, the author had complimented her on her passion and self-abandonment, and going home she had thought, "I might even go through the first performance, and then give it all up. If I had a success, that would be beautiful, splendid, almost heroic — it would be thrilling to abandon everything!" Not hearing from John, she told herself he must be angry, and she felt sorry for him. "He doesn't know yet how much I am going to do." Thus the other woman in her tempted and overcame her, and drew her on from day to day.

Mrs. Macrae sent Lord Robert to invite her to luncheon on Sunday. "There can be no harm in going there," she thought.

She went with Rosa, and was charmed with the lively, gay, and brilliant company. Clever and beautiful women, clever and handsome men, and nearly all of them of her own profession. The mistress of the mansion kept open house after church parade on Sunday, and she sat at the bottom of her table, dressed in black velvet, with the Archdeacon on her right and a famous actor on her left. Lord Robert sat at the head and talked to a lady whose remarks were heard all over the room; but Lady Robert was nowhere to be seen; there was a hush when her name was mentioned, and then a whispered rumour that she had differences with her husband, and had scandalised her mother by some act of indiscretion.

Glory's face beamed, and for the first half-hour she seemed to be on the point of breaking into a rapturous "Well!" Nearly opposite to her at the table sat a lady whose sleepy look and drowsy voice and airs of languor showed that she was admired, and that she knew it. Glory found her very amusing, and broke into little trills of laughter at her weary, withering comments. This drew the attention of some of the men; they found the contrast interesting. The conversation consisted first of hints, half signs, brilliant bits of by-play, and Glory rose to it like a fish to a May-fly. Then it fell upon bicycling and the costumes ladies wore for it. The languid one commented upon the female fetish, the skirt, and condemned "bloomers," whereupon Glory declared that they were just charming, and being challenged (by a gentleman) for her reasons, she said, " Because when a girl's got them on she feels as if she's an understudy for a man, and may even have a chance of playing the part itself in another and a better world."

Then there was general laughter, and the gentleman said, "You're in the profession yourself now, aren't you?"

"Just a stranger within your gates," she answered; and when the talk turned on a recent lawsuit, and the languid one said it was inconceivable that the woman concerned could have been such a coward in relation to the man, Glory protested that it was just as natural for a woman to be in fear of a man (if she loved him), as to be afraid of a mouse or to look under the bed.

"*Ma chère*," said a dainty little lady sitting next but one (she had come to London to perform in a silent play), "they tells me you's half my countrywoman. All right. Will you not speak de French to poor me?" And when Glory did so, the little one clapped her hands and declared she had never heard the English speak French before.

"Say French-cum-Irish," said Glory, "or rather French which begat Irish, which begat Manx!"

"Original, isn't she?" said somebody who was laughing.

"Like a sea-gull among so many pigeons!" said somebody else; and the hothouse airs of the languid lady were lost as in a fresh gust from the salt sea.

But her spirits subsided the moment she had recrossed the threshold. As they were going home in a cab past the hospital and down Piccadilly, Rosa, who was proud and happy, said, "There! All society isn't stupid and insipid, you see; and there are members of your own profession who try to live up to the ideal of moral character attainable by a gentleman in England even yet."

"Yes, no doubt. But, Rosa, there's another kind of man altogether, whose love has the reverence of a religion, and if I ever meet a man like that—one who is ready to trample all the world under his feet for me—I think—yes, I really think I shall leave everything behind and follow him."

"Leave everything behind, indeed! That *would* be pretty! When everything yields before you too, and all the world and his wife are waiting to shout your praises!"

Rosa had gone to her office, and Glory was turning over some designs for stage costumes, when Liza came in to say that the "Farver" was coming upstairs.

"He has come to scold me," thought Glory; so she began to hum, to push things about, and fill the room with noise. But when she saw his drawn face and wide-open eyes, she wanted to fall on his neck and cry.

"You have come to tell me you can't do what I suggested?" she said, "Of course, you can't."

"No," he said slowly, very slowly. "I have thought it all over, and concluded that I can—that I must. Yes, I am willing to go away, Glory; and when you are ready I shall be ready too."

"But where—where——?"

"I don't know yet; but I am willing to wait for the unrolling of the scroll. I am willing to follow step by step, not knowing whither. I am willing to go where God wills, for life or death."

"But your work in London—your great, great work——"

"God will see to that, Glory. He can do without any of us. None of us can do without Him. The sun will set without any assistance, you know;" and the pale face made an effort to smile.

"But, John, my dear, dear John, this is not what you expected, what you have been thinking of and dreaming of, and building your hopes upon."

"No," he said; "and for your sake I am sorry, very sorry. I

thought of a great career for you, Glory. Not rescue work merely—others can do that. There are many good women in the world—nearly all women are good, but few are great—and for the salvation of England, what England wants now is a great woman. . . . As for me—God knows best. He has His own way of weaning us from vanity and the snares of the devil. You were only an instrument in His hands, my child, hardly knowing what you were doing. Perhaps He has a work of intercession for us somewhere—far away from here—in some foreign mission-field—who can say?"

A feeling akin to terror caught her breath, and she looked up at him with fearful eyes.

"After all, I am glad that this has happened," he said. "It will help me to conquer self, to put self behind my back for ever, to show the world, by leaving London, that self has not entered into my count at all, and that I am thinking of nothing but my work."

A warm flush rose to her cheeks as he spoke, and again she wanted to fling herself on his neck and cry. But he was too calm for that, too sad and too spiritual. When he rose to go she held out her hands to him, but he only took them and carried them to his lips, and kissed them.

As soon as she was alone she flung herself down and cried, "Oh, give me strength to follow this man, who mistakes his love of me for the love of God!" But even while she sat with bent head and her hands over her face, the creeping sense came back as of another woman within her who was fighting for her heart. She had conquered again, but at what a cost! The foreign mission-field—what associations had she with that? Only the memory of her father's lonely life and friendless death.

She was feeling cold and had begun to shiver when the door opened and Rosa entered.

"So he *did* come again?"

"Yes."

"I thought he would," and Rosa laughed coldly.

"What do you mean?"

"That when religious feelings take possession of a man he will stop at nothing to gain the end he has in view."

"Rosa," said Glory, flushing crimson, "if you imply that my friend is capable of one unworthy act or thought, I must ask you to withdraw your words absolutely and at once!"

"Very well, dear. I was only thinking for your own good. We working women must not ruin our lives or let anybody else ruin them. 'Duty,' 'self-sacrifice'—I know the old formulas, but I don't believe in them. Obey your own heart, my dear, that is your first duty. A man like Storm would take you out of your real self, and stop your career, and——"

"Oh, my career, my career! I'm tired to death of hearing of it!"

"Glory!"

"And who knows? I may not go on with it after all."

"If you have lost your sense of duty to yourself, have you forgotten your duty to Mr. Drake? Think what Mr. Drake has done for you!"

"Mr. Drake! Mr. Drake! I'm sick of that too."

"How strange you are to-night, Glory!"

"Am I? So are you. It's Mr. Drake here and Mr. Drake there! Are you trying to force me into his arms?"

"Is it you that say that, Glory?—you! and to me, too? Don't you see that this is a different case altogether? And if I thought of my own feelings only—consulted my own heart——"

"Rosa!"

"Ah! is it so very foolish? Yes, he is young and handsome, and rich and brilliant, while I—I am ridiculous."

"No, no, Rosa; I don't mean that."

"I do, though; and when you came in between us—young and beautiful and clever—everything that I was not, and could never hope to be—and he was so drawn to you—what was I to do? Nurse my hopeless and ridiculous love—or think of him— his happiness?"

"Rosa, my poor dear Rosa, forgive me! forgive me!"

An hour later, dinner being over, they had returned to the drawing-room. Rosa was writing at the table, and there was no sound in the room except the scratching of her pen, the falling of her slips of "copy," and the dull reverberation of the bell of St. Clement's Danes, which was ringing for evening service. Glory was sitting at the desk by the window, with her head on her hands, looking down into the garden. Out of the dead load at her heart she kept saying to herself, "Could I do that? Could I give up the one I loved for his own good, putting myself back, and thinking of him only?" And then a subtle hypocrisy stole over her, and she thought, "Yes, I could, I could," and in a fever of nervous excitement she began to write a letter.

"'The wind bloweth where it listeth, and so with a woman's will. I cannot go abroad with you, dear, because I cannot allow myself to break up your life, for it *would* be that—it would, it would, you know it would! There are ten thousand men good enough for the foreign mission-field, but there is only one man in the world for your work in London. This is one of the things hidden from the wise and revealed to children and fools. It would be wrong of me to take you away from your great scene. I daren't do it. It would be too great a responsibility. My conscience must have been dead and buried when I suggested such a possibility! Thank God it has had a resurrection, and it is not yet too late."

But when the letter was sealed and stamped and sent out to the post, she thought, "I must be mad, and there is no method in my madness either. What do I want?—to join his life in London?" And then remembering what she had written, it seemed as if the other woman must have written it, the visionary woman, the woman she was making herself into day by day.

XVII

JOHN STORM had left home early on Monday morning. It was the last day of his tenancy of the clergy-house, and there was much to do at Soho. Towards noon he made his way to the church at Bishopsgate Street for the first time since he had left the Brotherhood. It was mid-day service, and the little place was full of business men with their quick eyes and eager faces. The Superior preached, and the sermon was on the religious life. We were each composed of two beings, one temporal, the other eternal; one carnal, the other spiritual. Life was a constant warfare between these two nearly-matched forces, and often the victory seemed to sway from this side to that. Our enemy with the chariots of iron was ourselves. There was a Judas in each one of us ready to betray us with a kiss if allowed. The lusts of the flesh were the most deadly sins, absolute chastity the most pleasing to God of all virtues. Did we desire to realise what the religious life could be? Then let us reflect upon the news which had come from the South Seas. What was the word that had fallen that morning on all Christendom like a thunderclap—say, rather, like the blast of a celestial trumpet? Father Damien was dead! Think of his lonely life in that distant island where doomed men lived out their days. Cut off from earthly marriage, with no one claiming his affection, in the same way as Christ, he was free to commit himself entirely to God and to God's afflicted children. He was truly married to Christ. Christ occupied his soul as Lord and spouse. Glorious life! Glorious death! Eternal crown of glory waiting for him in the glory everlasting!

When the service ended John Storm stepped up to speak to the Father. His wide-open eyes were flaming; he was visibly excited. "I came to ask a question," he said, "but it is answered already. I will follow Father Damien and take up his work. I was thinking of the mission-field, but my doubt was whether God had called me, and I had great fear of going uncalled. God brought me here this morning, not knowing what I was to do, but now I know, and my mind is made up at last."

The Father was not less moved. They went out into the courtyard together and walked to and fro, planning, scheming, contriving, deciding.

"You'll take the vows first, my son?"

"The vows?"

"The life vows."

"But—but will that be necessary?"

"It will be best. Think what a peculiar appeal it will have for those poor doomed creatures! They are cut off from the world by a terrible affliction, but you will be cut off by the graciousness of a Christ-fed purity. They are lepers made of disease; you will be as a leper for the kingdom of heaven's sake."

"But, Father, if that be so, how much greater the appeal will be if—if a woman goes out also. Say she is young and beautiful, and of great gifts."

"Brother Andrew may go with you, my son."

"Yes, Brother Andrew as well. But holy men in all ages have been bound by ties of intimacy and affection to good women who have lived and worked beside them."

"Sisters, my son, elder sisters always."

"And why not? Sister, indeed, and united to me by a great and spiritual love."

"We are none of us invincible, my son; let us not despise danger."

"Danger, Father! What is the worth of my religion if it does not enable me to defy that?"

"Well, well, do not decide too soon. I'll come to you at Soho this evening."

"Do; it's our last night there. I must tell my poor people what my plans are to be. Good-bye for the present, Father, good-bye."

"Good-bye, my son," and as John Storm went off with a light heart and bounding step the Father passed indoors with downcast face, saying to himself with a sigh, "Let him that thinketh he standeth take heed lest he fall."

It was Lord Mayor's Day again, the streets were thronged, and John Storm was long in forging his way home. Glory's letter was waiting for him, and he tore it open with nervous fingers, but when he had read it he laughed aloud. "God bless her! But she doesn't know everything yet." Mrs. Callender was out in the carriage. She would be back for lunch, and the maid was laying the cloth; but he would not wait. After scribbling a few lines in pencil to tell of his great resolve, he set off for Clement's Inn. The Strand was less crowded when he returned to it, and the newsboys were calling the evening papers with "Full memoir of Father Damien."

On coming home from rehearsal, Glory had found the costume for her third act, her great act, awaiting her. All day long she had been thinking of her letter to John, half ashamed of it, half regretting it, almost wishing it could be withdrawn. But the dress made a great tug at her heart, and she could not resist an impulse to try it on. The moment she had done so the visionary woman whose part she was to play seemed to take possession of her, and shame and regret were gone.

It was a magnificent stage costume, green as the grass in spring with the morning sun on it. The gown was a splendid brocade with gold-embroidered lace around the square-cut neck and about the shoulders of the tight-made sleeves. Round her hips was a sash of golden tissue, and its hanging ends were fringed with emeralds. A band of azure stones encircled her head, and her fingers were covered with turquoise rings.

She went to the drawing-room, shut the door, and began to rehearse the scene. It was where the imaginary Gloria, being vain and selfish, trampled everything under her feet that she might possess the world and the things of the world. Glory spoke the words aloud, forgetting they were not her own, until she heard another voice saying, "May I come in, dear?"

It was John at the door. She was ashamed of her costume then, but there was no running away. "Yes, of course, come in," she cried, trembling all over, half afraid to be seen, and yet proud too of her beauty and her splendour. When he entered she was laughing nervously and was about to say, "See, this has happened before——"

But he saw nothing unusual, and she was disappointed and annoyed. Coming in breathless, as if he had been running, he flung himself down on one end of the couch, threw his hat on the other end, and said, "What did I tell you, Glory? That a way would open itself, and it has!"

"Really?"

"Didn't you think of it when you saw the news in the papers this morning?"

"What news?"

"That Father Damien is dead."

"But can you—do you really mean that—do you intend——"

"I do, Glory—I do."

"Then you didn't get my letter this morning?"

"Oh yes, dear, yes; but you were only thinking for me—God bless you!—that I was giving up a great scene for a little one. But this this is the greatest scene in the world, Glory. Life is a small sacrifice; the true sacrifice is a living death, a living crucifixion."

She felt as if he had taken her by the throat and was choking her. He had got up and was walking to and fro, talking impetuously.

"Yes, it is a great sacrifice I am asking you to make now, dear. That far-off island, the poor lepers, and then life-long banishment. But God will reward you, and with interest too. Only think, Glory! Think of the effect of your mere presence out there among those poor doomed creatures! A young and beautiful woman! Not a melancholy old dolt like me, preaching and prating to them, but a bright and brilliant girl, laughing with them, playing games with them, making mimicry for them and singing to them in the voice of an angel. Oh, they'll love you, Glory, they'll worship you—you'll be next to God and His blessed Mother with them. And already I hear them saying among themselves, 'Heaven bless her! She might have had the world at her feet and made a great name and a great fortune, but she gave it all up—all, all, all—for pity and love of us!' Won't it be glorious, my child? Won't it be the noblest thing in all the world?"

And she struggled to answer, "Yes, no doubt—the noblest thing in all the world."

"Then you agree? Ah, I knew your heart spoke in your first letter, and you wanted to leave London. You shall, too, for God has willed it."

Then she recovered a little and made a nervous attempt to withdraw. "But the church at Westminster?"

He laughed like a boy. "Oh, Golightly may have that now, and welcome."

"But the work in London?"

"Ah, that's all right, Glory. Ever since I heard from you I have been dealing with the bonds which bound me to London one by one, unravelling some and breaking others. They are all discharged now, every one of them, and I need think of them no more. Self is put behind for ever, and I can stand before God and say, 'Do with me as you will; I am ready for anything —anything!'"

"Oh!"

"Crying, Glory? My poor, dear child! But why are you crying?"

"It's nothing!"

"Are you sure—quite sure? Am I asking too much of you? Don't let us deceive ourselves—think——"

"Let us talk of something else now." She began to laugh. "Look at me, John—don't I look well to-day?"

"You always look well, Glory."

"But isn't there any difference—this dress, for instance?"

Then his sight came back and his big eyes sparkled. "How beautiful you are, dear!"

"Really? Do I look nice then—really?"

"My beautiful, beautiful girl!"

Her head was thrown back, and she glowed with joy. "Don't come too near me, you know—don't crush me."

"Nay, no fear of that—I should be afraid."

"Not that I mustn't be touched exactly."

"What will they think, I wonder, those poor lost creatures, so ugly, so disfigured?"

"And my red hair. This colour suits it, doesn't it?"

"Some Madonna, they'll say; the very picture of the Mother of God herself!"

"Are you—are you afraid of me in this frock, dear? Shall I run and take it off?"

"No, no; let me look at you again."

"But you don't like me to-day, for all that."

"I?"

"Do you know you've never once kissed me since you came into the room?"

"Glory!"

"My love, my love!"

"And you," he said, close to her lips, "are you ready for anything?"

"Anything," she whispered.

At the next moment she was holding herself off with her arms stiff about his neck, that she might look at him and at her lace sleeves at the same time. Suddenly a furrow crossed his brow. He had remembered the Father's warning, and was summoning all his strength.

"But out there I'll love you as a sister, Glory."

"Ah!"

"For the sake of those poor doomed beings cut off from earthly love we'll love each other as the angels love."

"Yes, that is the highest, purest, truest love, no doubt. Still——"

"What does the old Talmud say? 'He who divorces himself from the joys of earth weds himself to the glories of Paradise.'"

Her lashes were still wet; she was gazing deep into his eyes.

"And to think of being united in the next world, Glory—what happiness, what ecstasy!"

"Love me in this world, dearest," she whispered.

"You'll be their youth, Glory, their strength, their loveliness!"

"Be mine, darling, be mine!"

But the furrow crossed his brow a second time, and he disengaged himself before their lips had met again. Then he walked about the room as before, talking in broken sentences. They would have to leave soon—very soon—almost at once. And now he must go back to Soho. There was so much to do —to arrange. On reaching the door he hesitated, quivering with love, hardly knowing how to part from her. She was standing with head down, half angry and half ashamed.

"Well, *au revoir*," he cried in a strained voice, and then fled down the stairs. "The Father was right," he thought. "No man is invincible. But, thank God, it is over! It can never occur again!"

Her glow had left her and she felt chilled and lost. There was no help for it now, and escape was impossible. She must renounce everything for the man who had renounced everything for her. Sitting on the couch, she dropped her head on the cushion, and cried like a child. In the lowest depths of her soul she knew full well that she could never go away, but she began to bid good-bye in her heart to the life she had been living. The charm and fascination of London began to pass before her like a panorama, with all the scenes of misery and squalor left out. What a beautiful world she was leaving behind her! She would remember it all her life long with useless and unending regret. Her tears were flowing through the fingers which were clasped beneath her face.

A postman's knock came to the door downstairs. The letter was from the manager, written in the swirl and rush of theatrical life, and reading like a telegram: "Theatre going on rapidly, men working day and night, rehearsals advanced and scenery progressing; might we not fix this day fortnight for the first performance?"

Enclosed with this was a letter from the author. "You are on the eve of an extraordinary success, dear Gloria, and I write to reassure and congratulate you. Some signs of inexperience I may perhaps observe, some lack of ease and simplicity, but already it is a performance of so much passion and power that I predict for it a triumphant success. A great future awaits you. Don't shrink from it, don't be afraid of it; it is as certain as that the sun will rise to-morrow."

She carried the letter to her lips, then rose from the couch, and threw up her head, closed her eyes, and smiled. The visionary woman was taking hold of her again with the slow grip and embrace of the glacier.

Rosa came home to dine, and at sight of the new costume she cried, "Shade of Titian! what a picture!" During dinner she mentioned that she had met Mr. Drake, who had said that the Prince was likely to be present at the production, having asked for the date and other particulars.

"But haven't you heard the *great* news, dear? It's in all the late editions of the evening papers."

"What is it?" said Glory; but she saw what was coming.

"Father Storm is to follow Father Damien. That's the report, at all events; but he is expected to make a statement at his club to-night, and I have to be there for the paper."

As soon as dinner was over Rosa went off to Soho, and then Glory was brought back with a shock to the agony of her inward struggle. She knew that her hour had arrived, and that on her action now everything depended. She knew that she could never break the chains by which the world and her profession held her. She knew that the other woman had come, that she must go with her, and go for good. But the renunciation of love was terrible. The day had been soft and beautiful. It was falling asleep and yawning now, with a drowsy breeze that shook the yellow leaves as they hung withered and closed on the thinning boughs like the fingers of an old maid's hand. She was sitting at the desk by the window, trying to write a letter. More than once she tore up the sheet, dried her eyes, and began again. What she wrote last was this:—

"It is impossible, dear John. I cannot go with you to the South Seas. I have struggled, but I cannot, I cannot! It is the greatest, noblest, sublimest mission in the world, but I am not the woman for these high tasks. I should be only a fruitless fig-tree, a sham, a hypocrite. It would be like taking a dead body with you to take me, for my heart would not be there. You would find that out, dear, and I should be ashamed.

"And then I cannot leave this life—I cannot give up London. I am like a child—I like the bustling streets, the brilliant thoroughfares, the crowds, the bands of music, the lights at night, and the sense of life. I like to succeed, too, and to be admired, and . . . yes, to hear 'the clapping of hands in a theatre.' You are above all this, and can look down at it as dross, and I like you for that also. But give it all up I can't; I haven't the strength; it is in my blood, dear, and if I part from it I must die.

"And then I like to be fondled and coaxed and kissed, and I want so much—oh, so much to be loved! I want somebody to tell me every day and always how much he loves me, and to praise me and pet me and forget everything else for me, everything, everything, even his own soul and salvation. You cannot do that; it would be sinful, and besides, it wouldn't be love as you understand it, and as it ought to be, if you are to go out to that solemn and awful task.

"When I said I loved you I spoke the truth, dear, and yet I didn't know what the word meant really, I didn't realise everything. I love you still—with all my heart and soul I love you; but now I know that there is a difference between us, that we can never come together. No, I cannot reach up to your austere heights. I am so weak; you are so strong. Your 'strength is as the strength of ten, because your heart is pure,' while I——

"I am unworthy of your thoughts, John. Leave me to the life I have chosen. It may be poor and vain and worthless, but it is the only life I'm fit for. And yet I love you . . . and you loved me. I suppose God makes men and women like that sometimes, and it is no use struggling.

"One kiss, dear—it is the last."

XVIII

John Storm went back to Victoria Square with a bright and joyful face, and found Mrs. Callender waiting for him, grim as a judge. He could see that her eyes were large and red with weeping, but she fell on him instantly with withering scorn.

"So you're here at last, are ye? A pretty senseless thing this is, to be sure! What are you dreaming about? Are you bewitched, or what? Do you suppose things can be broken off in this way? You to go to the leper islands indeed!"

"I'm called, auntie, and when God calls a man, what can he do but answer with Samuel——"

"Tut! Don't talk sic nonsense. Besides, Samuel had some sense. He waited to be called three times, and I havena heard this is your third time of calling."

John Storm laughed, and that provoked her to towering indignation. "Good God! what are you thinking of, man? There's that puir lassie—you're running away from her, too, aren't you? It's shameful, it's disgraceful, it's unprincipled, and *you* to do it too!"

"You needn't trouble about that, auntie," said John; "she is going with me."

"What?" cried Mrs. Callender, and her face expressed boundless astonishment.

"Yes," said John, "you women are brimful of courage, God bless you, and she's the bravest of you all."

"But you'll no have the assurance to tak' that puir bit lassie to yonder God-forsaken spot?"

"She wants to go . . . at least she wants to leave London."

"What! does she? Weel, weel! But didn't I say she was nought but one of your Sisters or sic-like? . . . And you're going to let a slip of a girl tak' you away frae your ain work and your ain duty . . . and you call yourself a man!"

He began to coax and appease her, and before long the grim old face was struggling between smiles and tears.

"Tut! get along wi' ye! I've a great mind, though . . . I'd be liking fine to see her anyway. . . . Now where does she bide in London?"

"Why do you want to know that, auntie?"

"What's it to you, laddie? Can't a body call to say 'Goodbye' to a lassie, and tak' her a wee present before going away, without asking a man's permission?"

"I shouldn't do it, though, if I were you."

"And why not, pray?"

"Because she's as bright as a star and as quick as a diamond, and she'd see through you in a twinkling. Besides, I shouldn't advise——"

"Keep your advice, like your salt, till you're asked for it, my man. . . . And to think of any reasonable body giving up his work in London for that . . . that——"

"Good men have gone out to the mission-field, auntie."

"Mission fiddlesticks! Just a barber's chair, fit for every comer."

"And then this isn't the mission-field exactly either."

"Mair's the pity, and then you wouldna be running bull-neck on your death before your time."

"None of us can do that, auntie, for Heaven is over all."

"High words off an empty stomach, my man, so you can just keep them to cool your parridge. But oh dear! oh dear! You'll forget your puir auld Jane Callender, anyway."

"Never, auntie!"

"Tut! don't tell me."

"Never!"

"It's the last I'm to see of you, laddie. I'm knowing that fine . . . and me that fond of you too, and looking on you as my ain son."

"Come, auntie, come; you mustn't take it so seriously."

"And to think a bit thing like that can make all this botherment!"

"Nay, it's my own doing—absolutely mine."

"Aye, aye! man's the head, but woman turns it."

They dined together and then got into the carriage for Soho. John talked continually, with an impetuous rush of enthusiasm; but the old lady sat in gloomy silence, broken only by a sigh. At the corner of Downing Street he got out to call on the Prime Minister, and sent the carriage on to the clergy-house.

A newsboy going down Whitehall was calling an evening paper. John bought a copy, and the first thing his eye fell upon was the mention of his own name. "The announcement in another column that Father Storm of Soho intends to take up the work which the heroic Father Damien has just laid down will be received by the public with mingled joy and regret—joy at the splendid heroism which prompts so noble a resolve, regret at the loss which the Church in London will sustain by the removal of a clergyman of so much courage, devotion, independence, and self-sacrifice. . . . That the son of a peer and heir to an earldom should voluntarily take up a life of poverty in Soho, one of the most crowded, criminal, and neglected corners of Christendom, was a fact of so much significance——"

John Storm crushed the paper in his hand and threw it into the street; but a few minutes afterwards he saw another copy of it in the hands of the Prime Minister as he came to the door of the Cabinet-room to greet him. The old man's face looked soft, and his voice had a faint tremor.

"I'm afraid you are bringing me bad news, John."

John laughed noisily. "Do I look like it, uncle? Bad news, indeed! No, but the best news in the world."

"What is it, my boy?"

"I'm about to be married. You've often told me I ought to be, and now I'm going to act on your advice."

The bleak old face was smiling. "Then the rumour I see in the papers isn't true, after all?"

"Oh, yes, it's true enough, and my wife is to go with me."

"But have you considered that carefully? Isn't it a terrible demand to make of any woman? Women are more religious than men, but they are more material also. Under the heat of religious impulse a woman is capable of sacrifices—great sacrifices —but when it has cooled——"

"No fear of that, uncle," said John; and then he told the Prime Minister what he had told Mrs. Callender—that it was Glory's proposal that they should leave London, and that without this suggestion he might not have thought of his present enterprise. The bleak face kept smiling, but the Prime Minister was asking himself, "What does this mean? Has she *her own* reasons for wishing to go away?"

"Do you know, my boy, that, with all this talk, you've not yet told me who she is?"

John told him, and then a faint and far-off rumour out of another world seemed to flit across his memory.

"An actress at present, you say?"

"So to speak, but ready to give up everything for this glorious mission."

"Very brave, no doubt, very beautiful; but what of your present responsibilities—your responsibilities in London?"

"That's just what I came to speak about," said John; and then his rapturous face straightened, and he made some effort to plunge into the practical aspect of his affairs at Soho. There was his club for girls and his home for children. They were to be turned out of the clergy-house to-morrow, and he had taken a shelter at Westminster. But the means to support them were still deficient, and if there was anything coming to him that would suffice for that purpose . . . if there was enough left . . . if his mother's money was not all gone——

The Prime Minister was looking into John's face, watching the play of his features, but hardly listening to what he said. "What does this mean?" he was asking himself, in the old habitual way of the man whose business it is to read the motives that are not revealed.

"So you are willing to leave London after all, John?"

"Why not, uncle? London is nothing to me in itself, less than nothing, and if that brave girl to whom it is everything——"

"And yet six months ago I gave you the opportunity of doing so, and then ——"

"Then my head was full of dreams, sir. Thank God they are gone now, and I am awake at last."

"But the Church—I thought your duty and devotion to the Church——"

"The Church is a chaos, uncle, a wreck of fragments without unity, principle, or life. No man can find foothold in it now without accommodating his duty and his loyalty to his chances of a livelihood. It is a career, not a crusade. Once I imagined that a man might live as a protest against all this, but it was a dream, a vain and presumptuous dream."

"And then your woman movement——"

"Another dream, uncle! A whole standing army marshalled and equipped to do battle against the world's sins toward woman could never hope for victory. Why? Because the enemy is ourselves, and only God can contend against a foe like that. He will, too! For the wrongs inflicted on woman by this wicked and immoral London, God will visit it with his vengeance yet. I see it coming, it is not far off, and God help those——"

"But surely, my boy, surely it is not necessary to fly away from the world in order to escape from your dreams? Just when it is going to be good to you, too. It was kicking and cuffing and laughing at you only yesterday——"

"And to-morrow it would kick and cuff and laugh at me again. Oh, it is a cowardly and contemptible world, uncle, and happy is the man who wants nothing of it! He is its master, its absolute master, and everybody else is its wretched slave. Think of the people who are scrambling for fame and titles and decorations and invitations to Court! They'll all be in their six feet by two feet some day. And then think of the rich men who hire detectives to watch over their children lest they should be stolen for sake of a ransom, while they themselves, like human mill-horses, go tramping round and round the safes which contain their securities! Oh, miserable delusion, to think that because a nation is rich it is therefore great! Once I thought the Church was the refuge from this worst of the spiritual dangers of the age, and so it would have been if it had been built on the Gospel. But it isn't; it loves the thrones of the world and bows down to the golden calf. Poverty! Give me poverty and let me renounce everything. Jesus, our blessed Jesus, He knew well what He was doing in choosing to be poor, and even as a man He was the greatest being that ever trod upon the earth."

"But this leper island mission is not poverty merely, my dear John it is death, certain death, sooner or later, and God knows what news the next mail may bring us."

"As to that, I feel I am in God's hands, sir, and He knows best what is good for us. People talk about dying before their time, but no man ever did or ever will or ever can do so, and it is blasphemy to think of it. Then which of us can prolong our lives by one day or hour or minute? But God can do everything. And what a grand inspiration to trust yourself absolutely to Him, to raise the arms heavenward, which the world would pinion to your side, and cry, 'Do with me as Thou wilt; I am ready for anything—anything.'"

A tremor passed over the wrinkles about the old man's eyes, and he thought, "All this is self-deception. He doesn't believe a word of it. Poor boy! his heart alone is leading him, and he is the worst slave of us all."

Then he said aloud, "Things haven't fallen out as I expected,

John, and I am sorry, very sorry. The laws of life and the laws of love don't always run together—I know that quite well."

John flinched, but made no protest.

"I shall feel as if I were losing your mother a second time when you leave me, my boy. To tell you the truth, I've been watching you and thinking of you, though you haven't known it. And you've rather neglected the old man. I thought you might bring your wife to me some day, and that I might live to see your children. But that's all over now, and there seems to be no help for it . . . They say the most noble and beautiful things in the world are done in a state of fever, and perhaps this fever of yours . . . H'm ! . . . As for the money, it is ready for you at any time."

"There can't be much left, uncle. I have gone through most of it."

"No, John, no; the money you spent was my money—your own is still untouched."

"You are too good, uncle, and if I had once thought you wished to see more of me——"

"Ah, I know, I know! It was a wise man who said it was hard to love a woman and do anything else, even to love God Himself."

John dropped his head and turned to go.

"But come again before you leave London—if you do leave it —and now good-bye and God bless you!"

The news of John Storm's intention to follow Father Damien had touched and thrilled the heart of London, and the streets and courts about St. Mary Magdalene's were thronged with people. In their eyes he was about to fulfil a glorious mission, and ought to be encouraged and sustained. "Good-bye, Father!" cried one. "God bless you!" cried another. A young woman with timid eyes stretched out her hand to him, and then everybody attempted to do the same. He tried to answer cheerfully, but was conscious that his throat was thick and his voice was husky. Mrs. Pincher was at the door of the clergy-house, crying openly and wiping her eyes. "Ain't there lepers enough in London, sir, without goin' to the ends of the earth for 'em?" He laughed and made an effort to answer her humorously, but for some reason both words and ideas failed him.

The club-room was crowded, and among the girls and Sisters there were several strange faces. Mrs. Callender sat at one end of the little platform, and she was glowering across at the other end, where the Father Superior stood in his black cassock, quiet and watchful, and with the sprawling, smiling face of Brother Andrew by his side. The girls were singing when John entered, and their voices swelled out as they saw him pushing his way through. When the hymn ended there was silence for a moment, as if it was expected that he would speak, but he did not rise, and the lady at the harmonium began again. Some of the young mothers from the Shelter above had brought down their little ones, and the thin, tuneless voices could be heard among the rest—

"There's a Friend for little children
Above the bright blue sky."

John had made a brave fight for it, but he was beginning to break down. Everybody else had risen; he could not rise. An expression of fear and at the same time of shame, had come into his face. Vaguely, half-consciously, half-reproachfully, he began to review the situation. After all, he was deserting his post, he was running away. This was his true scene, his true work, and if he turned his back upon it he would be pursued by eternal regrets. And yet he must go, he must leave everything—that alone he understood and felt.

All at once, God knows why, he began to think of something which had happened when he was a boy. With his father he was crossing the Duddon Sands. The tide was out, far out, but it had turned; it was galloping towards them, and they could hear the champing waves on the beach behind. "Run, boy, run! Give me your hand and run!"

Then he resumed the current of his former thoughts. "What was I thinking about?" he asked himself; and when he remembered, he thought, "I will give my hand to the Heavenly Father and go on without fear." At the second verse he rallied, rose to his feet, and joined in the singing. It was said afterwards that his deep voice rang out above all the other voices, and that he sang in rapid and irregular time, going faster and faster at every line.

They had reached the last verse but one when he saw a young girl crushing her way towards him with a letter. She was smiling, and seemed proud to render him this service. He was about to lay the letter aside when he glanced at it, and then he could not put it down. It was marked "Urgent," and the address was in Glory's handwriting. The champing waves were in his ears again. They were coming on and on.

A presentiment of evil crept over him, and he opened the letter and read it. Then his life fell to wreck in a moment. Its nullity, its hopelessness, its futility, its folly, the world with its elusive joys, love with its deceptions so cruel and so sweet, all, all came sweeping up on him like the sea-wrack out of a storm. In an instant the truth appeared to him, and he understood himself at last. For Glory's sake he had sacrificed everything, and deceived himself before God and man. And yet she had failed him and forsaken him, and slipped out of his hands in the end. The tide had overtaken and surrounded him, and the voices of the girls and the children were like the roar of the waters in his ears.

But what was this? Why had they stopped singing? All at once he became aware that everybody else was seated, and that he was standing alone on the edge of the platform with Glory's letter in his hand.

"Hush! hush!" There was a strained silence, and he tried to recollect what it was that he was expected to do. Every eye was on his face. Some of the strangers opened note-books and sat ready to write. Then, coming to himself, he understood what was before him, and tried to control his voice and begin.

"Girls," he said; but he was hardly able to speak or breathe. "Girls," he said again; but his strong voice shook, and he tried in vain to go on.

One of the girls began to sob. Then another and another. It was said afterwards that nobody could look on his drawn face, so hopeless, so full of the traces of suffering and bitter sadness, without wanting to cry aloud. But he controlled himself at length.

"My good friends all, you came to-night to bid me God-speed on a long journey, and I came to bid you farewell. But there is a higher Power that rules our actions, and it is little we know of our own future or our fate or ourselves. God bids me tell you that my leper island is to be London, and that my work among you is not done yet."

After saying this he stood a moment as if intending to say more, but he said nothing. The letter crinkled in his fingers; he looked at it, an expression of helplessness came into his face, and he sat down. And then the Father came up to him and sat beside him, and took his hand and comforted it as if he had been a little child.

There was another attempt to sing, but the hymn made no headway this time, for some of the girls were crying, they hardly knew why, and others were whispering, and the strangers were leaving the room. Two ladies were going down the stairs.

"I felt sure he wouldn't go," said one.

"Why so?" said the other.

"I can't tell you. I had my private reasons."

It was Rosa Macquarrie. Going down the dark lane she came upon a woman who had haunted the outside of the building during the past half-hour, apparently thinking at one moment of entering and at the next of going away. The woman hurriedly lowered her veil as Rosa approached her, but she was too late to avoid recognition.

"Glory! Is it you?"

Glory covered her face with her hands and sobbed.

"Whatever are you doing here?"

"Don't ask me, Rosa. Oh, I'm a lost woman! Lord forgive me! what have I done?"

"My poor child!"

"Take me home, Rosa; and don't leave me to-night, dear— not to-night, Rosa."

And Rosa took her by the arm and led her back to Clement's Inn.

Next morning before daybreak the brothers of the Society of the Holy Gethsemane had gathered in their church in Bishopsgate Street for Lauds and Prime. Only the chancel was lighted up, the rest of the church was dark, but the first gleams of dawn were now struggling through the eastern window against the candlelight on the altar and the gaslight on the choir.

John Storm was standing on the altar steps, and the Father was by his side. He was wearing the cassock of the Brotherhood, and the cord with the three knots was bound about his waist. All was silent round about, the city was still asleep, the current of life had not yet awakened for the day. Lauds and Prime were over, the brothers were on their knees, and the Father was reading the last words of the dedication service.

"Amen! Amen!"

There was a stroke of the bell overhead, a door somewhere was loudly slammed, and then the organ began to play—

"Holy, Holy, Holy, Lord God Almighty."

The brothers rose and sang, their voices filled the dark place, and the quivering sounds of the organ swelled up to the unseen roof.

"Holy, Holy, Holy! Merciful and Mighty,
God in Three Persons, Blessèd Trinity!"

The Father's cheeks were moist, but his eyes were shining and his face was full of a great joy. John Storm was standing with bowed head. He had made the vows of poverty, chastity, and obedience, and surrendered his life to God.

END OF THIRD BOOK

FOURTH BOOK.—SANCTUARY

I

Six months passed, and a panic terror had seized London. It was one of those epidemic frenzies which have fallen upon great cities in former ages of the world. The public mind was filled with the idea that London was threatened with a serious danger, that it was verging on an awful crisis, that it was about to be destroyed.

The signs were such as have usually been considered preparatory to the Second Coming of the Messiah—a shock of earthquake, which threw down a tottering chimney (somewhere in Soho), and the expected appearance of a comet. But this was not to be the second Advent: it was to be a disaster confined to London.

God was about to punish London for its sins. The dishonour lay at its door of being the wickedest city in the world. Side by side with the developments of mechanical science, lifting men to the power and position of angels, there was a moral degeneration degrading them to the level of beasts. With an apparent aspiration after social and humanitarian reform, there was a corruption of the public conscience and a hardening of the public heart. London was the living picture of this startling contrast. Impiety, iniquity, impurity, and injustice were at their height here, and either England must forfeit her position among the nations or the Almighty would interpose. The Almighty was about to interpose, and the consummation of London's wickedness was near.

By what means the destruction of London would come to pass was a matter on which there were many theories, and the fear and consternation of the people took various shapes. One of them was that of a mighty earthquake, in which the dome of St. Paul's was to totter, and the towers of Westminster Abbey to rock and fall amid clouds of dust. Another was that of an avenging fire, in which the great city was to light up the whole face of Europe and burn to ashes, as a witness of God's wrath at the sins of men. A third was that of a flood, in which the

Thames was to rise and submerge the city, and tens of thousands of houses and hundreds of thousands of persons were to be washed away and destroyed.

Concerning the time of the event the popular imagination had attained to a more definite idea. It was to occur on the great day of the Epsom races. Derby-day was the national day. More than any day associated with political independence, or with victory in battle, or yet with religious sanctity, the day devoted to sport and gambling and intemperance and immorality was England's day. Therefore the Almighty had selected that day for the awful revelation by which He would make His power known to man.

Thus the heart of London was once more stormed, and shame and panic ran through it like an epidemic. The consequences were the usual ones. In vain the newspapers published articles in derision of the madness, with accounts of similar frenzies which had laid hold of London before. There was a run on the banks, men sold their businesses, dissolved their partnerships, transferred their stocks, and removed to houses outside the suburbs. Great losses were sustained in all ranks of society, and the only class known to escape were the Jews on the Exchange, who held their peace and profited by their infidelity.

When people asked themselves who the author and origin of the panic was, they thought instantly, and with one accord, of a dark-eyed lonely man, who walked the streets of London in the black cassock of a monk, with the cord and three knots which were the witness of life vows. No dress could have shown to better advantage his dark-brown face and tall figure. Something majestic seemed to hang about the man. His big lustrous eyes, his faint smile with its sad expression always behind it, his silence, his reserve, his burning eloquence when he preached, seemed to lay siege to the imagination of the populace, and especially to take hold, as with a fiery grip, of the impassioned souls of women.

A certain mystery about his life did much to help this extraordinary fascination. When London as a whole became conscious of him, it was understood that he was in some sort a nobleman as well as a priest, and had renounced the pleasures and possessions of the world and given up all for God. His life was devoted to the poor and outcast, especially to the Magdalenes and their unhappy children. Although a detached monk still, and living in obedience to the rule of one of the monastic brotherhoods of the Anglican Church, he was also vicar of a parish in Westminster. His church was a centre of religious life in that abandoned district, having no fewer than thirty parochial organisations connected with it, including guilds, clubs, temperance societies, savings-banks, and, above all, shelters and orphanages for the girls and their little ones who were the vicar's especial care.

His chief helpers were a company of devoted women, drawn mainly from the fashionable fringe which skirted his squalid district, and banded together as a sisterhood. For clerical help he depended entirely on the brothers of his Society, and the money saved by these voluntary agencies he distributed among the poor, the sick, and the unfortunate. Money of his own he had none, and his purse was always empty by reason of his free-handedness. Rumour spoke of a fortune of many thousands which had been spent wholly on others, in the building or maintenance of school and hospital, shelter and refuge. He lived a life of more than Christian simplicity, and was seen to treat himself with constant disregard of comfort and convenience. His only home was two rooms (formerly assigned to the choir) on the ground-floor under his church, and it was understood that he slept on a hospital-bed wrapped in the cloak which in winter he wore over his cassock. His personal servant in these cell-like quarters was a lay brother from his Society,—a big, ungainly boy, with sprawling features,—who served him, and loved him, and looked up to him with the devotion of a dog. A dog of other kind he had also— a bloodhound, whose affection for him was a terror to all who awakened its jealousy or provoked its master's wrath. People said he had learnt renunciation, and was the most Christ-like man they had ever known. He was called "The Father."

Such was the man with whom the popular imagination associated the idea of the panic, but what specific ground there was for laying upon him the responsibility of the precise predictions which led to it none could rightly say. It was remembered afterwards that every new folly had been ascribed to him. "The Father says so and so," or "The Father says such and such will come to pass," and then came prophecies which were the remotest from his thoughts. No matter how wild or extravagant the assertion, if it was laid upon him there were people ready to believe it, so deep was the impression made on the public mind by this priest in the black cassock, with the bloodhound at his heels, so strong was the assurance that he was a man with the breath of God in him.

What was known with certainty was that the Father preached against the impurities and injustices of the age with a vehemence never heard before, and that when he spoke of the wickedness of the world towards woman, of the temptations that were laid

before her,—temptations of dress, of luxury, of false work and
false fame,—and then of the cruel neglect and abandonment of
woman when her summer had gone and her winter had come,
his lips seemed to be touched as by a live coal from the altar,
and his eyes to blaze as with Pentecostal fire. Cities and nations
which countenanced and upheld such corruptions of a false
civilisation would be overtaken by the judgment of God. That
judgment was near, it was imminent, and but for the many
instances in which the life of the rich, the great, and the powerful was redeemed by the highest virtue, this pitiful farce of a
national existence would have been played out already,—but for
the good men still found in Sodom the city of abominations
must long since have been destroyed. People there were to
laugh at these predictions, but they were only throwing cold
water on lime, the more they did so the more it smoked.

Little by little a supernatural atmosphere gathered about the
Father as a man sent from God. One day he visited a child
who was sick with a bad mouth, and, touching the child's mouth,
he said, "It will be well soon." The child recovered immediately, and the idea was started that he was a healer. People
waited for him that they might touch his hand. Sometimes
after service he had to stand half-an-hour while the congregation filed past him. Hard-headed persons, sane and cute in
other relations of life, were heard to protest that on shaking
hands with him an electric current passed through them. Sick
people declared themselves cured by the sight of him, and char-
latans sold handkerchiefs on pretence that he had blessed them.
He repeatedly protested that it was not necessary to touch or
even to see him. "Your faith alone can make you whole." But
the frenzy increased, the people crowded upon him, and he was
followed through the streets for his blessing.

Somebody discovered that he was born on the 25th of Decem-
ber, and was just thirty-three years of age. Then the madness
reached its height. A certain resemblance was observed in his
face and head to the traditional head and face of Christ, and it
was the humour of the populace to discover some mystical relations between him and the Divine figure. Hysterical women
kissed his hand, and even hailed him as their Saviour. He
protested and remonstrated, but all to no purpose. The delusion
grew, and his protestations helped it.

As the day approached that was to be big with the fate of
London, his church, which had been crowded before, was now
besieged. He was understood to preach the hope that in the
calamity to befall the city a remnant would be saved, as Israel
was saved from the plagues of Egypt. Thousands who were too

poor to leave London had determined to spend the night of the fateful day in the open air, and already they were going out into the fields and the parks, to Hampstead, Highgate, and Blackheath. The panic was becoming terrible, and the newspapers were calling upon the authorities to intervene. A danger to the public peace was threatened, and the man who was chiefly to blame for it should be dealt with at once. No matter that he was innocent of active sedition, no matter that he was living a life devoted to religious and humanitarian reforms, no matter that his vivid faith, his trust in God, and his obedience to the Divine will were like a light shining in a dark place, no matter that he was not guilty of the wild extravagance of the predictions of his followers,—"the Father" was a peril, he was a panic-maker, and he should be arrested and restrained.

The morning of Derby-day broke grey and dull and close. It was one of those mornings in summer which portend a thunder-storm and great heat. In that atmosphere London awoke to two great fevers—the fever of superstitious fear and the fever of gambling and sport.

II

But London is a monster with many hearts; it is capable of various emotions, and even at that feverish time it was at the full tide of a sensation of a different kind entirely. This was a new play and a new player. The play was "risky"; it was understood to present the fallen woman in her naked reality, and not as a soiled dove or sentimental plaything. The player was the actress who performed this part. She was new to the stage, and little was known of her, but it was whispered that she had something in common with the character she personated. Her success had been instantaneous: her photograph was in the shop-windows; it had been reproduced in the illustrated papers; she had sat to famous artists, and her portrait in oils was on the line at Burlington House.

The play was the latest work of the Scandinavian dramatist, the actress was Glory Quayle.

At nine o'clock on the morning of Derby-day Glory was waiting in the drawing-room of the Garden House, dressed in a magnificent outdoor costume of pale grey, which seemed to wave like a ripe hayfield. She looked paler and more nervous than before, and sometimes she glanced at the clock on the mantelpiece, and sometimes looked away in the distance before her while she drew on her long white gloves and buttoned them. Rosa Macquarrie came upstairs hurriedly. She was smartly dressed in black with red roses, and looked bright and brisk and happy.

"He has sent Benson with the carriage to ask us to drive down," said Rosa. "Must have some engagement surely. Let us be off, dear. No time to lose."

"Shall I go, I wonder?" said Glory with a strange gravity.

"Indeed yes, dear. Why not? You've not been in good spirits lately and it will do you good. Besides, you deserve a holiday after a six months' season. And then it's such a great day for *him* too——"

"Very well, I'll go," said Glory, and at that moment a twitch of her nervous fingers broke a button of one of the gloves. She drew it off, threw both gloves on to a side-table, took up another pair that lay there and followed Rosa down the stairs. An open carriage was waiting for them in the outer court of the Inn, and ten minutes afterwards they drew up in a narrow street off Whitehall, under a wide archway which opened into the large and silent quadrangle leading to the principal public offices. It was the Home Office; the carriage had come for Drake.

Drake had seen changes in his life too. His father was dead and he had succeeded to the baronetcy. He had also inherited a racing establishment which the family had long upheld, and a colt that had been entered for the Derby in his own name nearly three years ago was to run that day. Its name was Ellan Vannin, and it was not a favourite. Notwithstanding the change in his fortunes, Drake still held his position of private secretary to the Secretary of State, but it was understood that he was shortly to enter public life under the wing of the Government, and to stand for the first constituency that became vacant. Ministers predicted a career for him; there was nothing he might not aspire to, and hardly anything he might not do.

Parliament had adjourned in honour of the day on which the "Isthmian games" were celebrated, and the Home Secretary, as leader of the Lower House, had said that horse-racing was "a noble and distinguished sport deserving of a national holiday." But the Minister himself, and consequently his secretary, had been compelled to put in an appearance at their office for all that. There was urgent business demanding prompt attention.

In the large green room of the Home Office overlooking the empty quadrangle, the Minister, dressed in a paddock coat, received a deputation of six clergymen. It included Archdeacon

Wealthy, who served as its spokesman. In a rotund voice, strutting a step and swinging his glasses, the Archdeacon stated their case. They had come, most reluctantly and with a sense of pain and grief and humiliation, to make representations about a brother clergyman. It was the notorious Mr. Storm—"Father" Storm, for he was drawing the people into the Roman obedience. The man was bringing religion into ridicule and contempt, and it was the duty of all who loved their mother Church——

"Pardon me, Mr. Archdeacon, we have nothing to do with that," said the Minister. "You should go to your Bishop. Surely he is the proper person——"

"We've been, sir," said the Archdeacon, and then followed an explanation of the Bishop's powerlessness. The Church provided no funds to protect a Bishop from legal proceedings in inhibiting a vicar guilty of this ridiculous kind of conduct. "But the man comes within the power of the secular authorities, sir. He is constantly inciting people to assemble unlawfully to the danger of the public peace."

"How? How?"

"Well, he is a fanatic, a lunatic, and has put out monstrous and ridiculous predictions about the destruction of London, causing disorderly crowds to assemble about his church. The thoroughfares are blocked, and people are pushed about and assaulted. Indeed, things have come to such a pass that now . . . to-day——"

"Pardon me again, Mr. Archdeacon, but this seems to be a simple matter for the police. Why didn't you go to the Commissioner at Scotland Yard?"

"We did, sir; but he said—you will hardly believe it, but he actually affirmed—that as the man had been guilty of no overt act of sedition——"

"Precisely; that would be my view too."

"And are we, sir, to wait for a riot, for death, for murder, before the law can be put in motion? Is there no precedent for proceeding before anything serious . . . I may say alarming——"

"Well, gentlemen," said the Minister, glancing impatiently at his watch. "I can only promise you that the matter shall have proper attention. The Commissioner shall be seen, and if a summons——"

"It is too late for that now, sir. The man is a dangerous madman, and should be arrested and put under restraint."

"I confess I don't quite see what he has done, but if——"

The Archdeacon drew himself up. "Because a clergyman is well connected—has high official connections indeed . . . But surely it is better that one man should be put under control, whoever he is, than that the whole Church and nation should be endangered and disgraced."

"Ah . . . H'm! . . . H'm! I think I've heard that sentiment before somewhere, Mr. Archdeacon. But I'll not detain you now. If a warrant is necessary . . ." and with vague promises and plausible speeches the Minister bowed the deputation out of the room. Then he pisht and pshawed, swung a field-glass across his shoulder and prepared to leave for the day.

"Confound them! How these Christians love each other! I leave it with you, Drake. When the matter was mentioned at Downing Street the Prime Minister told us to act without regard to his interest in the young priest. If there's likely to be a riot let the Commissioner get his warrant . . . Heigho! Ten thirty! I'm off! Good-day!"

Some minutes afterwards Drake himself, having written to Scotland Yard, followed his chief down the private staircase to the quadrangle, where Glory and Rosa were waiting in the carriage under the arch.

In honour of the event in which his horse was to play a part Drake had engaged a coach to take a party of friends to the Downs. They assembled at a hotel in the Buckingham Palace Road. Lord Robert was there, dressed in the latest fashion, with boots of approved Parisian shape and a necktie of crying colours. Betty Bellman was with him, in a red and white dress and a large red hat. There was a lady in pale green with a light bonnet, another in grey and white, and another in brightest blue. They were a large, smart, and even gorgeous company, chiefly theatrical. Before eleven o'clock they were spinning along the Kennington Road on their way to Epsom.

Drake himself drove, and Glory occupied the seat of honour by his side. She was looking brighter now, and was smiling and laughing and making little sallies in response to her companion's talk. He was telling her all about the carnival. The Derby was the greatest race the world over. It was run for about six thousand sovereigns, but the total turn-over of the meeting was probably a million of money. Thus, on its business side alone, it was a great national enterprise, and the Puritans who would abolish it ought to think of that. A racehorse cost about three hundred a year to keep; but, of course, nobody maintained his racing establishment on his winnings. Nearly everybody had to bet, and gambling was not so great an offence as some people supposed. The whole trade of the world was of the nature of a gamble, life itself was a gamble, and the racecourse was the only market in the world where no man could afford to go bankrupt or be a defaulter and refuse to pay.

They were now going by Clapham Common with an unbroken stream of vehicles of every sort—coaches with outriders, landaus, hansom cabs, omnibuses, costers' spring-carts and barrows. Every coach carried its horn, and every horn was blown at the approach to every village. The sun was hot, and the roads were rising to the horses' fetlocks in dust. Drake was pointing out some of their travelling companions. That large coach going by at a furious gallop was the coach of the Army and Navy Club; that barouche with its pair of greys and its postilion belonged to a well-known wine merchant; that carriage, with its couple of leaders worth hundreds apiece, was the property of a prosperous publican; that was the coach which usually ran between Northumberland Avenue and Virginia Water, and its seats were let out at so much apiece, usually to clerks who practised innocent frauds to escape from the City; those soldiers on the omnibus were from Wellington Barracks on " Derby leave;" and those jolly tars with their sweethearts, packed like herrings in a car, were the only true sportsmen on the road, and probably hadn't the price of a glass of rum on any race of the day. Going by road to the Derby was almost a thing of the past, smart people didn't often do it, but it was the best fun anyway, and many an old sport tooled his team on the road still.

Glory grew brighter at every mile they covered. Everything pleased or amused or astonished her. With the charm born of a vivid interest in life she radiated happiness over all the company. Some glimpses of the country girl came back, her soul thrilled to the beauty of the world around, and she cried out like a child at sight of the chestnut and red hawthorn, and at the scent of spring with which the air was laden. From time to time she was recognised on the road, people raised their hats to her, and Drake made no disguise of his beaming pride. He leaned back to Rosa, who was sitting on the seat behind, and whispered, " Like herself to-day, isn't she ? "

" Why shouldn't she be, with all the world at her feet and her future on the knees of the gods ? " said Rosa.

But a shade of sadness came over Glory's face, as if the gay world and its amusements had not altogether filled a void that was left somewhere in her heart. They were drawing up to water the horses at the old "Cock" at Sutton, and a brown-faced woman, with big silver earrings and a monster hat and feather, came up to the coach to tell the " quality " their fortunes.

"Oh, let us, Glo," cried Betty. " I'd love it of all things, doncher know ! "

The gipsy had held out her hand to Glory. "Let me look at your palm, pretty lady."

"Am I to cross it with silver first?"

"Thank you kindly. But must I tell you the truth, lady?"

"Why, yes, mother. Why not?"

"Then you're going to lose money to-day, lady; but never mind, you shall be fortunate in the end, and the one you love shall be yours."

"That's all right," cried the gentlemen in chorus.

The ladies tittered, and Glory turned to Drake and said, "A pair of gloves against Ellan Vannin."

"Done!" said Drake, and there was general laughter.

The gipsy still held Glory's hand, and, looking up at Drake out of the corner of her eyes, she said, "I won't tell you what colour he is, pretty lady; but he is young and tall, and though he is a gorgio he is the kind a Romany girl would die for. Much trouble you'll have with him, and because of his foolishness and your own unkindness you'll put seven score miles between you. You like to live your life, lady, and as men drown their sorrows in drink so do you drown yours in pleasure. But it will all come right at last, lady, and those who envy and hate you now will kiss the ground you walk on."

"Glo," said Betty, "I'm surprised at ye, dearest, listenin' to such clipperty clapper."

Glory did not recover her composure after this incident until they came near the Downs. Meantime the grooms had blown their horns at many villages hidden in the verdure of charming hollows, and the coaches had overtaken the people who had left London earlier in the day to make the journey afoot. Boy tramps looking tired already—"Wish ye luck, gentlemen"— fat sailors and mutilated colliers playing organs—"'Twas in Trafalgar Bay" and "Come whoam to thee childer and me"— tatterdemalions selling the "Creet Card—on'y fourpence and I've slep' out on the Downs last night, s'elp me"—and all the ragged army of the maimed and the miserable who hang on the edge of a carnival.

Among this wreckage as they skimmed over it on the coach there was one figure more grotesque than the rest, a Polish Jew in his long kaftan and his worn sabbath hat, going along alone, triddle-traddle, in his slippers without heels. Lord Robert was at the moment teasing Betty into a pet by christening her "The Elephant" in allusion to her stoutness. But somebody called his attention to the Jew, and he screwed his glass to his eye, and cried, "Father Storm, by Jove!"

The nickname was taken up by other people on the coach,

and also by people on other coaches, and "Father Storm!" was thrown at the poor scarecrow as a missile from twenty quarters at once. Glory's colour was rising to her ears, and Drake was humming a tune to cover her confusion. But Betty was asking "Who was Father Storm, if you please?" and Lord Robert was saying. "Bless my stars, this is something new, don't you know! Here's somebody who doesn't know Father Storm! Father Storm, my dear Elephant, is the prophet, the modern Jonah who predicts that Nineveh, that is to say London, is to be destroyed this very day!"

"He must be balmy," said Betty, and the lady in blue went into fits of laughter.

"Yes," said Lord Robert, "and all because wicked men like ourselves insist on enjoying ourselves on a day like this with pretty people like you."

"Well, he *is* a cough-drop!" said Betty. The lady in blue asked what was "balmy" and a "cough-drop," and Lord Robert said—

"Betty means that the good father is crazy . . . silly . . . stupid . . . cracked in the head, in short——"

But Glory could bear no more. It was an insult to John Storm to be sat upon in judgment by such a woman. With a fiery jet of temper she turned about and said, "Pity there are not more heads cracked, then, if it would only let a little of the light of heaven into them."

"Oh, if it's like that . . . " began Betty, looking round significantly, and Lord Robert said, "It *is* like that, dear Elephant, and if our charming hurricane will pardon me, I'm not surprised that the man has broken out as a Messiah, and if the authorities don't intervene——"

"Hold your tongue, Robert," cried Drake. "Listen everybody!"

They were climbing on to the Downs, and could hear the deep hum of the people on the course. "My!" said Betty. "Well!" said the lady in blue. "It's like a beehive with the lid off," said Glory.

As they passed the railway station the people who had come by train poured into the road, and the coach had to slow down. "They must have come from the four winds of heaven," said Glory.

"Wait, only wait," said Drake.

Some minutes afterward everybody drew breath. They were on the top of the common, and had a full view of the course. It was a vast sea of human beings stretching as far as the eye could reach—a black moving ocean without a glimpse of soil or grass. The race track itself was a river of people; the grand stand, tier on tier, was black from its lawns at the bottom to its sloping gallery on top, and the "hill" opposite was a rocky coast of carriages, booths, carts, and clustering crowds. Glory's eyes seemed to leap out of her head. "It's a nation!" she said with panting breath. "An empire!"

They were diving into these breaking, plashing, plunging waters of human life with their multitudinous voices of laughter and speech, and Glory was looking at a dark figure in the hollow below which seemed to stand up above the rest, when Drake cried.

"Sit hard everybody! We'll take the hill at a gallop."

Then to the crack of the whip, the whoop of the driver, and the blast of the horn, the horses flew down like the wind. Betty screamed, Rosa groaned, and Glory laughed and looked up at Drake in her delight. When the coach drew up on the other side of the hollow, the bell was ringing at the grand stand as signal for another race, and the dark figure had disappeared.

III

That morning when John Storm went to take seven-o'clock celebration, the knocker-up with his long stick had not yet finished his rounds in the courts and alleys about the church, but the costers with their barrows and donkeys, their wives and their children, were making an early start for Epsom. There were many communicants, and it was eight o'clock before he returned to his rooms. By that time the postman had made his first delivery, and there was a letter from the Prime Minister. "Come to Downing Street as soon as this reaches you. I must see you immediately."

He ate his breakfast of milk and brown bread, said, "Goodbye, Brother Andrew; I shall be back for evening service," whistled to the dog and set out into the streets. But a sort of superstitious fear had taken hold of him, as if an event of supreme importance in his life was impending, and before answering his uncle's summons he made a round of the buildings in the vicinity which were devoted to the work of his mission. His first visit was to the school. The children had assembled, and they were being marshalled in order by the Sisters, and prepared for their hymn and prayer.

"Good-morning, Father."

"Good-morning, children."

Many of them had presents for him, one a flower, another a biscuit, another a marble, and yet another an old Christmas card. "God bless them, and protect them," he thought, and he left the school with a full heart.

His last visit was to the men's shelter, which he had established under the management of his former "organ-man," Mr. Jupe. It was a bare place, a shed which had been a stable and was now floored and ceiled. Beds resembling the bunks in the foc's'le of a ship lined the walls. When these were full the lodgers lay on the ground. A blanket only was provided. The men slept in their clothes, but rolled up their coats for pillows. There was a stove where they might cook their food if they had money to buy any. A ha'porth of tea and sugar mixed, a ha'porth of bread and a ha'porth of butter made a royal feast.

Going through the square in which his church stood he passed a smart gig at the door of a public-house that occupied the corner of a street. The publican in holiday clothes was stepping up to the driver's seat, and a young soldier, smoking a cigarette, was taking the place by his side. "Morning, Father, can you tip us the winner?" said the publican with a grin, while the soldier, with an impudent smile cried "Ta-ta" over his shoulder to the second storey of a tenement house where a young woman with a bloated and serious face and a head mopped up in curl-papers was looking down from an open window.

It was nine o'clock when John Storm reached the Prime Minister's house. A small crowd of people had followed him to the door. "His Lordship is waiting for you in the garden, sir," said the footman, and John was conducted to the back.

In the little shady enclosure between Downing Street and the Horse Guards Parade the Prime Minister was pacing to and fro. His head was bent, his step was heavy, he looked harassed and depressed. At sight of John's monkish habit he started with surprise and faltered uneasily. But presently sitting by John's side on a seat under a tree, and keeping his eyes away from him, he resumed their old relations and said—

"I sent for you, my boy, to warn you and counsel you. You must give up this crusade. It is a public danger and God knows what harm may come of it. Don't suppose I do not sympathise with you. I do to a certain extent. And don't think I charge you with all the follies of this ridiculous distemper. I have followed you and watched you, and I know that ninety-nine hundredths of this madness is not yours. But in the eye of the public you are responsible for the whole of it, and that is the way of the world always. Enthusiasm is a good thing, my boy; it is the rainbow in the heaven of youth, but it may go too far.

It may be hurtful to the man who nourishes it and dangerous to society. The world classes it with lunacy and love and so forth, among the nervous accidents of life, and the humdrum healthy-minded herd always call that man a fool and a weakling, or else a fanatic and a madman, in whom the grand errors of human nature are due to an effort—may I not say a vain effort?—to live up to a great ideal."

There were nervous twitchings over the muscles of John's face.

"Come, now, come, for the sake of peace and tranquillity, lest there should be disorder and even death, let this matter rest. Think, my boy, think, we are as much concerned for the world's welfare as you can be, and we have higher claims and heavier responsibilities. *I* cannot raise a hand to help you, John. In the nature of things I cannot defend you. I sent for you because . . . because you are your mother's son. Don't cast on me a heavier burden than I can bear. Save yourself and spare me."

"What do you wish me to do, uncle?"

"Leave London immediately and stay away until this tumult has settled down."

"Ah, that is impossible, sir."

"Impossible?"

"Quite impossible, and though I did not make these predictions about the destruction of London, yet I believe we are on the eve of a great change."

"You do?"

"Yes, and if you had not sent for me I should have called on you, to ask you to set aside a day for public prayer that God may in His mercy avert the calamity that is coming, or direct it to the salvation of His servants. The morality of the nation is on the decline, uncle, and when morality is lacking the end is not far off. England is given up to idleness, pomp, dissolute practices, and pleasure—pleasure, always pleasure. The vice of intemperance, the mania for gambling, these are the vultures that are consuming the vitals of our people. Look at the luxury of the country—a ludicrous travesty of national greatness! Look at the tastes and habits of our age—the deadliest enemies of true religion! And then look at the price we are paying in what the devil calls 'the priestesses of society' for the tranquillity of the demon of lust."

"But my boy, my dear boy——"

"Oh, yes, uncle, yes, I know, I know—many humanitarian schemes are afloat and we think we are not indifferent to the condition of the poor. But contrast the toiling women of East London with the idlers of Hyde Park in a London season. Other nations have professed well with their lips while their hearts have been set on wealth and pleasure. And they have fallen. Yes, sir, in ancient Asia as well as in modern Europe they have always fallen. And unless we unglue ourselves from the vanities which imperil our existence we shall fall too. The lust of pleasure and the lust of wealth bring their own revenges. In the nation as well as the individual the Almighty destroys them as of old."

"True—true!"

"Then how can I hold my peace or run away while it is the duty of Christians, of patriots, to cry out against this danger? On the soul of every one of us the duty rests, and who am I that I should escape from it? Oh, if the Church only realised her responsibility, if she only kept her eyes open——"

"She has powerful reasons for keeping them closed, my son," said the Minister, "and always will have until the Establishment is done away with. It is coming to that some day, but meantime have a care. The clergy are not your friends, John. Statesmen know too well the clerical cruelty which shelters itself behind the secular arm. It is an old story, I think, and you may find instances of that also in your ancient Palestine. But beware, my boy, beware——"

"Marvel not, my brethren, if the world hate you. Ye know that it hated me before it hated you!"

The exaltation of John's manner was increasing, and again the Prime Minister became uneasy, as if fearing that the young monk by his side would ask him next to kneel and pray.

"Ah, well," he said, rising, "I suppose there is no help for it, and matters must take their own course." Then he broke into other subjects, talked of his brother, John's father, whom he had lately heard from. His health was failing, he could not last very long, a letter from his son now might make all things well.

John was silent, his head was down, but the Prime Minister could see that his words took no effect. Then his bleak old face smiled a wintry smile as he said—

"But you are not mending much in one way, my boy. Do you know you've never once been here since the day you came to tell me you were to be married, and intended to follow in the footsteps of Father Damien!"

John flinched, and the muscles of his face twitched nervously again.

"That was an impossible enterprise, John. No wonder the lady couldn't suffer you to follow it. But she might have allowed you to see a lonely old kinsman for all that." John's pale face was breaking and his breath was coming fast. "Well,

well," taking his arm, "I'm not reproaching you, John. There are passions of the soul which eat up all the rest, I know that quite well, and when a man is under the sway of them he has neither father nor uncle, neither kith nor kin. Good-bye! . . . Ah, this way out—this way."

The footman had stepped up to the Minister and whispered something about a crowd in front of the house, and John was passed out of the garden by the back-door into the Park.

Three hours afterwards the frequenters of Epsom racecourse saw a man in a black cassock get up into an unoccupied waggonette and make ready to speak. He was on the breast of "The Hill," directly facing the grand stand, in a close pack of carriages, four-in-hands, landaus, and hansoms, filled with gaily-dressed women in pink and yellow costumes, drinking champagne and eating sandwiches, and being waited upon by footmen in livery. It was the interval between two events of the race-meeting, and beyond the labyrinth of vehicles there was a line of betting men in outer garments of blue silk and green alpaca, standing on stools under huge umbrellas and calling the odds to motley crowds of sweltering people on foot.

"Men and women," he began, and five thousand faces seemed to rise at the sound of his voice. The bookmakers kept up their nasal cries of "I lay on the field!" "Five to one bar one!" But the crowd turned and deserted them. "It's the Father, Father Storm," the people said, with laughter and chuckling, loose jests and some swearing, but they came up to him with one accord until the space about him, as far as to the roadway by which carriages climbed the hill, was an unbroken pavement of rippling faces.

"Good old Father!" and then laughter. "What abart the end of the world, old gel?" and then references to the "petticoats," and more laughter. "'Ere, I'll 'ave five bob each way Resurrection," and shrieks of wilder laughter still.

The preacher stood for some moments silent and unshaken. Then the quiet dignity of the man and the love of fairplay in the crowd secured him a hearing. He began amid general silence.

"I don't know if it is contrary to regulations to stand here to speak, but I am risking that for the urgency of the hour and message. Men and women, you are here under false pretences. You pretend to yourselves and to each other that you have come out of a love of sport, but you have not done so, and you know it. Sport is a plausible pleasure; to love horses and take delight in their fleetness is a pardonable vanity, but you are here to practise an unpardonable vice. You have come to gamble, and your gambling is attended by every form of intemperance and immorality. I am not afraid to tell you so, for God has laid upon me a plain message, and I intend to do my duty. These racecourses are not for horse-racing, but for reservoirs of avarice and drunkenness and prostitution. Don't think," he was looking straight into the painted faces of the women in pink and yellow, who were trying to smile and look amused, "don't think I am going to abuse the unhappy girls who are forced by a corrupt civilisation to live by their looks. They are my friends, and half my own life is spent among them. I have known some of them in whose hearts dwelt heavenly purity, and when I think of what they have suffered from men, I feel ashamed that I am a man. But, my sisters, for you too I have an urgent message. It is full summer with you now, as you sit here in your gay clothes on this bright day, but the winter is coming for every one of you, when there will be no more sunshine, no more luxury and pleasure and flattery, and when the miry wallowers in troughs and sties who are now taking the best years of your lives from you——"

"Helloa there! Whoop! Tarara-ra-ra-rara!"

A four-in-hand coach was dashing headlong up the hill amid clouds of dust, the rattling of wheels, the shouts of the driver, and the blasts of the horn, and the people who covered the roadway were surging forward to make room for it.

"It's Gloria!" said everybody, looking up at the occupants of the coach and recognising one of them.

The spell of the preacher was broken. He paused and turned his head and saw Glory. She was sitting tall and bright and gay on the box-seat by the side of Drake; the rays of the sun were on her, and she was smiling up into his face.

The preacher began again, then faltered, and then stopped. A bell at the grand stand was ringing. "Numbers goin' up," said everybody, and before any one could be conscious of what was happening John Storm was only a cipher in the throng and the crowd was melting away.

IV

The great carnival completely restored Glory's spirits. She laughed and cried out constantly, and lived from minute to minute like a child. Everybody recognised her, and nearly everybody saluted her. Drake beamed with pride and delight. He took her about the course, answered her questions, punctuated her jests, and explained everything, leaving Lord Robert to entertain his guests. Who were "those dwellers in tents"? They were the Guards' Club; and the service was also represented by artillerymen, king's hussars, and a line regiment from Aldershot. This was called "The Hill," where jovial rascaldom usually swarmed, looking out for stray overcoats and the lids of luncheon dishes left unprotected on carriages. Yes, the pickpocket, the card-sharper, the "lumberer," the confidence man, the blarneying beggar, and the faker of every description laid his snares on this holy spot. In fact, this is his sanctuary, and he peddles under the eye of the police. "Holy Land?" Ha, ha! "All the patriarchs out of the Bible here?" Oh, the vociferous gentlemen with patriarchal names in velveteen coats, under the banners and canvas signboards—Moses, Aaron, and so forth? They were the "bookies," otherwise bookmakers, generally Jews, and sometimes welshers.

"Here, come along, some of you sportsmen. I ain't made the price of my railway fare, s'elp me!" "It's a dead cert, gents." "Can't afford to buy thick 'uns at four quid apiece." "Five to one on the field!" "I lay on the field!"

A "thick 'un"? Oh, that was a sovereign, half a thick 'un half a sovereign, twenty-five pounds a "pony," five hundred a "monkey," flash notes were "stumers," and a bookmaker who couldn't pay was "a welsher." That? That was "the great Brockton," gentleman and tipster. "Amusement enough?" Yes; niggers, harpists, Christy minstrels, strong men, acrobats, agile clowns and girls on stilts, and all the ragamuffins from "the Burrer" bent on "making a bit." African Jungle? A shooting-gallery with model lions and bears. Fine Art Exhibition? A picture of the hanging of recent murderers. Boxing ring? Yes, for women—they strip to the waist, and fight like fiends. Then look at the lady auctioneer selling brass sovereigns a penny apiece.

"Buy one, gentlemen, and see what they're like, so as the 'bookies' can't pawse 'em on ye unawares."

"Food enough!" Yes, at Margett's, Patton's, Hatton's, and "The Three Brooms," as well as the barrows for stewed eels, hard-boiled eggs, trotters, coker-nuts, winkles, oysters, cockles, and all the luxuries of the New Cut. Why were they calling that dog "Cookshop"? Because he was pretty sure to go there in the end!

By this time they had ploughed over some quarter of a mile of the hill-side, fighting their way among the carriages that stood six deep along the rails, and through a seething mass of ruffianism, in a stifling atmosphere, polluted by the smell of ale and the reeking breath of tipsy people.

"Whoo! I feel like Shadrach, Meshach, and Abednego rolled into one," said Glory.

"Let us go into the paddock," said Drake, and they began to cross the race track.

"But wasn't that somebody preaching as we galloped down the hill?"

"Was it? I didn't notice," and they struggled through.

It was fresh and cool under the trees, and Glory thought it cheap even at ten shillings a head to walk for ten minutes on green grass. Horses waiting for their race were being walked about in clothes with their names worked on the quarter-sheets, and breeders, trainers, jockeys, and clerks of the course mingled with gentlemen in silk hats and ladies in smart costumes.

Drake's horse was a big bay colt, very thin, almost gaunt, and with long, high-stepping legs. The trainer was waiting for a last word with his owner. He was cool and confident. "Never better or fitter, Sir Francis, and one of the grandest three-year-olds that ever looked through a bridle. Improved wonderful since he got over his dental troubles, and does justice to the contents of his manger. Capital field, sir, but it's got to run up against summat smart to-day. Favourite, sir? Pooh! A coach-horse! Not stripping well—light in the flank and tucked up. But this colt fills the eye as a first-class one should. Whatever beats him will win, sir, take my word for that."

And the jockey, standing by in his black and white jacket, wagged his head, and said in a cheery whisper, "Have what ye like on 'im, Sir Francis. Great horse, sir! Got a Derby in 'im or I'm a Slowcome."

Drake laughed at their predictions, and Glory patted the creature while it beat its white feet on the ground and the leather of its saddle squeaked. The club stand from there looked like a sea of foaming laces, feathers, flowers, and sunshades. They turned to go to it, passing first by the judge's box, whereof Drake explained the use; then through the Jockey Club enclosure, which was full of peers, peeresses, judges, members of Parliament, and other turfites; and finally through the betting-ring, where some hundreds of betting-men of the superior class proclaimed their calling in loud voices and loud clothes and the gold letters on their betting-books. To one of these pencillers Drake said—

"What's the figure for Ellan Vannin?"

"Ten to one market price, sir."

"I'll take you in hundreds," said Drake, and they struggled through the throng.

Going up the stairs Glory said, "But wasn't the Archdeacon

at your office this morning? We saw him coming out of the square with little Mr. Golightly."

"Oh, did you? How hot it is to day!"

"Isn't it? I feel as if I should like to play Ariel in gossamer. . . . But wasn't it?"

"You needn't trouble about that, Glory. It's an old story that religious intolerance likes to throw the responsibility of its acts on the civil government."

"Then John Storm——"

"He is in no danger yet— none whatever."

"Oh, how glorious!" They had reached the balcony, and Glory was pretending that the change in her voice and manner came of delight at the sudden view. She stood for a moment spell-bound, and then leaned over the rail and looked through the dazzling haze that was rising from the vast crowd below. Not a foot of turf was to be seen for a mile around, save where at the jockeys' gate a space was kept clear by the police. It was a moving mass of humanity, and a low indistinguishable murmur was coming up from it such as the sea makes on the headlands above.

The cloud had died off Glory's face, and her eyes were sparkling. "What a wonderfully happy world it must be after all!" she said.

Just then the standard was hoisted over the royal stand to indicate that the Prince had arrived. Immediately afterwards there was a silent movement of hats on the lawn below the boxes, and then somebody down there began to sing "God save the Queen." The people on the grand stand took up the chorus, then the people on the course joined in, then the people on the "Hill," until, finally, the whole multitude sang the national hymn in a voice that was like the voice of an ocean.

Glory's eyes were now full of tears; she was struggling with a desire to cry aloud, and Drake, who was watching her smallest action, stood before her to screen her from the glances of gorgeously-attired ladies who were giggling and looking through lorgnettes. The fine flower of the aristocracy was present in force, and the club stand was full of the great ladies who took an interest in sport, and even kept studs of their own. Oriental potentates were among them in suits of blue and gold, and the French language was being spoken on all sides.

Glory attracted attention, and Drake's face beamed with delight. An illustrious personage asked to be introduced to her, and said he had seen her first performance and predicted her extraordinary success. She did not flinch. There was a slight tremor, a scarcely perceptible twitching of the lip, and then she bore her honours as if she had been born to them. The Prince entertained a party to luncheon, and Drake and Glory were invited to join it. All the smart people were there, and they looked like a horticultural exhibition of cream colour and rose pink and grey. Glory kept watching the great ones of the earth, and she found them very amusing.

"Well, what do you think?" said Drake.

"I think most people at the Derby must have the wrong make-up on. That gentleman, now—he ought to be done up as a stable-boy. And that lady in mauve—she's a ballet girl really, only——"

"Hush, for Heaven's sake!" But Glory whispered, "Let's go round the corner and laugh."

She sat between Drake and a ponderous gentleman with a great beard like a waterfall.

"What are the odds against the colt, Drake?"

Drake answered, and Glory recalled herself from her studies and said, "Oh yes, what did you say it was?"

"A prohibitive price—for you," said Drake.

"Nonsense! I'm going to do a flutter on my own, you know, and plunge against you."

It was explained to her that only bookmakers bet against horses, but the gentleman with the beard volunteered to reverse positions, and take Glory's ten to one against Ellan Vannin.

"In what?"

"Oh—h'm—in thick 'uns, of course."

"But what is the meaning of this running after strange gods?" said Drake.

"Never mind, sir! 'Out of the mouths of babes and sucklings,' you know . . ." and then the bell rang for the race of the day, and they scurried back to the stand. The numbers were going up, and a line of fifty policemen abreast were clearing the course. Some of the party had come over from the coach, and Lord Robert was jotting down in a note-book the particulars of betting commissions for his fair companions.

"And am I to be honoured with a commission from the Hurricane?" he asked.

"Yes; what's the price for Ellan Vannin?"

"Come down to five to one, pretty lady."

"Get me one to five that he's going to lose."

"But what in the world are you doing, Glory?" said Drake—his eyes were dancing with delight.

"Running a race with that old man in the box which can find a loser first."

At that moment the horses were sent out for the preliminary canter and parade before the royal stand, and a tingling electrical atmosphere seemed to come from somewhere and set every tongue wagging. It seemed as if something unexpected was about to occur, and countless eyes went up to the place where Drake stood with Glory by his side. He was outwardly calm, but with a proud flush under his pallor; she was visibly excited, and could not stand on the same spot for many seconds together. By this time the noise made by the bookmakers in the enclosure below was like that of ten thousand seafowl on a reef of rock, and Glory was trying to speak above the deafening clangour.

"Silver and gold have I none, but if I had   What's that?"

A white flag had fallen as signal for the start, there was a hollow roar from the starting-post point, and people were shouting "They're off!" Then there was a sudden silence, a dead hush, below, above, around, everywhere, and all eyes, all glasses, all lorgnettes were turned in the direction of the runners.

The horses got well away, and raced up the hill like cavalry charging in line, then at the mile-post the favourite drew to the front, and the others went after him in an indistinguishable mass. But the descent seemed not to his liking, he twisted a good deal, and the jockey was seen sawing the reins and almost hanging over the horse's head. When the racers swung round Tattenham Corner and came up like mice in the distance, it was seen that another horse had taken advantage of an opening and was overhauling the favourite with a tremendous rush. His colours were white and black. It was Ellan Vannin. From that moment Drake's horse never relinquished his advantage, but came down the straight like a great bird with his wings ceasing to flap, passed the stand amid great excitement, and won handsomely by a length.

Then, in the roar of delight that went up from the crowd, Glory with her hand on Drake's shoulder was seen to be crying, laughing, and cheering at the same moment.

"But *you've* lost," said Drake.

"Oh, bother that," she said, and when the jockey had slipped from his saddle and Drake had taken his horse into the weighing-room, and the "All right" was shouted, she started the cheering again, and said she meant to make a dead heat of it with Tennyson's brook.

"But why did you bet against me?" said Drake.

"You silly boy," she answered with a crow of happiness and gaiety, "didn't the gipsy tell me I should lose money to-day? And how could I bet on your horse unless you lost the race?"

Drake laughed merrily at her delicious duplicity, and could hardly resist an impulse to take her in his arms and kiss her. Meantime, his friends were slapping him on the back, and people were crushing up to offer him congratulations. He turned to take his horse into the paddock, and Lord Robert took Glory down after him. The trainer and jockey were there, looking proud and happy, and Drake, with a pale and triumphant face, was walking the great creature about as if reluctant to part with it. It was breathing heavily, and sweat stood in drops on its throat, head, and ears.

"Oh you beauty! How I should love to ride you!" said Glory.

"But dare you?" said Drake.

"Dare I! Only give me the chance."

"I will, by —— I will, or it won't be my fault."

Somebody brought champagne and Glory had to drink a bumper to "the best horse of the century, bar none." Then her glass was filled afresh, and she had to drink to the owner, "the best fellow on earth, bar none," and again she was compelled to drink "to the best bit of history ever made at Epsom, bar none." With that she was excused while the men drank at Drake's proposal, "to the loveliest, liveliest, leeriest, little woman in the world, God bless her," and she hid her face in her hands and said with a merry laugh, "Tell me when it's over, boys, and I'll come again."

After Drake had despatched telegrams and been bombarded by interviewers, he led the way back to the coach on the Hill, and the company prepared for their return. The sun had now gone, a thick veil of stagnant clouds had gathered over the place of it, the sky looked sulky, and Glory's head had begun to ache between the eyes. Rosa was to go home by train in order to reach her office early, and Glory half wished to accompany her. But an understudy was to play her part that night and she had no excuse. The coach wormed its way through the close pack of vehicles at the top of the hill, and began to follow the ebbing tide of humanity back to London.

"But what about my pair of gloves?"

"Oh, you're a hard man, reaping where you have not sowed, and gathering——"

"There, then, we're quits," said Drake, leaning over from the box-seat and snatching a kiss of her. It was now clear that he had been drinking a good deal.

V

Before the race had been run a solitary man with a dog at his heels had crossed the Downs on his way back to the railway station. Jealousy and rage possessed his heart between them, but he would not recognise these passions; he believed his emotions to be horror and pity and shame. John Storm had seen Glory on the racecourse in Drake's company, under Drake's protection: he proud and triumphant, she bright and gay and happy.

"O Lord, help me! Help me, O Lord!"

And now dragging along the road, in his mind's eye he saw her again as the victim of this man, his plaything, his pastime to take up or leave, no better than any of the women about her, and where they were going she would go also. Some day he would find her where he had found others, outcast, deserted, forlorn, lost, down in the trough of life, a thing of loathing and contempt.

"O Lord, help her! Help her, O Lord!"

There were few passengers by the train going back to London, nearly all traffic at this hour being the other way, and there was no one else in the compartment he occupied. He threw himself down in a corner, consumed with indignation and a strange sense of dishonour. Again he saw her bright eyes, her red lips, the glow of her whole radiant face, and a paroxysm of jealousy tore his heart to pieces. Glory was his. Though a bottomless abyss was yawning between them, her soul belonged to him, and a great upheaval of hatred for the man who possessed her body surged up to his throat. Against all this his pride as well as his religion rebelled. He crushed it down and tried to turn his mind to another current of ideas. How could he save her? If she should go down to perdition, his remorse would be worse to bear than flames of fire and brimstone. The more unworthy she was, the more reason he should strive to rescue her soul from the pangs of eternal torment.

The rattling of the carriage broke in upon these visions, and he got up and paced to and fro like a bear in a cage. And like a bear with its slow, strong grip he seemed to be holding her in his wrath and saying, "You shall not destroy yourself, you shall not, you shall not, for I—I—I forbid it!" Then he sank back in his seat exhausted by the conflict which made his soul a battlefield of spiritual and sensual passions. Every limb shook and quivered. He began to be afraid of himself, and he felt an impulse to fly away somewhere. When he alighted at Victoria his teeth were chattering, although the atmosphere was stifling and the sky was now heavy with black and lowering clouds.

To avoid the eyes of the people who usually followed him in the streets, he cut through a narrow thoroughfare and went back to Brown's Square by way of the Park. But the Park was like a vast camp. Thousands of people seemed to cover the grass as far as the eye could reach, and droves of workmen, followed by their wives and children, were trudging to other open spaces farther out. It was the panic terror. Afterwards it was calculated that fifty thousand persons from all parts of London had quitted the doomed city that day to await the expected catastrophe under the open sky.

The look of fierce passion had faded from his face by the time he reached his church, but there another ordeal awaited him. Though it still wanted an hour of the time of evening service, a great crowd had gathered in the square. He tried to escape observation, but the people pressed upon him, some to shake his hand, others to touch his cassock, and many to kneel at his feet, and even to cover them with kisses. With a sense of shame and hypocrisy he disengaged himself at length, and joined Brother Andrew in the sacristy. The simple fellow was full of marvellous stories. There had been wondrous manifestations of the workings of the Holy Spirit during the day. The knocker-up, who was a lame man, had shaken hands with the Father on his way home that morning, and now he had thrown away his stick and was walking firmly and praising God.

The church was large and rectangular and plain, and looked a well-used edifice, open every day and all day. The congregation was visibly excited, but the service appeared to calm them. The ritual was full, with procession and incense, but without vestments, and otherwise monastic in its severity. John Storm preached. The Epistle for the day had been from 1st Corinthians, and he took his text from that source also: "Deliver him up to Satan for the destruction of the flesh, that the spirit may be saved in the day of the Lord."

People said afterwards that they had never heard anything like that sermon. It was delivered in a voice that was low and tremulous with emotion. The subject was love. Love was the first inheritance that God had given to His creatures, the purest and highest, the sweetest and best. But man had degraded and debased it, at the temptation of Satan and the lust of the world. The expulsion of our first parents from Eden was only the poetic figure of what had happened through all the ages. It was happening now. And London, the modern Sodom, would as surely pay its penalty as did the cities of the ancient East. No need to think of flood or fire or tempest, of any given day or hour. The judgment that would fall on England like the plagues that fell on Egypt would be of a kind with the offence. She had wronged the spirit of love, and who knows but God would punish her by taking out of the family of man the passion by which she fell—lifting it away with all that pertained to it, good and bad, spiritual and sensual, holy and corrupt?

The burning heat-clouds of the day seemed to have descended into the church, and in the gathering darkness the preacher, his face just visible, with his eyes full of smouldering fire, drew an awful picture of the world under the effects of such a curse. A place without unselfishness, without self-sacrifice, without heroism, without chivalry, without loyalty, without laughter, and without children! Every man standing alone, isolated, self-centred, self-cursed, outlawed, loveless, marriageless, going headlong to degeneracy and death! Such might be God's punishment on this cruel and wicked city for its sensual sins.

Then the preacher lost control of his imagination and swept his hearers along with him as he fabricated horrible fancies. The people were terror-stricken, and not until the last hymn was given out did they recover the colour of their blanched faces. Then they sang as with one voice, and after the benediction had been pronounced, and they were surging down the aisles in close packs, they started the hymn again.

Even when they had left the church they could not disperse. Out in the square were the thousands who had not been able to get inside the doors, and every moment the vast proportions of the crowd were swelled. The ground was covered, the windows round about were thrown up and full of faces, and people had clambered on to the railings of the church, and even on to the roofs of the houses.

Somebody went to the sacristy and told the Father what was happening outside. He was now like a man beside himself, and going out on to the steps of the church, where he could be seen by all, he lifted his hands and pronounced a prayer in a sonorous and fervent voice—

"How long, O Lord, how long? From the bosom of God where Thou reposest, look down on the world where Thou didst walk as a man. Didst Thou not teach us to pray, 'Thy kingdom come'? Didst Thou not say Thy kingdom was near; that some who stood with Thee should not taste of death till they had seen it come with power; that when it came the poor should be blessed, the hungry should be fed, the blind should see, the heavy-laden should find rest, and the will of Thy Father should be done on earth even as it is done in heaven? But nigh upon two thousand years have gone, O Lord, and Thy kingdom hath not come. In Thy name now doth the Pharisee give alms in the streets to the sound of a trumpet going before him. In Thy name now doth the Levite pass by on the other side when a man has fallen among thieves. In Thy name now doth the priest buy and sell the glad tidings of the kingdom, giving for the gospel of God the commandments of men, living in rich men's houses, faring sumptuously every day, praying with his lips, ' Give us this day our daily bread,' but saying to his soul, ' Soul, thou hast much goods laid up for many years; take thine ease: eat, drink, and be merry.' How long, O Lord, how long?"

Hardly had John Storm stepped back when the heavy clouds broke into mutterings of thunder. So low were the sounds at first that in the general tumult they were scarcely noticed; but they came again and again, louder and louder with every fresh reverberation, and then the excitement of the people became intense and terrible. It was as if the heavens themselves had spoken to give sign and assurance of the calamity that had been foretold.

First a woman began to scream as if in the pains of labour. Then a young girl cried out for mercy, and accused herself of countless and nameless offences. Then the entire crowd seemed to burst into sobs and moans and agonising expressions of despair, mingled with shouts of wild laughter and mad thanksgiving: " Pardon, pardon!" " O Jesus, save me!" " O Saviour of sinners!" " O God, have mercy upon me!" "Oh, my heart, my heart!" Some threw themselves on the ground, stiff and motionless and insensible as dead men. Others stood over the stricken people and prayed for their relief from the power of Satan. Others fell into convulsions; and yet others, with wild and staring eyes, rejoiced in their own salvation.

It was now almost dark, and some of the people who had been out to the Derby were returning home in their gigs and coster's carts, laughing, singing, and nearly all of them drunk. There were wild encounters. A young soldier (it was Charlie Wilkes) came upon Pincher the pawnbroker. " Wot tcher, myte? Wot's yer amoosemint now?"

"Silence, you evil liver, you gambler, you son of Belial!"

"Stou thet, now; d'ye want a kepple er black eyes or a pench on the nowze?"

At nine o'clock the police of Westminster, being unable to disperse the crowd, sent to Scotland Yard for the mounted constabulary.

VI

MEANTIME the man who was the first cause of the tumult sat alone in his cell-like chamber under the church, a bare room, without carpet or rug, and having no furniture except a block bed, a small washstand, two chairs, a table, a prayer-stool and crucifix, and a print of the Virgin and Child. He heard the singing of the people outside, but it brought him neither inspiration nor comfort. Nature could no longer withstand the strain he had put upon it, and he was in deep dejection. It was one of those moments of revulsion which come to the strongest soul when at the crown, or near the crown, of his expectations he asks himself, "What is the good?" A flood of tender recollections was coming over him. He was thinking of the past, the happy past, the past of love and innocence which he had spent with Glory; of the little green island in the Irish Sea, and of all the sweetness of the days they had passed together before she had fallen to the temptations of the world, and he had become the victim of his hard if lofty fate. Oh, why had he denied himself the joys that came to all others? To what end had he given up the rewards of life which the poorest and the weakest and the meanest of men may share? Love, woman's love! why had he turned his back upon it? Why had he sacrificed himself? O God! if indeed it were all in vain?

Brother Andrew put his head in at the half-open door. His brother, the pawnbroker, was there, and had something to say to the Father. Pincher's face looked over Andrew's shoulder. The muscles of the man's eyes were convulsed by religious mania.

"I've just sold my biziness, sir, and we 'aven't a roof to cover us now," he cried, in the tone of one who had done something heroic.

John asked him what was to become of his mother.

"Lor, sir, ain't it the beginning of the end? That's the gawspel, ain't it? 'The foxes hev 'oles and the birds of the air hev nests——'"

And then close behind the man, interrupting him and pushing him aside, there came another, with fixed and staring eyes, crying, "Look 'ere, Father! Look! Twenty years I 'obbled on a stick, and look at me now! Praise the Lawd, I'm cured, en' no bloomin' error! I'm a brand as was plucked from the burnin' when my werry ends 'ad caught the flames. Praise the Lawd, Amen!"

John rebuked them and turned them out of the room, but he was almost in as great a frenzy. When he had shut the door, his mind went back to thoughts of Glory. She, too, was hurrying to the doom that was coming on all this wicked city. He had tried to save her from it, but he had failed. What could he do now? He felt a desire to do something—something else, something extraordinary.

Sitting on the end of the bed, he began again to recall Glory's face as he had seen it at the racecourse. And now it came to him as a shock, after his visions of her early girlhood. He thought there was a certain vulgarity in it which he had not observed before; a slight coarsening of its expression, an indescribable degeneracy, even under the glow of its developed beauty. With her full red lips and curving throat and dancing eyes she was smiling into the face of the man who was sitting by her side. Her smile was a significant smile, and the bright and eager look with which the man answered it was as full of meaning. He could read their thoughts. What had happened? Were all barriers broken down? Was everything understood between them?

This was the final madness, and he leapt to his feet in an outburst of uncontrollable rage. All at once he shuddered with a feeling that something terrible was brewing within him. He felt cold, a shiver was running over his whole body. But the thought he had been in search of had come to him of itself. It came first as a shock, and with a sense of indescribable dread, but it had taken hold of him and hurried him away. He had remembered his text, "Deliver him up to Satan for the destruction of the flesh, that the Spirit may be saved in the day of the Lord."

"Why not?" he thought. "It is in the Holy Book itself. There is the authority of St. Paul for it. Clearly the early Christians countenanced and practised such things." But then came a spasm of physical pain. That beautiful life so full of love and loveliness, radiating joy and sweetness and charm! The thing was impossible! It was monstrous! "Am I going mad?" he asked himself.

And then he began to be sorry for himself as well as for Glory. How could he live in the world without her? Although he had lost her, although an impassable gulf divided them, although he had not seen her for six months until to-day, yet it was something to know she was alive, and that he could go at night to the place where she was, and look up and think, "She is there." "It is true I am going mad," he thought, and he trembled again.

His mind oscillated among these conflicting ideas until the

more hideous thought returned to him of Drake and the smile exchanged with Glory. Then the blood rushed to his head, and strong emotion paralysed his reason. When he asked himself if it was right in England, and in the nineteenth century, to contemplate a course which might have been proper to Palestine and the first century, the answer came instantaneously that it *was* right. Glory was in peril. She was tottering on the verge of hell. It would not be wrong, but a noble duty, to prevent the possibility of such a hideous catastrophe. Better a life ended than a life degraded and a soul destroyed.

On this the sophism worked. It was true that he would lose her; she would be gone from him, she who was all his joy, his vision by day, his dream by night. But could he be so selfish as to keep her in the flesh, and thus expose her soul to eternal torment? And, after all, she would be his in the other world, his for ever, his alone. Nay, in this world also, for, being dead, he would love her still. "But, O God, must *I* do it?" he asked himself at one moment, and at the next came his answer, "Yes, yes, for I am God's minister."

That sent him back to his text again. "Deliver him up to *Satan* . . ." But there was a marginal reference to Timothy, and he turned it up with a trembling hand. *Satan* again; but the Revised Version gave "the Lord's servant," and thus the text should read, "Deliver him up to the Lord's servant for the destruction of the flesh, that the spirit may be saved in the day of the Lord." This made him cry out. He drank it in with inebriate delight. The thing was irrevocably decided. He was justified, he was authorised, he was the instrument of a fixed purpose. No other considerations could move him now.

By this time his heart and temples were beating violently, and he felt as if he were being carried up into a burning cloud. Before his eyes rose the vision of Isaiah, the meek lamb converted into an inexorable avenger descending from the summit of Edom. It was right to shed blood at the Divine command, nay, it was necessary, it was inevitable. And as God had commanded Abraham to take the life of Isaac whom he loved, so did God call on him, John Storm, to take the life of Glory, that he might save her from the risk of everlasting damnation.

There may have been intervals in which his sense of hearing left him, for it was only now that he became conscious that somebody was calling to him from the other side of the door.

"Is anybody there?" he asked, and a voice replied—

"Dear heart, yes, this five minutes and better, but I didna dare come in, thinking surely there was somebody talking with you. Is there no somebody here, then? No?"

It was Mrs. Callender, who was carrying a small Gladstone bag.

"Oh, it's you, is it?"

"Aye, it's mysel', and sorry I am to be bringing bad news to you."

"What is it?" he asked; but his tone betrayed complete indifference.

She closed the door, and answered in a whisper, "A warrant! I much misdoubt but there's one made out for you."

"Is that all?"

"Bless me, what does the man want? But come, laddie, come, you must tak' yoursel' off to some spot till the storm blows over."

"I have work to do, auntie."

"Work! You've worked too much already—that's half the botherment."

"God's work, auntie, and it must be done."

"Then God will do it Himself, without asking the life of a good man, or He's no just what I've been takin' Him for. But see," opening the bag and whispering again, "your auld coat and hat! I found them in your puir auld room that you'll no come back to. You've been looking like another body so long that naebody will ken you when you're like yoursel' again. Come, now, off with these lang ugly things."

"I cannot go, auntie."

"Cannot?"

"I will not. While God commands me I will do my duty."

"Eh, but men are kittle cattle! I've often called you my ain son; but if I were your ain mother I ken fine what I'd do with you—I'd just slap you and mak' you. I'll leave the clothes anyway. Maybe you'll be thinking better of it when I'm gone. Good-night to you! Your puir head's that hot and moidered! But what's wrang with you, John, man? What's come over ye, anyway?"

He seemed to be hardly conscious of her presence, and after standing a moment at the door, looking back at him with eyes of love and pity, she left the room.

He had been asking himself for the first time how he was to carry out his design. Sitting on the end of the bed with his head propped on his hand, he felt as if he were in the hold of a great ship, listening to the plash and roar of the stormy sea outside. The excitement of the populace was now ungovernable, and the air was filled with groans and cries. He would have to pass through the people, and they would see him and detain him, or perhaps follow him. His impatience was now feverish. The thing he had to do must be done to-night, it must be done immediately. But it was necessary in the first place to creep out unseen. How was he to do it?

When he came to himself he had a vague sense of some one wishing him good-night. "Oh, good-night, good-night!" he cried with an apologetic gesture. But he was alone in the room, and on turning about he saw the bag on the floor, and remembered everything. Then a strange thing happened. Two conflicting emotions took hold of him at once, the first an enthusiastic religious ecstasy, the other a low criminal cunning.

Everything was intended! He was only the instrument of a fixed purpose! These clothes were proof of it. They came to his hand at the very moment when they were wanted, when nothing else would have helped him. And Mrs. Callender had been the blind agent in a higher hand to carry out the Divine commands. Fly away and hide himself? God did not intend it. A warrant? No matter if it sent him like Cranmer to the stake! But this was a different thing entirely, this was God's will and purpose, this——

Yet even while thinking so he laughed an evil laugh, tore the clothes out of the bag with trembling hands, and made ready to put them on. He had removed his cassock when some one opened the door.

"Who's there?" he cried in a husky growl.

"Only me," said a timid voice, and Brother Andrew entered, looking pale and frightened.

"Oh, you! Come in; close the door; I've something to say to you. Listen! I'm going out, and I don't know when I shall be back. Where's the dog?"

"In the passage, Brother."

"Chain him up at the back, lest he should get out and follow me. Put this cassock away, and if anybody asks for me, say you don't know where I've gone—you understand?"

"Yes, but are you well, Brother Storm? You look as if you had just been running."

There was a hand-glass on the washstand, and John snatched it up and glanced into it, and put it down again instantly. His nostrils were quivering, his eyes were ablaze, and the expression of his face was shocking.

"What are they doing outside? See if I can get away without being recognised;" and Brother Andrew went out to look.

The passage from the chambers under the church was into a dark and narrow street at the back; but even there a group of people had gathered, attracted by the lights in the windows.

Their voices could be heard through the door which Brother Andrew had left ajar, and John stood behind it and listened. They were talking of himself—praising him, blessing him—telling stories of his holy life and gentleness.

Brother Andrew reported that most of the people were at the front, and they were frantic with religious excitement. Women were crushing up to the rail which the Father had leaned his head upon for a moment after he had finished his prayer, in order to press their handkerchiefs and shawls on it.

"But nobody would know you now, Brother Storm—even your face is different."

John laughed again, but he turned off the lights, thinking to drive away the few who were still lingering in the back street. The ruse succeeded. Then the man of God went out on his high errand, crept out, stole out, sneaked out, precisely as if he had been a criminal on his way to commit a crime.

He followed the lanes and narrow streets and alleys behind the Abbey, past the "Bell," the "Boar's Head," and the "Queen's Arms"—taverns that have borne the same names since the days when Westminster was Sanctuary. People home from the races were going into them with their red ties awry, with sprigs of lilac in their button-holes and oak leaves in their hats. The air was full of drunken singing, sounds of quarrelling, shameful words and curses. There were some mutterings of thunder and occasional flashes of lightning, and over all there was the deep hum of the crowd in the church square.

Crossing the bottom of Parliament Street he was almost run down by a squadron of mounted police, who were trotting into Broad Sanctuary. To escape observation he turned on to the Embankment, and walked under the walls of the gardens of Whitehall, past the back of Charing Cross Station to the street going up from the Temple.

The gate of Clement's Inn was closed, and the porter had to come out of his lodge to open it.

"The Garden House!"

"Garden House, sir? Inner court, left-hand corner."

John passed through. "That will be remembered afterwards," he thought. "But no matter; it will all be over then."

And coming out of the close streets with their clatter of traffic into the cool gardens with their odour of moistened grass, the dull glow in the sky and the glimpse of the stars through the tree-tops, his mind went back by a sudden bound to another night when he had walked over the same spot with Glory.

At that there came a spasm of tenderness, and his throat thickened. He could almost see her and feel her by his side, with her fragrant freshness and buoyant step. "O God, must I do it—must I—must I ?" he thought again.

But another memory of that night came back to him: he heard Drake's voice as it floated over the quiet place. Then the same upheaval of hatred which he had felt before he felt again. The man was the girl's ruin; he had tempted her by love of dress, of fame, of the world's vanities and follies of every sort. This made him think for the first time of how he might find her. He might find her with *him*. They would come back from the Derby together. He would bring her home, and they would sup in company. The house would be lit up, the windows thrown open; they would be playing and singing and laughing, and the sounds of their merriment would come down to him into the darkness below.

All the better, all the better! He would do it before the man's face! And when it was done, when all was over, when she lay there . . . lay there . . . there . . . he would turn on the man and say, "Look at her, the sweetest girl that ever breathed the breath of life, the dearest, truest woman in all the world! You have done that—you—you—you—and God damn you!"

His tortured heart was afire and his brain was reeling. Before he knew where he was he had passed from the outer court into the inner one. "Here it is; this is the house," he thought. But it was all dark, just a few lights burning, but they had been carefully turned down. The windows were closed, the blinds were drawn, and there was not a sound anywhere. He stood some minutes trying to think, and during that time the mood of frenzy left him and the low cunning came back. Then he rang the bell.

There was no answer, so he rang again. After a while he heard a footstep that seemed to come up from below. Still the door was not opened, and he rang a third time.

"Who's there?" said a voice within.

"It is I; open the door," he answered.

"Who are you?" said the voice; and he replied impatiently—

"Come, come, Liza; open and see."

Then the catch-lock was shot back. At the next moment he was in the hall, shutting the door behind him, and Liza was looking up into his face with eyes of mingled fear and relief.

"Lor, sir, why ever didn't you say it was you?"

"Where's your mistress?"

"Gone to the office, and won't be back till morning; and Miss Gloria isn't home from the races yet."

"I must see her to-night; I'll wait upstairs.'

"You must excuse me, sir—Farver I mean; but I wouldn't a'known your voice—it seemed so different. And me that sleepy too, being on the go since six in the mornin'——."

"Go to bed, Liza. You sleep in the kitchen, don't you?"

"Yes, sir, thank you; I think I will too. Miss Gloria can let herself in anyway, same as comin' from the theatre. But can I git ye anythink? No? Well, you know your wye up, sir, down't ye?"

"Yes, yes, good-night, Liza!"

"Good-night, Farver!"

He had set his foot on the stair to go up to the drawing-room when it flashed upon him that though he was the minister of God he was using the weapons of the devil. No matter! If he had been about to commit a crime it would have been different. But this was no crime, and he was no criminal. He was the instrument of God's mercy to the woman he loved. *He was going to slay her body that he might save her soul!*

VII

The journey home from the Derby had been a long one, but Glory had enjoyed it. When she had settled down to the physical discomfort of the blinding and choking dust, the humours of the road became amusing. This endless procession of good-humoured ruffianism sweeping through the most sacred retreats of nature, this inroad of every order of the Stygian demi-monde on to the slopes of Olympus, was intensely interesting. Men and women merry with drink, all laughing, shouting, and singing; some in fine clothes and lounging in carriages, others in striped jerseys and yellow cotton dresses huddled up on donkey-barrows; some smoking cigarettes and cigars and drinking champagne, others smoking clay pipes with the bowls downwards and flourishing bottles of ale; some holding rhubarb leaves over their heads for umbrellas and pelting the police with confetti, others wearing executioners' masks, false moustaches, and red-tipped noses, and blowing bleating notes out of penny-trumpets—but all one family, one company, one class.

There were ghastly scenes as well as humorous ones— an old horse, killed by the day's work and thrown into the ditch by the roadside, axle-trees broken by the heavy loads and people thrown out of their carts and cut, boy tramps dragging along like worn-out old men, and a welsher with his clothes torn to ribbons stealing across the fields to escape a yelping and infuriated crowd.

But the atmosphere was full of gaiety, and Glory laughed at nearly everything. Lord Robert, with his arm about Betty's waist, was chaffing a coster who had a drunken woman on his back-seat. "Got a passenger, driver?" "Yuss, sir, and I'm agoin' 'ome to my wife to-night, and thet's more nor you dare do." A young fellow in pearl buttons was tramping along with a young girl in a tremendous hat. He snatched her hat off, she snatched off his, he kissed her, she smacked his face, he put her hat on his own head, she put on his hat, and then they linked arms and sang a verse of the "Old Dutch."

Glory reproduced a part of this love passage in pantomime, and Drake screamed with laughter.

It was seven o'clock before they reached the outskirts of London. By that time a hamper on the coach had been emptied and the bottles thrown out; the procession had drawn up at a dozen villages on the way; the perspiring tipsters, with whom "things hadn't panned out well," had forgotten their disappointments and "didn't care a tinker's cuss;" every woman in a barrow had her head-gear in confusion, and she was singing in a drunken wail. Nevertheless, Drake, who was laughing and talking constantly, said it was the quietest Derby night he had ever seen, and he couldn't tell what things were coming to.

"Must be this religious mania, don't you know," said Lord Robert, pointing to a new and very different scene which they had just then come upon.

It was an open space covered with people, who had lit fires as if intending to camp out all night, and were now gathered in many groups, singing hymns and praying. The drunken wails from the procession stopped for a moment, and there was nothing heard but the whirring wheels and the mournful notes of the singers. Then "Father Storm" rose like the cry of a cormorant from a thousand throats at once. When the laughter that greeted the name had subsided Betty said—

"'Pon my honour, though, that man must be off his dot," and the lady in blue went into convulsions of hysterical giggling. Drake looked uneasy, and Lord Robert said, "Who cares what an elephant says?" But Glory took no notice now, save that for a moment the smile died off her face.

It had been agreed, when they cracked the head off the last bottle, that the company should dine together at the Café Royal or Romano's, so they drove first to Drake's chambers to brush the dust off and to wash and rest. Glory was the first to be ready, and while waiting for the others she sat at the organ in the sitting-room and played something. It was the hymn they had heard in the suburbs. At this there was laughter from the other side of the wall, and Drake, who seemed unable to lose sight of her, came to the door of his room in his shirt-sleeves. To cover up her confusion she sang a "coon" song. The company cheered her, and she sang another, and yet another. Finally, she began "My Mammie," but floundered, broke down, and cried.

"Rehearsal ten in the morning," said Betty.

Then everybody laughed, and while Drake busied himself putting Glory's cloak on her shoulders, he whispered—

"What's to do, dear? A bit off colour to-night, eh?"

"Be a good boy and leave me alone," she answered, and then she laughed also.

They were on the point of setting out when somebody said, "But it's late for dinner now—why not supper at the Corinthian Club?" At that the other ladies cried "Yes" with one voice. There was a dash of daring and doubtful propriety in the proposal.

"But are you game for it?" said Drake, looking at Glory.

"Why not?" she replied, with a merry smile, whereupon he cried "All right," and a look came into his eyes which she had never seen there before.

The Corinthian Club was in St. James's Square, a few doors from the residence of the Bishop of London. It was now dark, and as they passed through Jermyn Street a line of poor children stood by the poulterer's shop at the corner waiting for the scraps that are thrown away at closing time. York Street was choked with hansoms, but they reached the door at last. There were the sounds of music and dancing within. Officials in uniform stood in a hall examining the tickets of membership and taking the names of guests. The ladies removed their cloaks, the men hung up their coats and hats, a large door was thrown open, and they looked into the ball-room. The room was full of people as faultlessly dressed as at a house in Grosvenor Square. But the women were all young and pretty, and the men had no surnames. A long line of gilded youths in dress clothes occupied the middle of the floor. Each held by the waist the young man before him as if he were going to play leap-frog. "Helloa there!" shouted one of them, and the band struck up. Then the whole body kicked out right and left, while all sang a chorus, consisting chiefly of "Tra-la-la-la-la-la!" One of them was a lord, another a young man who had lately come into a fortune, another a light comedian, another belonged to a big firm on the Stock Exchange, another was a mystery, and another was one of "the boys," and lived by fleecing all the rest. They were executing a dance from the latest burlesque. "Helloa there!" the conductor shouted again, and the band stopped.

Lord Robert led the way upstairs. Pretty women in light pinks and blues sat in every corner of the staircase. There was a balcony from which you could look down on the dancers as from the gallery of a playhouse. Also there was an American bar, where women smoked cigarettes. Lord Robert ordered supper, and when the meal was announced they went into the supper-room.

"Helloa there!" greeted them as they entered. At little tables, lit up by pink candles, sat small groups of shirt fronts and butterfly ties, with fair heads and pretty frocks. Waiters were coming and going with champagne and silver dishes; there was a clatter of knives and forks, and a jabber of voices and laughter. And all the time there came the sounds of the band, with the "Tra-la-la," from the ballroom below.

Glory sat by Drake. She realised that she had lowered herself in his eyes by coming there. He was drinking a good deal and paying her endless compliments. From time to time the tables about them were vacated and filled again by similar shirt fronts and fair heads. People were arriving from the Derby, and the talk was of the day's racing. Some of the new arrivals saluted Drake, and many of them looked at Glory. "A rippin' good race, old chappie. Didn't suit my book exactly, but the bookies will have smiling faces at Tattersall's on Monday."

A man with a big beard at the next table pulled down his white waistcoat, lifted his glass, and said, "To Gloria!" It was her acquaintance of the racecourse.

"Who is Blue Beard?" she asked in a whisper.

"They call him the Faro King," said Drake. "Made all his money by gambling in Paris, and now he is a squire with a living in his gift."

Then over the laughter and voices, the band and the singing, with an awful suddenness there came a crash of thunder. The band and the comic song stopped, and there was a hush for a moment. Then Lord Robert said—

"Wonder if this is the dreadful storm that is to overwhelm the nation, don't you know!"

That fell on the house of frivolity like a second thunder-bolt, and people began to look up with blanched faces.

"Well, it isn't the first time the *storm* has howled—it's been howling all along," said Lord Robert, but nobody laughed.

Presently the company recovered itself, the bands and the singing were heard again, louder and wilder than before, the men shouted for more champagne, and nicknamed every waiter "Father Storm."

Glory was ashamed. With her head on her hand she was looking at the people around, when the "Faro King," who had been making eyes at her, leaned over her shoulder and said in a confidential whisper, "And what is Gloria looking for?"

"I am looking for *a man*," she answered. And as the big beard turned away with "Oh, confound it," she became aware that Drake and Lord Robert were at high words from opposite sides of the table.

"No, I tell you no, no, *no!*" said Drake. "Call him a weakling and a fool and an ass, if you will, but does that explain everything? This is one of the men with the breath of God in him, and you can't judge of him by ordinary standards."

"Should think not, indeed, dear chap," said Lord Robert. "Common sense laughs at the creature."

"So much the worse for common sense. When it judges of these isolated beings by the standards of the common herd then common sense is always the greatest nonsense."

"Oho! Oho!" came in several voices, but Drake paid no attention.

"Jesus Christ Himself was mocked at and ridiculed by the common sense of His time, by His own people, and even His own family; and His family and people and time have been gibbeted by all the centuries that have come after them. And so it has been with every ardent soul since who has taken up His parable and introduced into the world a new spirit. The world has laughed at him, and spat upon him, and, only for its fear of the sublime banner he has borne, it would have shut him up in a madhouse."

They were strange words in a strange place. Everybody listened.

"But these sombre giants are the leaders of the world for all that, and one hour of their Divine madness is worth more to humanity than a cycle of our sanity. And yet we deny them friendship and love, and do our best to put them out of the pale of the human family! We have invented a new name for them too—degenerates—pigmies and pigs as we are, who ought to go down on our knees to them with our faces buried in the dirt! Gentlemen," he cried, filling his glass and rising to his feet, "I give you a toast—the health of Father Storm!"

Glory had sat trembling all over, breathing hard, blushing, and wide-eyed until he had done. Then she leapt up to where he stood beside her, threw her arms about his neck and kissed him.

"And now you ring down quick, my dear," said Betty, and everybody laughed a little.

Drake was laughing with the rest, and Glory, who had dropped back to her seat in confused embarrassment, was trying to laugh too.

"Another bottle of fizz anyway," cried Drake. He had mistaken the meaning of Glory's kiss and was utterly intoxicated by it. She could have cried with shame and rage, seeing he thought such conduct came naturally to her, and perhaps imagined it wasn't the first time she had done as much. But to carry off the situation she laughed a good deal with him and when the wine came they jingled glasses.

"I'm going to see you home to-night," he whispered, smiling slily and looking her full in the eyes. She shook her head, but that only provoked him to fresh effort.

"I must—I will—you *shall* allow me," and he began to play with her hand and ruffle up the lace that covered her round arm.

Just then his man Benson, looking hot and excited, came up to him with a message. Glory overheard something about "the office," "the Secretary," and "Scotland Yard." Then Drake turned to her with a smile, over a look of vexation, and said, "I'm sorry, dear—very—I must go away for a while. Will you stay here until I return, or . . ."

"Take me out and put me in a cab," said Glory. Their getting up attracted attention and Lord Robert said—

"Is it, perhaps, something about that——"

"It's nothing," said Drake, and they left the room.

The band in the ballroom was still playing the dance out of the burlesque, and half a hundred voices were shouting "Tra-la-la-la," as Glory stepped into a hansom.

"I'll follow on though," whispered Drake, with a merry smile.

"We shall all be in bed and the house locked up . . . How magnificent you were to-night!"

"I couldn't see the man trodden on when he was down . . . But how lovely you've looked to-day, Glory! I'll get in to-night if I have to ring up Liza or break down the door for it."

As the cab crossed Trafalgar Square it had to draw up for a procession of people coming up Parliament Street singing hymns. Another and more disorderly procession of people, decorated with oak leaves and hawthorns and singing a music-hall song, came up and collided with it. A line of police broke up both processions and the hansom passed through.

VIII

On entering the drawing-room John Storm was seized with a weird feeling of dread. The soft air seemed to be filled with Glory's presence and her very breath to live in it. On the side-table a lamp was burning under a warm red shade. A heap of petty vanities lay about, articles of silver, little trinkets, fans, feathers, and flowers. His footsteps on the soft carpet made no noise. It was all so unlike the place he had come from, his own bare chamber under the church.

He could have fancied that Glory had that moment left the room. The door of a little ebony cabinet stood half-open and he could see inside. Its lower shelves were full of shoes and little dainty slippers, some of them of leather, some of satin, some black, some red, some white. They touched him with an indescribable tenderness and he turned his eyes away. Under the lamp lay a pair of white gloves. One of them was flat and had not been worn, but the other was filled out with the impression of a little hand. He took it up and laid it across his own big palm, and another wave of tenderness broke over him.

On the mantelpiece there were many photographs. Most of them were of Glory and some were very beautiful, with their gleaming and glistening eyes and their curling and waving hair. One looked even voluptuous with its parted lips and smiling mouth; but another was different—it was so sweet, so gay, so artless. He thought it must belong to an earlier period, for the dress was such as she used to wear in the days when he knew her first, a simple jersey and a sailor's stocking-cap. Ah, those days that were gone, with their innocence and joy! Glory! His bright, his beautiful Glory!

His emotion was depriving him of the free use of his faculties, and he began to ask himself why he was waiting there. At the next instant came the thought of the awful thing he had come to do and it seemed monstrous and impossible. "I'll go away," he told himself and he turned his face towards the door.

On a whatnot at the door-side of the room another photograph stood in a glass stand. His back had been to it, and the soft light of the lamp left a great part of the room in obscurity, but he saw it now, and something bitter that lay hidden at the bottom of his heart rose to his throat. It was a portrait of Drake, and at the sight of it he laughed savagely and sat down.

How long he sat he never knew. To the soul in torment there is no such thing as time; an hour is as much as eternity, and eternity is no more than an hour. His head was buried in his arms on the table, and he was a prey to anguish and doubt. At one time he told himself that God did not send men to commit murder; at the next, that this was not murder but sacrifice. Then a mocking voice in his ears seemed to say, "But the world will call it murder, and the law will punish you." To that he answered in his heart, "When I leave this house I will deliver myself up. I will go to the nearest police-court, and say, 'Take me; I have done my duty in the eye of God, but committed a crime in the eye of my country.'" And when the voice replied, "That will only lead to your own death also," he thought, "Death is a gain to those who die for their cause; and my death will be a protest against the degradation of women—a witness against the men who make them the creatures of their pleasure, their playthings, their victims, and their slaves." Thinking so, he found a strange thrill in the idea that all the world would hear of what he had done. "But I will say a mass for her soul in the morning," he told himself; and a chill came over him, and his heart grew cold as a stone.

Then he lifted his head and listened. The room was quiet, there was not a sound in the gardens of the Inn, and, through a window which was partly open, he could hear the monotonous murmur of the streets outside. A great silence seemed to have fallen on London, a silence more awful than all the noise and confused clamour of the evening. "It must be late," he thought; "it must be the middle of the night." Then the thought came to him that perhaps Glory would not come home that night at all, and, in a sudden outburst of pent-up feeling, his heart cried, "Thank God! thank God."

He had said it aloud, and the sound of his voice in the silent room awakened all his faculties. Suddenly he was aware of other sounds outside. There was a rumble of wheels and the rattle of a hansom. The hansom came nearer and nearer. It stopped in the outside courtyard. There was the noise of a curb-chain, as if the horse were shaking its head. The doors of the hansom opened with a creak and banged back on their spring. A voice—a woman's voice—said, "Good-night!" and another voice—a man's voice—answered, "Good-night, and thank you, Miss!" Then the cab-wheels turned and went off.

All his senses seemed to have gone into his ears, and in the silence of that quiet place he heard everything. He rose to his feet and stood waiting.

After a moment there was the sound of a key in the lock of the door below; the rustle of a woman's dress coming up the stairs, an odour of perfume in the air, an atmosphere of freshness and health, and then the door of the room, which had been ajar, was swung open, and there on the threshold, with her languid and tired but graceful movements, was she herself, Glory. Then his head turned giddy, and he could neither hear nor see.

When Glory saw him standing by the lamp, with his deadly pale face, she stood a moment in speechless astonishment, and passed her hand across her eyes as if to wipe out a vision. After that she clutched at a chair and made a faint cry.

"Oh, is it you?" she said, in a voice which she strove to control. "How you frightened me! Whoever would have thought of seeing you here!"

He was trying to answer, but his tongue would not obey him, and his silence alarmed her.

"I suppose Liza let you in—where *is* Liza?"

"Gone to bed," he said, in a thick voice.

"And Rosa—have you seen Rosa?"

"No."

"Of course not! How could you? She must be at the office, and won't be back for hours. So, you see, we are quite alone!"

She did not know why she said that, and, in spite of the voice which she tried to render cheerful, her lip trembled. Then she laughed, though there was nothing to laugh at, and down at the bottom of her heart she was afraid. But she began moving about, trying to make herself easy, and pretending not to be alarmed.

"Well, won't you help me off with my cloak? No? Then I must do it for myself, I suppose."

Throwing off her outer things, she walked across the room and sat down on the sofa near to where he stood.

"How tired I am! It's been such a day! Once is enough for that sort of thing, though! Now, where do you think I've been?"

"I know where you've been, Glory—I saw you there."

"You? Really? Then, perhaps, it *was* you who . . . Was it you in the hollow?"

"Yes."

He had moved to avoid contact with her, but now, standing by the mantelpiece looking into her face, he could not help recognising in the fashionable woman at his feet the features of the girl once so dear to him, the brilliant eyes, the long lashes, the twitching of the eyelids, and the restless movement of the mouth. Then the wave of tenderness came sweeping over him again, and he felt as if the ground were slipping beneath his feet.

"Will you say your prayers to-night, Glory?" he said.

"Why not?" she answered, trying to laugh.

"Then why not say them now, my child?"

"But why?"

He had made her tremble all over; but she got up, walked straight across to him, looked intently into his face for a moment, and then said, "What is the matter? Why are you so pale? You are not well, John!"

"No; I am not well either," he answered.

"John, John, what does it all mean? What are you thinking of? Why have you come here to-night?"

"To save your soul, my child. It is in great, great peril."

At first she took this for the common, everyday language of the devotee, but another look into his face banished that interpretation, and her fear rose to terror. Nevertheless she talked lightly, hardly knowing what she said. "Am I, then, so very wicked? Surely heaven doesn't want me yet, John. Some day, I trust . . . I hope——"

"To-night, to-night, *now!*"

Then her cheeks turned pale and her lips became white and bloodless. She had returned to the sofa, and half rose from it, then sat back, stretching out one hand as if to ward off a blow, but still keeping her eyes riveted on his face. Once she looked round to the door and tried to cry out, but her voice would not answer her.

This speechless fright lasted only a moment. Then she was herself again, and looked fearlessly up at him. She had the full use of her intellect, and her quick instinct went to the root of things. "This is the madness of jealousy," she thought. "There is only one way to deal with it. If I cry out—if I show that I am afraid—if I irritate him, it will soon be over." She told herself in a moment that she must try gentleness, tenderness, reason, affection, love.

Trembling from head to foot, she stepped up to him again, and began softly and sweetly, trying to explain herself. "John, dear John, if you see me with certain people and in certain places, you must not think from that——"

But he broke in upon her with a torrent of words. "I can't think of it at all, Glory. When I look ahead, I see nothing but shame, and misery, and degradation for you in the future. That man is destroying you, body and soul. He is leading you on to the devil, and hell, and damnation, and I cannot stand by and see it done."

"Believe me, John, you are mistaken—quite mistaken."

But with a look of sombre fury, he cried, "Can you deny it?"

"I can protect and care for myself, John."

"With that man's words in your ears still, can you deny it?"

Suddenly she remembered Drake's last whisper as she got into the hansom, and she covered her face with her hands.

"You can't! It is the truth! The man is following you to ruin you, and you know it. You've known it from the first, therefore you deserve all that can ever come to you. Do you know what you are guilty of? You are guilty of soul-suicide. What is the suicide of the body to the suicide of the soul? What is the crime of the poor broken creature who only chooses death and the grave before starvation or shame, compared to the sin of the wretched woman who murders her soul for the sake of the lusts and vanities of the world? The law of man may punish the one, but the vengeance of God is waiting for the other."

She was crying behind her hands, and in spite of the fury into which he had lashed himself a great pity took hold of him. He felt as if everything were slipping away from him, and he was trying to stand on an avalanche. But he told himself that he would not waver, that he would hold to his purpose, that he would stand firm as a rock. Heaving a deep sigh he walked to and fro across the room.

"O Glory, Glory! Can't you understand what it is to me to be the messenger of God's judgment?"

She gasped for breath, and what had been a vague surmise became a certainty—thinking he was God's avenger, yet with nothing but a poor spasm of jealousy in his heart, he had come with a fearful purpose to perform.

"I did what I could in other ways, and it was all in vain. Time after time I tried to save you from these dangers, but you would not listen. I was ready for any change, any sacrifice. Once I would have given up all the world for you, Glory—you know that quite well—friends, kinsmen, country, everything, even my work and my duty, and, but for the grace of God, God himself!"

But his tenderness broke again into a headlong torrent of reproach. "You failed me, didn't you? At the last moment too—the very last! Not content with the suicide of your own soul, you must attempt to murder the soul of another. Do you know what that is? That is the unpardonable sin! You are crying, aren't you? Why are you crying?" But even while he said this something told him that all he was waiting for was that her beautiful eyes should be raised and their splendid light flash upon him again.

"But that is all over now! It was a blunder, and the breach

between us is irreparable. I am better as I am, far, far better. Without friends, or kin, or country, consecrated for life, cut off from the world, separate, alone!"

She knew that her moment had come, and that she must vanquish this man, and turn him from his purpose whatever it was, by the only weapon a woman could use—his love of her. "I do not deny that you have a right to be angry with me," she said, "but don't think that I have not given up something too. At the time you speak of, when I chose this life and refused to go with you to the South Seas, I sacrificed a good deal—I sacrificed love. Do you think I didn't realise what that meant? That whatever the pleasure and delight my art might bring me, and the flattery, and the fame, and the applause, there were joys I was never to know—the happiness that every poor woman may feel, though she isn't clever at all, and the world knows nothing about her—the happiness of being a wife and a mother, and of holding her place in life, however humble she is and simple and unknown, and of linking the generations each to each. And though the world has been so good to me, do you think I have ever ceased to regret that? Do you think I don't remember it sometimes when the house rises at me, or when I am coming home, or perhaps when I awake in the middle of the night? And notwithstanding all this success with which the world has crowned me, do you think I don't hunger sometimes for what success can never buy—the love of a good man who would love me with all his soul and his strength and everything that is his?"

Out of a dry and husky throat John Storm answered, "I would rather die a thousand, thousand deaths than touch a hair of your head, Glory . . . But God's will is His will!" he added quivering and trembling. The compulsion of a great passion was drawing him, but he struggled hard against it. "And then this success—you cling to it nevertheless!" he cried with a forced laugh.

"Yes, I cling to it," she said, wiping away the tears that had begun to fall. "I cannot give it up—I cannot, I cannot!"

"Then what is the worth of your repentance?"

"It is not repentance; it is what you said it was in this room long ago . . . We are of different natures, John, that is the real trouble between us, now and always has been. But, whether we like it or not, our lives are wrapped up together for all that. We can't do without each other. God makes men and women like that sometimes."

There was a piteous smile on his face. "I never doubted your feeling for me, Glory—no, not even when you hurt me most."

"And if God made us so——"

"I shall never forgive myself, Glory, though heaven itself forgives me!"

"If God makes us love each other in spite of every barrier that divides us——"

"I shall never know another happy hour in this life, Glory, never!"

"Then why should we struggle? It is our fate, and we cannot conquer it. You can't give up your life, John, and I can't give up mine, but our hearts are one."

Her voice sang like music in his ears, and something in his aching heart was saying, "What are the laws we make for ourselves compared to the laws God makes for us?" Suddenly he felt something warm. It was Glory's breath on his hand. A fragrance like incense seemed to envelop him. He gasped as if suffocating, and sat down on the sofa.

"You are wrong, dear, if you think I care for the man you speak of. He has been very good to me, and helped me in my career, but he is nothing to me—nothing whatever . . . But we are such old friends, John! It seems impossible to remember a time when we were not old chums, you and I! Sometimes I dream of those dear old days in the 'lil oilan'.' Aw, they were ter'ble—just ter'ble! Do you remember the boat—the *Gloria*—do you remember her?"

He clenched his hands as though to hold on to his purpose, but it was slipping through his fingers like sand.

"What times they were! Coming round the castle of a summer evening when the bay and the sky were like two sheets of silvered glass looking into each other, and you and I singing 'John Peel.'" (In a quavering voice she sang a bar or two.) "'D'ye ken John Peel with his coat so gay? D'ye ken John Peel? . . .' Do you remember it, John?"

She was sobbing and laughing by turns. It was her old self, and the cruel years seemed to roll back. But still he struggled. "What is the love of the body to the love of the soul?" he told himself.

"You wore flannels then, and I was in a white jersey—like this, see," and she snatched up from the mantelpiece the photograph he had been looking at. "I got up my first act in imitation of it, and sometimes in the middle of a scene—such a jolly scene too—my mind goes back to that sweet old time, and I burst out crying."

He pushed the photograph away. "Why do you remind me of those days?" he said. "Is it only to make me realise the change in you?" But even at that moment the wonderful eyes pierced him through and through.

"Am I so much changed, John? Am I? No, no, dear! It is only my hair done differently. See, see!" and with trembling fingers she tore her hair from its knot. It fell in clusters over her shoulders and about her face. He wanted to lay his hand on it, and he turned to her and then turned away, fighting with himself as with an enemy.

"Or is it this old rag of lace that is so unlike my jersey? There—there!" she cried, tearing the lace from her neck, and throwing it on the floor and trampling upon it. "Look at me now, John—look at me! Am I not the same as ever? Why don't you look?"

She was fighting for her life. He started to his feet and came to her with his teeth set and his pupils fixed. "This is only the devil tempting me. Say your prayers, child!"

He grasped her left hand with his right. His grip almost overtaxed her strength and she felt faint. In an explosion of emotion the insane frenzy for destroying had come upon him again. He longed to give his feelings physical expression.

"Say them, say them!" he cried. "God sent me to kill you, Glory."

A sensation of terror and of triumph came over her at once. She half closed her eyes and threw her other arm around his neck. "No, but to love me! . . . Kiss me, John!"

Then a cry came from him like that of a man flinging himself over a precipice. He threw his arms about her, and her disordered hair fell over his face.

IX

"I THOUGHT it was God's voice—it was the devil's!"

John Storm was creeping like a thief through the streets of London in the dark hours before the dawn. It was a peaceful night after the thunderstorm of the evening before. A few large stars had come out, a clear moon was shining, and the air was quiet after the cries, the crackling tumult, and all the fury of human throats. There was only the swift rattling of mail-cars running to the post-office, the heavy clank of country carts crawling to Covent Garden, the measured tread of policemen, and the muddled laughter of drunken men and women by the coffee-stands at the street corners. "'Ow's the deluge, myte? Not come off yet? Well, give us a cup of cawfee on the strength of it."

It seemed as if eyes looked down on him from the dark sky

and pierced him through and through. His whole life had been an imposture from the first—his quarrel with his father, his taking Orders, his entering the monastery and his leaving it, his crusade in Soho, his intention of following Father Damien, his predictions at Westminster—all, all had been false and the expression of a lie! He was himself a sham, a mockery, a whited sepulchre, and had grossly sinned against the light and against God.

But the spiritual disillusion had come at last, and it had revealed him to himself at an awful depth of self-deception. Thinking in his pride and arrogance he was the Divine messenger, the avenger, the man of God, he had set out to shed blood like any wretched criminal, any jealous murderer who was driven along by devilish passion. How the devil had played with him too! With him, who was dedicated by the most solemn and sacred vows! And he had been as stubble before the wind—as chaff that the storm carrieth away!

With such feelings of poignant anguish he plodded through the echoing streets. Mechanically he made his way back to Westminster. By the time he got there the moon and stars had gone, and the chill of daybreak was in the air. He saw and heard nothing, but as he crossed Broad Sanctuary a line of mounted police trotted past him with their swords clanking.

It was not yet daylight when he knocked at the door of his chambers under the church.

"Who's there?" came in a fierce whisper.

"Open the door," he said in a spiritless voice.

The door was opened, and Brother Andrew, with the affectionate whine of a dog who has been snarling at his master in the dark, said, "Oh, is it you, Father? I thought you were gone. Did you meet them? They've been searching for you everywhere all night long."

He still spoke in whispers, as if some one had been ill. "I can't light up. They'd be sure to see and perhaps come back. They'll come in the morning in any case. Oh, it's terrible! Worse than ever now! Haven't you heard what has happened? Somebody has been killed!"

John was struggling to listen, but everything seemed to be happening a long way off.

"Well, not killed exactly, but badly hurt, and taken to the hospital."

It was Charlie Wilkes. He had insulted the name of the Father, and Pincher the pawnbroker had knocked him down. His head had struck against the curb, and he had been picked up insensible. Then the police had come and Pincher had been taken off to the police station.

"But it's my mother I'm thinking of," said Brother Andrew, and he brushed his sleeve across his eyes. "You must get away at once, Father. They'll lay everything on you. What's to be done? Let me think! Let me think! How my head is going round and round! There's a train from Euston to the north at five in the morning, isn't there? You must catch that. Don't speak, Father! Don't say you won't."

"I will go," said John, with a look of utter dejection.

The change that had come over him since the day before startled the lay brother. "But I suppose you've been out all night. How tired you look! Can I get you anything?"

John did not answer, and the lay brother brought some brown bread and coaxed him to eat a little of it. The day was beginning to dawn.

"Now you must go, Father.'

"And you, my lad?"

"Oh, I can take care of myself."

"Go back to the Brotherhood; take the dog with you——"

"The dog!" Brother Andrew seemed to be about to say something, but he checked himself, and with a wild look he muttered, "Oh, I know what *I'll* do. Good-bye!"

"Good-bye," said John, and then the broken man was back in the streets.

His nervous system had been exhausted by the events of the night, and when he entered the railway station he could scarcely put one foot before another. "Looks as if *he'd* had enough," said somebody behind him. He found an empty carriage and took his seat in the corner. A kind of stupor had come over his faculties, and he could neither think nor feel.

Three or four young men and boys were sorting and folding newspapers at a counter that stood on trestles before the closed-up bookstall. A placard slipped from the fingers of one of them, and fell on to the floor. John saw his own name in monster letters, and he began to ask himself what he was doing? Was he running away? It was cowardly, it was contemptible! And then it was so useless! He might go to the ends of the earth, yet he could not escape the only enemy it was worth while to fly from. That enemy was himself.

Suddenly he remembered that he had not taken his ticket, and he got out of the train. But instead of going to the ticket-office, he stood aside and tried to think what he ought to do. Then there was confusion and noise, people were hurrying past him, somebody was calling to him, and finally the engine whistled and the smoke rose to the roof. When he came to himself the train was gone, and he was standing on the platform alone.

"But what am I to do?" he asked himself.

It was a lovely summer morning, and the streets were empty and quiet. Little by little they became populous and noisy, and at length he was walking in a crowd. It was nine o'clock by this time, and he was in the Whitechapel Road, going along with a motley troop of Jews, Polish Jews, Germans, German Jews, and all the many tribes of cockneydom. Two costers behind him were talking and laughing.

"Lor' blesh you, it's jest abart enneff to myke a corpse laugh."

"Ain't it? An acquyntince uv mine . . . d'ye know Jow 'Awkins? Him as kep' the frahd fish-shop off of Flower and Dean. Yus? Well, he sold his bit uv biziness lahst week for a song, thinkin' the world was acomin' to a end, and this morning I meets him on the 'Owben Viadeck lookin' as if 'e'd 'ad the smallpox or somethink!"

John Storm had scarcely heard them. He had a strange feeling that everything was happening hundreds of miles away.

"What am I to do?" he asked himself again. Between twelve and one o'clock he was back in the City, walking aimlessly on and on. He did not choose the unfrequented thoroughfares, and when people looked into his face he thought, "If anybody asks me who I am I'll tell him." It was eight hours since he had eaten anything, and he felt weak and faint. Coming upon a coffee-house, he went in and ordered food. The place was full of young clerks at their mid-day meal. Most of them were reading newspapers, which they had folded and propped up on the tables before them, but two who sat near were talking.

"These predictions of the end of the world are a mania, a monomania, which recurs at regular intervals of the world's history," said one. He was a little man with a turned-up nose.

"But the strange thing is that people go on believing them," said his companion.

"That's not strange at all. This big, idiotic, amorphous London has no sense of humour. See how industriously it has been engaged for the last month in the noble art of making a fool of itself!" And then he looked round at John Storm, as if proud of his tall language.

John did not listen. He knew that everybody was talking about him, yet the matter did not seem to concern him now, but to belong to some other existence which his soul had had.

At length an idea came to him, and he thought he knew what he ought to do. He ought to go to the Brotherhood and ask to be taken back. But not as a son this time; only as a servant, to scour and scrub to the end of his life. There used to be a man to sweep out the church and ring the church-bell—he might be allowed to do menial work like that. He had proved false to his ideal, he had not been able to resist the lures of earthly love; but God was merciful, He would not utterly reject him.

His self-abasement was abject, yet several hours had passed before he attempted to carry out this design. It was the time of Evensong when he reached the church, and the brothers were singing their last hymn—

"Jesus, lover of my soul,
Let me to Thy bosom fly."

He stood by the porch and listened. The street was very quiet, hardly anybody was passing.

"Hide me, O my Saviour, hide,
Till the storms of life be past."

His heart surged up to his throat, and he could scarcely bear the pain of it. Yes, yes, yes! Other refuge had he none!

Suddenly a new thought smote him, and he felt like a man roused from a deep sleep. Glory! He had been thinking only of his own soul and his soul's salvation, and had forgotten his duty to others. He had his duty to Glory above all others, and he could not and must not escape from it. He must take his place by her side, and if that included the abandonment of his ideals, so be it! He had been proved unworthy of a life of holiness; he must lower his flag; he must be content to live the life of a man.

But he could not think what he ought to do next, and when night fell he was still wandering aimlessly through the streets. He had turned eastward again, and even in the tumultuous thoroughfares of Mile End he could not help seeing that something unusual was going on. People in drink were rolling about the streets and shouting and singing, as if it had been a public holiday. "Glad you ain't in kingdom-come to-night, old gel!"
"Well, what do *you* think?"

At twelve o'clock he went into a lodging-house and asked if he could have a bed. The keeper was in the kitchen talking with two men who were cooking a herring for their supper, and he looked up at his visitor in astonishment.

"Can I sleep you, sir? We ain't got no accommodation for gentlemen . . ." and then he stopped, looked more attentively, and said, "Are you from the Settlement, sir?"

John Storm made some inarticulate reply.

"Thort ye might be, sir. We often 'as 'em 'ere sempling the

cawfee, but bless'd if they ever wanted to semple a bed afore. Still, if *you* down't mind——"

"It will be better than I deserve, my man. Can you give me a cup of coffee before I turn in?"

"With pleasure, sir! Set down, sir! Myke yourself at 'ome. Me and my friends were jest talking of a gentleman of your cloth, sir—the pore feller as 'as got into trouble acrost Westminster way."

"Oh, you were talking of him, were you?"

"Sem 'ere says the biziness pyze."

"It *must* py, or people wouldn't do it," said the man leaning over the fire.

"Down't you believe it. That little gime down't py. 'Cause why? Look at the bloomin' stoo the feller's in now. If they ketch him 'e'll get six months 'ard."

"Then what's 'e been doin' it for? I down't see nothink in it if it down't py."

"'Cause he believes in it, thet's why! What do you think, sir?"

"I think the man has come by a just fall," said John. "God will never use him again, having brought him to shame."

"Must hev been a wrong un certingly," said the man over the fire.

When John Storm awoke in his cubicle next morning he saw his way clearer. He would deliver himself up to the warrant that was issued for his arrest, and go through with it to the end. Then he would return to Glory a free man, and God would find work for him even yet, after this awful lesson to his presumption and pride.

"Thet feller as was took ter the awspital is dead," said somebody in the kitchen, and then there was the crinkling of a newspaper.

"Is 'e?" said another. "The best thing the Father can do is to 'ook it, then. Cause why? W'ether 'e done it or not they'll fix it on ter 'im, doncher know."

John's head spun round and round. He remembered what Brother Andrew had said of Charlie Wilkes, and his heart, so warm a moment ago, felt benumbed as by frost. Nevertheless, at nine o'clock he was going westward in the Underground. People looked at him when he stepped into the carriage. He thought everybody knew him, and that the world was only playing with him as a cat plays with a mouse. The compartment was full of young clerks, smoking pipes and reading newspapers.

"Most extraordinary!" said one of them. "The fellow has

disappeared as absolutely as if he had been carried up into a cloud."

"Why extraordinary?" said another, in a thin voice. This one was not smoking, and he had the startled eyes of the enthusiast. "Elijah was taken up to heaven in the body, wasn't he? And why not Father Storm?"

"What?" cried the first, taking his pipe out of his mouth.

"Some people believe that," said the thin voice timidly.

"Oh, you want a dose of medicine, you do," said the first speaker, shaking out his ash and looking round with a knowing air. The young men got out in the City. John went on to Westminster Bridge.

It was terrible. Why could he not take advantage of the popular superstition and disappear indeed, taking Glory with him? But no, no, no!

Through all the torment of his soul his religion had remained the same, and now it rose up before him like a pillar of cloud and fire. He would do as he had intended, whatever the consequences, and if he was charged with crimes he had not committed, if he was accused of the offences of his followers, he would make no defence—if need be, he would allow himself to be convicted, and being innocent in this instance, God would accept his punishment as an atonement for his other sins! Glorious sacrifice! He would make it! And Glory herself would be proud of it some day.

With the glow of this resolution upon him he turned into Scotland Yard, and stepped boldly up to the office. The officer in charge received him with a deferential bow, but went on talking in a low voice to an inspector of police who was also standing at the other side of a counter.

"Strange!" he was saying. "I thought he was seen getting into the train at Euston."

"Don't know that he wasn't, either, in spite of all he says."

"Thinking of the dog?"

"Well, the dog, too," said the inspector, and then seeing John, "Helloa! Who's here?"

The officer stepped up to the counter. "What can I do for you, sir?" he asked.

John knew that the supreme moment had come, and he felt proud of himself that his resolution did not waver. Lifting his head, he said in a low and rapid voice, "I understand that you have a warrant for the arrest of Father Storm."

"We *had*, sir," the officer answered.

John looked embarrassed. "What do you mean by that?"

"I mean that Father Storm is now in custody."

John stared at the man with a feeling of stupefaction. "In custody? Did you say in custody?"

"Precisely. He has just given himself up!"

John answered impetuously, "But that is impossible."

"Why impossible, sir? Are you interested in this case?"

A certain quivering moved John's mouth. "I am Father Storm himself."

The officer was silent for a moment. Then he turned to the inspector with a pitying smile. "Another of them," he said significantly. The psychology of criminals had been an interesting study to this official.

"Wait a minute," said the inspector, and he went hurriedly through an inner doorway. The officer asked John some questions about his movements since yesterday. John answered vaguely in broken and rather bewildering sentences. Then the inspector returned.

"You are Father Storm?"

"Yes."

"Do you know of anybody who might wish to personate you?"

"God forbid that any one should do that."

"Still there is some one here who says——"

"Let me see him."

"Come this way, quietly," said the inspector, and John followed him to the inner room. His pride was all gone, his head was hanging low, and he was a prey to extraordinary agitation.

A man in a black cassock was sitting at a table making a statement to another officer, with an open book before him. His back was to the door, but John knew him in a moment. It was Brother Andrew.

"Then why have you given yourself up?" the officer asked, and Brother Andrew began a rambling and foolish explanation. He had seen it stated in an evening paper that the Father had been traced to the train at Euston, and he thought it a pity . . . a pity that the police . . . that the police should waste their time——"

"Take care!" said the officer. "You are in a position that should make you careful of what you say."

And then the inspector stepped forward, leaving John by the door.

"You still say you are Father Storm?"

"Of course I do," said Brother Andrew indignantly. "If I was anybody else, do you think I should come here and give myself up?"

"Then who is this standing behind you?"

Brother Andrew turned and saw John with a start of surprise

and a cry of terror. He seemed hardly able to believe in the reality of what was before him, and his restless eyeballs rolled fearfully. John tried to speak, but he could only utter a few inarticulate sounds.

"Well?" said the inspector. And while John stood with head down and heaving breast, Brother Andrew began to laugh hysterically and to say—

"Don't you know who this is? This is my lay brother. I brought him out of the Brotherhood six months ago, and he has been with me ever since."

The officers looked at each other. "Good heavens!" cried Brother Andrew in an imperious voice, "don't you believe me? You mustn't touch this man. He has done nothing—nothing at all. He is as tender as a woman, and wouldn't hurt a fly. What's he doing here?"

The officers also were dropping their heads, and the heart-rending voice went on, "Have you arrested him? You'll do very wrong if you arrest . . . But perhaps he has given himself up! That would be just like him. He is devoted to me, and would tell you any falsehood if he thought it would . . . But you must send him away . . . Tell him to go back to his old mother—that's the proper place for him. Good God! do you think I'm telling you lies?"

There was silence for a moment. "My poor lad, hush, hush!" said John, in a tone full of tenderness and authority. Then he turned to the inspector with a pitiful smile of triumph. "Are you satisfied?" he asked.

"Quite satisfied, Father," the officer answered in a broken voice; and then Brother Andrew began to cry.

X

WHEN Glory awoke on the morning after the Derby and thought of John, she felt no remorse. A sea of bewildering difficulty lay somewhere ahead, but she would not look at it. He loved her, she loved him, and nothing else mattered. If rules and vows stood between them, so much the worse for such enemies of love.

She was conscious that a subtle change had come over her. She was not herself any longer, but somebody else as well; not a woman merely, but in some sort a man; not Glory only, but also John Storm. Oh, delicious mystery! Oh, joy of joys! His arms seemed to be about her waist still, and his breath to linger about her neck. With a certain tremor, a certain thrill, she reached for a handglass, and looked at herself to learn if there was any difference in her face that the rest of the world would see. Yes, her eyes had another lustre, a deeper light, but she lay back in the cool bed with a smile and a long-drawn sigh. What matter whatever happened? Gone were the six cruel months in which she had awakened every morning with a pain at her breast. She was happy, happy, happy!

The morning sun was streaming across the room when Liza came in with the tea.

"Did ye see the Farver last night, Miss Gloria?"

"Oh, yes; that was all right, Liza."

The day's newspaper was lying folded on the tray. She took it up and opened it, remembering the Derby, and thinking for the first time of Drake's triumph. But what caught her eye in glaring headlines was a different matter—"The Panic Terror: Collapse of the Farce."

It was a shriek of triumphant derision. The fateful day had come and gone, yet London stood where it did before! Last night's tide had flowed and ebbed, and the dwellings of men were not submerged. No earthquake had swallowed up St. Paul's; no mighty bonfire of the greatest city of the world had lit up the sky of Europe, and even the thunderstorm which had broken over London had only laid the dust and left the air more clear.

"London is to be congratulated on the collapse of this panic, which, so far as we can hear, has been attended by only one casualty—an assault in Brown's Square, Westminster, on a young soldier, Charles Wilkes, of the Wellington Barracks, by two of the frantic army of the terror-stricken. The injured man was removed to St. Thomas's Hospital, while his assailants were taken to Rochester Row Police Station; and we have only to regret that the clerical panic-maker himself has not yet shared the fate of his followers. Late last night the authorities, recovering from their extraordinary supineness, issued a warrant for his arrest, but up to the time of going to press he had escaped the vigilance of the police."

Glory was breathing audibly as she read, and Liza, who was drawing up the blind, looked back at her with surprise.

"Liza, have you mentioned to anybody that Father Storm was here last night?"

"Why, no, miss; there ain't nobody stirrin' yet, and besides——"

"Then don't mention it to a soul. Will you do me that great, great kindness?"

"Down't ye know I will, mum?" said Liza, with a twinkle of the eye and a wag of the head.

Glory dressed hurriedly, went down to the drawing-room and wrote a letter. It was to Sefton, the manager. "Do not expect me to play to-night. I don't feel up to it. Sorry to be so troublesome."

Then Rosa came in with another newspaper in her hand, and, without saying anything, Glory showed her the letter. Rosa read it and returned it in silence. They understood each other.

During the next few hours Glory's impatience became feverish, and as soon as the first of the evening papers appeared she sent out for it. The panic was subsiding, and the people who had gone to the outskirts were returning to the city in troops, looking downcast and ashamed. No news of Father Storm. Inquiry that morning at Scotland Yard elicited the fact that nothing had yet been heard of him. There was much perplexity as to where he had spent the previous night.

Glory's face tingled and burned. From hour to hour she sent out for new editions. The panic itself was now eclipsed by the interest of John Storm's disappearance. His followers scouted the idea that he had fled from London. Nevertheless he had fallen. As a pretender to the gift of prophecy his career was at an end, and his crazy system of mystical divinity was the laughing-stock of London.

"It does not surprise us that this second Moses, this mock Messiah, has broken down. Such men always do, and must collapse, but that the public should ever have taken seriously a movement which . . ." and then a grotesque list of John's followers—one pawnbroker, one waiter, one "knocker-up," two or three apprentices, &c.

As she read all this Glory was at the same time glowing with shame, trembling with fear, and burning with indignation. She dined with Rosa alone, and they tried to talk of other matters. The effort was useless. At last Rosa said—

"I have to follow this thing up for the paper, dear, and I'm going to-night to see if they hold the usual service in his church."

"May I go with you?"

"If you wish to, but it will be useless—he won't be there."

"Why not?"

"The Prime Minister left London last night—I can't help thinking there is something in that."

"He will be there, Rosa. He's not the man to run away. I know him," said Glory proudly.

The church was crowded, and it was with difficulty they found seats. John's enemies were present in force—all the owners of

vested interests, who had seen their livelihood threatened by
the man who declared war on vice and its upholders. There
was a dangerous atmosphere before the service began, and, notwithstanding her brave faith in him, Glory found herself praying
that John Storm might not come. As the organ played and
the choir and clergy entered the excitement was intense, and
some of the congregation got on to their seats in their eagerness
to see if the Father was there. He was not there. The black
cassock and biretta in which he had lately preached were nowhere
to be seen, and a murmur of disappointment passed over friends
and enemies alike.

Then came a disgraceful spectacle. A man with a bloated
face and a bandage about his forehead rose in his place and
cried, "No Popery, boys!" Straightway the service, which
was being conducted by two of the clerical brothers from the
Brotherhood, was interrupted by hissing, whistling, shouting,
yelling, and whooping indescribable. Songs were roared out
during the lessons, and cushions, hassocks and prayer-books
were flung at the altar and its furniture. The terrified choir
boys fled downstairs to their own quarters, and the clergy were
driven out of the church.

John's own people stole away in terror and shame, but Glory
leapt to her feet as if to fling herself on the cowardly rabble.
Her voice was lost in the tumult, and Rosa drew her out into
the street.

"Is there no law in the land to prevent brawling like this?"
she cried, but the police paid no heed to her.

Then the congregation, which had broken up, came rushing
out of the church and round to the door leading to the chambers
beneath it.

"They've found him," thought Glory, pressing her hand over
her heart. But no, it was another matter. Immediately afterwards there rose over the babel of human voices the deep music
of the bloodhound in full cry. The crowd shrieked with fear
and delight, then surged and parted, and the dog came running
through, with its stern up, its head down, its forehead wrinkled,
and the long drapery of its ears and flews hanging in folds about
its face. In a moment it was gone, its mellow note was dying
away in the neighbouring streets, and a gang of ruffians were
racing after it. "That'll find the feller if he's in London,"
somebody shouted—it was the man with the bandaged forehead
—and there were yells of fiendish laughter.

Glory's head was going round, and she was holding on to Rosa's
arm with a convulsive grasp.

"The cowards!" she cried. "To use that poor creature's

devotion to his master for their own inhuman ends—it's cowardly, it's brutal, it's——Oh, oh, oh!"

"Come, dear," said Rosa, and she dragged Glory away.

They went back through Broad Sanctuary. Neither spoke, but both were thinking, "He has gone to the monastery. He intends to stay there until the storm is over." At Westminster Bridge they parted. "I have somewhere to go," said Rosa, turning down to the Underground. "She is going to Bishopsgate Street," thought Glory, and they separated with constraint.

Returning to Clement's Inn, Glory found a letter from Drake:—

"DEAR GLORY,—How can I apologise to you for my detestable behaviour of last night? The memory of what passed has taken all the joy out of the success upon which everybody is congratulating me. I have tried to persuade myself that you would make allowances for the day and the circumstances, and my natural excitement. But your life has been so blameless that it fills me with anguish and horror to think how I exposed you to misrepresentation by allowing you to go to that place, and by behaving to you as I did when you were there. Thank God, things went no farther, and some blessed power prevented me from carrying out my threat to follow you. Believe me, you shall see no more of men like Lord Robert Ure and women like his associates. I despise them from my heart, and wonder how I can have tolerated them so long. Do let me beg the favour of a line consenting to allow me to call and ask your forgiveness. —Yours most humbly, F. H. N. DRAKE."

Glory slept badly that night, and as soon as Liza was stirring she rang for the newspaper.

"Didn't ye 'ear the dorg, mum?" said Liza.

"What dog?"

"The Farver's dorg. It was scratching at the front dawer afore I was up this morning. 'It's the milk,' sez I. But the minute I opened the dawer up it came ter the drawerin' room and went snuffling rahnd everywhere."

"Where is it now?"

"Gorn, mum."

"Did anybody else see it? No? You say no? You're sure? Then say nothing about it, Liza—nothing whatever—that's a good girl."

The newspaper was full of the mysterious disappearance. Not a trace of the Father had yet been found. The idea had been started that he had gone into seclusion at the Anglican monastery with which he was associated, but on inquiry at

Bishopsgate Street it was found that nothing had been seen of him there. Since yesterday the whole of London had been scoured by the police, but not one fact had been brought to light to make clearer the mystery of his going away. With the most noticeable face and habit in London, he had evaded scrutiny and gone into a retirement which baffled discovery. No master of the stage art could have devised a more sensational disappearance. He had vanished as though whirled to heaven in a cloud, and that was literally what the more fanatical of his followers believed to have been his fate. Among these persons there were wild-eyed hangers-on telling of a flight upwards on a fiery chariot, as well as a predicted reappearance after three days. Such were the stories being gulped down by the thousands who still clung with an undefinable fascination to the memory of the charlatan. Meantime the soldier Wilkes had died of his injuries, and the coroner's inquiry was to be opened that day.

"Unfeeling brutes! The bloodhound is an angel of mercy compared to them," thought Glory; but the worst sting was in the thought that John had fled out of fear, and was now in hiding somewhere.

Towards noon the newsboys were rushing through the Inn, crying their papers against all regulations, and at the same moment Rosa came in to say that John Storm had surrendered.

"I knew it!" cried Glory. "I knew he would!"

Then Rosa told her of Brother Andrew's attempt to personate his master, and with what pitiful circumstances it had ended.

"Only a lay brother, you say, Rosa?"

"Yes, a poor half-witted soul apparently—must have been, to imagine a subterfuge like that would succeed in London."

Glory's eyes were gleaming. "Rosa," she said, "I would rather have done what he did than play the greatest part in all the world."

She wished to be present at the trial, and proposed to Rosa that she should go with her.

"But dare you, my child? Considering your old friendship, dare you see him——"

"Dare I?" said Glory. "Dare I stand in the dock by his side!"

But when she got to Bow Street, and saw the crowds in the court, the line of distinguished persons of both sexes allowed to sit on the bench, the army of reporters and newspaper artists, and all the mass of smiling and eager faces without ruth or pity, gathered together as for a show, her heart sickened and she crept out of the place before the prisoner was brought into the dock.

Walking to and fro in the corridor, she waited the result of the trial. It was not a long one. The charge was that of causing persons to assemble unlawfully to the danger of the public peace. There was no defence. A man with a bandaged forehead was the first witness. He was a publican who lived in Brown's Square, and had been a friend of the soldier Wilkes. The injury to his forehead was the result of a blow from a stick given by the prisoner's lay brother on the night of the Derby, when, with the help of the deceased, he had attempted to liberate the bloodhound. He had much to say of the Father's sermons, his speeches, his predictions, his slanders, and his disloyalty. Other witnesses were Pincher and Hawkins. They were in a state of abject fear at the fate hanging over their own heads, and tried to save their own skins by laying all the blame upon the Father. The last witness was Brother Andrew, and he broke down utterly. Within an hour Rosa came out to say that John Storm had been committed for trial. Bail was not asked for, and the prisoner, who had not uttered a word from first to last, had been taken back to the cells.

Glory hurried home and shut herself in her room. The newsboys in the street were shouting, "Father Storm in the dock," and filling the air with their cries. She covered her ears with her hands and made noises in her throat that she might not hear.

John Storm's career was at an end. It was all her fault. If she had yielded to his desire to leave London, or if she had joined him there, how different everything must have been. But she had broken in upon his life and wrecked it. She had sinned against him who had given her everything that one human soul can give another.

Liza came up with red eyes, bringing the evening papers and a letter. The papers contained long reports of the trial, and short editorials reproving the public for its interest in such a poor impostor. Some of them contained sketches of the prisoner and of the distinguished persons recognised in court. "The stage was represented by ——," and then a caricature of herself.

The letter was from Aunt Rachel:—

"MY DEAR, MY BEST-BELOVED GLORY,—I know how much your kind *heart* will be lowered by the painful tidings I have to write to you. Lord Storm died on Monday and was buried to-day. To the last he declared he would never consent to make peace with John, and he has left nothing to him but his title, so that our dear friend is now a nobleman without an estate. Everybody about the old lord at the end was unanimous in favour of his son, but he would not listen to them, and the scene at the death-bed was shocking. It seems that, with his dying breath and many bursts of laughter, he read aloud his will, which

ordered that his effects should be sold, and the proceeds given to some society for the protection of the Established Church. And then he told old Chalse that as soon as he was gone a coffin was to be got, and he was to be screwed down at once, 'for,' said he, 'my son would not come to see me *living*, and he shan't stand grinning at me *dead*.' The funeral was at Kirkpatrick this morning, and *few* came to see the last of one who had left none to mourn him; but just as the remains were being deposited in the dark vault, a carriage drove up and an elderly gentleman got out. No one knew him, and he stood and looked down with his impassive face while the service was being read, and then without speaking to any one he got back into the carriage and drove away. The *minute* he was gone I told Anna he was somebody of consequence, and then everybody said it must be Lord Storm's brother, and no less a person than the Prime Minister of England. It seems that the sale is to come off immediately, so that Knockaloe will be a waste, as if sown with salt, and, so far as this island is concerned, all trace of the Storms, father and son, will be gone for good. I ever knew it must end thus! But I will more particularly tell you everything when we meet again, which I hope may be *soon*. Meantime I need not say how much I am, my dear child, your ever fond, nay, more than fond, *devoted* auntie
RACHEL."

XI

"Yes," said Rosa across the dinner-table, "the sudden fall of a man who has filled a large space in the public eye is always pitiful. It is like the fall of a great tree in the forest. One never realised how big it was until it was down."

"It's awful—awful!" said Glory.

"Whether one liked the man or not, such a downfall seems hard to reconcile with the idea of a beneficent Providence."

"Hard? Impossible, you mean!"

"Glory!"

"Oh, I'm only a pagan and always have been, but I can't believe in a God that does nothing—I won't, I won't!"

"Still we can't see the end yet. After the cross the resurrection, as the Church folks say, and who knows but out of all this——"

"What's to become of his church?"

"Oh, there'll be people enough to see to that, and if the dear Archdeacon . . . But he's busy with Mrs. Macrae, bless him!

She has gone to wreck at last, and is living hidden away in a farmhouse somewhere that she may drink herself to death without detection and interruption. But the Archdeacon and Lord Robert have found her out, and there they are hovering round like two vultures waiting for the end."

"And his orphanage?"

"Ah, that's another pair of shoes altogether, dear. Being an institution that asks for an income instead of giving one, there'll be nobody too keen to take it over."

"O God! O God! What a world it is!" cried Glory.

After dinner she went off to Westminster in search of the orphanage. It stood on a corner of the church square. The door was closed and the windows of the ground-floor were shuttered. With difficulty she obtained admission and access to the person in charge. This was an elderly lady in a black silk dress and with snow-white hair.

"I'm no the matron, miss," she said. "The matron's gone, fled awa like a' the lave o' the grand Sisters, thinking sure the mob would mak' this house their next point of attack."

"Then I know whom *you* are; you're Mrs. Callender," said Glory.

"Jane Callender I am, young leddy. And who may ye be yersel'?"

"I'm a friend of John's, and I want to know if there's anything——"

"You're no the lassie hersel', are ye? You are, though. I see fine you are. Come, kiss me—again, lassie! Oh dear, oh dear! And to think we must be meeting same as this! For a' the world it's like clasping hands ower the puir laddie's grave."

They cried in each other's arms, and then both felt better.

"And the children," said Glory. "Who's looking after them if the matron and Sisters are gone?"

"Just me and the puir bairns theirsels, and the wee maid of all wark that opened the door til ye. But come your ways and look at them."

The dormitory was in an upper storey. Mrs. Callender had opened the door softly, and Glory stepped into a large dark room in which fifty children lay asleep. Their breathing was all that could be heard, and it seemed to fill the air as with the rustle of a gentle breeze. But it was hard to look upon them and to think of their only earthly father in his cell. With full hearts and dry throats the two women returned to a room below.

By this time the square, which before had only shown people standing in doorways and lounging at street corners, was crowded with a noisy rabble. They were shouting out indecent jokes about "monks," "his reverend lordship," and "doctors of diwinity;" and a small gang of them had got a rope which they were trying to throw as a lasso round a figure of the Virgin in a niche over the porch. The figure came down at length amid shrieks of delight, and when the police charged the mob they flung stones which broke the church windows.

Again Glory felt an impulse to throw herself on the cowardly rabble, but she only crouched at the window by the side of Mrs. Callender, and looked down at the sea of faces below with their evil eyes and cruel mouths.

"Oh, what a thing it is to be a woman!" she moaned.

"Aye, lassie, aye, there's mair than ane of us has felt that," said Mrs. Callender.

Glory did not speak again as long as they knelt by the window holding each other's hands, but the tears that had sprung to her eyes at the thought of her helplessness dried up of themselves, and in their place came the light of a great resolution. She knew that her hour had struck at last—that this was the beginning of the end.

The theatres were emptying and carriages were rolling away from them as she drove home by way of the Strand. She saw her name on omnibuses and her picture on hoardings, and felt a sharp pang. But she was in a state of feverish excitement, and the pain was gone in a moment.

Another letter from Drake was waiting for her at the Inn:—

"I feel, my dear Glory, that you are entirely justified in your silence; but to show you how deep is my regret, I am about to put it in my power to atone, as far as I can, for the conduct which has quite properly troubled and hurt you. You will put me under an eternal obligation if you will consent to become my wife. We should be friends as well as lovers, Glory, and in an age distinguished for brilliant and beautiful women, it would be the crown of my honour that my wife was above all a woman of genius. Nothing should disturb the development of your gifts, and if any social claims conflicted with them, they, and not you, would suffer. For the rest, I can bring you nothing, dear, but—thanks to the good father who was born before me—such advantages as belong to wealth. But so far as these go there is no pleasure you need deny yourself, and if your sympathies are set on any good work for humanity, there is no opportunity you may not command. With this I can only offer you the love and devotion of my whole heart and soul, which now wait in fear and pain for your reply."

Glory read this letter with a certain quivering of the eyelids, but she put it away without a qualm. Nevertheless, the letter was hard to reply to, and she made many attempts without satisfying herself in the end. There was a note of falsehood in all of them, and she felt troubled and ashamed.

"When I remember how good you have been to me from the first, I could cry to think of the answer I must give you. But I can't help it—Oh, I can't, I can't! Don't think me ungrateful, and don't suppose I am angry or in any way hurt or offended, but to do what you desire is impossible—quite, quite impossible. Oh, if you only knew what it is to deny myself the future you offer me, to turn my back on the gladness with which life has come to me, to strip all these roses from my hair, you would believe it must be a far, far higher call than to worldly rank and greatness that I am listening to at last. And it is. A woman may trifle with her heart while the one she loves is well and happy or great and prosperous; but when he is down and the cruel world is trampling on him, there can be no paltering with it any longer. . . . Yes, I must go to *him* if I go to anybody. Besides, you can do without me and he cannot. You have all the world and he has nothing but me. If you were a woman you would understand all this; but you are loyal and brave and true, and when I look at your letter and remember how often you have spoken up for a fallen man, my heart quivers and my eyes grow dim, and I know what it means to be an English gentleman."

After writing this letter, she went up to her bedroom and busied herself there for an hour, making up parcels of her clothing and jewellery, and labelling them with envelopes bearing names. The plainer costumes she addressed to Aunt Anna, a fur-lined jacket to Aunt Rachel, an opera-cloak to Rosa, and a quantity of underclothing to Liza. All her jewels, and nearly all the silver trinkets from the dressing-table, were made up in a parcel by themselves, and addressed back to the giver—Sir Francis Drake.

The clock of St. Clement Danes was chiming midnight when this was done, and she stood a moment and asked herself, "Is there anything else?" Then there was a slippered foot on the stair, and somebody knocked.

"It's only me, miss, and can I do anythink for ye?"

Glory opened the door and found Liza there, half-dressed, and looking as if she had been crying.

"Nothing, Liza; nothing, thank you. But why aren't you in bed?"

"I can't sleep a blessed wink to-night somehow, Miss," said Liza. And then, looking into the room, "But are ye goin' away somewhere, Miss Gloria?"

"Yes, perhaps."

"Thort ye was I could hear ye downstairs."

"Not far, though—just a little journey. Go back to bed now. Good-night!"

"Good-night, Miss," and Liza went down with lingering footsteps.

Half-an-hour or so afterwards, Glory heard Rosa come in from the office, and pass up to her bedroom on the floor above. "Dear unselfish soul!" she thought, and then she sat down to write another letter.

"Darling Rosa,—I am going to leave you, but there is no help for it—I must. Don't you remember I used to say if I should ever find a man who was willing to sacrifice all the world for me, I would leave everything and follow him? I have found him, dear, and he has not only sacrificed all the world for my sake, but trampled on heaven itself. I can't go to him now—would to heaven I could—but neither can I go on living this present life any longer. So I am turning my back on it all, exactly as I said I would—the world, so sweet and so cruel; art, so beautiful and so difficult, and even 'the clapping of hands in a theatre.' You will say I am a donkey, and so I may be, but it must be a descendant of Balaam's old friend, who knew the way she ought to go.

"Forgive me that I am going without saying good-bye. It is enough to have to resist the battering of one's own doubts without encountering your dear solicitations. And forgive me that I am not telling you where I am going and what is to become of me. You will be questioned and examined, and I feel as much frightened of being overtaken by my old existence as the poor simpleton who took it into his head that he was a grain of barley, and as often as he saw a cock or a hen he ran for his life. Thank you, dearest, for allowing me to share your sweet rooms with you, for the bright hours we have spent in them, and all the merry jaunts we have had together. There will be fewer creature comforts where I am going to, and my feet will not be so quick to do evil, which will at least be a saving of shoe-leather.

"Good-bye, old girl—loyal, unselfish, devoted friend! God will reward you yet, and a good man who has been chasing a will-o'-the-wisp will open his eyes to see that all the time the star of the morning has been by his side. To-morrow, when I leave the house, I know I shall want to run up and kiss you as you lie asleep, but I mustn't do that—the little druggeted stairs to your room would be like the road to another but not a better place, which is also paved with good intentions. What a scatterbrain I am! My heart is breaking, too, with all this severing of my poor little riven cords.—Your foolish old chummie (the last of her), GLORY."

Next morning, almost as soon as it was light, she rose and drew a little tin box from under the bed. It was the box that had brought all her belongings to London when she first came from her island home. Out of this box she took a simple grey costume—the costume she had bought for outdoor wear when a nurse at the hospital. Putting it on, she looked at herself in the glass. The plain grey figure, so unlike what she had been the night before, sent a little stab to her heart, and she sighed.

"But this is Glory, after all," she thought. "This is the grand-daughter of my grandfather, the daughter of my father, and not the visionary woman who has been masquerading in London so long." But the conceit did not comfort her very much, and scalding tear-drops began to fall.

Tying up some other clothing into a little bundle, she opened the door and listened. There was no noise in the house, and she crept downstairs with a light tread. At the drawing-room she paused, and took one last look round at the place where she had spent so many exciting hours, and lived through such various phases of life. While she stood on the threshold there was a sound of heavy breathing. It came from the pug, which lay coiled up on the sofa asleep. Reproaching herself with having forgotten the little thing, she took it up in her arms, and hushed it when it awoke and began to whine. Then she crept down to the front door, opened it softly, passed out, and closed it after her. There was a click of the lock in the silent gardens, and then no sound anywhere but the chirrup of the sparrows in the eaves.

The sun was beginning to climb over the cool and quiet streets as she went along, and some cabmen at the stand looked over at the woman in nurse's dress, with the little bundle in one hand and the dog under the other arm. "Been to a death, p'raps. Some uv these nurses, they've tender 'earts, bless 'em, and when I was in the 'awspital . . ." But she turned her head and hurried on, and the voice was lost in the empty air.

As she dipped into the slums of Westminster the sun gleamed on her wet face, and a group of noisy, happy girls, going to their work in the jam-factories of Soho, came towards her laughing.

The girls looked at the Sister as she passed; their tongues stopped and there was a hush.

XII

John Storm's enemies had succeeded. He was committed for sedition, and there was the probability that he would be brought up again and charged with complicity in manslaughter. Throughout the proceedings at the police court he maintained a calm and dignified silence. Supported by an exalted faith, he regarded even death with composure. When the trial was over and the policeman who stood at the back of the dock tapped him on the arm, he started like a man whose mind had been occupied with other issues.

" Eh ? "

" Come," said the policeman, and he was taken back to the cells.

Next day he was removed to Holloway, and there he observed the same calm and silent attitude. His bearing touched and impressed the authorities, and they tried by various small kindnesses to make his imprisonment easy. He encouraged them but little.

On the second morning an officer came to his cell and said, " Perhaps you would care to look at the newspaper, Father ? "

" Thank you, no," he answered. " The newspapers were never much to me even when I was living in the world—they cannot be necessary now that I am going out of it."

" Oh, come, you exaggerate your danger. Besides, now that the papers contain so much about yourself——"

" That is a reason why I should not see them."

" Well, to tell you the truth, Father, this morning's paper has something about somebody else, and that was why I brought it."

" Eh ? "

" Somebody near to you—very near and . . . But I'll leave it with you . . . Nothing to complain of this morning ?—no ? "

But John Storm was already deep in the columns of the newspaper. He found the news intended for him. It was the death of his father. The paragraph was cruel and merciless. " Thus the unhappy man who was brought up at Bow Street two days ago is now a peer in his own right and the immediate heir to an earldom."

The moment was a bitter and terrible one. Memories of past years swept over him—half-forgotten incidents of his boyhood, when his father was his only friend and he walked with his hand in his—memories of his father's love for him, his hopes, his aims, his ambitions, and all the vast ado of his poor delusive dreams. And then came thoughts of the broken old man dying alone, and of himself in his prison cell. It had been a strangely familiar thought to him of late that if he left London at seven in the morning he could speak to his father at seven the same night. And now his father was gone, the last opportunity was lost, and he could speak to him no more.

But he tried to conquer the call of blood which he had put aside so long, and to set over against it the claims of his exalted mission and the spirit of the teaching of Christ. What had Christ said? "Call no man your father upon the earth; for one is your Father, which is in heaven!"

"Yes," he thought, "that's it—'for one is your Father, which is in heaven.'"

Then he took up the newspaper again, thinking to read with a calmer mind the report of his father's death and burial, but his eye fell on a different matter:—

"ANOTHER MYSTERIOUS DISAPPEARANCE.—Hardly has the public mind recovered from the perplexity attending the disappearance of a well-known clergyman from Westminster, when the news comes of a no less mysterious disappearance of a popular actress from a West-End theatre."

It was Glory!

"Although a recent acquisition to the stage and the latest English actress to come into her heritage of fame, she was already a universal favourite, and her sudden and unaccountable disappearance is a shock as well as a surprise. To the disappointment of the public, she had not played her part for nearly a week, having excused herself on the ground of indisposition, but there was apparently nothing in the state of her health to give cause for anxiety or to prepare her friends for the step she has taken. What has become of her appears to be entirely beyond conjecture, but her colleagues and associates are still hoping for the best, though the tone of a letter left behind gives only too much reason to fear a sad and perhaps fatal sequel."

When the officer entered the cell again an hour after his first visit, John Storm was pallid and thin and grey. The sublime faith he had built up for himself had fallen to ruins, a cloud had hidden the face of the Father which is in heaven, and the death he had waited for as the crown of his life seemed to be no better than an abject end to a career that had failed.

"Cheer up," said the officer; "I've some good news for you, at all events."

The prisoner smiled sadly and shook his head.

"Bail was offered and accepted at Bow Street this morning, and you will be at liberty to leave us to-day."

"When?" said John, and his manner changed immediately.

"Well, not just yet, you know."

"For the love of God, let me go at once. I have something to do—somebody to look for and find."

"Still, for your own security, Father——"

"But why?"

"Then you don't know that the mob sent a dog out in search for you?"

"No, I didn't know that, but if all the dogs of Christendom——"

"There are worse dogs waiting for you than any that go on four legs, you know."

"That's nothing, nothing at all, and if bail has been accepted surely it is your duty to liberate me at once. I claim—I demand that you should do so."

The officer raised his eyes in astonishment. "You surprise me, Father. After your calmness and patience and submission to authority too!"

John Storm remained silent for a moment, and then he said with a touching solemnity, "You must forgive me. You are very good—everybody is good to me here. Still, I am not afraid, and if you can let me go——"

The officer left him. It was several hours before he returned. By this time the long summer day had closed in, and it was quite dark.

"They think you've gone. You can leave now. Come this way."

At the door of the office, some minutes afterwards, John Storm paused with the officer's hand in his and said—

"Perhaps it is needless to ask who is my bail" (he was thinking of Mrs. Callender), "but if you can tell me——"

"Certainly. It was Sir Francis Drake."

John Storm bowed gravely and turned away. As he passed out of the yard his eyes were bent on the ground and his step was slow and feeble.

At that moment Drake was on his way to the Corinthian Club. Early in the afternoon he had seen this letter in the columns of an evening paper :—

"THE MYSTERIOUS DISAPPEARANCES.—Is it not extraordinary that in discussing 'the epidemic of mystery' which now fills the air of London, it has apparently never occurred to any one that the two mysterious disappearances which are the text of so many sermons may be really one disappearance only; that the 'man of God' and the 'woman of the theatre' may have acted in collusion, from the same impulse and with the same expectation, and that the rich and beneficent person who (according to latest reports) has come to the rescue of the one, and is an active agent in looking for the other, is in reality the foolish though well-meaning victim of both?—R. U."

For three hours Drake had searched for Lord Robert, with flame in his eyes and fury in his looks. Going first to Belgrave Square, he had found the blinds down and the house shut up. Mrs. Macrae was dead. She had died at a lodging in the country, alone and unattended. Her wealth had not been able to buy the devotion of one faithful servant at the end. She had left nothing to her daughter except a remonstrance against her behaviour, but she had made Lord Robert her chief heir and sole executor.

That amiable mourner had returned to London with all possible despatch, as soon as the breath was out of his mother-in-law's body and arrangements were made for its transit. He was now engaged in relieving the tension of so much unusual emotion by a round of his nightly pleasures. Drake had come up with him at last.

The Corinthian Club was unusually gay that night. "Helloa, there!" came from every side. The music in the ballroom was louder than ever, and, judging by the number of the dancers, the attraction of "Tra-la-la" was even greater than before. There was the note of yet more reckless license everywhere, as if that little world whose life was pleasure had been under the cloud of a temporary terror, and was determined to make up for it by the wildest folly. The men chaffed and laughed, and shouted comic songs and kicked their legs about; the women drank and giggled.

Lord Robert was in the supper-room with three guests, the "Three Graces." The women were in full evening-dress. Betty was wearing the ring she had taken from Polly, "just to remember her by, pore thing," and the others were blazing in similar brilliants. The wretched man himself was half drunk. He had been talking of Father Storm and of his own wife in a jaunty tone, behind which there was an intensity of hatred.

"But this panic of his, don't you know, was the funniest thing ever heard of. Going home that night, I counted seventeen people on their knees in the streets—'pon my soul, I did! Eleven old women of eighty, two or three of seventy, and one or two that might be as young as sixty-nine. Then the epidemic of piety in high life, too! Several of our millionaires gave sixpence apiece to beggars—were seen to do it, don't you know. One old girl gave up playing baccarat and subscribed to 'Darkest England.' No end of sweet little women confessed their pretty weaknesses to their husbands, and now that the world is wagging along as merrily as before, they don't know what the devil they are to do. . . . But, look here!"

Out of his trouser pockets at either side he tugged a torn and crumpled assortment of letters, and proceeded to tumble them on to the table.

"These are a few of the applications I had from curates-in-charge and such beauties for the care of the living in Westminster while the other gentleman lay in jail. It's the Bishop's right to appoint the creature, don't you know, but they think a patron's recommendation . . . Oh, they're a sweet team! Listen to this—'May it please your lordship——'"

And then in mock tones, flourishing one hand, the man read aloud, amid the various noises of the place—the pop of champagne bottles and the rumble of the dancing in the room below—the fulsome letters he had received from clergymen. The wretched women, in their paint and patches, shrieked with laughter.

It was at that moment Drake came up, looking pale and fierce.

"Helloa, there! Is it you? Sit down, and take a glass of fizz."

"Not at this table," said Drake; "I prefer to drink with friends."

Lord Robert's eyes glistened and he tried to smile. "Really? Thought I was counted in that distinguished company, don't you know."

"So you were; but I've come to see that a friend who is not a friend is always the worst enemy."

"What do you mean?"

"What does that mean?" said Drake, throwing the paper on to the table.

"Well, what of it?"

"The initials to that letter are yours, and all the men I meet tell me that you have written it."

"They do, do they? Well?"

"I won't ask you if you did or if you didn't."

"Don't, dear boy."

"But I'll require you to disown it publicly, and at once."

"And if I won't—what then?"

"Then I'll tell the public for myself that it's a lie—a cowardly and contemptible lie, and that the man who wrote it is a cur."

"Oho! So it's like that, is it?" said Lord Robert, rising to his feet as if putting himself on guard.

"Yes, it *is* like that, Lord Robert Ure, because the woman who is slandered in that letter is as innocent as your own wife, and ten thousand times as pure as those who are your constant company."

Lord Robert's angular and ugly face glistened with a hateful smile. "Innocent!" he cried hoarsely, and then he laughed out loud. "Go on! It's rippin' to hear you, dear boy! Innocent, by God! Just as innocent as any other ballet-girl who is dragged through the stews of London, and then picked up at last by the born fool who keeps her for another man."

"You liar!" cried Drake, and, like a flash of light, he had shot his fist across the table and struck the man full in the face. Then laying hold of the table itself, he swept it away with all that was on it, and sprang at Lord Robert and took him by the throat.

"Take that back, will you? Take it back!"

"I won't," cried Lord Robert, writhing and struggling in his grip.

"Then take that—and that—and that—damn you!" cried Drake, showering blow after blow, and finally flinging the man into the débris of what had fallen from the table with a crash.

The women were screaming by this time, and all the house was in alarm. But Drake went out with long strides and a ferocious face, and no one attempted to stop him.

XIII

RETURNING to St. James's Street, Drake found John Storm waiting in his rooms. The men had changed a good deal since they last met, and the faces of both showed suffering.

"Forgive me for this visit," said Storm. "It was my first duty to call and thank you for what you've done."

"That's nothing—nothing at all," said Drake.

"I had also another object. You'll know what that is?"

Drake bowed his head.

"She is gone, it seems, and there is no trace left of her."

"None!"

"Then *you* know nothing?"

"Nothing! And you?"

"Nothing whatever!"

Drake bowed his head again. "I knew it was a lie that she had gone after you. I never believed that story?"

"Would to God she had!" said Storm fervently, and Drake flinched, but bore himself bravely. "When did she go?"

"Two days ago, apparently."

"Has anybody looked for her?"

"*I* have—everywhere—everywhere I can think of. But this London——"

"Yes, yes; I know, I know!"

"For two days I have never rested, and all last night——"

Storm's eyes were watching the twitchings of Drake's face. He had been sitting uneasily on his chair, and now he rose from it.

"Are you going already?" said Drake.

"Yes," said Storm. Then, in a husky voice, he added, "I don't know if we shall ever meet again, you and I. When death breaks the link that binds people——"

"For God's sake, don't say that."

"But it *is* so, isn't it?"

"Heaven knows! Certainly the letter she left behind—the letter to Rosa . . . Poor child! she was such a creature of joy —so bright, so brilliant! And then to think of her . . . I was much to blame—I came between you. But if I had once realised——"

Drake stopped, and the men fixed their eyes on each other for a moment, and then turned their heads away.

"I'm afraid I've done you a great injustice, sir," said Storm.

"Me?"

"I thought she was only your toy, your plaything. But perhaps" (his voice was breaking), "perhaps you loved her too."

Drake answered, almost inaudibly, "With all my heart and soul!"

"Then—then we have *both* lost her?"

"Both!"

There was silence for a moment. The hands of the two men met and clasped, and parted.

"I must go," said Storm, and he moved across the room with a look of utter weariness.

"But where are you going to?"

"I don't know—anywhere—nowhere—it doesn't matter now."

"Well——"

"Good-night!"

"Good-night!"

Drake stood at the door below until the slow, uncertain footsteps had turned the corner of the street and died away.

John Storm was sure now. Overwhelmed by his own disgrace, ashamed of his downfall, and perhaps with a sense of her own share in it, Glory had destroyed herself.

Strange contradiction! Much as he had hated Glory's way of life, there came to him at the moment a deep remorse at the thought that he had been the means of putting an end to it. And then her gay and happy spirit clouded by his own disasters! Her good name stained by association with his evil one! Her pure soul imperilled by his sin and fall!

But it was now very late, and he began to ask himself where he was to sleep. At first he thought of his old quarters under the church, and then he told himself that Brother Andrew would be gone by this time, and that everything connected with the parish must be transferred to other keeping. Going by a hotel in Trafalgar Square, he stepped in and asked for a bed.

"Certainly, sir," said the clerk, who was polite and deferential.

"Can I have something to eat too?"

"Coffee-room to the left, sir. Luggage coming, sir?"

"I have no luggage to-night," he answered; and then he saw that the clerk looked at him doubtfully.

The coffee-room was empty and only half lit up, for dinner was long over, and the business of the day was done. John was sitting at his meal, eating his food with his eyes down, and hardly conscious of what was going on around, when he became aware that from time to time people opened the room door and looked across at him, then whispered together and passed out. At length the clerk came up to him with awkward manners and a look of constraint.

"I beg your pardon, sir, but are you Father Storm?"

John bent his head.

"Then I'm sorry to say we cannot accommodate you; we dare not—we must request you to leave."

John rose without a word, paid his bill, and left the place.

But where was he to go to? What house would receive him? If one hotel refused him, all other hotels in London would do the same. Then he remembered the Shelter which he had himself established for the undeserving poor. The humiliation of that moment was terrible. But no matter! He would drink the cup of God's anger to the dregs.

The lamp was burning in the Clock Tower of the Houses of Parliament, and as John passed by the corner of Palace Yard two bishops came out in earnest conversation and walked on in front of him.

"The State and the Church are as the body and soul," said one, "and to separate them would be death to both."

"Just that," said the other; "and therefore we must fight for the Church's temporal possessions as we should contend for her spiritual rights, and so these Benefice Bills———."

The Shelter was at the point of closing, and Jupe was putting out the lamp over the door as John stepped up to him.

"Who is it?" said Jupe in the dark.

"Don't you know me, Jupe?" said John.

"Father Jawn Storm!" cried the man in a whisper of fear.

"I want shelter for the night, Jupe. Can you put me up anywhere?"

"You, sir?"

The man was staggered, and the long rod in his hand shook like a reed. Then he began to stammer something about the Bishop and the Archdeacon and his new orders and instructions; how the Shelter had been taken over by other authorities, and he was now———

"But, d——— it all," he said, stopping suddenly, putting his foot down firmly, and wagging his head to right and left like a man making a brave resolution, "I'll tyke ye in, sir, and heng it!"

It was the bitterest pill of all, but John swallowed it and stepped into the house. As he did so he was partly aware of some tumult in a neighbouring street, with the screaming of men and women and the barking of dogs.

The blankets had been served out for the night, and the men in the Shelter were clambering up to their bunks. In addition to the main apartment, there was a little room with a glass front, which hung like a cage near to the ceiling at one end, and was entered by a circular iron stair. This was the keeper's own sleeping-place, and Jupe was making it ready for John, while John himself sat waiting with the look of a crushed and humiliated man, when the tumult in the street came nearer, and at last drew up in front of the house.

"Wot's thet?" the men asked each other, lifting their heads, and Jupe came down and went to the door. When he returned his face was white, the sweat hung on his forehead, and a trembling shook his whole body.

"For Gawd's sake, Father, leave the house at onct," he whispered in great agitation. "There's a gang outside as'll pull the place dahn if I keep you."

There was silence for a moment, save for the shouting outside, and then John said with a sigh and a look of resignation, "Very well, let me out then," and he turned to the door.

"Not that wye, sir—this wye," said Jupe, and at the next moment they were stepping into a dark and narrow lane at the back. "Turn to the left when ye get ter the bottom, Father—mind ye turn ter the left."

But John Storm had scarcely heard him. His heart had failed him at last. He saw the baseness and ingratitude of the people whom he had spent himself to relieve and uplift and succour and comfort, and he repented himself of the hopes and aims and efforts which had come to this bankruptcy in the end.

"My God! my God! why hast Thou forsaken me?"

Yes, yes, that was it! It was not this poor vile race merely, this stupid and ungrateful humanity—it was God! God used one man's ignorance, and another man's anger, and another man's hatred, and another man's spite, and worked out His own ends through it all. And God had rejected him, refused him, turned a deaf ear to his prayer and his repentance, robbed him of friends, of affection, of love, and cast him out of the family of man!

Very well! So be it! What should he do? He would go back to prison and say, "Take me in again—there is no room left for me in the world. I am alone, and my heart is dead within me!"

He was at the end of the dark lane by this time, and forgetting Jupe's warning, and seeing a brightly-lighted street running off to his right, he swung round to it and walked boldly along. This was Old Pye Street, and he had come to the corner at which it opens into Brown's Square, when his absent mind became conscious of the loud baying of a dog. At the next moment the dog was at his feet, bounding about him with frantic delight, leaping up to him as if trying to kiss him, and uttering meanwhile the most tender, the most true, the most pitiful cries of love.

It was his own dog, the bloodhound Don!

His unworthy thoughts were chased away at the sight of this one faithful friend remaining, and he was stooping to fondle the great creature, to pull at the long drapery of its ears and the pendulous folds of its glorious forehead, when a short sharp cry caused him to lift his head.

"That's 'im!" said somebody, and then he was aware that a group of men with evil faces had gathered round. He knew them in a moment: the publican with his bandaged head, Sharkey, who had served his time and been released from prison, and Pincher and Hawkins, who were out on bail. They had all been drinking. The publican, who carried a stick, was drunk, and the "knocker-up" was staggering on a crutch.

Then came a hideous scene. The four men began to taunt John Storm, to take off their hats and bow to him in mock honour. " His Lordship, I believe ! " said one. " His Reverend Lordship, if you please ! " said another.

" Leave me, for God's sake leave me ! " said John.

But their taunts became more and more menacing. " Wot abart the end uv the world, Father ? " " Didn't ye tell me to sell my bit uv biziness ? " " And didn't ye say you'd cured me, and look at me now ! "

" Don't, I tell you, don't ! " cried John, and he moved away.

They followed and began to push him. Then he stopped and cried in a loud voice of struggle and agony, " Do you want to raise the devil in me ? Go home—go home ! "

But they only laughed and renewed their torment. His hat fell off and he snatched at it to recover it. In doing so his hand struck somebody in the face. " Strike a cripple, will ye ? " said the publican, and he raised his stick and struck a heavy blow on John's shoulder. At the next moment the dog had leapt upon the man and he was shrieking on the ground. The " knocker-up " lifted his crutch, and with the upper end of it he battered at the dog's brains.

" Stop, man, stop, stop ! Don ! Don ! "

But the dog held on, and the man with the crutch continued to strike at it, until Pincher, who had run to the other side of the street, came back with a clasp knife and plunged it into the dog's neck. Then with a growl and a whine and a pitiful cry the creature let go its hold and rolled over, and the publican got on to his feet.

It was the beginning of the end. John Storm looked down at the dog in its death-throes, and all the devil in his heart came up and mastered him. There was a shop at the corner of the square, and some heavy chairs were standing on the pavement. He took up one of these and swung it round him like a toy, and the men fell on every side.

By this time the street was in commotion, and people were coming from every court and yard and alley, crying, " A madman ! " " Police ! " " Lay hold of him ! " " He'll kill somebody ! " " Down with him ! "

John Storm was also shouting at the top of his voice, when suddenly he felt a dull, stunning pain, without exactly knowing where. Then he felt himself moving up, up, up—he was in a train, the train was going through a tunnel and the guards were screaming—then it was hot, and the next moment it was cold, and still he was floating, floating—and then he saw Glory— he heard her say something—and then he opened his eyes and lo! the dark sky was above him, and some women were speaking in agitated voices over his face.

"Who is it?"

"It's Father Storm. The brutes, the beasts! And the pore dog too!"

"Oh, dear! Where's the p'lice? What are we goin' ter do with 'im, Aggie?"

"Tyke 'im to my room, thet's what."

Then he heard Big Ben strike twelve, and then . . . It was a long, long journey, and the tunnel seemed to go on and on.

XIV

Half-an-hour afterwards there came to the door of the Orphanage the single loud thud that is the knock of the poor. An upper window was opened, and a tremulous voice from the street below cried, "Glory! Miss Gloria!"

It was Agatha Jones. Glory hastened downstairs and found the girl in great agitation. One glance at her face in the candle-light seemed to tell all.

"You've found him?"

"Yes, he's hurt—he's——"

"Be calm, child; tell me everything," said Glory, and Aggie delivered her message.

Since leaving Holloway, Father Storm had been followed and found by means of the dog. The crowd had set on him and knocked him down and injured him. He was now lying in Aggie's room. There had been nowhere else to take him to, for the men had disappeared the moment he was down, and the women were afraid to take him in. The police had come at last, and they were now gone for the doctor. Mrs. Pincher was with the Father, and the poor dog was dead.

Glory held her hand over her heart while Aggie told her story. "I follow you," she said. "Did you tell him I was here? Did he send you to fetch me?"

"He didn't speak," said Aggie.

"Is he unconscious?"

"Yes."

"I'll go with you at once."

Hurrying across the streets by Glory's side, Aggie apologised for her room again. "I down't live thet wye now, you know," she said. "It may seem strange to you, but while my little boy was alive I couldn't go into the streets to save my life—

I couldn't do it. And when 'is pore father died lahst week——"

The stone stairs to the tenement house were thronged with women. They stood huddled together in groups like sheep in a storm. There was not a man anywhere visible, except a drunken sailor who was coming down from an upper storey whistling and singing. The women silenced him. Had he no feelings?

"The doctor's came, Sister," said a woman standing by Aggie's door. Then Glory entered the room.

The poor disordered place was lit by a cheap lamp, which threw splashes of light and left tracks of shadow. John lay on the bed, muttering words that were inaudible. His coat and waistcoat had been removed, and his shirt was open at the neck. The high wall of his forehead was marble white, but his cheeks were red and feverish. One of his arms lay over the side of the bed, and Glory took it up and held it. Her great eyes were moist, but she did not cry, neither did she speak or move. The doctor was bathing a wound at the back of the head, and he looked up and nodded as Glory entered. At the other side of the bed an elderly woman in a widow's cap was wiping her eyes with her apron.

When the doctor was going away Glory followed him to the door.

"Is he seriously injured, doctor?"

"Very." The doctor was a young man, quick, brusque, and emphatic.

"Not dange——"

"Yes. The brutes have done for him, nurse, though you needn't tell his friends so."

"Then—there is—no chance—whatever?"

"Not a ghost of a chance. By the way, you might try to find out where his friends are and send a line to them. I'll be here in the morning. Good-night!"

Glory staggered back to the room with her hand pressed hard over her heart, and the young doctor, going downstairs two steps at a stride, met a police-sergeant and a reporter coming up. "Cruel business, sir!" "Yes, but just one of those things that can't easily be brought home to anybody." "Sad, though!" "Very sad!"

The short night seemed as if it would never end. When daylight came, the cheerless place was cleared of its refuse—its withered roses, its cigarette-ends, and its heaps of left-off clothing. Towards eight o'clock Glory hurried back to the Orphanage, leaving Aggie and Mrs. Pincher in charge. John had been muttering the whole night through, but he had never once moved and he was still unconscious.

"Good-morning, Sister!"

"Good-morning, children!"

The little faces, fresh and bright from sleep, were waiting for their breakfast. When the meal was over Glory wrote by express to Mrs. Callender and to the Father Superior of the Brotherhood, then put on her bonnet and cloak and turned towards Downing Street.

The Prime Minister had held an early Cabinet Council that morning. It was observed by his colleagues that he looked depressed and preoccupied. When the business of the day was done he rose to his feet rather feebly and said—

"My Lords and Gentlemen, I have long had it in mind to say something—something of importance—and I feel the impulse to say it now. We have been doing our best with legislation affecting the Church to give due reality and true life to its relation with the State. But the longer I live the more I feel that that relation is in itself a false one, injurious and even dangerous to both alike. Never in history, so far as I know, and certainly never within my own experience, has it been possible to maintain the union of Church and State without frequent adultery and corruption. The effort to do so has resulted in manifest impostures in sacred things, in ceremonies without spiritual significance, and in gross travesties of the solemn worship of God. Speaking of our own Church, I will not disguise my belief that, but for the good and true men who are always to be found within its pale, it could not survive the frequent disregard of principles which lie deep in the theory of Christianity. Its epicureanism, its regard for the interests of the purse, its tendency to rank the administrator above the apostle, are weeds that spring up out of the soil of its marriage with the State. And when I think of the anomalies and inequalities of its internal government, of its countless poor clergy, and of its lords and princes; above all, when I remember its apostolic pretensions and the certainty that he who attempts to live within the Church the real life of the Apostles will incur the risk of that martyrdom which it has always pronounced against innovators, I cannot but believe that the consciences of many Churchmen would be glad to be relieved of a burden of State temptation which they feel to be hurtful and intolerable—to render unto Cæsar the things which are Cæsar's and unto God the things that are God's. Be that as it may, I have now to tell you that, feeling this question to be paramount, yet despairing of dealing with it in the few years that old age has left to me, I have concluded to resign my office. It is for some younger statesman to fight this battle of the separation between the spiritual and the temporal in the interests of true religion and true civilisation. God grant he may be a Christian man, and God speed and bless him."

The Cabinet broke up with many unwonted expressions of affection for the old leader and many requests that he should "think again" over the step he contemplated. But every one knew that he had set his heart on an impossible enterprise, and every one felt that behind it lay the painful impulse of an incident reported at length in the newspapers that morning.

Left alone in the Cabinet-room, the Prime Minister drew up his chair before the empty grate and gave way to tender memories. He thought of John Storm and the wreck his life had fallen to; of John's mother and her brave renunciation of love; and finally of himself and his near retirement. A spasm of the old lust of power came over him, and he saw himself— to-morrow, next day, next week—delivering up his seals of office to the Queen, and then, the next day after that, getting up from this chair for the last time, and going out of this room to return to it no more—his work done, his life ended.

It was at that moment the footman came to say that a young lady in the dress of a nurse was waiting in the hall. "A messenger from John," he thought. And as he rose to receive her, heavily, wearily, and with the burden of his years upon him, Glory came into the room, with her quivering face and two great tear-drops standing in her eyes, but glowing with youth, and health, and courage.

"Sit down, sit down. But," looking at her again, "have you been here before?"

"Never, my lord."

"I have seen you somewhere."

"I was an actress once. And I am a friend of John's."

"Of John's? Then you are——"

"I am Glory."

"Glory! And so we meet at last, dear lady! But I *have* seen you before. When he spoke of you, but did not bring you to see me, I took a stolen glance at the theatre myself——"

"I have left it, my lord."

"Left it?"

And then she told him what she had done. His old eyes glistened and his head sank into his breast.

"It wasn't that I came to talk about, my lord, but another and more painful matter."

"Can I relieve you of the burden of your message, my child? It has reached me already. It is in all the morning newspapers."

"I didn't think of that. Still, the doctor told me to——"

"What does the doctor say about him?"

"He says——"

"Yes?"

"He says we are going to lose him."

"I have sent for a great surgeon . . . But no doubt it is past help. Poor boy! It seems only yesterday that he came up to London so full of hope and expectation. I can see him now, with his great eyes, sitting in that chair you occupy, talking of his plans and purposes. Poor John! To think he should come to this! But these tumultuous souls whose hearts are battlefields, when the battle is over what can be left but a waste?"

Glory's eyes had dried of themselves, and she was looking at the old man with an expression of pain, but he went on without observing her.

"It is one of the dark riddles of the inscrutable power which rules over life, that the good man can go under like that, while the evil one lives and prospers."

He rose and walked to and fro before the fireplace. "Ah, well! The years bring me an ever-deepening sadness, an ever-increasing sense of our impotence to diminish the infinite sorrow of the world."

Then he looked down at Glory, and said, "But I can hardly forgive him that he has thrown away so much for so little. And when I think of you, my child, and of all that might have been, and then of the bad end he has come to——"

"But I don't call it coming to a bad end, sir," said Glory in a quivering voice.

"No? To be torn, and buffeted, and trampled down in the streets?"

"What of it? He might have died of old age in his bed, and yet come to a worse end than that."

"True; but still——"

"If that is coming to a bad end, I shall have to believe that my father, who was a missionary, came to a bad end too when he was killed by the fevers of Africa. Every martyr comes to a bad end, if that is a bad ending. And so does everybody who is brave and true, and does good to humanity, and is willing to die for it. But it isn't bad. It's glorious! I would rather be the daughter of a man who died like that than be the daughter of an earl; and if I could have been the wife of one who was torn and trampled down in the streets by the very people——"

But her face, which had been aflame, broke into tears again and her voice failed her. The old man could not speak, and there was silence for a moment. Then she recovered herself, and said quietly—

"I came to ask you if you could do something for me."

"What is it?"

"You may have heard that John wished me to marry him?"

"Would to God you had done so!"

"That was when everybody was praising him."

"Well?"

"Everybody is abusing him now and railing at him and insulting him."

"Well?"

"I want to marry him at last, if there is a way—if you think it is possible and can be managed."

"But you say he is a dying man?"

"That's why! When he comes to himself he will be thinking, as you think, that his life has been a failure, and I want somebody to be there and say, 'It isn't, it is only beginning; it is the grain of mustard-seed that *must* die, but it will live in the heart of humanity for ages and ages to come, and I would rather take up your name, injured and insulted as it is, than win all the glory the world has in it.'"

The tears were coursing down the old man's face, and for some minutes he did not attempt to speak. Then he said—

"What you propose is quite possible. It will be a canonical marriage, but it will take some little time to arrange. I must send across to Lambeth Palace. Towards evening I can go down to where he lies and take the license with me. Meantime speak to a clergyman and have everything in readiness."

He walked with Glory down the long corridor to the door, and there he kissed her on the forehead and said—

"I've long known that a woman can be brave, but meeting you this morning has taught me something else, my child. Time and again I thought John's love of you was near to madness. He was ready to give up everything for it—everything! And he was right! Love like yours is the pearl of pearls, and he who wins it is a prince of princes!"

Later the same day, when the Prime Minister was sitting alone in his room, a member of his Cabinet brought him an evening paper containing an article which was making a deep impression in London. It was understood to be written by a journalist of Jewish extraction :—

"'HIS BLOOD BE ON US AND ON OUR CHILDREN.'

"This prediction has been for eighteen hundred years the expression of an historical truth. That the whole Jewish nation, and not Pilate or the rabble of Jerusalem, killed Jesus is a fact which every Jew has been made to feel down to the present day. But let the Christian nation that is without sin towards the Founder of Christianity first cast a stone at the Jews. If it is true, as Jesus Himself said, that he who offers a cup of cold water to the least of His little ones offers it to Him, then it is also true that he who inflicts torture and death on His followers crucifies Him afresh. The unhappy man who has been miserably murdered in the slums of Westminster was a follower of Jesus if ever there lived one, and whosoever the actual persons may be who are guilty of his death, the true culprit is the Christian nation which has inflicted mockeries and insults on everybody who has dared to stand alone under the ensign of Christ.

"Let us not be led away by sneers. This man, whatever his errors, his weaknesses, his self-delusions, and his many human failings, was a Christian. He was the prophet of woman in relation to humanity as hardly any one since Jesus has ever been. And he is hounded out of life. Thus, after nineteen centuries, Christianity presents the same characteristics of frightful tyranny which disfigured the old Jewish law. 'We have a law, and by our law he ought to die.' Such is the sentence still pronounced on reformers in a country where civil and religious laws are confounded. God grant the other half of that doom may not also come true—'His blood be on us and on our children.'"

XV

THERE was a crowd of people of all sorts outside the tenement house when Glory returned to Brown's Square, and even the stairs were thronged with them. "The nurse!" they whispered as Glory appeared, and they made a way for her. Aggie was on the landing, wiping her eyes and answering the questions of strangers, being half afraid of the notoriety her poor room was achieving and half proud of it.

"The laidy 'as came, Miss Gloria, and she sent me to tell you to wyte 'ere for 'er a minute."

Then putting her head in at the open door she beckoned, and Mrs. Callender came out.

"Hush! He's coming to! The poor laddie! He's been calling for ye, and calling and calling. But he thinks ye're in heaven together seemingly, so ye must not say anything to shock him. Come your ways in now, and tak' care, lassie."

John was still wandering, and the light of another world was in his eyes, but he was smiling and he appeared to see.

"Where is she?" he said, in the toneless voice of one who talks in his sleep.

"She's here now. Look! She's close beside ye."

Glory advanced a step and stood beside the bed, struggling with herself not to fall upon his breast. He looked at her with a smile, but without any surprise, and said—

"I knew that you would come to meet me,'Glory! How happy you look! We shall both be happy now."

Then his eyes wandered about the poor, ill-furnished apartment, and he said—

"How beautiful it is here! And how lightsome the air is! Look! The golden gates! And the seven golden candlesticks! And the sea of glass like unto crystal! And all the innumerable company of the angels!"

Aggie, who had returned to the room, was crying audibly.

"Are you crying, Glory? Foolish child to cry! But I know, I understand! Put your dear hand in mine, my child, and we will go together to God's throne, and say, 'Father, you must forgive us two. We were but man and woman, and we could not help but love each other though it was a fault, and for one of us it was a sin.' And God will forgive us, because He made us so, and because God is the God of love."

Glory could bear no more. "John!" she whispered.

He raised himself on his elbow, and held his head aslant, like one who listens to a sound that comes from a distance.

"John!"

"That's Glory's voice."

"It *is* Glory, dearest."

The serenity in his face gave way to a look of bewilderment.

"But Glory is dead."

"No, dear, she is alive, and she will never leave you again."

"What place is this?"

"This is Aggie's room."

"Aggie?"

"Don't you remember Aggie? One of the poor girls you fought and worked for."

"Is it your spirit, Glory?"

"It is myself, dearest—my very, very self."

Then a great joy came into his eyes; his breast heaved, his breath came quick, and without a word more he stretched out his arms.

"It *is* Glory! She is alive! My God! Oh, my God!"

"Do you forgive me, Glory?"

"Forgive? There is nothing to forgive you for, except loving me too well."

"My darling! My darling!"

"I thought I was in heaven, Glory; but I am like poor Buckingham—only half-way to it yet. Have I been unconscious?"

Glory nodded her head.

"Long?"

"Since last night."

"Ah, I remember everything now. I was knocked down in the streets, wasn't I? The men did it—Pincher, Hawkins, and the rest."

"They shall be punished, John," said Glory in a quivering voice. "As sure as heaven's above us and there's law in the land——"

"Aye, aye, laddie" (from somewhere by the door), "mak' yersel' sure o' that. There'll be never a man o' them but he'll hang for it, same as a pole-cat on a barn gate."

But John shook his head. "Poor fellows! They didn't understand. When they come to see what they've done . . . 'Lord, Lord, lay not this sin to their charge.'"

She had wiped away the tears that sprung to her eyes, and was sitting by his side and smiling. Her white teeth were showing, her red lips were twitching, and her face was full of sunshine. He was holding her hand, and gazing at her constantly, as if he could not allow himself to lose sight of her for a moment.

"But I'm half-sorry, for all that, Glory," he said.

"Sorry?"

"That we are not both in the other world, for there you were my bride, I remember, and all our pains were over."

Then her sweet face coloured up to the forehead, and she leaned over the bed and whispered, "Ask me to be your bride in this one, dearest."

"I can't! I daren't!"

"Are you thinking of the vows?"

"No," emphatically. "But—I am a dying man; I know that quite well. And what right have I——"

She gave a little gay toss of her golden head. "Pooh! nobody was ever married because he had a *right* to be exactly."

"But there is your own profession—your great career."

She shook her head gravely. "That's all over now."

"Eh?" reaching up on his elbow.

"When you had gone, and nearly everybody was deserting your work, I thought I should like to take up a part of it."

"And did you?"

She nodded.

"Blessed be God! Oh, God is very good!" and he lay back and panted.

She laughed nervously. "Well, are you determined to make me ashamed? Am I to throw myself at your head, sir? Or perhaps you are going to refuse me after all."

"But why should I burden all the years of your life with the name of a fallen man? I am dying in disgrace, Glory."

"No, but in honour—great, great honour! These few bad days will be forgotten soon, dearest—quite, quite forgotten. And in the future time people will come to me and say—girls, dearest, brave, brave girls, who are fighting the battle of life like men—they will come and say, 'And did you know him? Did you really, really know him?' And I will smile triumphantly and answer them, 'Yes, for he loved me, and he is mine and I am his, for ever and for ever.'"

"It would be beautiful! We could not come together in this world, but to be united for all eternity on the threshold of the next——"

"There! say no more about it, for it's all arranged anyhow. The Father has been persuaded to read the service, and the Prime Minister is to bring the Archbishop's license, and it's to be to-day—this evening—and—and I'm not the first woman who has settled everything herself!"

Then she began to laugh, and he laughed with her, and they laughed together in spite of his weakness and pain. At the next moment she was gone like a gleam of sunshine before a cloud, and Mrs. Callender had come back to the bedside, tying up the strings of her old-fashioned bonnet. "She's gold, laddie, that's what you Glory is—just gold."

"Ay, tried in the fire and tested," he replied, and then the back of his head began to throb fiercely.

Glory had fled out of the room to cry, and Mrs. Callender joined her on the landing. "I maun awa', lassie. I'd like fine to stop wi' ye, but I can't. It minds me of the time my Alec left me, and that's forty lang years the day, but he seems to have been with me ever syne."

"Where's Glory?"

"She's coming, Father," said Aggie, and at the sound of her name Glory wiped her eyes and returned.

"And was it by my being lost that you came here to Westminster and found me?"

"Yes, and myself as well."

"And I thought my life had been wasted! When one thinks of God's designs one feels humble— humble as the grass at one's feet. But are you sure you will never regret?"

"Never!"

"Nor look back?"

She tossed her head again. "Call me Mrs. Lot at once and have done with it."

"It's wonderful! What a glorious work is before you, Glory! You'll take it up where I have left it, and carry it on and on. You are nobler than I am, and stronger, far stronger, and purer and braver. And haven't I said all along that what the world wants now is a great woman! I had the pith of it all, though; I saw the true light, but I was not worthy. I had sinned and fallen, and didn't know my own heart, and was not fit to enter into the promised land. It is something, nevertheless, that I see it a long way off. And if I have been taken up to Sinai and heard the thunders of the everlasting law——"

"Hush, dear! somebody is coming."

It was the great surgeon whom the Prime Minister had sent for. He examined the injuries carefully, and gave certain instructions. "Mind you do this, Sister," and that and the other. But Glory could see that he had no hope. To relieve the pain in the head he wanted to administer morphia, but John refused to have it.

"I am going into the presence of the King," he said. "Let me have all my wits about me."

While the doctor was there the police sergeant returned with a magistrate and the reporter. "Sorry to intrude, but hearing your patient was now conscious . . ." And then he prepared to take John's deposition.

The reporter opened his notebook; the police magistrate stood at the foot of the bed, the doctor at one side of it, and Glory at the other side, holding John's hand and quivering.

"Do you know who struck you, sir?"

There was silence for a moment, and then came "Yes."

"Who was it?"

There was another pause, and then, "Don't ask me."

"But your own evidence will be most valuable, and indeed down to the present we have no other. Who was it, sir?"

"I can't tell you."

"But why?"

There was no answer.

"Why not give me the name of the scoundrel who took—I mean, attempted to take your life?"

Then in a voice that was hardly audible, with his head thrown back and his eyes on the ceiling, John said, "'Father, forgive them, for they know not what they do.'"

It was useless to go further. Glory saw the four men to the door.

"You must keep him quiet," said the doctor; "not that anything can save him, but he is a man of stubborn will——"

And the police magistrate said, "It may be all very fine to forgive your enemies, but everybody has his duty to society as well as to himself."

"Yes, yes," said Glory; "the world has no room for greater hearts than its own."

The police magistrate looked at her in bewilderment. "Just so," he said, and disappeared.

"Where is she now, my girl?"

"She's 'ere, Father."

"Hush!" said Glory, coming back to the room. "The doctor says you are not to talk so much."

"Then let me look at you, Glory. Sit here—here, and if I should seem to be suffering you must not mind that, because I am really very happy."

Just then an organ-man in the street began to play. Glory thought the music might disturb John, and she was going to send Aggie to stop it. But his face brightened, and he said, "Sing for me, Glory. Let me hear your voice."

The organ was playing a "coon" song, and she sang the words of it. They were simple words, childish words, almost babyish, but full of tenderness and love. The little black boy could think of nothing but his Loo-loo. In the night when he was sleeping he awoke and he was weeping, for he was always, always dreaming of his Loo-loo, his Loo-loo!

When the song was finished they took hands and talked in whispers, though they were alone in the room now, and nobody could hear them. His white face was very bright, and her moist eyes were full of merriment. They grew foolish in their tender-

ness, and played with each other like little children. There
were recollections of their early life in the little island home,
memories of years concentrated into an hour—humorous stories
and touches of mimicry. "O Lord! open Thou our lips ...
Where are you, Neilus?" 'Aw, here I am, your riverence, and
my tongue shall show forth Thy praise.'"

All at once John's face saddened and he said, "It's a pity,
though!"

"A pity?"

"I suppose the man who carries the flag always gets 'potted,'
as they say. But somebody must carry it."

Glory felt her tears gathering.

"It's a pity that I have to go before you, Glory."

She shook her head to keep the tears from flowing, and then
answered gaily, "Oh, that's only as it should be. I want a little
while to think it all out, you know, and then—then I'll pass
over to you, just as we fall asleep at night and pass from day
to day."

And then he lay back with a sigh and said, "Well, I have had
a happy end, at all events."

XVI

The day had been fine, with a rather fierce sun shining until
late in the afternoon, and long white clouds lying motionless
in a deep blue sky, like celestial sandbanks in a celestial
sea. But the tender and tempered splendour of the evening
had come at length, with the sun gone over the house-tops to
the north-west, and its solemn afterglow like the wings of
angels sweeping down. London was unusually quiet after
the roar and turmoil of the day. The great city lay like a tired
ocean, and like an ocean it seemed to sleep, full of its living as
well as its dead.

In a little square which stands on the fringe of the slums of
Westminster, and has a well-worn church in the middle, and
tenement-houses, institutions, and workshops around its sides, a
strange crowd had gathered. It consisted for the greater part
of persons who are generally thought to be beyond the sympathies of life—the "priestesses of society," who are the lowest
among women. But they stood there for hours in silence, or
walked about with dazed looks, glancing up at the window of
a room on the second storey which glittered with the rays
of the dying day. Their friend and champion was near to his

death in that room, and they were waiting for the last news of him.

The Prime Minister had kept his promise. Walking across from Downing Street his face had been clouded, as if he was thinking out the riddles of the inscrutable Power which stood to him for God. But when he came to the square and looked round at the people, his eyes brightened and he went on with resignation, and even content. The women made way for him with whispered explanations of who he was, and he walked through them to the room upstairs.

The room was nearly full already, for the Father Superior had come, bringing lay-brother Andrew along with him, and Aggie was sitting in a corner, and Mrs. Pincher was moving about, and there was also a stranger present. And though the little place was so mean and poor, it was full of soft radiance from the sky, and people walked about in it with a glow upon their faces.

Glory was by the bedside, standing erect and saying nothing. Her eyes were glistening with unshed tears and sometimes her mouth was twitching. John Storm was conscious and very quiet. Holding Glory's hand as if he could not part with it, he was looking around with the expression of the soldier who has done the fearful, perhaps the foolish and foolhardy thing, and scaled the walls of the enemy. He is lying with the enemy's shot in his breast now and with death in his eyes, but he is smiling proudly for all that, because he knows that the army is coming on. The Superior had brought from the Brotherhood the picture of the head of Christ in its crown of thorns to hang on the wall at the end of the bed, and the light from the window made flickering gleams on the glass and they were reflected on to his face.

Hardly anybody spoke. As soon as the Prime Minister arrived he took a paper from his pocket and gave it to the stranger, who glanced at it and bowed. Then they all gathered about the bed, and the Superior opened a book which he had carried in his hands, and in solemn accents began to read—

"Dearly beloved, we are gathered together in the sight of God——"

Brother Andrew, who was kneeling at the foot of the bed, whined like a dog, and some women on the landing, who were peering in at the open door, whispered among themselves, "It's the Holy Communion! Hush!"

John's power did not fail him. He made his responses in a clear voice, although his last strength was thrilling along the thread of life. And Glory, when her turn came, was brave too. There was just a touch of the old hoarseness in her glorious voice, a slight quivering of the lids of her glistening eyes, and then she went on to the end without faltering:—

 I, GLORY—
 —I, GLORY—
 —*take thee, JOHN—*
 —take thee, JOHN—
 —*to my wedded husband, to have and to hold from this day forward—*
 .... to have and to hold from this day forward—
 —*for better for worse, for richer for poorer, in sickness and in health—*
 .... in sickness and in health -
 —*to love, cherish and obey, till death us do part—*
 .... till death us do part——"
 .... AMEN!

AUTHOR'S NOTE

It will be seen that in writing this book I have sometimes used the diaries, letters, memoirs, sermons, and speeches of recognisable persons, living and dead. Also, it will be seen that I have frequently employed fact for the purposes of fiction. In doing so, I think I am true to the principles of art, and I know I am following the precedent of great writers. But being conscious of the grievous danger of giving personal offence, I would wish to say that I have not intended to paint anybody's portrait, or to describe the life of any known Society or to indicate the management of any particular Institution. To do any of these things would be to wrong the theory of fiction as I understand it, which is not to offer mock history or a substitute for fact, but to present a thought in the form of a story, with as much realism as the requirements of idealism will permit. In presenting the thought which is the motive of "The Christian," my desire has been to depict, however imperfectly, the types of mind and character, of creed and culture, of social effort and religious purpose which I think I see in the life of England and America at the close of the nineteenth century. For such a task my own observation and reflection could not be enough, and so I am conscious that in many passages of this book I have often been merely as the mould through which the metal has passed from the fires kept burning round about.

HALL CAINE.

Greeba Castle,
   Isle of Man, 1897.

Ballantyne Press
Printed by BALLANTYNE, HANSON & CO.
Edinburgh & London

Mr. William Heinemann's Autumn Announcements mdcccxcvii

The Books mentioned in this List may be obtained through any Bookseller

history and Biography
New Letters of Napoleon I.
OMITTED FROM THE COLLECTION PUBLISHED UNDER
THE AUSPICES OF NAPOLEON III.

TRANSLATED FROM THE FRENCH BY
LADY MARY LOYD.

In One Volume, demy 8vo, with Frontispiece, price 15s.

The monumental twenty-eight volumes of Napoleon I.'s letters, published under the direction of the Commission appointed by Napoleon III. to edit and arrange his uncle's correspondence, were by no means exhaustive. The *Correspondence*, as originally issued, contained, indeed, some 22,000 pieces. Many of these, however, were decrees, orders of the day, bulletins, &c., and the original minutes in the French archives show a total of over 30,000 letters. It is notorious that the Commission, of which Prince Napoleon was President, exercised its prerogative of suppression with great freedom. The reasons for its action in the matter are obvious. In some cases, letters were set aside as wanting in interest, or as going over ground already covered by other documents. But in the majority of instances, a pardonable zeal for the family glory came into play, urging the withholding of anything that might dim the lustre of Napoleon's fame, or reflect unpleasantly on his near relatives. Governed by considerations of this nature, the Commission set aside a series of letters of extraordinary historical interest—some dealing with the quarrels of Napoleon and his brothers, and the long struggle with the Pope, others containing trenchant criticisms of the capacity and conduct of eminent generals and officials, or bearing witness to the iron hand with which the greatest organiser the world has perhaps ever seen, carried out his "system," and ordered the affairs of the press, the police, and all the minutiæ of his vast economy.

The object of the two supplementary volumes recently published in France is to repair those deliberate omissions, and to make the former collection practically complete. A considerable part of these two volumes is naturally wanting in novelty and interest. But they contain so much that is fresh and new, so much of exceptional value historically, and they throw so many new lights on the actors of that wonderful drama of the First Empire, especially on the masterful character of its creator, that the English publisher is confident that a selection, with a view to the general interest felt for Napoleon I., is bound to be welcome.

History and Biography

WILLIAM SHAKESPEARE

A Critical Study. By GEORG BRANDES, Ph.D.
Translated from the Danish by WILLIAM ARCHER and DIANA WHITE.
In Two Volumes, demy 8vo. Price 24s.

Dr. Georg Brandes's "William Shakespeare" may best be called, perhaps, an exhaustive critical biography. He places the poet in his political and literary environment, and studies each play not as an isolated phenomenon, but as the record of a stage in Shakespeare's spiritual history. Dr. Brandes has achieved German thoroughness without German heaviness, and has produced what must be regarded as a standard work.

CATHERINE SFORZA.

A Study. By COUNT PASOLINI.
Adapted from the Italian by PAUL SYLVESTER.
Demy 8vo, with many Illustrations.

The sixteenth century memoir of Catherine Sforza, by Fabio Oliva, is comprised within too narrow a margin for so great a life; the later and more compendious history of the Spanish Abbé Burriel has the merit of being compiled from contemporary documents, but is lacking in critical and historical acumen. It has been left to the patient research of a lineal descendant of the hereditary enemies of the Attendoli-Sforza, to give to the world a vivid presentment of an historic figure, hitherto more famous than well-known. Count Pasolini's work is enriched by numerous illustrations, facsimiles of handwriting, seals, and quotations from some five hundred letters of the Madonna of Forli. It combines the charm of romance with the dignity of history, and brings within the reader's ken not only the militant princess who held the fort of St. Angelo against the Conclave (thus arresting the affairs of Europe until her own were settled), who circumvented Machiavelli and defied Cesar Borgia, but the private woman in her Court and home, her domestic and social relations.

A HISTORY OF THE LIVERPOOL PRIVATEERS

And Letters of Marque, including the Slave Trade.
By GOMER WILLIAMS.
In one volume, demy 8vo. Illustrated.

ROBERT, EARL NUGENT. A Memoir

By CLAUD NUGENT.
In one volume, demy 8vo, with a number of
Portraits and other Illustrations.

Literatures of the World

A SERIES OF SHORT HISTORIES.
Edited by EDMUND GOSSE.
Each volume large crown 8vo, cloth, **6s.**

A HISTORY OF FRENCH LITERATURE
By EDWARD DOWDEN, D.C.L., LL.D.,
Professor of Oratory and English Literature
in the University of Dublin.

In October.

A HISTORY OF ENGLISH LITERATURE
By EDMUND GOSSE,
Hon. M.A. of Trinity College, Cambridge.

In January.

A HISTORY OF ITALIAN LITERATURE
By RICHARD GARNETT, C.B., LL.D.,
Keeper of Printed Books in the
British Museum.

Already published.

A HISTORY OF ANCIENT GREEK LITERATURE
By GILBERT MURRAY, M.A.,
Professor of Greek in the University of Glasgow.

"A sketch to which the much-abused word 'brilliant' may be justly applied. Dealing in four hundred pages with a subject which is both immense and well-worn, Mr. Murray presents us with a treatment at once comprehensive, penetrating, and fresh. By dint of a clear, freely-moving intelligence, and by dint also of a style at once compact and lucid, he has produced a book which fairly represents the best conclusions of modern scholarship."—*The Times*

Literatures of the World

In preparation.

A HISTORY OF SPANISH LITERATURE. By J. FITZ-MAURICE KELLY.

A HISTORY OF JAPANESE LITERATURE. By WILLIAM GEORGE ASTON, C.M.G., M.A.

A HISTORY OF MODERN SCANDINAVIAN LITERATURE. By Dr. GEORG BRANDES.

A HISTORY OF SANSCRIT LITERATURE. By A. A. MACDONNELL, M.A.

A HISTORY OF HUNGARIAN LITERATURE. By Dr. ZOLTHAN BEÖTHY.

A HISTORY OF AMERICAN LITERATURE. By Professor MOSES COIT TYLER.

A HISTORY OF GERMAN LITERATURE. By Dr. C. H. HERFORD.

A HISTORY OF LATIN LITERATURE. By Dr. A. W. VERRALL.

Also volumes dealing with RUSSIAN, ARABIC, DUTCH, MODERN GREEK.

Philosophy

THE NON=RELIGION OF THE FUTURE

From the French of MARIE JEAN GUYAU.

In One Volume, demy 8vo, 17s. net.

The present work traces the connection between religion, æsthetics, and morals, and the inevitable decomposition of all systems of dogmatic religion; it also deals with the state of "non-religion," toward which the human mind seems to tend. It explains the exact sense in which one must understand the non-religion as distinguished from the "religion of the future," and sets forth the value and utility, for the time being, of religion.

Uniform with the above, price **17s.** *net each.*

By MAX NORDAU.
Paradoxes.
Conventional Lies of Our Civilisation.

By MAX NORDAU.
Degeneration.

By Dr. WILLIAM HIRSCH.
Genius and Degeneration.

Travel

CUBA IN WAR TIME
By RICHARD HARDING DAVIS,
Author of "Soldiers of Fortune."
With Numerous Illustrations by FREDERICK REMINGTON.
Crown 8vo.

WITH THE FIGHTING JAPS
Naval Experiences during the late Chino-Japanese War.
By J. CHALMERS.
Crown 8vo.

MY FOURTH TOUR IN WESTERN AUSTRALIA
By ALBERT F. CALVERT, F.R.G.S.
4to, with many Illustrations and Photographs.

Verse

POEMS FROM THE DIVAN OF HAFIZ
TRANSLATED FROM THE PERSIAN BY
GERTRUDE LOWTHIAN BELL.
Small crown 8vo,

A SELECTION FROM THE POEMS OF WILFRED SCAWEN BLUNT
With an Introduction by W. E. HENLEY.
Crown 8vo,

IN CAP AND GOWN
Three Centuries of Cambridge Wit.
Selected and arranged by CHARLES WHIBLEY.
A New Edition, with Frontispiece, price 3s. 6d.

Great Lives and Events

Uniformly bound in cloth, price 6s. each volume.

THE NEW VOLUME.

SIXTY YEARS OF EMPIRE

A Symposium.

With over 70 Portraits and Diagrams.

This volume gathers together the remarkable series of articles which attracted such general attention when they first appeared in the *Daily Chronicle*, on the occasion of the Queen's Jubilee. Embracing as they do the whole field of National and Imperial interests, written each by an expert in the subject of which he treats (Sir Charles Dilke, Mr. John Burns, Mr. A. B. Walkeley, and Mr. Joseph Pennell are among the contributors), illustrated with portraits and diagrams, the papers thus collected supply what this Jubilee year has hitherto failed to produce—a brief, comprehensive, and authoritative review of the period covered by Her Majesty's reign.

The following volumes have been published in this Series.

By K. WALISZEWSKI.
The Romance of an Empress. Catherine II. of Russia.

The Story of a Throne. Catherine II. of Russia.

By F. MASSON.
Napoleon and the Fair Sex.

The Memoirs of the Prince de Joinville.

By PAUL GAULOT.
A Friend of the Queen. Marie Antoinette and Count Fersen.

By ARTHUR WAUGH.
Alfred Lord Tennyson.

By E. GOSSE.
The Naturalist of the Seashore. The Life of Philip Henry Gosse.

LUMEN

Fcap. 8vo, cloth, price 3s. 6d.

By CAMILLE FLAMMARION.

M. Flammarion, the distinguished French astronomer, has in this volume entitled "Lumen" added to his exact scientific knowledge a new and interesting attempt to bring before his readers a speculative theory of life in another planet.

In France the volume has been widely read, for more than 50,000 copies have been sold in the original.

THE WORKS OF LORD BYRON

Edited by WILLIAM ERNEST HENLEY.

To be completed in Twelve Volumes.

The Letters, Diaries, Controversies, Speeches, &c., in Four, and the Verse in Eight.

Small crown 8vo, price 5s. net each.

VERSE VOLUME I. Containing "Hours of Idleness" and "English Bards and Scotch Reviewers." With a Portrait after SANDERS.

I. LETTERS, 1804-1813. With a Portrait after PHILLIPS.
[*Is now ready.*

Mr. W. E. Henley is not only steeped to the lips in Bryonic poetry, but he has also a very familiar acquaintance with the remarkable characters who formed "the Bryonic set," and he knows the manners and customs of the Regency epoch to an extent that gives him full mastery of his subject. There is originality in the very form of this edition.

"He manages to give, in a few vigorous sentences, vivid sketches of the wide circle of Byron's friends and enemies."—*Pall Mall Gazette.*

"The first volume is delightfully handy and the type excellent."—ANDREW LANG.

"Mr. Henley, so far as elucidation and illustration are concerned, is fully equipped."—*Athenæum.*

There will also be an Edition, limited to 150 sets, for sale in Great Britain, printed on Van Gelder's hand-made paper, price Six Guineas net, subscriptions for which are now being received.

STUDIES IN FRANKNESS
By CHARLES WHIBLEY.
Crown 8vo, with Frontispiece, price **7s. 6d.**

By the same Author, uniform with the above.

A BOOK OF SCOUNDRELS
Crown 8vo, buckram, price **7s. 6d.**

THE GENTLE ART OF MAKING ENEMIES
By JAMES McNEILL WHISTLER.

The continued demand for this unique work has enabled the publisher to induce Mr. Whistler to consent to the issue of another edition, which will be further enriched by the addition of much new material.

A few copies of the Large Paper Issue of the first edition are on sale, price £2, 2s. net.

The Drama

Admiral Guinea | Macaire
By W. E. HENLEY AND R. L. STEVENSON

Previously Published.

DEACON BRODIE. | BEAU AUSTIN.

The Princess and the Butterfly
By ARTHUR W. PINERO

Previously Published.

The Times.	The Benefit of the Doubt.
The Profligate.	Dandy Dick.
The Cabinet Minister.	Sweet Lavender.
The Hobby Horse.	The Schoolmistress.
Lady Bountiful.	The Weaker Sex.
The Magistrate.	The Amazons.
The Notorious Mrs. Ebbsmith.	The Second Mrs. Tanqueray.

The above 14 Volumes are now uniformly bound in *Leather*, in case. Price on application.

The Weavers | Lonely Folk
By GERHART HAUPTMANN

Previously Published, price 5s.

HANNELE: A DREAM POEM.
Translated by WILLIAM ARCHER.

New Fiction

In One Volume at 6s.

St. Ives
By ROBERT LOUIS STEVENSON.

By the same Author, price 6s.
The Ebb-Tide.

A New Novel
By SARAH GRAND.

By the same Author, price 6s. *each.*
The Heavenly Twins. | Ideala.
Our Manifold Nature.

Marietta's Marriage
By W. E. NORRIS.

By the same Author, price 6s. *each.*
The Dancer in Yellow. | A Victim of Good Luck.
The Countess Radna.

What Maisie Knew
By HENRY JAMES.

By the same Author, price 6s. *each.*
The Spoils of Poynton. | The Other House.
Embarrassments. | Terminations.

The War of the Worlds
By H. G. WELLS.

By the same Author.
The Island of Dr. Moreau. | The Time Machine.

The Master-Knot
By J. A. STEUART.

The Gad-Fly
By E. L. VOYNICH.

New Fiction

In One Volume at 6s.

The Gods Arrive
By ANNIE E. HOLDSWORTH.

By the same Author.

The Years that the Locust Hath Eaten. 6s. | Joanna Traill, Spinster. (*Pioneer Series*, cloth, 3s. net; paper, 2s. 6d. net.)

The Freedom of Henry Meredyth
By M. HAMILTON.

By the same Author, price 6s. each.

McLeod of the Camerons. | A Self-Denying Ordinance.

Pioneer Series, cloth, 3s. net; paper, 2s. 6d. net.

Across an Ulster Bog.

The Nigger of "The Narcissus"
By JOSEPH CONRAD.

The Drones Must Die
By MAX NORDAU.

By the same Author, price 6s. each.

The Malady of the Century. | A Comedy of Sentiment.

The Fourth Napoleon
By CHARLES BENHAM.

The Lake of Wine.
By B. E. J. CAPES.

Ezekiel's Sin
By J. H. PEARCE.

By the same Author, price 3s. 6d. each.

Eli's Daughter. | Inconsequent Lives.

New Fiction

In One Volume at 6s.

Mrs. John Forster
By CHARLES GRANVILLE.

A Champion of the Seventies
By EDITH A. BARNETT.

God's Foundling
By ALEC JOHN DAWSON.

The Londoners
By ROBERT HICHENS.

By the same Author, 6s. each.
An Imaginative Man. | The Folly of Eustace.
Flames.

Pioneer Series, paper, 2s. 6d. net; cloth, 3s. net.
The Green Carnation.

A New Volume
By STEPHEN CRANE.

By the same Author.

The Red Badge of Courage. | The Little Regiment.
(*Pioneer Series*, paper, 2s. 6d. net; | (*Pioneer Series*, paper, 2s. 6d. net;
cloth, 3s. net.) | cloth, 3s. net.)
Maggie. Price 2s. | The Black Riders. Price 3s. net.

A New Novel
By HAROLD FREDERIC.

By the same Author.

Illumination. Price 6s. | The Return of the O'Mahoney.
In the Valley. Price 3s. 6d. | Price 3s. 6d.
The Copperhead. Price 3s. 6d. | The New Exodus. Price 16s.

New Fiction

In One Volume at 6s.

A New Volume
By EDWIN PUGH.

By the same Author.

The Man of Straw.	A Street in Suburbia.
Price 6s.	(*Pioneer Series, paper*, 2s. 6d. net ; *cloth*, 3s. *net.*)

NEW VOLUMES OF SHORT STORIES

Dreamers of the Ghetto
By I. ZANGWILL.

By the same Author.

Children of the Ghetto.	The Premier and the Painter.
Price 6s.	Price 6s.
The King of Schnorrers.	The Old Maid's Club.
Price 6s.	Boards, 2s. ; cloth. 3s. 6d.

Last Studies
By HUBERT CRACKANTHORPE.

With an Introduction by HENRY JAMES, and a Portrait.

In the Permanent Way
By FLORA ANNA STEEL.

By the same Author, price 6s. each.

On the Face of the Waters.　|　From the Five Rivers.
The Potter's Thumb.

A Romance of the First Consul

From the Swedish of M. MALLING.

A New Volume of the Pioneer Series

Price 2s. 6d. net in paper, and 3s. net in cloth.

A MAN WITH A MAID
BY MRS. HENRY DUDENEY.

A complete List of this Series on application.

Two New Volumes of the International Library

Edited by EDMUND GOSSE.

In paper cover, 2s. 6d. ; cloth, 3s. 6d.

THE OLD ADAM AND THE NEW EVE
Translated from the German of RICHARD GOLM.

NIOBE
Translated from the Norwegian of JONAS LIE.

The Novels of Ivan Turgenev

Translated by CONSTANCE GARNETT.

Fcap. 8vo, cloth, 3s. net each Volume.

The New Volume
THE TORRENTS OF SPRING

Previously Published.

Rudin.
A House of Gentlefolk.
On the Eve.
Fathers and Children.
Smoke.

Virgin Soil. Two Vols.
A Sportsman's Sketches. Two Vols.
Dream Tales and Prose Fancies.

The Novels of Bjornstjerne Bjornson

Edited by EDMUND GOSSE.

Fcap. 8vo, cloth, 3s. net each Volume.

New Volumes.
Captain Mansana and Mother's Hands
Absalom's Hair and A Painful Memory

Previously Published.

Arne.
A Happy Boy.
The Fisher Lass.

The Bridal March and One Day.
Magnhild and Dust.

Books for Presentation

Meissonier. His Life and His Art.
By VALLERY C. O. GREARD, de l'Académie Française. Translated from the French by LADY MARY LOYD and FLORENCE SIMMONDS. In One Volume, with 38 full-page plates, 20 in photogravure and 18 in colour, and 200 text illustrations. Price £1, 16s. net.

Correggio. His Life, His Friends, and His Time.
By CORRADO RICCI. Translated by FLORENCE SIMMONDS. In One Volume, Imperial 8vo, with 16 photogravures, 21 full-page plates in colour, and 190 illustrations in the text. £2, 2s. net. Also an *Edition de Luxe*, limited to 100 copies, with duplicate set of the photogravure plates. Price £12, 12s. net.

Masterpieces of Greek Sculpture.
By ADOLF FURTWANGLER. Edited by EUGENIE SELLERS. With 19 full-page and 200 text illustrations, in One Volume 4to. Price £3, 3s. net. Also an *Edition de Luxe*, limited to 50 copies, on Japanese Vellum, in Two Volumes. Price £2, 12s. net.

Second Edition, enlarged and revised, now ready.
Rembrandt. His Life, His Work, and His Time.
By EMILE MICHEL (of the Institute of France). Edited by FREDERICK WEDMORE. Translated by Miss FLORENCE SIMMONDS. Two Volumes, Imperial 8vo, with 76 full-page plates, partly in photogravure and partly coloured, and hundreds of text illustrations. £2, 2s. net. A very few copies of the *Edition de Luxe*, containing a duplicate set of the photogravure plates. Price £12, 12s. net.

The Castles of England
Their Story and Structure.
By Sir JAMES D. MACKENZIE, Bart. In Two Volumes, Imperial 8vo, with 40 full-page plates, over 150 text illustrations, and 60 plans. Price £3, 3s. net.

AN ALPHABET
BY WILLIAM NICHOLSON.
*Will be Published in September 1897,
In Three Editions.*

1. *The Popular Edition.* Lithographed in Colours, on stout Cartridge Paper. Price **5s.**
2. *The Library Edition* (limited). Lithographed in Colours, on Dutch Hand-made Paper, mounted and bound in cloth, gilt top. Price **12s. 6d.**
3. *The Edition de Luxe* (limited). Printed from the Original Wood-blocks. Hand-coloured, and signed by the Artist. Price **£12, 12s.**

An Illustrated Prospectus on application.

AN ALMANAC OF TWELVE SPORTS FOR 1898
BY WILLIAM NICHOLSON.
*Will be Published in November 1897,
In Three Editions.*

1. *The Popular Edition.* Lithographed in Colours, on stout Cartridge Paper. Price **2s.**
2. *The Library Edition* (limited). Lithographed in Colours, on Japanese Vellum, and bound in cloth. Price **7s. 6d.**
3. *The Edition de Luxe* (limited). Printed from the Original Wood-blocks. Hand-coloured, and signed by the Artist. Price **£5, 5s.**

An Illustrated Prospectus on application.

These pictures, done by one of the most distinguished younger artists England can boast of, are English to the core, and will be delighted in, not only for a momentary perusal, but more so even if framed and daily seen, as indeed their subject, and assuredly also their artistic merit, warrants. The Art of the coloured woodcut, which was brought to its highest perfection in Japan, has been comparatively neglected of recent years in Europe, and its revival is due, probably, to the discovery of the inadequacy of all mechanical processes for certain artistic effects. Mr. Pennell has recently given enthusiastic testimony to the extraordinary merit of the few examples of Mr. Nicholson's art which have hitherto been published.

www.ingramcontent.com/pod-product-compliance
Lightning Source LLC
Chambersburg PA
CBHW022057300426
44117CB00007B/487